ISBN 978-1-5282-0586-3
PIBN 10915586

This book is a reproduction of an important historical work. Forgotten Books uses state-of-the-art technology to digitally reconstruct the work, preserving the original format whilst repairing imperfections present in the aged copy. In rare cases, an imperfection in the original, such as a blemish or missing page, may be replicated in our edition. We do, however, repair the vast majority of imperfections successfully; any imperfections that remain are intentionally left to preserve the state of such historical works.

1 MONTH OF
FREE
READING

at

www.ForgottenBooks.com

By purchasing this book you are eligible for one month membership to ForgottenBooks.com, giving you unlimited access to our entire collection of over 1,000,000 titles via our web site and mobile apps.

To claim your free month visit:

www.forgottenbooks.com/free915586

English
Français
Deutsche
Italiano
Español
Português

www.forgottenbooks.com

Mythology Photography **Fiction**
Fishing Christianity **Art** Cooking
Essays Buddhism Freemasonry
Medicine **Biology** Music **Ancient
Egypt** Evolution Carpentry Physics
Dance Geology **Mathematics** Fitness
Shakespeare **Folklore** Yoga Marketing
Confidence Immortality Biographies
Poetry **Psychology** Witchcraft
Electronics Chemistry History **Law**
Accounting **Philosophy** Anthropology
Alchemy Drama Quantum Mechanics
Atheism Sexual Health **Ancient History**
Entrepreneurship Languages Sport
Paleontology Needlework Islam
Metaphysics Investment Archaeology
Parenting Statistics Criminology
Motivational

WEST TILBURY: TILBURY FORT: GATEHOUSE; *c.* 1682.
South Front.

{ROYAL COMMISSION ON ⎫
HISTORICAL MONVMENTS ⎬
(*ENGLAND.*)

AN INVENTORY

OF THE HISTORICAL MONVMENTS

in

ESSEX

VOLUME IV. (South - East)

≈≈*ANNO* D̃NĪ∅·M·C·M·X·X·I·I·I ≈≈

LONDON:
PRINTED & PUBLISHED BY HIS MAJESTY'S STATIONERY OFFICE

To be purchased through any Bookseller or directly from H.M. STATIONERY OFFICE
at the following addresses: Imperial House, Kingsway, London, W.C.2, and
28 Abingdon Street, London, S.W.1; York Street, Manchester;
1 St. Andrew's Crescent, Cardiff; or 120 George Street,
Edinburgh.

Price £1 5s. 0d. net.

TABLE OF CONTENTS.

LIST OF PLANS AND ILLUSTRATIONS,

WITH TITLES AND PRINCIPAL DATES.

PREFACE.

I CAN do little more than repeat the words used by our late Chairman, Lord Plymouth, in explanation of the manner in which the monuments have been recorded.

This volume contains (in addition to the terms of appointment and official report) a Sectional Preface which, under subject headings, calls attention to any particularly interesting examples mentioned in the Inventory; an illustrated Inventory, with a concise account of the monuments visited; a list of monuments that the Commissioners have selected as especially worthy of preservation; a glossary of architectural, heraldic and archaeological terms; a map showing the topographical distribution of the scheduled monuments, and an index.

The foregoing are common to the earlier volumes. But, in addition, and in view of the fact that this is the concluding volume of the Essex series, we have thought it of interest to add a short review of the monuments of the county as a whole, together with an estimate of their relative position and value viewed from the wider standpoint of English archaeology. With this is combined a slight sketch of certain influences immediately affecting the county during the Roman and Saxon and Danish periods and a statement of the main lines upon which the Commission's system of dating mediaeval monuments is based. Further, at the end of the Inventory is given a list of those families whose arms, if anterior to 1550, are blazoned in this and in the preceding Essex volumes, while two pages of illustrations are devoted to some examples of mouldings grouped by centuries which were measured in the course of our enquiries, and another page gives examples of mason's marks drawn from Essex Churches. Lastly, the index is a combined index and covers all four volumes.

So far as the monuments in S.E. Essex are concerned they will be found, as before, under the heads of parishes arranged alphabetically, with an introductory paragraph calling attention to the more noticeable among them in each parish. The chronological sequence chosen is not perhaps scientifically perfect, but it has been found a workable basis for classification. The order adopted is as follows :—

     (1) Prehistoric monuments and earthworks.
     (2) Roman monuments and Roman earthworks.
     (3) English ecclesiastical monuments.
     (4) English secular monuments.
     (5) Unclassified monuments.

In addition to dwelling houses, the English secular class (4) includes all such earthworks as mount and bailey castles, homestead moats, etc. To the section of unclassified monuments (5) are assigned all undatable earthworks.

Each category of monuments has been under the care of separate Sub-Commissions.

The descriptions of the monuments are of necessity much compressed, but the underlying principle on which accounts of any importance are based is the same throughout.

In the first place, the Parish is located by letters in brackets which refer to the square where it is to be found in the map at the end of the volume; reference is also given where necessary to the Ordnance sheets (scale 6 inches to the mile) by small letters in front of the number of each monument. In the case of Churches. the description begins with a few words on the situation and material of the monument, together with a statement as to the development of its various parts. A second paragraph calls attention, when necessary, to its more remarkable features. This is followed by a concise description, mainly architectural, of its details. A fourth paragraph deals with the fittings in alphabetical order, while the concluding sentence gives a general statement as to structural condition. The accounts of less important buildings, whether secular or ecclesiastical, are still further compressed, and in the case of secular monuments consist of a single paragraph, or of a mere mention of their situation if they belong to a group with certain characteristics described in a covering paragraph.

The standardization of the spelling of proper names in the Commission's inventories has always presented considerable difficulties and almost any system is open to criticism. It is well known that during the period covered by our terms of reference, and indeed to a much later date, the art of spelling was in a very fluid state, proper names especially being subject to a wide variation, dictated partly by their phonetic values and partly by individual caprice. In the absence, therefore, of any final court of appeal, it has been thought best to abide, in the matter of place-names, by the spelling adopted by the Ordnance Survey, without prejudice as to its accuracy. In the matter of personal names, in treating of individual funeral monuments, etc., the actual spelling of the memorial has been reproduced, while in the rest of the text the normal spelling of the name has been adopted.

The illustrations are derived from photographs taken expressly for the Commission, and reproduced by H.M.'s Stationery Office, whose work, I think, deserves special recognition. They have been chosen both for their educational and for their æsthetic value. Had appearance alone been made the test of selection, many more might easily have been included. The map at the end of the Inventory shows the distribution of the monuments, and incidentally throws some light on the concentration of population in the county at various times before the year 1714.

To ensure clearness of description, all ancient churches not illustrated by historically hatched plans have been provided with key plans to a uniform scale of 48 feet to the inch, with the monumental portions shown in solid black. The dimensions given in the Inventory are internal unless otherwise stated.

It may also be well again to draw attention to the fact that our Record Cards may be consulted by any properly accredited persons who give notice of their intention to our Secretary, at 66, Victoria Street, Westminster, S.W.1. The cards contain drawings of tracery and mouldings as well as plans and sketches of the monuments—forming in truth the complete National Inventory—and will ultimately be deposited for reference in the Public Records Office.

As in the past, no monument has been or will be included in our Inventories that has not been actually inspected and the account checked in situ by a member of our own investigating staff. In a work of such intricate detail there must be mistakes. But I hope these are neither numerous nor serious. A further guarantee of accuracy lies in the fact that my fellow Commissioners Mr. Page and Mr. Peers have revised the reports of the Inventories of secular and ecclesiastical monuments, while Mr. Montgomerie has visited and supervised the reports on earthworks. Further, the heraldry of the Inventory has been checked by the Reverend E. E. Dorling, V.P.S.A. ;

the descriptions of armour by Mr. J. Murray Kendall, F.S.A. (Assistant to the Secretary of the Imperial War Museum) ; the descriptions of glass by Dr. M. R. James ; the description of brasses by Mr. Mill Stephenson, F.S.A. ; the spelling of names and descriptions of costumes by Mr. O. Barron, F.S.A. ; and the accounts of Roman monuments by Dr. R. E. Mortimer Wheeler, F.S.A. (Keeper of the Department of Archaeology in the Welsh National Museum). Nevertheless I shall welcome any corrections and criticisms that may be sent to me with a view to their possible inclusion in some future edition.

It is much to be regretted that, owing to the financial exigencies of the time, our staff has not yet been restored to its pre-war strength.

The success that has already attended the publication of the Commission's Inventories, and their value in securing the preservation of monuments of historical interest, that otherwise might have been destroyed, leads me to hope that the reduction of the work of investigation will be only temporary.

CRAWFORD AND BALCARRES.

7th May, 1923.

TERMS OF APPOINTMENT AND OFFICIAL REPORT.

WHITEHALL, 28TH OCTOBER, 1908.

The KING has been pleased to issue a Commission under His Majesty's Royal Sign Manual to the following effect :—

EDWARD, R. & I.

EDWARD THE SEVENTH, by the Grace of God, of the United Kingdom of Great Britain and Ireland and of the British Dominions beyond the Seas King, Defender of the Faith, to

Our right trusty and well-beloved Counsellor HERBERT COULSTOUN, BARON BURGHCLERE ;

Our right trusty and right well-beloved Cousin and Counsellor ROBERT GEORGE, EARL OF PLYMOUTH, Companion of Our Most Honourable Order of the Bath ;

Our right trusty and well-beloved Cousin HAROLD ARTHUR, VISCOUNT DILLON ; and

Our trusty and well-beloved :—

DAVID ALEXANDER EDWARD LINDSAY, Esquire, commonly called Lord Balcarres ;

SIR HENRY HOYLE HOWORTH, Knight Commander of Our Most Eminent Order of the Indian Empire, President of the Royal Archaeological Institute of Great Britain and Ireland ;

SIR JOHN FRANCIS FORTESCUE HORNER, Knight Commander of Our Royal Victorian Order ;

JAMES FITZGERALD, Esquire, Companion of the Imperial Service Order, Assistant Secretary in the Office of the Commissioners of Our Works and Public Buildings ;

JOHN GEORGE NEILSON CLIFT, Esquire, Honorary Secretary of the British Archaeological Association ;

FRANCIS JOHN HAVERFIELD, Esquire, Doctor of Laws, Camden Professor of Ancient History in the University of Oxford ;

EMSLIE JOHN HORNIMAN, Esquire ; and

LEONARD STOKES, Esquire, Vice-President of the Royal Institute of British Architects ;

GREETING !

Whereas We have deemed it expedient that a Commission should forthwith issue to make an inventory of the Ancient and Historical Monuments and Constructions connected with or illustrative of the contemporary culture, civilization and conditions of life of the people in England, excluding Monmouthshire, from the earliest times to the year 1700, and to specify those which seem most worthy of preservation :

Now know ye, that We, reposing great trust and confidence in your knowledge and ability, have authorized and appointed, and do by these Presents authorize and appoint you, the said Herbert Coulstoun, Baron Burghclere (Chairman) ; Robert George, Earl of Plymouth ; Harold Arthur, Viscount Dillon ; David Alexander Edward Lindsay (Lord Balcarres) ; Sir Henry Hoyle Howorth ; Sir John Francis Fortescue Horner ; James Fitzgerald ; John George Neilson Clift ; Francis John Haverfield ; Emslie John Horniman, and Leonard Stokes, to be Our Commissioners for the purposes of the said enquiry ;

And for the better enabling you to carry out the purposes of this Our Commission, We do by these Presents authorize you to call in the aid and co-operation of owners of ancient monuments, inviting them to assist you in furthering the objects of the Commission ; and to invite the possessors of such papers as you may deem it desirable to inspect to produce them before you.

And We do further give and grant unto you, or any three or more of you, full power to call before you such persons as you shall judge likely to afford you any information upon the subject of this Our Commission ; and also to call for, have access to and examine all such books, documents, registers and records as may afford you the fullest information on the subject, and to enquire of and concerning the premises by all other lawful ways and means whatsoever :

And We do by these Presents authorize and empower you, or any three or more of you, to visit and personally inspect such places as you may deem it expedient so to inspect for the more effectual carrying out of the purposes aforesaid :

And We do by these Presents will and ordain that this Our Commission shall continue in full force and virtue, and that you Our said Commissioners, or any three or more of you, may from time to time proceed in the execution thereof, and of every matter and thing therein contained, although the same be not continued from time to time by adjournment :

And We do further ordain that you, or any three or more of you, have liberty to report your proceedings under this our Commission from time to time if you shall judge it expedient so to do :

And Our further will and pleasure is that you do, with as little delay as possible, report to Us, under your hands and seals, or under the hands and seals of any three or more of you, your opinion upon the matters herein submitted for your consideration.

And for the purpose of aiding you in your enquiries We hereby appoint Our trusty and well-beloved George Herbert Duckworth, Esquire, to be Secretary to this Our Commission.

Given at Our Court at *St. James's* the twenty-seventh day of *October*, one thousand nine hundred and eight, in the eighth year of Our Reign.

By His Majesty's Command,

H. J. GLADSTONE.

EDWARD, R. & I.

Edward the Seventh, by the Grace of God, of the United Kingdom of Great Britain and Ireland and of the British Dominions beyond the Seas King, Defender of the Faith, To Our trusty and well-beloved Sir Schomberg Kerr McDonnell (commonly called the Honourable Sir Schomberg Kerr McDonnell), Knight Commander of Our Most Honourable Order of the Bath, Commander of Our Royal Victorian Order, Secretary to Our Commissioners of Works and Public Buildings,

GREETING !

Whereas We did by Warrant under Our Royal Sign Manual bearing date the twenty-seventh day of October, one thousand nine hundred and eight, appoint Commissioners to make an inventory of the Ancient and Historical Monuments and Constructions connected with or illustrative of the contemporary culture, civilization and conditions of life of the people in England, excluding Monmouthshire, from the earliest times to the year 1700, and to specify those which seem most worthy of preservation :

And Whereas a vacancy has been caused in the body of Commissioners appointed as aforesaid by the death of James Fitzgerald, Esquire :

Now know ye that We, reposing great confidence in you, do by these Presents appoint you the said Sir Schomberg Kerr McDonnell to be one of Our Commissioners for the purpose aforesaid, in the room of the said James Fitzgerald, deceased.

Given at Our Court at *St. James's*, the tenth day of *April*, 1909, in the ninth year of Our reign.

By His Majesty's Command,

H. J. GLADSTONE.

WHITEHALL, 30TH MAY, 1910.

The KING has been pleased to issue a Warrant under His Majesty's Royal Sign Manual to the following effect :—

GEORGE R. I.

GEORGE THE FIFTH, by the Grace of God, of the United Kingdom of Great Britain and Ireland and of the British Dominions beyond the Seas King, Defender of the Faith, to all to whom these Presents shall come,

GREETING !

Whereas it pleased His late Majesty from time to time to issue Royal Commissions of Enquiry for various purposes therein specified :—

And whereas, in the case of certain of these Commissions, namely; those known as—

The Ancient Monuments (England) Commission,

....

the Commissioners appointed by His late Majesty, or such of them as were then acting as Commissioners, were at the late Demise of the Crown still engaged upon the business entrusted to them :

And whereas we deem it expedient that the said Commissioners should continue their labours in connection with the said Enquiries notwithstanding the late Demise of the Crown :

Now know ye that We, reposing great trust and confidence in the zeal, discretion and ability of the present Members of each of the said Commissions, do by these Presents authorize them to continue their labours, and do hereby in every essential particular ratify and confirm the terms of the said several Commissions.

And We do further ordain that the said Commissioners do report to Us under their hands and seals, or under the hands and seals of such of their number as may be specified in the said Commissions respectively, their opinion upon the matters presented for their consideration ; and that any proceedings which they or any of them may have taken under and in pursuance of the said Commissions since the late Demise of the Crown and before the issue of these Presents shall be deemed and adjudged to have been taken under and in virtue of this Our Commission.

> Given at Our Court at *St. James's,* the twenty-sixth day of *May,* one thousand nine hundred and ten, in the first year of Our Reign.
>
> By His Majesty's Command,
>
> R. B. HALDANE.

GEORGE R. I.

GEORGE THE FIFTH, by the Grace of God, of the United Kingdom of Great Britain and Ireland and of the British Dominions beyond the Seas King, Defender of the Faith, to

Our right trusty and well-beloved Counsellor HERBERT COULSTOUN, BARON BURGHCLERE ;

Our right trusty and right well-beloved Cousin DAVID ALEXANDER EDWARD, EARL OF CRAWFORD ;

Our right trusty and right well-beloved Cousin and Counsellor ROBERT GEORGE, EARL OF PLYMOUTH, Companion of our Most Honourable Order of the Bath ;

Our right trusty and well-beloved Cousin HAROLD ARTHUR, VISCOUNT DILLON ; and

Our trusty and well-beloved :—

SIR SCHOMBERG KERR MCDONNELL (commonly called the Honourable Sir Schomberg Kerr McDonnell), Knight Grand Cross of Our Royal Victorian Order, Knight Commander of Our Most Honourable Order of the Bath ;

SIR HENRY HOYLE HOWORTH, Knight Commander of Our Most Eminent Order of the Indian Empire, President of the Royal Archaeological Institute of Great Britain and Ireland ;

SIR JOHN FRANCIS FORTESCUE HORNER, Knight Commander of Our Royal Victorian Order ;

JOHN GEORGE NEILSON CLIFT, Esquire, late Honorary Secretary of the British Archaeological Association ;

FRANCIS JOHN HAVERFIELD, Esquire, Doctor of Laws, Camden Professor of Ancient History in the University of Oxford ;

EMSLIE JOHN HORNIMAN, Esquire ; and

LEONARD STOKES, Esquire, Past President of the Royal Institute of British Architects ;

GREETING !

Whereas We have deemed it expedient that the proceedings of the Royal Commission on the Ancient and Historical Monuments and Constructions of England shall cover the period up to the year 1714, instead of up to the year 1700, and that a new Commission should issue for this purpose :

Now know ye that We have revoked and determined, and do by these Presents revoke and determine, the Warrants whereby Commissioners were appointed on the twenty-seventh day of October, one thousand nine hundred and eight, and the tenth day of April, one thousand nine hundred and nine, and every matter and thing therein contained.

And we do by these Presents authorize and appoint you, the said Herbert Coulstoun, Baron Burghclere (Chairman) ; David Alexander Edward, Earl of Crawford ; Robert George, Earl of Plymouth ; Harold Arthur, Viscount Dillon ; Sir Schomberg Kerr McDonnell ; Sir Henry Hoyle Howorth ; Sir John Francis Fortescue Horner ; John George Neilson Clift ; Francis John Haverfield ; Emslie John Horniman, and Leonard Stokes, to be Our Commissioners to make an inventory of the Ancient and Historical Monuments and Constructions connected with or illustrative of the contemporary culture, civilization and conditions of life of the people in England, excluding Monmouthshire, from the earliest times to the year 1714, and to specify those which seem most worthy of preservation.

And for the better enabling you to carry out the purposes of this Our Commission We do by these Presents authorize you to call in the aid and co-operation of owners of ancient monuments, inviting them to assist you in furthering the objects of the Commission ; and to invite the possessors of such papers as you may deem it desirable to inspect to produce them before you :

And We do further give and grant unto you, or any three or more of you, full power to call before you such persons as you shall judge likely to afford you any information upon the subject of this Our Commission ; and also to call for, have access to and examine all such books, documents, registers and records as may afford you the fullest information on the subject, and to enquire of and concerning the premises by all other lawful ways and means whatsoever :

And We do by these Presents authorize and empower you, or any three or more of you, to visit and personally inspect such places as you may deem it expedient so to inspect for the more effectual carrying out of the purposes aforesaid :

And We do by these Presents will and ordain that this Our Commission shall continue in full force and virtue, and that you, Our said Commissioners, or any three or more of you, may from time to time proceed in the execution thereof, and of every matter and thing therein contained, although the same be not continued from time to time by adjournment :

And We do further ordain that you, or any three or more of you, have liberty to report your proceedings under this Our Commission from time to time if you shall judge it expedient so to do :

And Our further will and pleasure is that you do, with as little delay as possible report to Us, under your hands and seals, or under the hands and seals of any three or more of you, your opinion upon the matters herein submitted for your consideration.

And for the purpose of aiding you in your enquiries We hereby appoint Our trusty and well-beloved George Herbert Duckworth, Esquire, to be Secretary to this our Commission.

Given at Our Court at *Saint James's*, the twenty-ninth day of *November*, one thousand nine hundred and thirteen, in the fourth year of Our Reign.

By His Majesty's Command,

R. McKENNA.

GEORGE R. I.

WHITEHALL, 11TH AUGUST, 1921.

The KING has been pleased to issue a Warrant under His Majesty's Royal Sign Manual to the following effect :—

GEORGE THE FIFTH, by the Grace of God, of the United Kingdom of Great Britain and Ireland and of the British Dominions beyond the Seas King, Defender of the Faith, to

Our trusty and well-beloved :—

SIR ARTHUR JOHN EVANS, Knight, Doctor of Letters, Doctor of Laws, Fellow of the Royal Society ;

SIR CHARLES HERCULES READ, Knight, Doctor of Laws, President of the Society of Antiquaries of London ;

MONTAGUE RHODES JAMES, Esquire, Doctor of Letters, Doctor of Laws, Provost of Eton College ;

DUNCAN HECTOR MONTGOMERIE, Esquire ;

WILLIAM PAGE, Esquire ; and

CHARLES REED PEERS, Esquire.

GREETING !

Know ye that We reposing great trust and confidence in your knowledge and ability do by these Presents appoint you the said Sir Arthur John Evans, Sir Charles Hercules Read, Montague Rhodes James, Duncan Hector Montgomerie, William Page and Charles Reed Peers to be members of the Royal Commission on Historical Monuments (England).

> Given at Our Court at *Saint James's*, the eighth day of *August*, one thousand nine hundred and twenty-one, in the twelfth year of Our Reign.

> By His Majesty's Command,

> EDWARD SHORTT.

ROYAL COMMISSION ON THE ANCIENT AND HISTORICAL
MONUMENTS AND CONSTRUCTIONS OF ENGLAND.

REPORT

TO THE KING'S MOST EXCELLENT MAJESTY.

1. May it please Your Majesty.

We, the undersigned Commissioners, appointed to make an Inventory of the Ancient and Historical Monuments and Constructions connected with or illustrative of the contemporary culture, civilization and conditions of life of the people in England, excluding Monmouthshire, from the earliest times to the year 1714, and to specify those which seem most worthy of preservation, humbly submit to Your Majesty the following Report on the Monuments in the S.E. Division of the County of Essex, being the 7th Interim Report on the work of the Commission since its appointment.

2. We tender to Your Majesty our respectful thanks for the gracious message which accompanied Your Majesty's acceptance of our Inventory of the Monuments in N.E. Essex.

3. It is with great regret that we place on record the sudden death of our Chairman, the Earl of Plymouth, Privy Councillor, Knight Grand Cross of the most excellent Order of the British Empire, Companion of the most honourable Order of the Bath, Lord Lieutenant of the County of Glamorgan, a Deputy Lieutenant of Worcestershire and of Shropshire, Sub-Prior of the Order of St. John of Jerusalem in England and a Trustee of the National Gallery, for whose wise direction and leadership the Commission since the death of our former Chairman, Lord Burghclere, owes a deep debt of gratitude.

We have also to record the severe loss suffered by the Commission through the death of Mr. R. P. L. Booker, M.A., F.S.A., who freely gave expert assistance to the Commission on all questions concerning Roman Monuments, and was primarily responsible for the Sections in Volume III (N.E. Essex) dealing with the important Roman remains in Colchester and its vicinity.

4. We have pleasure in reporting the completion of our enquiries into S.E. Essex, an area containing 658 monuments in 104 parishes, with an average of 6·3 monuments per parish. This Report is the fourth and concluding Report on the monuments of the county, and it is interesting to note that for the whole county the total number of monuments described in our illustrated Inventories amounts to 5,596 in 399

parishes, being an average of 15·5 per parish, which compares with averages of 24 monuments per parish in N.W. Essex (Volume I), 14·5 monuments in Central and S.W. Essex (Volume II), and 13 monuments per parish in N.E. Essex (Volume III).

5. Following our usual practice, we have prepared an illustrated volume containing the full Inventory of the monuments in the S.E. area of the county which, under the advice of the Lords Commissioners of Your Majesty's Treasury, will be issued as a separate Stationery Office publication.

6. No alteration has been found to be necessary in the order and method of describing the monuments scheduled. But, in view of the fact that Essex, Volume IV, is the concluding volume of a series which covers a most varied and interesting part of the country, we have added to the usual Sectional Preface dealing with S.E. Essex alone, a general review of the preceding volumes, with a statement calling attention to those monuments in the county, whether churches and their fittings, domestic monuments, Roman remains, or earthworks, that appear to be especially noteworthy.

We have also added a section in explanation of the types of monuments that are characteristic of the dates to which they have been assigned.

7. We desire to draw attention to the fact that our colleague, Mr. Page, is responsible for that part of the General Review which deals with Saxon and Danish times, while Mr. R. E. Mortimer Wheeler, M.C., D.Lit., F.S.A., is responsible for the sections dealing with Roman Essex, and Mr. A. W. Clapham, F.S.A., for the comparative review of the Mediaeval monuments and the description of the types of houses that are characteristic of the periods to which they belong.

The illustrations, which have throughout been selected for their educational as well as for their artistic value, are principally the work of one of our Senior Investigators, Mr. J. W. Bloe, F.S.A. We desire to congratulate him on the skill with which the difficulties inherent in taking photographs in places which are ill-lighted and from angles that demand almost acrobatic feats on the part of the photographer have been overcome, as well as for the skill in the selection of monuments for the comparative groups which are a feature of the Essex Inventories.

9. The index to this volume has again been the subject of special attention, and has been combined with the indices of previous volumes in such a way that in itself it forms a complete reference index to the monuments of the county. In view of the great accuracy required and the arduous nature of the work, we desire to express our special acknowledgments to Miss M. G. Saunders, a member of our executive staff, who has been primarily responsible for its compilation.

10. As in the previous volumes, the descriptions of monuments have been referred for revision to the incumbents of each parish, to special representatives of the Essex Archaeological Society, and to the principal owners of domestic buildings, and we are satisfied that no important monument dating from the earliest times to the year 1714 has been omitted. We have also inserted in this volume certain corrections and additions that have come to light as we passed from one part of the county to another.

11. Our special thanks are due to the Rev. Canon F. W. Galpin, M.A., President of the Essex Archaeological Society, to Mr. H. W. Lewer, F.S.A., to the

Rev. G. Montagu Benton, M.A., F.S.A., to Mr. C. F. D. Sperling and to the Rev. W. J. Pressey, M.A., for the time and trouble that they have devoted to checking the records of Church Plate and fittings contained in the four Essex volumes.

12. We humbly recommend to Your Majesty's notice the following monuments in S.E. Essex as " especially worthy of preservation " : —

EARTHWORKS AND ROMAN :—

2. ASHELDHAM.

(2) CAMP; a plateau camp with a mound on the line of the rampart.
Condition—Bad.

8. BRADWELL-JUXTA-MARE.

(1) FORT, probably OTHONA; remains of a Roman fort of the " Saxon Shore " type.
Condition—Poor, partly destroyed by the sea.

20. DANBURY.

(10) CAMP; a hill-top camp with a mound within the defences.
Condition—Bad.

67. PRITTLEWELL.

(13) CAMP; a plateau camp with a mound on the line of the rampart.
Condition—Bad.

73. RAYLEIGH.

(2) CASTLE; a mount and bailey castle, with strong defences.
Condition—Good.

84. SOUTH SHOEBURY.

(4) CAMP; remains of a fortified enclosure, probably that thrown up by the Danish leader Hasten c. 894.
Condition—Poor, partly destroyed by the sea.

101. WEST TILBURY.

(8) EARTHWORK; remains of works, perhaps of three periods.
Condition—Imperfect.

ECCLESIASTICAL :—

8. BRADWELL-JUXTA-MARE.

(3) CHAPEL OF ST. PETER-ON-THE-WALL; almost certainly the church built by Bishop Cedd in c. 654 at Ithancester.
Condition—Good.

17. CORRINGHAM.

(1) PARISH CHURCH; possibly dating from before the Conquest, with a good late 11th-century West Tower.
Condition—Good.

20. DANBURY.

(1) PARISH CHURCH; dating from the 13th century or earlier, with three oak effigies.
Condition—Good.

26. EAST TILBURY.

(2) PARISH CHURCH; dating from the 12th century; damaged by the Dutch fleet in 1667.
Condition—Good, some of the external stonework much decayed.

27. EASTWOOD.

(1) PARISH CHURCH; dating from the 12th century, with fine iron-work on door and 12th-century font.
Condition—Fairly good, but roofs defective.

31. GREAT BADDOW.

(1) PARISH CHURCH; dating from the 13th century, with good early 16th century brickwork.
Condition—Good.

33. GREAT STAMBRIDGE.

(1) PARISH CHURCH; dating probably from before the Conquest.
Condition—Good, much ivy on tower.

34. GREAT WAKERING.

(2) PARISH CHURCH; dating from c. 1100, with curious two-storeyed W. porch.
Condition—Fairly good, some stonework much decayed.

36. HADLEIGH.

(1) PARISH CHURCH; dating from the 12th century, with apsidal E. end and remains of paintings.
Condition—Good.

41. HORNCHURCH.

(1) PARISH CHURCH; dating from the 13th century, with a good 15th-century W. tower and some interesting brasses and monuments.
Condition—Structurally good, some of the stonework perished.

53. LITTLE WAKERING.

(1) PARISH CHURCH; dating from the 12th century and with a good W. tower of c. 1425.
Condition—Good.

56. MOUNTNESSING.

(1) Parish Church; dating from the 12th and 13th centuries, with remarkable timber-work to the bell-turret.
Condition—Good, largely rebuilt.

62. NORTH OCKENDON.

(1) Parish Church; dating from the 12th century, with good monuments and glass.
Condition—Good.

64. ORSETT.

(1) Parish Church; dating from the 12th century, with good detail, monument and pulpit.
Condition—Good.

67. PRITTLEWELL.

(1) Parish Church; dating from the 12th century, with a good 15th-century W. tower.
Condition—Good.

69. RAINHAM.

(1) Parish Church; dating from the second half of the 12th century, with good detail.
Condition—Good.

74. RETTENDON.

(1) Parish Church; dating from late in the 12th century, with good carved bench-ends and enriched 12th-century slab.
Condition—Good.

78. SANDON.

(1) Parish Church; dating from the 12th century, and with good early 16th-century brickwork; the piscina, communion table and pulpit are also of interest.
Condition—Good.

80. SOUTH BENFLEET.

(1) Parish Church; dating from the 12th century, with a very rich 15th-century roof to the S. porch.
Condition—Poor (recently repaired).

83. SOUTH OCKENDON.

(1) Parish Church; dating from the 12th century, with rich detail, a round tower and good brass.
Condition.—Good.

90. STOCK.

(1) Parish Church; dating from the 14th century or earlier, with a fine timber belfry of the 15th century.
Condition—Good, much restored.

100. WEST THURROCK.

Parish Church; dating from the 12th century, with foundations of former round nave.
Condition—Fairly good.

103. WOODHAM FERRERS.

(2) Bicknacre Priory; one 13th-century arch of the crossing of the Priory Church.
Condition—Good.

SECULAR :—

4. AVELEY.

(6) Belhus; a fairly large early 16th-century brick house with a courtyard, subsequently much altered and enlarged.
Condition—Good.

31. GREAT BADDOW.

(3) Great Sir Hughes; part of a larger early 17th-century house with a richly ornamented loggia.
Condition—Poor.

36. HADLEIGH.

(2) Castle; rebuilt in the 14th century, with extensive ruins of the curtain and other towers.
Condition—Ruinous, and in part dangerous.

41. HORNCHURCH.

(3) Nelmes; house dating from late in the 17th century, with very handsome carved staircase.
Condition—Good.

50. LITTLE BURSTEAD.

(4) Hatches Farm; a late 16th-century house with very good early 16th-century carved panelling.
Condition—Good.

54. LITTLE WARLEY.

(2) Hall; a 16th-century brick house with a good chimney-stack and staircase.
Condition—Good, except W. wall.

67. PRITTLEWELL.

(2) Priory; dating from late in the 12th century, remains of a Cluniac Priory.
Condition—Good.

(3) Porters; a complete 16th-century house of brick.
Condition—Good.

75. ROCHFORD.

(2) Hall; remains, partly ruined, of a very large 16th-century house of brick and rubble.
Condition—Poor, partly ruinous.

76. RUNWELL.

(2) FLEMING'S FARM; a fragment of a brick house of *c.* 1600.

Condition—Good.

89. STIFFORD.

(2) FORD PLACE; a 17th-century house with rich plaster ceilings.

Condition—Good.

98. WEST HANNINGFIELD.

(2) MEETING HOUSE; a much-restored house with extensive 17th-century painted decoration on plaster.

Condition—Good.

101. WEST TILBURY.

(3) TILBURY FORT; a late 17th-century stone gatehouse.

Condition—Good, but unequal settlement may cause trouble.

13. We offer our grateful thanks to the Rev. E. E. Dorling, V.P.S.A., for revision of the descriptions of Heraldry; to Mr. Oswald Barron, F.S.A., for revision of the descriptions of Costumes and spelling of names; to Mr. Mill Stephenson, F.S.A., for revision of descriptions of Brasses; to Mr. J. Murray Kendall, M.B.E., F.S.A., for revision of the descriptions of Armour; to Mr. R. E. Mortimer Wheeler, M.C., D.Lit., F.S.A., for revision of descriptions of Roman Remains; to Mr. Albany Major, O.B.E., F.S.A., Secretary to the Committee on Ancient Earthworks and Fortified Enclosures, for revision of the accounts of Earthworks; and to Mr. F. S. Eden for his descriptions and illustrations of the Ancient Glass in the county.

14. We desire again to call attention to the assistance given to our work by the Secretary (The Rev. T. H. Curling, M.A.) and members of the Essex Archaeological Society. We have also to thank the Bishop of Chelmsford for his letter of introduction to the clergy in his diocese, and the clergy who have freely opened their churches for investigation; and we have pleasure in acknowledging the hospitality extended to our staff by the clergy and owners of houses in the county.

15. We desire to express our acknowledgment of the good work accomplished by our Executive Staff in the persons of Mr. A. W. Clapham, F.S.A., Mr. J. W. Bloe, F.S.A., Mr. E. A. R. Rahbula, F.S.A., Mr. W. Byde Liebert, Mr. G. E. Chambers, F.S.A., Mr. M. L. Logan, Mr. P. K. Kipps and Miss M. G. Saunders; also by Miss M. V. Taylor, M.A., who has investigated the Roman Remains of this portion of the County of Essex.

16. We regret exceedingly that owing to loss of staff and its continued non-replacement owing to Treasury ruling, and, *a fortiori*, to the refusal to entertain any immediate prospect of its extension, it has not been possible to go forward with the pre-war intention of the Commission to train and place senior investigators in charge of separate counties or divisions of counties with competent staffs under them to report the results of their enquiries to a central office in London for final editing and publication; and, in addition, that it has been found necessary, in order still further to restrict expenditure on travel and subsistence, to postpone our proposed survey of Lincolnshire and confine our investigations in the immediate future to the counties of London and Middlesex.

17. The succeeding Inventories of the Commission will therefore deal in three volumes with the County of London, including the Cities of London and Westminster and the County of Middlesex.

18. In conclusion we desire to add that our Secretary, Mr. George H. Duckworth, C.B., F.S.A., has continued to afford invaluable and unremitting assistance to us, your Commissioners.

All of which we submit with our humble duty to Your Majesty.

Signed :

CRAWFORD & BALCARRES (*Chairman*).
DILLON.
HENRY H. HOWORTH.
J. F. F. HORNER.
J. G. N. CLIFT.
E. J. HORNIMAN.
LEONARD STOKES.
ARTHUR EVANS.
C. HERCULES READ.
M. R. JAMES.
D. H. MONTGOMERIE.
WILLIAM PAGE.
C. R. PEERS.

GEORGE H. DUCKWORTH,
Secretary.

21st March 1923.

GENERAL SURVEY OF ESSEX MONUMENTS.

PREHISTORIC AND ROMAN.

Essex has yielded a rich harvest of finds of the prehistoric era, but contains few structural remains which can with certainty be referred to pre-Roman times. Of the burial mounds which have survived the plough, those that have been scientifically opened and recorded are, for the most part, of the Roman period. In regard to the 'camps' our information is even more scanty; slight excavations have been carried out in the earthworks of Epping Upland and Loughton with inconclusive results, and it cannot be claimed that the casual discoveries of much Roman pottery in Uphall Camp, Great Ilford, throw any light on the date of that earthwork. It is a reasonable conjecture that some of the long lines at Colchester belong to the time when, under Cunobelinus, who died shortly after A.D. 40, Colchester was in effect the capital of south-eastern Britain. Here history, however, begins to supplement archaeology, and later, in connection with the camp at Shoeburyness and with the Burghs of Witham and Maldon, written records become increasingly circumstantial.

Shortly before the advent of Julius Caesar, the close inter-relationship inevitable at almost all periods between south-eastern Britain and the opposite shores of the Continent had been intensified by a renewed migration from north-eastern Gaul. Caesar states that in the districts near the coast he found people who had come over from Belgium to plunder and wage war, almost all of them being called by the names of the tribes from which they had first come thither. The first part of this statement is apparently supported by the distribution of certain distinctive types of pottery (notably, the pedestal-urn) which occur, with variations, in the valleys of the Seine and Marne, and, on this side of the Channel, mainly in Essex, Kent and Hertfordshire. When this pottery first reached Britain is not clear, but it was in use in the 1st century B.C., and the pedestal-urn itself, and its associated types, seem to have survived the Claudian invasion. The second part of Caesar's statement presents more difficulty; tribal names such as Atrebates, Catuvellauni and Parisii occur on both sides of the Channel, but the British Parisii lay to the N. of the pedestal-urn zone, and there seems to be no definite evidence that the Atrebates had reached this country before the invasion of Caesar. On the other hand, the distribution of the pedestal-urns in Gaul has been shown, by Mr. J. P. Bushe-Fox, to equate with the tribal area or sphere of influence of the Catalauni, and in his opinion, the distribution in this country forms an index to the extent of the occupation and influence of the same tribe (here called the Catuvellauni) shortly before and after the time of Caesar's expedition.

Other links between the two shores both before and after the Claudian conquest are important. The mysterious 'Red Hills' are found on the coasts both of Essex and of Brittany; and in Essex one of these contained a piece of Arretine ware, which probably came from the Continent at a time when discarded amphorae of Roman (or Mediterranean) origin found their way into pre-Roman graves between Colchester and Lexden. Much of the pre-Roman coinage found in Britain is now attributed to Gaulish mints; and the connection thus implied with the Continent was not weakened when, at the beginning of our era, British kings such as Tasciovanus and Cunobelinus produced their own currency with Latin inscriptions and even through the instrumentality of Roman moneyers. One of these coins, bearing the names CUNO(BELINUS) and CAMU(LODUNUM), displays an ear of corn and is reminiscent of the prosperity of agriculture in south-eastern Britain, both when Julius Caesar was able to supply his troops from the standing crops of Kent, and when, in the time of Strabo and in that of Ammianus Marcellinus, Britain was exporting corn to the Continent. Finally, the large 1st and 2nd-century burial-mounds of Ashdon (Bartlow Hills), West Mersea, and, possibly, Colchester (Lexden), Hockley and Foulness, together with other examples in Kent, are to be compared with those which in the same period were raised over the ashes of Belgic nobles in the neighbourhood of Bavai, Tongres and elsewhere in the continental Belgic area. It is indeed worthy of remark that, though these identical burials on both sides of the Channel clearly indicate a common native tradition, analogies of immediately pre-Roman date appear to be lacking. The pedestal-urn burials had not been marked by mounds, and the evidence of the tumuli in question has not yet been correlated with that of the pedestal-pottery.

In the generation preceding the Claudian invasion, the intrigues which, with occasional interference from Rome, had for years been carried on amongst the princelings of south-eastern Britain and their kinsfolk on the Continent, culminated in the hegemony of the Trinovantes under the famous Cunobelinus, described later by Suetonius as " Britannorum rex.' The tribal area of the Trinovantes coincided roughly with Essex and part of Middlesex, but the King himself was of the dynasty of the neighbouring Catuvellauni, whose capital was Verulamium (St. Albans), and history throws little light on the transfer of the seat of the Government from St. Albans to Colchester. As the native capital, Colchester became, in A.D. 43, the first goal of the invading legions, the official centre of the imperial cult, and (then or shortly afterwards) the converging point of at least two main roads. About A.D. 50 a colony was planted there, and, soon after the disasters which followed ten years later, the town was probably walled and assumed its permanent plan. With its 108 acres, it ranks in area considerably below several Romano-British towns, such as London, Wroxeter, Verulamium, Cirencester, and possibly Winchester. Its buildings, however, were commensurate with the status of the first Roman colony in the province, including, as they did, the Balkerne Gate and the vaulted sub-structure (? of a temple) under the Castle, buildings so far unparalleled, both in form and size, elsewhere in Britain. Moreover, in the neighbourhood of Colchester, West Mersea provides the foundations of a mausoleum which is equally without analogy in this country.

After the dramatic events of the 1st century, Colchester fades from Roman history. In fact, if not in name, York and London became respectively the military and the commercial headquarters of the province, and Colchester devolved into a prosperous country town, probably with a moderate foreign trade, but sufficiently far from the coast to stand aloof both from its immediate perils and from its responsibilities. To the period of the later Empire belongs the fort at Bradwell-juxta-Mare, a typical representative of the defensive works developed under Diocletian and Constantine I. It might be expected that Colchester would serve to some extent as a base-town for this new maritime frontier-system. But the forts established or reorganized under the Count of the Saxon Shore, unlike those of the earlier *limites*, were not based upon elaborate internal communications and permanent garrisons in reserve. In their case, supplies of men and provisions seem rather to have been carried coastwise, and the base-fortress was replaced (at least in intent) by a mobile field-force under the Count of Britain, who must also have relied partly upon sea-transport in case of emergency.

The Roman occupation of Essex seems to have led to no important displacement of the native·population. In the vicinity of Colchester, and in the north-western quarter of the county from Colchester to the Cambridgeshire border, country-houses of Roman provincial type sprang up immediately after the conquest, and were in many cases occupied probably by the wealthier of the natives, who were ready enough to submit to that Romanization which Tacitus calls "a part of their servitude.' The very remarkable richness of the contents of the burial-mounds at Ashdon (Bartlow Hills), already referred to, testifies to the prosperity of some of these native land-owners within the century following the conquest. In the same regions, apart from the Colony itself, a small walled town at Great Chesterford, and perhaps still smaller settlements at Chelmsford (? Caesaromagus), Brightlingsea and West Mersea are the only indications of anything approaching urban or village life. For the rest, the poorer natives seem to have continued to live in huts of their traditional type and to have carried on their industries, especially pottery-making, on the sites similarly used by their pre-Roman ancestors. At East Tilbury, the Thames mud has actually preserved the stumps of circular wooden huts occupied in the 1st, 2nd, and possibly the 3rd centuries A.D. At Great Burstead the trenches cut apparently by pre-Roman potters in search of clay were occupied by kilns built in the Roman manner but tended doubtless by the native workmen ; and at Shoeburyness a similar continuity seems to be indicated by kilns associated with Roman and pre-Roman pottery.

Apart from the remains of a 'villa' at Wanstead, no certain traces of any more highly civilized occupation are recorded in the southern half of the county. Towards the west, dense woodland must have obstructed agriculture and settle-ment. Towards the south-east, the low-lying marshlands, though shown by the sub-mergence of Red Hills, of the East Tilbury fort, and of part of the Bradwell fort to have been higher in Roman times than now, can have offered little attraction for settlement on any elaborate scale. In this respect the Essex shore differs markedly from that of Kent, where the remains of comfortable 'villas' are found in considerable numbers. It is probable, indeed, that the embanking and draining of some of the low lands bordering upon the Thames was begun by the Romans—Southwark, for example, was almost certainly protected by a series of dykes at this period. But the absence of buildings of Roman type from the Essex flats renders it tolerably certain that no attempt on any extensive scale was made by the Romans to reclaim them. It has been pointed out that certain low-lying settlements of early Norman date, such as West Thurrock, seem to imply the pre-existence of dykes, and that these are far less likely to have been built then than in Roman times ; but it must be remembered that the gradual lowering has very considerably aggravated the necessity for such protective measures.

In summary, it may be remarked that Essex is singularly representative of all phases of Romano-British life ; it contains a military site, two arterial roads, a town of colonial and at least one of inferior rank, several country houses of fully Romanized type, and some of the wattle huts, preserved by an unusual accident, of the simple peasantry who must have formed a large element in the population of the country.

R. E. M. WHEELER.

ANGLO-SAXON AND DANISH.

The change from Roman to Saxon rule is perhaps more obscure in Essex than in other parts of England. It might well be expected that the estuary of the Thames would form a safe and convenient haven for the disembarkation of the early Saxon immigrants, but if they used its northern shore, they passed on inland without leaving any distinct evidence of their presence. One reason, no doubt, for the sparse settle-ment of the district during the century or more after the withdrawal of the Roman legions was that much of the country was forest and marsh, unsuitable for the early settlers, who were agriculturists. The early Saxon cemeteries which have been discovered at Broomfield and Feering and the Saxon burials around Colchester are probably late in the pagan period of the Saxon settlement and may perhaps be assigned to the first half of the 7th century. They therefore throw little light on the subject. The villages of Essex are chiefly of a type which is considered Teutonic in origin, but their prevalence gives no precise date for their formation. This type, however, is interesting as explaining the lay-out of many of the villages in the county at the present day. The original settlement of this kind stands a little way off the high road surrounded by its territories which formed its open common fields. At one end of the village is the manor-house, adjoining which the lord in the 11th century built the church. In frequent instances the inhabitants migrated to the roadside to obtain the benefit of the traffic, and here a new village arose. Sometimes this migration has been so complete that the church has been left isolated.

No structural monuments of the East Saxons belonging to the period before their conversion to Christianity survive. In 604 St. Augustine sent Mellitus to convert them and to be their first bishop. Their conversion, however, at this time seems to have been merely formal and they soon returned to paganism. They were reconverted some fifty years later, when, in 654, Cedd, brother of St. Chad, was consecrated their bishop. To evangelize the country, according to the custom of the time, Cedd established two monasteries in Essex, in which he placed monks who went forth to preach the Gospel. One of these monasteries was founded at West Tilbury, of which no trace remains, and the other at Ithancester, the Roman station of Othona, the church of which has been identified with the chapel of St. Peter-on-the-Wall at Bradwell-juxta-Mare (*post*, p. 15). This chapel is one of the few examples existing in this country of a 7th-century church and is therefore of peculiar interest. It takes its name from its position on the site of the wall of the Roman fort and was almost wholly constructed from the Roman tiles and other materials found within the fort. Its original plan was of a type usually to be met with in Kent, and consisted of a sanctuary, formed by an apse, and a small oblong nave with western porch and possibly a porticus on the north and south sides. The chapel was for a long time used as a chapel-of-ease to the parish church and hence its preservation. For a time, however, it was desecrated and used as a barn, until it was recently restored to its original use after having been put in a condition of excellent repair. Erkenwald, bishop of the East Saxons, founded a monastery at Barking in 666 for the benefit of his sister Ethelburga ; and by tradition St. Osyth, granddaughter of Penda, established a monastery about 683 at Chich St. Osyth. Nothing remains of either of these churches, both of which were doubtless obliterated by the later buildings which arose on the sites.

At this early date London was the chief town of the East Saxons and the residence of their King and bishop. Its wealth attracted the cupidity of the Danish raiders in the 9th and 10th centuries, whose approach to it was through Essex. Hence the county was constantly devastated and there can be little doubt that many of the churches were robbed and destroyed by the pagan hosts from Denmark and Scandinavia. The monasteries of Barking and St. Osyth are said to have been then attacked and deserted, and a similar fate no doubt befell the other religious houses of the county. Thus for lengthy periods the organized services of the Church were interrupted and church building ceased. Unlike their treatment of the Danelagh, the Danes made few settlements in Essex ; it was to them merely a camping ground and a place of refuge when their hosts were hard pressed in other parts of the country. In this way they made use of many of the fortified enclosures of masonry and earth which they found ready to hand, for they had a much higher appreciation of the protective qualities of such forts than their opponents. They repaired the fortifications of the Roman walled towns and adapted the early camps to the more modern methods of warfare. In the opinion of the late Mr. Chalkley Gould, they utilized and altered the earlier camps of Wallbury in Great Hallingbury and Danbury and the entrenchments at Uphall near Barking (*V.C.H. Essex*, I, 281-3, 289). Earthworks at Benfleet and Shoebury, however, were thrown up as Danish forts. In 894 the Danes were defeated by King Alfred at Farnham in Kent, when they fled to an island in the Colne and thence to South Benfleet. Here Hasten built a fort, indications of the site of which still survive (*post*, p. 139). The Danes were again defeated here by the English army, which had been reinforced from London. The English took much booty and sent what Danish ships they could to London and burnt the rest. Charred remains have been found at Benfleet which it is suggested represent the Danish ships then destroyed. The survivors of this engagement fled to Shoebury where they threw up another fort, of which the remains of the earthen defences still survive (*post,* p. 144). This camp was probably of a more permanent character, for we learn from the Anglo-Saxon Chronicle that it served again as a place of refuge later in the same year. In 895 the Danes established themselves in Mersea Island, but no recognizable trace of their residence can be identified, nor can any remains be found on the east side of the Lea of the forts built there in the same year when the Danes were again compelled to abandon their ships.

 The Danes had taught the English the value of earthworks as a means of defence. During his long campaign against the Danes at the beginning of the 10th century, Edward the Elder spent some time in Essex carrying out his scheme for the erection of 'burhs' or forts throughout the country. In 913 he was at Maldon superintending the building of the ' burh ' at Witham, some fragmentary remains of which survive (*Essex*, II, p. 265). In 920 he visited Maldon again, where he built a ' burh,' of which no trace remains (*Essex*, II, p. 173) ; possibly it was destroyed after its capture from the Danes in 991.

 As might well be expected, no buildings belonging to this long unsettled period have survived in Essex to be scheduled in this Report. Houses for domestic use must have been erected to meet a periodical demand, but they were of an unsubstantial character only intended to meet the needs of the moment. It is unlikely that any churches would have been built at a time when they were the chief objects for plunder by pagan raiders. It was not until the religious revival in the latter part of the 10th century and the gradual conversion of the Danes and Northmen to Christianity that the building of churches commenced. The great era of church building began in the 11th century. Except the chapel of St. Peter-on-the-Wall at Bradwell-juxta-Mare, all the remains of pre-Conquest churches recorded in Essex probably belong to the fifty or sixty years preceding the Conquest. The entries in Domesday of priests and churches, which by no means form a complete summary of the total number of priests and churches in the county, indicate that in 1086 there was a considerable number of churches the majority of which were probably in existence before the Conquest.

 In a county which produces little building-stone probably most of the churches were originally built of wood and this may account for the scarcity of Saxon work which has survived. The timber-built churches would be replaced by stone structures in the latter part of the 11th and during the 12th century—whereby all traces of the earlier building would be lost. We are fortunate in having one example left us of a primitive timber structure. The church of Greensted (by Ongar), which it has been suggested is the wooden chapel (*lignea capella*) built in 1013 as a resting place for the body of St. Edmund on its way from London to St. Edmundsbury (Dugdale, *Mon.*

Angl., iii, 99n, 139), still retains its nave of split oak logs. It is in good preservation and forms an excellent and perhaps unique example in this country of a timber church of its date. Probably it indicates a method of construction commonly used both for ecclesiastical and domestic purposes in the early part of the 11th century.

The remaining pre-Conquest churches of the 11th century are all of masonry or of brick taken from some Roman site not far distant from the spot when the church was built. The most important is the cruciform church of Hadstock (*Essex*, I, p. 143) that has been identified with the minster ' of stone and lime ' which Cnut built in 1020 in memory of those who fell in the battle of ' Assandun,' where he obtained a victory over Edmund Ironside. The nave and north transept of the pre-Conquest church survive, but the chancel and south transept have been rebuilt, and the central tower, which probably formed a part of the original church, fell and was not built up again.

Most of the Saxon churches in Essex belong, however, to the type described in Professor Baldwin Brown's classification as consisting in plan of an oratory or nave with a rectangular chancel. Examples of this type of church are scattered over the county ; they are not confined to any particular district, for their survival is only a matter of chance. They may have been better built than others and so did not require to be rebuilt, or no pious benefactor arose who desired to leave his mark upon his parish church. The principal instances of this type of church are at Chickney (*Essex*, I, p. 62) and Inworth (*Essex*, III, pp. 138–9). The nave of Strethall church (*Essex*, I, p. 295) is a particularly interesting example of a date a little before the middle of the 11th century and the Saxon chancel-arch remains in good condition. Sturmer (*Essex*, I, p. 297) has a nave of about the same date as that at Strethall. At Corringham (*post*, p. 25), parts of the south walls of the chancel and nave are of pre-Conquest date, and at Great Stambridge (*post*, p. 58) the north walls of the chancel and nave contain work of the same period. The thinness of the north wall of the nave of Fobbing church (*post*, p. 44) suggests a pre-Conquest date, and indications of early work at the west end of the north wall of Wethersfield church (*Essex*, I, p. 332) may perhaps assign the original church to a like period.

Little Bardfield church (*Essex*, I, pp. 170–1), with its contemporary western tower, is a development of the same type. Its chancel has been rebuilt, but the nave with its windows in the north and south walls and north doorway, all now blocked, is original. The western tower is a good example of a fine 11th-century tower of five stages, the three upper stages having their original round-headed windows. Another example of a pre-Conquest western tower is to be found at Holy Trinity Church, Colchester (*Essex*, III, pp. 33–5). This tower is of three stages and is an addition to a pre-Conquest church of which only a small portion of the west wall remains. It is typically tall and slender and a contrast to the bolder design of Little Bardfield tower of about the same date.

Two further monasteries were founded towards the close of the Anglo-Saxon period, Mersea, a cell of St. Ouen at Rouen, by Edward the Confessor in 1046, and the famous minster at Waltham by Harold in 1060. At neither of them, however, are there any structural remains of a date definitely before the Conquest.

Only four stones with incised ornament of the pre-Conquest period are known to have been discovered in Essex. The earliest is a fragment of the shaft of a cross found built into the churchyard wall at Barking and now preserved in the church. It is ornamented on all four sides with plaits of true Anglian tradition which Mr. W. G. Collingwood, F.S.A., says are more elaborate than any he knows of before 870 and much more ingenious and regular than those of the 11th century. He attributes the date of the stone to the time of Edgar. It may well be that the cross was set up when

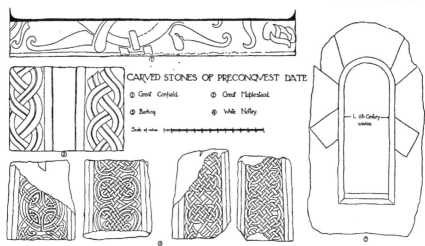

CARVED STONES OF PRECONQVEST DATE

① Great Canfield   ② Great Maplestead

③ Barking   ④ White Notley.

Scale of inches

the Abbey of Barking was restored by Edgar and Archbishop Dunstan about 970, after its destruction by the Danes a century before. Another stone at White Notley church has been used in the construction of a late 11th-century window in the north vestry. It was apparently part of a headstone and may be of the 10th century. It has some analogies with the pre-Conquest headstone at Whitchurch, Hants, and with a stone at Hexham. At Great Canfield church is a stone forming the abacus to the capital of the respond to the chancel-arch, upon the upper surface of which is zoomorphic ornament in low relief, of Danish workmanship. Its position prevents a complete examination of the ornament as a part of it is hidden by being bedded into the wall. It is probably a sepulchral stone of the early part of the 11th century, and closely resembles the Toui stone in St. Paul's Cathedral Library. The fourth carved stone was found not long ago on a rockery at Great Maplestead and has now been placed in the church. It was evidently part of a coped coffin-lid having a plain fillet running down the centre and sunk panels with interlaced ornament in relief on either side. When perfect the ridge would have formed a cross. It belongs probably to the end of the Saxon period and Mr. Collingwood would place it after the Conquest.

On the whole, Essex is not rich in Anglo-Saxon monuments. Danish influence, which for some time was strong, was destructive rather than constructive.

W. PAGE.

ARCHITECTURE : COMPARATIVE REVIEW.

The completion of the Commission's investigation of the County of Essex provides a suitable opportunity for a general review of the county as a unit and also of the methods and principles which are the foundation of the Commission's system of dating. A county, and more especially a large county like Essex, is in area sufficiently extensive to make a series of deductions from the information collected about its monuments a useful contribution to the study of comparative architecture and archaeology, though at the same time care has to be taken not to make the application too general.

The system of dating mediaeval, and, to a less extent, Renaissance architecture is, of course, primarily based on a series of examples all over the country of which the period or year of erection is recorded either in contemporary documents or on the buildings themselves, the vast majority of such buildings being of the class which comprises cathedrals, monastic and collegiate churches, castles and the larger houses of the country. The precise date of a parish church or small manor-house has been in too few instances preserved, and it is often dangerous to argue by analogy from the town to the country parish, from the main currents of contemporary life and thought to the backwaters, where new ideas may have taken long to penetrate. In the absence therefore of definite historical evidence, other tests have to be applied and it has been found that the character of the mouldings, the window-tracery and other ornamental details are the surest guides to the date of a building, though when these also fail, recourse must be had to such indications as may be provided by proportions of plan, thickness of walls and character of masonry.

Our investigations have shown that the pre-Conquest work of the county is probably nearly all of the later Saxon period, that is, they belong to the last 100 years of Saxon or Danish rule. The only exception is the chapel of St. Peter-on-the-Wall, Bradwell-juxta-Mare, which belongs architecturally to the class of church built in the early years of Saxon Christianity and of which the distinguishing features are the apsidal chancel, the triple arcade between the chancel and nave, the presence of rectangular 'porticus' (used as porches and chapels), and a relatively high level of constructional ability.

The later Saxon building has far less marked characteristics, though in Essex such characteristics are very uniform and not difficult to recognize. The plan generally is marked by an entire lack of care in setting out and the angles are seldom right-angles; the proportions of the nave are commonly rather less than two squares,* and the walls are, in nearly all the recorded instances, less than 3 feet thick, the average being about 2½ feet. The walls are always of rubble, and most frequently the quoins and dressings are of rubble also, but of rather larger stones than the rest of the wall. Long and short work, that is to say, freestone quoins placed alternately horizontally and on end, and generally accepted as a distinctive feature of late pre-Conquest work, is but little represented in the county, the only definite example being at Strethall. The windows are commonly of the double splay type, that is to say, the actual aperture (or plane represented in later ages by the glass-line) is placed more or less centrally in the thickness of the wall with equally splayed reveals both inside and out. This feature is exemplified at Holy Trinity, Colchester, Hadstock, Chickney, Strethall, Inworth and Little Bardfield, but is not present in the undoubted pre-Conquest work of Little Bardfield tower. Post-Conquest examples of double-splay windows occasionally occur, though not in Essex, but they are almost always in conjunction with detail which leaves no doubt as to their later date. Another pre-Conquest feature is found in the absence of a rebate or door-check on the jambs of the doorways, of which there is an example at Holy Trinity, Colchester, in conjunction with a triangular head, another pre-Conquest feature, probably borrowed from Carolingian work on the Continent.

---

* The uniformity in the proportions of width to length in five instances (all of late pre-Conquest date) is so remarkable and perhaps significant that the details are appended :—

	Length. Feet.	Width. Feet.	Proportion of Width to Length.
Inworth	33	19¾	·59
Strethall	26	15	·59
Chickney	31 (32 on N.)	18	·58
Hadstock	36½ (without former central tower)	21½	·59
Little Bardfield	33½	20	·59

BOWERS GIFFORD. Early 16th-century.
From the South-East.

TILLINGHAM. 12th-century and later.
From the South.

ASHINGDON. Early 14th-century and later.
From the North-East.

BURNHAM. 14th-century and later; S. Aisle, early 16th-century.
From the South.

DANBURY. W. Tower, 14th-century; Spire, 15th-century.
From the South-West.

BASILDON. 14th-century and later.
From the South.

NORTH SHOEBURY. 13th-century and later.
From the South-West.

SUTTON. Early 12th-century and later.
From the South-East.

CHURCH TOWERS.

RUNWELL. 15th-century.

GREAT BURSTEAD.
Late 14th-century.

FOBBING. c. 1500.

NORTH OCKENDON.
Late 15th-century.

RAYLEIGH. 15th-century.

UPMINSTER. c. 1200.
Bell-chamber later.

SOUTH OCKENDON. *c.* 1230-40.

HOCKLEY. 14th-century ; top probably later.

PITSEA. Early 16th-century.

PAGLESHAM. Early 16th-century.

CHURCHES IN POOR OR RUINOUS CONDITION.

EAST HANNINGFIELD.
13th-century and later.

HAZELEIGH.
16th-century and later. (Now destroyed.)

LATCHINGDON.
Dating from the 14th-century or earlier;
partly rebuilt, 1618.

LAINDON HILLS.
Early 16th-century and later.

Ruined Church:
Interior of W. half of S. Wall.

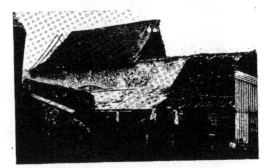

Ruined Church: S. Wall, from the South-East.

STEEPLE: (2). STANESGATE PRIORY. Early 12th-century and later.

Turning from the consideration of points of construction and form to that of architectural detail and ornament, the distinctive features are equally clear when contrasted with work of the succeeding period, though mouldings and ornament were but sparingly used by the earlier builders.   Late pre-Conquest mouldings are almost invariably distinguished by a lack of form, by a poverty of ideas and an amateurish execution which shows that the mason was attempting an unfamiliar task with little or nothing to guide him but a remote and distorted tradition of debased Roman work. The only exception to this is at the rather ambitious church at Hadstock, where the feeble mouldings, above described, are reinforced by carving on the imposts, which recalls the Greek honeysuckle ornament and is not without some merit.

The 7th-century church of Bradwell-juxta-Mare, as has been said, stands, so far as Essex is concerned, in a class by itself.   It is built almost entirely of Roman material from the adjoining station of Othona and conforms in plan to the type of the early churches to which SS. Pancras and Martin, Canterbury, the early churches at Rochester, Reculver and Lyminge, Kent, and South Elmham, Suffolk, belong.   It is remarkable for having retained some original windows which are of comparatively large dimensions and of simple rectangular form with wooden lintels to the heads.   The buttresses are of the simple pilaster type, weathered at the top, and the chancel formerly terminated eastwards in an apse.

Another presumably pre-Conquest building standing in a class by itself is the timber-built nave of Greensted (by Ongar).   This type of construction of split oak logs was no doubt common enough at the period, but Greensted appears to be now the sole surviving example of that age in the country.

Structural remains of the Saxon period have been noted in eleven or twelve churches in the county, a fairly high percentage (3 per cent.), compared to Hertford-shire with three churches (2 per cent.), and Buckingham with four churches (1¾ per cent.).

It is unnecessary to recapitulate here the distinguishing features of the succeeding periods of Romanesque and Gothic, but attention may be called to certain details not generally touched upon by the ordinary text-books.   Late 11th or early 12th-century churches are unusually common in Essex and in nearly every case they follow certain well-defined conventions.   The proportions of the nave of the Norman parish church in Essex were commonly two squares (*i.e.*, the length was double the width), and where this proportion is departed from by a large increase of length there is *primâ facie* evidence of the former existence of a central tower.   The Norman parish chancel was either square-ended or apsidal, and there is little evidence as to which termination was·the more popular, as in the great majority of cases the E. end was subsequently rebuilt.   The apsidal ends are of two chief types : (*a*) the simple type, of the same width as the nave and without a chancel-arch, and (*b*) the more advanced type, where there is an arch across the chord of the apse and generally a chancel-arch further west.   The first type either is or was exemplified at Little Tey, Little Braxted, Langford, Mashbury and Easthorpe, and the second type at East Ham, Copford, Hadleigh and White Notley.   The west apse at Langford is probably unique in this country.   Simple square E. ends survive at Castle Hedingham, Chipping Ongar, Elsenham, etc.   The churches of Copford and Great Clacton belong to a very small and highly interesting class of church (Chepstow Priory is the only other example in this country), of which the distinguishing feature is the groined stone vault, over the main body, divided into bays by cross-arches.   In all three instances the vaults have been removed.   The walls of a parish church of this period are almost invariably just under or just over 3 feet thick, and the rubble when of flint or septaria is commonly laid in regular courses; herringbone work is not uncommon, though this form of masonry may also be found in pre-Conquest work. The inclusion of Roman brick in the walls is more usual in this than in any other period. Twelfth-century ashlar may commonly be distinguished by the lines of the tooling running diagonally across the stone ; in the 13th century the tooling was almost invariably upright and parallel to the edge of the stone. The 13th century, judging from the architectural level attained, was a period of depression in the county. The only remarkable structure erected during the period is the triangular W. tower of All Saints, Maldon, but except for its plan it is undistinguished.

The 14th century gives evidence of some recovery of building activity and here and there work was produced of a richness and variety not generally met with in a parish church, as in the chancel at Lawford, the S. aisle of All Saints, Maldon, and the chancel at Fyfield. The erection of the handsome chancel at Tilty and the chapel at Little Dunmow are due to the adjoining monasteries of which they formed part.

The wave of church building which covered East Anglia in the 14th and 15th centuries with great parish churches extended into the northern part of Essex, and produced the great churches of Saffron Walden, Thaxted and Dedham, and the less important structures of Coggeshall and Great Bromley, while the handsome tower at Brightlingsea belongs to the same type. The peculiarly East Anglian practice of panelling with knapped flint incased in stone is also in evidence in Essex, chiefly in the northern part of the county.

In the 16th century Essex suffered architecturally, like the rest of England, from the dissolution of the monasteries ; of the churches of seven greater monasteries previously existing in the county only one, Waltham, has left substantial remains, though the nave of St. Botolph's, Colchester, shows that even some of the lesser monasteries had churches of considerable extent and magnificence.

The entire absence of freestone in the county of Essex necessitated its importation from elsewhere or the substitution of some other material. In the 12th century a certain amount of Barnack-stone, and other Northamptonshire oolites, was in use, but this material gave place later in the century to the soft limestone of Merstham and Reigate. A little Caen stone is observable in the remains of the larger monastic churches, and there are numerous instances of the use of Purbeck and Petworth marbles for decorative work, shafting and monumental masonry. Clunch or Totternhoe stone (a chalk stratum) is used for internal work in the northern part of the county. The rubble is normally of flint, but towards the east there is considerable use of pudding-stone (conglomerate of clay and pebbles) and septaria (hardened clay), both found locally. Of the substitutes, brick and timber, the former will be dealt with under domestic work, the latter was mainly used for towers only, though there are three instances in the county of timber churches. The towers of this material form a somewhat remarkable group, which it would be difficult to equal in any other part of England. The finest of these towers are at Blackmore, Margaretting, Navestock and Stock. In the most usual type the tower rests on massive angle posts with cross-beams, braces and framing, and is surrounded on three sides by a lower ' aisle ' with a pent roof, and of which the framing serves to support and buttress the main structure.

The church fittings in Essex do not call for any very lengthy or particular mention. The woodwork is generally undistinguished, and the screen-work in no instance rises above a very moderate level of excellence. Only one rood-screen (North Weald Basset), complete with its loft, survives in the county. In monumental art the county takes a much higher place. There are eight oak effigies of the 13th and 14th centuries, a high proportion for any one county, and the series of Vere monuments at

CREEKSEA.
(4). Grove Cottage; 16th or early 17th-century.

ORSETT.
(20). Hall Farm; early 16th-century. E. wing.

GREAT BURSTEAD.
(10). Highbury; late 16th or early 17th-century.

HORNDON-ON-THE-HILL.
(2). Bell Inn; 15th-century.

W. end of South Front. South Front.
UPMINSTER: (4). Great Tomkyns; 15th-century.

NEVENDON.
(4). Great Bromfords; 15th-century and later.

RUNWELL.
(3). Gifford's Farm; 16th-century.

EAST HANNINGFIELD.
(4). Rails Farm; 16th-century and later.

NEVENDON.
(5). Little Bromfords; late 16th-century.

EASTWOOD.
(6). Blatches; 16th-century and later.

MOUNTNESSING.
(9). Wardroper's Farm; 16th-century.

LEIGH.

(8). House, S. side of High Street;
late 16th-century.

ROCHFORD.

(8). House, opposite N. end of North Street; 17th-century.

WOODHAM FERRERS.

(7). House, E. of churchyard; 16th-century.

CORRINGHAM.

(2). Bull Inn; 15th-century; main block, 17th-century.

UPMINSTER.

(3). Upminster Hall; late 16th-century. W. Front.

Part of S. Front.

S. Front.

WEST HANNINGFIELD. (9). Elm's Farm; 16th and 17th-century.

BULPHAN.

(5). Appleton's Farm ; 15th-century and later.

LITTLE BURSTEAD.

(4). Hatches Farm ; second half of 16th century.

TILLINGHAM.

(4). Reddings ; early 16th-century.

ROCHFORD.

(6). House, E. side of South Street;
15th-century and later.

SOUTHCHURCH.

(4). Bournesgreen Farm ; 16th-century and later.

WEST TILBURY.

(5). Marshall's Farm ; 16th-century.

Earls Colne and of Marney monuments at Layer Marney are equally interesting. Fine series of Renaissance memorials to the Smiths at Theydon Mount and to the Petres at Ingatestone also deserve mention. Essex is a good county for brasses both from their number and interest. Four brasses belong to the first half of the 14th century, and are consequently among the 25 earliest in the country. Eleven more examples have canopies more or less complete. Of individual fittings, perhaps the only ones of more than local significance are the carved 13th-century rood in the Gatehouse at Barking, the carved late 12th-century slab at Runwell, of which the original form is uncertain, and the painted 13th-century chest at Newport.

From the point of view of comparative archaeology the domestic buildings of Essex are of much greater importance than the ecclesiastical. Probably in few of the other counties of England can so great a mass of mediaeval building be found, while on the continent of Europe this class is practically non-existent except in towns. The Commission has inventoried in the county some 750 secular buildings of a date anterior to the Reformation. There are no definite examples of the 12th century and only one (Manor House, Little Chesterford) of the 13th, but the 14th, 15th and early 16th centuries are represented by so great a number of examples as to render the deductions drawn from so large a mass of evidence of more than local value. The vast majority of these buildings are of timber and belong to the small manor-house, farm-house and cottage classes, and as such form a remarkable commentary on the social and economic history of the country. The 13th-century and nearly all the 14th-century examples belong to the type of which the distinctive feature is the timber-aisled hall, which can be traced back to the earliest Saxon times and perhaps even earlier. Of this type there survive in Essex some six or seven examples, all with the same external characteristics—the central hall open to the roof, which is carried down over the side aisles to within 6 or 8 feet of the ground,

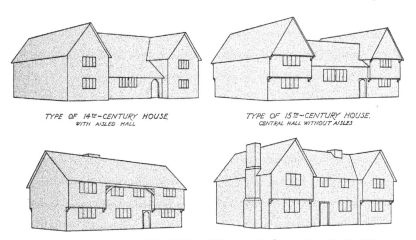

TYPE OF 14ᵀᴴ-CENTURY HOUSE.
WITH AISLED HALL

TYPE OF 15ᵀᴴ-CENTURY HOUSE.
CENTRAL HALL WITHOUT AISLES

TYPE OF LATE 15ᵀᴴ & EARLY 16ᵀᴴ-CENTURY HOUSE
WITH CONTINUOUS EAVES

TYPE OF LATE 16ᵀᴴ & EARLY 17ᵀᴴ-CENTURY HOUSE
WITH TWO-STOREYED MAIN BLOCK

and the gabled cross-wings at each end of the hall, two storeys in height, one containing the solar and the other the buttery and offices. The roof construction is always of the king-post type, except in the case of Gatehouse Farm, Felsted, which has a roof of queen-post type, probably arrived at by the desire to dispense with the oak columns of the aisles. No instance of the aisled hall has been found later than the 14th century, and the type had no doubt been generally abandoned before the close of the century. A 15th-century building in Essex can generally be distinguished by its outline, a central hall (still open to the roof) with two storeyed cross-wings at the ends, the eaves of the hall being thus at a much lower level than the eaves of the cross-wings. The upper storey of the cross-wings generally projects at one or both ends, a feature which is not found in the previous period. The roofs are of the king-post type, except in the few instances where the hammer-beam or the curved principal is preferred. The timbers and joists are heavy and set close together, the floor joists being commonly laid flat instead of upright in the modern and more scientific manner.

Late 15th and early 16th-century buildings show little variation from this type except that there is a more frequent occurrence of the hall block divided into two storeys. A not uncommon feature of small early 16th-century houses is the lack of gables to the cross-wings, the eaves being carried continuously across the whole front and their deeper projection over the hall block being supported by curved braces from the wings. The windows of the early houses seem to have been divided into lights by oak upright bars set diagonally in the frame and with no provision for glazing. This feature, however, seems to have been occasionally used down to the 17th century and is consequently no safe criterion of an early date.

After the Reformation timber domestic building seems to have gradually lost its standard form; the timber studs and joists are set wider and wider apart and the individual timbers become less and less substantial. A late 16th or 17th-century house of the early plan can generally be distinguished from a 15th-century example by the lower pitch of the roofs and by the general level of the eaves being maintained throughout the building.

With the Reformation and the advent of the new Tudor aristocracy began an era of domestic building on a large scale. Essex is well provided with examples of of this and the succeeding periods, among which may be mentioned Audley End, Moyns Park, Hill Hall, Layer Marney Hall, Gosfield Hall, Belhus and New Hall, Boreham. Other great houses of the 16th century, such as Little Leighs, Rochford Hall and St. Osyth's Priory, have suffered more or less from demolition. Of large houses of the mediaeval period only Faulkbourne Hall and fragments of Nether Hall (Roydon) survive, though there were extensive domestic buildings of the Veres at Castle Hedingham, a royal palace at Havering and a palace of the Bishops of London at Orsett.

The use of brickwork in Essex became very common in the 15th century, but before that time there is ample evidence of the occasional use of this material from the 12th century downwards. This early use of brick is perhaps commoner in East Anglia, and its comparatively frequent occurrence in the webs of 14th-century vaulting and similar positions where chalk would have been equally efficacious seems to negative the possibility of importation. The shaped bricks used in the late 12th-century columns at Coggeshall Abbey were evidently made for their present positions and consequently are almost certainly of local manufacture.

A. W. CLAPHAM.

From the South.

From the North-West.
EAST TILBURY. Oven in Hut-circle II (*see* Plan) on foreshore of the Thames.

CHADWELL: (1). Oven, 700 yards S.E. of Parish Church.

EARTHWORKS.

The Ditch between the Mount and Bailey.

The Keep-mound.

RAYLEIGH : (2). THE CASTLE. End of 11th century.

DOWNHAM : (2). BARN HALL.
Part of Moat.

HOCKLEY : (9). PLUMBEROW MOUNT.

SOUTH-EAST ESSEX.

SECTIONAL PREFACE.

(i) EARTHWORKS, ETC., PREHISTORIC AND LATER.

The earthworks of interest in the S.E. quarter of Essex are few and most of them are in a fragmentary condition.

There are three 'camps,' at Asheldham, Danbury and Prittlewell respectively, all in a poor state of preservation. At Bradwell-juxta-Mare slight undulations in the ground near St. Peter's Chapel mark the site of the foundations of the N. and W. walls of the Roman Station.

The church at South Benfleet stands on the probable site of the camp built by Hasten, *c.* 894, and near the Artillery Barracks at South Shoebury are slight remains of a work which has been ascribed to the same period.

There are entrenchments near West Tilbury church consisting of a rampart and internal ditch, probably on the site of an earlier work, and at East Tilbury earthworks apparently not of a defensive nature and locally known as " Soldiers' Graves."

A large moated mound of low elevation near Purleigh church is not shown on the Ordnance maps. Rayleigh Castle (Plan p. 123), probably built by Suene, the son of Robert Fitz Wimarc, is a good example of the mount and bailey type of earthwork, but the masonry of the castle has long since been removed. The ring and bailey at Orsett is shown on the O.S. maps as " the site of Bishop Bonner's Palace," and retains traces of foundations along the edge of the 'ring.' At Hadleigh the castle built by Hubert de Burgh, Earl of Kent in the reign of Henry III, was much altered and largely rebuilt by Edward III, and has practically no defensive earthworks.

About eighty homestead moats have been located. The best are at Mucking Hall (Barling), Moat House (Basildon), Bowers Hall (Bowers Gifford), Scotts' Hall (Canewdon), Barn Hall (Downham), Laindon Ponds (Laindon), Bacon's Farm (Mountnessing), Chichester Hall (Rawreth), Chitham's Farm (Ramsden Bellhouse), Butler's Farm (Shopland), the Hall (S. Ockendon), and a double moat at Edwin's Hall (Woodham Ferrers).

Unclassified earthworks include a large number of pits in Hangman's Wood, Little Thurrock. They are known locally as Deneholes, and consist of shafts sunk to a depth of from 50 to 100 feet down to the chalk, and, in most cases, enlarged at the bottom into several chambers. Similar pits have been found near Bexley, in Kent, and elsewhere, and they are generally considered to be disused chalk mines. An ancient track on the Maplin Sands, known as the Broomway, is also of interest. Starting in Great Wakering parish it runs parallel to and about half a mile from the coast, past Havengore to a point on

Foulness Island known as Fisherman's Head. Several branch roads leave the main track for points on the shore. The track is submerged for about twelve hours of the day. Other unclassified earthworks are Plumberow Mount (Hockley parish), opened in 1914 and assigned to the Romano-British period; two mounds and some banks in Norsey Wood (Great Burstead); a number of large mounds of irregular shape situated close to the River Crouch (opened and described as being connected with mediaeval salt workings) and some Red Hills, the latter being low mounds of burnt earth which are found generally along the line of the old high-water mark or at the sides of creeks.

(ii) Roman Remains.

South-east Essex contains one Roman monument of importance. The remains of the Roman fort (Plan p. 14) at Bradwell-juxta-Mare, destroyed by erosion on the seaward side and largely destroyed or buried on the landward, are yet sufficient to show that it may be included amongst the forts built on the southern and eastern coasts at various times between the end of the 3rd and the beginning of the 5th centuries. All or most of the coins found in the fort during the excavations of 1864 fall within this period, and there is no sufficient evidence of any earlier settlement on the site. Whether we may go further and accept the specious identification of the fort with the Othona of the *Notitia Dignitatum* is less certain. The Saxon chapel which lies across the west wall is satisfactorily identified with Cedd's foundation at " Ythancaestir," stated by Beda (*Hist. Eccl.*, III, Ch. XXII) to have been in the province of the East Angles and on the banks of the Pante—a name still retained for the upper reaches of the Blackwater. The derivation, however, of Ythan from Othona presents difficulties, and is not accepted by Mr. W. H. Stevenson. The variant " Othana " given by the Vienna MS. may be disregarded, and, in any case, does not solve the problem; but the evidence, both as to the Roman and the Saxon forms of the name, is too limited to form an adequate basis for conjecture. The difficulty is not reduced by the fact that Walton Castle, a fort of similar type, which stood until the eighteenth century on the shore near Felixstowe, has not been fitted into the list of the *Notitia*, and must at present remain a possible claimant to the name.

The other Roman remains in this region, though individually of little importance, have a definite historical value. Houses of Roman type are apparently absent, and the occurrence of Roman bricks, and possibly of Roman masonry in mediaeval structures, such as the parish church of South Benfleet or the destroyed Rayleigh Castle, may perhaps be attributed to the later plundering of the numerous 'villas' on or near the Kentish shore of the Thames. The population on the Essex side seems to have consisted of natives who were content with their traditional round huts of timber or turves, such as those which a happy chance has preserved in the Thames mud at East Tilbury. Similar huts have been preserved but ill-recorded on the Kentish flats; and it may be assumed that the potters whose kilns have been found at South Shoebury, Buttsbury and Great Burstead lived in dwellings of equally primitive and evanescent type. The area is rich in pottery of the latest pre-Roman period, and it is evident that the local craft survived the Roman conquest until the close of the first century, if not later. Its products—the so-called ' Upchurch ' and other wares—retained native characteristics but

GREAT BADDOW CHURCH.
South Porch; 17th-century.

RAYLEIGH CHURCH.
South Porch; early 16th-century.

SANDON CHURCH.
South Porch; early 16th-century.

DOWNHAM CHURCH.
West Tower; late 15th or early
16th-century.

EAST HORNDON CHURCH.
West Tower; c. 1500 and 17th-century.

GREAT BURSTEAD:
(5). BILLERICAY CHURCH.
West Tower; late 15th-century.

PARISH CHURCHES WITH WOODEN BELL-TURRETS.

EASTWOOD. From the South-East.

SOUTH HANNINGFIELD. From the South.

LAINDON. From the South-West.

STOW MARIES. From the North-West.

WEST HANNINGFIELD.
From the South.

RAMSDEN BELLHOUSE.
From the South-West.

HORNDON-ON-THE-HILL.
From the West.

LAINDON CHURCH. 15th-century.

WEST HANNINGFIELD CHURCH.
15th-century.

NORTH BENFLEET CHURCH.
16th-century.

MOUNTNESSING CHURCH.
15th-century.

HORNDON-ON-THE-HILL CHURCH.
15th-century.

RUNWELL.
S. Porch ; late 15th-century.

RUNWELL.
N. Porch ; late 15th-century.

MUNDON.
N. Porch ; early 16th-century.

BULPHAN.
S. Porch ; c. 1500.

showed increasing Roman influence, and the occurrence of a Romano-Celtic cordoned urn with pottery apparently of 3rd-century date in an oven recently found at Chadwell represents an exceptionally late survival of a distinctively native type.

The endurance of native traditions is further exemplified by the mound-burial, apparently of early 2nd-century date, found many years ago in the parish of Foulness. This burial should probably be included with the better-known series already referred to in Volumes I and III of the present Inventory. Incineration-burials of more normal type have been noted at West Tilbury, opposite Low Street Manor House in Mucking Marsh (*Arch. Journ.*, XLII, 276–7; XXIX, 187), Great Burstead, Grays Thurrock, where Roman burials are said to have been found in a denehole (*V.C.H., Essex*, I, 309–11; *cf. Illus. Lond. News*, 1857, II, 267; *Arch. Journ.*, XXVI, 192), and possibly at Canewdon; whilst inhumation burials have been discovered at South Shoebury in the immediate neighbourhood of Roman remains.

To what extent, if any, the dykes which drain and protect the marshes bordering upon the Thames may be ascribed to a period as early as that of the Roman occupation is quite uncertain. The submergence of the Bradwell fort and the East Tilbury huts, and analogous evidence elsewhere round the Essex coast, show that the land-level was higher there in Roman times; but it is not impossible that such settlements, with others in the neighbourhood of London (see *Surrey Arch. Collections*, XXVIII, p. 111) were to some extent protected by dykes similar to those which have yielded a Roman centurial stone on the flats of Monmouthshire.

Apart from the arterial road from London to Colchester (see Volume II), no road certainly of Roman origin has been identified in south-east Essex. The lack of any well-defined approach to Bradwell suggests that the fort may throughout its history have been supplied principally by sea; and in the remainder of this region absence of roads is the natural corollary of the absence of Roman structural remains.

(iii) Ecclesiastical and Secular Architecture.

Building Materials: Stone, Flint, Brick, Etc.

The general characteristics of building in the S.E. district follow very closely the local Essex types, and there is little variation in the methods and material employed. In ecclesiastical work, proximity to the Thames Estuary and consequent freedom of communication with Kent and the Medway are reflected by the much freer use of Kentish ragstone, which is very largely employed for rubble-walling in place of the flint-work of the northern and central parts of the county. Reuse of Roman material is comparatively infrequent and very little septaria and pudding-stone is apparent. None of the brickwork is of earlier date than the 15th century, except for the unusual glazed bricks in Purleigh church. Secular building, when not of timber, is almost invariably of brick, except for some rubble-work used in the core of the walls of Rochford Hall, and the walls of certain dissolved religious houses such as Prittlewell and Thoby Priories, adapted as dwelling-houses.

ECCLESIASTICAL BUILDINGS.

The churches of S.E. Essex do not include any buildings of the first class, but though most of them are of small size they are by no means lacking in architectural interest. Chronologically all the mediaeval periods are sufficiently represented, but the examples of the 14th century are generally undistinguished.

In the chapel (Plate p. 17) of St. Peter-on-the-Wall (Bradwell-juxta-Mare), Essex possesses a pre-Conquest building of the highest interest. It may be identified, almost certainly, with the church built by St. Cedd at Ithancester *c.* 654, and the nave (Plate p. 16) of this date is still standing almost intact.

Part of the church of Great Stambridge may be definitely assigned to the late pre-Conquest period, and work of the same date is probably preserved in the churches at Corringham and Fobbing though the evidence is inconclusive.

Of late 11th and 12th-century churches the most complete are at Hadleigh (Plate p. 61), Rainham (Plate p. 115), Sutton and Chadwell. Good Romanesque detail survives at S. Ockendon (Plate p. 120), Sutton, S. Shoebury and E. Tilbury, and there is a good transitional doorway at Prittlewell Priory (Plate p. 121). The W. tower at Corringham (Plate p. 28) is an interesting late 11th-century structure, with blind arcading resembling that at Great Tey.

The proportion of 13th-century work is considerably larger in the S.E. than in the other parts of the county, but none of it is of marked distinction. The best examples occur at Stifford, Thundersley, Mountnessing, E. Tilbury and Horndon-on-the-Hill. There is a richly moulded S. doorway at Sutton (Plate p. 121) and the surviving arch (Plate p. 173) of Bicknacre Priory (Woodham Ferrers) is of this period.

Work of the 14th century is meagre in extent and comparatively poor in quality. The arcades (see Plates) at Danbury, Orsett, Purleigh and Stanford-le-Hope have fairly good detail, and Great Burstead and Rochford have window-tracery of some interest.

The 15th and early 16th centuries are best represented by a series of handsome W. towers (see Plates), of which those at Prittlewell, Hornchurch, Little Wakering, Canewdon and Barling are executed in stone, and those at Rochford, Downham, Sandon and Billericay in brick. Great Baddow, Sandon, E. Horndon and Burnham churches possess other good work of the period, the first three being mainly examples of brickwork.

Very little post-Reformation ecclesiastical work has survived, but parts of the towers of E. Horndon (Plate p. xxxviii) and W. Thurrock (Plate p. 167) and the porch at Great Baddow (Plate p. xxxviii) may be mentioned.

Turning to peculiarities of plan Hadleigh is the only church possessing an apse and S. Ockendon the only one with a round tower. The foundations of the round nave at W. Thurrock are no longer visible.

The belfries of Stock (Plate p. 156) W. Hanningfield, Ramsden Bellhouse (Plate pp. xxxviii-ix), Mundon and Bulphan are entirely of timber and the bell-turrets (Plate pp. xxxviii-ix) at Horndon-on-the-Hill, Mountnessing and Laindon rest on elaborate timber-construction within the walls of the nave. At Laindon there is also an interesting timber annexe (Plate pp. xxxviii-ix) at the W. end of the nave. At Nevendon there is structural evidence for an early nave of timber, subsequently replaced by the existing building.

HORNDON-ON-THE-HILL.
Main Street, E. side, showing Monument (2) in distance.

EAST HORNDON.
(4). Boar's Head Inn ; late 17th-century.

ROCHFORD.
South Street, E. side, showing Monument (5).

HORNDON-ON-THE-HILL.
Main Street, W. side, showing Monuments (6), (7) and (8).

PRITTLEWELL.
(4). House, W. side of North Street ; early 16th-century.

GREAT BADDOW.
(6). House and Shop, 50 yards W. of church ;
15th-century and later.

High Street, Billericay : W. side,
showing Monument (12) ; 16th-century.

High Street, Billericay : E. side, showing
the Church (5), etc.

GREAT BURSTEAD.

HOUSES AND COTTAGES WITH THATCHED ROOFS.

STIFFORD.
(7). Cottage, 90 yards W. of church ; early 18th-century.

ORSETT.
(4). Birch Terrace ; 16th and 17th-century.

FOBBING.
(4). House, 500 yards N.N.W. of church ; 15th-century.

CANVEY ISLAND.
(1). Dutch Cottage ; dated 1621.

STIFFORD.
(8). Cottage, 70 yards W.N.W. of church ; 17th-century.

STIFFORD.
(10). Cottage, 120 yards W. of church ; 17th-century.

TILLINGHAM.
(3). West Hyde ; 17th-century.

FOBBING.
(3). Wheelers House ; late 15th-century and later.

PRITTLEWELL.
(6). Deeds Cottages ; 16th-century.

LITTLE BURSTEAD.
(7). St. Margaret's Farm ; 16th-century or earlier.

TILLINGHAM.
(6). Bridgemans ; 17th-century.

RUNWELL.
(4). Church End ; 17th-century.

ORSETT.
(17). Mill House ; 17th-century.

WICKFORD.
(6). Shot Farm ; late 16th-century.

VANGE.
(3). Merricks: Barn; late 16th or early 17th-century.

WICKFORD.
(6). Shot Farm: Barn; late 16th-century.

HORNDON-ON-THE-HILL.
(12). Linsteads Farm: Barn; 17th-century.

RETTENDON.
(2). Rettendon Place: Barn; 16th-century.

GREAT BURSTEAD.
(21). Chantry Barn, Billericay; probably mediaeval.

SOUTH OCKENDON.
(3). South Ockendon Hall: Interior of Barn
late 15th or early 16th-century.

UPMINSTER.
(4). Great Tomkyns: Interior of Barn; 17th-century.

The only roof of particular excellence is the handsome carved example over the S. porch at S. Benfleet (Plate p. 140). Other roofs of interest occur at Laindon (Plate p. 48) and Wickford.

The porches are mostly of timber, and of these the best are at S. Benfleet, Shopland, Stock, Mundon and Fobbing (see Plates). Stone or brick porches of interest exist at Southminster, Sandon, Rayleigh, Prittlewell and Great Wakering (Plate p. 60). The last named is W. of the tower and has a chamber above it. Stone or brick vaulting occurs only in the porches at Southminster (Plate p. 146) and Sandon, mentioned above.

MONASTIC AND COLLEGIATE BUILDINGS.

The .monastic houses of S.E. Essex were of little importance and have left only inconsiderable remains. Of two small Cluniac houses the Priory of Prittlewell retains parts of the Frater and western range, while at Stanesgate Priory (Steeple) the shell of the 12th and 14th-century nave of the church (Plate p. xxxiii) is still standing but threatens to fall in the near future. The Austin Canons possessed two small houses at Bicknacre (Woodham Ferrers) and Thoby (Mountnessing) ; the first is evidenced by one arch of the crossing only and the second by part of the S. wall of the church and some portions of the W. range (Plate p. 96). There are no remains, except the parish church, of the alien hospital or priory of Hornchurch.

Small 17th-century almshouses are scheduled under Rochford and Stock, and there are remains of late 16th-century work in the Pennant Almshouses at Hornchurch.

SECULAR BUILDINGS.

The high proportion of pre-Reformation houses is maintained in S.E. Essex ; the number scheduled is 75 ; but comparatively few are in any way remarkable, and only one (Bretts, Aveley) may possibly go back to the 14th century. The best examples of timber-framed building are Great Sir Hughes, Great Baddow (Plate p. 52) ; W. Hanningfield (9) ; Slough House, Danbury (Plate p. 32) ; and Upminster (4).

Of larger houses (see Plates) nearly all are built of brick. The remains of Rochford Hall, now partly ruinous, indicate a very extensive building of early 16th-century date. Belhus is a fairly large courtyard house of the same period. Creeksea Place, Little Warley Hall and Flemings, Runwell, are fragments of 16th-century houses of some distinction. Edwins Hall, Woodham Ferrers ; Porters, Prittlewell (Plate p. 114) ; and Woodham Mortimer Hall are fair examples of the lesser houses of the 16th and 17th centuries. Of later work of the 17th century there are examples (see Plates) with features of interest at Fremnells, Downham ; Ford Place, Stifford ; and at Nelmes, Hornchurch. The Manor House, S. Shoebury, is a fair example of a dwelling of the period of Queen Anne. On Canvey Island are two early 17th-century octagonal houses (Plate pp. xl–i) of timber, built probably by the Dutch settlers.

Of military works there are extensive remains of the 14th-century curtain and towers of Hadleigh Castle (Plate pp. 64–5) and the late 17th-century gatehouse (Frontispiece) and other works at Tilbury Fort.

FITTINGS.

Altars.—The only mediaeval altar-slabs noted are those at Canewdon and Stock.

Bells.—Thirty-five bells are of pre-Reformation date. Of these six are of the 14th century, including one at Southchurch probably by Geoffrey of Edmonton, two at Rawreth by John of Hadham, and three (one at Bowers Gifford and two at Eastwood) by William Burford. There are also four bells of *c.* 1400 by Robert Burford.

Brasses (Plates pp. 25, etc.). — The district contains eight 14th-century brasses and of these the most interesting are the Flemish plate (Plate p. 160) to Ralph de Knevynton, 1370, at Aveley, and the fine but mutilated figure (Plate p. 56) at Bowers Gifford. Half-figures of two priests and a lady remain at Corringham, Stifford (Plate p. 160) and West Hanningfield respectively. There is also a mutilated armed figure (Plate p. 56) with remains of a canopy to Sir I. Bruyn, 1400, at South Ockendon, and a smaller armed figure of 1371 at Shopland.

Of later brasses the most important are the figures (Plate p. 78) with heraldic mantles and tabard at Ingrave (formerly at West Horndon). The earliest 16th-century brass at Althorne includes the figure of a nun in the group of daughters.

There are two interesting early 14th-century indents formerly with half-figures at Hornchurch and West Thurrock, and other indents of the same period at Stifford, Basildon, Southchurch, Corringham and elsewhere.

Ceilings and *Plaster-work.* — The finest plaster ceilings (Plates pp. 97, 153) in the district are those at Ford Place, Stifford, where one of the rooms has figures representing the four seasons, and at Orsett Hall. There is also an enriched ceiling at Beauchamps, Shopland, and the front of the same house has good pargeting dated 1688.

Chairs (Plate p. xlii).—Several churches possess 17th or early 18th-century chairs of more than usual richness. The best examples are at Aveley, Chadwell, Paglesham and Grays Thurrock.

Chests (Plate p. xliii).—The chests of the district include a 13th-century example at Wennington and another early example of similar type at Eastwood. There are 'dug-out' chests at Great Burstead, Mountnessing and Rayleigh, and massive iron-bound chests at South Ockendon, Rainham and West Hanningfield. The poor-box at Runwell is cut in the solid.

Consecration Crosses.—The only definite consecration crosses in position are at Rayleigh and Southminster. South Benfleet and Great Stambridge have crosses of brick on the buttresses of the towers.

Doors.—The most interesting door in the district is at Eastwood (Plate p. 45); it is elaborately enriched with ironwork of two distinct dates. A second door at Eastwood and another at Buttsbury have interesting ironwork of more ordinary character (Plate pp. 4–5). There are carved or traceried doors at Hornchurch and Prittlewell, and at Belhus, Aveley, is a richly carved early 16th-century screen with doors, not *in situ* and of foreign workmanship. The doors at Hatches Farm, Little Burstead, have fine carved panels of the same period.

AVELEY. *c.* 1620.

CHADWELL. Late 17th-century.

PAGLESHAM. Late 17th-century.

GRAYS THURROCK. Possibly late 17th-century.

EASTWOOD.
Late 12th-century.

SHOPLAND.
Early 13th-century.

ALTHORNE. *c.* 1400.
From the North-East.

ALTHORNE. *c.* 1400.
From the South-West.

FONTS.

VANGE.
12th-century.

LAINDON.
Bowl; early 13th-century.

EAST HORNDON.
Bowl; c. 1200.

HOCKLEY.
Early 13th-century.

HORNDON-ON-THE-HILL.
14th-century.

BRADWELL-JUXTA-MARE.
14th-century.

WEST HANNINGFIELD.
14th-century.

GREAT STAMBRIDGE.
Late 15th-century.

ORSETT.
c. 1500.

GRAYS THURROCK.
15th· or early 16th-century.

WEST HANNINGFIELD. Dug-out; 13th or 14th-century.

WENNINGTON.
13th-century; part of lid, later.

SOUTH OCKENDON.
In N. Chapel; 14th-century or earlier.

GREAT BURSTEAD.
Dug-out; 12th or 13th-century.

RAINHAM. In N. Aisle; 16th-century.

ORSETT. Late 16th or early 17th-century;
lid, 13th-century.

Fireplaces (Plate p. 65).—The best stone fireplaces are at Orsett Hall; Porters, Prittlewell; South Ockendon (10); and Horndon-on-the-Hill (18); of these the first has carved figures of Hope and Charity, the two next are of late 16th-century date and of semi-Gothic character; the fourth of somewhat coarse Renaissance design. There are wooden overmantels of interest at Belhus, Aveley; Stockwell Hall, Little Burstead; Horndon-on-the-Hill (18); Upminster (8); and Danbury (2), all of late 16th or 17th-century date.

Fonts (Plates pp. xlii–iii).—Of early fonts the best is the well-preserved round bowl with interlacing arcading at Eastwood; square 12th-century fonts with varied enrichment occur at Vange, East Horndon, Tillingham and Aveley, Of similar character, but of early 13th-century date, are the examples at Shopland, Laindon and North Benfleet. Fourteenth-century fonts with features of interest occur at Horndon-on-the-Hill and Bradwell-juxta-Mare, the latter carved with grotesque faces. The finest 15th-century font is at Althorne; it has a series of carved figures. There are other 15th or early 16th-century fonts of more ordinary type at Great Stambridge, Grays Thurrock, Mountnessing and Orsett.

Glass (Plates pp. xliv–v).—Ancient painted glass in the churches of south-east Essex is mainly represented by fragments of borders, quarries and tabernacle-work. At South Hanningfield (13th and 14th-century) and North Shoebury (both 14th-century) there are interesting examples of grisaille-foliage with borders *in situ*.

Of single figures, there are two complete, though restored, examples, probably SS. Helen and Mary Magdalene, at North Ockendon, under canopies. At Hornchurch there is a mutilated 15th-century Crucifixion and a tracery light with a figure of our Lord, both in grisaille.

Of subject panels there are some fine examples (16th and 17th-century) at Prittlewell, not native to the church but formerly part of the Neave Collection of old painted glass at Dagnam Park, Noak Hill.

Of heraldry there are a few good examples at Great Burstead, Woodham Ferrers and North Ockendon of the 14th century, and at Sandon and East Horndon of the 15th century, the last an especially good shield of the arms of Tyrrell impaling Marney. At Upminster is some interesting, though much mutilated, heraldry of the Lathom family.

The fine heraldic domestic glass with the arms of Fiennes and Barrett formerly at Belhus, Aveley, has recently been removed.

Monuments.—There are no monuments of outstanding interest in the district except the three oak effigies (Plate p. 29) in armour at Danbury, all of the end of the 13th or the beginning of the 14th century. An interesting and unusual memorial is the wall-tablet with incised 14th-century inscription (Plate p. 48) at Fobbing. At East Horndon is a handsome incised slab (Plate p. 40) with figure and canopy, to Alice Tyrell, 1422. There is a fragment of a late 12th or early 13th-century carved head-stone or coffin-lid at North Shoebury, and a slab (Plate p. 25) with carved edges of late 12th-century date at Rettendon. Of late mediaeval monuments the only ones of interest are an altar-tomb at Hornchurch, the recessed and canopied tomb at Rayleigh, and an altar-tomb at Stanford-le-Hope, set in a 14th-century recess (Plate p. 105).

Most of the Renaissance monuments of interest date from early in the 17th century. They include tombs with recumbent figures (Plate p. 100) at North Ockendon, Little Warley, Orsett (Plate p. 105) and West Thurrock (Plate p. 172), and wall-monuments with kneeling figures at Woodham Ferrers (Plate p. 105), North Ockendon, South Ockendon and Hornchurch. At North Ockendon is a curious series erected by Gabriel Pointz to the memory of his ancestors, and the monument (Plate p. 141) at South Ockendon represents a Lord Mayor of London in robes of office. The monument (Plate p. 85) at Little Warley has a superstructure in the form of the draped canopy of a bed.

Paintings.—Ecclesiastical paintings on plaster are uncommon and mostly very badly preserved. There are remains of a ' Doom ' at Woodham Ferrers, various subjects in panels at East Hanningfield (Plate p. 104), a figure of St. Thomas of Canterbury at Hadleigh, and a Nativity at Little Wakering. Domestic painted decoration is represented by the elaborate 17th-century scheme at West Hanningfield (2) and remains of a figure - subject at Belhus, Aveley.

Panelling.—Panels of foreign origin, enriched with carved heads, etc., are preserved at Porters, Prittlewell ; Hatches Farm, Little Burstead ; and Belhus, Aveley.

Piscinae (Plate p. xlv).—There are 12th-century pillar-piscinae at Sandon and Aveley, the former elaborately enriched. Of 13th-century piscinae examples are to be found at West Thurrock, Rettendon, Woodham Ferrers, etc. None of the later piscinae are particularly noteworthy, but there are 14th-century examples at Little Thurrock and Purleigh.

Plate (Plate p. xliv).—The stem of the cup at Mundon may be of pre-Reformation date, but the cup itself is of the 17th century. The district contains an unusually large number of Elizabethan cups, 39 in all ; of these one is of 1561, eight of 1562, four of 1563, and six of 1564. None of the later plate is of great interest, but there is a good flagon of 1665 at Stifford.

Pulpits.—The only pre-Reformation pulpit is at Sandon (Plate p. 79), but there are good late 16th or early 17th-century examples (Plate p. 4) at Great Baddow, North Ockendon, Wennington, East Tilbury and Aveley ; the first of these is richly ornamented and retains its sounding board. There is a late 17th-century pulpit with carved cherub-heads, etc., at Canewdon, and one of slightly later date at Purleigh.

Royal Arms.—There is a handsome painting of the Royal Stuart Arms (Plate p. 79) on plaster in the church of Laindon Hills. There are remains of another painted Royal Arms at East Tilbury.

Screens (Plate pp. 4–5).—Mediaeval screenwork is uncommon in the district ; there is, however, an interesting 14th-century screen at Corringham, with turned shafts, and 14th or 15th-century examples at Bulphan and Stanford-le-Hope.

Seating (Plate p. 5).—There are good bench-ends with carved popey-heads at Rettendon and Danbury, the former with heraldic devices. The benches and ends at Great Burstead have traceried panelling.

RETTENDON CHURCH.
Paten, 1641 ; Cup, 1562.

NORTH OCKENDON CHURCH.
Paten and Cup, 1646 ; Cup and Cover Paten, 1561.

RUNWELL CHURCH.
Cup and Cover Paten, 1562.

HORNCHURCH CHURCH.
Cup with Cover Paten, 1563 ; Flagon, 1699 ; others later.

HORNDON-ON-THE-HILL CHURCH.
Flagon, 1700 ; Cup, 1567 ; Pewter Plates, 17th-century.

FOULNESS CHURCH.
Cup, 1612 ; Cup and Cover Paten, 1712.

NORTH SHOEBURY CHURCH.
In N.W. window of Nave ; 14th-century.

WOODHAM WALTER CHURCH.
In middle window of N. Aisle ; 15th-century.
(*See* Volume II.)

PRITTLEWELL CHURCH.
Part of E. window of S. Chapel. The Temptation ;
16th-century ; foreign.

NORTH OCKENDON CHURCH.
Figure in E. window of N. Chapel ;
late 13th-century.

GLASS.
(Approximately one-eighth full size—from drawings.)

PURLEIGH CHURCH.
In E. window of
S. Aisle ; 14th-century.

CORRINGHAM
CHURCH.
In W. window of
N. Aisle ; possibly
14th-century.

SANDON CHURCH.
In S.E. window of Chancel :
Arms of St. Gregory ;
15th or early 16th-century.

EAST HORNDON CHURCH.
In E. window of S. Chapel :
Arms of Tyrell impaling
Marney ; 15th-century.

SANDON CHURCH.
In S.E. window of
Chancel ; 15th-century.

SANDON CHURCH.
In S.E. window of
Chancel ; date uncertain.

GREAT BURSTEAD CHURCH.
In S.W. window, S. Aisle : Arms of Grey of Wilton ;
14th-century.

Arms of Poyntz and Beauchamp ; 14th-century.

Arms of Poyntz, with quarterings ;

PISCINAE AND SEDILIA.

RETTENDON CHURCH.
Piscina and Sedilia in Chancel ; 13th-century.

WOODHAM FERRERS CHURCH.
Double Piscina in Chancel ; mid 13th-century.

SANDON CHURCH.
Pillar-Piscina in Chancel ;
12th-century.

DANBURY CHURCH.
Piscina in Chancel ;
late 13th-century.

WEST THURROCK CHURCH.
Piscina in Chancel ; 13th-century.

LITTLE THURROCK CHURCH.
Piscina and Sedilia in Chancel ; 14th-century.

Sedilia.—Sedilia, generally ranging with a piscina, occur at Tillingham, Rettendon (Plate p. xlv), Stanford-le-Hope, Orsett and Little Thurrock (Plate p. xlv); the first two are of the 13th and the remainder of the 14th century.

Staircases.—The finest staircase in the district is the handsome late 17th-century example at Nelmes, Hornchurch (Plate p. 71); the pierced carving is disposed in raking panels between the string and the rail. Seventeenth-century staircases of minor interest occur at Little Warley Hall, Eastwood (8), etc.

Miscellanea.—There are wrought iron *hour-glass stands* at South Ockendon, Wennington (Plate p. 104) and Stifford. At Great Burstead is a late 17th-century *reredos* (Plate p. 53) said to have been brought from a London church. Portions of two carved alabaster ' *tables* ' are preserved at Barling (Plate p. 25).

CONDITION.

Mediaeval Churches, etc.—Of the hundred churches included in the Inventory, fourteen have been entirely rebuilt, and two others except for small portions of old walling which have been incorporated in the new work; four others have been entirely rebuilt except for the tower; of the remaining eighty, three retain little old work beyond the tower, and the majority have been restored and in some cases partly rebuilt. Five are in fairly good condition, five poor and five bad. The church at East Hanningfield (Plate p. 33) is now a ruin, Hazeleigh, owing to its ruinous state, has been pulled down, and Laindon Hills is now only used occasionally and through neglect is rapidly becoming ruinous (Plate p. xxxiii). There are bad cracks in the tower at East Horndon, and Ashingdon is in a serious state through the shifting subsoil. The tower at Downham is badly cracked, and with those at South Shoebury and Stifford is threatened by the growth of ivy. With these exceptions the growth of ivy on the walls is only serious at Mucking.

The parishes of Havengore, Lee Chapel, Little Stambridge and West Horndon have no churches.

About seven per cent. of the secular buildings are in poor or bad condition; most of them, however, are small cottages. Great Sir Hughes, Great Baddow, is in a badly neglected state and Rochford Hall in a poor condition and partly in ruins. The more important houses, however, are generally in a good state of preservation, but, among others, Belhus, Aveley, has suffered in the hands of restorers. Hadleigh Castle is in ruins and the existing work is in some danger owing to the unstable condition of the subsoil.

The earthworks generally, including the camps at Asheldham, Danbury and Prittlewell, have suffered under the plough and are in a poor state of preservation; the site of the camp at South Shoebury has been largely built over by barracks. A notable exception is Rayleigh Castle, an exceptionally good and well-preserved example of the mount and bailey type.

ESSEX.

LIST OF HUNDREDS, HALF-HUNDREDS AND PARISHES.

(The Parishes printed in Italics are included in Volume 4. The figures in brackets refer to the volumes in which the other parishes are described.)

CLAVERING.

Berden (1)
Clavering (1)
Farnham (1)
Langley (1)
Manuden (1)
Ugley (1)

UTTLESFORD.

Arkesden (1)
Birchanger (1)
Chrishall (1)
Debden (1)
Elmdon (1)
Elsenham (1)
Great Chesterford (1)
Henham (1)
Littlebury (1)
Little Chesterford (1)
Newport (1)
Quendon (1)
Rickling (1)
Saffron Walden (1)
Stansted Mountfitchet
          (1)
Strethall (1)
Takeley (1)
Wenden Lofts (1)
Wendens Ambo (1)
Wicken Bonhunt (1)
Widdington (1)
Wimbish (1)

FRESHWELL.

Ashdon (1)
Bardfield Saling (1)
Bartlow End (1)
Great Bardfield (1)
Great Sampford (1)
Hadstock (1)
Helion Bumpstead (1)
Hempstead (1)
Little Bardfield (1)
Little Sampford (1)
Radwinter (1)

DUNMOW.

Aythorpe Roding (2)
Barnston (2)
Berners Roding (2)
Broxted (1)
Chickney (1)
Good Easter (2)

DUNMOW—cont.

Great Canfield (2)
Great Dunmow (1)
Great Easton (1)
High Easter (2)
High Roding (2)
Leaden Roding (2)
Lindsell (1)
Little Canfield (2)
Little Dunmow (1)
Little Easton (1)
Margaret Roding (2)
Mashbury (2)
Pleshey (2)
Shellow Bowells (2)
Thaxted (1)
Tilty (1)
White Roding (2)
Willingale Doe (2)
Willingale Spain (2)

HINCKFORD.

Alphamstone (3)
Ashen (1)
Belchamp Otton (1)
Belchamp St. Paul's (1)
Belchamp Walter (1)
Birdbrook (1)
Bocking (1)
Borley (1)
Braintree (2)
Bulmer (1)
Castle Hedingham (1)
Felsted (2)
Finchingfield (1)
Foxearth (1)
Gestingthorpe (1)
Gosfield (1)
Great Henny (3)
Great Maplestead (1)
Great Saling (1)
Great Yeldham (1)
Halstead Rural (1)
Halstead Urban (1)
Lamarsh (3)
Liston (1)
Little Henny (3)
Little Maplestead (1)
Little Yeldham (1)
Middleton (3)
Northwood (1)
Ovington (1)
Panfield (1)

HINCKFORD—cont.

Pebmarsh (3)
Pentlow (1)
Rayne (1)
Ridgewell (1)
Shalford (1)
Sible Hedingham (1)
Stambourne (1)
Stebbing (1)
Steeple Bumpstead (1)
Stisted (3)
Sturmer (1)
Tilbury-juxta-Clare (1)
Toppesfield (1)
Twinstead (3)
Wethersfield (1)
Wickham St. Paul's (1)

HARLOW.

Great Hallingbury (2)
Great Parndon (2)
Harlow (2)
Hatfield Broad Oak (2)
Latton (2)
Little Hallingbury (2)
Little Parndon (2)
Matching (2)
Netteswell (2)
Roydon (2)
Sheering (2)

LEXDEN.

Aldham (3)
Birch (3)
Boxted (3)
Bures (3)
Chapel (3)
Colne Engaine (3)
Copford (3)
Dedham (3)
Earls Colne (3)
East Donyland (3)
Easthorpe (3)
Feering (3)
Fordham (3)
Great Coggeshall (3)
Great Horkesley (3)
Great Tey (3)
Inworth (3)
Langham (3)
Little Horkesley (3)
Little Tey (3)

LEXDEN—cont.

Marks Tey (3)
Markshall (3)
Messing (3)
Mount Bures (3)
Pattiswick (3)
Stanway (3)
Wakes Colne (3)
West Bergholt (3)
White Colne (3)
Wivenhoe (3)
Wormingford (3)

COLCHESTER.

Colchester (3)

WITHAM.

Black Notley (2)
Bradwell-
   (juxta-Coggeshall) (3)
Cressing (3)
Fairsted (2)
Faulkbourne (2)
Great Braxted (3)
Hatfield Peverel (2)
Kelvedon (3)
Little Braxted (3)
Little Coggeshall (3)
Rivenhall (3)
Terling (2)
Ulting (2)
White Notley (2)
Witham (2)

CHELMSFORD.

Buttsbury
Danbury
East Hanningfield
Great Baddow
Mountnessing
Rettendon
Runwell
Sandon
South Hanningfield
Stock
West Hanningfield
Woodham Ferrers
Boreham (2)
Blackmore (2)
Broomfield (2)
Chelmsford (2)
Chignall (2)

CHELMSFORD—cont.

Great Leighs (2)
Great Waltham (2)
Ingatestone and
  Fryerning (2)
Little Baddow (2)
Little Leighs (2)
Little Waltham (2)
Margaretting (2)
Roxwell (2)
Springfield (2)
Widford (2)
Writtle (2)

TENDRING.

Alresford (3)
Ardleigh (3)
Beaumont-cum-Moze (3)
Bradfield (3)
Brightlingsea (3)
Dovercourt (3)
Elmstead (3)
Frating (3)
Frinton (3)
Great Bentley (3)
Great Bromley (3)
Great Clacton (3)
Great Holland (3)
Great Oakley (3)
Harwich (3)
Kirby-le-Soken (3)
Lawford (3)
Little Bentley (3)
Little Bromley (3)
Little Clacton (3)
Little Holland (3)
Little Oakley (3)
Manningtree (3)
Mistley (3)
Ramsey (3)
St. Osyth (3)
Tendring (3)
Thorpe-le-Soken (3)
Thorrington (3)
Walton-le-Soken (3)
Weeley (3)
Wix (3)
Wrabness (3)

WINSTREE.

Abberton (3)
East Mersea (3)
Fingringhoe (3)
Great Wigborough (3)
Langenhoe (3)
Layer Breton (3)
Layer de la Haye (3)
Layer Marney (3)
Little Wigborough (3)
Peldon (3)

WINSTREE—cont.

Salcott (3)
Virley (3)
West Mersea (3)

THURSTABLE.

Goldhanger (3)
Great Totham (3)
Heybridge (3)
Langford (2)
Little Totham (3)
Tollesbury (3)
Tolleshunt D'Arcy (3)
Tolleshunt Knights (3)
Tolleshunt Major (3)
Wickham Bishops (2)

DENGIE.

Althorne
Asheldham
Bradwell-juxta-Mare
Burnham
Cold Norton
Creeksea
Dengie
Hazeleigh
Latchingdon
Mayland
Mundon
North Fambridge
Purleigh
St. Lawrence
Southminster
Steeple
Stow Maries
Tillingham
Woodham Mortimer
Maldon All Saints (2)
Maldon St. Mary (2)
Maldon St. Peter (2)
Woodham Walter (2)

ROCHFORD.

Ashingdon
Barling
Canewdon
Eastwood
Foulness
Great Stambridge
Great Wakering
Hadleigh
Havengore
Hawkwell
Hockley
Leigh
Little Stambridge
Little Wakering
North Shoebury
Paglesham
Prittlewell

ROCHFORD—cont.

Rayleigh
Rawreth
Rochford
Shopland
South Fambridge
South Shoebury
Southchurch
Sutton

BARSTABLE.

Basildon
Bowers Gifford
Bulphan
Canvey Island
Chadwell
Corringham
Downham
Dunton (Wayletts)
East Horndon
East Tilbury
Fobbing
Great Burstead
Horndon-on-the-Hill
Hutton
Ingrave
Laindon
Laindon Hills
Lee Chapel
Little Burstead
Little Thurrock
Mucking
Nevendon
North Benfleet
Orsett
Pitsea
Ramsden Bellhouse
Ramsden Crays
South Benfleet
Stanford-le-Hope
Thundersley
Vange
West Horndon
West Tilbury
Wickford
Brentwood (2)
Doddinghurst (2)
Shenfield (2)

ONGAR.

Abbess Roding (2)
Beauchamp Roding (2)
Bobbingworth (2)
Buckhurst Hill (2)
Chigwell (2)
Chipping Ongar (2)
Fyfield (2)
Greensted (juxta-Ongar)
                (2)
High Laver (2)

ONGAR—cont.

High Ongar (2)
Kelvedon Hatch (2)
Lambourne (2)
Little Laver (2)
Loughton (2)
Magdalen Laver (2)
Moreton (2)
Navestock (2)
North Weald Bassett (2)
Norton Mandeville (2)
Shelley (2)
Stanford Rivers (2)
Stapleford Abbots (2)
Stapleford Tawney (2)
Stondon Massey (2)
Theydon Bois (2)
Theydon Garnon (2)
Theydon Mount (2)

CHAFFORD.

Aveley
Childerditch
Cranham
Grays Thurrock
Great Warley
Little Warley
North Ockendon
Rainham
South Ockendon
Stifford
Upminster
Wennington
West Thurrock
South Weald (2)

HAVERING.

Hornchurch
Havering-atte-Bower (2)
Noak Hill (2)
Romford Rural (2)
Romford Urban (2)

WALTHAM.

Chingford (2)
Epping (2)
Epping Upland (2)
Nazeing (2)
Waltham Holy Cross (2)

BECONTREE.

Barking (2)
Dagenham (2)
East Ham (2)
Great Ilford (2)
Little Ilford (2)
Low Leyton (2)
Walthamstow (2)
Wanstead (2)
West Ham (2)
Woodford (2)

AN INVENTORY OF THE ANCIENT AND HISTORICAL MONUMENTS IN SOUTH-EAST ESSEX.

ACCREDITED TO A DATE ANTERIOR TO 1714,

arranged by Parishes.

(Unless otherwise stated, the dimensions given in the Inventory are internal. Monuments with titles printed in italics are covered by an introductory sentence, to which reference should be made. The key plans of those churches which are not illustrated by historically hatched plans are drawn to a uniform scale of 48 ft. to the inch, with the monumental portions shown in solid black.)

1. ALTHORNE. (F.b.)

(O.S. 6 in. lxii. S.E.)

Althorne is a parish on the left bank of the Crouch, 3 m. N.W. of Burnham. The church is the principal monument.

Ecclesiastical :—

(1). PARISH CHURCH OF ST. ANDREW stands towards the W. side of the parish. The walls are of flint and stone-rubble, those of the chancel are of brick; the dressings are of limestone and brick and the roofs are tiled. The *Nave* was built probably late in the 14th century. Early in the 16th century the *Chancel* was rebuilt. About 1500 the *West Tower* was added. The church has been restored in modern times. The *South Porch* is probably of the 18th century. Among the fittings the font is noteworthy.

Architectural Description—The *Chancel* (20¾ ft. by 15¾ ft.) has a modern E. window. In the N. wall is a much restored early 16th-century window of two cinquefoiled lights with vertical tracery in a square head with a moulded label, all covered with cement. In the S. wall is a similar window and further E. is a doorway of the same date, also covered with cement and with moulded jambs and four-centred arch. The chancel-arch is modern except for the stone responds which are possibly of the 14th century.

The *Nave* (38¼ ft. by 20 ft.) has in the N. wall three windows, the two eastern are of 15th-century date, partly restored, and each of two trefoiled lights in a four-centred head with a moulded label; the western window is of late 15th-century date,

partly restored, and of two pointed lights in a square head with a moulded label; the heads of all three windows have been rebuilt; between the two western windows is the late 14th-century N. doorway with moulded jambs and two-centred arch; it is now blocked; at the E. end of the wall are the late 15th or early 16th-century upper and lower doorways to the rood-loft staircase, which is enclosed in a projection; the upper doorway has a segmental-pointed head. In the S. wall are three windows uniform with those in the N. wall; the late 14th-century S. doorway has moulded jambs and a four-centred arch.

The *West Tower* (12 ft. by 10¾ ft.) is of c. 1500 and of three stages with an embattled parapet, enriched with flint-inlay in a trellis-work of ashlar. The two-centred tower-arch is of three chamfered orders, but has been filled in and the responds rebuilt. The W. window is modern; flanking it are two plain crosses in brick; the W. doorway has moulded jambs and segmental-pointed arch with a moulded label enriched with carved flowers. The S. and W. walls of the second stage have each a window with a trefoiled head and jambs carved with flowers. The bell-chamber has in each wall a window of two cinquefoiled lights under a four-centred head with a moulded label, some partly broken away.

Fittings—Bells : two; 1st by Thomas Harrys, late 15th-century and inscribed " Vox Augustine Sonet in Aure Dei " ; 2nd by Miles Graye, 1638. *Brasses :* In nave—(1) of William Hyklott, 1508, " which paide for the werkemanship of the wall' of this churche," figure in civil costume, Trinity and indents of two children ; (2) to Margaret Hyklott, 1502, figures of two daughters, one habited as a nun, a Virgin and child, indent only of main figure. *Bracket :* In nave—on splay of window, moulded bracket, 15th - century. *Font* (Plate, p. xlii–iii): octagonal bowl with sunk panels carved with figures—(*a*) baptism of a king, (*b*) man and woman, (*c*) king and queen, (*d*) seraph, (*e*) two men with scrolls, (*f*) martyrdom of St. Andrew, (*g*) two

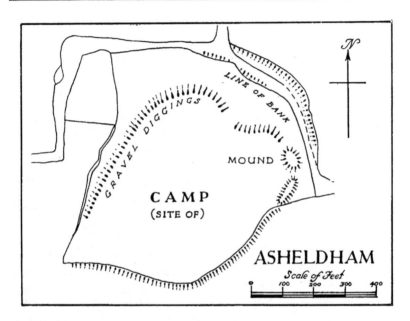

figures of men, moulded under-edge carved with angels, panelled stem, with two ranges of cusped panels divided by an embattled band, moulded base carved with square flowers, *c.* 1400. *Inscription :* On tower—above W. doorway, in black-letter, " + Orate pro animabus dominorum Johannis Wylson et Johannis Hyll quorum animabus propicietur deus amen." *Piscina :* In nave—in S. wall, with rounded head and round drain, 15th-century. *Plate :* includes cup of 1599 with baluster stem. *Sundial :* On buttress on S. side of nave scratched sundial.

Condition—Of tower, bad.

Secular :—

(2). Homestead Moat at Warner's Farm, 400 yards E.S.E. of the church.

(3). Cottage, 170 yards S. of the church, is of two storeys, timber-framed and weather-boarded ; the roofs are tiled. It was built probably in the 16th century with a cross-wing at the E. end. Inside the building are exposed ceiling-beams.

Condition—Fairly good.

2. ASHELDHAM. (G.b.)

(O.S. 6 in. lxiii. N.E.)

Asheldham is a small parish 4 m. N.N.E. of Burnham-on-Crouch.

Ecclesiastical :—

(1). Parish Church of St. Laurence stands on the S. side of the parish. The walls are of septaria with some Roman bricks ; the dressings are of limestone ; the roofs are tiled. The whole church including *Chancel, Nave* and *West Tower* was rebuilt early in the 14th century, the tower being rather later in date than the rest of the building. The chancel was restored in the 19th century when the E. wall was rebuilt and the *South Porch* added.

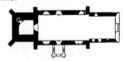

Architectural Description—The *Chancel* (19½ ft. by 17½ ft.) has a modern E. wall and window.

In the N. wall is a 14th-century window of a single trefoiled light. In the S. wall is a 14th-century window of one trefoiled ogee light with moulded jambs, splays and rear-arch ; further E. is a doorway of the same date with moulded and shafted jambs, moulded two-centred arch, rear-arch and labels with head-stops ; the capital of one shaft is foliated. There is no chancel-arch. The *Nave* (38¼ ft. by 18¾ ft.) has in the N. wall two windows, the eastern is of the 14th century and of one cinquefoiled ogee light with a moulded label ; in the E. splay is the 14th-century doorway to the rood-loft staircase ; it has a two-centred head ; the western window is modern ; further E. is the 14th-century N. doorway, with double chamfered jambs and moulded two-centred arch and label. In the S. wall are two windows both modern except for the splays and rear-arches which are probably of 14th and 13th-century date respectively ; between them is the 14th-century S. doorway, similar to the N. doorway.

The *West Tower* (11 ft. square) is of three stages with a modern embattled parapet and undivided externally except by a band of flints above the ground-stage. In the E. wall is a 14th-century doorway with double-chamfered jambs and two-centred head. In the W. wall is a 14th-century window, of one trefoiled ogee light. The second stage has in the N. wall a small loop of Roman brick. The bell-chamber has in each wall a 14th-century window of one trefoiled light.

Fittings—*Communion Table :* with carved and ' gouty' reeded legs with Ionic capitals and fluted top-rail, *c.* 1600. *Floor-slab :* In chancel — to Philip, son of Rev. Philip ' Ranshaw, 1691. *Piscinae :* In nave—in N. wall, with two-centred head and octofoiled drain, 14th-century ; in S. wall, with trefoiled ogee head and octofoiled drain, 14th-century. *Plate :* includes small cup of 1563 with band of. engraved ornament and a mid 17th-century stand-paten. *Sedile :* In chancel—with moulded two-centred arch, label cut back, shafted jambs with moulded capitals and bases, early 14th-century. *Stoup :* In nave—in splay of S. doorway, with trefoiled ogee head and round basin, 14th-century. *Scratchings :* On N. doorway —mason's marks. On jamb of S. doorway—date 1609, etc. *Miscellanea :* Incorporated in N. wall of chancel, fragments of window tracery.

Condition—Good.

Unclassified :—

(2). PLATEAU CAMP, 600 yards W. of the church, appears to have been of irregular shape but the original plan has been much obscured by gravel digging. There is a large mound on the E. side and a rampart continuing to the S.W. The northern boundary is probably represented by the road which makes a detour at this ' point

and the southern side is represented by a slight bank and scarp.

Condition—Bad.

---

3. ASHINGDON. (F.c.)

(O.S. 6 in. lxx. N.W.)

Ashingdon is a small parish about 5 m. N. of Southend-on-Sea. The church is the principal monument.

Ecclesiastical :—

(1). PARISH CHURCH OF ST. ANDREW (Plate, p. xxxii) stands near the middle of the parish. The walls are of ragstone and flint-rubble with septaria, Roman and 16th-century brick ; the dressings are of various limestones and brick ; the roofs are tiled. The *Chancel* and *Nave* were built early in the 14th century and the *West Tower* was added late in .the same century. Early in the 16th century the E. wall of the chancel was rebuilt in brick and the *South Porch* added ; the chancel-arch was perhaps removed at the same time. The church was restored in the 18th century when the S.E. angle of the nave was rebuilt, and again in modern times when the *North Vestry* was added.

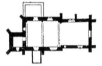

Architectural Description—The *Chancel* (21 ft. by 17½ ft.) has an E. wall of brick with black brick diapering ; the E. window is all modern except the splays and rear-arch which are probably of the 14th century. In the N. wall is an early 16th-century brick window of two four-centred lights with a square moulded label. In the S. wall are two windows, the eastern is of the 15th century and of two cinquefoiled lights in a square head with a moulded label ; the western window is a 14th-century ' low-side' with a plain pointed head. The chancel-arch has been removed except the early 14th-century N. respond of trefoiled plan with moulded capitals and bases.

The *Nave* (25 ft. by 19 ft.) has in the N. wall an early 14th-century window of two pointed lights in a two-centred head with a moulded label ; the rear-arch is of 16th-century brick ; the 14th-century N. doorway has moulded jambs, two-centred arch and label. In the S. wall is an 18th-century window and further W. is the early 14th-century S. doorway with moulded jambs, two-centred arch and label. In the W. wall N. of the tower is a 14th-century window of one trefoiled light.

The *West Tower* (7 ft. by 7½ ft.) is of late 14th-century date and of three stages with a low pyramidal roof with a small saddle at the top. In the E. wall is a doorway with chamfered jambs and two-centred arch. In the S. wall is a plain square-headed window. The second stage has in the S. wall a similar window. The bell-chamber has in the E. wall a square-headed window and the N., S. and W. walls have each a window of two cinquefoiled lights with tracery in a two-centred head with a moulded label; the mullions and tracery of the S. and W. windows are missing.

The *South Porch* is of timber and of early 16th-century date partly restored. It has a flat three-centred outer archway, chamfered wall-plates, wall-posts, plates, tie-beam and curved braces.

The *Roof* of the chancel is of early 16th-century date and of two bays with braced principals forming almost semi-circular arches and an inserted tie-beam; the wall-plates are moulded. The 15th-century roof of the nave is of two bays with moulded wall-plates and tie-beams with king-posts; on the N. side the trusses rest on oak posts, owing to the insecurity of the N. wall.

Fittings—Book : Bible of 1683, oak leather-covered binding with pierced brass mountings. *Font :* octagonal bowl with concave faces and moulded under-edge, plain stem and moulded base, early 16th-century. *Piscinae :* In chancel—with chamfered jambs and pointed head, round drain cut back, 14th-century, reset. In nave—in N. wall, with octofoiled drain and trefoiled head from a former window, 14th-century. *Plate :* includes cup of 1564 with band of engraved ornament, cup of 1640 with baluster stem and a late 17th-century paten; the two last belonged to South·Fambridge. *Recess :* In chancel—in N. wall, square-headed recess with oak lintel, date uncertain, now covered by modern panelling. *Royal Arms :* In nave—on N. wall, Stuart arms painted on wood with moulded frame. *Sundial :* In porch—loose stone with roughly cut sundial. *Miscellanea :* In nave—damaged moulded capital, 14th-century.

Condition—Good, recently restored.

Secular :—

(2). ROUNCEFALL, house, about ½ m. W.S.W. of the church, is of one storey with attics, timber-framed and weather-boarded; the roofs are tiled. It was built in the 17th century on a rectangular plan and has an original central chimney-stack, square on plan with rebated angles. Inside the building the timber-framing and ceiling-beams are exposed.

Condition—Good.

Unclassified :—

(3). RED HILLS, at Beckney Farm, about 2 m. N.W. of the church.

4. AVELEY. (B.e.)

(O.S. 6 in. lxxxiii. N.W.)

Aveley is a parish and small village on the N. bank of the Thames, 6 m. N.W. of Tilbury. The church and Belhus are the principal monuments.

Ecclesiastical :—

(1). PARISH CHURCH OF ST. MICHAEL stands in the village. The walls are of roughly coursed flint and ragstone with some Roman and 16th-century bricks; the tower and the dressings are of limestone; the roofs are covered with tiles, slates and lead. The *Nave* was built early in the 12th century and c. 1160 the *South Aisle* was added. The *North Aisle* was added c. 1220 and about the middle of the 13th century the *Chancel* was rebuilt and the *North Chapel* added; the *West Tower* is of almost the same date. In the 14th century the S. aisle was much altered and partly rebuilt. In the 15th century the N. aisle was extended one bay to the W., the *North Porch* added and the upper part of the tower rebuilt. The clear-storey is probably of 15th-century date but has been largely rebuilt. The church was restored in the 19th century and the chancel partly refaced or rebuilt.

The church is of considerable architectural interest and among the fittings the Flemish brass and the early 17th-century pulpit are noteworthy.

Architectural Description—The·*Chancel* (34 ft. by 16 ft.) has a modern E. window incorporating some·old stones. The N. arcade is of c. 1240 and of two bays with two-centred arches of two chamfered orders; the cylindrical column has a moulded bell-capital and base, and the responds have attached half-columns. In the S. wall are three windows, the easternmost is modern except the 13th-century E. splay and the 15th-century W. splay and rear-arch; the middle window is modern except for the 13th-century splays and rear-arch; the westernmost window is of the 15th century and of three cinquefoiled lights in a square head with a moulded label; below the middle window is a doorway with chamfered jambs and two-centred arch, probably of the 15th century. There is no chancel-arch.

The *North Chapel* (37 ft. by 9¾ ft.) has a modern window in the E. wall. In the N. wall are two windows mostly modern except the splays and rear-arches, which are of 13th-century material, rebuilt in the 15th century.

The *Nave* (41 ft. by 18 ft.) (Plate. p. 8) has a N. arcade of c. 1220 and of three bays with two-centred arches of two chamfered orders; the cylindrical columns have moulded bases and bell-capitals; the responds have each a semi-octagonal attached shaft with moulded imposts; the E. impost is modern; E. of the arcade is a round-

WENNINGTON CHURCH.
17th-century.

GREAT BADDOW CHURCH.
Pulpit with Sounding-board, dated 1639.

ORSETT CHURCH.
Pulpit and Panelling; dated 1630.

NORTH OCKENDON CHURCH.
Mid 17th-century.

EAST TILBURY CHURCH.
Early 17th-century.

BULPHAN CHURCH.
Chancel Screen ; part of W. side ; 15th-century.

CORRINGHAM CHURCH.
Screen to N. Chapel ; early 14th-century.

RAYLEIGH CHURCH.
Screen in W. Arch of N. Chapel ; c. 1500.

STANFORD-LE-HOPE CHURCH.
Screen in W. Archway of S. Chapel ; late 14th or early 15th-century.

PRITTLEWELL CHURCH.
Door in S. Doorway ; early 16th-century.

EASTWOOD CHURCH.
Ironwork on disused N. door; late 12th or
early 13th-century.

BUTTSBURY CHURCH.
Ironwork on N. door of Nave; early
13th-century and later.

STIFFORD CHURCH.
N· door, 16th-century, with re-set ironwork,
early 13th-century.

SOUTH HANNINGFIELD CHURCH.
South door with ironwork; late 14th or early
15th-centur .

RETTENDON CHURCH.
Carved Popey-heads to bench-ends in Chancel; late 15th-century.

GREAT BURSTEAD CHURCH.
Seats in S. Aisle; 15th-century.

EAST HORNDON CHURCH.
Gallery Front, N. side of Nave;
early 17th-century.

DANBURY CHURCH.
Seats in Nave; 15th-century.

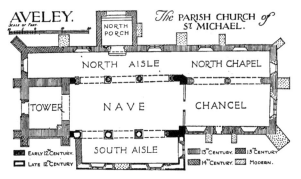

AVELEY. *Scale of Feet.*

The PARISH CHURCH *of* S⸆ MICHAEL.

NORTH PORCH

NORTH AISLE — NORTH CHAPEL

TOWER — NAVE — CHANCEL

SOUTH AISLE

Early 12ᵗʰ Century. — Late 12ᵗʰ Century. — 13ᵗʰ Century. — 14ᵗʰ Century. — 15ᵗʰ Century. — Modern.

headed opening to the rood-loft, covered with modern plaster. The S. arcade is of *c.* 1160 and of three bays with round arches; the two easternmost are of two plain orders but the westernmost has been rebuilt with the original material and is of one wide chamfered order; the piers and responds are of the same section as the arches and have moulded imposts at the springing level; the impost of the W. respond is continued a short distance along the wall and the W. wall of the S. aisle is built against it; over the E. arch is part of the round head of an early 12th-century window. The clearstorey has three modern windows on each side.

The *North Aisle* (9¾ ft. wide) has in the N. wall two partly restored 15th-century windows each of two cinquefoiled lights in a square head with a moulded label; between them is the modern N. doorway. In the W. wall is a window similar to those in the N. wall.

The *South Aisle* (9¼ ft. wide) has a 14th-century E. window, entirely modern externally and of two cinquefoiled lights with a quatrefoil in a two-centred head. In the S. wall are two windows all modern except the splays and rear-arches which are probably of the 14th century; between them is the 14th-century S. doorway with a two-centred head and now blocked.

The *West Tower* (12½ ft. by 15½ ft.) is of two stages with an embattled parapet. The 13th-century tower-arch is two-centred and of one continuous chamfered order. The 15th-century W. window. is of three cinquefoiled lights in a square head with a moulded label and modern mullions; the 15th-century W. doorway has moulded jambs and two-centred arch. The bell-chamber has in the E. wall a window all modern except the splays and rear-arch; the N., S. and W. walls have each a two-light window modern externally but with 15th-century splays and rear-arches.

The *North Porch* is probably of the 15th century but has no ancient features.

The *Roof* of the nave is of the 16th century and of three bays but the trusses have been cased except the westernmost which has a tie-beam with curved braces forming a four-centred arch. The tower has the framing for the old roof.

Fittings—*Bells:* five; 1st and 2nd by John Waylett, 1712; 3rd by William Culverden, early 16th-century and inscribed "Sancte Petre Ora Pro Nobis"; 4th by James Bartlet, 1692; 5th by Thomas Bartlet, 1618. *Bracket:* In nave—on S.W. respond, moulded corbel for image, 15th-century. *Brasses:* In chancel—(1) groups of six sons and two daughters and four shields-of-arms, (a) and (d) *crusily fitchy three lions*, (b) *a fesse and a pierced molet in chief* impaling *three eagles*, (c) (a) impaling the two coats of (b), indents of figures of man and wife, and marginal inscription, *c.* 1520; (2) (Plate, p. 160) of Ralph de Knevynton, 1370, rectangular plate with figure wearing mail hauberk with pointed skirt, rivet-studded haketon on breeches; plate pauldrons, arm-pieces, knee-cops, bainbergs, and sollerets with chains attaching the hilts of the sword and dagger to the plastron of the haketon, head bare, feet on dog, cusped canopy with traceried spandrels, Flemish work, indents of two shields; (3) of Nathaniell and Elizabeth, infant children of Edward Bacon, 1588, with small figures of children, shield-of-arms and two crests; (4) to Edward Barette, 1585, with one shield and one lozenge-of-arms. In N. chapel—(5) to Charles Barett, 1584, with shield-of-arms; palimpsest on the reverse of inscription, part of a Flemish inscription of *c.* 1420. See also Monuments. *Chair* (Plate, p. xlii): In chancel— with carved back, shaped arms and turned front legs, *c.* 1620. *Coffin-lid:* In nave—with raised ornamental cross, late 13th or early 14th-century. *Communion Table:* In tower—with turned legs, cut down, 17th-century, modern top. *Font:*

square bowl with four shallow round-headed panels on each face, cylindrical stem with a small detached shaft at each angle, late 12th-century. *Glass :* In tower—in W. window, four quarries with small quatrefoils and fragments of tabernacle work, head, etc., 14th-century and later. *Monuments* and *Floor-slab.* Monuments : In N. chapel —on E. wall, (1) of Elizabeth, infant daughter of Edward Bacon, 1583, Purbeck marble tablet with side columns of Gothic type with round arch, initials E.B. in spandrels, at back brass of a swaddled infant, head and feet missing, indent of a small lozenge-shaped plate ; on N. wall, (2) Purbeck marble tablet with side columns and round moulded arch, indents of man and woman, one son and one daughter, inscription-plate, Trinity, scrolls and two shields-of-arms, *c.* 1520. In churchyard—W. of tower, (3) to James Jefferȳ, 1703, and seven children, head-stone. Floor-slab : In nave—to Rafe (R ?)ingsall, 1632. *Niche :* In nave—in S.E. respond, with trefoiled head and moulded sill, late 14th or early 15th-century. *Piscinae :* In chancel—sunk in wall, pillar-piscina with scalloped capital, 12th-century, trefoiled ogee recess, 14th-century. In N. chapel—in S. wall, with moulded jambs and unusually cusped head, octofoiled drain partly broken, 14th-century. In S. aisle—in S. wall, with moulded jambs and trefoiled head, 14th-century. *Plate :* includes cup and cover-paten of 1620 and late 17th-century alms-dish given by Thomas Latham, who died 1726. *Pulpit :* hexagonal, pilasters at the angles with strap-ornament, moulded cornice with carved frieze, on S.E. face reversed panel with date 1621, stem springing from hexagonal fluted shaft with moulded base ; hexagonal sounding-board with strap-work frieze and consoles at the angles, panelled soffit with arabesque panel in the middle. *Screen :* Between chancel and nave—moulded head, middle doorway with modern posts, moulded middle rail, on either side of doorway five open panels with cinquefoiled and traceried heads, similar head divided and reused under lintel of doorway, early 15th-century, lower part modern. *Stoup :* In nave—W. of N. doorway, round bowl with triangular brick head, early 16th-century.
Condition—Good.

(2). CHAPEL DE LA LEE, about 150 yards N.E. of the church, has been completely demolished except for a length of about 50 ft. of the N. wall adjoining the main road. It is built of ragstone-rubble repaired with brickwork of varying dates and has a chamfered stone plinth. It is possibly of 14th-century date.

Secular :—

(3). HOMESTEAD MOAT, immediately E. of the church.

(4). KENNINGTONS, house and moat, about 1 m. N.N.W. of the church. The *House* is of two storeys, timber-framed and plastered ; the roofs are tiled. It is possibly the end wing of a 15th-century house, the major part of which has been demolished, and has 17th-century alterations, and modern additions at the back. The central chimney-stack is of 17th-century brickwork. Inside the building some of the timber-construction is exposed and on the first floor is a heavy cambered tie-beam with curved braces.
The *Moat* is fragmentary.
Condition—Of house, good.

(5). BRETTS, house and moat, about 1¼ m. N.N.W. of the church. The *House* is of two storeys ; the walls are of plastered timber-framing and brick and the roofs are covered with slate. It was built possibly in the 14th century and is of half H-shaped plan with the cross-wings extending towards the E. Alterations were made in the 16th and 17th centuries. Modern work includes the one-storey addition on the E. front and considerable alterations to the roof. The reset 15th-century entrance doorway has a four-centred head with trefoiled spandrels, within a square moulded frame. The 17th-century chimney-stacks are rectangular and have moulded stringcourses just above the ridge of the roof. Inside the building some of the main ceiling-beams are exposed and the passage in the N. wing has the joists showing, and a four-centred archway. In the E. wall of the original hall are two blocked windows, each of two cinquefoiled lights in a square head with a moulded label ; they have stone dressings and are of 15th-century date. There are two moulded batten doors of early 17th-century date and the N.W. room has a fireplace with a segmental-pointed head. On the first floor some of the timber-construction is exposed. In the E. wall are two blocked windows with diamond-shaped mullions and two of the rooms have open fireplaces with four-centred heads. The hall was divided into three bays and had curved braces to the roof-trusses, forming two-centred arches. The wall-plates to the middle bay are richly moulded but are apparently not *in situ.* The roof over the N.E. wing is of central-purlin type with curved braces.
The *Moat* is incomplete. The N. and W. arms remain and are still filled with water and on the E. side is a sunk wall of old brickwork which was possibly a retaining wall to the E. arm.
Condition—Of house, good.

(6). BELHUS, house, stables and outbuildings, ¾ m. N.N.E. of the church. The *House* is mainly of three storeys ; the walls are of brick with some stone dressings ; the roofs are tiled. The building to which reference is made in the will of John Barrett, who died in 1526, as " my place called Bellhouse Hall, alias Barretts, which I have

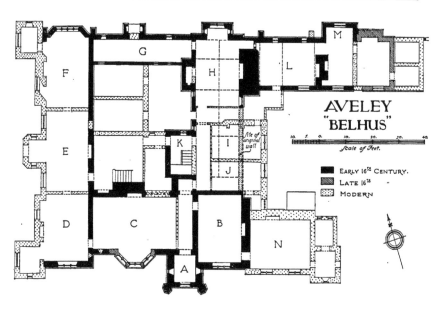

AVELEY
"BELHUS"

Scale of Feet.

EARLY 16th CENTURY.
LATE 16th "
MODERN

newly builded," forms the nucleus of the present house, but it seems probable that only part of the building was completed at the time of his death. It was built round a rectangular court-yard with the principal front facing the S. and the N. range extending eastwards some distance beyond the E. wall of the main building. The Hall was in the middle of the S. range and had at the S.E. corner a tower ; in the S.E. angle of the courtyard was the staircase-block. Late in the 16th century an extension or rebuilding was made of the N.E. wing and about the same time a bay-window of two storeys was built on the S. side of the Hall, when it is probable that the S. wall of the original building was raised to its present height. Very considerable alterations and additions were made during the 18th and 19th centuries which include the rebuilding of the whole of the W. wall and redecoration of the rooms in the W. range, the building of a staircase and rooms on the S. and W. sides of the courtyard, the extending eastwards of the S. range and the widening of the middle part of the E. range by the removal and rebuilding of the E. wall further towards the E. In recent years one storey additions have been made at the E. end of the N. and S. ranges.

The house is interesting as an example of an early Tudor mansion, but the mid 18th-century and later alterations in the 'Gothic style' have robbed the building of its original character.

The *S. Front* (Plate, p. 9) is flanked at either end by modern towers and includes, at the E. end, the modern S.E. addition. The rest of the front, including the tower in the middle, is mainly of 16th-century date and of red brick with the original walling diapered with black headers. It has a plinth with a moulded stone offset, and, on either side of the tower, a plain continuous parapet with a moulded brick coping. The S. walls of the side ranges project beyond the face of the Hall block and were originally gabled ; the moulded brick corbelling which carries the upper part of the return wall on the E. side of the W. wing probably indicates the eaves-level of the original gable. The tower is of four storeys, undivided externally, and has at the N.W. corner an octagonal stair-turret leading from the second floor and carried up above the parapet ; it rests on a four-centred arch across the external N.W. angle. At the other angles are polygonal clasping buttresses which rise above the parapet and terminate in conical caps. The windows to the ground-storey are modern, the southern one replacing the original entrance-doorway; the remaining windows are original and each of one or two four-centred lights. The stair-turret has nine small loops, mostly blocked. The bay-window to the hall is of late 16th-century date and has two four-centred lights in each face; the remaining windows are modern except for some small blocked lights. Inserted in the plinth W. of the tower are five square panels of plastered brick with heraldic figures in relief; two with a double-headed spread-eagle, two with a swan and one with a fleur-de-lis.

The *N. Elevation* (Plate, p. 9) is unsymmetrical and of two storeys except the modern N.W. tower and the N. ends of the cross-ranges which are of three stages. The W. bay is semi-hexagonal on plan and is flanked on either side by a buttress which is surmounted by a twisted shaft with a moulded capping; the parapet of the N. wall has a finial of a similar twisted form. On the remainder of the front are three original projecting bays each with crow-stepped gables, the westernmost forming a porch with a four-centred entrance-archway, internal side-recesses or seats, and an inner doorway, now blocked. Most of the small single-light windows are original and have four-centred heads but only two of the larger ones are entirely of 16th-century date.

The E. wall of the *N.E. Wing* is gabled and the S. wall has some diaper-work on the early 16th-century part of the wall. The windows are square-headed and in the S. wall are two doorways, one blocked, the other which has a four-centred head is covered by a modern porch. The E. wall of the E. cross-wing is modern but, inside the building, part of the original wall remains and has in the N. end a blocked square-headed window to the kitchen (H). Reset in the modern porch is a 16th-century doorway (Plate, p. 64) with richly carved frame and head; the frame has two female figures, one holding a bird, the other a looking-glass and both standing on corbels; carved on the head of the doorway is a cherub and various emblematic figures, now much defaced. The door is divided into eight panels by moulded and nail-studded rails and muntins and is hung on three strap-hinges with fleur-de-lis ends. The elevations to the original courtyard have been almost completely covered by later additions but in the S. wall is a large window of four four-centred lights in a four-centred head and now blocked.

Interior. The *Ground Storey* of the tower (A) originally formed the main entrance porch and has a quadripartite vault now plastered over. The original Hall (C) contains some fragments of 16th and 17th-century panelling but the screen is modern. Between room (E) and the W. porch are two large doors of *c.* 1540; they are remarkably fine examples of Flemish workmanship with the lower part of carved and linen-fold panels and the

upper divided into open trefoiled lights by richly carved posts. At the sides are reused panels carved with tracery and figures. In room (F) is some reused panelling and some tapestry of *c.* 1700. The original main beams are exposed in the ceilings of the Kitchen (H) and the rooms adjoining on the S.; the W. fireplace in (H), though partly bricked up, retains an original four-centred arch-recess. In the N. wall of room (I) is a reused mantelpiece and overmantel of *c.* 1600 (Plate, p. 65). The overmantel is carried on two fluted pilasters and is divided into two main panels by tapering pilasters supporting a moulded cornice and frieze carved with strap-work ornament; each panel has a raised and arched recess containing a small obelisk. Room (J) has some 17th-century panelling and incorporated in the window of the staircase (K) are some fragments of carved woodwork from a doorway or fireplace. The projecting bay (M) originally contained a staircase, since removed. On the *First Floor*, in the room over (F), is some early 18th-century tapestry and on the N. wall of the passage or gallery, on the N. side of the courtyard, are the remains of an early 16th-century painting in black and red probably historical and representing numerous mounted figures of men and women in contemporary costume; some of the men carry shields one of which has *a double-headed eagle*. Only part of the painting is exposed the remainder being covered with plaster. The room over the W. end of (L) is entered from the adjoining passage through a four-centred doorway and there is a blocked doorway in the E. wall, the timber-framing of which is exposed. There is some 17th-century panelling in the modern staircase leading to the second floor of the tower and the staircase between the third and fourth stage has its original treads and circular newel. The *Roof* over the Hall block has tie-beams with curved struts supporting purlins with curved wind-braces and collar-beams; the roof over the N.E. wing is of similar construction. The roof of the W. range is now inaccessible.

A considerable amount of glass of varying dates is incorporated in the windows. In the Library (B) is a panel with an early 17th-century portrait and arms of Sir Francis Bacon. In the ground-floor of the Tower in the S. window (brought from Hurstmonceaux) are two shields (*a*) Fiennes impaling Holland; (*b*) France; in the E. window are two roundels with the Fiennes badge, a wolf-hound, contained in a wreath of foliage and pomegranates; set in fragmentary quarries with the initials R. and E. (for Roger Fiennes and Elizabeth Holland), all within a border of dog collars and chains and fragments of the Fiennes motto. In the W. window is similar glass, all 15th-century. In the Hall (C) in four middle lights of bay-window are (1) a roundel within a

AVELEY : PARISH CHURCH OF ST. MICHAEL.
Interior, showing S. Arçade, *c.* 1160 ; N. Arçade, *c.* 1220, etc.

South Front.

North Front.

AVELEY : BELHUS. Early 16th-century and later.

bay chaplet with the quartered shield of Norris and Mountfort impaling Vere quartering Howard ; some of the glass is diapered, and some has small modern repairs ; (2) a strap-work medallion with the arms of Barrett, *parted palewise barry of four argent and gules counterchanged* quartering Belhouse *argent crusily fitchy sable with three lions gules ;* (3) similar medallion to (2) with the arms of Norris quartering Mountford and impaling Lovell quartering Deyncourt, Burnell and Holland ; (4) a circular medallion of green bay-leaves with the quartered arms of Lovell impaling Beaumont quartering Comyn of Badenoch, Bardolf and Phelips Lord Bardolf, all 16th-century. In the Dining room (D) are (a) a repaired 16th-century shield with the arms of Barrett and Belhouse quarterly impaling Dineley ; (b) a medallion with a Tudor rose on a shield within a chaplet and a strap-work frame, 16th-century ; (c) quartered shield of Barrett and Belhouse, mainly 16th-century ; in the heads of two lights are figures of cherubs, 17th-century. In the windows of the modern S.W. tower are some fragments of 15th-century heraldic glass incorporated in a modern setting and in the S. drawing room is a gartered shield of Vere, 16th-century, but partly modern. In the W. porch are two circular medallions, (a) a representation of the Marriage at Cana, probably Flemish ; (b) a domestic scene of unknown significance ; both 16th-century. In Room (N) is a 17th-century quartered shield of Barrett. In Room (F), some fragments of canopy-work in brown line on white glass, green diapered glass, 15th-century and some older pieces of ruby. On the first floor in room above (D) are two 15th-century roundels with the Fiennes badge, a large subject panel of *c.* 1630–40 and of foreign workmanship, and some miscellaneous glass. In the small room above (E) are two medallions, probably of German origin and representing (a) Joseph's brethren casting him into a pit, 16th-century, and (b) a nimbed saint, probably St. Matthew, 17th-century.

The *Stable* (Plate, pp. 56–7), to the S.E. of the house, is a rectangular building of two storeys with attics. The walls are of brick ; the roofs are tiled. It was built late in the 16th century with N. and S. gabled walls and is now connected on the E. by a modern addition with another stable. It has a plain plinth, projecting string-courses of brick at the floor-levels and shaped kneelers of moulded bricks to both gables. The clock-turret and chimney-stack are modern. Inside, the building is divided into three bays by heavy ceiling-beams.

The *Stable* adjoining on the E. is also of two storeys with attics and has brick walls and a tiled roof. It was remodelled early in the 18th century and has a projecting plinth and plain string-course at the first-floor level. The roof is hipped and has a modillioned cornice at the eaves. With the exception of a five-light window with diamond-shaped mullions in the W. wall all the windows are 18th-century or later insertions. The roof is of collar-beam construction.

The *Stable* to the S. is of brick and timber-framing and though almost entirely rebuilt incorporates some reused 17th-century timber and moulded tie-beams.

Condition—Of house and stables, good but much altered.

MONUMENTS (7–19).

The following monuments, unless otherwise described, are of the 17th century and of two storeys, timber-framed and plastered ; the roofs are tiled. Many of the buildings have exposed ceiling-beams and original chimney-stacks. Condition—Good or fairly good.

MAIN STREET, S. side :—

(7). *House*, now two shops, 60 yards N. of the church, is part of a 16th-century house and has a modern addition at the back. The upper storey projects on the N. front and is gabled at the E. end, it also projected at the E. end of the S. elevation but has been underbuilt.

(8). *House*, now three tenements, 20 yards E. of (7), has gabled cross-wings at either end and has been much altered and partly refaced with brick.

(9). *House*, now two tenements, E. of (8), is of two storeys with attics. The walls are of brick and the house was built probably late in the 16th century. The entrance door to the W. tenement is of three vertical moulded panels. In the S. wall are two blocked windows each of a single light with chamfered jambs and the S. chimney-stack is original and has two diagonal shafts set on a rectangular base.

(10). *House*, now tenements, E. of (9), has modern additions at the back.

(11). *House*, now tenements, E. of (10), has walls of weather-boarded timber-framing and was built probably in the 16th century on an L-shaped plan with the wings extending towards the S. and E. The upper storey projects at the W. end of the N. front on three brackets. The original W. chimney-stack has three diagonal shafts. Inside the building some of the timber-construction is exposed.

(12). *House*, 20 yards E.N.E. of (11), is of two storeys with attics. It was built probably in the 16th century and has modern additions. The upper storey of the original building projects along the whole of the N. front and has a bracket at either end.

(13). *House*, now two tenements, 60 yards E.N.E. of (12), was originally of the central-chimney type but has a later S.W. extension and a modern addition at the back.

Main Street, N. side :—

(14). *Prince Albert Inn*, 60 yards N.W. of (7), is of two storeys with attics and was built in the 16th century on an L-shaped plan with the wings extending towards the N. and E.; it has been added to on the N. and E. The roof over the front block has been raised and in it are three gabled dormers. The main chimney-stack is of cruciform plan, set diagonally on a square base.

(15). *House*, now three tenements, and garden wall, 20 yards W. of (14). The *House* was built on an L-shaped plan with the wings extending towards the N. and E. but a later addition in the angle and modern additions on the N. make the existing plan very irregular. The W. wing is gabled at either end and the E. end of the S. front has been refaced with modern brick. Inside the building, on the first floor, is some early 17th-century panelling. The *Wall* running N. from the W. end of the house for a length of about 20 ft. is of old flint-rubble.

(16). *House*, now two tenements, at W. corner of road running N., ¼ m. W.N.W. of the church, is of one storey with attics. It is of the central-chimney type with a modern addition on the N. and has a thatched roof.

---

(17). *Courts*, house, ¼ m. N.E. of the church, was built probably in the 16th century on an L-shaped plan with the wings extending towards the N. and W. It has a later extension on the E. and modern additions on the N. The upper storey of the original building projects on the S. front and is supported on three heavy carved brackets. Inside the building in the entrance passage is some early 17th-century panelling.

(18). *Cottage*, near Vicarage, 950 yards N.W. of the church, is roofed partly with tiles and partly with slates. It is of central-chimney type and has modern additions on the N. and E.

(19). *Lennard Arms Inn*, on border of parish, nearly 1½ m. W.N.W. of the church, is a small building of the central-chimney type, possibly of 16th-century date, with modern additions on the N. and E.

BADDOW, see GREAT BADDOW.

5. BARLING. (F.c.)

(O.S. 6 in. (a)lxx. S.E. (b)lxxi. S.W. (c)lxxviii. N.E. (d) lxxix. N.W.)

Barling is a small parish about 4 m. N.E. of Southend-on-Sea. The church is the principal monument.

Ecclesiastical :—

d(1). PARISH CHURCH OF ALL SAINTS, stands near the middle of the parish. The walls are of ragstone-rubble with some flint in the nave; the dressings are of various limestones, the roofs are tiled and the spire boarded. The S. wall of the *Nave* is possibly of the 12th century as indicated by its thickness and the rear-arch of the S. doorway. The Chancel was subsequently lengthened and probably early in the 15th century a N. vestry was added; the base of the walls are probably of this date; the *West Tower*, also, was added early in the 15th century. The *Chancel* was rebuilt except the N. wall and the *North Aisle* with its arcade added *c.* 1500; a S. porch was perhaps added at the same date. The upper part of the *South Porch* is of late 16th or 17th-century date. The *Vestry* was rebuilt early in the 19th century and the church was restored in 1863–4. Amongst the fittings the carved alabaster 'tables' from a former reredos are noteworthy.

Architectural Description—The *Chancel* (30 ft. by 16½ ft.) has an E. window all modern except the 15th-century splays. In the N. wall is a 15th-century doorway with chamfered jambs and two-centred head; further W. is an arch for which see Nave arcade. In the S. wall are two windows and a doorway all modern except the splays of both and the rear-arch of the western window. The side walls have a moulded string-course, at the eaves-level, and carried across the E. wall as a string to the former low-pitched gable. There is no chancel-arch.

The *North Vestry* has the base of the walls of ragstone-rubble.

The *Nave* (35¾ ft. by 17¾ ft.) has a N. arcade of *c.* 1500 and of four bays with two-centred arches of two moulded orders; the octagonal columns have concave faces and moulded capitals and bases; the E. arch is higher than the rest and springs, on the E., from a moulded corbel-capital with concave faces and a boss of foliage at the bottom; the W. respond has an attached half-column. In the S. wall are two windows, the eastern modern and the western of the 14th century and of two cinquefoiled lights with a cusped spandrel in a two-centred head; between the windows is the S. doorway all modern except the plastered semi-circular rear-arch which may be of the 12th century.

The *North Aisle* and *Chapel* (12 ft. wide) is entirely of *c.* 1500 and has in the E. wall a window of three cinquefoiled lights in a segmental-pointed head. In the N. wall are three windows each of two cinquefoiled lights in a segmental-pointed head with a moulded label; between the two eastern windows is the rood-loft staircase, the lower doorway having a four-centred and the upper a rough triangular head; between the two western windows is the N. doorway, now blocked, with moulded jambs, two-centred arch and label with reused head-stops. In the W. wall is a window uniform with that in the E. wall, but with a moulded label.

The *West Tower* (10 ft. by 9½ ft.) (Plate, p. 12) is of early 15th-century date and of three stages with an embattled parapet and on the E. face the marks of the former steep-pitched roof of the nave. The two-centred tower-arch is of two hollow-chamfered orders, the inner continuous and the outer dying on to the square responds. The W. doorway has moulded jambs, two-centred arch and label; the W. window is of two cinquefoiled lights with vertical tracery in a two-centred head with a moulded label. The N., S. and W. walls of the second stage have each a single pointed light. The bell-chamber has in each wall a window of two trefoiled lights in a square head with a defaced label. Between the first and second stages on the W. face is a band of flint and stone chequerwork continued round the side walls as a band of flint. On the E. wall are traces of the former high-pitched roof of the nave.

The *South Porch* is probably of late 16th-century date and is timber-framed and stands on stonerubble walls of earlier date. It has a squareheaded outer entrance with a moulded frame and two cambered tie-beams with curved braces.

The *Roof* of the chancel has two moulded tiebeams of *c.* 1500 and an old tie-beam at the W. end. The gabled roof of the N. aisle has old moulded tie-beams reused, the four westernmost tie-beams being moulded and of *c.* 1500.

Fittings—Bells: two; 1st by John Dier, late 16th-century; 2nd by John Hodson, 1666. *Brass Indent:* Outside W. doorway—of inscription-plate and probably figure. *Chest:* In tower —front only, with four panels of conventional foliage, late 16th-century. *Coffin-lid:* In N. aisle—with incised cusped cross and stepped calvary, late 13th or early 14th-century. *Door:* In N. doorway—of ridged battens with fillets over joints, *c.* 1500. *Font:* octagonal, four sides panelled with blank shields in squares, three with quatrefoils in circles and one blank, moulded under-side and base, buttressed stem, *c.* 1500. *Glass:* In N. aisle—loose against E. window, roundel with interlacing pattern and roses, 15th-century. *Locker:* In chancel—in N. wall, rectangular with chamfered edges, date uncertain. *Monuments* and *Floor-slabs.* Monuments: In churchyard—S.E. side, (1) to George Asser, 1674, and Susanna, his wife, 1658, table-tomb of stone,

with carved sides and moulded slab, hour-glass and skull at ends; S.W. of tower; (2) to Susanna, wife of William Cripps, 1714, also to William Cripps, 1752, stone table-tomb. Floor-slabs: In chancel— (1) to George Asser, 1683, and ——, his wife, 1686, late the wife of Thomas Wright; (2) to Richard Bateman, 1668, with achievement-of-arms. *Niches:* On W. face of tower—three, two lower with trefoiled and upper with cinquefoiled head, 15th-century. *Piscina:* In chancel—with trefoiled head and round drain, probably 14th-century reset. *Plate:* includes cup of 1562 with two engraved bands, paten of 1566 or 1568 and two pewter plates. *Pulpit:* hexagonal, with bolection-moulded panelled sides, cornice and lower rail, shaped and moulded standard against wall with carved consoles, sounding-board with panelled soffit and five carved rosettes as pendants, late 17th-century. *Reredos:* In vestry—from former reredos, two alabaster carvings (Plate, p. 25), both headless, probably of St. Dominic, in monastic habit, and a seated figure, with remains of colour, early 15th-century. *Sedile:* In chancel— sill of S.E. window carried down to form seat. Condition—Good.

Secular :—

c(2). HOMESTEAD MOAT, at Mucking Hall, about 1 m. W. of the church.

MONUMENTS (3–9).

The following monuments, unless otherwise described, are of the 17th century, and of two storeys, timber-framed and plastered or weatherboarded; the roofs are tiled. Many of the buildings have original chimney-stacks and exposed ceiling-beams.
Condition—Good, or fairly good.

d(3). *House,* two tenements, 100 yards S.W. of the church, has on the W. front remains of ornamental pargeting including a panel with the date 167(8) and a circle surrounded by hearts. The chimney-stack at the S. end has two restored diagonal shafts.

d(4). *House,* 500 yards S.S.W. of the church, has modern additions at the back and side.

d(5). *House,* 600 yards W. of the church, is modern but incorporates a small portion of a 15th-century building. The original roof is of the central-purlin type with king-posts, struts and cambered tie-beams in the end walls.

b(6). *Roper's Farm,* house, about 1,100 yards N.W. of the church, has a modern addition at the back. There are curved brackets to an exposed ceiling-beam on the first floor.

a(7). *Trumpions,* house, 300 yards S.W. of (6), was built possibly in the 15th century, with a central Hall and E. and W. cross-wings. The

Hall roof has been raised and a first floor inserted. In the E. wall is a blocked two-light window with diamond-shaped mullions.

*(8). *Cottage*, 100 yards N.W. of Trumpions, has modern additions at the E. and W. ends.

*(9). *Jail Farm*, house and walling, about ¾ m. W.S.W. of the church. The *House* incorporates a portion of a 15th-century house which originally extended further E. The W. end was altered in the 17th century. The centre part of the building was originally the W. end of the hall and open to the roof but has had a first floor inserted ; the E. end is modern. Inside the building is an original roof-truss ; the king-post has a plain capital and base and four-way strut.

N. of the house is a length of about 15 ft. of rubble *Walling* said to have been part of a jail of the Bishops of London.

---

6. BASILDON.   (D.c.)

(O.S. 6 in. (a)lxviii. S.E. (b)lxxvi. N.E.)

Basildon is a parish 4 m. S.E. of Billericay.

Ecclesiastical :—

*(1). PARISH CHURCH OF HOLY CROSS (Plate, p. xxxii) stands near the middle of the parish. The walls are of ragstone-rubble and brick with dressings of Reigate and other limestone : the roofs are tiled. The *Nave* was built in the 14th century and about the middle of the 15th century the *South Porch* was added, followed by the *West Tower* c. 1500. The *Chancel* was rebuilt in brick in 1597. In 1702 the church was extensively repaired, most of the N. wall of the nave being rebuilt in brick. The church has been restored in modern times.

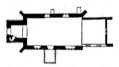

Architectural Description—The *Chancel* (17½ ft. by 18 ft.) is of red 16th-century brick and has a modern E. window. Above it is an inscription recording the building of the chancel by Arthur Den[ham 1597]. The S. wall has been rebuilt above the plinth and has two modern windows. There is no chancel-arch.

The *Nave* (41¼ ft. by 20½ ft.) has in the N. wall a reset 15th-century window of two trefoiled lights in a square head with a moulded label ; further W. is the 14th-century N. doorway with moulded jambs, two-centred arch and defaced label ; it is

now blocked ; W. of the doorway .the wall is probably of the 14th century but E. of it the wall, as indicated in a painted inscription on a framed board, is of 1702. In the S. wall are two windows, the eastern of the 15th century and of three cinquefoiled lights in a square head with a moulded label ; the western window is similar but of two lights ; between them is the 14th-century S. doorway with moulded jambs and two-centred head.

The *West Tower* (9 ft. by 9½ ft.) is of c. 1500 and of three stages, divided externally into two by a string-course. The two-centred tower-arch is of two orders, the outer moulded and continuous and the inner chamfered and dying on to the side walls. The W. window is of two cinquefoiled lights in a square head with a moulded label ; the W. doorway has moulded jambs, two-centred arch and label. The N., S. and W. walls of the second stage have each a window of one trefoiled light with a square moulded label. The bell-chamber has in each wall a window of two trefoiled lights in a square head with a moulded label.

The *South Porch* is of mid 15th-century date and is timber-framed. The four-centred outer archway has spandrels carved with defaced foliage. The barge-boards of the S. gable have rather elaborate trefoiled cusping. The side walls have been much restored and have each two bays, each bay divided into four lights by moulded mullions. The roof has moulded wall-plates and a cambered tie-beam with curved braces ; the spandrels are carved with a bear and ragged staff (Plate, p. 84) and a dragon.

The *Roof* of the chancel is of early 16th-century date and has moulded and embattled purlins, moulded ridge and rafters and principals with curved braces forming three-centred arches. The nave has five chamfered tie-beams probably of early 18th-century date.

Fittings—*Bells:* three, inaccessible but said to be; 2nd by William Land, 1634 ; 3rd by Henry Jordan, 15th-century and inscribed " Sancta Margareta Ora Pro Nobis." *Brass Indents:* In nave—partly under pulpit, (1) of figure with remains of marginal inscription in Lombardic letters, 14th-century ; (2) of half figure of priest and inscription-plate. *Communion Rails:* with moulded and carved rail and turned and twisted balusters, c. 1700. *Communion Table:* In tower—with turned baluster legs, c. 1700. *Door:* In S. doorway—of moulded overlapping battens, 16th-century. *Monument:* In churchyard—S.E. of chancel, to Mary, daughter of John Betts, 1662, head-stone. *Plate:* includes cup of 1709 with the date 1710 and the arms of Queen Anne. *Royal Arms:* In nave—on N. wall, of Queen Anne before the union, painted on wood. *Weather-vane:* On tower—with initials and date F.A. 1702.

Condition—Good.

BARLING : PARISH CHURCH OF ALL SAINTS. From the North-West.
West Tower, early 15th-century ; North Aisle, *c.* 1500.

BRADWELL-JUXTA-MARE: ROMAN STATION OR FORT.

Secular :—

a(2). HOMESTEAD MOAT and fish-ponds at Moat House on site of Botelers, 250 yards S.E. of the church.

b(3). HOMESTEAD MOAT at Basildon Hall, nearly 1 m. S.S.W. of the church.

BENFLEET, see NORTH BENFLEET and SOUTH BENFLEET.

7. BOWERS GIFFORD. (D.d.)

(O.S. 6 in. lxxvii. N.W.)

Bowers Gifford is a parish 8 m. W.N.W. of Southend-on-Sea.

Ecclesiastical :—

(1). PARISH CHURCH OF ST. MARGARET (Plate, p. xxxii) stands near the middle of the parish. The walls are of ragstone-rubble with some flint and Roman brick ; the dressings are of Reigate stone and the roofs are covered with slate. The whole church, including *Chancel, Nave* and *West Tower*, was rebuilt early in the 16th century except for the S. wall of the nave which is thicker than the other walls and is of uncertain date. The church has been restored in modern times when the chancel has been largely refaced and the *South Porch* added.

Among the fittings the 14th-century brass is noteworthy ; this brass has been ascribed without sufficient evidence to Sir John Gifford, 1348.

Architectural Description—The *Chancel* (21 ft. by 19 ft.) has no ancient features and is structurally undivided from the nave.

The *Nave* (40½ ft. by 18½ ft.) has in the N. wall two early 16th-century windows each of two trefoiled lights in a square head with a moulded label ; further W. is the N. doorway, of the same date and with moulded jambs, two-centred arch and label. In the S. wall are two early 16th-century windows each of three cinquefoiled lights in a square head with a moulded label ; the S. doorway is similar to the N. doorway in date and detail.

The *West Tower* (10 ft. square) is of early 16th-century date and of two stages surmounted by a boarded timber superstructure and a low octagonal spire also boarded. The two-centred tower-arch is of two orders the outer moulded and continuous and the inner hollow-chamfered and dying on to

the responds. In the W. wall is part of the rear-arch and the external relieving-arch of a former W. doorway ; above it is a window of one cinque-foiled light with a square moulded label. The N., S. and W. walls of the second stage have each a window of one trefoiled light with a square moulded label ; the floor of the second stage has hollow-chamfered joists and is supported by braced posts.

Fittings—*Bells :* two ; 1st by Robert Burford, *c.* 1400, inscribed " Sancta Katerina Ora Pro Nobis," and 2nd by William Burford, 14th-century, and inscribed " Sit Nomen Domini Benedictum." *Brass :* In chancel—*c.* 1340, figure (Plate, p. 56) of man wearing surcoat, and mail hauberk with skirts to knee and loose sleeves to mid forearm, gambeson with fluted sleeves, fluted breeches, shell shoulder pieces and elbow roundels fastened with points ; no plate below knee cops, rowel spurs ; heater-shaped shield with diapered field and *six fleurs-de-lis*, head and part of right leg missing. *Door :* In S. doorway—of two folds with overlapping nail-studded battens, early 16th-century. *Font :* octagonal bowl with moulded under-edge, plain stem and hollow-chamfered base, early 16th-century ; font-cover : old finial with facets and lozenge-ornament painted gold, red and white, 16th or 17th-century. *Piscina :* In chancel — with moulded jambs and trefoiled head, 15th-century.

Condition—Good.

Secular :—

HOMESTEAD MOATS.

(2). At Bowers Hall, 600 yards N. of the church.

(3). At the Rectory, about ½ m. N.N.W. of the church.

8. BRADWELL-JUXTA-MARE. (G.a.)

(O.S. 6 in. *(a)*lv. N.E. *(b)*lv. S.E. *(c)*lvi. N.W.)

Bradwell-juxta-Mare is a parish 10 m. E. of Maldon. The remains of the Roman station of Othona and the chapel of St. Peter-on-the-Wall are the principal monuments.

Roman :—

e(1). FORT, probably OTHONA. The remains of a Roman fort, largely destroyed by the sea, are still partly visible 2 m. E.N.E. of the parish church. The plan, as revealed by excavation in 1864, shows the W. wall, 522 ft. long, and fragments of the N. and S. walls, 290 ft. and 150 ft. long respectively. The corners are rounded. At the N.W. corner is a horse-shoe bastion, 16 ft. in diameter, and 115 ft. further S. is a similar bastion ; a third was

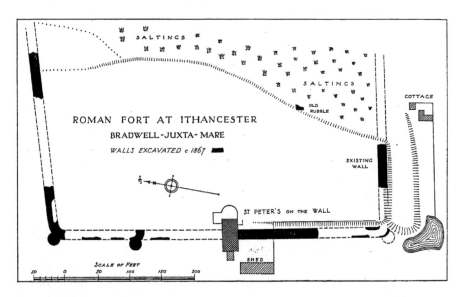

ROMAN FORT AT ITHANCESTER
BRADWELL-JUXTA-MARE
WALLS EXCAVATED c 1867

SALTINGS

SALTINGS

OLD RUBBLE

COTTAGE

EXISTING WALL

ST PETER'S ON THE WALL

SHED

SCALE OF FEET

thought to have existed at the S.W. corner. The wall seems to have been about 12 ft. thick, and a fragment still existing on the S. side shows a triple layer of bricks (measuring 10–10¾ in. long by 1–1¾ in. thick), four courses of septaria (measuring 4½–6 in. by 3–3½ in.), surmounted by a second triple layer of bricks, with lavish use of mortar. The fragment (Plate, p. 13) stands to a height of 4 ft., and the interior of the fort is now level with the top of it. No gateways are known, but the line of the road approaching the site from the W. indicates the position of one approximately on the site of St. Peter's Chapel. Traces of a ditch have been observed on the W. and N. sides ; on the S. side the line is marked by a wide ditch and by a pond at the S.W. corner. Traces of seaweed 5 ft. above the present high-water mark, apparently on the S. side, suggested to the excavators a Roman wharf, but without reason. Within the fort, the only structure noted was a short fragment of "old rubble-work" about 4 ft. high near the S. wall. No structural remains or burials are known outside the fort.

Many small objects were turned up during the excavations and are preserved by Mr. Christopher Parker at Faulkbourne Hall. Potsherds, coins and other small objects can be picked up on the surface. The coins date from Gallienus to

Arcadius but are commonest for the Constantinian period. The pottery is mostly of the same date though a little appears to be of the second century as does also one brooch.

In character the fort resembles others of the series defending the 'Saxon Shore.' On the supposition that it was originally square, it would have contained rather more than 6 acres and so would have approximated in size, as in character, to the fort at Burgh in Suffolk. If its identification with the 'Othona' of the *Notitia Dignitatum* be accepted, it was garrisoned by irregular troops called Fortenses. (See *Sectional Preface*, p. xxxviii ; and *Arch.*, XLI, 440 ; *Arch. Journ.*, XXII, 64, and XXIII, 60 ; C. R. Smith in *Gent.'s Mag.*, 1865, II, 403–8 ; *Coll. Antiq.*, VII, 155–6 ; Laver, *Essex Arch. Soc.*, XI, 85 ; Raven, *Ibid.*, VI, 291, 352. Further note by Chancellor in *Arch. Journ.*, XXXIV, 212–3. C. R. Peers on the Chapel, *Ibid.*, LVIII, 420, with plan.)

Ecclesiastical :—

ᵃ(2). PARISH CHURCH OF ST. THOMAS stands in the village. The walls of the chancel are of flint and septaria-rubble, those of the nave are of brick and stone and the tower is of brick ; the dressings are of limestone ; the roofs are tiled. The *Chancel* was built probably early in the 14th century. The *Nave* was rebuilt in 1706 and the *West Tower* added. The church has been restored in modern times, the N. *Organ Chamber* added and the chancel partly rebuilt.

Architectural Description—The *Chancel* (37½ ft. by 19 ft.) has a modern E. window. In the N. wall is a window all modern except the splays ; further W. is a modern archway. In the S. wall are two windows uniform with that in the N. wall. The early 14th-century chancel-arch is two-centred and of two moulded orders ; the responds have each three attached shafts with moulded capitals.

The *Nave* (65¼ ft. by 25 ft.) is of *c.* 1706 except the E. gable, which is partly of early 16th-century brick with trefoiled corbelling ; all the windows and the doorway are modern.

The *West Tower* (10¼ ft. square) is of red brick and of three stages with an embattled parapet. It is entirely of *c.* 1706. In the E. wall is a modern doorway. The N. and S. walls have each a window with a rounded head, wooden frame, mullion and transom. In the S. wall is a doorway with a segmental head. The W. doorway is modern. The second stage has windows in the N. and S. walls, and the bell-chamber a window in each wall, all similar to those in the ground-stage.

Fittings—*Brasses* and *Indents*. Brasses : In chancel—on N. wall, (1) of Margaret Wyott, 1526, figure of woman in pedimental head-dress, etc. ; (2) shield-of-arms—*three owls and a sinister quarter impaling four bars on a bend three scallops,* early 16th-century ; (3) to John Debanke, rector, 1601, inscription only ; (4) to Thomas Debanck, 1606, inscription only. Indents : In nave—(1) and (2) of inscription-plates ; (3) of two figures, two groups of children, inscription-plate and shield ; (4) of figure, inscription-plate and shield. *Chair :* In chancel—with turned legs and carved back, early 18th-century. *Font* (Plate, pp.xlii–iii) : octagonal bowl with moulded under-edge and four large heads, one of a priest and one with a bandeau, projecting from alternate faces and formerly with a shaft beneath each, round stem, 14th-century. *Monuments :* In chancel—in N. wall, (1) two stone panels, from former monument, with cusped heads and shields—(a) *a cheveron engrailed between three roundels each charged with a cross, a crescent for difference,* (b) *a cheveron between three scallops,* early 16th-century ; on S. wall, (2) to John Sherman, S.T.P. Rector of the parish, 1666, alabaster and

black marble tablet with side pilasters and shield-of-arms. *Plate :* includes cup of 1626, dated 1626, and an early 18th-century pewter flagon and plate. *Scratching :* On S. wall of nave—date 1707. *Miscellanea :* Incorporated in walls of nave— many worked stones and 14th-century head-stops.

Condition—Good, but tower overgrown with ivy.

*(3). CHAPEL OF ST. PETER-ON-THE-WALL stands nearly 2 m. E.N.E. of the parish church. The walls are almost entirely of reused Roman material including ashlar, septaria and brick ; the roof is tiled. The chapel is almost certainly that built by Bishop Cedd in *c.* 654 at Ithancester. It stands astride the former W. wall of the Roman station and originally consisted of an apse, *Nave* and W. porch and possibly ' porticus ' on the N. and S. A tower was subsequently added above the porch. It was a chapel-of-ease to Bradwell in the Middle Ages, but was eventually desecrated and used as a barn ; the apse and tower were destroyed. It has recently been restored and is now again used as a chapel (Plates, pp. 16, 17).

The building is of extreme interest as one of the earliest surviving churches in England.

Architectural Description—The *Apse* has been destroyed to the foundations but the plan has been recovered by excavation ; it projected about 17 ft. to the E. of the present E. wall and the side walls rose to a height of 21 ft. The stump of the N. wall retains the W. jamb of a former doorway.

The *Nave* (49½ ft. by 21½ ft.) has walls 2½ ft. thick and rising to a height of 24 ft. under the eaves. In the E. wall are the Roman brick springers and responds of two arches about 2 ft. within the side walls, the rest of the wall is comparatively modern and built of reused material. The arrangement indicated is that of the usual three arches as at St. Pancras, Canterbury, Reculver, etc., but the existing remains of the curves of the two side arches hardly allow of a central arch of the same span. The N. and S. walls were apparently divided into bays by tabled buttresses and there were pairs of similar buttresses at the western corners leaving the angles of the building free. In the middle of the N. and S. walls is a large modern section showing the position of the entrances when the building was used as a barn. At the E. end of the S. wall are remains of an original doorway, perhaps opening into a ' porticus ' and further W. are the foundations of an added wall. The two windows, two on each side, have original jambs and splays and modern lintels replacing original lintels ; they have been much altered ; the N.W. window is blocked and partly destroyed and all are set high in the wall. In the W. wall is an original doorway with a modern lintel ; above it is an original window with a round head of Roman brick and jambs partly of brick and partly of stone. Flanking the doorway are traces

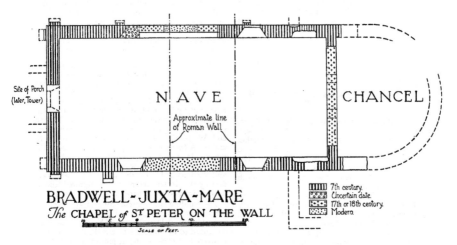

BRADWELL~JUXTA~MARE
The CHAPEL *of* S^T PETER ON THE WALL

7th century.	
Uncertain date.	
17th or 18th century.	
Modern.	

Scale of Feet.

of the junction of the walls of the former porch. Foundations of this porch have been discovered and also those of an annexe on the S. side of the nave.

Condition—Good.

Secular :—

c(4). RECTORY, S. of the church, is of two storeys, timber-framed and plastered ; the roofs are tiled. The N. wing is of early 16th-century date ; it was extended S. at some uncertain date and *c.* 1780 a large S. wing in the Adam style was built. Inside the building one room of the old wing has original moulded ceiling-beams and joists ; the room at the N. end of the same wing has an open-timbered ceiling.

Condition—Good.

c(5). MUNKIN'S FARM, house, ¾ m. S.W. of (3), is of two storeys, timber-framed and weather-boarded ; the roofs are tiled. It was built in the 15th or 16th century with cross-wings at the E. and W. ends. Inside the building are some exposed ceiling-beams and one room is lined with early 18th-century panelling.

Condition—Fairly good.

b(6). BRADWELL HALL, 1¼ m. S.W. of the parish church, is of two storeys, timber-framed and plastered ; the roofs are tiled. It was built early in the 17th century and has a cross-wing at the E. end. The original central chimney-stack has the bases of four grouped diagonal shafts.

Condition—Good.

a(7). CAGE and WHIPPING POSTS, at S. E. corner of churchyard. The cage is an 18th-century structure of brick and built into it are the oak whipping posts.

---

9. BULPHAN. (C.d.)

(O.S. 6 in. ^(a)lxxv. S.E. ^(b)lxxvi. N.W.)

Bulphan is a parish 5½ m. S.S.E. of Brentwood. The church is the principal monument.

Ecclesiastical :—

b(1). PARISH CHURCH OF ST. MARY stands towards the centre of the parish. The walls are of limestone and flint-rubble, modern brick and timber-framing. The *Chancel, Nave, Belfry* and *South Porch* are apparently of late 15th-century date but the church was very considerably repaired and partly rebuilt in the 19th century when the *Vestry* was added and the external walls were refaced so that little of the earlier building remains.

Amongst the fittings the screen, which is said to have been brought from Barking, is of interest.

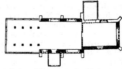

Architectural Description—The *Chancel* (25 ft. by 17¼ ft.) has in the E. wall a modern window.

BRADWELL-JUXTA-MARE : CHAPEL OF ST. PETER-ON-THE-WALL ; *c.* 654.
From the North-West.

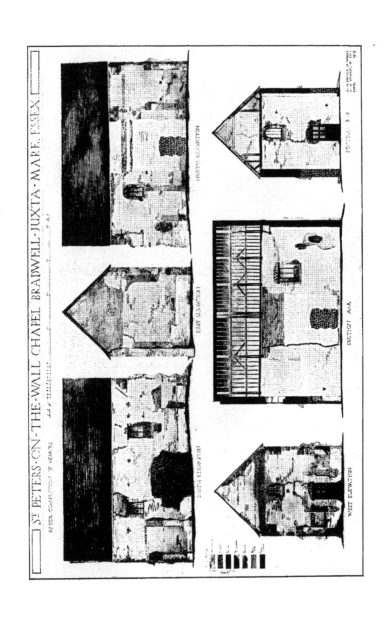

ST PETERS-ON-THE-WALL CHAPEL BRADWELL-JUXTA-MARE, ESSEX

AFTER COMPLETION OF REPAIRS

NORTH ELEVATION

EAST ELEVATION

SOUTH ELEVATION

SECTION A-A

WEST ELEVATION

The N. wall is modern but incorporates a partly restored square-headed window of *c.* 1500 and of two trefoiled lights with a moulded label. In the S. wall, in the refacing of which some old material has been reused, is a similar window. There is no chancel-arch.

The *Nave* (32 ft. by 20¼ ft.) has been largely rebuilt. Reset in the N. wall are two square-headed windows of *c.* 1500 each of two cinque-foiled lights with a moulded label; externally only the head and labels are old. In the S. wall is a doorway of *c.* 1500 with hollow-chamfered jambs, four-centred head and moulded label; the W. jamb has been partly restored.

The *Belfry* (about 24 ft. square) at the W. end of the nave is enclosed within modern timber-framed and plastered walls standing on a brick plinth. It is a heavy timber structure supporting the bell-turret and is of late 15th-century date and divided by oak posts into four bays with side aisles; the curved cross-braces from N. to S. form wide two-centred arches and support the square framework of the modern turret. The N. and S. sides are divided horizontally by cross-beams with diagonal framing above; supporting the cross-beams to the two middle bays are curved braces forming arches into the aisles.

The *South Porch* (Plate, p. xxxix) is of *c.* 1500 and of timber-framing on a modern plinth. The entrance archway has moulded jambs and four-centred head with spandrels carved on both sides with symbols of the Evangelists. On either side the framing is moulded in the form of vertical panels; above is a moulded bressummer and a panelled gable with cusped barge-boards terminating at the apex in an ogee. The sides have each five lights with four-centred heads, traceried spandrels carved with foliage, and grotesques and moulded mullions. The roof is in one bay with a moulded tie-beam at either end supporting a king-post with moulded and curved braces carrying a moulded ridge-piece. Under the N. tie-beam are curved braces forming a four-centred arch with a Tudor rose and conventional foliage carved in the spandrels. The gable at the S. end is panelled and the rafters and wall-plates are moulded.

Fittings—Bell: one, uninscribed. *Brass Indents:* Outside W. doorway—(1) with traces of inscription-plate, probably 16th-century. At entrance to S. porch—(2) of civilian with inscription-plate, late 15th-century. *Font:* In churchyard, by lych-gate, circular stem with moulded edge. *Plate:* includes cup of 1650 and a pewter alms-dish, with shield-of-arms, 17th-century. *Royal Arms:* At W. end of nave—of Queen Anne, in wooden frame. *Screen* (Plates, pp. 4–5, 20): Between chancel and nave—of four bays, two on each side of the entrance, upper panels open with two-centred heads, each subdivided into two trefoiled and sub-cusped lights with open traceried heads; middle rail

moulded and embattled; close lower panels, moulded and having circular and triangular piercings with traces of colour in imitation of tracery on W. face; entrance with cusped and sub-cusped heads and on S. side part of a carved eagle; main spandrels below cornice traceried on E. side and plain on W. side for fixing of former loft, 15th-century, slightly repaired and not *in situ*, cornice modern. *Miscellanea:* Brick panel on outside of S. wall of nave with date and initials in relief $\frac{W}{H S}$ 1686. Part of hollow-chamfered stone window-jamb by lych-gate, probably 15th-century.

Condition—Good, much altered.

Secular :—

HOMESTEAD MOATS.

a(2). At Spring Farm, ¾ m. S.S.W. of the church.

b(3). N. of Noke Hall, nearly 1 m. E.N.E. of the church.

b(4). GARLESTERS, house, 700 yards W. of (3), is of two storeys with attics, timber-framed and plastered; the roofs are tiled. It was built probably in the 16th century. Inside the building some of the timber-framing is exposed.

Condition—Good.

b(5). APPLETON'S FARM, house (Plate, p. xxxv), 100 yards W. of (4), is of two storeys, timber-framed and plastered; the roofs are tiled. It was built in the 15th century with a central Hall and cross-wings at the E. and W. ends. In the 17th century the Hall was divided into two storeys and late in the same century the E. wing was extended N. The upper storey projects at the S. end of both cross-wings, on curved brackets. There is a blocked window to the staircase with bar-mullions, set diagonally. The 17th-century W. chimney-stack has four grouped shafts, set diagonally. Inside the building the ceiling-beams are exposed. The Hall has an original king-post roof with moulded wall-plates. The king-post roof of the E. wing is also original.

Condition—Good.

10. BURNHAM. (G.c.)

(O.S. 6 in. (*a*)lxiii. S.W. (*b*)lxxi. N.W. (*c*)lxxi. N.E.)

Burnham is a parish and small town 9 m. S.E. of Maldon. The church is the principal monument.

Ecclesiastical :—

a(1). PARISH CHURCH OF ST. MARY (Plate, p. xxxii) stands about 1 m. N. of the town. The E. wall of the chancel is of squared diaper of flints, ragstone and 17th-century brick. The S. chapel is of roughly coursed flints; the S. aisle of flint-rubble; the N. aisle of rag-rubble; and the S. porch of flint and rag-rubble. The lower stage of the W.

B

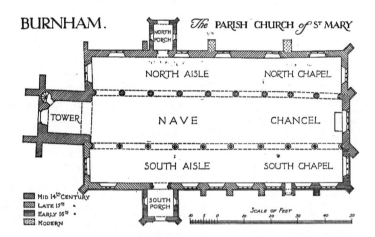

BURNHAM. *The* PARISH CHURCH *of* S^T MARY

NORTH PORCH

NORTH AISLE   NORTH CHAPEL

TOWER

NAVE   CHANCEL

SOUTH AISLE   SOUTH CHAPEL

MID 14TH CENTURY
LATE 15TH "
EARLY 16TH "
MODERN

SOUTH PORCH

SCALE OF FEET
10 5 0   10   20   30   40   50

tower is of septaria with some Roman brick and flint ; the upper stages are of ragstone-rubble. The N. porch is of brick. The dressings are of limestone and the roofs are tiled, except those of the N. and S. aisles which have lead flats. The *Chancel, Nave, North Aisle*, and lower stage of *West Tower* were built towards the middle of the 14th century. In the middle of the 15th century the two upper stages of the tower were added or rebuilt. Late in the same century the N. aisle was lengthened towards the E., forming a *North Chapel*. The *South Aisle* was added *c.* 1500, and lengthened eastward a few years later to form a *South Chapel* and the *South Porch* was also built. The church has been restored in modern times and the upper part of the tower partly rebuilt.

Architectural Description — The *Chancel* and *Nave* (93 ft. by 16½ ft.) are structurally undivided. The 14th-century E. window is modern externally and is of three trefoiled lights in a four-centred head ; the splays have attached shafts with modern capitals and bases. The N. arcade is of nine bays of which the three eastern are of late 15th or early 16th-century date and the six western are of the 14th century ; the arches of the later bays are lower than the rest ; all the arches are two-centred and of two chamfered orders ; the columns are octagonal and have moulded capitals and bases differing in the earlier and later work ; the responds have attached half-columns. The S. arcade is also of nine bays, the six westernmost of *c.* 1500 and the three easternmost of early 16th-century date ; each arch is two-centred and of two moulded orders ;

the columns have each four attached shafts, filleted on the outer face and with moulded capitals and bases ; the responds have attached half-columns.

The *North Aisle* (12 ft. wide) has in the E. wall a late 15th-century window of three cinquefoiled lights in a pedimental head with a moulded label. In the N. wall are five windows, the easternmost is of the 14th century reset, restored externally, and of two trefoiled lights with tracery in a segmental head with a moulded rear-arch ; the second and third windows are of the 14th century, partly restored and each of two trefoiled lights with a moulded label. The two westernmost windows are of mid 14th-century date and have trefoiled ogee lights and moulded rear-arches. The head-stops to the labels are modern and the tracery has been restored. Between these windows is the 14th-century N. doorway with moulded jambs, two-centred arch and label with head-stops. In the W. wall is a window all modern except for parts of the splays and rear-arch which are of late 15th-century date.

The *South Aisle* (12 ft. wide) has a late 15th-century E. window of three cinquefoiled lights in a square head with a moulded label. In the S. wall are seven windows, the three easternmost of *c.* 1520 and the others of late 15th-century date ; each window has three cinquefoiled lights with tracery in a four-centred head with a moulded label ; all have modern repairs ; between the two western windows is the early 16th-century S. doorway with chamfered jambs and three-centred arch and between the second and third windows is a doorway in the buttress with moulded jambs and four-centred head. In the W. wall is a 15th-century window of three cinquefoiled lights in a square head with a label.

The *West Tower* (12 ft. square) is of three stages with an embattled parapet. The 14th-century two-centred tower-arch is of two chamfered orders ; the responds are plain. The W. window of *c.* 1360 is of three trefoiled ogee lights with net-tracery in a two-centred head, repaired in the 16th or 17th century and having a moulded label with head-stops. The internal label has a head-stop on the S. side and the moulded rear-arch springs from attached shafts with foliated capitals and moulded bases. The W. doorway has chamfered jambs, two-centred arch and moulded label ; it is now partly blocked. The N. and S. walls of the second stage have each a 15th-century window of one cinquefoiled light. The bell-chamber has in each wall a 15th-century window of two cinque-foiled lights in a square head. In the W. wall above the window is a large cross in knapped flints.

The *North Porch* is of early 16th-century brick-work with a crow-stepped N. gable. The outer archway has chamfered jambs and a four-centred head. The side walls have each a window of one four-centred light with a square moulded label and now blocked. The E. and W. walls have brick diapering.

The *South Porch* has an early 16th-century outer archway with moulded head and jambs, four-centred arch and label ; above is a shield-of-arms, *a cross between four stars* probably for Dunmow Priory ; round it is a much weathered inscription perhaps reading '' Hoc opus erat quod dominus Johannes Harvy vicarius fieri curavit cujus animae et animabus omnium fidelium deus propicetur Amen 1523.'' Above are two shields-of-arms and a badge (*a*) Fitzwalter ; (*b*) the quartered coat of Radcliff, Lord Fitzwalter impaling the quartered coat of Stafford, Duke of Buckingham ; (*c*) square stone with a star. The side walls have each a window with a four-centred moulded head and moulded label. The parapet wall is embattled.

The *Roof* of the S. Porch has moulded wall-plates of early 16th-century date.

Fittings—*Bells :* five ; 1st and 2nd by Anthony Bartlet, 1673 ; 3rd by John Walgrave, 15th-century and inscribed '' Sancta Katerina Ora Pro Nobis.'' *Brass Indent :* In N. Porch—cracked and broken, 16th-century. *Doors :* In N. doorway —with moulded fillets planted on, trellis-framing, 15th-century. In S. doorway of S. Porch—of linen-fold panels with moulded fillets, early 16th-century. In turret-staircase to tower, with nail-studded iron bands, 15th-century. *Font :* square bowl of Purbeck marble with moulded under-edge, worked round heads of side shafts, cylindrical stem and four small angle shafts, late 12th-century ;

plinth modern. *Glass :* In W. window of tower—portions of kneeling male and female figures, yellow white and ruby, 14th-century. *Monument* and *Floor-slab.* Monument : E. of N. porch—to Sarah, wife of Josiah Kingsman, 1703, table-tomb with moulded edge and achievement-of-arms. Floor-slab : In N. aisle—with inscription illegible except for the date 1678. On same stone to —— (M)iddleston, 1680. *Niche :* In N. aisle—now in N. wall, but not *in situ*, with moulded jambs and triangular head with carved crockets and finial, border of carved fruit and foliage bosses and two shields-of-arms, (*a*) Fitzwalter, (*b*) a *cross formy*, late 14th-century. *Piscina :* In N. aisle—in E. wall, with moulded jambs and trefoiled head, 15th-century. *Plate :* includes cup and stand-paten of 1638. *Scratching :* On S. door of S. aisle —1623 W.M. ; on buttress W. of door to S. chapel, scratched dial.

Condition—Fairly good.

Secular :—

a(2). HOMESTEAD MOAT at Burnham Hall, N. of the church.

MONUMENTS (3–8).

The following monuments, unless otherwise described, are of the 17th century and of two storeys, timber-framed and plastered or weather-boarded ; the roofs are tiled or covered with slates. Some of the buildings have original chimney-stacks and exposed ceiling-beams.

Condition—Good or fairly good, unless noted.

a(3). *Cobbin's Farm*, house, 750 yards N. of the church, has an original chimney-stack with two diagonal shafts.

a(4). *Cherrygarden*, house, ½ m. W. of the church, is built of red brick. The porch on the N. has a gable with concave sides and a moulded pediment. The original chimney-stack at the E. end has four diagonal shafts.

a(5). *Pinner's Farm*, house, 600 yards N.W. of (5).

a(6). *Cottage*, 100 yards S.E. of the church. Inside the building are original shaped brackets.

b(7). *House* on N. side of High Street, 150 yards W. of the end of the street, was built probably in the 16th century and has cross-wings at the E. and W. ends. The walls have been partly refaced with brick.

b(8). *House* opposite (7).

Condition—Poor.

Unclassified :—

c(9). RED HILL at Coleward Farm, 2 m. E.S.E. of the church, and another at Redward Farm, about ½ m. N.E. of Coleward Farm.

———

BURSTEAD, see GREAT BURSTEAD
and LITTLE BURSTEAD.

———

11. BUTTSBURY. (C.c.)

(O.S. 6 in. [a]lx. N.W. [b]lx. N.E. [c]lx. S.W. [d]lx. S.E.)

Buttsbury is a parish immediately N. of Billericay.

Roman :—

[a](1) A kiln was found about 1860 in the garden immediately north of the Workhouse, on the hill north of Billericay, in the south-eastern corner of this parish. It consisted of a circular basin of baked clay, 2½ ft. across and 3 ft. deep, with a rectangular flue running in a north-easterly direction, probably the stoke-hole or chimney. Fragments of vessels were found in and around it and fragments of ' brown jars ' and amphoræ were dug up in the same field. The tradition that a bath and flue with a tessellated pavement were unearthed here is probably a distortion of the above facts. Whatever structure there was could not have occupied a large area, for trenches and pits dug close by for a variety of reasons during the last twenty years have revealed nothing more. Burials with ' Samian ' saucers, a bronze lamp and beads were discovered in widening the neighbouring road in 1863–6 (*Essex Arch. Soc. Trans.*, II, 1863, 72 ; V, 1873, 211 ; hence *Arch. Journ.*, XXXVI, 73 ; and *Soc. of Antiq. Proc.*, VII, 371).

Ecclesiastical :—

[a](2). PARISH CHURCH OF ST. MARY stands on the W. side of the parish. The walls are probably of rubble but are largely covered with cement ; the dressings are of limestone and the roofs are tiled. The *North* and *South Aisles* are perhaps of the 14th century but there is little evidence and they may be of the same date as the arcades, with the two doorways reset. The *Nave* with its N. and S. arcades, was built late in the 15th century. Late in the 18th or early in the 19th century the *Chancel* was rebuilt and the *West Tower* and *South Porch* added.

Architectural Description—The *Nave* (26 ft. by 16½ ft.) has 15th-century N. and S. arcades each of two bays and with two-centred arches of two chamfered orders, the outer continuous and the inner springing from attached semi-octagonal shafts with moulded capitals.

The *North Aisle* (7½ ft. wide) has in the N. wall a modern window and a N. doorway probably

of early 14th-century date and with jambs and two-centred arch of two chamfered orders with a moulded label.

The *South Aisle* (7 ft. wide) has in the S. wall a modern window and a doorway probably of the 14th century and similar to the N. doorway.

The *Roof* of the chancel is of late 15th-century date and of king-post type ; the middle tie-beam is modern.

Fittings—*Bells :* one, probably by Henry Jordan, 15th-century. *Chests :* In nave—at W. end, small framed chest with two old lock-plates and slot for coins, 16th-century. In tower—similar, with horizontal iron bands, probably 17th-century. *Doors :* In N. doorway (Plate, pp. 4–5)—of wide battens with remains of two ornamental hinges, early 13th-century, three added straps with similar ornament, one piece of purely ornamental iron-work and handle, 14th or 15th-century, iron grille in upper part, later. In S. doorway—of four wide battens with iron grille, date uncertain. *Monument* and *Floor-slabs.* Monument : In churchyard —N. of chancel, to Thomas Tyrell, 1638, table-tomb. Floor-slabs : In nave—(1) to Edward Francklin, 1680 ; (2) to Ann (Francklin), wife of John Lockey, 1688. *Plate :* includes cup of 1563 and cover-paten of 1567, both with bands of engraved ornament.

Condition—Bad, cracks in walls and much damp.

Secular :—

[b](3). GREAT BLUNTS, 1½ m. S.E. of the church, is of two storeys with attics, timber-framed and plastered ; the roofs are tiled. It was built probably late in the 16th or early in the 17th century on an irregular half H-shaped plan, the wings projecting towards the W. ; there are later additions at the back. The three original chimney-stacks have, respectively, three diagonal, three octagonal and four square shafts. Inside the building the ceiling-beams are exposed.

Condition—Good.

[b](4). BEAR INN, in Stock village, nearly 1¾ m. E. of the church, is of two storeys, timber-framed and plastered ; the roofs are tiled. It was built in the 16th century on a T-shaped plan, with the cross-wing at the E. end ; at the back are modern additions. The gable on the N. front of the E. wing has original carved barge-boards with moulded pendants.

Condition—Good.

[c](5). HANAKIN'S FARM, house, nearly 1¾ m. S. of the church, is of two storeys, timber-framed and plastered ; the roofs are tiled. It was built in the 16th century on a T-shaped plan with the cross-wing at the E. end. The main block is of one storey only and has an original central chimney-stack.

Condition—Fairly good.

BULPHAN : PARISH CHURCH OF ST. MARY.
East side of Chancel-screen : 15th-century.

CANEWDON : PARISH CHURCH OF ST. NICHOLAS.
West Tower ; early 15th-century.

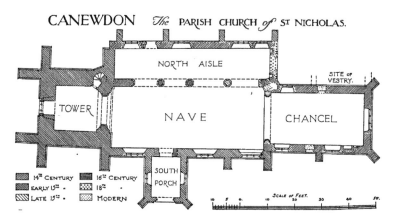

CANEWDON *The* PARISH CHURCH *of* ST NICHOLAS.

14ᵗʰ CENTURY   16ᵗʰ CENTURY
EARLY 15ᵗʰ .   18ᵗʰ .
LATE 15ᵗʰ .   MODERN

SCALE OF FEET.

12. CANEWDON. (F.c.)

(O.S. 6 in. (a)lxx. N.E. (b)lxxi. N.W. (c)lxxi. N.E.)

Canewdon is a parish and village on the S. of the Crouch estuary, 6 m. N. of Southend-on-Sea. The church is the principal monument.

Roman :—

ᵃ(1). A Roman building of some kind is possibly indicated by Roman tiles "excavated on the S. side of the churchyard" about 1848, but no further information is available. Burial-urns, recorded to have been discovered in a gravel-pit near Canewdon Hall about 1712, may have been either Roman or Saxon.

(For the tiles, *B.A.A.*, IV (1849), 74. For the urns, Salmon, *Hist. of Essex* (1743), 385 ; Morant, *Hist. of Essex* (1768), I, 313—both apparently from Holman, quoted *Essex Arch. Soc. Trans.* (N.S.), XII, 113–5. Marked Roman on O.S. 6 in. lxx. N.E.)

Ecclesiastical :—

ᵃ(2). PARISH CHURCH OF ST. NICHOLAS stands near the middle of the parish. The walls are mainly of ragstone-rubble with some septaria and flint ; the dressings are of limestone ; the roofs are covered with tiles and lead. The *Nave, Chancel* and *North Aisle* were built in the 14th century. Early in the 15th century the *West Tower* and *South Porch* were added and the S. wall of the nave rebuilt ; a N. vestry was probably added at the same time. Later in the same century the two eastern bays of the N. arcade were rebuilt

and the N. aisle largely rebuilt. Late in the 18th century the N. vestry was pulled down. The church has been restored in modern times when the chancel was largely rebuilt.

The Tower is a good example of its period and among the fittings the altar-slab and pulpit are noteworthy.

Architectural Description—The *Chancel* (34½ ft. by 19 ft.) has an E. window all modern except the 15th-century rear-arch and parts of the splays, jambs and head. In the N. wall is a modern window with reused stones in the splays ; E. of it is a 15th-century doorway to the former vestry of which the toothing of the E. wall remains ; the doorway has hollow-chamfered jambs and two-centred arch and is now blocked. In the S. wall are two windows, the eastern of the 15th century but mainly modern externally and of two cinquefoiled lights in a segmental head ; the western window is of late 15th-century date and of two cinquefoiled and transomed lights in a segmental-pointed head, much restored ; between the windows is a 14th-century doorway, now blocked, with moulded jambs, two-centred arch and label with defaced stops. The chancel-arch is modern.

The *Nave* (56½ ft. by 22½ ft.) has a N. arcade (Plate, p. 24) of four bays originally of the 14th century with the two eastern bays rebuilt and widened by the cutting back of the respond late in the 15th century ; the first bay has a reset two-centred arch of three chamfered orders ; the second arch is two-centred and of two chamfered orders, the inner of the 15th and the outer of the 14th century, reset ; the remaining two arches are each of three chamfered orders, two-centred and of the 14th century. The outer orders spring from carved figures including a woman's head, beasts and a bird all much defaced, a beast holding a shield *a cheveron between three rings* for Chanceaux and a shield *seven lozenges and a border* (perhaps voided lozenges for Robert Braybroke, Bishop of London). The octagonal columns of the arcade have moulded capitals all of the 14th century, the first column having been reset ; the 15th-century E. respond is square with a moulded impost ; the 14th-century W. respond has an attached half-column. At the E. end of the wall is the 15th-century rood-loft staircase, now blocked but with the N. jamb of the lower doorway exposed. In the S. wall are three early 15th-century windows, the two eastern-most are of three pointed lights with uncusped tracery in a two-centred head with a moulded label and head-stops ; the westernmost window is modern except for the splays and part of the rear-arch and a label with grotesque stops ; further E. is the early 16th-century S. doorway with moulded jambs and two-centred arch in a square head with moulded labels and traceried spandrels enclosing blank shields.

The *North Aisle* (11¼ ft. wide) is said to have a blocked window in the E. wall. In the N. wall are four windows, the easternmost is of the 14th century much restored and of three cinquefoiled lights with intersecting tracery in a two-centred head ; the second window is of the 15th century and of three pointed lights with uncusped vertical tracery in a two-centred head with a moulded label and head-stops ; the third window is similar to the second but partly restored ; the westernmost window is all modern except the heads of the two 15th-century cinquefoiled lights ; further E. is the 15th-century N. doorway with moulded jambs and two-centred arch.

The *West Tower* (16 ft. square) (Plate, p. 21) is of dressed ragstone, of early 15th-century date and of three stages with an embattled parapet of flint and stone chequer-work with crosses in the merlons. The two-centred tower-arch is of four orders ; the three inner are chamfered and of these the outer is continuous and the inner two rest on attached shafts with moulded capitals and bases. The W. window is of three cinquefoiled lights with vertical tracery in a two-centred head with a moulded label and head-stop ; below the window are three moulded panels (Plate, p. 84) containing shields-of-arms (*a*) defaced ; (*b*) France modern quartering England ; (*c*) *a bend cotised between six lions* for Bohun impaling *a lion* for Fitzalan quartering *checky* for Warrenne ; the W. doorway has moulded jambs and two-centred arch in a square head with a moulded label, angels holding shields, as stops, and traceried spandrels enclosing defaced shields. The E., N. and S. walls of the second stage have

each a window of one trefoiled light with a moulded label ; in the W. wall is a window of two cinque-foiled lights with tracery in a two-centred head with moulded jambs and label. The bell-chamber has in each wall a window of two cinquefoiled lights with vertical tracery in a two-centred head with a square outer order and label.

The *South Porch* is of early 15th-century date and has an embattled parapet of flint and stone chequer-work with plain crosses on the merlons. The outer archway has moulded and shafted jambs and a two-centred arch in a square outer order with a defaced label ; the traceried spandrels enclose small blank shields. The side walls have each a window of two cinquefoiled lights in a square head with a moulded label.

The *Roof* of the nave is of the 15th century and of four bays with plain king-post trusses ; the third tie-beam is inscribed R.H., T.D. 1698, the date of some repair. The N. aisle has a plain lean-to roof of uncertain date with main timbers dividing it into eight bays. The 15th-century ceiling of the ground-stage of the tower has heavy chamfered braces crossing in the middle and formerly having a boss at the intersection. The flat-pitched 15th-century roof of the S. porch is of two bays with chamfered main timbers.

Fittings—*Altar :* In N. aisle—at E. end, slab with chamfered under-edge and broken in two, four consecration crosses remaining. *Bells :* Five ; 1st by John and Christopher Hodson, 1678 ; 3rd by Miles Graye, 1634 ; 5th by John Waylett, 1707 ; bell-frame old. *Brass Indents :* In nave —(1) of figures, scroll and inscription-plate. In S. porch—(2) of man and two small figures and inscription-plate ; (3) of inscription-plate ; (4) of man, three wives and children ; (5) of marginal inscription. *Chests :* In chancel—small, with hutch-type with moulded edge to lid, early 17th-century. In N. aisle—with panelled front and ends and moulded edge to lid, 17th-century. *Doors :* In nave —in S. doorway, of overlapping battens with trellis-framing and strap-hinges, 15th-century. In tower —in W. doorway, of nail-studded battens with hollow-chamfered fillets, mostly missing, 15th-century ; in bell-chamber doorway, of overlapping battens with strap-hinges, 15th-century. *Glass :* In nave—in middle S. window, remains of border of crowns and ruby glass, fragments of black-letter inscription, etc., early 15th-century. *Monuments :* In churchyard—S. of nave, (1) to John Bishop, 1709, brick and stone table-tomb ; (2) to John Allen, 1691, headstone with skull and cross-bones. *Niches :* In N. aisle—in E. wall, (1) with cinquefoiled head from former window, 15th-century, remains of red and black paint ; (2) with cinquefoiled ogee head and broken sill, 14th-century, with painted red stars on a black ground. On W. tower—flanking W. doorway, two with moulded jambs and cinquefoiled heads and square moulded labels, moulded pedestals, early 15th-century ; on W. buttress, two with moulded jambs and trefoiled ogee heads, and pedestals, early 15th-century. *Painting :* In N. aisle—on E. splay of N.E. window, remains of black border, etc. ; see also Niches and Miscellanea. *Piscinae :* In chancel—with moulded jambs and cinquefoiled square head, early 15th-century, round drain partly broken, above it a shield-of-arms—*a cheveron between three rings,* 15th-century. In N. aisle—in E. wall, with moulded jambs and trefoiled head with defaced label, quatrefoiled drain, 14th-century. *Plate :* includes cup of 1665, dated 1665. *Poor-boxes :* In N. aisle—(1) small iron-bound box with strap-hinges and two straps, 15th-century ; (2) cylindrical box with concave lid and iron lock, probably 17th-century. *Pulpit :* hexagonal, panelled sides with carved and moulded cornice, cherub-heads and swags of fruit and foliage, pendants of foliage at the angles, late 17th-century. *Sedile :* In chancel—in S. wall, with hollow-chamfered jambs, 15th-century, modern head. *Miscellanea :* In N. aisle—a collection of objects including part of a circular base of font-stem ; late 17th-century twisted baluster from communion rails, 15th-century popey-head and traceried panel. In W. tower is a 15th-century head-stop. In chancel—built into S. wall, parts of panelled buttresses or shafts of a tabernacle and also a painted head belonging to the same work, original red, dark green and gold colour, 15th-century.

Condition—Poor, cracks in walling and stone-work much decayed.

Secular :—

a(3). HOMESTEAD MOAT, at Canewdon Hall, N.E. of the church.

b(4). LAMBOURNE HALL, house and moat, about 1 m. E.S.E. of the church. The *House* is of two storeys with attics ; the walls are timber-framed and plastered ; the roofs are tiled. It was built possibly late in the 15th or early in the 16th century but the S.E. end was rebuilt in the 17th century when a two-storeyed porch was added on the S.W. front and a chimney-stack inserted at the W. end of the original hall. There are 18th-century and modern additions. On the S.W. front the upper storey of the porch projects and is gabled. The upper storey projected on the N.E. side of the main door, but has been underbuilt. One chimney-stack has a 17th-century hexagonal shaft. Inside the building a few of the curved braces supporting the main beams are exposed as are also some of the ceiling-beams.

The *Moat* formerly surrounded the house.

Condition—Of house, good.

a(5). SCOTT'S HALL, house and moat, about ¾ m. S. of the church. The *House* is of two storeys,

timber-framed and weather-boarded ; the roofs are tiled. It was built in the 17th century on a rectangular plan but has later additions. Inside the building there are exposed ceiling-beams.

The *Moat* N. of the house is now dry.

Condition—Of house, good.

MONUMENTS (6–9).

The following monuments, unless otherwise described, are of the 17th century, and of two storeys, timber-framed and plastered or weather-boarded ; the roofs are tiled. Some of the buildings have exposed ceiling-beams and original chimney-stacks.

Condition—Good or fairly good.

a(6). *House,* now three tenements, on S. side of road, about 350 yards E. of the church, was built possibly in the 15th century. It has been much altered and partly refaced with modern brick. The upper storey projects at the E. end of the N. front.

a(7). *House,* 200 yards E. of (5), was built possibly in the 16th century and has later additions. The upper storey of the W. wing projects on the N. front.

a(8). *White House,* about 380 yards S.W. of the church, is of two storeys with attics. It is of the central-chimney-type and has low additions at the E. end.

a(9). *Sturgeon's,* house, 750 yards S. of the church, is of one storey with attics and was built in the 16th century. Inside the building is an original fireplace and the roof has exposed wind-braces.

Unclassified :—

a and c(10). RED HILLS, S. of and following line of the River Crouch, at Norpits Farm, 1½ m. N.W. of the church, and some others further E. in detached portion of parish.

---

13. CANVEY ISLAND. (D.d.)

(O.S. 6 in. lxxvii. S.W.)

Canvey Island is a parish on the N. side of the Thames estuary, about 6 m. W. of Southend-on-Sea.

Secular :—

(1). DUTCH COTTAGE (Plate, pp. xl–i), in village, 200 yards S.E. of the church, is of two storeys, and of plastered timber-framing and brick ; the roofs are thatched. It is dated 1621 and is octagonal on plan with a central chimney-stack. Inside the building the timber-framing is exposed.

(2). DUTCH COTTAGE, S.E. of Hill Hall, 700 yards N.W. of the church, is of two storeys and is similar in plan and construction to (1). It is dated 1618.

(3). TREE FARM, house, about 1½ m. W.N.W. of
the church, is of one storey with attics, timber-
framed and weather-boarded; the roofs are
thatched. It was built in the 17th century and
is of the central-chimney type with modern
additions at the back. The square chimney-stack
is original.

_____

14. CHADWELL. (C.e.)

(O.S. 6 in. lxxxiv. S.W.)

Chadwell is a parish 2 m. E. of Grays Thurrock.
The church is the principal monument.

Roman :—

(1). In Messrs. Christian and Neilson's gravel-pit,
700 yards S.E. of the parish church, an oven
(Plate, p. xxxvi) was found in July, 1922, together
with several urns. The oven had apparently been
circular and domed, with a diameter of over 5 ft.
A flue projected from it for a distance of at least
4 ft. and was 1 ft. 3 in. wide. When the structure
was discovered three complete vessels were found
within it, and others, more or less fragmentary,
together with a decorated clay lamp, were found
in the same area. The pottery, which is now in the
Colchester Museum, presents unusual features, but
most of it is probably of 3rd to 4th-century date.
Some of it retains traces of Late Celtic traditions.
There is no evidence that it was made on the
present site; the purpose for which the oven was
originally used was not apparent.

Roman coins of all dates have been found in the
parish, and a site about 100 yards E. of the oven
has yielded a large quantity of Samian sherds,
mostly of late 1st or early 2nd-century date,
including a large number of stamps. No traces of
buildings were, however, noticed.

Ecclesiastical :—

(2). PARISH CHURCH OF ST. MARY stands in
the village. The walls are of flint-rubble with some
ragstone; the dressings are of Reigate stone;
the roofs are tiled. The *Nave* was built early in
the 12th century and the western parts of the
side walls of the *Chancel* are of the same date.

The chancel was lengthened in the 14th century.
At the end of the 15th century the nave was
lengthened towards the W., the rood-loft staircase
inserted and the *West Tower* added. The church
has been restored in modern times when the
South Vestry was added.

Architectural Description—The *Chancel* (31 ft.
by 13 ft.) has an E. window all modern except the
14th-century splays and rear-arch and part of
the jambs. In the N. wall are two windows, the
eastern of the 14th century and of one trefoiled
light; the western window is modern. In the
S. wall are two windows, each of two cinquefoiled
lights with tracery in a two-centred head and
probably of the 14th century but covered with
paint. There is no chancel-arch.

The *Nave* (44½ ft. by 17¼ ft.) has in the N. wall
two modern windows; between them, set within
the 12th-century one, is the early 15th-century
N. doorway with moulded jambs and two-centred
head; above it is the round head of the 12th-
century doorway with diapered voussoirs and a
diapered tympanum of small stones (Plate, p. 84);
both E. and W. of the doorway is a blocked
12th-century window with a round head; the
western is visible only internally. In the S. wall
are two windows both modern except the 14th-
century rear-arch of the first and the splays and
rear-arch of the second; between them is the
12th-century S. doorway of one plain round
order enclosing a plastered tympanum supported
on a segmental arch; there are two blocked 12th-
century windows similar to those in the N. wall;
at the E. end of the wall is the 15th-century
rood-loft staircase with upper and lower doorways
having three-centred heads.

The *West Tower* (12½ ft. square) is of late 15th-
century date and of three stages with an embattled
parapet decorated with brick and flint chequer-
work. The two-centred tower-arch is of three
chamfered orders, the outer continuous and the
two inner resting on semi-octagonal responds with
moulded capitals and chamfered bases. The
W. window is of three four-centred lights in a
segmental head with a moulded label; the W.
doorway has moulded jambs, four-centred arch
and label. The N. and S. walls of the second stage
have each a single-light window, much weathered.
The bell-chamber has in each wall a window of two
four-centred lights and all in square heads except
the W. window which has a four-centred head;
all have moulded labels.

The *Roof* of the chancel has at the W. end some
old trussed-rafters without collar-beams. The
roof of the nave is ceiled but has some old shaped
sprocket-pieces.

Fittings—*Bells :* Three; 1st probably by John
Wood, 1694, badly broken; 3rd by Thomas
Bartlet, 1628; bell-frame, 17th-century. *Brass
and Indent.* Brass: In chancel—to Cicilye, wife
of Thomas Owen, 1603, with shield-of-arms.
Indent: Outside N. doorway—of figure, broken.
Chair (Plate, p. xlii): In chancel—with carved
back, shaped arms, moulded legs with carved rail
and claw-feet, late 17th-century, probably French.
Chest : In vestry—oak chest-of-drawers with

DANBURY: PARISH CHURCH OF ST. JOHN THE BAPTIST.
Interior, showing N. Arcade, late 13th-century; N. Aisle, etc.

CANEWDON: PARISH CHURCH OF ST. NICHOLAS.
Interior, showing N. Arcade, 14th-century, altered in the 15th century, etc.

NORTH OCKENDON CHURCH.
Brasses of Thomasyn Badby, 15[32], William
Poyntz and Elizabeth, his wife, 1502.

RETTENDON CHURCH.
Slab in N. Aisle; late 12th-century, with Brasses
of c. 1535.

FOBBING CHURCH.
The Virgin and Child; 15th-century.

NORTH SHOEBURY
CHURCH.
Fragment of Slab: late

BARLING CHURCH.
Small alabaster figures; early 15th-century.

panelled fronts and brass fittings, 17th-century. *Door :* In W. doorway—of moulded battens with strap-hinges, late 15th-century. *Glass :* In top and south tracery-lights of E. window, 14th-century fragments of borders, foliage and coloured glass. *Monument :* In churchyard—N.E. corner, to M.G., 1691, cut on a piece of sarsen stone. *Niche :* S. of W. doorway, externally, with trefoiled ogee head and rebated jambs with holes for fastenings, possibly stoup, 14th-century. *Panelling :* In chancel—in S.E. window-recess, eight 17th-century carved panels. *Pictures :* In chancel—two, " The Finding of Moses," ascribed to (?) Agostino Caracci, and " Christ at the House of Simon Peter," ascribed to Paul Veronese. *Piscina :* In chancel—with trefoiled head and sexfoiled drain, 14th-century. *Sundials :* On E. jamb of S. doorway and on quoin of S.E. angle of nave—two scratched dials. *Table :* In vestry—oval gate-leg table, 17th-century. *Miscellanea :* Used as quoin of S.E. angle of nave, part of head of 12th-century window.
Condition—Good, but stonework of tower much perished.

Secular :—

(3). SLEEPERS FARM, house 50 yards W.S.W. of the church, is of two storeys, timber-framed and plastered ; the roof is thatched. It was built in the 15th century and has a cross-wing at the S. end and a modern extension at the W. The upper storey projects at both ends of the cross-wing and is supported on curved brackets. The central chimney-stack is of the 17th century. Inside the building some of the timber-construction is exposed and some of the rooms have open-timbered ceilings. There is an original doorway in the N. wall of the S. cross-wing with a four-centred head and now blocked by the inserted chimney-stack ; a 17th-century battened door also remains. The original roof over the S. wing is of two bays with a heavy cambered tie-beam, curved braces and a king-post with four-way struts and there is an original cambered tie-beam with curved braces across the middle of the main block.
Condition—Good.

15. CHILDERDITCH. (B.d.)
(O.S. 6 in. lxvii. S.E.)

Childerditch is a parish 5 m. S.W. of Billericay.

Ecclesiastical :—

(1). PARISH CHURCH OF ALL SAINTS AND ST. FAITH was rebuilt in 1869 and contains from the old church the following :—
Fittings—*Font :* octagonal bowl with quatrefoiled panels enclosing carved rose, leopards' heads, pomegranate, rose and pomegranate dimidiated,

fleur-de-lis and foliage ; round upper edge black-letter inscription, " This is the cost of Jhon Throsscher and Ceceli his wiffe," moulded base, early 16th-century.
Condition—Rebuilt.

Secular :—

(2). HOMESTEAD MOAT, at Tillingham Hall, nearly 1¼ m. S.S.E. of the church.

(3). COTTAGE, on E. wide of road, nearly 800 yards N.N.E. of the church, is of two storeys, timber-framed and plastered ; the roofs are tiled. It was built in the 17th century and has an original chimney-stack of cruciform plan.
Condition—Fairly good.

(4). HOUSE, on W. side of road, 250 yards N.N.W. of (3), is of two storeys and of timber-framing, partly plastered and partly weather-boarded ; the roofs are tiled. It was built probably in the 16th century and is of L-shaped plan with the wings extending towards the S. and W. The upper storey projects at the N. end of the E. front.
Condition—Good.

16. COLD NORTON. (E.b.)
(O.S. 6 in. lxii. N.W.)

Cold Norton is a small parish 4½ m. S. of Maldon.

Ecclesiastical :—

PARISH CHURCH OF ST. STEPHEN was entirely rebuilt in 1855. It contains from the old church the following :—
Fittings—*Brass* and *Indents.* Brass : In nave —of woman in pedimental head-dress, etc., *c.* 1520. Indents : Outside S. porch—(1) of figure. At entrance to churchyard—(2) of two figures and inscription-plate. *Monuments :* In chancel— in N. wall, (1) to Maude (Tasburghe), wife of Robert Cammocke, 1599, and her daughter, inscribed slab. In churchyard—(2) to William Walker, J.P., 1708, table-tomb. *Plate :* includes cup and cover-paten of 1568, the latter dated.
Condition—Of church, rebuilt.

17. CORRINGHAM. (D.d.)
(O.S. 6 in. ⁽ᵃ⁾lxxvi. S.E. ⁽ᵇ⁾lxxxv. N.W.)

Corringham is a parish and small village on the N. bank of the Thames estuary, 7 m. N.E. of Tilbury. The church is the principal monument.

Ecclesiastical :—

ᵃ(1). PARISH CHURCH OF ST. MARY stands in the village. The walls are of ragstone-rubble and flint ; the dressings are of Reigate and other limestone and the roofs are tiled. The S. walls of

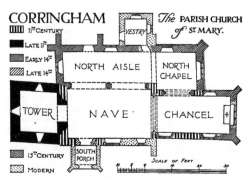

the *Chancel* and *Nave* are of the 11th century, the thickness in each case favouring a pre- rather than a post-Conquest date. The *West Tower* was added late in the 11th century and stands partly on the earlier W. wall of the nave. Early in the 14th century a *North Chapel* and *North Aisle* were added and the chancel was extended to the E. in the same century and the walls heightened ; in the 17th century the chancel-arch fell. The church has been restored in modern times when the chancel-arch and part of the S. wall of the nave were rebuilt and the *North Vestry* and *South Porch* added.

The church is of interest from its early date and amongst the fittings the 14th-century screen is noteworthy.

Architectural Description—The *Chancel* (28 ft. by 13½ ft.) has a modern E. window. In the N. wall is an early 14th-century arch, two-centred and of two chamfered orders the outer continuous and the inner resting on attached shafts with moulded capitals and bases ; further E. is a 14th-century window, partly restored and of two trefoiled ogee lights with tracery in a two-centred head with a moulded label. The lower part of the western half of the S. wall is built of roughly coursed herring-bone rubble possibly of pre-Conquest date. In the S. wall are two windows, the eastern of the 14th century and similar to that in the N. wall ; the western window is of the 15th century and of two cinquefoiled lights in a square head with a moulded label. The chancel-arch is modern.

The *North Chapel* (14½ ft. by 13½ ft.) has external wall-faces of bands of flint and freestone. The 14th-century E. window is partly restored and of three trefoiled ogee lights with modern tracery in a segmental head with a moulded label. In the N. wall is a 14th-century window of two trefoiled ogee lights with a quatrefoil in a two-centred head.

The 14th-century W. archway is two-centred and of two chamfered orders dying on to the side walls.

The *Nave* (31 ft. by 17½ ft.) has an early 14th-century N. arcade of two bays with two-centred arches of two chamfered orders ; the octagonal column has a moulded capital and base and the responds have attached half-columns ; the responds show evidence of rebuilding and the arches may have been widened. In the S. wall are two modern windows and further W. is the late 14th-century S. doorway with sunk-chamfered jambs and moulded arch of two orders with a moulded label. The western part of the S. wall is similar in date and character to the older walling on the S. of the chancel.

The *North Aisle* (10¾ ft. wide) has in the N. wall a 14th-century window similar to the N. window in the N. chapel ; E. of it is a modern doorway and W. of it is the 14th-century N. doorway with jambs and two-centred arch of two chamfered orders. In the W. wall is a window similar to that in the N. wall.

The *West Tower* (13¾ ft. by 14¾ ft.) (Plate, p. 28) is of late 11th-century date and of three stages with a pyramidal roof. The round tower-arch is of one plain order with chamfered imposts ; the keystone on the E. side is carved with a small head. The N., S. and W. walls have each a window of one narrow light, modern externally. The N., S. and W. walls of the second stage have each a window similar to those in the stage below but with 14th-century trefoiled heads. The bell-chamber is divided externally into two sub-stages by an offset, the lower has on each face three round-headed recesses of rubble ; above these on each face is a series of five similar recesses but the middle one on the N., S. and W. sides is pierced for a window and fitted with a modern central shaft with old cushion-capital and base and supporting two small round sub-arches of rubble ; the corresponding opening on the E. face formerly opened into the nave roof ; the roof on this side also covered the lower range of recesses.

The *Roofs* are modern except for the 15th-century moulded and embattled wall-plates on the N. of the N. chapel and aisle and on both sides of the nave.

Fittings—*Bells :* three ; 1st by John Dier, 1580 ; 2nd and 3rd by Thomas Bartlet, 1629 and 1617 respectively. *Brasses* and *Indents.* Brasses : In chancel—(1) of Richard de Beltoun, *c.* 1340, half-effigy of priest in mass vestments ; (2) of civilian, *c.* 1460, much worn and reset ; (3) to Alice Greyve, 1453, inscription only. In N. chapel —(3) to Robert Draper, 1595, parson of Corringham, inscription only. In nave—(4) to Thomas at Lee, 1464, and Margaret his wife, inscription only. Indents : In N. chapel—(1) later used for brass (3), marginal inscription in separate capitals to (Is)abelle Baud, 14th-century. In nave—(2) of figure and inscription-plate, possibly of brass (2) ; (3) tapering slab with traces of marginal inscription in separate capitals, late 13th or early 14th-century. *Chests :* In N. chapel—(1) plain, of hutch-type with square lock-plates, 17th-century. In N. vestry—(2) of oak, iron-bound with three strap-hinges and one old drop-handle, mediaeval. *Glass :* In N. chapel—in E. window, two angels and part of yellow rays. In N. window, foliage, probably *in situ*. Both 15th-century. In N. aisle— W. window, a dragon (Plate, pp. xliv–v), possibly 14th-century. *Panelling :* In nave—incorporated in bench, traceried panel in three tiers with foliated spandrels and embattled rail, 15th-century. *Piscina :* In chancel—with chamfered jambs and trefoiled head, round drain, 14th-century. *Plate :* includes 17th-century cup with altered rim and dated 1685, cover-paten of 1684. *Screen* (Plate, pp. 4–5) : In N. chapel—with middle doorway and four lights on each side divided by shafts with moulded capitals, bands and bases and with cusped intersecting tracery above, close lower panels, early 14th-century, 17th-century scratched initials and dates on sill. *Stoup :* In nave—E. of S. doorway, recess with cinquefoiled head and broken bowl, 14th or 15th-century. *Miscellanea :* Reset in N. respond of chancel-arch, corbel or bracket of ogee form. The churchyard wall incorporates old stones and has a weathered coping.
Condition—Good.

Secular :—

MONUMENTS (2–7).

The following monuments, unless otherwise described, are of the 17th century and of two storeys, timber-framed and weather-boarded ; the roofs are tiled. Some of the buildings have original chimney-stacks and exposed ceiling-beams.
Condition—Good.

ᵃ(2). Bull Inn (Plate, pp. xxxiv–v), 40 yards N.E. of the church, is of two storeys with attics and of plastered timber-framing. It has an E. cross-wing and modern additions on the N.W. and N.E. The cross-wing is probably of 15th-century date but the main block was rebuilt in the 17th century. The upper storey of the cross-wing projects on the S.W. front. The 17th-century chimney-stack is of cruciform plan set diagonally.

ᵃ(3). House and *Shop,* on W. side of the road, 120 yards N.N.W. of the church, was of half H-shaped plan with the cross-wings extending towards the S.W. but a modern addition makes the present plan rectangular. The S.E. wing is possibly of 15th-century date but the main block and N.W. wing are later.

ᵃ(4). Giffords' Cross, house, 650 yards W.N.W. of the church, is of two storeys with attics. It was built probably in the 16th century on an L-shaped plan with the wings extending towards the N.W. and S.W. but a later addition of *c.* 1700 makes the present plan rectangular ; the roof was rebuilt and heightened at the same time. The original chimney-stack has grouped diagonal shafts. Inside the building is some early 17th-century panelling.

ᵃ(5). Northlands Farm, house, about 1¾ m. N.W. of the church, is of two storeys with attics and cellars. The N. and S. doors are panelled and of 17th-century date, the latter has a hood supported on shaped brackets. Inside the building some of the timber-framing is exposed. The main staircase is original and has turned balusters and newel posts.

ᵃ(6). Cottage, now two tenements, ½ m. N.E. of the church, is of the central-chimney type.

ᵇ(7). Reedham, farmhouse, about 1½ m. E.S.E. of the church, is of two storeys with attics ; the walls are partly timber-framed and partly of brick. It has been much altered and has a modern addition at the back. Inside the building some of the timber-framing is exposed.

----

18. CRANHAM. (B.d.)

(O.S. 6 in. lxxv. N.W.)

Cranham is a parish 4 m. E.S.E. of Romford.

Ecclesiastical :—

(1). PARISH CHURCH OF ALL SAINTS was rebuilt in 1874 but contains from the old church the following :—

Fittings—*Bells :* three ; 1st and 2nd by John Danyell, 15th - century and both inscribed " Johannes Est Nomen Eius " ; 3rd by Henry Jordan, 15th-century and inscribed " Sancta Petre Ora Pro Nobis." *Brass :* In chancel—to

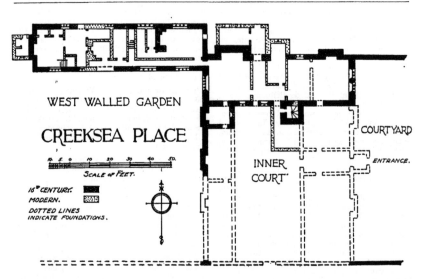

WEST WALLED GARDEN

CREEKSEA PLACE

SCALE OF FEET.

15ᵗʰ CENTURY.
MODERN.
DOTTED LINES
INDICATE FOUNDATIONS.

COURTYARD

ENTRANCE.

INNER
COURT

Nathan Wright, 1657, inscription and achievement-of-arms. *Floor-slab:* In chancel—to Susannah (Wright), wife successively of Charles Potts and Francis Drake, 1664, with achievement-of-arms.

The churchyard wall on the S. and W. is of 16th-century brick.

Condition—Rebuilt.

Secular :—

(2). COTTAGE, on E. side of main road, 1 m. N. of the church, is of one storey with attics, timber-framed and weather-boarded; the roofs are thatched. It was built in the 17th century on a rectangular plan and has an original chimney-stack at the W. end.

Condition—Good.

(3). WALL round the garden of Cranham Hall is of 16th-century brickwork.

Condition—Good.

----

19. CREEKSEA. (F.c.)

(O.S. 6 in. lxiii. S.W.)

Creeksea is a small parish on the left bank of the Crouch and adjoining Burnham on the W. Creeksea Place is the principal monument.

Ecclesiastical :—

(1). PARISH CHURCH OF ALL SAINTS was entirely rebuilt in 1878 but has from the old church the 14th-century S. doorway with moulded jambs, two-centred arch and label. The S. porch incorporates the 14th-century jambs of the outer archway and a cinquefoiled ogee light on each side.

Fittings—Brass: In chancel—to Sir Arthur Herris, 1631, inscription and three shields-of-arms. *Floor-slab:* In nave — to John Cooch, 1711. *Font:* octagonal bowl with panelled sides, two carved with a saltire and one with a coiled serpent or whorl, 15th-century, base modern. *Plate:* includes cup and paten of 1699, the latter dated.

Condition—Rebuilt. ·

Secular :—

(2). CREEKSEA PLACE, ½ m. S.S.E. of the church, is partly of two storeys with attics and partly of one with attics ; the walls are of red brick ; the roofs are tiled. The house was probably completed *c.* 1569 and then consisted of three, or possibly four, ranges surrounding a courtyard and a long wing projecting W. from the N. end. About 1740 the S. part of the house together with the enclosing walls of the gardens was destroyed, leaving standing only the outer courtyard enclosure, the N. range and the W. wing. The house has been restored in modern times, a range built on the foundations of the original E. range and various additions made.

CORRINGHAM: PARISH CHURCH OF ST. MARY.
West Tower, from the South-West ; late 11th-century.

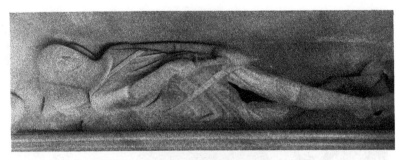

Oak effigy of Knight in eastern recess, N. Aisle ; late 13th-century.

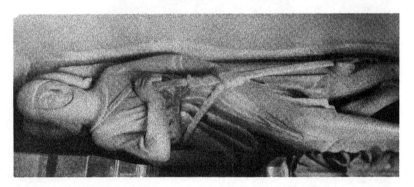

Oak effigy of Knight in western recess, N. Aisle ; late 13th-century.

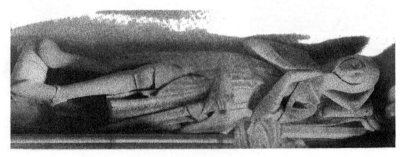

Oak effigy of Knight in recess in S. Aisle ; *c.* 1300.

DANBURY : PARISH CHURCH OF ST. JOHN THE BAPTIST.

The house is of interest as a fragment of a large 16th-century building.

Elevations—The *N. Front* has several original windows with brick mullions and transoms and square moulded labels; they are all partly restored. The two chimney-stacks are original, one is embattled and has octagonal shafts with moulded bases; the other has moulded bases but 17th-century shafts, set diagonally. The modern doorway has an original moulded oak frame, reset. There is an original lead rain-water head dated 1569. The E. end of the N. range has original windows, partly restored and similar to those on the N. front; the gable has a moulded pinnacle at the apex. Similar windows and gable are at the W. end of the same range (Plate; pp. 56–7), and S. of it is an original chimney-stack with an embattled offset. Some remains of the former W. range adjoin this stack. The S. side of the N. range has a square original staircase-wing and several original windows. The *W. Wing* is of one storey with attics and has original windows; at the W. end (Plate, pp. 56–7) is a chimney-stack with tabled offsets and grouped diagonal shafts. The middle portion of this range is modern and may mark the position of a former entrance archway.

Interior—The original arrangement of the house is uncertain, but the Hall occupied either the N. or the destroyed W. range. One room on the ground-floor has an elaborately carved stone fireplace and some 17th-century panelling, all brought from elsewhere. On the first floor are two original fireplaces with four-centred heads and plain spandrels and one room is lined with late 16th-century panelling. The newel staircase is original and at the top are two original doorways with moulded oak frames.

The *Courtyard*, E. of the house, has octagonal brick turrets at the outer angles and in the middle of the E. side is an original archway with a four-centred arch and pinnacles at the base of the gable.

The *Foundations* of two walled gardens to the S. and W. of the house have been uncovered and the angles of the walls are still exposed.

Condition—Of house, good, much altered.

(3). CREEKSEA HALL, 100 yards E. of the church, has been rebuilt except the N. wing which is of two storeys, timber-framed and plastered; the roofs are tiled. It was built probably in the 16th century and the timber-framing and ceiling-beams are exposed.

Condition—Good.

(4). GROVE COTTAGE (Plate, p. xxxiv), about ¼ m. S.W. of (2), is of two storeys, timber-framed and plastered; the roofs are tiled. It was built probably in the 16th or early in the 17th century and has exposed timber-framing. The front doorway has a chamfered frame and square head.

Inside the building are some original wide fireplaces and exposed ceiling-beams; there is also a little panelling of *c.* 1700.

20. DANBURY. (D.b.)

(O.S. 6 in. liii. S.E.)

Danbury is a parish 5 m. E. of Chelmsford. The church and the camp are the principal monuments.

Ecclesiastical :—

(1). PARISH CHURCH OF ST. JOHN THE BAPTIST (Plates, pp. xxxii, 24) stands on the S. side of the village. The walls are of iron pudding-stone-rubble except the tower which is of pebble-rubble; the dressings are mostly of Reigate stone and the roofs are tiled. The earliest part of the building appears to be the *North Aisle*, the base of the N. wall of which is of coursed rubble, possibly of 12th-century date. It is possible that this aisle was the early nave. It was much altered in the latter part of the 13th century when the *Chancel* was built. The N. arcade is of about the same date. The *Nave* and a S. aisle were built early in the 14th century and probably in the order named; the *West Tower* was added about the middle of the same century. The spire fell in 1402, destroying some of the roofs; it was restored in the 15th century and the *North Vestry* added about the same time. The *South Chapel* was added in 1837, the chancel-arch rebuilt in 1846, and the church restored in 1866–7 when the *South Aisle* was rebuilt, and the *North Porch* added. Among the fittings the three oak effigies are noteworthy.

Architectural Description—The *Chancel* (32¼ ft. by 20½ ft.) has an E. window, modern except for the 15th-century splays and two-centred rear-arch. In the N. wall is a 15th-century window partly restored and of three cinquefoiled lights in a square head with a moulded label; further E. is the early 15th-century doorway to the vestry, with moulded jambs and two-centred head; E. of it is a small 15th-century piercing, set low in the wall and trefoiled at the top and bottom with splays towards the vestry. The S. arcade and chancel-arch are modern.

The *North Vestry* (14 ft. by 9 ft.) has in the E. wall a modern window. In the W. wall is a doorway with chamfered jambs and two-centred head, said to be modern but possibly of reused material.

The *South Chapel* is modern but has a reset buttress at the S.E. angle and two 15th-century windows reset in the S. wall; the eastern is of two cinquefoiled lights in a square head and modern externally; the second is similar, but of three lights with a moulded label and one old head-stop; this window is much restored.

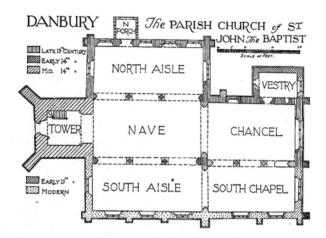

DANBURY. *The* PARISH CHURCH *of* S^T JOHN *The* BAPTIST

LATE 13TH CENTURY
EARLY 14TH "
MID. 14TH "

NORTH AISLE

VESTRY

TOWER

NAVE

CHANCEL

EARLY 15TH "
MODERN

SOUTH AISLE

SOUTH CHAPEL

The *Nave* (39½ ft. by 20¼ ft.) has late 13th and early 14th-century N. and S. arcades of three bays (Plate, p. 24), with two-centred arches of two orders, both hollow-chamfered on the N. and one chamfered and one hollow-chamfered on the S.; the columns are of quatrefoiled plan with moulded capitals and bases; the base-moulds differ slightly on the two sides and the bases of the N. arcade stand on square plinths; the responds have attached half-columns; the N. arcade is of rather earlier date than the S.

The *North Aisle* (16¾ ft. wide) has an E. window all modern except the splays; S. of it is a 14th-century squint to the chancel, with a two-centred head. In the N. wall are four late 13th-century windows, all much restored internally and each of two trefoiled lights with a quatrefoil in a two-centred head; between the two western windows is a doorway of the same date with moulded two-centred arch and label; the jambs have each an attached shaft with a moulded capital and base. In the W. wall is a window all modern except the late 13th-century splays, rear-arch and moulded label with head-stops.

The *West Tower* (12½ ft. square) is of mid 14th-century date and of three stages with an embattled parapet and a spire covered with shingles and lead. The two-centred tower-arch is of one chamfered order. The W. window, restored externally, is of two trefoiled ogee lights and tracery in a two-centred head; the W. doorway (Plate, p. 84) has moulded jambs, two-centred arch and label returned as a string-course and with another string-course at the level of the crown of the arch; between the

string-courses and flanking the doorway are two niches each with moulded jambs, cinquefoiled head and moulded label. The second stage has in the E. and N. walls a single-light window, the latter covered by the clock. In the S. wall is a window of one cinquefoiled light with a square moulded label. In the W. wall is a similar window of one trefoiled light. The bell-chamber has in the E. wall a defaced window with a square head. In the N. wall is a 16th-century window, partly of brick and of two round-headed lights with a square defaced label. The S. wall has a similar window but restored in the 18th century except the W. jamb. In the W. wall is a plain single-light.

The *Roof* of the chancel is probably of the 15th century and is of plain trussed-rafter type with moulded plates. The Vestry has a pent-roof with a moulded plate of the 15th century. The roof of the nave appears to have been reconstructed but incorporates old timbers. The roof of the N. aisle has a high-pitched trussed-rafter roof; the eastern part was subsequently wainscoted and has moulded ribs finished with moulded bases, resting on oak corbels carved with the heads of two kings and two women of late 14th or early 15th-century date; the moulded plates are of the same date partly restored, but the rest of the roof is probably of *c.* 1300. The 15th-century spire has a centre-post resting on four curved braces and with massive tie-beams at the base.

Fittings—*Bells:* five; 3rd and 5th by Miles Graye and dated 1642 and 1622 respectively. *Brasses* and *Indent.* Brasses: In N. aisle— (1) to Edward Mildmay, 1635, inscription and shield-of-arms ; (2) to Humfrey Mildmay, 1613, inscription and two shields-of-arms. Indents : In N. aisle—of cross with foiled ends, inscription-plate and two shields, *c.* 1420. *Chair :* In chancel —modern but incorporating rough carving of St. Catherine, 16th or 17th-century. *Chest :* Small, hide-bound, with cambered lid, 17th-century. *Funeral-helm :* In N. aisle—on E. wall, combed funeral-helm with vizor, carved lion crest, late 16th or early 17th-century. *Gallery :* In tower—with hollow-chamfered arches, 15th-century and turned balusters, *c.* 1600. *Monuments* and *Floor-slabs.* Monuments : In chancel—on N. wall, (1) to John Nicoll, 1690, plain white marble tablet with shield-of-arms. In N. aisle—in N. wall, (2) recess with shafted jambs and moulded segmental-pointed arch with a moulded label ; under it oak effigy (Plate, p. 29) in chain mail, surcoat to just below the knees, crossed legs, feet on lion, hand drawing sword, late 13th-century ; (3) adjoining (2) and with similar recess, head-stop between the two, oak effigy (Plate, p. 29) similar to last but sheathing sword and feet on lion, dragon biting scabbard, late 13th-century. In S. aisle—in S. wall, (4) similar recess, reset in modern wall, oak effigy (Plate, p. 29) similar to (2) and (3) but surcoat rather longer, knee-cops, hands in attitude of prayer, mail coif, feet on lion, *c.* 1300. In tower—(5) to George Wither, D.D., 1605, alabaster tablet with strap-ornament and shield-of-arms. In churchyard— S. side, (6) to John Lawrence and Alice his wife, also their children, John, Alice and Elizabeth, 1705, head-stone. Floor-slabs : In S. chapel— (1) to Thomas Langham, 1669, and Sarah Nicoll, 1683, with shield-of-arms ; (2) to Robert Cory, D.D., rector and prebendary of St. Paul's, 1704, with shield-of-arms. In N. aisle—(3) to John Mildmay, 1673, with shield-of-arms ; (4) to William Mildmay, 1682, with shield-of-arms. In S. aisle—(5) to Samuel Cooper, 1677, with shield-of-arms. *Niche :* In S. aisle—in E. wall, small, with lancet-head and chamfered jambs, 13th-century. *Painting :* In chancel—on S. wall, Jacobean strap-work in red, early 17th-century. In N. aisle—on walls, masoned lines and on E. wall, interlacing foliage in brown, yellow and black, late 13th-century, much restored. *Piscinae :* In chancel (Plate, p. xlv) —with hollow-chamfered jambs and cinquefoiled head with moulded label and mask-stops, round drain partly restored, late 13th-century. In N. aisle—in E. wall, square-headed recess, with damaged round drain, date uncertain. In S. aisle—reset in S. wall, round drain, date uncertain. *Plate :* includes paten of 1667 and brass alms-dish of foreign workmanship with repoussé figures of Adam and Eve, inscription " Humfri Tailler 1631 " and a meaningless succession of letters in two bands. *Seating :* In nave—four benches (Plate, p. 5) with moulded rails and three popey-heads, remains of beasts on shoulders, 15th-century.

Scratching : On jamb on N. doorway—the name Ysabel and a cross, mediaeval. *Sloup :* In N. aisle—in N. wall, with reset drain from a piscina and segmental head, probably 15th-century. *Miscellanea :* Incorporated in backs of benches and cupboard in tower, traceried panels and desk front, 15th-century.

Condition—Good.

Secular :—

(2). FRETTONS, house (Plate, pp. 56–7), 100 yards N.E. of the church, is of two storeys ; the walls are timber-framed and refaced with brick ; the roofs are tiled. It was built probably early in the 16th century and consisted of a central hall with E. and W. cross-wings. Later in the same century a wing was added to the S.W. of the building. A kitchen block was built parallel to this addition at the S.E. corner of the house late in the 17th century, and there are small modern additions. The chimney-stack on the S. side of the hall is original and has an embattled offset and a single diagonal shaft. The S.W. wing has two late 16th-century chimney-stacks with grouped diagonal shafts. Inside the building the Hall is lined with 17th-century panelling and has an overmantel of two square carved panels divided by a pair of tapering pilasters with a narrow round-headed panel between them and supporting a carved frieze. The lower part of the walls of another room are lined with 16th-century panelling.

Condition—Good, much altered.

MONUMENTS (3–8).

The following monuments, unless otherwise described, are of late 16th-century date and of two storeys, timber-framed and plastered or weather-boarded ; the roofs are tiled. Some of the buildings have exposed ceiling-beams and original chimney-stacks.

Condition—Good or fairly good.

(3). *Griffin Inn*, 130 yards N. of the church, has cross-wings at the E. and W. ends. It has been considerably altered and has a modern addition at the back. One chimney-stack has two diagonal shafts. Inside the building are some fragments of 15th-century quatrefoil carving, said to have been brought from the church.

(4). *House*, opposite (3), was built early in the 16th century with a cross-wing at the W. end. The upper storey projects on the N. The main doorway has a four-centred head with spandrels carved with foliage.

(5). *Elmgreen Farm*, house, 500 yards N.W. of the church, with modern additions on the S. It has a gabled cross-wing at the N.W. end with a projecting upper storey.

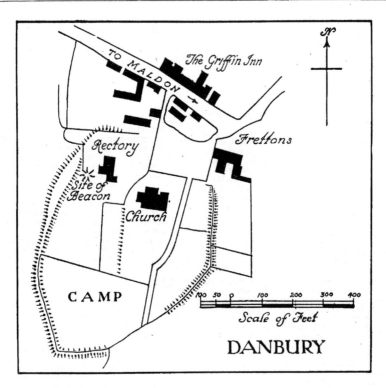

(6). *Cottage*, ¼ m. S. by W. of the church, is of L-shaped plan with the wings extending towards the S. and E. The S. end of the W. wing has a projecting upper storey. In the W. wall is an original doorway with moulded jambs, four-centred head and sunk spandrels.

(7). *House*, now tenements, at Russell Green, about 1 m. E. of the church, was built probably early in the 17th century.

(8). *Slough House* (Plate, p. 32), at Slough Bridge, 2 m. S.E. of the church, was built late in the 15th or early in the 16th century and consists of a central-hall block with gabled cross-wings at the N. and S. ends. The central block and the N. wing were largely rebuilt probably in the 17th century. It has a modern addition at the back. On the N. and S. sides of the original building are large mid 16th-century brick chimney-stacks each with two octagonal shafts. Inside the building on the upper floor is a stone fireplace with a four-centred head ; the roof retains a central purlin and a rough king-post with two-way struts.

Part of the garden wall is built of blocks of pudding-stone and ragstone, probably reused material.

(9). *Douglas House*, about 400 yards E. of the church, was built in the 15th century with a hall and cross-wings at the E. and W. ends. The hall was subsequently divided into two storeys. Inside the building the hall has an original roof truss with curved braces and octagonal king-post with moulded capital and base. At the W. end of the hall is an original doorway with a two-centred head.

WEST HANNINGFIELD: (2). THE MEETING HOUSE (formerly Fullers);
late 16th-century. From the South-West.

DANBURY: (8). SLOUGH HOUSE.
Late 15th or early 16th-century, altered in the 17th century.

From the South-East, showing Chancel, early 16th-century, and ruined Nave.

Interior of ruined Nave, showing N. Arcade ; early 16th-century.

EAST HANNINGFIELD : PARISH CHURCH OF ALL SAINTS.

Unclassified :—

(10). DANBURY CAMP, is a roughly oval earthwork, situated on high ground at the W. end of a promontory, between the Rivers Blackwater and Crouch, and enclosing the church and churchyard. Though much denuded, the entire outline of the work can still be traced, but on the N. a slight dip, towards the road, is all that remains. The defences consisted, apparently, of a single rampart and ditch, with a slight mound (shown on Morant's 18th-century plan as 'site of beacon') at the N.W. corner. There are slight traces of transverse banks inside the camp.
Condition—Poor.

21. DENGIE. (G.b.)

(O.S. 6 in. lxiii. N.E.)

Dengie is a parish 5 m. N.E. of Burnham.

Ecclesiastical :—

(1). PARISH CHURCH OF ST. JAMES stands on the W. side of the parish. The walls are of septaria, flint and pebble-rubble with yellow 14th-century and red Roman brick ; the dressings are of limestone and the roofs are tiled. The *Chancel* and *Nave* were apparently rebuilt early in the 14th century but the walls of the nave may be substantially of earlier date. The church has been restored in modern times when the bell-turret was' rebuilt and the *North Vestry* and *South Porch* added.

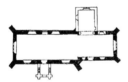

Architectural Description—The *Chancel* (26¼ ft. by 16¼ ft.) has an E. window, all modern except the 14th-century splays and reset rear-arch. In the N. wall is a large blocked window with a smaller modern window, with reused 14th-century material, set in the blocking ; further W. is a modern archway. In the S. wall are two windows, the eastern is uniform with that in the N. wall, the western window is modern except for the splays and rear-arch which are probably of the 14th century ; it is set low in the wall ; between them is a modern doorway incorporating some old stones in the jambs and rear-arch. There is no chancel-arch.

The *Nave* (45 ft. by 18¼ ft.) has in the N. wall two 14th-century windows partly restored and each of two trefoiled lights with tracery in a two-

centred head with a moulded label ; between them is the much restored N. doorway of the same date and now blocked ; it has moulded jambs, two-centred arch and a modern label. In the S. wall are two much restored windows similar to those in the N. wall ; the S. doorway is modern. In the W.wall is a 14th-century window, much restored and of three trefoiled ogee lights with tracery in an ogee head with a moulded label and head-stops ; further N. is a small blocked 14th-century doorway with hollow-chamfered jambs and a two-centred head.

Fittings—*Bells :* two ; 2nd by Thomas Bullisdon, *c.* 1500, inscribed " Sancta Maria Ora Pro Nobis " and " Sur Thomas Morys Vekery." *Brass :* In nave—figure of woman, two groups of children, indent of inscription-plate, *c.* 1520. *Coffin-lid :* In churchyard—with hollow-chamfered edge and traces of Lombardic inscription. *Plate :* includes cup of 1565 with two bands of engraved ornament. *Stoup :* E. of S. doorway, with plain pointed head and broken bowl, date uncertain.
Condition—Good.

Secular :—

(2). DENGIE HALL, W. of the church, was rebuilt in the 18th century except for part of a 17th-century building at the back. It is of two storeys, timber-framed and plastered ; the roofs are tiled.
Condition—Good.

(3). KEELINGS, house, 600 yards E. of the church is of two storeys, timber-framed, with modern brick; the roofs are tiled. It was built early in the 17th century and has a modern block on the S. side. There are two original chimney-stacks with diagonal shafts. Inside the building the ceiling-beams and joists are exposed.
Condition—Good.

22. DOWNHAM. (D.c.)

(O.S. 6 in. (a)lx. S.E. (b)lxi. S.W. (c)lxix. N.W.)

Downham is a parish, about 3½ m. E. of Billericay. The principal monument is Fremnells.

Ecclesiastical :—

c(1). PARISH CHURCH OF ST. MARGARET stands about the middle of the parish. ·The W. tower is of red brick. The church has been entirely rebuilt except the *West Tower* which is of late 15th or early 16th-century date ; the chancel and nave incorporate some reused material.

Architectural Description — The *Chancel* has reset in the S. wall an early 14th-century window of two trefoiled ogee lights with a quatrefoil in a two-centred head with a moulded label and modern stops ; it has been partly restored.

C

The *Nave* has reset in the N. wall two windows, the eastern of late 14th-century date, partly restored and of one cinquefoiled light in a square head with a moulded label and jambs ; the western window is similar to that in the S. wall of the chancel but with old head-stops ; the 13th-century N. doorway has jambs and two-centred arch of two chamfered orders, partly restored. The 14th-century S. doorway is partly restored and has double chamfered jambs and two-centred arch with a moulded label and head-stops.

The *West Tower* (10½ ft. by 11 ft.) is of late 15th or early 16th-century date and of red brick with black brick-diapering (Plate, p. xxxviii) ; it is of three stages with a restored embattled parapet and S.E. stair-turret. The two-centred tower-arch is mostly covered with modern plaster but the two chamfered orders on the E. are of stone and probably 13th or 14th-century material reused. The W. window has been completely restored ; the W. doorway has chamfered jambs and four-centred arch, the latter mostly restored. The second stage has in the N., (S. ?) and W. walls a single-light opening. The bell-chamber has in each wall a window of two four-centred lights in a four-centred head.

The modern timber-framed S. Porch incorporates some old timbers.

Fittings—Bells : four ; 2nd by John Clarke, 1621 ; 4th by Miles Graye, 1677. *Brasses :* In chancel—on N. wall, (1) to "good" Sir Henrie Terrell and Thomassin his wife, 1588, inscription only ; (2) to Joyce (Baker), wife of John Tyrrell, 1594, inscription only. In nave—on N. wall, (3) to Thomas Tyrell, 14th-century, inscription only, in French ; (4) to Alice, wife of Thomas Tyrell, 14th-century, inscription also in French, with shield-of-arms, *checky* for Adeleigh. *Chest :* In vestry—with plain panelled front, made up of 17th or 18th-century panelling. *Communion Table :* In vestry—with heavy turned legs, fluted top rails with carved brackets, 17th-century, modern rails, etc. *Door :* In turret-staircase to tower—of nail-studded battens, early 16th-century. *Glass :* In nave—in N.E. window, various fragments including several crowns four in a border, pieces of tabernacle work and foliage, mostly 14th-century ; fragment of black-letter inscription, 15th-century. *Monument* and *Floor-slabs.* Monument : In W. tower—to Sarah (Norden), wife of Benjamin Disbrowe, 1692, and to Benjamin Disbrowe, 1707–8, altar-tomb, stone sides carved with emblems of mortality and two achievements-of-arms, black marble slab with inscription and shield-of-arms. Floor-slabs : In tower—(1) to Sir Thomas Raymond, 1683, with achievement-of-arms ; (2) to Rebekah, wife of Francis Platt, 1703, and to Francis Platt, 1714 ; (3) to Sir William Andrew, 1684. *Plate :* includes a small cup and cover-paten of 1562, both with modern lining. *Scratchings :* On jambs of S. door-way, various scratchings, including a cross low down on the E. jamb, letters, etc., various dates. *Stoup :* In S. porch—with depressed elliptical head and restored basin, probably early 16th-century.

Condition—Of W. tower, bad cracks in E. wall and much ivy.

Secular :—

e(2). HOMESTEAD MOAT (Plate, p. xxxvii), at Barn Hall, ¾ m. S.E. of the parish church.

a(3). FREMNELLS, house (Plate, pp. 56–7), out-house and moat, about 1¼ m. N.N.W. of the church. The *House* is of two storeys with attics ; the walls are partly of plastered timber-framing and partly of brick ; the roofs are tiled. It was built *c.* 1670 on an H-shaped plan with the cross-wings on the N. and S. and has modern additions on the E. The house is an interesting example of its period.

On the W. front the cross-wings are gabled and there is a similar gable rising above a central projecting bay. At the first-floor level is a heavy moulded cornice but a cornice at the attic level has been cut off flush with the general face. Above it, connecting the gables, is a plain panelled parapet and there are similar panels between the windows. The windows have solid moulded frames, transoms and mullions ; most of these are original but a few have been renewed. There are three original chimney-stacks, two plain but the third has three diagonal shafts. Inside the building the main hall is panelled with late 16th-century panelling and in one of the rooms in the N. wing are some panels of the same date. A room in the S. wing is lined with linen-fold panelling.

In front of the house is a garden enclosure within a brick wall entered between two brick pillars with ball finials (Plate, p. 64). In each pillar is a sunk panel, one with initials $\frac{R}{TA}$ &c., the other with the date 1676.

An *Outhouse* to the E. is timber-framed, of two storeys and tiled. It contains heavy beams and is probably of 17th-century date.

The *Moat* is imperfect.

Condition—Of house, good.

MONUMENTS (4 and 5).

The following monuments are of the 17th century, of two storeys, timber-framed and weather-boarded, and have tiled roofs. They have original chimney-stacks and exposed ceiling-beams.

b(4). *Cottage,* at road-fork, ½ m. N. of the church, was built on a T-shaped plan with the cross-wing at the W. end. The central chimney-stack has three diagonal shafts.

Condition—Fairly good.

(5) *Castledon,* house, now tenements, nearly 1 m. S. by E. of the church.

Condition—Poor (now demolished.)

23. DUNTON (WAYLETTS). (C.c.)

(O.S. 6 in. (ª)lxviii. S.W. (ᵇ)lxxvi. N.W.)

Dunton is a parish 5 m. S.E. of Brentwood.

Ecclesiastical :—

ᵇ(1). PARISH CHURCH OF ST. MARY stands towards the S. end of the parish. It was rebuilt in 1873, except for a part of the N. wall of the chancel which is of 16th-century brick, and a 15th-century framed truss, with a cambered tie-beam and curved braces forming part of the bell-turret ; part of the old chamfered wall-plates are incorporated in the chancel-roof.

Fittings—*Bell :* probably of 1712 but uninscribed. *Chairs :* two, one broken, with carved backs and front rails, shaped legs, early 18th-century. *Coffin :* In churchyard—S. of the church, stone coffin with shaped head, much damaged and lower part of cover with stem of cross, 13th-century. *Plate :* includes cup of 1563 with bands of engraved ornament and cover-paten of 1567. *Table :* In vestry—with turned legs cut down and incised top rail, 17th-century.

Condition—Poor.

Secular :—

ᵇ(2). HOMESTEAD MOAT, N. of the Rectory, about ¼ m. N. of the church.

ª(3). WAYLETTS, house, about 1 m. N. by E. of the church, is of two storeys with attics. The walls are of plastered timber-framing ; the roofs are tiled. It was built in the 16th century on a rectangular plan and the upper storey probably projected on the W. side but has been underbuilt in brick at a later period. There is an original chimney-stack on the S., diapered in black headers and, towards the N. end of the building, a chimney-stack with a single diagonal shaft. Inside the building some of the rooms have exposed ceiling-beams and there is some 17th-century panelling on both floors. On the first floor is a blocked window of two lights with a moulded mullion. The roof is of the queen-post type.

Condition—Fairly good.

ª(4). SOUTHFIELDS, house, about 1 m. N.E. of the church, is of two storeys with attics. The walls are of brick, and the roofs are tiled. It was built early in the 18th century on an L-shaped plan with the wings extending towards the N. and W. The principal fronts were symmetrical, but some of the windows have been blocked and others altered ; there is a plain projecting string-course at the first floor level. The dormer windows have hipped roofs. On either side of the blocked windows above the entrance doorway are two sunk panels, one with the initials C.T. and the other with the date 1710.

Condition—Good.

24. EAST HANNINGFIELD. (D.b.)

(O.S. 6 in. lxi. N.W.)

East Hanningfield is a parish and small village 5 m. S.E. of Chelmsford. The ruined church is interesting.

Ecclesiastical :—

(1). PARISH CHURCH OF ALL SAINTS (Plates, pp. xxxiii, 33) stands 1 m. S.S.W. of the village. The walls of the nave are of pudding-stone and pebble-rubble ; the rest of the building is of brick ; the dressings are mainly of brick ; the roof of the chancel is slate-covered. The *Nave* judging from the thickness and materials of the walls and the presence of a wall-painting of *c.* 1300, must be of the 13th century or earlier. Early in the 16th century the *Chancel* was rebuilt and the *North Aisle* added. The church was burnt in 1883 and since that date the whole building, except the chancel, has remained roofless and ruinous ; the chancel was cut off by a modern wall and re-roofed.

Among the fittings the wall-paintings are noteworthy.

Architectural Description—The *Chancel* (23 ft. by 17½ ft.) is of early 16th-century date and of red brick. The E. window has moulded jambs, four-centred arch and label ; the rest of the window is modern. The side walls have each a broad flat projection about the middle of the length and finished with a crenelated top. In the N. wall is a two-centred brick archway ; the responds have each an attached shaft with moulded capital and base, covered with cement ; the arch is now blocked. In the S. wall are two windows both of two four-centred lights, the eastern with a square head and a moulded label and the western with a four-centred head ; between them is a blocked doorway with jambs and four-centred arch of two chamfered orders. There is no chancel-arch.

The *Nave* (41 ft. by 22½ ft.) has an early 16th-century N. arcade (Plate, p. 33) of brick and of two bays with four-centred arches of three orders, the two outer plain and the inner chamfered ; the middle octagonal column or double respond has a moulded capital and base ; the responds have attached half-round shafts. In the S. wall is an early 16th-century brick window of four four-centred lights in a square head with a moulded label. The S. doorway is modern and on the external wall are the marks of the gable of a former porch. In the W. wall is a window, modern except for the splays and two-centred rear-arch probably of the 14th century.

The *North Aisle* (13¼ ft. wide) is of early 16th-century date, and has in the E. wall a window of three four-centred lights in a square head with a moulded label ; one mullion has been destroyed. In the N. wall are two windows, the eastern of stone and of two cinquefoiled lights in a square head with a moulded label, all 15th-century work reset ; the western window is similar but all of modern stone. In the W. wall is a brick window with a segmental-pointed head, much restored and without a mullion.

Fittings—Brass : Loose in chancel—to Richard Brydges, 1606, Councellor at Law, inscription only ; slab with indent on floor. *Painting :* In nave— on S. wall, extensive remains (Plate, p. 104) of figure-subjects in red or brown lines on white plaster ; on E., Adam and Eve and the same figures with spade and spindle ; remains of large figure of St. Catherine crowned, with her wheel, and a gabled canopy with side shafts ; further W., the sacrifices of Cain and Abel with flames rising from a lamb and sheaves of corn ; small remains of other figures and two pieces of a band of running-foliage ornament, late 13th or early 14th-century. *Piscinae :* In chancel—double recess of reused 15th-century window-material, with cinquefoiled heads, no drains. In nave—in S. wall, with chamfered two-centred head, possibly 14th-century, no drain. *Plate :* includes a large cup of late 17th-century date and an old brass alms-bason of foreign origin. *Stoup :* In nave— E. of S. doorway, recess with roughly plastered two-centred head, bowl broken, early 16th-century.

Condition—Of chancel, bad ; of nave, roofless and ruinous.

Secular :—

(2). HOMESTEAD MOAT, at Great Claydons Farm, 1,100 yards W. of the modern church.

(3). WILLIS FARM, house (Plate, p. 57), 400 yards S. of the modern church, is of two storeys ; the walls are timber-framed and plastered ; the roofs are tiled. It was built probably in the 16th century on an L-shaped plan with the wings extending towards the S. and W. and a staircase-block in the angle. A modern addition makes the plan roughly rectangular. The upper storey projects at the N. end of the S. wing. On the E. side is an original chimney-stack with two diagonal shafts on an embattled base.

Condition—Good.

(4). RAILS FARM, house (Plate, pp. xxxiv–v), on opposite side of the road and 100 yards S.E. of (3). The house is of two storeys, timber-framed

and plastered ; the roofs are tiled. It was built probably in the 16th century on a T-shaped plan with the cross-wing at the N. end. It appears to have originally extended further S. where there is now a low modern addition. The upper storey projects on the W. side of the main block and at the E. end of the cross-wing ; at the S. end of the W. front is a gabled two-storeyed porch. On the N. side is an original chimney-stack with two diagonal shafts.

———

25. EAST HORNDON: (C.c.)

(O.S. 6 in. (a)lxvii. S.E. (b)lxviii. S.W.)

East Horndon is a parish 4 m. S.W. of Billericay. The church is the principal monument.

Ecclesiastical :—

a(1). PARISH CHURCH OF ALL SAINTS (Plates, pp. 36, 37) stands near the middle of the parish. The walls are of red brick with some dressings of reused stone ; the roofs are tiled.

The *Chancel, Nave, Transeptal Chapels* and the *North Chapel*, which contains the Tyrell tomb of 1476, were built probably in the last quarter of the 15th century, but the presence of reused material and the divergence in the axis indicate the existence of a previous building on the site. Early in the 16th century the *South Chapel, West Tower* and *South Porch* were added, probably in the order named. The W. tower fell and was partly reconstructed early in the 17th century.

The church is interesting as a complete brick building and the two-storeyed transeptal chapels are an unusual feature. Among the fittings incised slab is noteworthy.

Architectural Description—The Chancel (26½ ft. by 13½ ft.) has an E. window all modern except the two-centred rear-arch. The N. wall has at the E. end, externally, a shallow recess finished at the top with a trefoiled corbel-table. In the internal N.E. angle is an irregular projection of doubtful purpose ; further W. is an archway with moulded responds and four-centred arch opening into a small sepulchral *Chapel* without windows, but with the internal walls decorated with two ranges of trefoil and cinquefoil-headed sunk panels ; the roof is arched from E. to W. and has chamfered ribs with blank shields at the intersections ; the external face of the N. wall has two crosses on stepped bases, in black headers ; W. of the chapel is a modern window incorporating some old stones. The S. arcade is of two bays with four-centred arches of two moulded orders ; the column is of quatrefoil plan with moulded capitals and bases and the responds have attached half-columns. There is no chancel-arch.

EAST HORNDON: PARISH CHURCH OF ALL SAINTS. From the South-East.
Chancel and S. Transept, late 15th-century; S. Chapel, S. Porch and W. Tower, early 16th-century;
W. Tower reconstructed in the 17th century.

ORSETT: PARISH CHURCH OF ST. GILES AND ALL SAINTS.

EAST HORNDON: PARISH CHURCH OF ALL SAINTS.

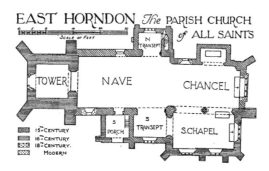

EAST HORNDON *The* PARISH CHURCH *of* ALL SAINTS

The *South Chapel* (22¾ ft. by 12¼ ft.) has in the
E. wall a stone window of three cinquefoiled lights
in a segmental-pointed head with a moulded label.
In the S. wall are two windows, the eastern of two
and the western of three cinquefoiled lights in a
square head with a moulded label. In the W. wall
is a segmental-pointed arch of two continuous
chamfered orders.

The *Nave* (33½ ft. by 19 ft.) has in the N. wall an
opening to the N. transeptal chapel and extending
up to the roof-plate ; further W. is a reset late
14th-century doorway with chamfered jambs, two-
centred arch and moulded label ; it is now blocked ;
E. of the opening to the transept are traces of the
doorway to the rood-loft. In the S. wall is an
opening to the S. transeptal chapel, similar to that
in the N. wall ; the early 16th-century S. doorway
is of stone and has moulded jambs and two-centred
arch in a segmental head with a moulded label and
quatrefoiled spandrels enclosing a shield and a
Tudor rose ; above it is a pointed brick arch ;
further W. is a 17th-century window of one three-
centred light.

The *North Transeptal Chapel* (12 ft. by 8 ft.) has
a wooden floor dividing it into two storeys. The
lower storey has in the E. wall a staircase to the
upper storey and to the rood-loft ; the doorway
has a segmental-pointed head and the staircase is
lit by a quatrefoiled opening at the N. end. In the
N. wall is a window of three cinquefoiled lights in
a square head with a moulded label. The upper
storey has in the N. wall a single-light window
with a four-centred head, widened at a later date.

The *South Transeptal Chapel* (8½ ft. by 6 ft.) is
also of two storeys. The head-beam of the archway
to the nave shows the mortices of the former doorway from the rood-loft. The lower storey has a
S. window uniform with the corresponding window
in the N. transept. The upper storey has in the

S. wall a window with a triangular head and a
modern frame ; W. of it is a fireplace with a
four-centred head.

The *West Tower* (12¼ ft. square) is of two stages,
the lower mainly of *c.* 1500 and the upper of the
17th century (Plate, p. xxxviii). In the E. wall is
an opening with a plain bressummer in place of the
tower-arch. In both the N. and S. walls is a small
round-headed window. In the W. wall is a segmental-headed window and below it a window of
two lights with elliptical heads ; the W. doorway
is probably of the 18th century. The bell-chamber
has a crow-stepped embattled parapet, a moulded
cornice below it and pilaster buttresses at the
angles. The N., S., and E. walls have each an
elliptical-headed window set in a rectangular
projecting panel.

The *South Porch* is covered by a continuation of
the S. transept roof. The outer archway has a
two-centred head and above it is a small niche
with a trefoiled head. In the W. wall is a small
loop.

The *Roof* of the chancel is of trussed-rafter type,
boarded on the soffit and with moulded ribs
dividing it into square panels and having bosses
carved with birds, flowers and shields at the intersections. The roof of the nave has king-post
trusses with moulded tie-beams and moulded and
embattled wall-plates. The low-pitched roof of the
S. chapel has moulded beams, joists and wall-plates.

Fittings—*Bells :* four ; 1st and 2nd by Thomas
Bartlet, 1621 ; 3rd by John Clifton, 1635. *Brasses
and Indent.* Brasses : In N. chapel—set on
modern brick tomb, to Sir Thomas Tyrell [1476]
and Anne (Marney), his wife, late 15th century
figure of woman, mutilated marginal inscription,
and indents of second figure, inscription-plate and
four shields. See also Monument (2). Indent : In
nave—in N. doorway, of figure, and shield, much

defaced. *Coffin-lid :* In upper storey of N. transept—fragment with foliated cross-head, 13th-century. *Door :* In S. doorway—of overlapping nail-studded battens, with strap-hinges, drop-handle and grille, early 16th-century. *Font* (Plate, pp. xlii–iii): square bowl, two sides carved with ornamental cross and other two with simple interlacing arcade of round arches, *c.* 1200, stem and base modern. *Funeral-helms :* In S. chapel—two helmets both with vizors and combs, 16th-century. *Galleries :* To front of upper storeys of transepts, balustrades (Plate, p. 5) with turned balusters, some early 17th-century and some modern. *Glass :* In S. chapel—in E. window, shield-of-arms (Plate, pp. xliv–v) *argent two cheverons azure and an engrailed border gules,* for Tyrell impaling *gules a leopard rampant argent* for Marney, 15th-century. *Monuments* and *Floor-slabs.* Monuments : In S. chapel—on S. wall, (1) to Sir John Tyrell, 1676, and Martha (Washington), his wife, 1679, also to Sir Charles Tyrell, 1714, and Martha, his wife, 1690, marble wall-monument with fluted pilasters, broken pediment and achievement-of-arms. In S. transept—(2) altar-tomb, recessed in wall, with moulded slab and panelled base, with remains of shields in front, recess with flat cusped arch and foliated spandrels and quatrefoiled soffit, on slab brass of headless figure of man in plate-armour, *c.* 1520, eight sons, indents of Trinity, wife and daughter, inscription-plate and fillet. *Floor-slabs :* In S. chapel—now a modern raised tomb, (1) of Alice (Cogesale), wife of Sir John Tyrell, 1422, incised slab (Plate, p. 40) of hard limestone with figure of woman in horned head-dress and fur-lined cloak, under vaulted canopy with shafts containing figures of children with their names on scrolls, two shields—(*a*) *a cross between four scallops* for Coggeshall, and (*b*) Coggeshall dimidiating *two cheverons and an engrailed border* for Tyrell, marginal inscription with symbols of the Evangelists ; (2) to Sir John Tyrell, 1675, " once decimated, twice imprisoned, thrice sequestrated," with achievement-of-arms ; (3) to Martha, wife of Sir Charles Tyrell, 1690, with shield-of-arms. *Plate :* includes cup of 1564 and cover-paten of 1567. *Pulpit :* semi-octagonal, with two tiers of moulded panels, 17th-century, rail modern. *Seating :* In chancel—two bench-ends with popey-heads, early 16th-century. *Stoup :* In nave—in S. wall, recess with part of basin and trefoiled head, early 16th-century. *Miscellanea :* In upper storey of N. transept—fragments of windows and oak screen ; other fragments of moulded stonework in churchyard.

Condition—Building shows signs of settlement and tower has bad cracks in W. wall, etc.

Secular :—

b(2). BARNS, MOAT and FISH-PONDS at Heron Hall, 1½ m. N.N.E. of the church. The small

Barn to the S. of the moat is of two storeys and of brick with a tiled roof. It was built in the 16th century and has window-openings with four-centred heads on both floors. The large *Barn* to the N.E. of the former is of the same materials. It is of ten bays with a porch on the E. and was built early in the 18th century. Built into the N. end of the W. wall are two stone gate-piers with moulded caps and bases.

The *Moat* is complete and surrounds a large and strongly defended site. On the E. side is a strong retaining bank and on the W. three small fish-ponds. About ¼ m. N.W. of the moat is a large area enclosed on three sides by a strong retaining bank and known as the Heron pond. A small stream runs through the middle.

Condition—Of barns and earthworks, good.

b(3). MOUNT THRIFT, house and moat, 1 m. N.N.E. of the church. The *House* is of two storeys, timber-framed and plastered ; the roofs are tiled. It was built probably in the 16th century, but has been considerably altered by insertion of later partitions and by additions on both the E. and W. sides. The central chimney-stack has four shafts, set diagonally on a cruciform plan with a square base. Inside the building some of the rooms have exposed ceiling-beams. On the first floor are two doors of moulded battens and on the ground-floor is a cupboard door of 16th-century panelling. There is a blocked window on the first floor of three lights with moulded mullions.

The *Moat* is fragmentary.

Condition—Of house, good.

a(4). BOAR'S HEAD INN (Plate, p. xl), at Heron Gate, about 1 m. N. by E. of the church, is of two storeys, timber-framed and plastered ; the roofs are tiled. It was built probably late in the 17th century but has been much altered.

Condition—Good.

---

26. EAST TILBURY. (C.e.)

(O.S. 6 in. ^(a)lxxxiv. S.W. ^(b)lxxxiv. S.E. ^(c)lxxxix. N.W.)

East Tilbury is a river-side parish 3 m. E. of Tilbury town and docks. The church and the Romano-British huts are the principal monuments.

Roman :—

c(1). Adjoining the western boundary of the parish, on the foreshore of the Thames, below the present high-tide level, are fragmentary remains (Plate, p. xxxvi) of a small settlement of circular huts associated with very numerous potsherds of the 1st and 2nd centuries A.D. In 1920 the remains visible in the mud at low-tide represented three adjacent huts, and fragments of a fourth were detected about 20 yards further W. The interior

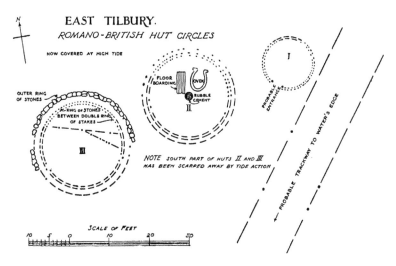

EAST TILBURY.

ROMANO-BRITISH HUT CIRCLES

NOW COVERED AT HIGH TIDE

NOTE SOUTH PART OF HUTS II AND III HAS BEEN SCARPED AWAY BY TIDE ACTION

SCALE OF FEET

diameter of the smallest was about 11½ ft., that of the largest about 20 ft. The two largest circles consisted of three rings of pointed stakes, each 1½–2 in. in diameter, mostly in their original round state but sometimes roughly squared. They were employed either singly or in pairs, and formed the framework for interlacing wattlework which still remains in excellent preservation below the mud. The two innermost rings of stakes are about 8 in. apart, and between them are remains of a ring of stones (Kentish rag with some chalk), whilst a similar ring of stones appears to have surrounded the outermost ring of stakes. One hut (III on plan) retains traces of a partition. Another (II) has in the middle a small circular platform, 1½ ft. in diameter, of rubble; this shows no signs of burning and was therefore not a hearth, but probably supported a stout central roof-pole. In the same hut is a piece of original wood-flooring, about 5 ft. by 2 ft., made up of 1 in. by 5 in. planking; and close to this are the foundations of an oval or omega-shaped oven, with hard clay walls 6 in. thick and an opening on the N. side. The ground in and around the opening is burnt black and hard to a considerable depth, but no indication remains of the original use of the oven. In the smallest circle (I) the entrance appears to be marked by two thick posts, each 2½ in. in diameter, set 2 ft. 10 in. apart. In and around the huts were fragments of the clay daub with which

the timber walls had been covered. The rings of stone cannot have been carried up to any considerable height. Numerous fragments of roofing tile may indicate the nature of the roofing.

Immediately E. of the huts is a shallow channel, running N.E. and S.W., with some traces of flanking stakes. This may represent a former trackway leading from the old river-edge.

The foreshore for about 100 yards on each side of the huts is covered with potsherds, including the following 1st and 2nd-century Samian forms: 15/17, 18, 18/31, 27, 30, 31, 37, 38, 54 (plain), 78, and 79. Mr. F. Lambert, F.S.A., has noted the following potter's stamps: DAGOM[ARVS] (on form 18/31), OF VIRIL (on form 18), AVITI-MA (on form 33), ANISATV[S] (on form 33), [CINT]VSMIM (on form 31), and INDERCILLIOF (on form 33). Most of the pottery, however, is of native type, with marked Late Celtic elements such as cordons, bosses and incised linear patterns, and represents the production of native manufacturers working under Roman influence.

No 'wasters' have yet been noticed from this site, and there is no evidence that any of the pottery was made on the spot. The site may have been a landing-place for traffic from Kent or elsewhere; the amount of pottery certainly seems excessive for the ordinary requirements of a small hut-settlement.

(Slight mention of the site in *Arch. Journ.*, XLII (1885), pp. 276–7.)

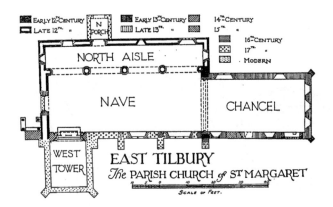

EARLY 12TH CENTURY   EARLY 13TH CENTURY   14TH CENTURY
LATE 12TH "   N PORCH   LATE 13TH "   15TH "
  16TH CENTURY
  17TH "
  MODERN

NORTH AISLE

NAVE

CHANCEL

WEST TOWER

EAST TILBURY
The PARISH CHURCH *of* ST MARGARET

SCALE of FEET.

Ecclesiastical :—

[b](2). PARISH CHURCH OF ST. MARGARET, now St. Katherine, stands at the S. end of the village. The walls are of flint and ragstone-rubble with some Roman and later bricks ; the dressings are mostly of Reigate stone ; the roofs are tiled. The *Nave* was built early in the 12th century and late in the same century the N. arcade was built and the *North Aisle* added. The *Chancel* was rebuilt and probably enlarged in the first half of the 13th century. In the 14th century the S. arcade was built and a S. aisle and tower added ; the chancel-arch was also rebuilt and widened. The S. aisle and tower are said to have been destroyed by the Dutch fleet in 1667 and the S. arcade was then blocked. A N. porch was built in 1704. The church has been restored in modern times when the *North Porch* was rebuilt. A new *West Tower* has been begun but not completed.

Architectural Description—The *Chancel* (35½ ft. by 19¼ ft.) has in the E. wall three early 13th-century graduated lancet-windows (Plate, p. 41) with moulded internal labels and intermediate mask-stops. In the N. wall are two windows, the eastern is similar to those in the E. wall ; the western window is of early 14th-century date probably reset and is of two cinquefoiled lights in a two-centred head ; the W. half of the wall externally is faced with knapped flints, probably 16th-century work. In the S. wall (Plate, p. 84) are four windows, the easternmost is of early 16th-century date and of two four-centred lights in a four-centred head with a moulded label ; it is set in a taller two-centred opening probably of the 14th century and is now blocked with 17th-century

brick ; the second window is similar to the eastern window in the N. wall and had an external label ; the third window is a late 13th-century lancet without a label ; the westernmost window is a 13th-century lancet partly blocked and with a 15th-century cinquefoiled light inserted ; the window is carried down below a transom as a 'low-side' and rebated for a shutter. Below and to the E. of the third window is a late 13th-century doorway with chamfered jambs and two-centred arch ; W. of the same window is a blocked doorway with a roughly two-centred head, probably of early 13th-century date. Below the windows of the chancel runs a moulded string-course, of which the western half has been cut away. The distorted 14th-century chancel-arch is two-centred and of two moulded orders, the outer dying on the chamfered N. respond and the S. side wall and the inner springing from attached shafts with moulded capitals and bases.

The *Nave* (56½ ft. by 21¼ ft.) has a late 12th-century N. arcade (Plate, p. 41) of four bays with two-centred arches of one plain order ; the middle column is octagonal and the others round ; the two eastern have carved and scalloped capitals with square abaci ; the third capital is similar but uncarved and perhaps unfinished ; all have moulded bases ; the semi-octagonal responds have grooved and chamfered abaci and the eastern has volutes at the angles of the capital ; above the W. half of the first arch are the remains of an early 12th-century window, now blocked. The quoins of the original N.E. angle of the nave remain *in situ*. In the S. wall are remains of the two eastern arches of the early 14th-century S. arcade with two-centred arches ; part of the E. respond shows

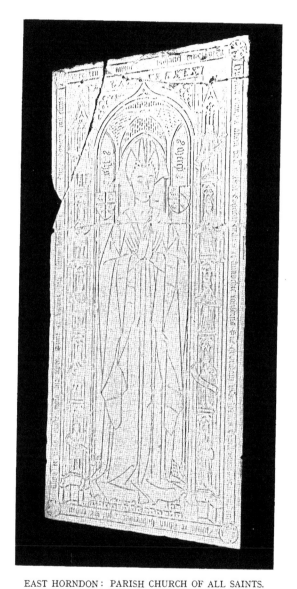

EAST HORNDON: PARISH CHURCH OF ALL SAINTS.
Incised slab to Alice (Cogesale), wife of Sir John Tyrell, 1422.

externally and has a moulded capital and base ; reset in the blocking of the arcade are two 14th-century windows, the eastern of three trefoiled ogee lights with tracery in a four-centred head and the western of two similar lights with tracery in an elliptical head ; in the W. bay is the 14th-century tower-arch, two-centred and of three chamfered orders, the two outer continuous and the inner springing from attached shafts with moulded capitals and bases ; the archway is partly blocked. In the W. wall is a 13th-century lancet window and below it a large W. doorway, probably of the same date with shafted and moulded jambs and abaci and moulded two-centred arch, much defaced.

The *North Aisle* (7¾ ft. wide) has in the E. wall a 15th-century window of one cinquefoiled light. This wall is faced with knapped flints like the N. wall of the chancel. In the N. wall are three windows, the easternmost is of three trefoiled ogee lights in a square head, all of wood and probably of early 16th-century date partly restored ; the second window is a small late 12th-century light with a later lancet-head ; the westernmost window is modern ; the 14th-century N. doorway has moulded jambs and two-centred arch with defaced label and head-stops ; the N. wall has been largely refaced in the 17th century. In the W. wall is a 16th-century window of one four-centred light with some reused 12th-century stones in the splays.

The *North Porch* is modern but incorporates old material. Adjoining the W. wall of the nave externally is a timber bell-cote, all modern except the 17th-century vertical posts.

The *Roof* of the chancel is modern except for three tie-beams which are probably of the 17th century.

Fittings—Bell : one, by William Oldfield, 1629. *Brass Indents :* In chancel—(1) of small figure, probably of priest, and inscription-plate. In tower —(2) of inscription-plate. *Coffins* and *Coffin-lids :* In tower—part of shaped head of a coffin and part of the lower end of another, also two lids with moulded edges and raised crosses, 13th-century. *Doors :* Loose in N. aisle—of two folds with strap-hinges, 17th-century. In N. doorway—of feathered battens, probably 16th or 17th-century. *Font :* octagonal bowl, with moulded under-edge, plain stem and moulded base, early 16th-century. *Monument* and *Floor-slab.* Monument : In church-yard—S. of chancel, to Abigail, wife of Thomas Bland, 1713, head-stone. Floor-slab : In chancel—to John Rawlinson, 1698. *Piscina :* In chancel—with trefoiled head with projecting sexfoiled drain, foliated on the underside, shallow shelf and grooves for later shelf, late 13th-century. *Pulpit* (Plate, p. 4) : hexagonal, each face with enriched arcaded panel with arabesque spandrels, fluted and enriched pilasters at angles and dentilled cornice, early

17th-century. *Royal Arms :* Above chancel-arch—remains of painted 16th-century Royal Arms in garter with supporters. *Miscellanea :* Reused in walls and filling of arcade, various worked and moulded stones, 14th and 15th-century. In tower, reset, two dished angle-stones with drains, mediaeval.

Condition—Good, some of the external stonework much decayed.

Secular :—

MONUMENTS (3–6).

The following monuments, unless otherwise described are of two storeys, timber-framed and plastered or weather-boarded ; the roofs are tiled. Some of the buildings have original chimney-stacks. Condition—Good or fairly good.

ᵃ(3). *Black Cottage,* on E. side of road, 550 yards N.W. of the church, was built in the 17th century and is of central-chimney type. The walls have been partly rebuilt in brick. The chimney-stack has four shafts built on a cruciform plan.

ᵃ(4). *East Tilbury Place,* house, about ¾ m. N.W. of the church, is of two storeys with attics. It was built probably early in the 18th century but has been much altered. Inside the building is an original staircase with moulded string, turned balusters and square newels surmounted by ball-finials.

ᵃ(5). *Gravelpit Farm,* house and outbuildings, 1 m. W.N.W. of the church. The *House* was built early in the 17th century ; later alterations include the rebuilding of parts of the walls in brick.

The *Barn* is of late 17th-century date and of weather-boarded timber-framing open at the ends and carried at the sides on brick walls.

ᵃ(6). *Smithy,* cottage, at the junction of the road to the church and the Muckingford Road, 1¾ m. N.N.W. of the church, is a rectangular building of late 17th or early 18th-century date.

Unclassified :—

ᵇ(7). EARTHWORK locally known as "Soldiers' Graves." Running W. of the church and traceable for a distance of ½ m. or more, is an abrupt partly artificial scarp with a ditch and external rampart at the foot. It faces S. and overlooks the river. It was probably not a defensive work.

---

27. EASTWOOD. (E.d.)

(O.S. 6 in. ⁽ᵃ⁾lxx. S.W. ⁽ᵇ⁾lxxviii. N.W.)

Eastwood is a small parish 2 m. N.W. of Southend-on-Sea. The church is interesting.

ᵇ(1). PARISH CHURCH OF ST. LAURENCE AND ALL SAINTS (Plate, pp. xxxviii–ix) stands towards the S.E. corner of the parish. The walls are of ragstone-rubble with some pudding-stone, flint and Roman

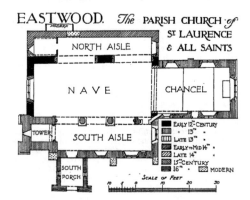

EASTWOOD. *The* PARISH CHURCH *of* S.⸵ LAURENCE & ALL SAINTS

NORTH AISLE

NAVE

CHANCEL

TOWER

SOUTH AISLE

SOUTH PORCH

EARLY 12.⸵ CENTURY
13.⸵ "
LATE 13.⸵ "
EARLY TO MID 14.⸵ "
LATE 14.⸵ "
15.⸵ CENTURY
16.⸵ "   MODERN

SCALE OF FEET

brick, they are now covered with cement. The dressings are of Reigate and other limestone and the roofs are tiled. The *Nave* was built early in the 12th century. Early in the 13th century the S. arcade was built and the *South Aisle* and *West Tower* added; the *Chancel* was rebuilt probably about the same time. In the 14th century the N. wall was pierced by an arcade and the *North Aisle* added. Early in the 16th century the *South Porch* was added. The upper part of the tower fell or was destroyed at some uncertain date. The church was restored in the 19th century and the timber bell-turret of the tower is modern.

The church is of considerable architectural interest; the priest's room is an unusual feature and amongst the fittings the font and N. and S. doors are noteworthy.

Architectural Description—The *Chancel* (29 ft. by 16 ft.) has an E. window all modern except the 14th-century splays and rear-arch. In the N. wall are two windows, the eastern of mid 14th-century date and of two cinquefoiled ogee lights with tracery in a two-centred head with a moulded label; the western window is of the 13th century, possibly widened, and of a single lancet-light. In the S. wall are two windows, the eastern uniform with the corresponding window in the N. wall and the western a 'low-side' of 13th or 14th-century date and of one pointed light; it is set in a wide 14th-century recess with a two-centred arch of one chamfered order; at the W. end of the recess is an early 16th-century squint with a rough rounded head; E. of the recess is a doorway probably of the 14th century and with chamfered jambs and segmental-pointed arch. The late 14th-century chancel-arch (Plate, p. 44) is two-centred and of two chamfered orders dying on to

the side walls; below it are the two ends of the rood-beam cut off flush with the walls; above the arch on the E. are the marks of an earlier gable roof.

The *Nave* (44 ft. by 20 ft.) (Plate, p. 44) has in the N. wall two wide 14th-century arches, two-centred and of one chamfered order; higher up are remains of three 12th-century windows, the middle one almost complete and the other two with parts of the rear-arches, etc.; they were round-headed and each of a single light; the easternmost has an ashlar rear-arch. On the S. side of the E. respond of the arcade is part of a moulded 13th-century capping probably of a former recess now cut away. The early 13th-century S. arcade is of three bays with two-centred arches of two chamfered orders with a moulded label on the N. side; the octagonal columns have moulded capitals and bases and added plinths of brick; the angles of the piers have been partly cut away; the responds have each a round attached shaft with moulded capital and base; above the W. haunch of the third arch is part of the rear-arch of a 12th-century window; E. of the arcade and in the adjoining E. wall are remains of two 13th-century recesses, the arches springing from a common moulded impost in the angle; the E. recess has been mostly cut away and blocked and the S. recess has a two-centred arch and has been pierced through at the back to communicate with the S. aisle. In the W. wall is a 15th-century window of three cinquefoiled and sub-cusped lights with vertical tracery in a segmental-pointed head with a moulded label.

The *North Aisle* (6½ ft. wide) has in the E. wall a partly restored 14th-century window of two cinquefoiled ogee lights with tracery in a segmental head. In the N. wall is a 14th-century doorway, now blocked and with plain jambs and a later oak lintel. In the W. wall is a 15th-century square-headed loop divided into two stages and lighting the two apartments partitioned off at the end of the aisle ; the 15th-century partition is of oak with a moulded and embattled head and rail, chamfered posts and ridged muntins ; the doorway has a four-centred head ; the floor of the upper chamber has chamfered joists and rests on braced corner-posts ; the trap-door is of feathered battens with strap-hinges.

The *South Aisle* (9¾ ft. wide) has in the E. wall a window of two lights and of doubtful date with a modern head. In the S. wall are two windows, the eastern is of the 14th century and of two trefoiled ogee lights with tracery in a square head ; the western window is of the 13th century and of one wide pointed light ; further W. is the 13th-century S. doorway with hollow-chamfered jambs and modern head. The walls of the S. aisle were heightened or the upper part rebuilt probably in the 17th century.

The *West Tower* (6½ ft. square) is of two stages, the lower of early 13th-century date and the upper modern. The tower-arch is two-centred and of two chamfered orders ; the responds are similar to the responds of the S. arcade. In the W. wall is a small lancet-window.

The *South Porch* is of brick and of the 16th century and has an outer archway with chamfered jambs and four-centred arch ; the gable has foiled barge-boards. The side walls have each a window of one light with a segmental head.

The *Roof* of the chancel is probably of the 14th century and is of braced collar-beam type with two moulded tie-beams and moulded wall-plates ; the eastern bay may be of later date. The 15th-century roof of the nave has four trusses with octagonal king-posts having moulded capitals and bases, and one truss with a plain king-post. The roofs of the aisles are ceiled. The porch has reused timbers.

Fittings—*Bells:* three ; said to be, 1st by Charles Newman, 1693 ; 2nd by William Burford, 14th-century, and inscribed "Sancta Katerina Ora Pro Nobis" ; 3rd by the same founder and inscribed "Sancte Gregori Ora Pro Nobis." *Bier:* of oak with turned legs and shaped brackets and the initials and date C.F. 1706. *Brackets :* In chancel —flanking E. window, two, moulded and cut back to wall-face, late 14th-century. *Brass* and *Indent.* Brass : In chancel—of Thomas Burrough, 1600, figure of man in civil dress. Indent : In N. aisle— of civilian, two wives and inscription-plate, c. 1480. *Chest :* At vicarage—of hutch-type with plain styles, two lock-plates, 13th or early 14th-century, lid later. *Doors :* In N. aisle—now unhung, of three battens with elaborate ironwork (Plate, pp. 4–5) including two hinges with crescent-shaped enrichments and scrolled ends, also separate straps and

crescent-shaped pieces similarly ornamented, late 12th or early 13th-century; in doorway of partition, of overlapping battens with chamfered frame and strap-hinges, 15th-century. In S. aisle—in S. doorway, of three battens covered with extensive remains of scrolled and foliated ironwork (Plate, p. 45), nail-studded, on this has been applied two hinges and a strap similar to those on the door in the N. aisle, one of these is defective and the strap has remains of an inscription in Lombardic letters probably reading " Pax regat intrantes eadem regat egredientes," cross-shaped scutcheon with foliated ends and a straight border with enrichment of cheverons or crossed lines, late 13th-century with late 12th or early 13th-century hinges, etc., applied. *Font* (Plate, pp. xlii–iii) : round tapering bowl with round interlacing arcade with simply foliated spandrels and resting on tall pilasters with crudely moulded capitals and bases, plain stem and moulded base, late 12th-century. *Monuments* and *Floor-slab.* Monuments : In churchyard—on S.E., (1) to Elizabeth, wife of Thomas Dighton, 1708, Thomas her son and Mary her granddaughter, head-stone ; E. of chancel, (2) to Thomas Purchas, 1657 (?), table-tomb. Floor-slab : In N. aisle— to Elizabeth Hooker, 1666. *Niches :* In S. aisle —in E. wall, with moulded jambs and modern head, probably 14th-century. On S. porch—above outer archway, of brick with trefoiled head and square label, early 16th-century. *Paintings :* Traces of paintings on piers of S. arcade, date uncertain. *Panelling :* Incorporated in modern framing in porch, 17th-century. *Piscinae :* In S. aisle—in S. wall, with square head and quatrefoiled drain, 14th-century. Loose in N. aisle—square bowl and drain, said to have come from chancel. *Plate :* includes cup and cover-paten of 1562, the former with band of engraved ornament. *Stoup :* In S. porch—rough recess partly broken away and covered with plaster. *Miscellanea :* In S. aisle— forming sill of S.E. window, stone slab with moulded edge from tomb or altar, possibly 14th-century.

Condition—Fairly good, but roofs defective.

Secular —:

MONUMENTS (2–11).

The following monuments, unless otherwise described, are of the 17th century, and of two storeys, timber-framed and plastered or weather-boarded ; the roofs are tiled. Some of the buildings have exposed ceiling-beams and original chimney-stacks.

Condition—Good.

b(2). *House,* now two tenements, 300 yards W.S.W. of the church, was built in the 16th century and has a later addition at the S. end. Inside the building some of the timber-framing is exposed.

^b(3). *Old Workhouse*, 550 yards W.S.W. of the church.

^b(4). *Bellhouse Farm*, house, about 1½ m. W. of the church, is of two storeys with attics. It was built in the 16th century on an L-shaped plan with the wings extending towards the S. and W. and a staircase in the angle. Modern additions have been built on the W. side of both wings. The upper storey projects on the N. front and has an original moulded fascia and curved brackets. In the roof are two gabled dormers. The S. front of the E. wing of the original house is gabled and has a projecting upper storey with curved brackets. The chimney-stack at the W. end of the original house has stepped offsets. Inside the building a ceiling-beam in the N. wing is supported on moulded brackets.

^b(5). *Dandies Farm*, house, at Noblesgreen, about 1 m. W.N.W. of the church.

^b(6). *Blatches*, house (Plate, pp. xxxiv–v), about 1m. W. of the church, is of two storeys with attics. It was built in the 16th century on an L-shaped plan with the wings extending towards the E. and N. There is a modern addition on the W. At the end of the S. front the upper storey projects and has an original moulded bressummer with curved brackets. In the E. end of the S. wall is an original window, now blocked, of three lights with moulded frame and mullions. On the N. front the W. wing has two similar blocked windows ; E. of the staircase is an original chimney-stack with stepped offsets. Inside the building is an original staircase with a central newel. The roof is of collar-beam type and has curved wind-braces.

^a(7). *Eastwood Lodge*, house, nearly 2¼ m. W.N.W. of the church, is of two storeys with cellars. It was built early in the 16th century on a modified half H-shaped plan with the cross-wings extending westwards. In the 17th century a staircase was added in the angle formed by the N. and central blocks. There are modern additions on the N. side and the house has been much altered. On the S. side of the N. wing the upper storey projects but has been partly cut into by the staircase. Inside the building, in the walls of the N.E. cellar are four brick niches, three with shaped heads and one with a two-centred head.

^b(8). *Westbarrow Hall*, house, now two tenements, ½ m. N.N.E. of the church, was built in the 15th century with a central hall and cross-wings at the E. and W. ends. The W. wing was rebuilt in the 17th century and has since been largely refaced with brick. The roofs to the hall and W. wing have been partly rebuilt, and smoke-blackened timbers in the former suggest that the first floor of the central block is an insertion. There is a modern addition on the N. On both the N. and S. fronts the upper storey of the W. wing projects. In the W. wall of the E. wing is a partly blocked window with diamond-shaped mullions. Inside the building, in the E. wing, is a 17th-century staircase with flat-shaped moulded rail and square newel posts with shaped tops. The roof of the E. wing is original and of three bays with cambered tie-beams, and octagonal king-posts with moulded capitals and bases. The roof over the W. wing retains one old tie-beam with queen-posts ; the side purlins have curved wind-braces.

^b(9). *Old Workhouse*, on E. side of the main road to Rochford, 1 m. E.N.E. of the church. The N. end of the building is of 15th-century date and is probably all that remains of a fairly large house, the existing building on the S. being of 18th-century date. On the E. the upper storey projects and has one curved bracket. On the N. is an original chimney-stack with crow-stepped offsets. Inside the building on the ground-floor the timber-framing is exposed.

^b(10). *Three Ashes Inn*, now a shop and two tenements, 300 yards N.N.E. of (9), was built late in the 16th century. Late 17th-century and modern additions on the E. make the existing building L-shaped on plan with wings projecting to the S. and W.

^a(11). *Cottage*, on E. side of the main road to Rochford, about 1¼ m. N.E. of the church, was built probably in the 16th century as the W. wing of a larger house ; it has been very much altered. On the S. front the upper storey projects and has a moulded barge-board to the gable. Inside the building the timber-framing is exposed.

FAMBRIDGE, see NORTH FAMBRIDGE and SOUTH FAMBRIDGE.

28. FOBBING. (D.d.)

(O.S. 6 in. lxxvi. S.E.)

Fobbing is a parish and village 7 m. N.E. of Tilbury. The church is interesting.

Ecclesiastical :—

(1). PARISH CHURCH OF ST. MICHAEL stands in the S.W. corner of the parish. The walls are of ragstone-rubble with some flint, septaria, tile, etc. ; the dressings are mainly of Reigate stone ; the roofs are tiled. The *Nave* was built in the 11th century, possibly before the Conquest, as the N. wall is only 2½ ft. thick. Early in the 14th century the *Chancel* was rebuilt and the *South Chapel* added. Towards the middle of the 14th century the nave was extended W., the S. arcade built and a S.W. tower and *South Aisle* added ; this aisle appears to have extended only to the E. face of the tower. Late in the 15th century this tower was destroyed and the existing *West Tower* built ;

EASTWOOD: PARISH CHURCH OF ST. LAURENCE AND ALL SAINTS.
Interior, showing Chancel-arch, late 14th-century, and Nave, 12th-century, with N. arches, 14th-century, and S. Arcade, early 13th-century. Nave roof, 15th-century.

EASTWOOD : PARISH CHURCH OF ST. LAURENCE AND ALL SAINTS.
S. Door, showing iron-work, late 13th-century, with late 12th or early 13th-century
hinges, etc., applied.

FOBBING *The* PARISH CHURCH *of* St MICHAEL.

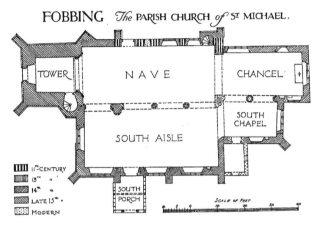

at the same time the S. aisle was largely rebuilt, and extended W. to cover the site of the former tower ; the rood-stair turret was built and the E. arch of the arcade rebuilt to accommodate the rood-loft. The *South Porch* is also of late 15th-century date. The church has been restored in modern times when the *South Vestry* was added.

The church is of some architectural interest.

Architectural Description—The *Chancel* (29 ft. by 15¾ ft.) has a 15th-century E. window of three cinquefoiled lights with vertical tracery in a two-centred head with a moulded label. In the N. wall are two windows, the eastern is a reset 13th-century lancet-light and the western is of *c.* 1500 and of three cinquefoiled lights in a square head with a moulded label. In the S. wall is a window all modern except the E. splay and rear-arch which are possibly of the 14th century ; further W. is an early 14th-century arcade of two bays with two-centred arches of two, hollow-chamfered orders, partly restored ; the pier and W. respond are modern ; the E. respond has an attached semi-octagonal shaft with moulded capital and base. The early 14th-century chancel-arch is two-centred and of two chamfered orders dying on to the walls.

The *South Chapel* (20 ft. by 12½ ft.) has an E. window all modern except the 15th-century jambs, sill, splays and rear-arch. In the S. wall is an early 14th-century window of two lights with tracery in a two-centred head with a defaced label ; further W. is a modern doorway. In the W. wall is a 14th-century two-centred arch of two hollow-chamfered orders, dying on to the responds.

The *Nave* (49 ft. by 20½ ft.) has in the N. wall two 14th-century windows, the eastern is of two cinquefoiled ogee lights with tracery in a square head ; the western window is also of two cinquefoiled ogee lights with different tracery in a three-centred head ; to the W. of this window is a blocked 11th-century window with a wide external opening (1½ ft.) and a round head ; the 14th-century N. doorway has moulded jambs and two-centred arch with a moulded label and head-stops ; at the E. end of the N. wall is the rood-loft staircase of *c.* 1500 ; the lower doorway has a two-centred and the upper a four-centred head. The 14th-century S. arcade is of four bays of which the eastern was heightened and rebuilt *c.* 1500, the arches are two-centred and of two chamfered orders and the columns are octagonal with moulded capitals and bases ; the W. respond of the third bay has an attached half-column ; the westernmost bay is separated from the third by a solid pier and formerly opened into the S.W. tower ; both orders of the arch are continued down the E. respond and the inner order down the W. respond.

The *South Aisle* (21¼ ft. wide) has, adjoining the pier just described, part of the base of the respond of an arch formerly opening from the aisle into the S.W. tower. In the S. wall are three windows of *c.* 1500, each of three cinquefoiled lights in a square head with a moulded label ; high up in the wall further E. is a small square-headed window probably of the same date ; the late 15th-century S. doorway has moulded jambs, two-centred arch and label. In the W. wall is a late 15th-century window of three cinquefoiled lights with vertical tracery in a two-centred head with a moulded label.

The *West Tower* (14 ft. by 12½ ft.) is of *c.* 1500 and of three stages with an embattled parapet and a stair-turret rising above it (Plate, pp. xxxii–iii). The two-centred tower-arch is of three hollow-chamfered orders, the two outer dying on to the splayed responds and the inner resting on attached shafts with moulded capitals and bases. The W. window is of three pointed lights with plain transomed tracery in a two-centred head with a moulded label; the W. doorway has moulded jambs and two-centred arch in a square head with a moulded label and traceried spandrels enclosing rosettes. The N., S. and W. walls of the second stage have each a window of one four-centred light with a square moulded label. The bell-chamber has in each wall a window of two pointed and transomed lights in a four-centred head with a moulded label.

The *South Porch* (Plate, p. 96) is of late 15th-century date and is timber-framed on dwarf brick and rubble walls. The four-centred outer archway has spandrels carved with foliage, the head of a king and a seated man opening the mouth of a dragon; the carved and cusped barge-boards of the gable are much defaced. The E. and W. sides have been restored except for the main posts. The roof is of two bays with moulded wall-plates and king-post trusses.

The *Roof* of the chancel is of the 15th century and of braced collar-beam type with a moulded and embattled wall-plate on the N. side. The roof of the S. chapel is of similar type with a similar wall-plate on the S. side; the N. wall-plate is probably of the 17th-century. The 15th-century roof of the nave is of four bays with moulded and embattled wall-plates and king-post trusses; the tie-beams have curved braces with traceried spandrels. The 15th-century roof of the S. aisle is of four bays with moulded and embattled wall-plates and plain king-post trusses. The first floor of the tower is of *c.* 1500 and has moulded and embattled wall-plates.

Fittings—*Bells*: five; 1st to 4th by Thomas Bartlet, 1629; bell-frame, 17th-century, much restored. *Bracket*: In S. chapel—in E. wall, piece of 13th-century coffin-lid used as bracket. *Brass Indents*: In S. aisle—(1) of figure of man, scroll and inscription-plate. In W. tower—(2) of man and wife, inscription-plate and groups of children; (3) of woman and inscription-plate; (4) of man and wife with inscription-plate. *Doors*: In N. doorway—of feathered battens on trellis-framing, 15th-century, two strap-hinges with ornamental prongs, possibly 13th-century. In S. doorway—of ridged battens on trellis-framing, old drop-handle and lock, 15th-century. In tower—in W. doorway, panelled, with drop-handle, strap-hinges and lock, 17th-century; in turret-staircase, three battened doors, *c.* 1500. *Font*: octagonal bowl of Purbeck marble with two shallow-pointed panels in each face, eight small shafts and hollow-chamfered base, 13th-century, stem modern. *Glass*: In E. window of chancel, fragments of tabernacle-work, 15th-century; in E. window of S. chapel, 14th and 15th-century fragments of quarries with foliated and trellised designs. In nave—in N.E. window, foliated quarries, borders and foliated spandrels, 14th-century, *in situ*. In N.W. window, foliage, borders and fragments including tabernacle-work and Lombardic letter T, 14th and 15th-century. In S. aisle—in middle S. window, 14th and 15th-century fragments of quarries, borders and tabernacle-work. *Image*: In S. chapel—on bracket, seated stone figure of the Virgin and Child (Plate, p. 25), both heads gone, 15th-century. *Monument* and *Floor-slab*. Monument: In chancel—on N. wall, to Thomas de Crawedene, *c.* 1340, stone sunk-panel (Plate, p. 48) with Lombardic inscription "+Pur lamur Jesu Crist priez pur sa alme ki ci gist pater noster et ave Thomas de Crawedene fut apelle." *Floor-slab*: In tower, to Sarah, wife of James Foxon, 1712, and James their son. *Piscinae*: In chancel—with two-centred head and square drain, 13th or 14th-century. In S. chapel—in S. wall, with two-centred head and multifoiled drain, 14th-century. In S. aisle—in S. wall, with trefoiled head and round drain, 15th-century. *Plate*: includes cup of 1633 dated 1633. *Scratchings*: On stonework of S. aisle and W. tower, mason's marks; on W. respond of S. arcade, graffito. *Seating*: In S. aisle—seven benches, five with traceried bench-ends, two with shaped tops, early 16th-century, restored; also two early 17th-century benches with shaped finials to the posts. In tower—one bench with traceried ends, 16th-century. *Sedile*: In chancel, one bay with moulded jambs and two-centred head and label, 14th-century. *Stoup*: In S. aisle—E. of S. doorway, large bowl recessed into wall, early 16th-century. *Weather-vane*: with letters A.A., possibly 17th-century. *Miscellanea*: In E. wall of chancel, internally, two carved head-stops, 14th-century; in S. respond of chancel-arch, part of coffin-lid, used as corbel.

Condition—Good.

Secular :—

MONUMENTS (2–9).

The following monuments, unless otherwise described, are of two storeys, timber-framed and plastered or weather-boarded; the roofs are tiled. Some of the buildings have original chimney-stacks and exposed ceiling-beams.

Condition—Good.

(2). *The Rectory*, 50 yards N. of the church, is of two storeys with attics and has been partly refaced with modern brickwork. It is possibly a 16th-century house enlarged at a later date and has modern additions on the N.E. and S.E.

(3). *Wheelers House* (Plate, pp. xl–i), now two tenements, on E. side of road, 300 yards N.N.W. of the church, was built late in the 15th century but has been much altered. It has a small modern addition on the S. The upper storey projects at both ends of the W. front, and the southern projection, which at some later date has been extended partly along the main block, has curved brackets. The eaves are continuous and are supported over the middle block by a curved bracket springing from the upper storey of the N. wing. The early 17th-century main chimney-stack has a shaft of cruciform plan set diagonally on a square base. Inside the building on the first floor of the main block is a heavy cambered tie-beam with curved braces but the upper part is hidden by a modern ceiling.

(4). *House* (Plate, pp. xl–i), now three tenements, on W. side of road, 500 yards N.N.W. of the church, has a thatched roof. It was built probably in the 15th century with a central hall and N. and S. cross-wings and has a modern addition at the back. The upper storeys of the cross-wings project on the E. front and are supported on heavy curved brackets.

(5). *House*, now two tenements, opposite (3), is the central hall of a 15th-century dwelling, the cross-wings of which have been demolished. The first floor and central chimney-stack were inserted in the 17th century. In the W. wall is an original four-centred doorway. Inside the building is a king-post truss, with a heavy moulded tie-beam with curved braces forming a four-centred arch below, octagonal king-post with a moulded base and necking and curved four-way struts ; the wall-plates are also moulded.

(6). *White Lion Inn*, 150 yards W.N.W. of the church, was built possibly in the 15th century with a central hall and N.E. and S.W. cross-wings. In the 17th century a first floor was inserted in the hall and the roof raised ; there is a modern addition at the back. The upper storeys of the cross-wings project on the S.E. front. Inside the building is a 17th-century open fireplace and one original cambered tie-beam is exposed.

(7). *House* (Plate, pp. 56–7), 90 yards N.W. of the church, is of two storeys with attics and has been refaced with 18th-century brick. It was built in the 16th century on an L-shaped plan with the wings extending towards the N.W. and N.E. and has a modern addition in the angle. At the end of the N.W. wing is a large chimney-stack of early 17th-century date surmounted by three grouped diagonal shafts. Inside the building is some early 17th-century panelling and an original winding-stair with a central newel.

(8). *House*, now two tenements, 50 yards S. of the church, is modern except for the 17th-century chimney-stack.

(9). *Fobbing Hall*, house, now two tenements, 200 yards S.E. of the church, was built probably in the 16th century and has a cross-wing at the W. end and modern additions at the back. The main chimney-stack is of early 17th-century date. Inside the building in the W. wing is a cambered tie-beam with curved braces.

---

29. FOULNESS. (G.c.)

(O.S. 6 in. lxxi. S.W.)

Foulness is an island and parish on the S. side of the Crouch, 8 m. N.E. of Southend-on-Sea.

Roman :—

(1). A tumulus on Loading Marsh, Little Shelford, was found to contain a large urn enclosing burnt bones and surrounded by seven or eight other vessels of which two were 'Samian,' apparently of early 2nd-century date. The mound was destroyed. Another tumulus was said to exist close by.

(*Brit. Arch. Assoc. Journ.*, IV, 74. For similar burials of Roman date, see *Essex Inventory*, Vol. I, Sectional Preface, p. xxiv.)

Ecclesiastical :—

(2). PARISH CHURCH OF ST. MARY was entirely rebuilt in 1850 but retains the following fitting from the old church :—

Plate (Plate, p. xliv) : includes two cups of 1612 and 1712 respectively and a cover-paten of 1712.

Secular :—

(3). HOUSE, 160 yards S.W. of the church, is of one storey with attics, timber-framed and weather-boarded ; the roofs are tiled. It was built in the 17th century and has modern additions at each end. Inside the building are some exposed ceiling-beams.

Condition—Good.

(4). WHITE HOUSE, 1 m. W.S.W. of the church, is of two storeys, timber-framed and weather-boarded and partly refaced with brick, the roofs are tiled. The S.E. wing was built early in the 17th century ; the N.W. wing was added later in the same century making the building of modified L-shaped plan. Modern extensions have been made to both blocks. The timber-framing is exposed on the E. side of the S.E. wing ; on this side is a blocked door. Inside the building the timber-framing and ceiling-beams are exposed.

Condition—Unoccupied and falling into disrepair.

Unclassified :—

(5). RED HILL, at Little Shelford Farm, nearly 2¼ m. S.W. of the church.

30. GRAYS THURROCK. (B.e.)

(O.S. 6 in. lxxxiii. S.E.)

Grays Thurrock or Grays is a town on the N. bank of the Thames, 2 m. N.W. of Tilbury.

Ecclesiastical :—

(1). PARISH CHURCH OF SS. PETER AND PAUL stands in the town. The walls are of ragstone and flint-rubble, with dressings of limestone ; the roofs are tiled. The church, consisting of the *Chancel* and *Nave*, perhaps with provision for a central tower, was built probably in the first years of the 13th century or earlier ; the cross-arches of the chancel although apparently modern may be copies or restorations of the original arches of that date. The *Tower* N. of the crossing was built *c.* 1230 and the *South Chapel* opposite was added *c.* 1280–90. The whole structure was largely rebuilt in 1846 when the nave was considerably lengthened westward, the *North Aisle, South Porch* and *Vestry* added, the upper part of the tower rebuilt, and most of the dressings, especially of the chancel, were renewed.

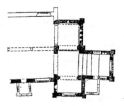

Architectural Description—The *Chancel* (23 ft. by 15¾ ft.) has been largely rebuilt and retains no ancient architectural features.

The *Crossing* (15½ ft. by 19 ft.) has E. and W. arches of late 12th or early 13th-century design but apparently entirely of modern stonework. The N. and S. arches are described below.

The *North Tower* (15¼ ft. square) is of three stages ; the top stage is modern. The early 13th-century archway from the crossing is two-centred and of two chamfered orders ; the restored responds are chamfered and have moulded imposts. The E. and N. walls of the ground-stage have wall-arches of similar design and date. In the E. wall are three original graduated lancets and in the N. wall a similar lancet, all restored externally. In the W. wall is a modern archway. The second stage has both in the E. and N. walls an original lancet-window, modern externally, and in the W. wall is a similar window, now blocked. In the S.W. angle are two doorways, both probably original and now blocked; one has a later oak lintel and the other has the head cut away.

The *South Chapel* or *Transept* (18¼ ft. by 9¼ ft.) has in the N. wall a late 13th-century archway from the crossing ; it is two-centred and of two chamfered orders ; the responds, partly restored, have original moulded capitals, of which the abaci have been cut away, and moulded bases. In the S. wall is a modern window, and in the W. wall a partly restored 13th-century lancet.

The *Nave* is modern except the E. half of the S. wall, in which is the S. doorway with moulded jambs and two-centred arch, probably of the 13th century.

Fittings—*Brasses :* In chancel—on S. wall, figures of two women in pedimental head-dresses and group of six children, early 16th-century. *Chairs :* In chancel—two (Plate, p. xlii) with pierced and carved backs, shaped and carved arms and turned legs with carved and turned rails, possibly late 17th-century. *Floor-slab :* In tower—to Jeremiah Watts, 1711. *Font* (Plate, pp. xlii–iii) : octagonal, with moulded top and under-side, each face with square panel carved with blank shields, roses, a flower, irradiated Agnus Dei, and a shield—*a cheveron between three cinqfoils*, two of the blank shields have later scratchings ; stem with pointed panels and moulded base, 15th or early 16th-century. *Funeral-helm,* etc. : In chancel—on N. wall, combed helm with vizor, late 16th-century ; on S. wall, gauntlet and short sword. *Lockers :* In N. wall of chancel, twin lockers with rebated jambs and round heads, date uncertain, probably early 13th-century. *Niche :* In S. transept—in W. wall, square and plastered, date uncertain. *Panelling :* Used in door in second stage of tower, 17th-century. *Piscina :* In S. transept—in S. wall, with moulded jambs and trefoiled head, round drain, 13th-century. *Plate :* includes cup dated 1663, paten dated 1628 and larger paten dated 1685. *Screen :* Under S. arch to N. tower—with entrance having multifoiled and traceried head, half modern, four bays on each side each with cinquefoiled ogee heads and tracery, moulded mullions and moulded and embattled cornice, early 16th-century. *Tiles :* In vestry—black and yellow glazed tiles laid in patterned bands, found on site of cottage N. of the church and relaid here.

Condition—Good, mostly rebuilt.

Secular :—

MONUMENTS (2–6).

The following monuments, unless otherwise described, are of the 17th century and of two storeys, timber-framed and weather-boarded ; the roofs are tiled. Some of the buildings have original chimney-stacks and exposed ceiling-beams.

Condition—Good.

LAINDON : PARISH CHURCH OF ST. NICHOLAS.
Chancel-roof, late 15th-century ; Nave-roof, 15th-century.

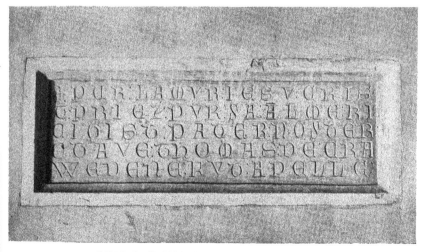

FOBBING : PARISH CHURCH OF ST. MICHAEL.
Tablet in Chancel to Thomas de Crawedene ; *c.* 1340.

GREAT BADDOW: PARISH CHURCH OF ST. MARY.
From the South-East, showing Clearstorey, early 16th-century ; W. Tower, 14th-century and later, etc.

High Street, W. Side :—

(2). *Bull Inn,* and range of tenements, 80 yards S. of the church, are of two storeys with attics and form a long rectangular building of late 17th-century date which is of plastered brickwork ; at the back is a modern addition. Above an open carriage-way running through the middle of the inn is an original three-light window divided by pilasters having moulded capitals and bases ; the centre light has a semi-circular head. On the E. and W. sides of the building is a modillioned eaves-cornice. The attics are lighted by five gabled dormer-windows on the W. front and four on the E.

(3). *House,* now two tenements, 100 yards S. of (2), is of two storeys with attics. It is of L-shaped plan with the wings extending towards the S. and E. The S. wall is of brick and there are modern additions at the back. Inside the building, against the chimney-stack, is an original circular staircase leading up to the attics.

E. Side :—

(4). *House,* now two tenements, opposite (3), is of L-shaped plan with the wings extending towards the N. and E. It has modern additions at the back. ·

(5). *House,* 40 yards N. of (4), is built of brick and faced with plaster. The front block, facing the street, is of early 17th-century date but has later modern additions at the back.

(6).¹ *Shop,* on S. side of Argent Street, 60 yards S.W. of (3), is of two storeys with attics. It is a fragment of a larger building.

31. GREAT BADDOW. (D.b.)

(O.S. 6 in. ⁽ᵃ⁾lii. S.E. ⁽ᵇ⁾liii. S.W.)

Great Baddow is a parish and village due S. of Chelmsford. The principal monuments are the church and Great Sir Hughes.

Ecclesiastical :—

ᵇ(1). Parish Church of St. Mary (Plate, p. 49) stands in the village. The walls are of flint-rubble with some fragments of Roman brick ; the chapels, clearstorey and porch are of brick ; the dressings are of limestone and brick ; the roofs are covered with tiles, slates and lead.

The *Chancel, Nave* and a N. Aisle were built about the middle of the 13th century probably on the site of an earlier church, and at a rather later date a *South Aisle* was added. In the first half of the 14th century the *Aisles* were widened and the *West Tower* was begun, the upper half of the Tower being completed later in the same century. Early in the 16th century the *South Chapel* and

the clearstorey of the Nave were added and a little later the *North Chapel* was built. The *South Porch* was added in the 17th century. The church has been restored in modern times when the dormer-windows were added to the chancel and the *North Vestry* added or rebuilt.

The clearstorey is a handsome example of early 16th-century brickwork and among the fittings the 17th-century pulpit is noteworthy.

*Architectural Description—*The *Chancel* (28½ ft. by 22½ ft.) has a modern E. window of four lights and tracery ; the gable-head is of early 16th-century brick. In the N. wall is a 13th-century lancet now mostly restored, and further W. is a modern doorway into the vestry ; the early 16th-century brick arch opening into the N. Chapel is two-centred and of one chamfered order resting on attached shafts with moulded capitals and bases ; the chamfered outer order of the responds is carried up vertically to the wall-plates and is plastered. In the S. wall is a window originally a 13th-century lancet, afterwards widened to the W. in the 15th century and now all modern except the splays and four-centred rear-arch ; further W. is an archway similar to that in the N. wall but four-centred and of larger detail. The 15th-century chancel-arch is two-centred and of two chamfered orders, the outer continuous and the inner resting on attached shafts with moulded capitals and bases.

The *North Chapel* (11½ ft. by 14½ ft.) is of brick with an embattled parapet. In the E. wall an early 16th-century brick window of one three-centred light. In the N. wall is a brick window of three four-centred lights in a square head with a moulded label, all cemented externally. In the W. wall is a four-centred arch of two chamfered orders, the inner carried on shafts with moulded capitals and tall bases.

The *South Chapel* (15 ft. by 14½ ft.) is of brick with a crow-stepped embattled parapet. In the E. wall is an early 16th-century brick window of three four-centred lights in a square head with a moulded label, all cemented externally, and with a four-centred plastered rear-arch. In the S. wall is a modern doorway inserted in the blocking of an original window. In the W. wall is an archway nearly uniform with that to the N. chapel.

The *Nave* (46½ ft. by 23½ ft.) has 13th-century N. and S. arcades of three bays, with two-centred arches of two chamfered orders ; the columns are cylindrical except the second on the N., which is octagonal, and all have moulded capitals and bases. The N. arcade is the earlier and has square responds, the eastern having an attached square shaft with moulded capital and base and the western a carved head-corbel and capital carrying the inner orders of the arches. The S. arcade has chamfered responds and the inner orders are carried on corbel-capitals, the eastern partly restored. The early 16th-century clearstorey is of red brick with diaper

GREAT BADDOW *The* PARISH CHURCH *of* ST MARY.

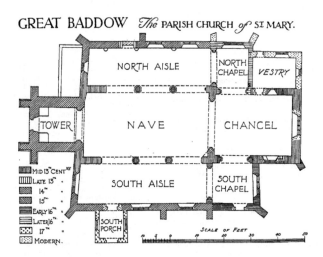

NORTH AISLE

NORTH CHAPEL

VESTRY

TOWER

NAVE

CHANCEL

SOUTH AISLE

SOUTH CHAPEL

SOUTH PORCH

Mid 13ᵗʰ Centᵞ
Late 13ᵗʰ "
14ᵗʰ "
15ᵗʰ "
Early 16ᵗʰ "
Later 16ᵗʰ "
17ᵗʰ "
Modern.

Scale of Feet

patterns in black bricks, and has a crow-stepped embattled parapet resting on a trefoiled corbel-table ; a series of octagonal pinnacles with conical moulded caps divides it into five bays length-wise and two cross-wise. In the E. wall are two windows each of two round-headed lights under a four-centred head ; the side walls have each five windows each of two cinquefoiled lights under a three-centred head with a moulded label.

The *North Aisle* (14 ft. wide) has an early 16th-century embattled parapet. In the N. wall are two windows each of two lights and tracery all modern except the moulded splays and chamfered rear-arches which are of the 14th century. Further W. is a blocked doorway with a two-centred head and segmental-pointed rear-arch of the 13th or 14th century. In the W. wall is a single-light window all modern except the 14th-century moulded splays and rear-arch.

The *South Aisle* (14½ ft. wide) has an early 16th-century crow-stepped embattled parapet of brick. In the S. wall are two windows each of three lights and tracery all modern except the 14th-century splays and rear-arches. Further W. is the S. doorway with modern shafted and moulded jambs and a moulded two-centred arch of the 13th century reset in the 14th century and having a chamfered outer order and moulded label. In the W. wall is a 14th-century window of three lights and tracery in a two-centred head, all much restored.

The *West Tower* (13½ ft. by 12½ ft.) is of the 14th century ; the upper half, which is probably a little later than the lower half, has an embattled parapet, and is surmounted by a leaded spire. The two-centred tower-arch is of three chamfered orders, the outermost continuous from the responds, the inner two carried on large attached semi-octagonal shafts with moulded capitals and bases. The W. window is of two trefoiled ogee-headed lights with partly restored tracery in a two-centred head with a moulded label and defaced head-stops. The W. doorway has moulded jambs, two-centred arch and label with defaced head-stops. The second storey has in each wall a window of one pointed light ; the E. window looking into the nave. The bell-chamber has 18th-century windows of brick. On the E. face of the tower are the weatherings of the former steep-pitched roof of the nave.

The *South Porch* (Plate, p. xxxviii) is of the first half of the 17th century and is built of brick. The outer archway is of two orders, the outer square, the inner semi-circular with imposts and a pendant key-block. Above it is a moulded entablature and the gable-head has a moulded coping and, at the base and apex, the remains of circular pinnacles. The side walls have each a window of two round-headed lights, covered with cement.

The *Roof* of the S. chapel has hollow-chamfered transverse rafters of the 16th or 17th century, the rest is modern. The low-pitched roof of the nave is of early 16th-century date and is of five bays ;

the principal beams are moulded and carved with twisted running foliage and have curved braces below their ends springing from moulded corbel-capitals enriched with carved cresting; the moulded ridge and smaller ribs divide each half bay into six compartments; the ceiling is boarded; the wall-plates are moulded and have carved cresting. The flat lean-to roof of the N. Aisle has three tie-beams carrying posts and two-way curved struts under a central purlin, all the timbers being moulded and of the 14th century; the curved struts are carried on the sides of the tie-beams by small moulded corbel-capitals, two of which are now missing; the S. wall-plate is also moulded and of the same date; the N. wall-plate is moulded and carved with plain bosses and is probably of the 17th century; above it is a fascia-board inscribed "HUMFERI LOW ET HENRY STILEMAN CHURCHWARDENS ANO D 1639"; under the N. ends of the principals are chamfered wall-posts from the floor, with plain capitals probably of the 16th or 17th century. The roof of the S. Aisle has old square rafters probably of the 17th century or later. The floor of the ringing-chamber of the tower has old timbers, possibly 14th or 15th-century.

Fittings—*Brass* and *Indents*. Brass: In chancel—of Jane (Lewkenor), wife of John Paschall [1614], figure of woman, inscription, and shield-of-arms. Indents: In S. porch—four slabs and fragments of a fifth with rivets and much-defaced indents. *Glass:* In nave—in spandrels of clearstorey windows, fragments of black and yellow border, 14th-century and later reset. *Monument* and *Floor-slabs*. Monument: In S. chapel—on S. wall, to Hellen Sydnor, 1651, and Elizabeth Hubert, 1625, daughters of Thomas Leventhorpe, marble wall-monument with side-pilasters, cornice and two shields-of-arms. Floor-slabs: In nave—(1) to John Ingram, 1694; (2) to the Reverend Charles Adams M.A., 1683. In N. aisle—(3) to John Everard, 16(14?). In tower—(4) to Abigall, wife of John —— (name defaced), 1692. *Piscinae:* In chancel—with trefoiled heads in front and side-opening into sedile, octofoiled drain, late 13th-century. In N. chapel—in E. wall, with four-centred head and round drain, early 16th-century. In S. aisle—in S. wall, with chamfered jambs and two-centred head, round drain, 14th-century. *Plate:* includes flagon of 1627, with shield-of-arms, and alms-dish of 1675 with shield-of-arms. *Pulpit* (Plate, p. 4): octagonal with alternate wide and narrow sides, all panelled; larger panels with representations of arches in perspective with side-columns, pediments and carved frames, smaller and lower panels with foliage and jewel-ornaments; base modern except central post; sounding-board with panelled soffit having carved rose in centre, carved frieze, moulded cornice, carved strap-work cresting, and at the angles, consoles with pinnacles above and small

pendants below; the back standard has three panels, one carved with a cross and another with the Sacred Heart, shaped and carved borders; on a rail is carved the date 1639. *Recess:* In N. chapel—in E. wall, with two-centred head, 16th century. *Royal Arms:* Over chancel-arch—painted board, with initials C R and date 1660; all in a moulded wood frame surmounted by a broken pediment. *Sedile:* In chancel—sill of former S.E. lancet carried down to form a seat, of same date as piscina.

Condition—Good.

. **Secular :—**

b(2). HOMESTEAD MOAT at Mascalls, about 1 m. S.S.E. of the church.

b(3). GREAT SIR HUGHES, house (Plate, p. 52), 1¾ m. S.S.E. of the church, is of two storeys with attics, timber-framed and plastered; the roofs are tiled. It was built early in the 17th century and appears to have been the N. wing of a much larger house. There is an 18th-century kitchen addition on the W.

The exceptional amount of external carved wood-work is of interest.

The plan is rectangular and consists of two parallel blocks, the lower part of the northern block forming an open loggia divided into five bays with square fluted columns standing on panelled pedestals and having moulded capitals and bases and carved brackets supporting the carved bressummer to the upper storey. Below the bressummer, between the brackets, each bay is subdivided by two elliptical arches separated by moulded pendants and having sunk spandrels. The upper storey has three oriel-windows, each supported on three carved brackets and of five lights with moulded mullions and carved transoms. The timber-framing is exposed, the vertical members between the windows being in the form of tapering pilasters with moulded capitals above which are carved brackets supporting a widely projecting eaves. The chimney-stack has two octagonal shafts with moulded bases. The entrance door is original and is divided into small panels enriched with lozenges by moulded and nail-studded rails and muntins. It has an original knocker and lozenge-shaped plate; at the side are the remains of an iron bracket. The E. end has original moulded barge-boards and pendant. The S. block has a three-storeyed bay-window. Inside the building two of the rooms are lined with 17th-century panelling and one of the attics has an original panelled door. A carved newel-post and a few of the balusters to the staircase are original.

Condition—Poor.

MONUMENTS (4–16).

The following monuments, unless otherwise described, are of the 17th century and of two storeys, timber-framed and plastered or weather-boarded ; the roofs are tiled. Many of the buildings have original chimney-stacks and exposed ceiling-beams.

Condition—Good or fairly good, unless noted.

[b](4). *House*, 30 yards N.W. of the church, has been refaced with brick and much altered.

[b](5). *White Horse Inn*, 70 yards S.W. of the church, has an original chimney-stack of grouped shafts but is otherwise modern.

[b](6). *House and Shop* (Plate, p. xl), on W. side of road, 50 yards W. of the church, was built probably in the 15th century. A central chimney-stack was inserted late in the 16th or early in the 17th century ; the S. end of the house has been converted into a shop and the building has been added to and much altered. On the E. front the whole of the upper storey projects. The chimney-stack has four grouped octagonal shafts. Inside the building the shop has moulded ceiling-beams ; the principal cross-beam has curved braces which spring from moulded brackets and have sunk spandrels.

[b](7). *House*, 60 yards N.W. of (6), is built on an L-shaped plan and has wings extending towards the N. and W. and a projecting bay in the centre of the E. front. The window in the upper storey of the centre bay is original and is of four lights with moulded mullions and transoms. There are two original chimney-stacks ; one has two diagonal shafts. A modern scratching on the plaster at the N. end gives the date 1675.

[b](8). *House*, 50 yards N.W. of (7), has a central chimney-stack with grouped diagonal shafts. Inside the building is an early 17th-century panelled door.

[b](9). *House* (Plate, p. 57), on N. side of road, 350 yards N.N.W. of the church, was built probably in the 16th century with a cross-wing at the W. end. The main chimney-stack has three octagonal shafts with moulded bases.

[b](10). *Manor Farm*, house, 20 yards E. of (9), has on the S. front an original door divided into small panels by wide, nail-studded rails and muntins.

[b](11). *Cottage*, 100 yards E. of (10), was built probably early in the 16th century but has been added to and much altered. Inside the building is a richly moulded beam.

[a](12). *Lathcoats*, cottage, about 1 m. W.S.W. of the church, was built probably late in the 16th century. It has modern extensions at the back. The upper storey projects at the N. end of the E. front.

[a](13). *Oakman's Farm*, house, about 1¾ m. S.W. of the church, was built probably in the 16th

century, on an L-shaped plan with the wings extending towards the N. and W. At the S. end of the E. front the upper storey projects.

Condition—Poor.

[a](14). *Bareman's Farm*, house, 50 yards S.W. of (13), was built probably in the 16th century. The upper storey projects at the S. end of the W. front.

[b](15). *Cottage*, opposite Brook Farm, nearly 1¼ m. S. of the church, has a projecting storey at the S. end.

[b](16). *Duffield's Farm*, house ¾ m. S.S.W. of the church, has been much altered. The principal chimney-stack is original and has two diagonal shafts. Inside the building the timber-framing in one of the rooms is exposed and there is a wide fireplace, now partly blocked.

[b](17). The *garden-wall* enclosing the grounds of Baddow House is largely of 17th-century date.

----

32. GREAT BURSTEAD. (C.c.)

(O.S. 6 in. [a]lxviii. N.W. [b]lxviii. N.E.)

Great Burstead is a parish 8 m. S. of Chelmsford. The small town of Billericay, at the N. end of the civil parish, was formed into a separate ecclesiastical parish in 1844. The church in Great Burstead village is the principal monument.

Roman :—

[a](1). OVENS OR KILNS. In 1724, " a place made like an oven, of hard dark clay, large enough to hold 6 half-peck loaves " was found 3 ft. below the surface " at the windmill on a high hill near Billericay." This site is usually identified with that on which a windmill now stands, about 1 m. N. of the parish church of Great Burstead ; formerly, however, another windmill existed close by but on the W. side of the Rayleigh road. With the oven was a large bed of black earth or ashes containing Roman potsherds, fibulae, two denarii of Trajan and Hadrian, and other coins (Morant, *Hist. of Essex*, I, 196 ; Salmon, *Hist. of Essex* (1743), 264, 303, 334, and MS. note in Gough's interleaved copy of Salmon in the Bodleian Library, quoting Soc. Ant. MS. Minutes for 1725).

In the middle of the 19th century, in gravel-digging, similar finds of dark earth, potsherds and " the remains of an oven" were found (*Essex Arch. Soc. Trans.* (O.S.), II, 70), and near it " subterranean masonry," thought to be part of a hypocaust but perhaps connected with a kiln. Close by was a pit 25 ft. deep full of potsherds, and a number of incineration burials with a British gold coin and coins of Trajan, Hadrian, Pius and Constantine (*B. A. A. Journ.*, III, 249–50 ; IV, 74, 155–6 ; *Essex Arch. Soc. Trans.* (O.S.), II, 70–1 ; V, 209–11 ; *Proc. Soc. Ant.* (2nd S.), VII, 370–2).

GREAT BADDOW: (3). GREAT SIR HUGHES. Early 17th-century.
North side.

STIFFORD.
PARISH CHURCH OF ST. MARY THE VIRGIN.
E. end of S. Chapel, showing mid 13th-century windows, etc.

GREAT BURSTEAD:
PARISH CHURCH OF ST. MARY MAGDALEN.
Communion Rails and Reredos; late 17th-century, brought from elsewhere.

a(2). About 500 yards W. of (1), in digging for a gasometer (now removed) in 1877, a " pavement or platform " of mortar or concrete 3 in. thick and 6 ft. square was found. On it lay a number of broken vessels, including ' Samian ' (one said to have been stamped DACMVS) and, it is said, some cinerary urns (*Arch. Journ.*, XXXVI, 76). Burials were also discovered in the Dissenters' Burial Ground, Billericay, about ¼ m. N. of (1), and a vault containing stone-coffins, probably post-Roman, was also found there (*Arch. Journ.*, XXXVI, 75 ; *Essex Arch. Soc. Trans.* (O.S.), II, 72).

b(3). Norsey Wood, at the N.E. corner of the parish, contains various earthworks including trenches of different sizes which run in different directions without coherent plan. These have been partially disturbed by the digging of gravel. One was 8 ft. deep, 300 yards long and 4–5 ft. wide, ending in a circular pit 15 ft. in diameter ; the largest was 10–12 ft. deep, twice as wide, and curved at the bottom. Many had been filled with dark soil containing broken Roman pottery and tiles. In one of the eastern group of trenches was a primitive smelting-furnace containing a little slag, black ashes and lumps of gritty substance like mortaria. " Two rods " from it in the same trench a kiln was found 3–4 ft. in diameter, domed and built of square bricks (6–8 in. square and about 2 in. thick). When found, " a score or two " of black pots, apparently whole, were in it. Other kilns were also found and cinerary deposits associated with flanged tiles were encountered in great numbers. Some of the urns were apparently of Late Celtic type, and it is in any case clear that the wood was a pre-Roman site, the occupation of which was continued into the Roman period. At least some of the trenches must have been made before the kilns, since these were built in them. Good clay is found below the gravel in the neighbourhood, and it was perhaps for this that the trenches were cut. It may here be noted that a hoard of 1,000 bronze coins was found about 1820 at Tylde Hall, Ramsden Crays, just outside the wood and parish, but is not recorded in detail (*Essex Arch. Soc. Trans.* (O.S.), II, 70).

(See *Sectional Preface*, p. xxxviii ; and *Essex Arch. Soc. Trans.* (O.S.), V, 212 ; V.C.H. Essex, I, 284 ; and MS. notes by the late Col. Branfill, R.E., of Billericay.)

Ecclesiastical :—

a(4). PARISH CHURCH OF ST. MARY MAGDALEN stands towards the S. end of the parish. The walls are mixed rubble partly covered with cement ; the tower is of ragstone ; the dressings are of limestone ; the roofs are tiled. The *Nave* was built in the 12th century. Late in the 14th century the *West Tower* was added. The *Chancel* was probably rebuilt and enlarged in the 14th or 15th century. In the 15th century the *South Aisle* was added, incorporating reused 14th-century work ; late in the same century or early in the 16th the *South Chapel* and *North* and *South Porches* were added probably in the order given.

Architectural Description—The *Chancel* (31 ft. by 21¼ ft.) has in the E. wall a window with a two-centred head and probably of the 15th century, but now blocked. In the N. wall are two windows, the eastern of early 16th-century date and of three four-centred lights in a square head with a moulded label ; the western is probably of late 15th-century date and is of three cinquefoiled lights in a four-centred head with a moulded label ; below the eastern window is an early 16th-century doorway with a moulded rear-arch and now blocked. The late 15th or early 16th-century S. arcade is of two bays with two-centred arches of two moulded orders, the outer continuous and the inner springing from attached shafts with moulded capitals and bases. There is no chancel-arch.

The *South Chapel* (31 ft. by 16 ft.) is of early 16th-century date. The E. wall has two courses of flint and stone chequer-work above the plinth ; the E. window is of three cinquefoiled lights in a four-centred head with a moulded label. In the S. wall are two windows similar to that in the E. wall but of smaller size ; between them is a doorway with moulded jambs and two-centred head with a moulded label ; it is now blocked.

The *Nave* (44 ft. by 23½ ft.) has in the N. wall three windows ; the easternmost is of late 14th-century date and of three trefoiled ogee lights with tracery in a two-centred head with a moulded label and one defaced head-stop ; the middle window is a small 12th-century light with a round head ; the westernmost window is probably of early 16th-century date and is of three four-centred lights in a square head with a moulded label ; the late 15th or early 16th-century N. doorway has moulded jambs and two-centred arch in a square head with a moulded label and crowned head-stops ; the spandrels (Plate, p. 84) are carved with the Annunciation. The figure of Gabriel holds a scroll inscribed "Ave Maria [gratia] plena dominus tecum." The 15th-century S. arcade is of three bays with two-centred arches of two chamfered orders ; the octagonal columns have moulded capitals and bases and the responds have attached half-columns ; E. of the arcade is a cutting, through the wall, of doubtful date with an arched head.

The *South Aisle* (15 ft. wide) has in the S. wall two reset early 14th-century windows each of two trefoiled lights with a quatrefoil in a two-centred head ; the 15th-century S. doorway has double hollow-chamfered jambs and two-centred arch with a moulded label. The W. wall has been largely rebuilt and contains a modern window.

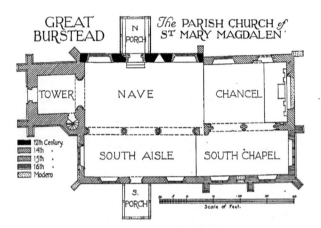

GREAT BURSTEAD

The PARISH CHURCH *of* S^T MARY MAGDALEN

N PORCH

TOWER   NAVE   CHANCEL

SOUTH AISLE   SOUTH CHAPEL

S. PORCH

12th Century.
14th "
15th "
16th "
Modern

Scale of Feet.

The *West Tower* (14 ft. square) was built late in the 14th century and is of three stages with a moulded plinth and embattled parapet; it is finished with a timber spire of some height (Plate, pp. xxxii–iii). The two-centred tower-arch is of two chamfered orders; the responds have attached semi-octagonal shafts with moulded capitals and bases. The W. window is of two cinquefoiled lights with tracery in a two-centred head; the label, jambs and mullion are modern; the W. doorway has moulded jambs and two-centred arch. The N. and S. walls of the second stage have each a partly restored window of one trefoiled light. The bell-chamber has in each wall a much restored window of two trefoiled lights in a square head with a moulded label.

The *North Porch* is of c. 1500, timber-framed and of two bays; the outer archway is four-centred and is flanked by openings with remains of traceried heads; the gable has foiled barge-boards, carved with foliage. The mullions and heads of the lights of the side bays have been removed. The roof is of king-post type with curved braces, forming four-centred arches.

The *South Porch* is of early 16th-century date, partly restored; it is timber-framed and of two bays; the outer archway is two-centred. The side bays are each of two lights with modern three-centred heads. The roof is of similar character to that of the N. porch.

The *Roof* of the chancel is of the 15th century and of two bays with moulded and embattled tie-beams and wall-plates and square rebated king-posts with four-way struts. The early 16th-century roof of the S. chapel is similar to that of the

chancel; the curved braces of the tie-beams rest on stone corbels, one carved with an angel holding a blank shield; the spandrels of one truss are carved with a quatrefoil and a grotesque face. The 15th-century roof of the nave is of four bays, with moulded and embattled plates and moulded tie-beams supporting octagonal king-posts with moulded capitals and bases. The late 15th or early 16th-century roof of the S. aisle is of four bays with king-post trusses, moulded wall-plates and hollow-chamfered tie-beams.

Fittings—*Bells*: five; 4th by John Walgrave, early 15th-century, inscribed "Vox Augustini Sonet In Aure Dei." *Chairs*: In chancel—two, one with carved back and rails, twisted legs and posts, and arms; the second with carved back, curved legs and twisted rails, late 17th-century. *Chest* (Plate, p. xliii): heavy 'dug-out' of oak, bound with iron, seven hinges and three hasps, 12th or 13th-century. *Communion Rails* (Plate, p. 53): with moulded upper and lower rails, panelled uprights and turned balusters, gates now in belfry, quadrant-shaped corners, late 17th-century, said to have come from a London Church. *Doors*: In S. doorway of S. chapel—of battens with strap-hinge and two drop-handles, 15th-century. In N. doorway—of overlapping battens with trellis-framing, strap-hinges and drop-handle, 15th-century. In S. doorway—similar to that in N. doorway, with ornamental pierced scutcheon-plate, 15th-century. *Font*: octagonal bowl with moulded under-side, plain stem and moulded base, 15th-century. *Glass*: In chancel—in N.W. window, foliated quarries, a sun, stars, rose and fragments, 15th and 16th-century. In nave—in

N.E. window, various fragments, 14th and 16th-century. In S. aisle—in S.E. window, fragments including borders of crowns, foliage, etc., partly *in situ ;* in S.W. window, similar ornament and *in situ* in head, foliage and a shield (Plate, pp. xliv–v) *barry argent and azure a label of five points gules* for Grey of Wilton, 14th-century. In W. window of tower—two foliated roundels, 14th-century. *Monuments* and *Floor-slabs.* Monuments : In chancel—on S. wall, (1) to Ursula (Thresher), wife of John Cooke, 1705, and to their daughter Ursula, 1703, marble tablet with cherub-head and shield-of-arms. In churchyard—N. side, (2) to Robert Chignall, 1695, head-stone ; S. side, (3) to Eliza Hewes, 1694, head and foot-stones ; (4) to Thomas Price, 1714, head-stone ; (5) to Samuel Finch, 1713, head-stone. Floor-slabs : In chancel—(1) to Thomas Stokes, 1701 ; (2) to Samuel Thresher, 1702. In S. chapel—(3) to John Tyrell, 1712, with achievement-of-arms. In nave —(4) to Samuel Bridge, 1661, preacher ; (5) to Joseph Fis . . . , and Ann, his wife, late 17th-century. *Piscinae :* In chancel—with moulded jambs and trefoiled ogee arch in a square head, 15th-century. In S. chapel—on S. wall, with moulded jambs and four-centred head, broken round drain, 15th-century. *Reredos* (Plate, p. 53) : of oak in three bays, divided by fluted Corinthian pilasters, middle bay with two round-headed panels and a curved pediment with the sacred name, irradiated, and above a pelican in her piety, side bays each with rectangular panels and above them small panels filled with carved foliage, late 17th-century, said to have come from a London church. *Scratchings :* On arcade on S. of chancel—various masons' marks. *Seating :* In S. aisle—ten pews (Plate, p. 5) and one front, of oak with buttressed ends each with a cinquefoiled and traceried head, the back of one pew and the single front have similar buttresses and heads, 15th-century. *Stoup :* In N. porch—recess with moulded four-centred arch in a square head with rosettes in the spandrels and a moulded label, 15th-century. *Miscellanea :* In S. aisle—a length of moulded and embattled beam, probably from a roof, 15th-century.
Condition—Good.

ᵃ(5). CHURCH OF ST. MARY MAGDALEN, BIL-LERICAY, stands on the E. side of the High Street. (Plate, p. xl). The *West Tower* was built late in the 15th century, but the rest of the church was rebuilt in the 18th century and the two staircases flanking the tower are modern additions.

Architectural Description—The *West Tower* (8 ft. by 8½ ft.) is entirely of red brick (Plate, p. xxxviii). It is of three stages, the lowest divided into two storeys internally ; the tower is finished with a crow-stepped parapet projecting on trefoiled corbelling ; at the angles are small hexagonal pinnacles. The tower-arch is two-centred and of two hollow-chamfered orders ; the responds have each an attached shaft with moulded capitals ; the lower part of the tower-arch is blocked and has an 18th-century archway inserted in the blocking. The N. and S. walls have each an opening, both probably modern. The W. doorway has moulded jambs and two-centred arch in a square head with a moulded label ; above it is a window of two cinquefoiled lights with tracery in a two-centred head with a moulded label. The second stage has in the E. wall a pointed opening. The N. and W. walls have each a window of one four-centred light. In the S. wall is a doorway with a two-centred head, now blocked. The bell-chamber has in each wall two windows, both with two-centred heads.

Fittings—*Recess :* In second stage—in S. wall, plain rectangular recess with corbelled head, late 15th-century. *Stoup :* S. of W. doorway, externally, recess with square head and stone sill, basin destroyed, late 15th-century.
Condition—Good.

Secular :—

MONUMENTS (6–31).

The following monuments, unless otherwise described, are of the 17th century and of two storeys, timber-framed and plastered or weather-boarded ; the roofs are tiled. Some of the buildings have original chimney-stacks and exposed ceiling-beams.
Condition—Good or fairly good unless noted.

CHURCH STREET :—

ᵃ(6). *House*, formerly an inn, at W. end of the churchyard, is of two storeys with attics. It was built on an L-shaped plan with the wings extending towards the S. and W. but has been added to on the S. The upper storey originally projected at the N. end of the E. front but has been underbuilt by the modern additions. The original chimney-stack at the W. end of the house has two diagonal shafts. Inside the building is an original battened door.

ᵃ(7). *House*, on opposite side of the road to (6), has an original chimney-stack of three diagonal shafts.

ᵇ(8). *House* and barn, on N.W. side of the road, 50 yards N. of the church. The *House* is a small building of late 16th or early 17th-century date with later additions. The lower part of the main chimney-stack is original but the upper part has been rebuilt. Inside the building· some of the timber-construction is exposed and there is a blocked two-light window with a moulded frame and mullion in the S. wall. There is a small portion of early 17th-century panelling and an original doorway with a four-centred head.

The *Barn*, N. of the house, is possibly of the 17th century but has undergone later repairs.

---

b(9). *King's Head Inn*, at Slicesgate, nearly ¾ m. N.E. of the church, has been added to and much altered.

b(10). *Highbury*, house (Plate, p. xxxiv), 1 m. N.E. of the church, was built late in the 16th or early in the 17th century on an L-shaped plan with the wings extending towards the N.E. and N.W. but later additions make the present plan T-shaped. The timber-framing is exposed both externally and internally. Inside the building is a heavy battened door.

b(11). *Bullstead Farm*, house, ¾ m. N.N.E. of the church, is a long 17th-century building which has been slightly altered and added to at later dates. The chimneys have been rebuilt but most of the first floor windows retain their original lead casements and iron fastenings.

BILLERICAY : *High Street, W. side :—*

a(12). *Chantry House* (Plate, p. xl), with shop and tenement adjoining on the N., 300 yards S. of the railway bridge, was originally one building of the central-hall type with N. and S. cross-wings and a S. extension. It was built probably early in the 16th century but a floor has since been inserted in the Hall and considerable modern alterations have been made. On the E. front the timber-framing is exposed at the S. end ; the date 1510 below the S. gable is said to have been discovered when this was done. In the upper floor of the S. wing are two blocked two-light windows divided vertically by iron bars and in the roof over the central block is a gabled dormer. Inside the building some of the timber-construction is exposed. The two blocked doorways in the N. wall of the S. cross-wing suggest this to have been the buttery wing. The ground-floor room is lined with 16th-century panelling and the two disused doors are panelled in a similar manner. A late 17th-century moulded wood cornice runs round the room and by the fireplace is a panelled cupboard of the same date with a segmental head and archivolt supported by fluted pilasters with moulded caps. In the room above is some 16th-century panelling and a late 17th-century cornice and fireplace. On the same floor are two battened doors and a 16th-century door with wrought-iron cocks'-head hinges.

a(13). *Red Lion Inn*, 240 yards S.S.W. of (12), is a fragment of a late 15th-century house, but has been considerably altered and added to. Some of

the original roof-timbers are visible in the bedroom ceilings. The purlins are moulded and have curved wind-braces and the collar-beams are cambered.

a(14). *Burstead House* and tenement adjoining on the N., 10 yards S. of (13), are of two storeys with attics. Originally one house, the present building has been refronted in brick and considerably altered ; it now forms a rectangular block with two modern additions at the back. The main chimney-stack is of grouped diagonal shafts. Inside the building, three of the first-floor rooms have late 17th-century fireplaces with panelled overmantels and one room has a panelled dado. The main staircase is of the same date and of massive character with square newels, moulded, string and handrail and twisted balusters.

E. side :—

a(15). *House*, now two tenements, 150 yards S. of the railway bridge, has a cross-wing at the S. end and is of early 17th-century date or possibly earlier. The roof of the N. block is much lower than that of the cross-wing which has a slightly projecting upper storey. There are two early 17th-century chimney-stacks, the one to the S. wing having three diagonal shafts.

a(16). *House*, now two tenements, 80 yards S. of (15), is of weather-boarded timber-framing. Inside the building is a battened door ; the original newel at the top of the stairs has a shaped head.

a(17). *House*, adjoining (16) on the S., is a late 16th-century rectangular building with a later addition at the back. In the E. wall of the original building is a moulded beam inscribed "THE : YEAR : OF : OUR : LORDE : 1577 (?) ELIZABETH . . ." ; the rest of the inscription is hidden by the floor-beams in the back addition. There is a battened door on the first floor.

a(18). *House*, adjoining (17) on the S., is of two storeys with attics. The upper storey projected on the W. front but has been underbuilt by a modern shop-window.

a(19). *House*, incorporating tenements and the N. end of the Chequers Inn, 5 yards S. of (18), has been altered and added to on the E.

a(20). *Chequers Inn* and baker's shop, adjoining on the S. immediately S. of (19), were built probably in the 16th century as one house with a central Hall and N. and S. cross-wings. Additions have been made both on the back and front and in adapting the building to its present purposes the interior has been completely altered. The upper storey of the S. cross-wing originally projected on the street front but has been underbuilt by the modern shop-window.

a(21). *Barn* (Plate, p. xli) at back of (20) is built partly of split logs, and is probably of mediaeval date.

BOWERS GIFFORD :
PARISH CHURCH OF ST. MARGARET.
Brass of man in armour ; *c.* 1340.

SOUTH OCKENDON :
PARISH CHURCH OF ST. NICHOLAS,
Brass [of Sir Ingram Bruyn ; 1400].

(Approximately one-tenth full size.)

BRICK HOUSES.

DANBURY.
(2). Frettons; early and late 16th-century. From the South-East.

DOWNHAM.
(3). Fremnells; *c.* 1670. From the South-West.

STIFFORD.
(2). Ford Place; 1655. From the North-East.

RAINHAM.
(2). Daymns Hall; 17th-century.

FOBBING.
(7). House, 90 yards N.W. of church; 16th-century and later.

S. side of N.W. extension.

N. range from the South-West.

CREEKSEA : Creeksea Place ; *c.* 1569.

HORNDON-ON-THE-HILL.
(16). Arden Hall: Dovecot; 17th-century.

STOCK.
(2). Almshouses founded by Richard Twedye; 16th-century.

ROCHFORD.
(3). Almshouses, N. side of Church Street; early 17th-century.

AVELEY : BELHUS.
Stable, S.E. of house; late 16th-century.

Turret, etc., in N.E. angle of N.E. Courtyard.

S.W. angle of Middle Block.

ROCHFORD : ROCHFORD HALL ; c. 1540–50.

WOODHAM MORTIMER.
(4). Nursery Farm ; late 16th
or early 17th-century.

WOODHAM MORTIMER.
(5). Tyndales ; 16th-century.

SANDON.
(3). Cottage, E. of church ;
16th-century.

STOW MARIES.
(2). Stow Hall ; early
17th-century.

NORTH BENFLEET.
(6). Great Fanton Hall ;
early 17th-century.

GREAT BADDOW.
(9). House, 350 yards N.N.W. of
church ; 16th-century.

WOODHAM FERRERS.
(11). Quilter's Farm ; 17th-century.

EAST HANNINGFIELD.
(3). Willis Farm ; 16th-century.

HORNDON-ON-THE-HILL.
(17). The Gables ; 17th-century.

STANFORD-LE-HOPE.
(5). House, N. of Hassenbrook Hall ; 16th-century.

STEEPLE.
(4). Stanesgate Abbey Farm ; 16th-century and later.

ª(22). *Two tenements*, in Chapel Street, adjoining (21) on the S., were built late in the 16th or early in the following century and were probably parts of the same house. The southernmost is of two storeys with attics. Both have been added to at the back and otherwise altered. The upper storey of the N. tenement projects on the street front and is carried on curved brackets at either end. Inside the building is an original door and the stairs to the attics are probably of the same date.
Condition—Poor.

ª(23). *Shop*, 80 yards S. of the church, is of two storeys with attics. It has been much altered.
Condition—Poor.

ª(24). *Conservative Club*, adjoining (23) on the S., has a modern front to the lower storey.
Condition—Poor.

ª(25). *House*, adjoining (24) on the S., is modern but has over the back door a reused door-head carved with a simple enrichment and the date 1588, 13 (?) and the letter M.

ª(26). *House* and shop, 25 yards S. of (25) has a cross-wing at the N. end.

ª(27). *Council Offices*, 140 yards S. of (26) has a central block, N. and S. cross-wings. The lower storey of the N. cross-wing forms an open carriage-way to the yard at the back; the S. wing has been extended. Both internally and externally the building has been much altered.

ª(28). *House*, 25 yards S. of (27) is of two storeys with attics and cellars. It is of early 18th-century date but has been much altered.

ª(29). *Dryden House*, adjoining (28) on the S., is of two storeys with attics and cellars. The roofs are covered with slates. It was built early in the 18th century on an L-shaped plan with the wings extending towards the N. and E., but later additions make the present plan rectangular. The street front has a wooden modillioned cornice.

ª(30). *House*, now three tenements, 20 yards S. of (29), has additions at the back. The main chimney-stack has three diagonal shafts.

ª(31). *House*, now two tenements, 50 yards S. of (30), has a cross-wing at the S. end with a projecting upper storey on the street front. There are modern additions at the back. Inside the building are some moulded battened doors.

Unclassified :—

b(32). BURIAL-MOUNDS, ETC., in Norsey Wood, 1 m. N.W. of Billericay Church. The wood is thickly planted and partly enclosed within a strong bank from 5 ft. to 6 ft. high. In it are two burial-mounds which were opened in 1865. (*Essex Arch. Soc. Trans.*, V, p. 214 (1873), N.S.,

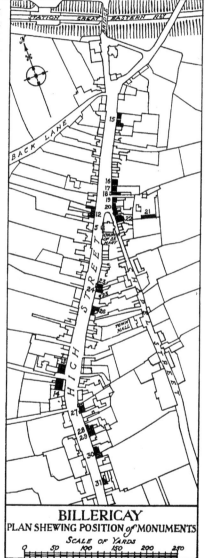

BILLERICAY
PLAN SHEWING POSITION *of* MONUMENTS
SCALE OF YARDS

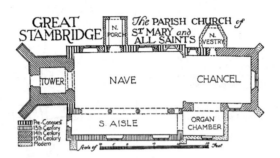

GREAT STAMBRIDGE — The PARISH CHURCH of ST MARY and ALL SAINTS

V, p. 227.)   The S. burial-mound is 45 ft. in diameter and 5 ft. high and was found to contain "a British urn of rude workmanship and three large burial urns with ashes and calcined bones in them."

The N. burial-mound is about 50 ft. in diameter and 5 ft. high and contained seven similar urns all within 3 ft. of the summit.   Across the S. end of the wood is a bank about ½ m. long shown on the O.S. sheets as "The Deerbank."   There are several shallow pits in the wood of doubtful origin but of considerable antiquity.   (See also Roman (3).)

Condition—Of burial-mounds, fairly good.

33. GREAT STAMBRIDGE.   (F.c.)

(O.S. 6 in. [a]lxx. S.E. [b]lxxi. S.W.)

Great Stambridge is a small parish on the estuary of the River Roach, 4 m. N.E. of Southend-on-Sea. The church is the principal monument.

Ecclesiastical :—

[a](1). PARISH CHURCH OF ST. MARY AND ALL SAINTS stands in the S.W. corner of the parish. The walls are of ragstone, flint and septaria-rubble with some pudding-stone and brick and with dressings of Reigate and other limestone ; the roofs are covered with tiles and slates.   Parts of the *Nave* and *Chancel* are of pre-Conquest date. The *South Aisle* was added *c.* 1300, and in the 14th century or earlier the greater part of the chancel was rebuilt.   The *West Tower* is a 15th-century addition and the *North Porch* is probably of the same date.   The chancel-arch has been removed and a modern *Vestry* and *Organ-chamber* erected on the N. and S. side of the chancel respectively.

The pre-Conquest origin of the church gives it some architectural interest.

Architectural Description—The *Chancel* (24 ft. by 17 ft.) has an E. window, all modern except the splays and chamfered two-centred rear-arch which are probably of the 14th century.   In the N. wall is a 14th-century doorway with chamfered jambs and two-centred head with a moulded label.   W. of the doorway the wall is of pre-Conquest date with an external set-back about 9 ft. from the ground ; high up in the wall is the relieving-arch or head of a pre-Conquest window.   The existing window is modern except for the splays.   In the S. wall is a modern arch and window.

The *Nave* (40¾ ft. by 20½ ft.) has in the N. wall three windows, the easternmost a much repaired square-headed window, probably of 13th-century origin ; the other two windows are of the 15th century and each of two cinquefoiled lights in a square head with a moulded label ; between them is a late 14th or early 15th-century doorway with moulded jambs and two-centred head with a moulded label.   The N. wall is of rag and pudding-stone and is of pre-Conquest date.   At about 9 ft. from the ground is a rough external offset, continued along from the chancel.   Immediately E. of the second window of the nave and above the offset are the remains of one external splay of a pre-Conquest window and immediately W. of the porch is a patch of yellow septaria-filling which suggests the previous existence of a similar window. The S. arcade is of *c.* 1300 and of three bays with two-centred arches of two hollow-chamfered orders resting on octagonal piers and semi-octagonal responds with moulded capitals and bases of varying detail, the arches have on the N. side a moulded label.   The S.W. angle of the nave retains the pre-Conquest walling of rag and pudding-stone.

The *South Aisle* (7¾ ft. wide) has been partly refaced and partly cemented over externally ; the windows are modern.

The *West Tower* (about 9 ft. square) is of 15th-century date and of three stages with an 18th-century embattled brick parapet and two courses of flint and stone chequer-work above the plinth. The tower-arch is pointed and of two continuous chamfered orders, the inner interrupted by moulded capitals. In the W. wall is a 15th-century doorway with chamfered jambs and two-centred head and external label now covered with modern cement. Above is a 15th-century window of three cinque-foiled lights with vertical tracery in a two-centred head with a moulded label. The bell-chamber has in the E. wall a single-light window with a two-centred head and moulded label; in the S. wall is a similar window. There are probably other windows in the N. and W. walls, and a second in the E. wall, now obscured by a thick growth of ivy. On the face of the S.W. buttress is a cross of red and yellow bricks.

The *North Porch* (9½ ft. by 7¾ ft.) has a two-centred and chamfered outer archway in a square moulded outer order, probably of 15th-century date. The walls have been refaced externally with modern brick and plaster. The roof is of the 15th century and of two bays with cambered tie-beams supported by four-centred arched braces carrying king-posts with curved struts and a central purlin.

Fittings—*Font* (Plate, pp. xlii–iii): octagonal bowl with concave sides, one blank, the others each with a quatrefoiled circle enclosing (*a*) a four-leafed flower, (*b*) shield with fleur-de-lis, (*c*) a four-leafed rose, (*d*) shield with the letter W surmounted by a crown, (*e*) eight-leafed flower, (*f*) shield with *four bars*, (*g*) shield with *three pierced molets and a border;* moulded under-edge and hollow-chamfered base, late 15th-century. *Monuments:* In churchyard—on N. side, (1) to Samuel, son of Samuel and Sarah Sharp, 1680, head-stone; (2) to Sarah, daughter of the above, 1680, head-stone. *Niche:* By W. door of tower—with chamfered jambs and four-centred head, probably 15th-century. *Piscina:* In chancel—with moulded ogee head and jambs and corbelled-out basin resting on a man's head and having tapering trefoiled traceried panels, 14th-century. *Plate:* includes an Elizabethan cup, date-mark obliterated. *Recess:* In N.E. corner of nave across the angle—with rounded chamfered head, of 15th-century date, probably formerly part of rood-stairway.

Secular :—

HOMESTEAD MOATS.

ᵃ(2). At Great Stambridge Hall, ¼ m. S.E. of the church.

ᵃ(3). At Hampton Barns, nearly 1 m. E.N.E. of the church.

ᵃ(4). SHEPHERD AND DOG INN, at Ballards Gore, nearly 1½ m. N.N.E. of the church, is of two storeys, timber-framed and plastered; the roofs are tiled. It was built in the 15th century and is of T-shaped plan with the cross-wing at the E. end. In the 17th century the roof to the W. wing was raised and an upper floor and chimney-stack inserted; modern additions have been made on the N. and W. The S. end of the E. wing has a projecting upper storey and the main chimney-stack is of 17th-century date. Inside the building some of the rooms have exposed ceiling-beams.

Condition—Good.

ᵃ(5). COTTAGE, 100 yards W. of (4), is of two storeys, timber-framed and weather-boarded; the roofs are tiled. It was built in the 16th century and has modern additions on the S. The E. end of the original building has a projecting upper storey with a moulded bracket at the N. end.

Condition—Good.

Unclassified :—

ᵇ(6). RED HILLS, two on Wallsea Island, S.W. of Oldpool Farm. Another has been located at the E. end of the island.

---

34. GREAT WAKERING. (G.d.)

(O.S. 6 in. lxxix. N.W.)

Great Wakering is a small parish on the coast, 4 m. E.N.E. of Southend-on-Sea. The church is the principal monument.

Roman :—

(1). Roman tiles from Great Wakering, possibly from brick-earth pits near Wakering Stairs, are in Prittlewell Priory Museum, and may indicate continued occupation in a place known, by the discovery of many Late Celtic burial-urns, now in the Colchester Museum, to have been inhabited just before the Roman occupation.

Ecclesiastical :—

(2). PARISH CHURCH OF ST. NICHOLAS (Plate, p. 60) stands at the E. end of the village. The walls are of roughly coursed ragstone-rubble with some septaria and flint; the dressings are of Reigate and other limestone; the roofs are tiled and the spire boarded. The *Chancel* and *Nave* were built *c.* 1100. The ground-stage of the *West Tower* was added *c.* 1130, the upper part of the tower being completed towards the end of the same century. The chancel-arch was rebuilt in the 15th century reusing older material and late in the 15th century the *West Porch* with the room over were built. The *South Porch* was added early in the 16th century. The *North Chapel* or annexe was built in 1843 and the church has been restored in modern times.

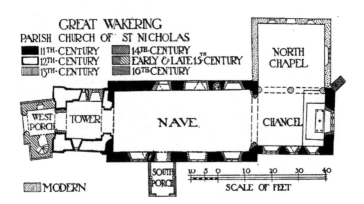

GREAT WAKERING
PARISH CHURCH OF ST NICHOLAS
■ 11TH-CENTURY   ▨ 14TH-CENTURY
□ 12TH-CENTURY   ▨ EARLY & LATE 15TH CENTURY
▨ 13TH-CENTURY   ▨ 16TH CENTURY

NORTH
CHAPEL

WEST
PORCH   TOWER   NAVE.   CHANCEL

SOUTH
PORCH

▨ MODERN

SCALE OF FEET

The 12th-century W. Tower is interesting and the W. Porch is an unusual feature.

Architectural Description—The *Chancel* (25 ft. by 19 ft.) has an E. window all modern except the splays and segmental-pointed rear-arch which are probably of the 14th century. The N. arcade is modern. In the S. wall are three windows, the two eastern are early 13th-century lancets restored externally in Roman cement; the westernmost window is of late 15th-century date and of two cinquefoiled lights with vertical tracery in a square head; E. of the middle window is the E. jamb and part of the head of a single-light window of *c*. 1100. The 15th-century chancel-arch is two-centred and of two chamfered orders, the outer continuous and the inner resting on attached semi-octagonal shafts with moulded capitals and hollow-chamfered bases; the responds, except the capitals, are of the 13th century, possibly reset.

The *Nave* (50½ ft. by 22¼ ft.) has in the N. wall three windows, the easternmost is of early 14th-century date and of two trefoiled ogee lights with a quatrefoil in a two-centred head with a moulded label; the W. jamb and the rear-arch are modern; the second window has late 14th-century splays, cut back for wider lights, two-centred rear-arch and moulded external label; it is fitted with an 18th-century wooden frame; the westernmost window is of the 18th century, set high in the wall and blocked internally; W. of the easternmost window is the 15th-century rood-loft staircase with a lower doorway having rebated jambs and two-centred head; a wooden beam set in the W. splay of the adjoining window was possibly part of the construction of the rood-loft; the 14th-century N. doorway has chamfered jambs and two-centred arch; it is now blocked; above it

is a blocked window of *c*. 1100 with a round head; part of a similar window is visible above the middle window in the same wall. In the S. wall are three windows, the two eastern are similar to the easternmost in the N. wall but the second of these is modern externally and the splays have been cut back; the westernmost window is of early 14th-century date and of two plain pointed lights with a spandrel in a two-centred head with a moulded label, partly restored; the mid 13th-century S. doorway has jambs and a two-centred arch of two chamfered orders, moulded imposts and a moulded label with mask-stops; above the W. wall of the porch is the E. jamb of a window of *c*. 1100. In the W. wall above the tower-arch is a window of *c*. 1100 with a round head and is now blocked internally.

The *West Tower* (about 13½ ft. square) is of three stages, the lowest of *c*. 1130, with flat pilaster buttresses of rubble at the angles; while the two upper stages are of late 12th-century date and without buttresses. The semi-circular tower-arch is of two plain orders with chamfered imposts; the wall was probably thickened when the tower was added. In the N. wall is a 15th-century window of two cinquefoiled lights in a square head with a moulded label; W. of it is a round-headed window of *c*. 1130, blocked externally. In the S. wall is a similar 12th-century window also blocked and hardly visible externally. The early 15th-century W. doorway has moulded jambs and two-centred arch in a square head with a moulded label; the spandrels have quatrefoiled circles enclosing foliage; the jambs and label are much defaced. The N., S. and W. walls of the second stage have each a window with late 12th-century splays and slightly pointed rear-arch; the N. window is partly blocked and fitted with a 16th-century window; the S.

GREAT WAKERING : PARISH CHURCH OF ST. NICHOLAS ; *c.* 1100 and later.
From the South-West, showing W. Tower, 12th-century (with later windows) ; W. Porch, late 15th-century, etc.

HADLEIGH: PARISH CHURCH OF ST. JAMES THE LESS; mid 12th-century and later.
From the North-East.

window is blocked externally ; the W. window is covered by the added porch-building. The bell-chamber has in each wall a window with late 12th-century splays and two-centred rear-arch ; the E. window has 16th-century jambs of brick, a four-centred head, remains of a label and an inner order of 18th-century brickwork ; the other three windows have each two trefoiled 15th-century lights and a three-centred head with a moulded label.

The *West Porch* is of late 15th-century date and has an outer archway with splayed responds and two-centred arch with a moulded label. In the N. wall is a small square-headed window now blocked. In the S. wall is the doorway to the large projecting turret-staircase, it has hollow-chamfered jambs and four-centred head. The room over the porch has in the W. wall a plain square-headed window and below it is what appears to be a small niche, now blocked.

The *South Porch* is of early 16th-century date and of timber-framing on dwarf rubble walls ; the outer archway has moulded jambs, three-centred arch and sunk spandrels ; above it is a moulded and embattled beam at the base of the gable. The openings in the side walls are now blocked.

The *Roof* of the chancel is of trussed-rafter type, ceiled on the soffit. The late 14th or early 15th-century roof of the nave is of three bays with king-post trusses ; the wall-plates are moulded and the king-posts have moulded capitals and bases ; the two eastern trusses rest on carved stone corbels.

Fittings—*Brass Indents :* In chancel—of priest with crocketed canopy and inscription-plate, *c.* 1400. In nave—as threshold of S. doorway, defaced. *Chest :* In N. chapel—of oak with cambered lid, iron-bound, probably 16th-century. *Door :* In S. doorway of nail-studded battens with fillets planted on and strap-hinges, probably 15th-century. *Monuments :* In churchyard— S. side—(1) to John Fitzlewes, 1699, and John, his father, 1701, table-tomb ; (2) to Priscilla Skinner, 1711, head-stone ; (3) to Nicholas Kennett, 1713, head-stone ; (4) to . . . Coll . . . , 170., head-stone. *Paintings :* In nave—on N. and S. walls, remains of black-letter inscriptions in rectangular frames, 17th-century ; on chancel-arch, remains of red and black colour. *Piscina :* In chancel— under S.E. window, recess with reset moulded head, possibly piscina, 13th-century. *Stoup :* In S. porch—rough recess, date uncertain.

Condition—Fairly good, some stonework much decayed.

Secular :—

MONUMENTS (3–6).

The following monuments, unless otherwise described, are of two storeys, timber-framed and

plastered or weather-boarded ; the roofs are tiled. Some of the buildings have original chimney-stacks and exposed ceiling-beams.

Condition—Good.

(3). *House*, now two tenements, on S. side of road, 300 yards W. of the church, was built in the 17th century on an L-shaped plan with the wings extending towards the E. and S. ; there are modern additions on the S. of both wings.

(4). *House*, now three tenements, on N. side of road, 230 yards W. of (3), was built in the 17th century on an L-shaped plan with the wings extending towards the N. and W. There is a modern addition at the back.

(5). *House*, at Samuel's Corner, ½ m. E. of the church, was built possibly in the 16th century on an L-shaped plan with the wings extending towards the S. and W. Chimney-stacks were added early in the following century and there is a modern extension on the W. side of the S. wing.

(6). *Friends Farm*, house, 750 yards S.E. of the church, was built in the 16th century on an L-shaped plan with the wings extending towards the N. and W. There is a modern addition on the S. side of the S. wing. The upper storey originally projected at the W. end of the S. wing but has now been underbuilt.

---

35. GREAT WARLEY. (B.d.)

(O.S. 6 in. [a]lxvii. S.W. [b]lxxv. N.E.)

Great Warley is a parish and village 2 m. S.S.W. of Brentwood.

Ecclesiastical :—

[b](1). PARISH CHURCH OF ST. MARY has recently been pulled down with the exception of the modern *West Tower*, which contains the following :—

Fittings—*Brass :* In tower—to Margaret, wife of John Agmondesham, 1582, inscription only, with indent of shield. *Monuments* and *Floor-slabs.* Monuments : (1) On W. wall, of Gyles Fleming, 1623, and Gyles Fleming, his son, 1633, with Susanna, his wife, alabaster wall-monument with bust of man in ruff and cloak. In churchyard— S.E. of tower, (2) to John Stevens, 1711, head-stone ; (3) to Robert Stanes, 1712, head-stone. E. of tower, (4) to Elizabeth, wife of Cornelius Rockliff, 1714, head-stone. *Floor-slabs :* (1) to John Stedman, 169(3 ?), rector of the parish ; (2) to John Wetherell, 1661, with shield-of-arms. *Plate :* includes cup, cover-paten and stand-paten, all of 1700 and dated 1701, also early 18th-century pewter plate.

Secular :—

MONUMENTS (2–8).

The following monuments, unless otherwise described, are of two storeys, timber-framed and plastered ; the roofs are tiled. Some of the buildings have original chimney-stacks and exposed ceiling-beams.

Condition—Good or fairly good.

b(2). *Franks*, house, nearly 1 m. S.W. of the church, was built probably in the 15th century on an L-shaped plan with the wings extending towards the N. and W. Later alterations include a 17th-century eastern extension of the middle part of the N. wing and considerable modern additions. The two main chimney-stacks are of early 17th-century date ; the stack in the middle of the E. wing has two diagonal shafts. Inside the building is an original doorway with a two-centred head, and two rooms on the upper floor are lined with late 16th-century panelling divided by shallow fluted pilasters supporting small carved brackets. There are two doors of about the same date, one of which has 'cock's-head' hinges. The roof over the middle part of the N. wing is of central-purlin type and, above the W. wing, the original king-post with central-purlin two-way struts is visible. A fire-back, recently imported, has the initials $\frac{P}{T\ E}$ and the date 1690.

b(3). *Bolens and Herds*, farmhouse, 1¾ m. S.S.E. of the church, is a long rectangular building, probably of 16th-century date, with modern additions at the back.

GREAT WARLEY STREET :—

a(4). *Wallets*, house, at S. corner of the cross-roads, was built in the 15th century with a central hall and N.E. and S.W. cross-wings. Late in the 16th century an upper floor was inserted in the hall and modern alterations include the addition of the staircase and the extension of the S.E. wing. The upper storeys of both the cross-wings project on the N.E. front. The chimney-stack at the S. end of the original hall is of late 16th-century date and of four shafts set diagonally on a cruciform plan with a square base. Inside the building one room is lined with panelling of c. 1600. The staircase is of 17th-century date and has turned balusters and moulded handrail but is not *in situ*. The original roof over the northernmost wing has a heavy tie-beam with square king-post and curved braces.

b(5). *House*, now Post Office and tenement, on opposite side of the road and 30 yards W. of (4), was built in the 15th century with a central hall and E. and W. cross-wings. An upper floor has been inserted in the hall and there are considerable modern alterations. The upper storey of the E. cross-wing projects on the S. front and in the roof

of the central block are two gabled dormers. The central chimney-stack was built probably when the upper floor was inserted but has been rebuilt above the roof. Inside the building the main tie-beam to the roof over the original hall is exposed and is supported by curved braces carrying a king-post ; the curved braces to the main tie-beam of the roof are also exposed.

a(6). *Cottage*, on S. side of the road to the church, 50 yards E. of (4), was built probably in the 16th-century on a rectangular plan with a cross-wing at the N. end ; there is a modern addition at the back. The upper storey of the N. cross-wing projects on the W. front.

a(7). *House*, now two tenements, N. of (6), was built probably in the 15th century on an L-shaped plan with the wings extending towards the S. and E. The insertion of partitions and alterations at a later date have obscured the original plan ; there is a modern extension at the back. Inside the building is an original doorway with a two-centred head and in the upper storey of the N. wing an original tie-beam supported by rough braces.

———

a(8). *Cottage*, on W. side of Brock Street, about 550 yards N. of the cross-roads, is of one storey with attics. It was built probably early in the 17th century and has a modern extension on the W. There are two gabled dormers in the roof and at the N. end an original chimney-stack with two diagonal shafts.

———

36. HADLEIGH.   (E.d.)

(O.S. 6 in. (*a*)lxxvii. N.E. (*b*)lxxvii. S.E.)

Hadleigh is a small parish and village on the N. side of the River Thames, N. of Canvey Island and 4 m. W. of Southend-on-Sea. The church and the Castle are the only monuments, the latter being of exceptional interest.

Ecclesiastical :—

a(1). PARISH CHURCH OF ST. JAMES THE LESS (Plate, p. 61) stands in the village. The walls are of mixed rubble with limestone dressings and the roofs are tiled. The whole church, including *Apse*, *Chancel* and *Nave*, was built about the middle of the 12th century. The bell-turret is probably of the 16th century. The church has been restored in modern times and the *South Porch* is of late 18th-century date.

The building is interesting as a complete 12th-century church with an apse and among the fittings the paintings are noteworthy.

HADLEIGH
The PARISH CHURCH *of* ST JAMES THE LESS

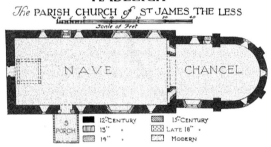

Scale of Feet

■ 12ᵀᴴCENTURY   ▨ 15ᵀᴴCENTURY
▨ 13"   "   ▨ LATE 18" .
▨ 14" .   ▨ MODERN

Architectural Description—The *Apse* (17¼ ft. by 20½ ft.) has flat pilaster buttresses and three round-headed windows, completely restored externally, but with old splays. Between the apse and the chancel are plain responds with moulded imposts. The *Chancel* (14 ft. by 20½ ft.) has in the N. wall a round-headed 12th-century window much restored; E. of it is a blocked doorway, all of modern stonework. In the S. wall is a partly restored early 14th-century window of two cinque-foiled lights with tracery in a two-centred head with a moulded label. The 12th-century chancel-arch is semi-circular and of two plain orders; the responds have moulded imposts; flanking it are two round-headed arches, each having a squint (Plate, p. 104) with a circular foiled opening of the 15th century on the E. face.

The *Nave* (56¼ ft. by 24¼ ft.) has in the N. wall four windows; the easternmost is an early 13th-century lancet-window; the second window is of the 15th century and of two cinquefoiled lights with vertical tracery in a square head with a moulded label and head-stops; the two western windows are single round-headed 12th-century lights and between them is the late 13th-century N. doorway with chamfered jambs and two-centred arch; it is now blocked; on the E. splay is a small diapered design. In the S. wall are four windows, the easternmost and the two western are similar to the western windows in the N. wall, but the easternmost is much restored; the second window is of early 15th-century date, much restored and of two trefoiled ogee lights with vertical tracery in a square head; the early 15th-century S. doorway has moulded jambs and two-centred arch with a moulded label and defaced head-stops, the round rear-arch is of the 12th century. In the W. wall is a 12th-century round-headed doorway of two plain orders, much restored; above it is a 12th-century window similar to those

in the N. wall; in the gable is a blocked opening. The bell-turret at the W. end of the nave stands on four oak posts and framing, probably of the 17th century.

Fittings—*Bell :* one, inaccessible, but said to be by John Wilnar, 1636. *Bracket :* In apse—with double roll on the soffit, 12th-century. *Door :* In N. doorway—of overlapping nail-studded battens, probably 16th-century. *Font :* made up of octagonal bowl, separate lower part carved with stiff-leaf foliage, probably recut, 13th-century, stem and base modern. *Niches :* In apse—in E. wall, with cinquefoiled and sub-cusped head and sunk spandrel, 15th-century unfinished. In nave—in E. wall, small with cusped head, 15th-century. *Paintings :* In nave—on W. splay of N.E. window, upper part of figure of St. Thomas of Canterbury, with early mitre, pall and cross-staff, inscription above, " Beate Tomas," c. 1200. In head of third window in N. wall, remains of figure, possibly angel, etc., probably 13th-century. On wall-face further W., traces of a trefoiled canopy and a nimbed head, 14th-century. *Plate :* includes cup and cover-paten, the latter of 1568, the cup without date-mark but of same period, both with band of engraved ornament. *Royal Arms :* In nave—at W. end, of Queen Anne after the Union, painted on canvas. *Stoup :* in S. porch—with cinquefoiled head, 15th-century, basin removed.

Condition—Good.

Secular :—

(2). HADLEIGH CASTLE (Plates, pp. 64–5) stands 1,100 yards S. of the church and is built at the end of a spur projecting from the rising ground overlooking the River Thames and Canvey Island from the N. It evidently consisted of a strongly fortified bailey, polygonal on plan and enclosing an area 350 ft. from

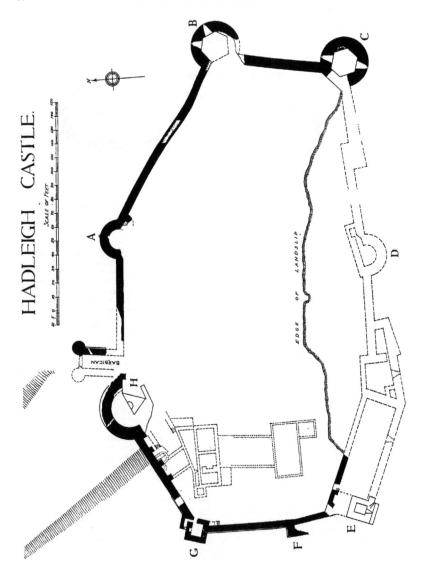

WEST TILBURY. Tilbury Fort:
Gatehouse, c. 1682 : north side.

HORNDON-ON-THE-HILL.
(3). Gates at house 70 yards E. of church ;
late 17th or early 18th-century.

DOWNHAM : (3). FREMNELLS.
Gate-posts ; dated 1676.

AVELEY : (6). BELHUS.
Doorway in E. Front ; 16th-century, reset.

STANFORD-LE-HOPE : (4). HASSENBROOK HALL.
Doorway and Wall to Garden ; early 17th-century.

From the East, showing S.E. Tower (C) and N.E. Tower (B).

S.E. Tower (C) from the N.W.

S.E. Tower (C) from the S.W.

N.E. Tower (B) from the S.

HADLEIGH CASTLE; 14th-century.

Entrance, with remains of Barbican and N.W. Tower;
from interior.

Stair in W. Wall and Turret (G).

Entrance from exterior   Tower (C) in distance.

S.W. Tower (E).

S. Wall from interior, and S.E. Tower (C).

S. Wall from exterior.

Part of W. side of S.E. Tower (C).

E. side of N.W. Barbican.

HADLEIGH CASTLE; 14th-century.

LITTLE BURSTEAD.
(2). Stockwell Hall : Overmantel in Dining Room; *c.* 1600.

AVELEY.
(6). Belhus : Fireplace on ground floor; *c.* 1600.

LITTLE BURSTEAD.
(4). Hatches : Door; early 16th-century.

PRITTLEWELL
(3). Porters : Fireplace in Hall; late 16th-century.

HORNDON-ON-THE-HILL.
(8). Old Market Hall : Timber construction; 16th-century.

UPMINSTER.
(4). Great Tomkyns : Interior of Hall; 15th-century.

E. to W. and 150 ft. wide, and surrounded by a thick curtain wall with projecting towers at the angles. The entrance was on the N. side and the approach was protected towards the S. by a wedge-shaped ramp, partly artificial, which projected to the N.W. The site, which slopes away from the walls on all sides, added greatly to the strength of the Castle as a fortified building. No part of the existing structure appears to be earlier than the 14th century, when the whole Castle was reconstructed. There is documentary evidence of the progress of the work in 1365–6 (E.A.S.T., N.S., i, 86 et seq.).

The Castle is of exceptional interest, being the only work of its type in the county.

The walls and towers are of Reigate stone and ragstone, with some chalk, used internally. The original height of the towers and walls is uncertain ; none of the buildings is now complete, and in places the foundations only remain.

The Castle was entered through a *Barbican* at the W. end of the N. wall, and on the W. of the barbican was a strong tower (H.) commanding the approach. The entrance gateway was 10 ft. wide and flanked on either side by a small circular turret, but only the lower part of the E. wall of the barbican and E. turret remain, though the position of the W. wall is marked by a slight rise in the ground and the entrance by two stones with rebates for the gate or portcullis. The lower part of the walls of the barbican were battered externally, and in the E. wall immediately S. of the entrance tower is a square-headed, splayed loop. Nothing definite can be said about the plan or height of the *Tower* H. immediately S.W. of the entrance, but part of the outer wall remains and projects in a semi-circle beyond the curtain-wall, and within the area are remains of platforms and possibly of the base of a pier to carry the vault. The E. side has been pulled down to within a few feet of the ground, but the springing of a vault is indicated in the upper part on the W. side with traces of an internal string-course below and a window above. E. of the barbican at the angle of the N. and N.E. curtain-walls is the *Tower* A., projecting outwards in a semi-circle of 28 ft. in diameter, but little more than the foundations of both the N. wall, and the tower with the two lowest steps of a stair at the S.E. corner remain above the ground. The N.E. curtain-wall is in places 6 ft. high, but has been stripped of the greater part of its facings.

The *Tower* B. at the junction of the N.E. and E. walls is internally hexagonal on plan and projects outwards in a three-quarter circle of 36 ft. diameter. The greater part of the wall on the N. and E. is standing and is of three storeys with a slightly projecting plinth having a band of knapped flint above it, and a plain string-course marking the

upper storeys. On the ground-floor are two small square-headed windows only visible externally, and on the first floor are two similar windows with wide internal splays and segmental rear-arches. On the top stage is a single window, similar to the others and a wide recess for a fireplace. In the thickness of the wall on the E. side is a flue, and on the W. side are traces of a stair-turret.

The *Tower* C. at the S. end of the E. curtain-wall is of three storeys and is similar to tower B., though practically the whole of the outer wall remains. On the ground-stage are two square-headed windows and in each of the two upper storeys are four windows and traces of a fifth. On the top storey the segmental rear-arches retain their original dressings. In the N.E. side of the wall are two flues and on the S. side a garde-robe shaft or shafts discharging through three square-headed openings with steeply sloped sills in the outer face of the plinth. On the same side are indications of a former stair-turret. A landslide has carried practically the whole of the S. side of the bailey down the hill for a distance of about 40 ft. The foundation of the S. walls and structure, however, can here be traced, including the semi-circular *Tower* D. (which was immediately opposite and apparently of similar design to the corresponding tower A. on the N. side of the bailey), the lower parts of the walls of several buildings situated at the S.W. corner of the castle and the basement of the small square *Tower* E. at the S. end of the W. curtain-wall. These buildings projected on the S. beyond the inner face of the building. The basement of the *Tower* E. consisted of two rooms, part of the northernmost one of which is still *in situ* and has a floor paved with yellow brick. In the wall of the fallen portion are two small openings, now facing S., and on the E. side is a small garde-robe chute. Under the floor is a cavity. The curtain-wall on the W. is considerably thinner than those on the N.E. and S. of the building and stands only a few feet above the ground. At the S. end are the lower parts of the walls of the rectangular projection F., the purpose of which is doubtful, and at the N. end, at the junction with the N.W. wall, the lowest storey of the small square *Tower* G. This has one room, with traces of a fireplace in the N. wall, and, opening out of it on the N., a smaller chamber, probably a garde-robe. Against the curtain-wall, at the S.E. corner of the tower are the lower steps of a staircase leading to the parapet walk. The N.W. curtain-wall, between the towers G. and H., is preserved to a considerable height, and has, projecting from the S.E. face, three buttresses. Adjoining this wall extensive foundations of kitchen buildings, shown in the plan, were uncovered about 1863 and the lines of an adjoining hall and solar wing were visible in the turf in 1921–2.

Condition—The whole work is now in a ruinous condition and the tower B. is in imminent danger of collapse, owing to the unstable nature .of the underlying London clay.

HANNINGFIELD, see EAST HANNINGFIELD, SOUTH HANNINGFIELD, and WEST HANNINGFIELD.

37. HAVENGORE. (G.d.)

No monuments known.

38. HAWKWELL. (E.c.)

(O.S. 6 in. lxx. S.W.)

Hawkwell is a parish 2 m. N.W. of Rochford.

Ecclesiastical :—

(1). PARISH CHURCH OF ST. MARY stands near the E. end of the parish. The walls are of plastered ragstone and flint-rubble, with limestone dressings ; the roofs are tiled. The *Nave* and *Chancel* were built in the 14th century, but the chancel was altered in the 15th century and the bell-turret is of the same period. The church was restored in the 19th century, when the *North Vestry* and *South Porch* were added.

Architectural Description—The *Chancel* (16 ft. by 18 ft.) has an E. window, all modern except the 15th-century rear-arch and splays. In the S. wall are two windows, the eastern is modern except the 15th-century rear-arch and splays ; the western window is a 'lowside' of one trefoiled light and probably of the 14th century. The 15th-century chancel-arch is two-centred and of two chamfered orders, the outer continuous and the inner resting on attached shafts with moulded capitals.

The *Nave* (30½ ft. by 17¾ ft.) has in the N. wall a window, all modern except the splays and rear-arch, which are probably of the 14th century ; further W. is the 14th-century N. doorway, with moulded jambs and two-centred arch. In the S. wall is a window similar to that in the N. wall ; further W. is the 14th-century S. doorway, with jambs and two-centred arch of two orders, the outer moulded and the inner chamfered. In the W. wall is a window, all modern except the splays.

The bell-turret at the W. end of the nave stands on four oak posts with cross-beams and curved braces supporting the square framing of the turret.

The *Roof* of the chancel is plastered, but has 15th-century moulded wall-plates. The 15th-century roof of the nave has moulded wall-plates, and a middle truss with an octagonal king-post having moulded capital and base.

Fittings—*Door :* In S. doorway—of overlapping nail-studded battens with strap-hinges and cinque-foiled handle-plate, 15th-century. *Piscina :* In chancel—with hollow-chamfered jambs and square head, 14th or 15th-century, square drain with chamfered under-edge, probably earlier. *Plate :* includes cup of 1662.

Condition—Good.

Secular :—

(2). HOMESTEAD MOAT, at Parsonage Farm, 550 yards S.W. of the church.

(3). CLEMENTS HALL, house, ½ m. N.W. of church, is of two storeys, timber-framed and weather-boarded. It was built probably in the 16th century on a L-shaped plan with the wings extending to the N. and W. In the middle of the E. front is a two-storeyed projecting bay with an entrance porch in front. The house has been much altered and there are modern additions on the N. and W. The upper storey projects at the W. end of the S. front. Inside the building one of the ground-floor rooms has a restored fireplace of *c.* 1600, with a carved wooden overmantel of three semi-circular arches springing from imposts and divided by pilasters carved with strapwork ornament and caryatides and supporting a continuous moulded cornice. Flanking the jambs of the fireplace are panels carved with similar caryatides and strap-ornament. A modern door in the same room incorporates some 17th-century panelling.

Condition—Good.

39. HAZELEIGH. (E.b.)

(O.S. 6 in. liv. S.W.)

Hazeleigh is a small parish 2½ m. S.W. of Maldon.

Ecclesiastical :—

(1). PARISH CHURCH OF ST. NICHOLAS (Plate, p. xxxiii) stands near the middle of the parish. The walls are of plastered timber-framing and the roofs are tiled. The *Chancel* was built in the 16th century or perhaps earlier. The *Nave* was rebuilt in the 17th and 18th century but incorporates much material of an earlier date. The *Vestry* and *South Porch* were perhaps added at the same time.

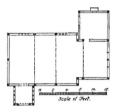

Scale of Feet.

Architectural Description—The *Chancel* (11½ ft. by 13¼ ft.), *North Vestry* and *South Porch,* have no ancient features except the timber-framing.

The *Nave* (25½ ft. by 17¾ ft.) has in the N. wall two original windows, each of three lights in a square head with moulded frame and mullions. Over the W. end is a timber bell-turret.

The *Roofs* of the chancel and nave are ceiled and have principals with curved braces ; the purlins of the chancel have curved side braces.

Fittings — *Communion Rails :* with heavy moulded rail and symmetrically turned balusters, *c.* 1600.

Condition—Ruinous (since demolished).

Secular :—

(2). HAZELEIGH HALL, house and moat, E. of the church. The *House* is of two storeys with attics, timber-framed and plastered ; the roofs are tiled. The main block was built probably in the 16th century, and there are 17th-century and later additions at the back. Inside the building is some early 17th-century panelling and a door of moulded battens. The roof, of five bays, has curved wind-braces.

The *Moat* is incomplete.

Condition—Of house, good.

40. HOCKLEY. (E.c.)

(O.S. 6 in. [a]lxi. S.E. [b]lxix. N.E. [c]lxx. N.W. [d]lxix. S.E. [d]lxx. S.W.)

Hockley is a parish and small village on the River Crouch 4 m. N.W. of Rochford.

Ecclesiastical :—

[e](1). PARISH CHURCH OF ST. PETER stands near the middle of the parish. The walls are of mixed rubble mainly covered with plaster ; the S. porch is of red brick ; the dressings are of limestone ; the roofs are tiled. The *Nave* is possibly of the 12th century, but there is little evidence of this except the thickness of the S. wall. The *Chancel* was probably rebuilt in the 13th century and *c.* 1210–20 the N. arcade and *North Aisle* were built. The *West Tower* was added in the 14th

century, but the top stage is perhaps of later date. In the 16th or 17th century the *South Porch* was added and in the 17th century the E. wall of the chancel was rebuilt. The church has been restored in modern times, when the *North Vestry* was added.

Architectural Description—The *Chancel* (29¾ ft. by 16 ft.) has a modern E. window. In the N. wall are the jambs of a blocked window ; further W. is a modern doorway. In the S. wall is a blocked window with a two-centred head and probably of the 14th century ; at the W. end of the wall is a window of one round-headed light, possibly of the 13th century and subsequently widened ; further E. is a 13th-century doorway with chamfered jambs and two-centred arch. Between the chancel and nave is a plain braced tie-beam resting on two posts against the walls.

The *Nave* (42½ ft. by 18½ ft.) has a N. arcade of *c.* 1210–20 and of four bays with two-centred arches of two orders, the outer plain and the inner chamfered ; the cylindrical columns have moulded bases and capitals carved with conventional foliage of varying design ; the responds have attached half-columns. In the S. wall are three windows, the easternmost and westernmost are modern except for the splays and rear-arches which are possibly of the 15th century ; the middle window is of the 15th century and of three cinquefoiled lights with vertical tracery in a two-centred head with a moulded label ; further W. is the early 13th-century S. doorway with jambs and two-centred arch of two chamfered orders.

The *North Aisle* (11 ft. wide) has in the E. wall a 15th-century window of one cinquefoiled light. In the N. wall are two windows, both of the 14th century and one with a trefoiled and one with a plain pointed head ; between them is the 13th-century N. doorway with plain jambs and two-centred arch. In the W. wall is a 13th-century lancet-window, now covered externally with cement.

The *West Tower* (12½ ft. square) is of two stages, the lower square and the upper with the angles cut back to form an irregular octagon (Plate, pp. xxxii–iii) ; it has an embattled parapet and a small spire. The 14th-century tower-arch is two-centred and of two continuous chamfered orders ; higher up on the W. side is an outer order springing from stone corbels. In the N. wall is a 14th-century recess with a segmental-pointed head of brick and tile.

In the S. wall are two 14th-century windows, one above the other, the lower of one cinquefoiled ogee light and the upper of one trefoiled light. The 14th-century W. doorway has cemented jambs and a cinquefoiled ogee head badly weathered and repaired with cement. In the angles of the tower are oak posts supporting an inserted floor. The N., S. and W. sides of the bell-chamber have each a 15th-century window of two trefoiled lights in a square head; the mullions have been destroyed and the windows are much decayed; in the E. wall is a window of one pointed light.

The *South Porch* is of the 16th or 17th century and of red brick. The outer archway has a square 18th-century wooden frame. The side walls have each a window of one four-centred light.

The *Roof* of the nave is of the 14th century and of three bays with king-post trusses; the king-posts have moulded capitals and one bay has 14th-century moulded wall-plates. The N. aisle has a plain pent roof of doubtful date. The S. porch has a 16th or 17th-century roof of collar-beam type with one cambered tie-beam.

Fittings—*Bells:* three; 1st by John Hodson, 1657; 2nd by James Bartlet, 1684; 3rd by Miles Graye, 1626. The bell-frame is old. *Font* (Plate, pp. xlii–iii): octagonal bowl of Purbeck marble, each face with two shallow pointed panels, octagonal stem with attached shafts at the angles, early 13th-century, much weathered and stem cut down. *Glass:* In N. aisle—in E. window, four quarries (made up of fragments of an inscription) with the word "deus" in black-letter and two with the word "...ictus," 15th-century. *Monuments:* In churchyard—S. side, (1) to Elizabeth, wife of William Richman, 1711, head-stone; (2) to Elizabeth, daughter of William Richman, 1714, head-stone. *Piscina:* In chancel—with chamfered jambs widened out to the square head, round drain, probably 13th-century. *Plate:* includes cup of 1562 with band of engraved ornament. *Stoup:* In S. porch—with trefoiled head, 14th-century, much mutilated. *Miscellanea:* Incorporated in S. and W. walls of churchyard, numerous worked stones.

Condition—Poor, cracks in various places and some stonework much weathered.

Secular :—

[b](2). HOMESTEAD MOAT, at Shepherd's Farm, about ½ m. N.W. of the church.

MONUMENTS (3–8).

The following monuments, unless otherwise described, are of the 17th century, and of two storeys, timber-framed and plastered or weather-boarded; the roofs are tiled. Some of the buildings have original chimney-stacks and exposed ceiling beams.

Condition—Good.

[c](3). *Hockley Hall*, 100 yards S.S.W. of the church, is of two storeys with attics. It was built on an L-shaped plan with the wings extending towards the S. and W., but has been much altered and added to on the N. and S.

[c](4). *Lower Hockley Hall*, nearly 1 m. N.E. of the church, has modern additions on the S., E. and W.

[a](5). *Bett's Farm*, 1,450 yards S.E. of the church, was originally of the central-chimney type of plan, but modern additions on the N.E. and S.E. makes the present plan T-shaped. It has been entirely refaced with modern brick and weather-boarding.

[c](6). *Cottage*, ¼ m. W.S.W. of (5), is of the central-chimney type, with a projecting gabled bay in the centre of the E. front carried on modern columns; there is a modern addition at the back. In the gable of the bay is painted the date 1611. Inside the building one of the ground-floor rooms has an early 17th-century door and the staircase on the ground-floor has some late 17th-century balusters, an old newel and a short length of moulded handrail.

[a](7). *Whitbreads*, house, 1,600 yards S.S.W. of the church, has been much altered and added to.

[a](8). *White House*, 450 yards W. of (7), is a small cottage of the central-chimney type, much altered, on to which has been built a modern house.

Unclassified :—

[c](9). PLUMBEROW MOUNT (Plate, p. xxxvii), about 1 m. E.N.E. of the church, is circular, about 76 ft. in diameter at the base and 14 ft. high. Excavations undertaken in 1914, though inconclusive, yielded a coin of Domitian, much Roman and some Saxon pottery (all fragmentary), but no certain indication either of the purpose or of the date of the mound, save that it is obviously not pre-Roman. (See *Essex Arch. Soc. Trans.*, N.S., XIII, 224–237.)

Condition—Good.

[a](10). MOUNDS, ten or more, N. of the Crouch and about 1¾ m. N. of the church. They vary greatly in size and height, and near them are several depressions or pans. The mounds have been excavated and were assumed to have been connected with mediaeval salt workings.

Condition—Good.

---

41. HORNCHURCH. (A.d.)

(O.S. 6 in. [a]lxvii. S.W. [b]lxxiv. N.E. [c]lxxiv. S.E. [d]lxxv. N.W.)

Hornchurch is a parish and village about 2 m. S.E. of Romford. The principal monuments are the church and Nelmes.

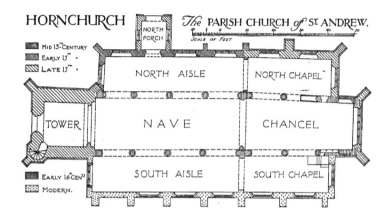

HORNCHURCH *The* PARISH CHURCH *of* S.^T ANDREW.

SCALE OF FEET

MID 13.TH CENTURY

EARLY 15TH ·

LATE 15TH ·

EARLY 16.TH CEN^Y

MODERN.

NORTH PORCH

NORTH AISLE

NORTH CHAPEL

TOWER

NAVE

CHANCEL

SOUTH AISLE

SOUTH CHAPEL

Ecclesiastical :—

^a(1). PARISH CHURCH OF ST. ANDREW (Plate, p. 70) stands on the E. side of the village. The walls are of septaria and ragstone-rubble, with some brick ; the dressings are of limestone ; the roofs are covered with lead. The *Chancel* and *Nave*, with N. and S. aisles, were built about the middle of the 13th century. Early in the 15th century the *North* and S. *Aisles* were rebuilt ; later in the same century the *North* and S. *Chapels*, the *West Tower* and the *North Porch* were added ; the clearstorey of the nave was built about the same time. The church has been restored in modern times, the *South Chapel* and *Aisle* being rebuilt in brick.

The tower is a fairly good example of its period, and among the fittings are some interesting brasses and monuments.

Architectural Description—The *Chancel* (40¼ ft. by 16½ ft.) has a modern E. window. In the N. wall is a window, all modern except the 15th-century splays and rear-arch ; further W. is a 15th-century doorway with chamfered jambs and two-centred arch ; the 15th-century N. arcade is of two bays with two-centred arches of two hollow-chamfered orders ; the column is octagonal, with moulded capital and base, and the responds have attached half columns ; above the arcade is an early 16th-century clearstorey window of three trefoiled lights in a square head and now partly blocked. The S. wall has windows and arcade uniform with those in the N. wall ; the clearstorey window is entirely blocked. In the back of the westernmost bay of the sedilia (see Fittings) is a squint from the S. chapel. The chancel-arch is

modern except for the N. respond, which is of mid 13th-century date and has three attached shafts divided by small rolls.

The *North Chapel* (31 ft. by 13¼ ft.) is of late 15th-century date and has an E. and two N. windows, each of three cinquefoiled lights with vertical tracery in a two-centred head with a moulded label. In the W. wall is an early 16th-century archway, four-centred and of two hollow-chamfered orders, the outer continuous and the inner resting on attached shafts with moulded capitals and bases.

The *South Chapel* has been almost entirely rebuilt and has, reset in the E. wall, a late 15th-century window of three cinquefoiled lights in a four-centred head. In the S. wall are two reset windows of late 15th-century date and each of three cinquefoiled lights with vertical tracery in a segmental-pointed head, patched with cement.

The *Nave* (53½ ft. by 18¼ ft.) has mid 13th-century N. and S. arcades, each of four bays with two-centred arches of two chamfered orders ; the cylindrical columns have moulded capitals and bases and the responds have attached half columns ; the S.E. respond and the capital of the N.E. respond are modern ; above the third column on the N. is a round panel enclosing a quatrefoil and five carved flowers. The 15th-century clearstorey has on each side four much restored windows, each of three cinquefoiled lights in a segmental-pointed head.

The *North Aisle* (13 ft. wide) has in the N. wall three windows similar to those in the N. chapel ; between the two western is the 15th-century N.

doorway with moulded jambs and two-centred arch in a square head with a moulded label ; the spandrels have defaced carving. In the W. wall is a window uniform with those in the N. wall.

The *South Aisle* has been rebuilt, but reset in the S. wall are three windows uniform with the S. windows in the S. chapel. In the W. wall is a reset window uniform with the E. window of the S. chapel.

The *West Tower* (16 ft. square) is of late 15th-century date and of three stages with an embattled parapet and embattled turrets rising above each angle ; on the tower is a short copper-covered spire. The two-centred tower-arch is of two moulded orders, the outer continuous and the inner resting on attached shafts with moulded capitals and bases. The W. window, restored externally, is of three cinquefoiled lights with vertical tracery in a two-centred head ; the W. doorway has moulded jambs and two-centred arch in a square head with a moulded label and plain shields in the spandrels, all restored in cement ; above the window is a stone carved with the letter M or a reversed W in relief. The ground stage is divided into two storeys by a ringing gallery. The second stage has in each wall a window of one trefoiled light in a square head, all partly restored ; the N. window is covered by a clock-face and the S. and W. windows have moulded labels. The bell-chamber has in each wall a partly restored window of three trefoiled lights in a four-centred head with a moulded label. The W. face of the parapet has a stone with the initials R F carved in relief. On the stair-turret is a niche and figure, see *Niche* under Fittings.

The *North Porch* is of the 15th century and has a two-centred outer archway of two moulded orders with double chamfered jambs. The side walls have each a window, all modern except the splays and rear-arches.

The *Roof* of the chancel is flat-pitched and of early 16th-century date ; it is of three bays with moulded main timbers and stunted king-posts ; one tie-beam is modern. The 15th-century roof of the N. chapel is of two bays with moulded main timbers and curved braces to the tie-beams, forming four-centred arches. The N. aisle has a similar roof of four bays. The roof of the nave is similar to that of the chancel, but the tie-beams are carved with grotesque faces. The 15th-century roof of the N. porch is similar to that of the N. chapel and has moulded rafters and hollow-chamfered braces and wall-posts. The modern roof of the S. chapel and aisle incorporate some old timbers and one or two old stone corbels.

Fittings—*Bell* : clock-bell said to be by Anthony Bartlet, 1674. *Brasses* and *Indents*. Brasses : In chancel—(1) to George Reede, LL.B., vicar of the parish, 1530, inscription and scroll with indents of figure and four roundels ; (2) to James Pollexfen,

B.C.L., Fellow, etc., of St. Mary's College, Oxford, 1587, inscription only ; (3) in same slab, of two wives of [William Drywode, 1602], figures of two women in hats, etc., rest of brass lost ; (4) to Homphry Drywood, 1595, inscription only, on same slab ; (5) group of five boys, *c.* 1500, on same slab ; (6) a shield of *c.* 1500, *on a cheveron three hawk's heads razed* (?), on same slab ; (7) to Peerce Pennaunte,. 1590, inscription with achievement-of-arms reset in another slab ; (8) probably to Thomas Scargile, 1475, and Elizabeth, his wife, shield-of-arms *a saltire charged with a fleur-de-lis and a border* for Scargile, indents of figure of man in armour, wife, inscription-plate and three shields ; (9) to [Katherine (Powlet), wife of William Fermor, 1510], all lost except two shields reset in indents of (8), (*a*) *a fess between three lions' heads with three anchors on the fess* for Fermor impaling a quartered shield of Powlet as (*b*), (*b*) Powlet quartering Ereby, Delamore and Skelton ; (10) of Thomas Drywood, 1591, and Anne, his wife, with figures of man and wife and groups of eight sons and three daughters, original indent of this brass with fragment of marginal inscription partly covered by organ ; (11) to Sire Boneface de Hart, canon of 'Oste' (? Aosta), late 13th or early 14th-century, indents of foliated cross, half figures of two ecclesiastics, three shields and marginal inscription in separate capitals, two letters (N and F) only remain. In N. chapel—on N. wall, (12) of Thomas Hone, 1604, with groups of six sons and six daughters, figures of man and wife reset in slab in chancel with earlier indents, shield-of-arms belonging to this brass, in another slab in chancel (see Indent (5)). Indents : In chancel—(1) of two figures and inscription-plate, early 16th-century ; (2) of figure of woman and inscription-plate, *c.* 1520 ; (3) to (?) Philip de Dovre, early 14th-century, marginal inscription in separate capitals ; (4) of figures of man and wife, two groups of children, and inscription-plate, 16th-century ; (5) of figures of man and wife, inscription-plate, and two shields, *c.* 1480 ; (6) of figure of man, inscription-plate and two shields, probably 15th-century ; (7) of inscription-plate and shield-of-arms ; (8) of figures of man and wife, two groups of children and inscription-plate, late 15th-century. In W. tower—(9) of inscription-plate ; (10) of figures of man and wife, two groups of children, inscription-plate and one shield, mid 16th-century ; (11 and 12) defaced indents. *Coffin-lids* : On N. of tower, foliated cross on stepped base, 13th-century ; on S. of tower, fragment with part of stem of cross. *Doors* : In N. doorway—of two folds, each with four vertical panels with traceried heads, moulded rail at springing level of arch and plain panels above, early 15th-century. In W. doorway—of two folds each with vertical panels, moulded rail at springing of arch ; early 16th-century. In doorway to turret-staircase of tower,

HORNCHURCH: PARISH CHURCH OF ST. ANDREW.
From the North-West.
West Tower; late 15th-century.

LITTLE WAKERING:
PARISH CHURCH OF ST. MARY.
West Tower; c. 1425.

HORNCHURCH: (3). NELMES.

Main Staircase, late 17th-century; Upper flight.

with vertical chamfered fillets and strap-hinges, early 16th-century. *Glass :* In N. chapel—in E. window, a fragmentary Crucifixion (with later female head) and Christ enthroned, and parts of two shields-of-arms (a) probably *argent billetty sable a fesse dancetty sable* for Deyncourt, (b) Deyncourt impaling *a cheveron between three wheatsheaves,* numerous fragments of a border of leopards' heads and coloured glass, tabernacle work, portions of figures, white roses, and quarries with conventional designs, 15th and 16th-century. *Image :* see Niche. *Monuments* and *Floor-slabs.* Monuments : In chancel—under N. arcade, (1) to [William Ayloffe, 1517, and Audrey (Shaa), his wife], altar-tomb with moulded slab and base, sides and end with quatrefoiled and sub-cusped panels, each enclosing a shield—(a) *a collared lion between three crosses formy,* for Ayloffe, (b) Ayloffe impaling *a cheveron ermine between three lozenges ermine,* for Shaa, (c) *a cross charged with a leopard's head a crescent for difference* for Bruges or Bridges impaling Ayloffe, (d) Ayloffe, (e) Ayloffe impaling Shaa, (f) Shaa impaling *a fesse engrailed between three cinquefoils* for Darcy, sinking for brass fillet round slab. In S. chapel—on E. wall, (2) of Humfrey Pye, 1625, alabaster and marble wall-monument with kneeling figure in civil costume at prayer-desk, carved side-pilasters, cornice and two shields-of-arms. In N. aisle—on N. wall, (3) of Richard Blakstone or Blaston, 1638, alabaster and marble wall-monument with kneeling figures of man and wife in recess with draped and curtained canopy flanked by headless female figures, achievement and two shields-of-arms. In S. chapel—on S. wall (4) to Sir Francis Prujean, 1666, marble tablet with Ionic side columns, entablature and broken pediment, achievement and two shields-of-arms. In tower—on N. wall (5) to Thomas Withring, 1651, chief Postmaster of Great Britain, marble tablet with side pilasters and obelisks, round arch and segmental pediment, achievement and two shields-of-arms, below tablet two small recumbent skeletons ; (6) to Charles Pratt, 1624, marble tablet with Corinthian side columns and broken pediment ; on S. wall (7) of Francis Rame, 1617, and Helen, his wife, 1613, marble wall-monument with kneeling figures of man and wife in recess with side pilasters and entablature, on base figures in relief of nine sons and a daughter ; (8) to Charles Ryves (Ryvius) S.T.P.; vicar of the parish, 1610, marble tablet with carved frame. In churchyard—W. of tower (9) name illegible, but of 1698, head-stone with fluted pilasters. Floor-slabs : In chancel—(1) to Sir Edward Jackman, 1650 ; (2) to Sir John Sudbury, Bart., 1691, and Bridget (Exton), his wife, also to Ann, their daughter, 1691, with achievement-of-arms. In N. chapel—(3) probably to (Richard Bl)akeston, 1638 ; (4) with name hidden, *c.* 1650, with lozenge-of-arms. In tower—(5) to George Thorowgood, 1648,

with shield-of-arms. In churchyard—E. of chancel (6) to Francis Shaw, vicar of the parish, 1696, also to Jane, 1697, Edward 1697, and Elizabeth, 1697, his children. *Niche :* On W. tower—on W. face of stair-turret, with square head and carved seated figure of bishop in mass vestments, much weathered, 15th-century. *Piscina :* In chancel—modern, but incorporating W. side of cinquefoiled arch in a square head, spandrel carved with rose and foliage, 15th-century. *Plate* (Plate, p. xliv) : includes cup and cover-paten of 1563, with bands of engraved ornament, and flagon of 1699, given in 1700, with locking-lid and whistle. *Paintings :* In nave—on S. respond of tower-arch, outline of shield, 16th or 17th-century. *Sedilia :* In chancel—of three bays divided by shafts with moulded capitals and bases, jambs with attached shafts, cinquefoiled heads, *c.* 1270, but very much restored. *Stoup :* On tower—S. of W. doorway, with stone jambs and segmental brick head, now filled in, 15th-century, repaired in the 16th century.

Condition—Structurally good, but some dressings perished and roof not altogether weather-proof.

Secular :—

c(2). HOMESTEAD MOAT, at Dovers, 3 m. S.S.W. of the church.

a(3). NELMES, house, outbuildings and moat, about 1 m. N. of the church. The *House* is of three storeys ; the walls are of brick and plastered timber-framing ; the roofs are tiled. The S.E. wing was built in the 16th century on a half H-shaped plan, with wings extending towards the S., and has a 17th-century addition on the N. At the same time the E. kitchen-wing was built. Subsequent alterations include the demolition of the kitchen-wing and a modern addition between the wings of the original house.

The main staircase is a rich example of an unusual type.

The S. front was refaced *c.* 1720. The W. elevation has a moulded string on the S. block and the 17th-century addition has rusticated angles. The N. elevation is of rusticated brick-work and has a brick eaves-cornice. The lower part of the N. wall of the kitchen-wing remains ; it is of similar rusticated brickwork and has a moulded brick plinth. Inside the building the back staircase is of early 17th-century date and has moulded handrail and strings, turned balusters and square newels with moulded knobs and pendants. In the adjoining passage is some late 16th-century panelling and there are some doors of the same date. The main staircase (Plates, pp. 71, 75) to the first floor is of late 17th-century date. It has panelled and carved newel posts, with moulded tops surmounted by spherical knobs carved with acanthus leaf, heavy moulded hand-rail and carved moulded string, and in place of balusters are large moulded panels with elaborate pierced carving of conventional foliage and flowers. The staircase is partly supported by an Ionic column standing on a shaped pedestal. In the hall is a doorway with a round moulded head, a tympanum with radial flutings and a panelled door. At the top of the stairs are some turned and twisted balusters, which are said to have been taken from the church.

The *Outbuilding*, about 100 yards S.W. of the house, is now a dwelling known as Capel Nelmes, and is said to have been the stables. It is of brick and of two storeys with attics. It was built in the 16th century and has in the N. wall two original two-light windows and one of four lights, each light having a four-centred head; in the attic is an original square-headed window of two lights. The 17th-century staircase was removed here from Nelmes in recent years and has moulded hand-rail, string and newels and heavy turned balusters.

The *Moat* is fragmentary.

Condition—Of house and outbuilding, good.

MONUMENTS (4–27).

The following monuments, unless otherwise described, are of the 17th century, and of two storeys, timber-framed and plastered or weather-boarded; the roofs are tiled or thatched. Many of the buildings have exposed ceiling-beams and original chimney-stacks.

Condition—Good, or fairly good.

High Street, N. side :—

d(4). *Dury Falls*, house, 300 yards E. of the church, was built in the 16th century, on an L-shaped plan with the wings extending towards the S.E. and N.E.; the S.E. wing was extended in the 18th century and there are large modern additions. The 17th-century main chimney-stack has six grouped diagonal shafts on a rectangular base and that at the N.E. end of the original block has two diagonal shafts on a moulded base.

d(5). *The Vicarage*, N. of the church, has modern additions on the N., E. and W., and has otherwise been much altered.

d(6). *The Hall*, 120 yards N. of the church, was built in the 16th century and has a large modern addition on the S. front. One 17th-century chimney-stack has two diagonal shafts on a rectangular buttressed base. Inside the building the dairy has a red brick floor divided into patterns by lines of bones. Another room has its floor lined with stone slabs, the centre of each slab being cut out and filled with a square of small bricks. One

room has some original panelling. There is some 17th-century brick walling in the garden N. of the house.

d(7). *The King's Head Inn*, 300 yards W.N.W. of the church, is of two storeys with attics. The original building was on an L-shaped plan, but has been added to and much modernized.

d(8). *Plough House*, shop and tenement, 500 yards N.W. of the church, was built early in the 16th-century and has modern additions on the E. and S.

The upper storey projected on the S. and W. fronts, but on the W. has been underbuilt and on the S. incorporated in the modern extension. There is a 16th-century doorway, with a four-centred head, to the shop. Inside the building is a similar doorway.

d(9). *House*, now tenements, and shop, 30 yards S.W. of (8), is of two storeys with attics; it is partly faced with brick. It was built in the 16th century on an L-shaped plan, with the wings extending towards the W. and N.; the N. wing was extended N. in the 17th century. A projecting chimney-stack on the E. front is partly of stone.

d(10). *The Bull Inn*, 100 yards W. of (9), was built probably in the 16th century and has an 18th-century block on the E. The 17th-century chimney-stack on the N. side has three diagonal shafts on a buttressed base.

d(11). *Pennant's Almshouses*, 50 yards W. of (10), were built probably *c.* 1597, but have been almost entirely rebuilt in the 18th century.

S. side :—

b(12). *House*, now three tenements, 100 yards W. of (11), was built probably in the 16th century on an L-shaped plan, with the wings extending towards the E. and S. A 17th-century chimney-stack on the S. side has two diagonal shafts.

d(13). *House*, now three tenements, 60 yards E. of (12), was built in the 16th century and has an 18th-century extension on the E. The upper storey projects in front and has a piece of a 17th or 18th-century carved fascia on the bressummer.

d(14). *House*, now two tenements and cartway, opposite (9), was built in the 15th century and was probably an inn. The upper storey of the gateway and E. wing projects on both sides; the gateway forms a gabled cross-wing and retains at the back, its original curved braces.

d(15). *House*, now two tenements, opposite (9), was built possibly in the 16th century. The upper storey at the N.E. end of the house originally projected at the back, but has now been under-built.

^d(16). *House*, 60 yards S.E. of No. 15, is of two storeys with attics. It is of L-shaped plan, with the wings extending towards the S.E. and S.W. ; the S.W. wing was built probably in the 15th century and the S.E. in the 16th century. Below the eaves in the N.W. wall of the original building is a blocked four-light window. The 17th-century chimney-stack of the S.E. wing has three diagonal shafts.

^d(17). *Cottage*, 650 yards N.W. of the church.

^d(18). *White House*, on E. side of North Street, 50 yards N. of (17), is of two storeys with attics and has modern additions on the E. The original central chimney-stack is of a cross-shaped plan, set diagonally on a square moulded base. On the E. side of the central stack is a gabled stair-turret with a central newel.

^d(19). *Hacton Farm*, house and barn, about 1,100 yards S. of the church. The *House* is of T-shaped plan, with the cross-wings at the N. end, and was built late in the 16th century and extended S. in the 17th century. The original central chimney-stack is of four grouped shafts set diagonally, and there is a blocked attic window, with moulded head, jambs and mullion in the S. wall of the 16th-century building.

The *Barn*, N. of the house, is a large building of brick, with chimney projections on the N. side, and was originally the wing of a 16th-century house. There are several original windows, now blocked, and three original fireplaces, one with a four-centred head and one blocked.

^e(20). *Brittons*, house and barns, 2 m. S.W. of the church. The *House*, though practically re-built in the 18th century, incorporates some fragments of mediaeval coursed limestone and septaria-masonry, and some 16th and 17th-century brickwork in its walls, indicating a former building of considerable size. In the attics is some 16th and 17th-century linen-fold and moulded panelling with a carved figure ; there is a reset staircase to the third storey of *c*. 1700, with a moulded handrail and string and carved and twisted balusters.

The *Barn*, S.E. of the house, is of brick. The N. wall has a moulded plinth and is of 16th-century date, but the rest of the building is modern, though some old timbers have been reused in the roof. Running E. from the barn is an old wall, the lower part of which is of flint-rubble, the upper of 16th-century brickwork and reused ashlar. The top is modern. The *Barn* S. of the above is of 16th-century brick with a moulded plinth, the E. and W. walls are gabled and have weathered copings and stepped terminals, and the N. wall is divided into nine bays by weathered buttresses. In the E. wall are the remains of an original doorway and window, with a four-centred head, above

which runs a moulded string-course. The middle entrance in the N. wall is modern, but on either side are four narrow square-headed lights with wide internal splays and there are corresponding original lights in the wall opposite. In the centre of the S. wall is a blocked doorway, with a wide four-centred head and towards the W. end of the wall is a rough heart-shaped diaper in black headers. The roof is divided into nine bays by queen-post trusses having cambered tie-beams supported by curved braces which spring off stepped brick corbels. The roof has been very much repaired.

S. of the barn is a 16th-century garden-wall enclosing a square garden. In the centre of the N. wall is a doorway with a four-centred head, to the E. of which is a V in black headers. W. of the doorway are five niches with four centred heads and there are also five niches in the W. wall. Part of the W. wall retains its original plaster.

^b(21). *Wyebridge Farm*, house, about 1¾ m. W.S.W. of the church, was built in the 16th century on an L-shaped plan with wings extending towards the S.E. and N.E. A 17th-century chimney-stack and modern extensions have been built on the N.E. side. The upper storey of the N.E. wing projects on the S.W. front, and on the N.W. front the timber-framing is exposed. An original chimney-stack in the centre of this wall is of three diagonal shafts and the two shafts of the 17th-century stack are similar ; there are two original windows with moulded frames, now blocked.

^b(22). *Crown Inn*, about 1½ m. W.N.W. of the church, is of two storeys with attics ; although it incorporates some old timbers, possibly of 17th-century date, it has been almost entirely rebuilt in modern brick. On the W. side is a modern plaster panel with the date A.D. 1433.

^b(23). *Bush Elms*, house, nearly 1¼ m. N.W. of the church, is of two storeys with attics. The E. cross-wing was built in the 15th century, but the Hall and the W. cross-wing were rebuilt in the 17th century. There are modern additions on the N. and S.W. The upper storey projects at the S. end of the original wing. The 17th-century central chimney-stack has two diagonal shafts. Inside the building the screen dividing the original wing from the former Hall remains and has two four-centred doorways, one of which is blocked. In the roof is a king-post truss with central purlin and four-way struts.

There are some fragments of worked masonry in the garden, including a piece of a 15th-century semi-octagonal respond with its moulded capital and base, and in the greenhouse are a few 13th-century glazed tiles.

^d(24). *Burnt Houses*, cottage, about 1 m. N.N.W. of the church.

d(25). *House*, now four tenements, on E. side of North Street, about 1,200 yards N.N.W. of the church, was originally of T-shaped plan ; it has been considerably added to. The original chimney-stack has two diagonal shafts.

d(26). *Lillyputs*, house, about 1 m. N.E. of the church is built partly of brick. The original house was extended S. late in the 17th century and has a modern addition on the N.

d(27). *Fairkytes*, house, 800 yards N.W. of the church, was built *c.* 1700, but has been much altered. Inside the building is an early 18th-century staircase, with turned balusters and cut string.

———

HORNDON, see HORNDON-ON-THE-HILL, EAST HORNDON and WEST HORNDON.

42. HORNDON-ON-THE-HILL. (C.d.)

(O.S. 6 in. *(a)*lxxvi. S.W. *(b)*lxxxiv. N.W.)

Horndon-on-the-Hill is a parish and village 5 m. N.N.E. of Tilbury. The church and the Old Market Hall are the principal monuments.

Ecclesiastical :—

a(1). PARISH CHURCH OF SS. PETER AND PAUL (Plates, pp. xxxviii–ix, 74) stands in the village. The walls are of ragstone and flint-rubble, with some Roman and later brick ; the dressings are of Reigate and other limestone ; the roofs are tiled. The *Chancel*, *Nave* and *North* and *South Aisles* were built early in the 13th century ; shortly afterwards a N. chapel was added. In the 15th century the chancel was lengthened towards the E., the *North Chapel*, *North Aisle* and the W. wall of the nave largely rebuilt, and the *South Porch* and *Bell-turret* added. In the 17th century the walls of the N. chapel and aisle were lowered and the main roof carried down over them. The church has been extensively restored in modern times, when much of the S. wall of the chancel was rebuilt, the N. wall refaced and the S. porch largely rebuilt.

The church is of some architectural interest and amongst the fittings the font is noteworthy.

Architectural Description—The *Chancel* (35 ft. by 18½ ft.) has an early 15th-century E. window, partly restored, and of four cinquefoiled lights with vertical tracery in a two-centred head with a moulded label and one grotesque and one defaced stop ; N. of the window and set low in the wall is a small opening (2 in. by 4 in.) ; it is square internally and of doubtful purpose. In the N. wall is a reset 13th-century lancet-window, with shafted splays and modern externally ; further W.

is an arcade of *c.* 1240, of two bays with two-centred arches of two chamfered orders ; the restored octagonal column has a moulded capital and ' hold-water ' base ; the responds have attached half columns. In the S. wall are two 15th-century windows, the eastern of two four-centred lights in a square head and the western of two trefoiled lights in a square head with a moulded label ; it is partly restored and reset in the rebuilt wall ; between the windows is a modern doorway. The 13th-century chancel-arch is two-centred and of two continuous hollow-chamfered orders, much restored.

The *North Chapel* (18½ ft. by 12 ft.) has in the E. wall a window probably of the 15th century, but much altered when the roof was lowered in the 17th century and fitted with a wooden frame. In the N. wall is a window incorporating some 17th-century bricks, with an oak frame partly of the 17th century. In the W. wall is a modern arch.

The *Nave* (50½ ft. by 16½ ft.) has early 13th-century N. and S. arcades (Plate, p. 74) of four bays with two-centred arches of four orders, the inner chamfered and the outer plain except in the fourth bay on the N. and the third on the S., where both orders are chamfered ; three of the voussoirs of the first bay on the N. have carved rosettes ; the columns are cylindrical, except the middle one on each side, which is octagonal ; the responds are semi-circular and they and the columns have moulded capitals and bases ; the capitals of both E. responds and of the two western columns on the N. are carved with conventional foliage of varying design. Above the two eastern columns of the N. arcade are two 13th-century clearstorey windows, both originally quatrefoiled ; the eastern one has now a modern external head of brick. In the W. wall is a window with a modern frame and 15th-century splays ; the 15th-century W. doorway has moulded jambs and two-centred arch in a square head with a moulded label and two-centred arch in a square head with a moulded label enclosing small heads. The 15th-century *Bell-turret* (Plate, pp. xxxviii–ix), at the W. end of the nave, stands on four posts supporting cross-beams with curved braces ; the N. and S. cross-beams are cantilevered towards the E. and support struts to the superstructure ; above the cross-beams is trellis-framing.

The *North Aisle* (12½ ft. wide) has in the N. wall three windows ; the two eastern of the 15th century and of two lights with the head cut down when the roof was lowered, and otherwise altered ; the westernmost window is a 13th-century lancet with a modern head and 17th-century repair ; the 14th or 15th-century N. doorway has a two-centred hollow-chamfered head and a moulded label ; it was blocked in the 17th century. In the W. wall is a 15th-century window of two cinquefoiled lights in a square head with a moulded label.

HORNDON-ON-THE-HILL: PARISH CHURCH OF SS. PETER AND PAUL.
Interior, showing Arcades, early 13th-century; Nave-roof, 15th-century, etc.

STAIRCASES.

LITTLE WARLEY.
Little Warley Hall; c. 1600.

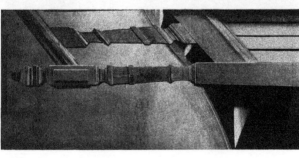

Lower Flight.

Upper Flight.

HORNCHURCH. (3) Nelmes; late 17th-century.

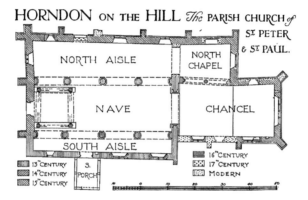

HORNDON ON THE HILL *The* PARISH CHURCH *of*
S^{T} PETER
& S^{T} PAUL.

NORTH AISLE

NORTH CHAPEL

NAVE

CHANCEL

SOUTH AISLE

13THCENTURY   14THCENTURY   15THCENTURY   S. PORCH   16THCENTURY   17THCENTURY   MODERN

The *South Aisle* (5 ft. wide) has in the S. wall
three windows, the two eastern are of the 14th
century and each of two trefoiled ogee lights with
a flowing quatrefoil in a two-centred head with
a moulded label ; the westernmost window is an
early 13th-century lancet with moulded splays and
rear-arch, carved and foliated imposts of curious
design and a restored head ; the early 13th-
century S. doorway has a round head of two
moulded orders ; the jambs have each two attached
shafts with moulded capitals and bases, all much
defaced.

The *South Porch* has been rebuilt except for the
brick plinth, but incorporates some 15th-century
timber, including the sills of the side windows and
the cusped barge-boards to the gable. The roof
is of two bays and has moulded wall-plates partly
restored and curved and moulded principals
forming two-centred arches.

The *Roof* of the chancel is of the 15th century
and of braced collar-beam type with moulded
wall-plates and one old tie-beam. The roof of
the nave was altered in the 18th century, but
incorporates two 15th-century king-post trusses
and other timbers. The modern roofs of the
N. chapel and S. aisle incorporate some old timbers.

Fittings—Bells : five, inaccessible, but said to
be : 3rd by John Waylett, 1706 ; 5th by John
Clifton, 1640. *Brass :* In chancel—to Daniel
Caldwell [1634], inscription with shield-of-arms.
Font (Plate, pp. xlii–iii): square bowl, cusped panels
cut at each end of each side, square stem with similar
panelling, hollow - chamfered base, 14th - century.
Glass : In E. window—quarries with yellow and
black design, fragment of border, and three irradiated roundels, two with "ihc," 15th-century.
Monuments and *Floor - s'abs.* Monuments : In

chancel—on N. wall (1) to Daniel Caldwell, 1634
and Alice (Mayn), his wife, alabaster and marble
wall-monument with Corinthian side columns, two
angels and three shields-of-arms. In N. aisle—on
N. wall (2) to Thomas Ashen, 1684, and Frances, his
wife, 1694, white marble tablet with broken pediment and urn. Floor-slabs : In chancel—(1) to
Susan, daughter of Jonas Sandford, 163(7 ?), with
achievement-of-arms ; (2) to Laurence Caldwell,
1631 ; (3) to Phillip Newport, 1686 ; (4) to Phillip
Newport, jun., 1690 ; (5) to Frances, only daughter
of William Grant, 1706, with achievement-of-arms ;
(6) to Jasper Kingsman, jun., 1686, with achievement-of-arms ; (7) to Jasper Kingsman, 1704,
with achievement-of-arms. In N. chapel—(8)
Susanah Sto . . ., 16(6 ?)8 ; (9) to Ann,
daughter of Thomas Caldwell, 1652. In N. aisle—
(10) to Thomas, John, William, John and Richard,
sons of Thomas Ashen, 17th-century. In churchyard—W. side (11) to Samuel Banks, 1711, and
Hannah Wilkinson, his daughter, 1703. *Niche :*
In chancel—in S. wall, with two-centred head of
reused window-tracery. *Painting :* In nave—
remains of red and black colour on columns of
both arcades, traces of foliage above N. arcade
at W. end and of scroll design above S. arcade.
Above S. doorway, scroll with text, restored.
Piscina : In chancel—with four-centred head
towards chancel and smaller opening into recess
of S.E. window, round drain, possibly early 16th-
century. *Plate* (Plate, p. xliv) : includes cup of
1567, flagon of 1700 and two 17th-century pewter
plates. *Recesses :* In nave—in E. respond of N.
arcade, small square recess. Outside W. doorway,
two square recesses, one above the other. *Sedile :*
In chancel—sill of S.E. window carried down to
form seat. *Stoup :* In S. aisle—E. of S. doorway,

THE MONUMENTS OF SOUTH-EAST ESSEX.

with square head and mutilated bowl, possibly 16th-century. *Miscellanea :* Set on corbels on N. wall of aisle, externally, parts of head of 15th-century window ; other worked stones used as borders to paths in churchyard.
Condition—Good.

Secular :—

MONUMENTS (2–18).

The following monuments, unless otherwise described, are of the 17th century and of two storeys, timber-framed and plastered or weather-boarded ; the roofs are tiled. Many of the buildings have exposed ceiling-beams and original chimney-stacks.
Condition—Good, or fairly good.

Main Street, E. side :—

ᵃ(2). *Bell Inn* (Plates, pp. xxxiv, xl), about 100 yards S.E. of the church, was built in the 15th century with wings projecting E. from the N. and S. ends. The S. wing was rebuilt in the 17th century and has a modern extension. The cart-way, with the storey above, was also rebuilt in the 17th century. The upper storey projects on the whole of the E. side, with exposed joists and timber-framing. The upper storey also projects on the S. part of the W. front. In the N. wall are three blocked windows and a blocked original door-way with a four-centred head. There is a similar doorway at the back of the N.E. wing. Inside the building the N.E. wing has an original wall-post, with a shaped head and an original king-post roof.

ᵃ(3). *Gates* (Plate, p. 64), at house, 50 yards N. of (2), are of wood and of two folds with quadrant-shaped tops and deeply moulded panels. They date from late in the 17th or early in the 18th century.

W. side :—

ᵃ(4). *Cottage,* about 200 yards S.S.E. of the church, is thatched and probably formed part of a 16th-century house. Inside the building is a 17th-century battened door.

ᵃ(5). *Old Vicarage,* 50 yards N. of (4), has been much altered and added to.

ᵃ(6). *House* (Plate, p. xl), two tenements, at N. corner of street, 100 yards N. of (5), was built in the 15th century on an L-shaped plan, with the wings extending towards the N. and W. The W. wing has a later extension. The upper storey projects on the S. side of the original W. wing. Inside the building both wings have remains of the original roof-construction.

ᵃ(7). *House* (Plate, p. xl), N. of (6), was built in the 16th century. Inside the building is an original cambered tie-beam with curved braces.

ᵃ(8). *Old Market Hall* (Plates, pp. xl, 65), now club-room, N. of (7), was built in the 16th century and originally had an open ground-storey three bays from N. to S. and two bays wide. It has now been closed in and the upper storey which projects has been largely rebuilt. The former open market hall has heavy posts and cross-beams with curved braces forming four-centred arches. Some of the curved brackets under the projecting upper storey remain.

ᵃ(9). *House,* four tenements, 50 yards N. of (8), is of L-shaped plan, with the wings extending towards the W. and N. The upper storey projects on the S. side.

ᵃ(10). *House,* two tenements, N. of (9), was built probably in the 16th century, but has been refaced with modern brick.

———

ᵃ(11). *Gore Ox* Farm, house, two tenements and barn, 550 yards W.S.W. of the church. The *House* has modern additions on the W. and N.
The *Barn,* N. of the house, is of five bays, with a roof of queen-post type.

ᵃ(12). *Linsteads Farm,* house, two tenements, and barn, 1,500 yards S.W. of the church. The *House* was built probably in the 16th century and is of L-shaped plan, with the wings extending towards the W. and S. Inside the building is an original queen-post roof-truss.
The *Barn* (Plate, p. xli), E. of the house, is cf five bays, with a roof of queen-post type.

ᵃ(13). *Great Malgraves,* house, about 1 m. N. of the church, was built probably in the 16th century, with cross-wings at the N. and S. ends. The N. wing was extended W. in the 17th century. The upper storey projects at the end of this extension and the central chimney-stack has grouped diagonal shafts.

ᵃ(14). *Wrens Park,* house, 1,100 yards N.N.E. of the church, was built late in the 17th or early in the 18th century and has a modern addition on the N.

ᵃ(15). *Rucks Farm,* house, ¼ m. N.E. of (14), was built in the 15th century, to which period the middle portion and the N.E. cross-wing belong. The S.W. part was added or rebuilt in the 16th century and the original main block raised. The upper storey projects at the S.E. end of the original cross-wing. Inside the building the cross-wing has an original king-post roof-truss. The 16th-century part has curved wind-braces to the roof.

ᵃ(16). *Arden Hall,* house, outhouses and barns, ¼ m. N.E. of the church. The *House* is of three storeys and was much altered and refronted in brick about the middle of the 18th century.

The *Outbuilding*, E. of the house, is part of a 15th-century house and has an original king-post roof-truss. S. of the house is a square building (Plate, pp. 56–7) of brick, with a pyramidal roof and built as a pigeon-house.

The *Barn*, N.E. of the house, is of five bays with a W. porch. A second barn, N.W. of the first, is also of five bays, with a S. porch ; the roof is thatched.

ᵃ(17). *The Gables* (Plate, p. 57) (formerly *Myrtle Cottage*), house, 600 yards S.S.E. of the church, has a late 17th-century and a modern addition at the back. The central chimney-stack is original and has grouped diagonal shafts and pilasters. Inside the building the main chimney-stack has a small trefoil-headed niche on the S. side. In the N.E. room is some original panelling and there are some panelled doors in the attics. The staircase, of *c.* 1700, has turned balusters and some flat shaped balusters of earlier date.

ᵇ(18). *Saffron Gardens*, house and outbuilding, about 1,100 yards S.S.W. of the church. The *House* is of L-shaped plan, with the wings extending towards the N. and E. In the 18th century two small bays were added to the S. front, probably to contain two powdering closets. In the angle of the wings is a small turret, formerly containing a newel staircase. Inside the building two rooms have original panelling and one of them has a fireplace of stone with a moulded lintel carved with figures and conventional foliage, with a shield-of-arms in the middle ; the lintel is supported by two helmeted terminal figures ; flanking the fireplace are fluted Doric pilasters of oak supporting a panelled overmantel divided into two bays ; the various parts do not fit and are evidently not *in situ*.

---

43. HUTTON. (C.c.)

(O.S. 6 in. ⁽ᵃ⁾lix. S.E. ⁽ᵇ⁾lxviii. N.W.)

Hutton is a small parish 2½ m. E.N.E. of Brentwood.

Ecclesiastical :—

ᵇ(1). PARISH CHURCH OF ALL SAINTS stands near the middle of the parish. The walls are of flint-rubble, with limestone dressings ; the roofs are tiled. The church was apparently rebuilt in the 14th century, when it consisted of a chancel, *Nave* and N. and S. aisles. The *North Porch* was added late in the same century, and the timber *Bell-turret* built in the 15th century. The church was very largely rebuilt in 1873, the *Chancel*, *Aisles* and *North* and *South Chapels* being entirely modern.

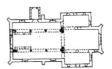

Architectural Description—The *Nave* (36 ft. by 12½ ft.) has in the E. wall a 14th-century two-centred chancel-arch of one moulded and one chamfered order ; the responds have each three attached shafts with moulded capitals and bases. The N. and S. arcades are both of the 14th century and are each of three bays with two-centred arches of one moulded and one chamfered order ; the columns are of quatrefoiled plan with moulded capitals and bases and the responds have attached half columns ; the work has been considerably scraped and repaired. The W. window is modern.

The *Bell-turret* at the W. end of the nave is of the 15th-century and stands on six oak posts with cross-beams and curved braces.

The *North* and *South Aisles* are modern, but have windows incorporating old material. The N. doorway is of late 14th-century date reset and much restored ; it has moulded jambs and two-centred arch with a moulded label and one modern and one defaced head-stop.

The *North Porch* is of late 14th-century date and of timber standing on modern dwarf walls. The three-centred outer archway has a beam over it carved with trefoils. The barge-boards are cusped. The side walls have each four lights with trefoiled ogee and traceried heads ; the wall-plates are moulded.

The *Roof* of the nave is probably of late 14th-century date and is of two bays with moulded wall-plates and king-post trusses. The roofs of the aisles are continued down from the main roof and have moulded wall-plates.

Fittings—*Bells :* five ; 2nd by Anthony Bartlet, 1655 ; 3rd by William Land, 1637. *Brasses :* In S. chapel—on S. wall (1) of man in plate-armour and woman in pedimental head-dress, groups of eight sons and eight daughters, *c.* 1525 ; on W. wall (2) to George White, 1584, inscription only. *Monument :* In S. aisle—on W. wall, to Thomas Cory, 1656, prothonotary of the Court of Common Pleas, also to Judith (Clitherow), his wife, 1663, black and white marble tablet with pediment and shield-of-arms. *Piscinae :* In N. vestry—in E. wall, with trefoiled head, no drain, probably late 14th-century, reset. In rectory garden — with cinquefoiled head and broken drain, late 14th-century. *Plate :* includes cover-paten of 1567, and stand-paten, probably of 1648, with the arms of Cory. *Recess :* In S. aisle—in S. wall, small square-headed recess.

Condition—Good, much restored.

Secular :—

b(2). HOMESTEAD MOAT, at Hutton Hall, N.W. of the church.

b(3). HOUSE, on S. side of road, 700 yards N.E. of the church, is of two storeys with attics, timber-framed and plastered ; the roofs are tiled. It was built probably in the 17th century and has an original coved eaves-cornice of plaster and a central chimney-stack also original.
Condition—Good.

a(4). CRUSH'S FARM, house, ¾ m. N.N.W. of the church, is of two storeys, timber-framed and plastered ; the roofs are tiled. It was built probably early in the 16th century and has a cross-wing at the N. end. The upper storey projects at both ends of the cross-wing, but the projection at the W. end has been underbuilt. Inside the building the original ceiling-beams and joists are exposed and the cross-wing has an original cambered tie-beam with curved braces.
Condition—Good.

———

44. INGRAVE. (B.c.)

(O.S. 6 in. *(a)*lxvii. N.E. *(b)*lxvii. S.E.)

Ingrave is a small parish 2 m. S.E. of Brentwood.

Ecclesiastical :—

a(1). PARISH CHURCH OF ST. NICHOLAS was entirely rebuilt on a new site about 1734. The site of the old church is indicated by a depression in the ground S.W. of Ingrave Hall. The new church contains the following :—
Fittings—*Brasses* and *Indents*. Brasses : In chancel—(1) (Plate, p. 78) of [Margaret, daughter of Sir Lewis John, wife successively of Sir William Lucy and . . . Wake, 1466], figure of woman in butterfly head-dress, fragment of marginal inscription and four shields-of-arms—(*a*) *a cheveron between three trefoils*, for FitzLewes, impaling Montagu and Monthermer quarterly ; (*b*) *crusilly three luces*, for Lucy impaling FitzLewes ; (*c*) Wake impaling FitzLewes ; (*d*) *crusilly a cross*, for Goshalm, impaling FitzLewes, indent of inscription and scroll ; (2) (Plate, p. 78) cf [Sir Richard FitzLewes, 1528, and his four wives (*a*) Alice (Harleston) ; (*b*) unknown ; (*c*) Elizabeth (Sheldon) ; and (*d*) Joan (Hornby)], figure of man in plate-armour with tabard of arms, FitzLewes quartering Goshalm, head on crested helm, feet on dog, figures of four wives with pedimental head-dresses and (*a*), (*c*) and (*d*) with heraldic mantles—(*a*) *a leaping goat* for Bardwell quartering *three roundels* for Heath, *quarterly* for Pagenham, and *a bend between two dancetty cotices with an ermine tail on the bend*, for Clopton, all impaling FitzLewes ; (*c*) FitzLewes impaling *a cross* for Sheldon ; (*d*) FitzLewes

impaling *three bugle-horns* for Hornby quartering *ermine*, indents of two groups of children. Both brasses formerly in the church of West Horndon (now destroyed). Indents : In front of S. door-way—defaced. *Communion Table :* In vestry—with turned legs, 17th-century. *Font :* Octagonal bowl with quatrefoiled panels, moulded edge and base, early 16th-century. *Monument :* In front of W. doorway—slab of former altar-tomb.
Condition—Rebuilt.

Secular :—

a(2). BARN and moat, at Ingrave Hall, nearly ¾ m. N. of the church. The *Barn* was built probably in the 16th century and is timber-framed and weather-boarded. It is of six bays, with a roof of queen-post type and a N. porch.
The *Moat* E. of the barn is well preserved.
Condition—Of barn, good.

a(3). SALMOND'S FARM, house, 160 yards N.E. of the church, is of two storeys, timber-framed and plastered ; the roofs are tiled. It was built probably in the 15th century, with a central Hall and cross-wings at the N. and S. ends. The hall was divided into two storeys probably late in the 16th century, when the central chimney-stack was inserted. The upper storey projects at the W. end of the N. cross-wing and the main chimney-stack has two diagonal shafts. Inside the building some of the ceiling-beams are exposed and there are remains of the original roof-construction.
Condition—Good.

———

45. LAINDON. (C.c.)

(O.S. 6 in. *(a)*lxvii. S.W. *(b)*lxviii. S.E.)

Laindon is a parish 3 m. S. of Billericay. The church is interesting.

Ecclesiastical :—

b(1). PARISH CHURCH OF ST. NICHOLAS stands in the middle of the parish. The walls are of ragstone-rubble, with some pudding-stone, brick and flint ; the W. annexe is timber-framed ; the dressings are of Reigate and Barnack-stone ; the roofs are tiled. The *Nave* is possibly of 12th-century origin, though the proportions and thickness of the walls are the only evidence of this date. The *South Chapel* was added *c.* 1330 and about the same time the nave and chancel were perhaps largely rebuilt. The *South Porch* was added in the 15th century and the *Bell-turret* is probably of the same date. Early in the 17th century the *West Annexe* was added or rebuilt, probably for use as a school. The church has been restored in modern times.

Sir Richard FitzLewes, 1528, and his four wives.

Margaret, wife of Sir William Lucy, and
afterwards of . . . Wake, 1466.

INGRAVE: PARISH CHURCH OF ST. NICHOLAS.

Brasses in Chancel-floor: brought from West Horndon Church.   (Approximately one-twelfth full size.)

SANDON : PARISH CHURCH OF ST. ANDREW.
Pulpit : late 15th century.

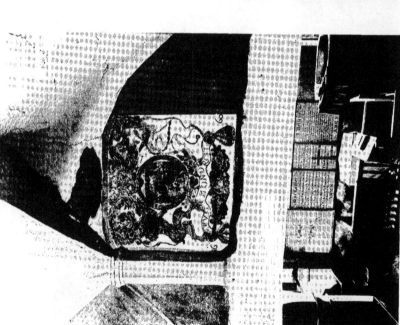

LAINDON HILLS : PARISH CHURCH OF ALL SAINTS.
Interior, showing painted Royal Arms : 1660.

LAINDON
The PARISH CHURCH *of* S^T NICHOLAS

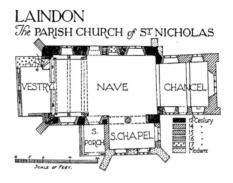

NAVE

VESTRY CHANCEL

S. PORCH S.CHAPEL

12 Century
14 ·
15 ·
16 ·
17 ·
Modern

SCALE OF FEET.

Architectural Description—The *Chancel* (19 ft. by 16 ft.) has an E. window, all modern except the 14th-century splays and rear-arch. In the N. wall are two windows, the eastern modern except for the 15th-century splays and rear-arch, and the western of the 15th century; both are of two trefoiled lights in a square head with a moulded label. In the S. wall are two 15th-century windows, both partly restored, and similar to the windows in the N. wall; between them is a 16th-century doorway with a three-centred head and restored jambs. There is no chancel-arch.

The *Nave* (38½ ft. by 22 ft.) has in the N. wall three windows, the easternmost is of the 15th century, partly restored, and of two cinquefoiled lights in a square head; the second window is of the 14th century and of one light, now blocked; the westernmost window is modern except for the 15th-century splays and rear-arch and part of one jamb; the partly restored 15th-century N. doorway has moulded jambs and two-centred arch. In the E. half of the S. wall is an arcade of c. 1330 and of two bays with two-centred arches of two chamfered orders dying on to the responds; the octagonal column has a moulded capital and base; the S. doorway is similar to the N. doorway, except that the head is modern; further W. is a partly restored 15th-century window of two cinque-foiled lights in a square head with a moulded label and head and grotesque stops.

The *Bell-turret*, at the W. end of the nave, rests on posts with heavy curved braces, forming a two-centred arch, and subsidiary struts (Plate, pp. xxxviii–ix); above the cross-beams the framing is of trellis-form; the turret itself has two cinque-foiled lights of wood in each face and supports a shingled spire (Plate, pp. xxxviii–ix).

The *South Aisle* or *Chapel* (17 ft. by 9 ft.) has in the E. wall a partly restored 15th-century

window of two cinquefoiled lights in a square head with a moulded label. In the S. wall, which has been rebuilt, are two similar windows, all modern except the 15th-century splays and rear-arches.

The *West Annexe* (10¾ ft. by 15 ft.) is timber-framed and of two storeys with an attic; it is roofed with a gable towards the W. (Plate, pp. xxxviii–ix). Part of the N. wall and the N.W. angle are of 18th-century brick. The ceiling-beams are plain and the windows and doorways are modern. On the E. face of the E. wall is a 16th-century moulded cornice or string. The W. wall of the nave has been mostly removed, its place being taken by a timber-framed partition.

The *South Porch* has been rebuilt, but incorporates the 15th-century outer archway of oak, with a four-centred head and spandrels carved with foliage and rosettes. Against the S. doorway of the nave is a similar archway, the spandrels are carved with a dragon and a scallop-shell, etc., on one side, and a beast pierced with a patriarchal cross on the other.

The *Roof* of the chancel (Plate, p. 48) is of late 15th-century date and of two bays with moulded main timbers, embattled purlins and wall-plates with carved cresting; the principals have curved braces springing from wall-posts and forming three-centred arches; the wind-braces have traceried spandrels. The 15th-century roof of the nave is of two bays with king-post trusses, the middle tie-beam is moulded and has curved braces; the E. truss is modern. The 15th-century roof of the S. chapel is of braced collar-beam type.

Fittings — *Bells:* five, said to be: 2nd by Thomas Bartlet, 1619, with the name "James Harris"; 3rd and 4th by John Bird, 15th-century, and inscribed respectively "Johannes Cristi Care Dignare Pro Nobis Orare" and "Sum Rosa

Pulsata Mundi Katerina Vocata" ; 5th by Robert Mot, 1588. *Brasses* and *Indents.* Brasses: In chancel—on N. wall (1) of priest in mass vestments with chalice and wafer, *c.* 1480 ; on S. wall (2) of priest in mass vestments with chalice and wafer, *c.* 1510. Indents : In chancel—(1) of brass (1) ; in nave (2) of brass (2) ; both with indent of inscription-plate ; (3) of priest and inscription-plate. *Chest :* In annexe—lid with moulded edge and three straps, two straps at angles and two old locks, 17th-century. *Door :* In S. doorway—of nail-studded battens with strap-hinges, 15th-century. *Font* (Plate, pp.xlii–iii): square bowl, each face with five shallow pointed panels, early 13th-century, stem modern. *Glass :* In E. window, fragments, including a fleur-de-lis growing out of a leopard's head, 16th-century ; other small fragments in windows of chancel, nave and S. chapel. *Inscriptions :* In nave—on W. wall, five painted panels with cherubs in the angles, some with texts and inscription recording benefactions of John Puckle, 1617. *Monument :* In S. chapel—in S. wall, recess with chamfered and segmental-pointed arch, 14th-century, probably tomb-recess. *Panelling :* In annexe—some early 17th and 18th-century panelling not *in situ. Piscinae :* In chancel—with trefoiled ogee head and round drain, partly broken, 14th-century. In S. chapel—in S. wall, with two-centred head, drain missing, probably 15th-century. *Plate :* includes cup of 1656, with baluster stem and a paten of 1672, probably of secular origin and with repoussé work of flowers and a hound chasing a lion. *Stoup :* In nave—E. of S. doorway, with two-centred head, bowl cut away, probably 15th-century. *Table :* In annexe—with turned baluster legs and shaped brackets, late 17th-century. *Miscellanea :* In nave—at W. end, piece of woodwork carved with guilloche ornament and the date 1630.

Condition—Good.

Secular :—

a(2). HOMESTEAD MOAT, at Great Gubbins Farm, about ¾ m. W.S.W. of the church.

b(3). LAINDONPONDS, house and moat, about 1¼ m. N.E. of the church. The *House* is of two storeys, timber-framed and plastered ; the roofs are tiled. It is a long rectangular building, with a cross-wing at the S. end and was built probably early in the 17th century and extended northwards at a later date. Two of the chimney-stacks are original. Inside the building some of the rooms have exposed ceiling-beams.

The *Moat* surrounds the house and is in an excellent state of preservation.

Condition—Of house, poor.

MONUMENTS (4–7).

The following monuments, unless otherwise described, are of the 17th century, and of two storeys, timber-framed and plastered or weather-boarded ; the roofs are tiled. Some of the buildings have original chimney-stacks and exposed ceiling-beams.

Condition—Good, unless noted.

b(4). *Laindon Hall,* house, a few yards E. of the church, is of T-shaped plan, with the cross-wing at the N. end ; it was built probably in the 15th century, but has been considerably altered. The upper storey of the S. wing originally projected on the E. front, but has been underbuilt.

b(5). *Prince of Wales Inn,* 1,200 yards N.N.E. of the church, is of central-chimney type. It has a modern W. extension.

b(6). *Petchey's Farm,* 100 yards E. of (5), is of central-chimney type. A modern addition has been added to the two diagonal shafts of the original chimney-stack.

Condition—Poor.

b(7). *Puckles Farm,* 500 yards E.N.E. of (6), is of central-chimney type. An early 18th-century addition and a modern extension on the N.W. makes the plan L-shaped.

---

46. LAINDON HILLS. (C.d.)

(O.S. 6 in. *(a)*lxxvi. N.W. *(b)*lxxvi. N.E.)

Laindon Hills is a parish on the high ground 7 m. N.N.E. of Tilbury. The church is the principal monument.

Ecclesiastical :—

a(1). PARISH CHURCH OF ALL SAINTS (Plate, p. xxxiii) stands towards the S.W. corner of the parish. The walls are partly of ragstone and flint-rubble and partly of red brick ; the dressings are of limestone ; the roofs are tiled. The *Nave* and *Chancel* were built in brick early in the 16th century, but the flint-rubble in the lower part of the walls and the jamb-stones of the S. doorway indicate the existence of an earlier building. Early in the 17th century a N. chapel was added and later in the same century the *South Porch* was built. The *North Chapel* was rebuilt about 1834 and the W. wall and bell-turret are also modern.

Among the fittings the Royal Arms painted on plaster are noteworthy.

Architectural Description—The *Chancel* (15 ft. square) has an early 16th-century E. window of brick and of three four-centred lights with vertical tracery in a two-centred head with a moulded label. In the N. wall is an early 17th-century arcade of two bays with round arches of two chamfered orders and an octagonal column and semi-octagonal responds with moulded capitals; the whole is in plastered brick; on the S. face, between the arches are the initials and date R.E. 1621, in plaster. In the S. wall is an early 16th-century window of brick and of two four-centred lights in a four-centred head. The chancel is structurally undivided from the nave.

The *Nave* (32¾ ft. by 14½ ft.) has in the N. wall an early 16th-century window with a four-centred head, now blocked; further W. is the modern N. doorway. In the S. wall is a window similar to the S. window of the chancel; further W. is the S. doorway with mediaeval chamfered lower jambs of stone and early 16th-century segmental arch and upper jambs of brick, with a square moulded label. In the W. wall is a modern window.

The *South Porch* is of 17th-century brick and has an outer archway with a plain wooden lintel.

The *Roof* of the chancel is plastered, but has a central purlin and a tie-beam at the W. end with mortices for a former screen in the soffit and plastered framing above it. The early 16th-century roof of the nave is also plastered, but has one king-post truss and above the wall-plate on the N. side is the inscription in plaster "Thomas Richardson John Elliett Nov 1666"; the W. bay of the roof is modern. The S. porch has a 17th-century collar-beam roof.

Fittings—*Bells:* two, 1st uninscribed; 2nd by Thomas Lawrence, early 16th-century. *Brass Indent:* In nave—of heads of man and woman (?), and marginal inscriptions, early 14th-century. *Communion Table:* In chancel—with turned legs and shaped brackets under top rails, late 17th-century. *Communion Rails:* with turned balusters and square posts, moulded rail with initials and date S.S.R. 1686 W.E.C. *Font:* In stables at rectory—octagonal bowl with moulded upper and lower edge, trefoil-headed panels in each face and on stem, moulded base, 15th-century. *Monument* and *Floor-slabs.* Monument: In churchyard—S. side, to Robert Benton, 1712, head-stone. Floor-slabs: In chancel—(1) to Thomas Richardson, 1669; (2) to Ann, wife of Thomas Richardson, 1630, also to Elizabeth, wife of Thomas Richardson, son of the above, 1666, and George and Elizabeth, two of her children. *Panelling:* In nave—incorporated in pew, 17th-century. *Royal Arms* (Plate, p. 79): on plastered framing between nave and chancel, painted arms dated 1660, and below it black-letter inscription from Proverbs 24, 21 and the name John Elliett, Churchwarden.

Condition — Disused and rapidly becoming ruinous.

Secular :—

a(2). LITTLE MALGRAVES, house and barn, ½ m. W.S.W. of the church. The *House* is of two storeys with attics; the walls are of plastered brick; the roofs are tiled. It was built late in the 17th century on a square plan and has half-hipped gables on the N. and S. On the E. front is an original door of moulded battens; inside the building some of the ceiling-beams are exposed. The *Barn* S. of the house is of the same date; the walls are of brick and the roofs are tiled. It has a projecting porch on the E. side and is eight bays long.

Condition—Fairly good.

b(3). NORTHLANDS HOUSE, ¾ m. E.S.E. of the church, is modern but incorporates the following pieces of old glass in its windows. (1) An oval cartouche of the arms of Henry VII. with supporters, and a 'black-letter' inscription. (2) A panel inscribed "Gulielm d'Albini Seigneur de Molbray, ceu de Mowbray, Robert de Roos, Radulp de Giffard Vicecomes, Gualter de Thany Vicecomes, Johannes de Chauncey 1479, Dom. Joannes Gore Miles Praetor Urbis 1624," all 17th-century. (3) An oval bay-chaplet with clasps and bands, the shield missing, 16th-century, partly restored. (1) and (2) are parts of a series painted in the 17th century, probably for Sir John Gore, Lord Mayor of London, in 1624.

---

47. LATCHINGDON. (F.b.)

(O.S. 6 in. (*a*)lxii. N.E. (*b*)lxii. S.E.)

Latchingdon is a parish on the left bank of the Crouch, 5 m. S.S.E. of Maldon.

Ecclesiastical :—

b(1). OLD PARISH CHURCH OF ST. MICHAEL (Plate, p. xxxiii) stands about the middle of the parish. The walls are of rubble and brick, with dressings of limestone; the roofs are tiled. The *Nave* is of uncertain date, but possibly of the 14th century, when the *South Porch* was added. At some uncertain period the former chancel or apse was destroyed. About 1618 part of the N. wall of the nave was rebuilt in brick. The church has been restored in modern times, the E. wall rebuilt and the W. wall largely refaced.

Architectural Description—The *Nave* (38½ ft. by 19½ ft.) has in the N. wall a 17th-century window of brick and of three round-headed lights in a

F

square head, with modern mullions ; further W. is a doorway of the same date, with a three-centred rear-arch, and now blocked. In the S. wall are two windows ; the eastern is of the 15th century and of two cinquefoiled lights in a square head with a moulded label ; the western window is of doubtful date and is a single narrow light with a square 17th-century head of brick ; between the windows is the late 14th-century S. doorway with double chamfered jambs and two-centred arch. In the W. wall is a modern window. At the W. end of the nave are four posts and framing to carry a former bell-turret and gallery.

The *South Porch* has a late 14th-century outer archway with moulded jambs and two-centred arch.

The *Roof* of the nave has two old tie-beams, one moulded and of 15th-century date. The 17th-century roof of the porch has plain rafters and purlins.

Fittings—Bell : one, uninscribed, date uncertain. *Brass Indents :* (1) of three figures, inscription-plate and two shields ; (2) of two figures and inscription-plate. *Communion Table :* with turned legs and enriched top rail, late 17th-century. *Inscriptions :* On stones in N. wall of nave— "Mathew Bets and Robert Peirc mad this wall 1618" and "Mathew Drakes Edmund Catmur churchwardenes when this wall was built 1618 IRIX." *Plate :* includes cup of 1639. *Stoup :* In porch—with chamfered jambs and two-centred head, 14th-century, basin partly destroyed.

Condition—Fairly good.

^a(2). SITE OF ST. PETER'S CHURCH, SNOREHAM, about ½ m. N.N.W. of (1), is marked by a rectangular area in a meadow S. of Snoreham Hall.

Secular :—

HOMESTEAD MOATS.

^a(3). At Good Hares, 1 m. N.N.E. of the church.

^a(4). At Lawling Hall, ¾ m. N.E. of (3).

^a(5). At Greenlane Farm, ¾ m. S.E. of (4).

^b(6). TYLE HALL, house and moat, 500 yards E. of the church. The *House* is of two storeys, timber-framed and plastered ; the roofs are tiled. It was built probably in the 16th century, with cross-wings at the E. and W. ends. There is a modern addition on the W.

The *Moat* surrounds the house.

Condition—Of house, good, much altered.

^a(7). LONDONHAYS, house, ¾ m. W. of (2), is of two storeys, timber-framed and partly plastered and partly weather-boarded ; the roofs are tiled. It was built probably in the 17th century and has an addition on the E. The upper storey projects at the N. end of the main block.

Condition—Fairly good.

^a(8). BROOK HALL, formerly Lawling Smiths, house, ¼ m. S. of (4), is of two storeys, timber-framed and weather-boarded ; the roofs are tiled. It was built probably in the 17th century and has a cross-wing at the E. end. Inside the building the ceiling-beams are exposed.

Condition—Fairly good.

Unclassified :—

^a(9). RED HILL, N.E. of Butterfield's Farm, ⅜ m. N. of the modern church.

48. LEE CHAPEL. (C.d.)

No monuments known.

49. LEIGH. (E.d.)

(O.S. 6 in. lxxviii. S.W.)

Leigh is a parish and town on the N. bank of the Thames estuary, 2 m. W. of Southend-on-Sea.

Ecclesiastical :—

(1). PARISH CHURCH OF ST. CLEMENT stands in the town. The walls are of ragstone and flint-rubble, except the S. porch which is of brick ; the dressings are of ragstone and limestone ; the roofs are tiled. The whole church, including *Chancel, Nave, North Aisle* and *Chapel* and *West Tower* appears to have been rebuilt late in the 15th or early in the 16th century. Shortly after the *South Porch* and the rood stair-turret were added. The church was restored in the 19th and 20th centuries, when the chancel was extended about 16 ft. to the E., *North Vestries, South Chapel* and *Aisle* added.

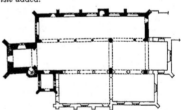

Architectural Description—All the ancient details are of late 15th or early 16th-century date.

The *Chancel* (41 ft. by 20½ ft.) is entirely modern E. of the arcades. The N. arcade is of two bays, with two-centred arches of two hollow-chamfered orders ; the first arch is low and narrow, the second is wide and struck from below the springing-level ; the column is octagonal with moulded capital and base ; the responds have attached half-columns ; the arcade has been restored in plaster. The S. arcade is modern. The chancel-arch is of modern plaster, but the N. respond may be old but is covered with plaster.

The *Nave* (53¼ ft. by 20¼ ft.) has a N. arcade of four bays, with arches, columns and responds of similar detail to those of the N. arcade of the chancel. The S. arcade is modern, but W. of it is the old S. doorway with moulded jambs and two-centred arch and label.

The *North Chapel* and *Aisle* (16¼ ft. wide) has an E. window of four cinquefoiled lights with vertical tracery in a two-centred head with a moulded label. In the N. wall are four windows, each of three cinquefoiled lights in segmental-pointed heads; further W. is the N. doorway, now blocked, with moulded jambs, two-centred arch and label, much weathered; between the second and third windows is the lower part of the doorway to the rood stair-turret, with rebated jambs and now blocked. In the W. wall is a window of four cinquefoiled lights, with vertical tracery in a two-centred head.

In the modern S. aisle, the S. doorway incorporates some 15th-century moulded jamb-stones.

The *West Tower* (14 ft. by 13 ft.) is of three stages, with a moulded plinth and an embattled parapet with an embattled turret rising above its S.E. angle. The two-centred tower-arch is of three hollow-chamfered orders; the splayed responds have each an attached shaft with moulded capital and base. In the N. wall is a modern window. In the S. wall is a doorway to the turret-staircase, with hollow-chamfered jambs and two-centred head. The W. window is of two cinque-foiled and one trefoiled light with tracery in a two-centred head with a moulded label; all restored in cement; the W. doorway has moulded jambs and two-centred arch in a square head with a moulded label and blank shields in the spandrels, all restored in cement. The second stage has a single-light window in the W. wall. The bell-chamber has in each wall a window of three trefoiled lights in a four-centred head with a moulded label, all restored in cement.

The *South Porch* is of red brick with a moulded plinth having trefoil-headed panels of flint-inlay. The outer archway has moulded jambs and four-centred arch with a double label, the outer being square-headed and enclosing foiled spandrels. The side walls have each a window of two four-centred lights in a four-centred head with a moulded label.

The *Roof* of the N. aisle is of five bays plastered under the rafters, but with curved and moulded principals springing from corbels carved with figures holding shields; the wall-plates are moulded and embattled.

Fittings—*Bells*: six; 3rd by Miles Graye, 1674. *Brasses*: In chancel—(1) of Richard Chester, 1632, elder brother and master of Trinity House, figure of man in civil dress, and wife, four sons and one daughter; (2) to Captain John Price, 1709, and Martha (Godman), his wife, 1696, with

(8220)

achievement-of-arms; (3) figure of man and wife in civil dress, c. 1640; (4) to Thomas Saman, and Thomas, his grandson, 1576, inscription only. In N. chapel—(5) to Robert Salmon, 1641, inscription only; (6) to Robert Salmon, 1591, inscription only. In nave—(7) to George Ireland, 1570, inscription only. In N. aisle—(8) of Richard Haddok, 1453, and Cristine, his wife, and to John, their son, and Alice, his wife, also to Margaret, second wife of Richard, figures of two men in civil dress and their wives and groups of seven sons and three daughters and eight sons and three daughters. *Door*: In tower—in doorway of turret-staircase, of nail-studded battens with moulded fillets, late 15th-century. *Monuments* and *Floor-slabs*: In N. aisle—on N. wall (1) to Anne, wife of Sir Edward Whitaker, 1705, white marble tablet with side-columns, voluted pediment and achievement-of-arms; (2) of Robert Salmon (see Brass (3)), 1641, master of Trinity House and sheriff of London, alabaster and black marble, tablet with half figure, side pilasters, cornice and achievement-of-arms. In churchyard—E. end (3) to Capt. Richard Haddock, 1660(?), Capt. William Haddock, 166–, Anna Haddock, 1688, Elizabeth Haddock, 1709, and Sir Richard Haddock, 1714, Controller of the Navy, table-tomb; (4) to Capt. William Goodlad, 1639, "chief commander of the Greenland fleet 20 years" and master of Trinity House, panelled table-tomb with scroll borders and rusticated arched enrichment; (5) to Richard Goodlad, 1690, and Elizabeth, his wife, 1712, table-tomb; S. side (6) to Sarah, wife of Richard Goodlad, 1685, table-tomb with panelled sides and ornamental pilasters; (7) to Sarah, widow of Joseph Cadman, 1710, head-stone. *Floor-slabs*: In chancel—(1) to Elizabeth Stevens, 1700, and to Mary, wife of Capt. Whitaker, 1698; (2) to James Moyer, 1661. In S. chapel—(3) to John Burdocke, 1601, and John, his son, and others later, with mariner's compass at top. In nave—(4) to Thomas Printer (?), c. 1700; (5) to Ann Thomson, 1712, and others later. In churchyard—S. side (6) to William Hampton, 1624. *Poor-box*: In nave—square oak box, with three hasps and lid inscribed "I pray you the pore remember," square baluster stem, c. 1630.

Condition—Good.

MONUMENTS (2–8).

The following monuments, unless otherwise described, are of the 17th century and of two storeys, timber-framed and plastered or weather-boarded; the roofs are tiled. Some of the buildings have original chimney-stacks and exposed ceiling-beams.

Condition—Good.

(2). *Leigh House*, 20 yards N.W. of the church, is of two storeys with attics. It has been much altered and refaced and has modern additions at the back and N. side.

High Street, N. side :—

(3). *Cooksplace,* house, now three tenements, 300 yards W.S.W. of the church, is of two storeys with attics. It is rectangular on plan, with a N. staircase block on either side of which are modern additions. Inside the building part of the staircase is original, and has moulded handrail, turned balusters and a square newel with a carved top.

(4). *House,* 30 yards W.N.W. of (3). The N. end was built in the 15th century and is possibly a fragment of a larger house. The S. end being a 16th-century addition. The upper storey originally projected along the whole of the E. side, but has now been underbuilt, and the S. front has been refaced with brick. Inside the building in the wall between the original building and the 16th-century addition, on the ground-floor is a blocked two-light window. In the roof of the N. block is an original cambered tie-beam with curved braces and a two-way king-post.

(5). *Crooked Billet Inn,* 150 yards W.N.W. of (4), is of two storeys with attics and was built probably late in the 16th century. It has been much altered and added to. There are two original chimney-stacks, each with three grouped diagonal shafts. Inside the building on the ground-floor is an original fireplace with a four-centred head.

S. side :—

(6). *House,* now three tenements, 40 yards E.S.E. of (5), has modern additions at the back.

(7). *House,* now four tenements, 120 yards E.S.E. of (6), is of two storeys with attics and was built in the 16th century on a half H-shaped plan, with the cross-wings extending towards the E. The space between the wings has been filled in by a modern extension and there are modern additions at both ends of the building. Inside the building is an original staircase with a central newel and the roof retains a queen-post truss with cambered tie-beams, curved wind-braces and octagonal queen-posts.

(8). *House* (Plate, pp. xxxiv–v), now two tenements, 50 yards W. of (7), is of two storeys with attics and was built late in the 16th century. The roof has since been heightened and the building altered and added to on the N.W. and S.W. The upper storey projects on the whole of the N.E. front.

---

50. LITTLE BURSTEAD. (C.c.)

(O.S. 6 in. (ᵃ)lxviii. N.W. (ᵇ)lxviii. S.W.)

Little Burstead is a parish 2 m. S. of Billericay. The church, Stockwell Hall and Hatches Farm are the principal monuments.

Ecclesiastical :—

ᵇ(1). PARISH CHURCH OF ST. MARY (?) stands a short distance S. of the village. The walls are of pudding-stone and ragstone-rubble, with limestone and brick dressings. The roofs are tiled. The church consisting of *Chancel* and *Nave* is probably of early 13th-century date. The S. wall of the chancel is probably of a later date. A S. porch and the *Bell-turret* were added probably in the 15th century. The church was altered in the 16th century, when the S.E. angle of the nave was rebuilt, and has been restored in modern times when the *South Porch* was rebuilt and the *North Vestry* added possibly on the site of an earlier building.

Architectural Description—The *Chancel* (21 ft. by 15½ ft.) has an early 16th-century E. window of brick and of three round-headed lights with vertical tracery in a two-centred head with a moulded label. In the N. wall is a modern doorway. In the S. wall are two 16th-century brick windows, each of two pointed lights in a four-centred head with a moulded label ; between them is a much restored early 16th-century doorway with chamfered jambs and two-centred arch in a square head with a moulded label and shield-stops, one charged with—*two cheverons and an engrailed border* for Tyrell. There is no chancel-arch.

The *North Vestry* is modern but reset in the N. wall is an early 16th-century window of brick and of one light with a moulded label.

The *Nave* (36½ ft. by 21½ ft.) has in the N. wall two windows ; the eastern is of the 14th century or later and of one pointed light ; it is set in a recess cut back in the wall, probably to provide more room for a nave-altar or for a rood or rood-loft staircase ; the western window is an early 13th-century lancet ; further W. is the 13th-century N. doorway, with chamfered jambs and two-centred arch, and now blocked. Against the E. wall, S. of the chancel, is a length of moulded oak beam, probably part of the reredos of a nave-altar. The S.E. angle of the nave is of 16th-century brick with black brick diapering ; in the S. wall is a 15th-century window of three cinquefoiled lights with vertical tracery in a square head and all modern externally except parts of the label ; the S. doorway is probably of the 13th century and has jambs and two-centred arch of two plain orders. In the W. wall is a partly restored early

CHADWELL.
N. Doorway; early 15th-century. Doorhead above; 12th-century.

BASILDON.
Spandrel of truss in roof of Porch, with bear and ragged staff; mid 15th-century.

GREAT BURSTEAD.
Spandrels of N. Doorway with the Annunciation; late 15th or early 16th-century.

LITTLE WAKERING.
Panel in West Tower with arms of John Wakering, Bishop of Norwich, 1416–25.

EAST TILBURY.
S. wall of Chancel: Doorways and Windows; 13th-century and later.

DANBURY.
Doorway and Niches in W. Tower; mid 14th-century.

CANEWDON.
Doorway, Niches and Panels in W. Tower; early 15th-century.

LITTLE WARLEY: PARISH CHURCH OF ST. PETER.
Monument of Sir Denner Strutt, Bart., and Dorothye, his wife, 1641.

14th-century window of two trefoiled ogee lights with a quatrefoil in a two-centred head with a moulded label and head-stops. The wall has been heightened and buttressed in 17th-century brickwork.

The *Bell-turret*, at the W. end of the nave, is of timber and of the 15th century. It rests on six posts, with cross-beams supported by curved braces forming two-centred arches. There is a shingled broach-spire.

The *Roof* of the chancel is of early 16th-century date and of two bays with cambered tie-beams and curved braces forming four-centred arches and having traceried spandrels. The 15th-century roof of the nave is of two bays with moulded wall-plates and king-post trusses with curved braces resting on stone corbels carved with angels. The roof of the S. porch is plain and of the 15th century. *Fittings—Bells:* two; 1st by John Clarke, 1620 ; 2nd by John Clifton, 1633. *Brasses :* In chancel—(1) to Anne (Crooke), wife of William Walton, 1639, inscription only ; (2) to Elizabeth, wife of William Sammes, 1617, inscription only (see also Floor-slabs (1) and (6)). *Chair :* In vestry—with carved back and arms, probably early 18th-century. *Doors :* In doorway to vestry, of nail-studded battens with moulded fillets, early 16th-century, partly restored. In S. doorway, of overlapping battens, with one strap-hinge and a double grille, 16th-century. *Floor-slabs :* In chancel—(1) to [John Beckman, parson, 1628], with . brass plate with verses, also to Elizabeth . . . , 1611 ; (2) to Elizabeth (Herris), wife of George Walton, 1666, with shield-of-arms ; (3) to George Walton, 1662, with shield-of-arms ; (4) to Christopher Herris, 1654, with shield-of-arms ; (5) to Sir Robert ——tin, 1707 ; (6) to George, 1663, and George, 1667, sons of George Walton, also a brass plate to Mary, their sister, 1678, and indent of square plate ; (7) to Charles Walton, 1714, with achievement-of-arms. In nave—(8) to Hezekiah Joscelyn, 1701 ; (9) to Mrs. Clare Pinlow (?), 170(5 ?). *Font :* plain octagonal bowl and stem, moulded base, 15th or early 16th-century. *Glass :* In nave—in N.E. window, achievement and one shield-of-arms, 17th-century, and fragments of border, 15th-century ; in next window, nine panels with figures of Christ-and eight apostles, probably foreign, late 17th or early 18th-century ; in W. window, small piece of foliage, probably 14th-century, *in situ. Locker :* In chancel—in N. wall, rectangular recess rebated for door. *Panelling :* In nave—on E. wall, S. of chancel, below moulded beam, panel of oak with remains of painting, probably early 16th-century. *Piscina :* In chancel—with shafted jambs and trefoiled head, early 13th-century. *Plate :* includes cup and cover-paten of 1629. *Screen :* between chancel and nave—close lower panels with moulded muntins, made up with modern work,

15th-century ; incorporated in modern reredos, five cinquefoiled heads of lights with tracery and head of entrance bay, probably from same screen. *Sundials :* On jambs of S. doorway, three scratched dials. *Miscellanea :* In vestry—on S. wall, verses and inscription to George Walton, 1662, his son, George, 1690, and his daughter, Elizabeth, 1690, and two shields-of-arms, illuminated on vellum and framed. Outside S. porch, two octagonal stones, possibly part of base of cross. Condition—Fairly good.

Secular :—

ᵃ(2). STOCKWELL HALL, house and moat, about ½ m. N.N.W. of the church. The *House* is of two storeys with attics, timber-framed and plastered, the roofs are tiled. It was built on a rectangular plan late in the 16th or early in the 17th century. A wing was added on the N. side at a rather later date. At the W. end is an original chimney-stack with two diagonal shafts. Inside the building the hall and dining-room are lined with panelling of *c.* 1600 and the latter room has an overmantel (Plate, p. 65) with two square, enriched and arcaded panels, divided and flanked by fluted pilasters. The drawing-room has an arcaded overmantel of four bays, with terminal figures and arabesque ornament. In the kitchen is a 17th-century panelled door. The two staircases are of the 17th century and both have twisted balusters and square newels. On the first floor is some original panelling similar to that below and two 17th-century doors. In the window of the staircase is an oval panel of painted glass dated 1610 with a shield without arms, a crest, mantling and various fragments.

The *Moat* is incomplete.

ᵇ(3). *Rectory,* house and moat, 550 yards N. of the church. The *House* is of two storeys ; the walls are of brick and the roofs are covered with slates. The N. corner was built probably late in the 17th-century, but the roof has been largely re-constructed, and the main building is of 18th-century date. On the N.W. front of the old portion are three casement windows with leaded glazing ; two retain their original wrought-iron fasteners. Inside the building are two large beams ; one room on the first floor has a moulded shelf over the fireplace.

The *Moat* is fragmentary.

Condition—Of house, good.

MONUMENTS (4-7).

The following monuments, unless otherwise described, are of two storeys, timber-framed and plastered or weather-boarded ; the roofs are tiled. Some of the buildings have original chimney-stacks and exposed ceiling-beams.

Condition—Good, unless noted.

[a](4). *Halches Farm*, house (Plate, p. xxxv), ¼ m. W. of (2), was built in the second half of the 16th century with a cross-wing at the S. end. The upper storey projects at the W. end of the cross-wing and has a moulded bressummer; under it is a bay-window, incorporating some original mullions. The door at the E. end of the cross-wing is of moulded battens and hangs on an original moulded frame. Inside the building the main room of the cross-wing is lined with early 17th-century panelling and over the fireplace are panels with conventional incised designs and two early 16th-century panels, very delicately carved with *amorini*, etc., and heads in round medallions. On the N. side of the room are two doors (Plate, p. 65), each of six panels, similarly carved with heads, *amorini*, beasts, etc.; all are of French type. Other parts of the house have some 17th-century doors and windows with moulded mullions.

[a](5). *Sudbury's Farm*, house, about ½ m. N.W. of (4), was built probably in the 16th century and extended eastwards in the 17th century. There are two original chimney-stacks, one cruciform on plan and one with three diagonal shafts. On the middle of the roof is a small bell-cot and bell.
Condition—Poor.

[b](6). *Botneyhill Farm*, house, 1 m. W. of the church, was built probably in the 16th century and has a modern extension on the W. It is of L-shaped plan, with the wings extending towards the W. and N.

[b](7). *St. Margaret's Farm*, house (Plate, pp. xl-i), ½ m. W. of the church, was built in the 16th century or earlier, with the cross-wings on the E. and W., and a staircase-wing between them on the N. The two 17th-century chimney-stacks have grouped diagonal shafts. Inside the building the staircase has early 17th-century flat-shaped balusters and plain rails and newels.

51. LITTLE STAMBRIDGE. (F.c.)

(O.S. 6 in. lxx. S.E.)

Little Stambridge is a small parish 1 m. N.E. of Rochford.

Secular :—

(1). HOMESTEAD MOAT, at Rectory, 650 yards N. of Little Stambridge Hall.

(2). LITTLE STAMBRIDGE HALL, house and moat, stands near the middle of the parish. The *House* is of two storeys with attics, the walls are of brick and the roofs are tiled. It was built in the 16th century and the central block, with the W. cross-wing, are of this date. The house was much altered and the walls almost entirely refaced when the present E. wing was built in the 18th century.

At the S. end of the W. front is an original chimney-stack, with stepped offsets and moulded corbelling to the heads of the shafts. The front of the stack is diapered with blue bricks. The chimney-stack on the N. side of the centre block is probably similar, but now completely covered with ivy. Inside, the building has been much altered, but the roof retains some old timbers, including collar-beams and curved wind-braces.
The *Moat* is incomplete.

(3). COOMBS, house, now three tenements, and moat, about ¾ m. S. of the Hall. The *House* is of two storeys timber-framed and weather-boarded; the roofs are tiled. It was built probably in the 16th century. The older part of the existing building is L-shaped on plan, with the wings extending towards the S. and W. In the 17th century the W. wing was heightened, and extending southwards from the W. end of this wing is a modern addition. The chimney-stack at the W. end of the W. wing is probably of 17th-century date. Inside the building some of the rooms have exposed ceiling-beams, one of the rooms has two exposed wall-posts with moulded heads, and in the roof over the W. wing is a cambered tie-beam.
The *Moat* is incomplete.
Condition—Of house, good.

52. LITTLE THURROCK. (C.e.)

(O.S. 6 in. lxxxiii. S.E.)

Little Thurrock is a parish on the N. bank of the Thames adjoining Tilbury on the W.

Ecclesiastical :—

(1). PARISH CHURCH OF ST. MARY stands near the middle of the parish. The walls are of flint and mixed rubble, with dressings of limestone and some Barnack stone; the roofs are tiled. The *Nave* was built c. 1170–80 and was extended westwards at a later date. In the 14th century the *Chancel* was rebuilt. The church has been extensively restored in modern times, when the *West Tower, South Vestry, Organ Chamber* and *North Porch* were added.

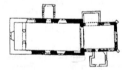

Architectural Description—The *Chancel* (22½ ft. by 16¾ ft.) has an E. window, all modern except the 14th-century splays and rear-arch. In the N. wall is a window also modern except for the

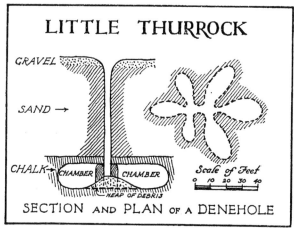

LITTLE THURROCK

GRAVEL

SAND →

CHALK → CHAMBER   CHAMBER   Scale of Feet
0 10 20 30 40

HEAP OF DEBRIS

SECTION and PLAN of a DENEHOLE

Reproduced with the permission of the Victoria County Histories.

14th-century splays and rear-arch ; further W. is a modern opening to the organ-chamber. In the S. wall are two windows similar to that in the N. wall ; between them is a doorway modern except for the 14th-century splays and rear-arch. The chancel-arch is modern except for part of the moulded and carved 12th-century abaci.

The *Nave* (40½ ft. by 20 ft.) has in the N. wall two windows ; the eastern is modern except for the partly restored 14th-century splays and rear-arch, the western window is modern ; E. of the eastern window, externally, is a straight joint, probably the jamb of a 12th-century window ; the N. doorway is modern except for part of the moulded two-centred head and label, with defaced head-stops, which are of the 14th century. In the S. wall is a window similar to the eastern window in the N. wall ; E. of it is one jamb of a window, probably of the 12th century ; the 12th-century S. doorway has plain jambs and round arch, covered with cement ; it is now blocked.

Fittings—Bell : inaccessible, but said to be by Richard Phelps, 1711. *Door :* In N. doorway—modern with 15th or 16th-century strap-hinges, drop-handle and scutcheon-plate. *Floor-slabs :* In chancel—(1) to Henry Withes (?), 164(3 ?). In churchyard—E. side, (2) to David La . . ., 1712 (?). *Piscina :* In chancel (Plate, p. xlv)—with trefoiled ogee head and label, defaced head-stops, foliated finial, and quatrefoiled drain, 14th-century. *Pulpit :* of oak, hexagonal with bolection moulded

panels, initials and date R 1700 C, cornice and legs modern. *Recesses :* In nave—in S. wall, at E. end, with segmental head and shafted W. jamb, reset, remains of recess in E. wall adjoining, with attached column to S. jamb with moulded capital and springing of arch, rest of work probably reused in recess in S. wall, early 13th-century. *Reredos :* Incorporated in modern work, some 15th-century tracery in panels. *Sedilia :* In chancel (Plate, p. xlv) —three bays with two-centred arches and moulded label with head-stops ; round shafts with moulded capitals and bases and attached shafts to jambs, 14th-century. *Stoup :* In nave—E. of N. doorway, with triangular head and modern sill, early 16th-century. *Sundial :* On E. jamb of S. doorway— scratched dial.

Condition—Good, much restored.

Unclassified :—

(2). DENEHOLES, in Hangman's Wood, partly in Orsett parish. There are over 70 of the pits in the neighbourhood. They each consist of a vertical shaft from 50 to 100 feet deep and from three to four feet wide ending in excavations in the chalk which in some cases open out into several chambers. Excavations undertaken by the Essex Field Club (Journal III) disclosed footholds in the sides of the shafts and marks apparently made by ropes at the edges.

Condition—Good.

53. LITTLE WAKERING.   (F.d.)
(O.S. 6 in. lxxviii. N.E.)

Little Wakering is a small parish on the estuary of the River Roach, 4 m. N.E. of Southend-on-Sea.

Ecclesiastical :—

(1). PARISH CHURCH OF ST. MARY stands in the village. The walls are of mixed rubble except the tower, which is of coursed ragstone-rubble; the dressings are of limestone and the roofs are tiled. The *Chancel* and *Nave* were built early in the 12th century. In the 15th century the chancel was widened towards the S. and perhaps lengthened. The chancel-arch was rebuilt in the 15th century and the *West Tower* added *c.* 1425. A S. porch was added in the 15th or 16th century of which the base of the walls remains. The church, particularly the chancel, has been restored in modern times and the *South Porch* rebuilt. ·

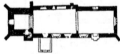

Architectural Description—The *Chancel* (26½ ft. by 16¼ ft.) has an E. window, all modern except the 15th-century rear-arch and splays. In the N. wall is a 12th-century window with a round head and modern externally; below it is a 14th-century doorway with jambs and two-centred arch of two moulded orders; it is set with the splays outward and is now blocked. In the S. wall is a modern window incorporating some old stones in the splays; E. of it is a recess with a modern arch, but old stones in the jambs. The 15th-century chancel-arch is of distorted two-centred form and of two chamfered orders; the chamfered responds have moulded capitals and bases, the N. base being cut away.

The *Nave* (32½ ft. by 18 ft.) has in the N. wall two windows; the eastern is a single 12th-century round-headed light, partly restored; the western window is of the 15th century and of two cinquefoiled lights in a square head with a moulded label. Below it, externally, is a blocked opening of uncertain date, with a rough segmental head and rising only about 4 ft. above the ground level; at the E. end of the wall is the 15th-century rood-loft staircase with upper and lower doorways having rebated jambs and two-centred heads; at the sill level of the upper doorway is a section of the former rood-beam, cut flush with the wall. In the S. wall are two windows, both modern except for the rear-arch and splays of the eastern, which are possibly of the 14th century; further W. is the 14th-century S. doorway, partly restored and with jambs and two-centred arch of two moulded orders with a moulded base.

The *West Tower* (11 ft. square) is of *c.* 1425 and of three stages with a moulded plinth and an embattled parapet of flint and stone chequer-work surmounted by a slender shingled spire (Plate, p. 70). The two-centred tower-arch is of two chamfered orders; the responds have each an attached semi-octagonal shaft with moulded capital and hollow-chamfered base. The W. doorway has moulded jambs and two-centred arch in a square head with a defaced moulded label and blank shields in the spandrels; flanking the doorway are two square sunk panels, each enclosing a shield (Plate, p. 84), (*a*) *a pelican in chief a mitre* for John Wakering, Bishop of Norwich (1416–1425); (*b*) *a cheveron* for Stafford impaling France, quartering England and Bohun, all within a border, for Anne, Countess of Stafford; the W. window is of three cinquefoiled lights with vertical tracery in a two-centred head with a defaced label; flanking it are four niches, the upper pair with pointed heads and the lower pair with cinquefoiled heads, square moulded labels and blank shields in the spandrels. The N., S. and W. walls of the second stage have each a window of one cinquefoiled light with a square moulded label. The bell-chamber has in each wall a window of two cinquefoiled lights in a square head with a moulded label.

The *Roof* of the nave is of the 15th century with two king-post trusses, with chamfered main beams and one king-post with moulded capital and base.

Fittings—*Bells:* three; all by John Waylett, 1707. *Doors:* In tower—in lower doorway to turret, of nail-studded battens with strap-hinges and foiled scutcheon-plate, 15th-century; in doorway of second stage, of nail-studded battens with strap-hinges and foiled scutcheon-plate, 15th-century; in doorway of second stage, of nail-studded battens with ring-handle, 15th-century; in W. doorway, of two folds with overlapping nail-studded battens with strap-hinges, 15th-century, repaired. *Locker:* In W. wall of turret-staircase in tower—rectangular recess with rebated reveals, 15th-century. *Monuments* and *Floor-slab.* Monuments: In churchyard—S. of chancel (1) to Thomas Wiggins, 1708, head-stone; (2) to William Archer, 1694, flat slab; (3) to Sarah, wife of William Archer, 1672, flat slab.   Floor-slab: In nave—to Bradford Bury, 1675, with shield-of-arms. *Painting:* In chancel—on splays of N. window, on E. splay, remains of a Nativity under a round arch, on W. splay remains of a figure, possibly the Virgin, under arch, also bands of red on yellow ground, 12th or 13th-century, almost effaced. *Piscina:* In chancel—with chamfered jambs and cinquefoiled head, 15th-century, projecting octofoiled drain on moulded corbel, 13th-century, restored. *Plate:* includes cup of 1566. *Recess:* In nave—in N. wall, with moulded, two-centred arch, moulded and shafted jambs with moulded bases and foliated capitals, early 13th-century, possibly tomb-recess. *Stoup :* In nave—in E. splay of S. doorway, funnel-shaped recess with mortar of hard oolite or marble, set in it.

Condition—Good.

Secular :—

HOMESTEAD MOATS.

(2). N. of Habits Hall and 600 yards W.N.W. of the church.

(3). At Barrow Hall, 1,500 yards W. of the church.

———

(4). LITTLE WAKERING HALL, house and outbuilding and garden-wall, 750 yards E. of the church. The *House* is of two storeys, timber-framed and plastered ; the roofs are tiled. It was built in the 15th century with a central hall and E. and W. cross-wings, but was considerably altered *c.* 1599, when the hall roof was raised, a floor inserted and a staircase added at the N.E. corner of the hall. In the 18th century a two-storeyed S. porch was built in the angle between the hall and W. wing and modern alterations include additions on the N. side of the house. The upper storey of the E. wing projects on the S. and E. fronts and is carried on heavy curved brackets with a heavy corner-post and diagonal bracket at the S.E. angle. The entrance doorway in the W. end of the S. wall of the hall has a moulded square head and jambs ; it is now covered by the porch. The late 16th-century chimney-stack on the N. of the W. wing is rectangular and those to the hall are each of three grouped diagonal shafts. Inside the building some of the ceiling-beams are exposed. The beam across the middle of the hall is supported on shaped and panelled brackets ; on the northern one is the date 1599. The hall has a 16th-century open fireplace with a late 18th-century carved mantelpiece. In the room occupying the E. end of the original hall is some early 17th-century panelling. The stair has an original central newel and in the roof at the top are some moulded oak balusters, square on plan. The roof over the W. wing is constructed of heavy timbers and in three bays, with curved braces under the collar-beams forming two-centred arches; there are curved wind-braces to the purlins.

The *Outbuilding,* S.W. of the house, is of brick and was built in the 17th century on a L-shaped plan, with the wings extending towards the N. and W. The N. wing is divided into seven bays by tie-beams and has in the N. end of the E. wall a blocked square-headed window of two lights with moulded head, jambs and mullion, to the S. of it is a similar window of four lights.

The *Wall* enclosing the garden on the E. side of the house is of 17th-century date and of brick. It has blocked circular look-outs on the N. and E. sides.

Condition—Of house, good.

(5). COTTAGE, range of tenements, opposite the W. end of the church, was built in the 17th century and is of one storey with attics, timber-framed and plastered ; the roofs are tiled. The chimney-stack at the N. end is original and has stepped offsets and two diagonal shafts.

Condition—Good.

———

54. LITTLE WARLEY. (B.c.)

(O.S. 6 in. (a)lxvii. S.E. (b)lxxv. N.E.)

Little Warley is a parish 2 m. S. of Brentwood. The church and Little Warley Hall are the principal monuments.

Ecclesiastical :—

(b)(1). PARISH CHURCH OF ST. PETER stands near the middle of the parish. The walls are of ragstone-rubble and brick, with limestone dressings ; the roofs are tiled. The *Nave,* judging by the thickness of the walls, is of early date, but the earliest remaining detail is of the 15th century. A W. tower was probably added in the 15th century. The *Chancel* was rebuilt in brick in the 16th century and the *South Porch* is perhaps of the same date. The *West Tower* was rebuilt in brick in 1718, possibly on the old foundations and with some reused stonework. The church has been restored in modern times, when the E. wall was rebuilt.

Among the fittings the monuments are noteworthy.

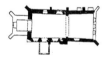

Architectural Description—The *Chancel* (18 ft. by 18 ft.) has a modern E. wall. In the S. wall is a modern window, all modern except the 16th-century splays and rear-arch. The early 16th-century chancel-arch is two-centred and of two chamfered orders dying on to splayed responds.

The *Nave* (26 ft. by 17 ft.) has in the N. wall an early 15th-century window of two cinquefoiled lights with vertical tracery in a two-centred head with a moulded label ; further W. is the 15th-century N. doorway, now blocked ; it has hollow-chamfered jambs and two-centred arch. The S. wall has at the E. end the projection enclosing the 15th-century rood-loft staircase ; the upper and lower doorways have two-centred heads and the former is rebated for a door ; further W. are two windows similar to that in the N. wall and between them is the 15th-century S. doorway, with double hollow-chamfered jambs, two-centred arch and moulded label.

The *South Porch* is of timber on modern dwarf walls. The early 16th-century outer archway has a four-centred arch in a square head with trefoiled spandrels. The side walls have moulded and embattled wall-plates.

The *Roof* of the nave is of late 15th-century date and of two bays with moulded wall-plates and king-post trusses ; the rebated middle king-post has four-way struts.

Fittings—*Bell :* possibly by William Wodewarde, 15th-century and inscribed " Johannes Cristi Care Dignare Pro Nobis Orare." *Brass and Indents.* Brass : In chancel—on S. wall, of Anne (Wolley), wife successively of Davye Hanmer and John Terrell, 1592, half figure of a woman in ruff, etc. Indents : In nave—(1) of half figure and inscription-plate, 15th-century ; (2) of brass in chancel. *Door :* In S. doorway—of overlapping nail-studded battens with strap-hinges and round engrailed scutcheon-plate, 15th-century. *Glass :* In nave—in N. window, border of crowned Ms and shield with device, *in situ,* also flowered quarries, 15th-century ; in S.E. window, borders of crowned Ms and IHC, flowered quarries, etc., 15th-century, *in situ. Monuments :* In chancel— N. side (1) of Sir Denner Strutt, Bart., and Dorothye (Staresmore), his wife, 1641, alabaster and marble altar-tomb (Plate, p. 85) in two stages, upper with effigy of lady in costume of period, flanked by cherubs drawing back the draped canopy, two cartouches of arms ; lower stage, probably added, with effigy of man in plate-armour ; on S. side (2) to Mary (Chapman), wife of [Sir Denner Strutt, Bart.] 1658, alabaster and marble altar-tomb with reclining effigy (Plate, p. 105) of woman in shroud, back-piece against wall, with pediment and achievement-of-arms, and supported by large voluted trusses. In nave—in blocked N. doorway, alabaster figure of Time, 17th-century, found in churchyard and probably from former monument. *Panelling :* In gallery— late 16th or early 17th-century, reset. *Pavement :* In chancel—black and white marble squares, late 17th-century, reset. *Plate :* includes cup of 1564 with band of engraved ornament. *Pulpit :* incorporates three stages of a 17th-century pulpit ; a fourth was probably the original door. *Seating :* In nave—three seats with moulded rails, early 16th-century, and one panelled back, late 16th or early 17th-century. In nave and chancel— eight box-pews of late 16th or early 17th-century panelling. *Stoup :* In nave—in S. wall, recess with two-centred head, 15th or early 16th-century, no basin. *Miscellanea :* Incorporated

in communion table, carved cresting from 15th-century screen. Loose in tower—gate with turned balusters and jewel ornament, 17th-century, probably from former communion rails.

Condition—Fairly good.

Secular :—

b(2). LITTLE WARLEY HALL, house and· moat, S. of the church. The *House* is of two storeys with attics. The walls are of brick and the roofs are tiled. It was built probably early in the 16th century and formerly extended further towards the W. The plan consists of a main or Hall block, with 'screens' at the E. end entered by a N. porch. E. of the main block is a kitchen-wing. The N. front (Plate, p. 90) has diapering in black bricks and a two-storeyed porch with a crow-stepped gable ; the outer archway has moulded jambs and two-centred arch with a square moulded label ; the inner doorway has moulded jambs and a four-centred arch in a square head of brick, with spandrels carved with a Tudor rose and a molet ; within the arch is a moulded oak frame ; the upper storey of the porch has an original window with a square head and moulded label and 'now partly blocked. The main block has a large projecting chimney-stack, with stepped offsets and two shafts with spiral enrichment and moulded bases resting on trefoiled corbelling. The other· windows on this front have been altered, but one in the kitchen-wing retains its original opening. The back eleva-tion has an original square-headed doorway at the S. end of the 'screens,' and further W. is an original garde-robe projection.

Inside the building the original hall has moulded ceiling-beams, joists and wall-plates. In the N. wall is an original fireplace of stone with moulded jambs and four-centred arch and spandrels carved with foliage and blank shields. There are three original oak doorways with moulded frames and four-centred arches in square heads ; the spandrels are carved, one having a Tudor rose and knot. The staircase (Plate, p. 75) is of *c.* 1600 and has flat balusters with raking mouldings, moulded rail and square moulded newels.

The *Moat* is fragmentary.

Condition—Of house, good, except the W. wall.

MONUMENTS (3–5).

The following monuments, unless otherwise described, are of the 17th century and of two storeys, timber-framed and plastered or weather-boarded ; the roofs are tiled.

Condition—Good.

b(3). *Old England,* house, nearly 1 m. S. of the church, is of L-shaped plan with the wings extend-ing towards the E. and S. Inside the building are some exposed ceiling-beams and joists.

LITTLE WARLEY: (2). LITTLE WARLEY HALL. Early 16th-century.
North front.

MOUNTNESSING : PARISH CHURCH OF ST. GILES.
Interior, showing N. Arcade, mid 13th-century, and Framing of Bell-turret, 15th-century.

ª(4). *Farmhouse,* in the village, about 1 m. N. of the church, has an original central chimney-stack with grouped diagonal shafts.

ª(5). *Clapgate,* house, ¾ m. W. of (4), was built *c.* 1700 and has a modillioned eaves-cornice. Inside the building is an original staircase with turned balusters, close string and square newels.

---

55. MAYLAND. (F.b.)

(O.S. 6 in. lxiii. N.W.)

Mayland is a small parish 3½ m. N.W. of Burnham-on-Crouch.

Ecclesiastical :—

PARISH CHURCH OF ST. BARNABAS was entirely rebuilt in 1866 about 300 yards S. of the old site. It contains from the old church the following :—

Fittings—*Bell :* one, by Miles Graye, 1662. *Monument* and *Floor-slabs.* Monument : In old churchyard—to Robert Craske, 1712, Dorothy, his ·wife, and three children, head-stone. Floor-slabs : In church—(1) to Reuben Robinson, 1657 ; (2) to Thomas Fowle, 1666. *Plate :* includes Elizabethan cup with two bands of incised ornament and cover-paten dated 1568. Condition—Rebuilt.

---

56. MOUNTNESSING. (B.b.)

(O.S. 6 in. ⁽ᵃ⁾lix. N.E. ⁽ᵇ⁾lix. S.E. ⁽ᶜ⁾lx. S.W.)

Mountnessing is a parish and hamlet 3 m. N.W. of Billericay. The church and Thoby Priory are the principal monuments.

Ecclesiastical :—

ᶜ(1). PARISH CHURCH OF ST. GILES stands about 1½ m. S.E. of the village. The walls are of mixed rubble, with limestone dressings ; the roofs are tiled. The *Nave* was built in the 12th century, but the only definite evidence of this is the N.E. angle which has quoins of Roman brick. About the middle of the 13th century the *North* and *South Aisles* were added. In the 15th century the timber belfry was built within the W. end of the nave. The W. end of the nave was rebuilt in brick in 1653. The *Chancel* was rebuilt late in the 18th or early in the 19th century, and the rest of the church largely rebuilt, using the old materials in 1889, when the *South Porch* was rebuilt and the *Organ-Chamber* added. The timber-framed belfry is interesting.

Architectural Description — The *Chancel* is modern, but the chancel-arch may incorporate some 14th-century work retooled.

The *Nave* (40 ft. by 21½ ft.) has a mid 13th-century N. arcade (Plate, p. 91) of three bays, partly restored and reset, with two-centred arches of two chamfered orders ; the round columns have moulded bell-capitals, the eastern (Plate, p. 161) carved with ' stiff-leaf' foliage and a head ; the E. respond is semi-octagonal and has a moulded capital carved with ' stiff-leaf' foliage ; the W. respond is modern. The S. arcade is generally similar to the N. arcade, but probably of a·slightly later date ; the capital of the eastern column is modern and that of the western is simply moulded ; the E. respond is semi-circular and has a semi-octagonal moulded capital of 15th-century detail ; reset below it is a corbel carved with the half figure of an angel and much defaced ; the W. respond is semi-octagonal and has a moulded capital ; E. of the arcade is a cutting through the wall containing steps and having the rebate for a door on the W. jamb. The W. wall is of red brick and in the gable is a panel with a moulded sill, broken entablature and high-pitched pediment ; below it is the date 1653 ; the W. doorway is modern, and the W. window, probably of the 15th century, reset, is of two cinquefoiled lights in a square head.

The *North Aisle* (8½ ft. wide) has an E. window, all modern except the splays and rear-arch, which are possibly of the 14th century. In the N. wall are two single-light windows with trefoiled heads ; they are probably of the 13th century, but much restored and reset ; between them is the 13th or early 14th-century N. doorway, with chamfered jambs and two-centred head, now blocked. In the W. wall is a modern window.

The *South Aisle* (9½ ft. wide) has been mainly rebuilt and has no ancient features.

The *Belfry* at the W. end of the nave is of the 15th century and rests on heavy oak framing (Plates, pp. xxxviii–ix, 91), with four main posts, tie-beams and curved braces with side struts across the aisles ; the main braces on the E. side form a two-centred arch and rest on attached shafts (that on the S. modern) with moulded capitals ; the N. and S. sides have a middle post and a second and lower tie-beam with curved braces and trellis-framing ; there is also a lower tie-beam on the W. side supported on two intermediate posts having curved braces to the side bays ; the square weather-boarded turret rests on cross-beams with curved diagonal braces. The *Roof* of the nave is of the 15th century and has king-post trusses with octagonal king-posts, which have moulded capitals and bases. The pent-roof of the N. aisle incorporates some old timbers.

Fittings—*Bell :* one ; not accessible, but said to be by Thomas Bullisdon, *c.* 1500, and inscribed " Sancte Jacobe Ora Pro Nobis." *Brass :* In chancel — to John Peers, 1583, inscription only.

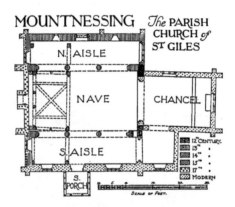

MOUNTNESSING *The* PARISH CHURCH *of* S.T GILES

N. AISLE

NAVE   CHANCEL

S. AISLE

S. PORCH

12.TH CENTURY.
13.TH
14.TH
15.TH
17.TH
MODERN

SCALE OF FEET.

Chest : In nave—long ' dug-out' with cambered lid and strap-hinges, probably 13th-century with later ironwork. *Font :* octagonal bowl, each face with square panel enclosing carvings of three fishes, compass, square and mallet, a formy cross, flowers and foliage, late 15th-century. *Monuments* and *Floor-slabs.* Monuments : In chancel—on N. wall (1) to Edmund Pert [1676], white marble tablet with achievement-of-arms. In nave—at W. end (2) fragments of two small kneeling figures of man and woman, from former monument of *c.* 1600. In churchyard—E. of S. aisle (3) to Henry Pert, 1671, flat stone ; S. of S. aisle (4) to John Bayley, 1702, flat stone ; (5) to J. B., 1712, head-stone. Floor-slabs : In chancel—(1) to Edmund Pert, 1676, with shield-of-arms ; (2) to Alexander Prescott, 1701, with shield-of-arms ; (3) to Alexander Prescott, 17–9, with shield-of-arms ; (4) to Mary, daughter of Francis Woolmer, 17(00 ?) ; (5) to Thomas Woolmer, 1707. *Panelling :* In N. aisle —incorporated in modern box, with jewelled ornament and carved frieze with strap-work, mid 17th-century. *Plate :* includes cup of 1564 with band of engraved ornament, and stand-paten of 1704 with the arms of Prescott. *Miscellanea :* In nave —in case, large rib-bone possibly of whale. Condition—Good, largely rebuilt.

Secular :—

HOMESTEAD MOATS.

a(2). At Bacons, 1 m. N. of the church.

b(3). At Woodlands, 2 m. N.W. of the church.

c(4). At Arnold's Farm, 1 m. W. of the church.

d(5). MOUNTNESSING HALL, house and moat, W. of the church. The *House* is of two storeys, timber-framed and refaced with brick ; the roofs

are tiled. It was built probably in the 17th century, but has been very much altered. At the E. end of the building is an original chimney-stack with grouped shafts.

The *Moat* is incomplete.

Condition—Of house, good.

e(6). THOBY PRIORY, house and ruins, nearly 2 m. N.W. of the church. The Priory was founded for Austin Canons sometime before the middle of the 12th century. It was suppressed by Wolsey in 1525. The ruins of the church (Plate, p. 96) consist only of the S. wall of the presbytery and the arch to the W. of it, which may have opened into a S. nave-arcade ; the wall extending W. from this point appears to consist entirely of reused material and to be of post-suppression date. The walls are of rubble and brick, with limestone dressings. The remaining arch is probably of 14th-century date and is two-centred and of two moulded orders ; the lower part is blocked. The presbytery was apparently rebuilt in the 15th century and has a diagonal buttress at the S.E. angle and a 15th-century window in the S. wall, with a four-centred arch, a brick rear-arch and a moulded label ; the mullions, etc., have been destroyed and the sill is carried down internally to form a sedile.

The *House* is of two storeys, with walls of brick or rubble plastered, and the roofs are tiled. It was evidently formed out of the W. range of the claustral block, but the walls of the hall are the only ones which appear to be of mediaeval date ; the building was burnt out late in the last century and the existing hall, now of one storey, has no ancient structural features except the mid 16th-century fireplace in the E. wall, with stop-moulded

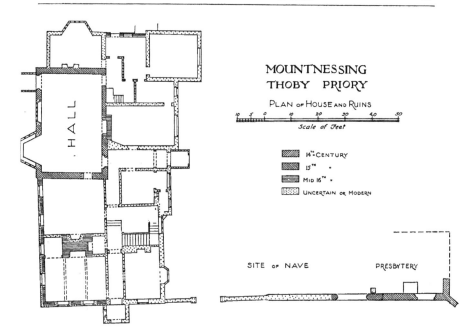

MOUNTNESSING
THOBY PRIORY

PLAN of HOUSE and RUINS

Scale of feet

14.th CENTURY

15 TH "

MID 16 TH "

UNCERTAIN or MODERN

SITE of NAVE   PRESBYTERY

jambs and four-centred arch in a square head with foliated spandrels; the doorway in the W. wall has a four-centred head and may perhaps be old, but is covered with cement. The S. block of the building is possibly of the 16th century, but has no ancient features except the fireplace in the S. room, which is generally similar to that in the hall and has foliage and blank shields in the spandrels. In this room and in the hall is a considerable quantity of late 16th-century panelling and the hall fireplace has an iron fire-back with the royal arms and the date and initials 1635 C.R.

Condition—Good; a wing has recently been added on the site of the W. part of the nave.

MONUMENTS (7–10).

The following monuments, unless otherwise described, are of the 16th century and of two storeys, timber-framed and plastered; the roofs are tiled. Some of the buildings have original chimney-stacks and exposed ceiling-beams.

Condition—Good.

b(7). *George and Dragon Inn*, on N.W. side of the main road, nearly 1½ m. W.N.W. of the church, has been much altered.

b(8). *Drury's Farm*, on S.E. side of the main road, nearly opposite (7), is built on a modified H-shaped plan with the cross-wings at the N.E. and S.W. ends. It has been refaced with modern brick and much altered, but retains an original chimney-stack with three grouped diagonal shafts.

c(9). *Wardroper's Farm* (Plate, pp. xxxiv–v), 1,100 yards E. of the church, is built on a modified L-shaped plan with the wings extending towards the S. and E. Except the E. end, which appears to be an addition to the original building, the upper storey projects along the whole of the N. front and has a moulded bressummer supported by curved brackets. Within the front door is the three-centred head of the original doorway.

c(10). *Cottage*, at Padham's Green, 1,100 yards N.N.W. of the church, is timber-framed, partly plastered and partly weather-boarded and is built on an L-shaped plan with the wings extending to the N. and W. The upper storey projects on the W. front of the S. wing.

57. MUCKING. (C.e.)

(O.S. 6 in. (ª)lxxxiv. N.W. (ᵇ)lxxxiv. N.E.)

Mucking is a parish on the N. bank of the Thames, 4 m. N.E. of Tilbury. The church is interesting.

Ecclesiastical :—

ᵇ(1). PARISH CHURCH OF ST. JOHN THE BAPTIST stands near the N.E. angle of the parish. The walls are of ragstone-rubble, with some flint and brick ; the dressings are of limestone ; the roofs are covered with tiles, slate and lead. The S. wall of the *Nave* may be of the 12th century, but the earliest remaining detail is the early 13th-century S. arcade. The *Chancel* was probably rebuilt in the same century with a N. chapel. The chapel was probably destroyed in the 14th century. In the 15th century the *West Tower* was added and the *South Aisle* probably rebuilt. The *South Chapel* was added c. 1500. The church has been extensively restored in modern times, the S. chapel, nave, S. aisle and W. tower being largely rebuilt about 1850.

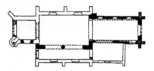

Architectural Description—The *Chancel* (33½ ft. by 14½ ft.) has a late 15th-century E. window, partly restored, of three trefoiled lights with vertical tracery in a two-centred head. In the N. wall is a wall-arcade of three bays with two-centred arches of one chamfered order ; the E. respond is plain, but the W. respond and the intermediate pier have each a Purbeck marble shaft with a moulded capital of varying form, the eastern of the 14th century and the western of the 13th century ; the abacus of the second capital appears on the outer face of the wall, and, externally, traces of two arches are visible ; at the back of the first column there is a straight joint showing externally ; these features seem to indicate that the two western bays opened into a N. chapel which was destroyed during the 14th century ; each bay of the arcade encloses a 14th or a reused 13th-century lancet-window. In the S. wall is a window of c. 1500 and of two trefoiled lights in a square head ; further W. is a two-centred arch-way of the same date and of two hollow-chamfered orders ; the responds have each an attached shaft with concave faces and a moulded capital and hollow-chamfered base. The chancel-arch is modern.

The *South Chapel* (22½ ft. by 12¾ ft.) has modern E. and S. walls. In the W. wall is a two-centred arch of c. 1500, partly restored, of one continuous chamfered order.

The *Nave* (36¾ ft. by 27½ ft.) has a modern N. wall incorporating some old material. The early 13th-century S. arcade is of two bays with two-centred arches of three chamfered orders on the N. side and two on the S. ; the responds are plain and partly restored and the circular column has a moulded base and capital (Plate, p. 161) carved with foliage, heads and devices.

The *South Aisle* (7½ ft. wide) has been rebuilt with some reused material. In the W. wall is a late 15th-century window of two cinquefoiled lights in a square head with a moulded label.

The *West Tower* (14 ft. square) is of two stages, the upper is entirely and the lower partly modern. In the S. wall the doorway incorporates part of the moulded head and jambs of a 15th-century doorway. Below the W. window is a straight joint probably indicating the position of the former window.

Fittings—Bells : three ; 1st dated 1579 ; 2nd by William Land, 1632 ; 3rd by John Hodson, 1665. *Brass Indents :* In S. aisle—(1) of figures of man, wife, two groups of children, shield and inscription-plate, 15th-century. As threshold to doorway of vicarage garden—(2) of civilian, wife, and inscription-plate. As step to cottage, S. of churchyard—(3) of man and two shields. *Font :* In S. aisle—disused bowl of semi-octagonal form with chamfered under edge, 15th-century. *Monument :* In S. chapel—of Elizabeth, wife successively of Eugeny Gatton, Thomas Gill, Dense Hartridge and Frauncis Downes, 1607, alabaster wall-monument with kneeling figure at prayer-desk, side pilasters, cresting and three shields - of - arms. *Piscina :* In chancel—with two-centred head and two round drains, 13th-century. *Plate :* includes 17th-century cup with lower half of stem modern. *Sedilia :* In chancel—three bays with chamfered jambs and two-centred heads, 13th-century. *Miscellanea :* In churchyard and vicarage garden, various worked and moulded stones.

Condition—Good, but much ivy on building.

MONUMENTS (2–7).

The following monuments, unless otherwise described, are of the 17th century and of two storeys, timber-framed and plastered or weather-boarded ; the roofs are tiled. Some of the buildings have original chimney-stacks and exposed ceiling-beams.

Condition—Good, or fairly good.

ᵇ(2). *Crown Inn*, now a farmhouse, 200 yards S.E. of the church, has been very extensively altered. It has an early 17th-century chimney-stack with three diagonal shafts, now partly covered by the roof.

b(3). *House,* now tenements, 250 yards S.S.E. of (2), was built probably late in the 15th or early in the 16th century with a central hall and N. and S. cross-wings. The N. cross-wing has been partly rebuilt and the roof of the central block has been continued over it. The upper storey of the S. wing projects on the W. front and is carried on curved brackets. Inside the building, the roof over the S. wing is of two bays with an original king-post truss.

a(4). *Gobions,* house, nearly 1¼ m. S. of the church, is a long rectangular building, much altered and having a small modern addition at the back. Inside the building is a door of moulded battens.

a(5). *George and Dragon Inn,* on N.E. side of road, about 1¼ m. S.S.W. of the church, was built probably in the 16th century, but has been added to and considerably altered. There is an original chimney-stack with two diagonal shafts. Inside the building some of the timber-construction is exposed.

a(6). *Sutton's Farm,* cottage, on N.W. side of road, about 1 m. S.W. of the church, is of two storeys with attics. It is of the central-chimney type and has an addition at the back.

a(7). *Walton's Hall,* house, 240 yards N.E. of (6), is possibly of early 18th-century date, but has been much altered.

---

58. MUNDON. (F.b.)

(O.S. 6 in. *(a)*liv. S.E. *(b)*lxii. N.E.)

Mundon is a parish 3 m. S.S.E. of Maldon. The church is the principal monument.

Ecclesiastical :—

a(1). PARISH CHURCH OF ST. MARY stands towards the S. side of the parish. The walls of the nave are of plastered rubble, those of the chancel of red brick; the belfry and porch are of timber; the roofs are tiled. The *Nave* is of uncertain date, the earliest existing detail being of the 14th century. The timber *Belfry* and *North Porch* were added early in the 16th century, and about the same time a small chapel, now destroyed, was added S.E. of the nave. The *Chancel* was rebuilt above the plinth early in the 18th century. The church has been restored in modern times.

The timber belfry and N. porch are of interest.

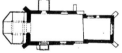

Architectural Description—The *Chancel* (20 ft. by 16 ft.) has an early 18th-century E. window of

three lights with a solid oak frame. In the N. wall is a similar window of two lights and a segmental-headed doorway.

The *Nave* (38 ft. by 20 ft.) has in the N. wall a 14th-century window of two roughly pointed lights with a plain spandrel in a two-centred head with a moulded label; further W. is the late 14th-century N. doorway, with double hollow-chamfered jambs and segmental-pointed arch with a moulded label and head-stops; the jambs, arch and label are carved with rosettes and square flowers; the E. end of the wall is of modern brick. At the E. end of the S. wall is an early 16th-century archway, now blocked, but formerly opening into a chapel; it is four-centred and the surrounding wall is of red brick; above it is a modern window; further W. is an early 16th-century window of two four-centred lights in a four-centred head with a moulded label; the S. doorway is of the 18th century. In the W. wall is an early 16th-century four-centred archway of brick; above it is an opening with a segmental-pointed head.

The *Belfry* is of early 16th-century date and timber-framed; it has four posts in the middle forming a square, and round it is a semi-octagonal aisle with a pent-roof; the bell-chamber is weather-boarded.

The *North Porch* (Plate, p. xxxix) is of early 16th-century date and timber-framed; the outer archway has a flat four-centred head with spandrels carved with twisted-leaf ornament; the gable has moulded barge-boards and a carved and moulded tie-beam; beneath it is a straining-beam of flat four-centred form and with carved spandrels similar to those of the archway; the straining-beam springs from moulded pendants and there is a square pendant at the apex of the gable; the close filling of the gable and lower parts of the side walls have moulded muntins. The sides of the porch are divided into lights by moulded mullions.

The *Roof* of the nave is probably of the 15th century and has plain tie-beams and central purlin; one of the king-posts is octagonal and the other two square and probably of 17th-century or later date. The early 16th-century roof of the porch has moulded rafters and tie-beams.

Fittings—*Bell:* one, probably by John Langhorne, *c.* 1400, and inscribed " Vincentius Reboat Ut Cunta Noxia Tollat." *Brass Indent:* In N. porch—of figures of man and two wives, inscription-plate and two groups of children, early 16th-century. *Coffin-lid:* In church-yard—fragment with hollow-chamfered edge and foliated cross, 13th-century. *Door:* On modern N. door —one 15th or 16th-century strap-hinge and a later foiled scutcheon-plate. *Font:* square bowl with angles cut off, circular stem with four small octagonal shafts having square moulded capitals and bases, *c,* 1200, much repaired. *Monument:*

In churchyard—S. side, to Richard Eve, 1712, head-stone. *Plate:* includes Jacobean, or later, cup with Greek and Latin inscriptions, stem possibly of pre-Reformation date. *Miscellanea:* In churchyard—fragments of window-jambs and tracery.
Condition—Fairly good.

Secular :—

ᵃ(2). MOATED SITE enclosing the church, Hall, etc. and now incomplete.

ᵇ(3). HOMESTEAD MOAT, at Limbourne Park Farm, ½ m. S.W. of the church.

ᵃ(4). BARN at Mundon Hall, 130 yards N. of the church, is probably of the 17th century, timber-framed and weather-boarded; the roofs are thatched. It is of eight bays with an aisle.
Condition—Fairly good.

ᵃ(5). WHITE HOUSE FARM, house, 1,100 yards N.N.W. of the church, is of two storeys, timber-framed and partly plastered and partly weather-boarded; the roofs are tiled. It was built in the 16th century and has an original chimney-stack at the E. end with a moulded base to the shaft. Inside the building are original moulded ceiling-beams and joists.
Condition—Poor.

Unclassified :—

ᵃ(6). RED HILL, W. of Pickworth's Farm, 1¼ m. E.N.E. of the church.

59. NEVENDON. (D.c.)

(O.S. 6 in. ⁽ᵃ⁾lxviii. S.E. ⁽ᵇ⁾lxix. S.W.)

Nevendon is a parish 4 m. S.E. of Billericay.

Ecclesiastical :—

ᵇ(1). PARISH CHURCH OF ST. PETER stands in the middle of the parish. The walls are of ragstone-rubble mixed with tile in the chancel and with dressings of limestone; the roofs are tiled. The *Chancel* was built in the 13th century, the nave at that time being probably of timber, as the stone W. quoins of the chancel are preserved. The *Nave* was rebuilt in stone in the 14th century. The bell-turret is of the 17th century or earlier. The church has been restored in modern times, when the walls were repointed and the *South Vestry* added.

Architectural Description—The *Chancel* (23½ ft. by 18 ft.) has an E. window all modern except for some reused stones in the splays. In the N. wall

are two 13th-century lancet-windows, modern externally; close to the W. end of the wall is a straight joint formed by the N.W. quoins of the chancel. In the S. wall are two 13th-century lancet-windows, the eastern modern externally; between them is a modern opening. There is a straight joint about 1½ ft. E. of the junction with the nave, similar to that in the N. wall.

The *Nave* (30 ft. by 20 ft.) has in the N. wall a modern window; further W. is the late 14th-century N. doorway with moulded jambs, two-centred arch and label with defaced head-stops. In the S. wall is a window and a doorway similar to those in the N. wall, but the doorway has no label. In the W. wall is a modern window.

The *Roofs* of the chancel and nave are of the 15th century with four king-post trusses with octagonal king-posts; at the W. end of the nave is the framing supporting the bell-turret.

Fittings—*Monument* and *Floor-slab*—Monument: In churchyard—to Thomas Blackmore, 1679, and to Elizabeth, 1690, and Ann, 1677, his daughters, table-tomb. Floor-slab: In chancel—to Thomas Hervey, rector of the parish, 1712. *Piscina:* In nave—in S. wall, with cinquefoiled head and sexfoiled drain, 15th-century. *Recess:* In chancel—in N. wall, extending to floor and with rebated jambs and segmental head, date uncertain. *Stoup:* In nave—E. of N. doorway—rough recess covered with modern cement.
Condition—Good.

Secular :—

ᵃ(2). HOMESTEAD MOAT, at Cranes, nearly ½ m. S.W. of the church.

ᵇ(3). FORE RIDERS, house and moat, 500 yards N.N.E. of the church. The house is of two storeys; the walls are of timber-framing partly plastered and partly weather-boarded; the roofs are tiled. It was built probably in the 16th century on an L-shaped plan with the wings extending towards the N. and W. The upper storey projected at the S. end of the W. front and is carried on a moulded bressummer with curved brackets.
The *Moat* is incomplete.

ᵇ(4). GREAT BROMFORDS, house (Plate, pp.xxxiv-v) and moat, nearly ¾ m. N.N.E. of the church. The *House* is of two storeys, timber-framed and plastered; the roofs are tiled. It was built in the 15th century on an L-shaped plan with the wings extending towards the S. and E. In the 17th century an addition was made on the N. side of the E. wing, and there is a modern extension at the N.W. corner. The upper storey projects on the S. front of both wings and on the E. side of the E. wing; at the S.E. corner of the E. wing is an exposed wall-post with a moulded

MOUNTNESSING : THOBY PRIORY.   14th-century and later.
Ruins of Church, from the North-East.

FOBBING : PARISH CHURCH OF ST. MICHAEL.
South Porch ;   late 15th-century.

ORSETT: ORSETT HALL.

Fireplace and Ceiling in S.E. room; mid 17th-century.

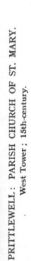

PRITTLEWELL: PARISH CHURCH OF ST. MARY.

West Tower; 15th-century.

cap. The base of one of the chimney-stacks is of thin bricks. Inside the building the ceiling-beams in the rooms of the original house are exposed and the principal beams are supported on curved brackets.

The *Moat* is incomplete.

Condition—Of house, good.

b(5). LITTLE BROMFORDS, house (Plate, pp. xxxiv–v) and moat, 150 yards N.N.E. of (4). The *House* is of two storeys with attics, timber-framed and plastered; the roofs are tiled. It was built probably late in the 16th century on a modified L-shaped plan with the wings extending towards the N. and E. and a small projecting bay (possibly originally a porch) extending westward at the S. end of the W. wing; there is a modern addition on the N. The gables to the E. wing and at the W. end of the S. front have moulded barge-boards, as has also the W. projecting bay; the upper storey of the latter projects on both sides and has moulded bres-summers supported on elaborately shaped brackets. In the upper storey is an original window of two lights with a moulded mullion. The main chimney-stack is original and of grouped diagonal shafts. Inside the building some of the timber-construction and ceiling-beams are exposed. One of the rooms on the ground-floor has two original doors divided into small panels by moulded rails and muntins, and there is a similar door on the first floor made up of old material. In one of the ground-floor fire-places is a fireback with the initials E.M. and the date 1641, brought from elsewhere. The roof is of collar-beam construction.

The *Moat* surrounds the house and garden but is partly filled in.

Condition—Of house, good.

(6). FRAMPTON'S FARM, house, 200 yards E.N.E. of the church, is of two storeys, timber-framed and plastered, the roofs are tiled. It was built probably in the 16th century with a gabled cross-wing at the E. end which has the upper storey projecting on both the N. and S. fronts. Inside the building the W. room on the ground-floor has exposed ceiling-beams.

Condition—Good.

---

60. NORTH BENFLEET. (D.c.)

(O.S. 6 in. lxix. S.W.)

North Benfleet is a small parish 8 m. W.N.W. of Southend-on-Sea.

Ecclesiastical :—

(1). PARISH CHURCH OF ALL SAINTS stands at the S. end of the parish. The walls are of rag-stone-rubble with some flint and brickwork; the

dressings are of Reigate stone and brick ; the roofs are tiled. The *Nave* was built early in the 13th century, but except for the W. bay it was largely reconstructed in the 17th century. Early in the 16th century the *North Porch* was added and a bell-turret built. The church has been restored in modern times, when the *Chancel* was rebuilt and the *Organ Chamber* and *West Tower* added.

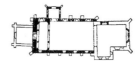

Architectural Description—The *Chancel* is modern, but incorporates the 14th-century moulded splays and rear-arch of the E. window and an early 16th-century brick window in the N. wall of two trefoiled lights with tracery in a two-centred head with a moulded label.

The *Nave* (41¼ ft. by 21 ft.) has been largely refaced both internally and externally except for the W. bay. In the N. wall are four modern windows and a modern doorway. In the S. wall are four windows, all modern externally but with 17th-century brick splays and rear-arches, except the westernmost which is plastered internally; the internal wall-face is of 17th-century white brick except the W. bay. In the W. wall is a modern doorway, and above it a window of *c.* 1200 and of one round-headed light. At the W. end of the nave is the timber framework (Plate, pp. xxxviii–ix) of the former bell-turret ; it has four main and four subsidiary posts and heavy curved braces.

The *North Porch* has been partly reconstructed. The early 16th-century outer archway has moulded jambs and two-centred head. The side walls have each a modern window.

Fittings—*Bells :* two ; both by Robert Burford, early 15th-century, and inscribed " Sancta Katerina Ora Pro Nobis." *Chest :* with moulded and panelled lid, front and ends, early 17th-century. *Font :* square bowl, each face with six shallow pointed panels, square base with seating for stem and four shafts at the angles, early 13th-century, stem modern. *Monument :* In churchyard—N. side, to Mary Smith, 1711, head-stone. *Piscina :* In chancel—recess with trefoiled head, 15th-century, much restored, set in it a shaft with 13th-century moulded capital, forming drain, and base. *Plate :* includes cup of 1564 and cover-paten, the former with a band of engraved ornament.

Condition—Poor, cracks in walls and buttresses falling away.

Secular :—

HOMESTEAD MOATS.

(2). At Coldblows, 600 yards W. of the church.

(3). At Smith's Farm, 700 yards N.W. of the church.

(4). At Bradfield's Farm, 1,000 yards N.W. of the church.

———

(5). NORTH BENFLEET HALL, house and moat, N. of the church. The *House* is of two storeys with attics ; the walls are of plastered timber-framing and brickwork, and the roofs are tiled. It is H-shaped on plan with a staircase block in the W. angle on the N. side. The E. wing is of 15th-century date, but the middle block and W. wing were built or rebuilt in the 16th century. Considerable alterations were made in the 17th century, when a cellar was formed under the E. wing, and modern alterations include the rebuilding of the roofs of the W. wing and middle block. Both ends of the cross-wings have been refaced with modern brickwork, and the projecting upper storey at the S. end of the E. wing has been underbuilt. On the S. front the wall of the middle block has a projecting gable at either end, carried on a moulded bressummer at the eaves-level, with moulded brackets below. The entrance door has big strap-hinges with foliated ends, and over it is a blocked two-light window with moulded jambs and mullions. On the upper floor of the E. front of the E. wing is a blocked 17th-century window, and in the W. wall of this wing is a blocked window of five lights with diamond-shaped mullions. On the N. front, over the entrance doorway is a blocked two-light window, and there is a similar window of five lights to the staircase ; there are also blocked windows to each floor of the E. wing. The two principal chimney-stacks are of 17th-century date. Inside the building the ground-floor rooms have exposed ceiling-beams and the timber-framing in the walls of the passage on the N. side of the central block and the main staircase is also exposed. There is a 17th-century door adjoining the N. entrance with moulded styles and strap-hinges. The staircase has a moulded handrail and square newel-post with shaped top of *c.* 1600. The bays of the roof over the E. wing are original, and the main truss has a cambered tie-beam with curved braces below forming a four-centred arch and a king-post with curved two-way struts to the central purlin. The roof over the central block is modern but retains one old cambered tie-beam.

The *Moat* is incomplete.

Condition—Of house, good.

(6). GREAT FANTON HALL, house, (Plate, p. 57) about 1 m. N. of the church, is of timber-framing, with attics ; the walls are of timber-framing, partly plastered and partly weather-boarded ; the

roofs are tiled. It was built early in the 17th century and repaired and altered *c.* 1787 ; there are modern additions on the N. and W. On the plastered E. front are the initials W.R. and the date 1787. The central chimney-stack is original and of six grouped octagonal shafts on a rectangular base. Inside the building some of the timber-construction and ceiling-beams are exposed.

Condition—Good.

———

61. NORTH FAMBRIDGE. (E.c.)

(O.S. 6 in. lxii. S.W.)

North Fambridge is a parish on the left bank of the Crouch, 6¼ m. S. of Maldon.

Ecclesiastical :—

(1). PARISH CHURCH OF HOLY TRINITY stands near the middle of the parish. It was entirely rebuilt in the first half of the 18th century in red brick, with round-headed windows. It contains from the old church the following :—

Fittings—*Brasses :* (1) of William Osborne, 1590, and Annes (Walker) his wife, figures of man and woman, with head missing, eight sons and eight daughters ; (2) to Ann, wife of above, 1607, inscription only. *Font :* octagonal bowl, faces carved with roses or shields, 15th-century ; square base with socket for four angle-shafts, probably late 12th-century.

Condition—Good.

Secular :—

(2). NORTH FAMBRIDGE HALL, E. of the church, is of two storeys, timber-framed and plastered, the roofs are tiled. It was built probably in the 16th century with cross-wings at the E. and W. ends, but has been very extensively altered.

Condition—Good.

———

62. NORTH OCKENDON. (B.d.)

(O.S. 6 in. (a)lxxv. S.W. (b)lxxv. S.E.)

North Ockendon is a parish 5¼ m. S.E. of Romford. The church is the principal monument.

Ecclesiastical :—

[b](1). PARISH CHURCH OF ST. MARY MAGDALENE stands about the middle of the parish. The walls are of ragstone and flint-rubble with dressings of Reigate stone ; the roofs are tiled. The *Nave* and *Chancel* are probably of *c.* 1170, the W. bay of the N. arcade being of the same date or shortly after. About 1240 the *North Aisle* and the three E. bays of the N. arcade were built or rebuilt ; the aisle may have been again rebuilt late in the

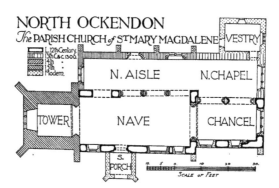

NORTH OCKENDON
The PARISH CHURCH *of* ST MARY MAGDALENE

N. AISLE   N.CHAPEL

TOWER   NAVE   CHANCEL

S. PORCH

Scale of Feet

14th century. About 1300 the *North Chapel* with its arcade was built. Early in the 15th century the E. bay of the N. arcade, and later in the same century the chancel arch, were rebuilt and the *West Tower* added. The church has been drastically restored in modern times, when the *North Vestry* and *South Porch* were added.

The S. doorway is a curious example of 12th-century work, and among the fittings the Poyntz monuments and the stained glass are noteworthy.

Architectural Description—The *Chancel* (22¼ ft. by 13 ft.) has a modern E. window. In the N. wall is an arcade of *c.* 1300 and of two bays with segmental-pointed arches of two chamfered orders, probably rebuilt subsequently; the column is of quatrefoiled plan with a moulded capital carved with vine and oak ornament, etc., and a moulded base; the E. respond has an attached shaft with a moulded base and capital carved with oak ornament; the W. respond has an attached half-column, but without carving; it was probably rebuilt when the chancel was altered. In the S. wall are two modern windows. The late 15th-century chancel-arch is two-centred and of two moulded orders, the outer continuous and the inner resting on attached shafts with moulded capitals and bases.

The *North Chapel* (22 ft. by 14 ft.) has an E. window, modern except for some stones in the splays. In the N. wall is a modern doorway.

The *Nave* (41¼ ft. by 18 ft.) has a N. arcade of four bays; the three eastern bays are of *c.* 1240 with two-centred arches of two chamfered orders; the easternmost bay was rebuilt in the 15th century and the first column is of this date; it is octagonal and has a moulded capital and base; the second column is of the 13th century and cylindrical with moulded capital and hold-water base; the W. respond of the third bay has an attached half-column of the same date; further W. is a late

12th-century arch, two-centred and of one plain chamfered order. In the S. wall are three windows, the easternmost and westernmost are modern; the middle window is of mid-15th-century date, restored externally and of three trefoiled ogee lights with vertical tracery in a four-centred head; further W. is the late 12th-century S. doorway with a round arch, very much stilted, of three orders, the innermost moulded and the outer two carved with cheveron and billet-ornament respectively; the jambs are of four orders, one of which has a round shaft with scalloped or foliated capital and much restored bases with spurs; the abaci are moulded and continued round the three outer orders; the inner order has a later segmental-pointed arch supporting the plain tympanum.

The *North Aisle* (11¼ ft. wide) has in the N. wall a window all modern except the splays and rear-arch, which are probably of late 14th-century date; further W. is the N. doorway, with jambs and two-centred arch of two chamfered orders with a moulded label; it contains much modern stonework, but is probably of late 14th-century date. In the W. wall is a window all modern except the late 14th-century splays and rear-arch.

The *West Tower* (13 ft. by 11½ ft.) is of late 15th-century date and of three stages with an embattled parapet (Plate, pp. xxxii–iii). The two-centred tower-arch is of two hollow-chamfered orders, the outer continuous and the inner resting on attached shafts with moulded capitals and bases. The W. window is of three cinquefoiled lights with tracery in a four-centred head with a moulded label. The N., S. and W. walls of the second stage have each a window of one four-centred light. The bell-chamber has in each wall a window of two cinquefoiled lights in a square head with a moulded label, that of the N. window being of brick.

The *Roof* of the N. chapel is of the 15th century and of trussed-rafter type with one tie-beam. The late 15th-century roof of the nave is of four bays with plain king-post trusses. The roof of the N. aisle is of similar date and construction to that of the nave.

Fittings—*Bells:* five; 1st, 2nd, 4th and 5th by Miles Graye, 1621; 3rd by Philip Wightman, 1695. *Brasses* and *Indents*—Brasses: In N. chapel—on S. wall (1) (Plate, p. 25) of Thomasyn (Ardall) wife of Roger Badby and widow of Robert Latham, 15[32], figure of woman in pedimental head-dress, three shields-of-arms—(*a*) *a chief indented charged with three roundels and a border gobony ermine and . . . a molet for difference* for Lathom; (*b*) Lathom impaling *argent a cheveron between three stars* for Ardall; (*c*) Lathom without the difference; (2) (Plate, p. 25) of William Poyntz (date not shown) and Elizabeth (Shaa) his wife, 1502, figures of man in armour and wife, groups of six sons and six daughters and three shields-of-arms all—*barry of eight in chief a molet* for Poyntz impaling *a cheveron between three lozenges ermine* for Shaa; (3) to John Poyntz, 1547, inscription and four shields-of-arms, two Poyntz and two Poyntz impaling *gyronny four martlets counter-coloured* for Sibles. Indents: In N. chapel—said to be covered by seating, (1) to William Baudwin, 1316, marginal inscription in separate capitals; position uncertain, perhaps lost, (2) to Johan Bauchon, 1323, (3) various broken fragments. *Chest:* In N. aisle—with moulded styles and panelled lid, inlaid front with initials and date W.P., M.P., 1557. *Glass:* In N. chapel —in E. window (Plate, p. 104), figure of St. Mary Magdalene with pot in hand, 15th-century, much repaired; figure of crowned female saint (Plate, pp. xliv-v), with staff-cross and book (probably St. Helen), late 13th-century; three elaborate tabernacled niches with spired canopies and crocketed gables, early 14th-century, fragments including leopards' heads, etc., the whole partly repaired and made up with modern glass. In W. window of tower—seven 14th-century shields-of-arms, Clare, Warenne, England, Old France, Poyntz (Plate, pp. xliv-v), Bohun of Hereford, and Beauchamp (Plate, pp. xliv-v), also an achievement of the quartered arms of Poyntz, dated 1603 (Plate, pp. xliv-v), and some portions of borders. *Monuments* and *Floor-slabs.*—Monuments: In N. chapel —beginning on the N. wall and continuing along the E. wall are a series of eight small monuments (Plate, p. 110) erected by Gabriel Poyntz in 1606 to himself, his son and his six direct ancestors, each monument consists of a kneeling figure of a man in armour and his wife, in a recess, flanked by pilasters of various designs and supporting a cornice with achievement and two shields-of-arms, a curious attempt has been made to make the costumes of the ancestors archaeologically correct;

the following are thus commemorated (1) Thomas Pointz, 1597, and Jane (Pybrian) his wife; (2) Gabriel Pointz and Audrey (Cutts) his wife, erected 1606; (3) Thomas Pointz, 1562, and Ann (van Calva) his wife; (4) John Poinz, elder brother of (3) and Anne (Sibles) his wife; (5) William Poinz, *temp.* Henry VII, and Elizabeth (Shaw) his wife; (6) John Poinz, *temp.* Henry VI, and Matilda (Pertte) his wife; (7) John Pointz, *temp.* Henry IV, and Allionora (Dancote) his wife; (8) Pointz Fitz Pointz, *temp.* Edward III, and Allionora (Bawdin) his wife. The other monuments are as follows—On N. wall of N. chapel (Plate, p. 110), (9) of Catherine (Pointz) wife of John Maurice, early 17th-century, alabaster and marble wall-monument with kneeling figure of man in armour and wife, side-pilasters, entablature and achievement-of-arms; (10) of Sir James Poyntz, alias Morice, 1623, and Richard his son, 1643, alabaster and marble wall-monument with kneeling figures of two men, one in armour, Corinthian side-columns, entablature and achievement-of-arms; (11) of Sir Thomas Poyntz, alias Littleton, Bart., 1709, white marble monument (Plate, p. 100) with bust, composite side-columns, segmental pediment, cherubs and an achievement-of-arms; (12) to Audrey Poyntz, 1594, wooden panel painted with strap-work and gilt; (13) of Sir Gabriel Poyntz, 1607, and Audrey (Cutts) his wife, 1594; marble altar-tomb (Plate, p. 100) with recumbent effigies (Plate, p. 101) of man in armour and wife, panelled-marble backing against wall with achievement and six shields-of-arms and above it a large oak canopy in the form of a tester with cornice and five pendants, soffit painted with clouds, sun, moon and stars. In churchyard—S. side (14) to John Cowland, Sarah his wife, Susannah Cowland and John Cowland, erected by Sarah Cowland, 1712, low table-tomb; (15) to Matthias Fox, 1714, head-stone; (16) to Matthias Fox, 1700, head-stone. Floor-slabs: In N. Chapel—(1) to Sir Thomas Poyntz, alias Littleton, Bart., 1709-10; (2) to Anne, widow of above (1), 1714. *Piscina:* In chancel—with moulded jambs and double two-centred head, corbelled back in the middle, late 13th-century. *Plate* (Plate, p. xliv): includes cup and cover-paten of 1561, cup of 1646, dated 1643, and stand-paten of the same date. *Pulpit:* (Plate, p. 4) hexagonal of three stages, top stage panelled and carved with flowers and foliage, middle stage with irregular panelling, mid 17th-century, bottom stage modern. *Staircase:* to first floor of tower—with solid treads and chamfered runners, 15th-century.

Condition—Good.

Secular :—

ᵇ(2). NORTH OCKENDON HALL, house, outbuilding and moat S. of the church. The *House* is of two

NORTH OCKENDON: PARISH CHURCH OF ST. MARY MAGDALENE.
Monuments of Sir Gabriel Poyntz, 1607, and Audrey, his wife, 1594, and of Sir Thomas Poyntz, 1709.

NORTH OCKENDON: PARISH CHURCH OF ST. MARY MAGDALENE.

Effigies of Sir Gabriel Poyntz, 1607, and Audrey, his wife, 1594.

storeys with attics and cellars ; the walls are of brick ; the roofs are tiled. The L-shaped block at the W. end is of the 16th century, but the upper part of its S. wing was rebuilt *c.* 1700. The E. block is modern. Inside the building the cellar has an original moulded ceiling-beam and a wide open fireplace. There is some early 17th-century panelling in the attics.

The *Outbuilding*, N.E. of the house, is of the 16th century and has brick walls. The E. wall has two original windows with chamfered jambs and four-centred heads and some black brick diapering. Inside the building are chamfered ceiling-beams and exposed timber-framing. The adjoining garden has 16th-century boundary walls containing arched recesses.

The *Moat* formerly enclosed a large area, but the N. and W. arms have been partly filled in.

Condition—Of house, fairly good, but some bad cracks in W. wing.

a(3). BALDWINS, house and moat, 1¼ m. S.W. of the church. The *House* is of two storeys, timber-framed and plastered ; the roofs are covered with slates. It was built in the 16th century. The central chimney-stack has an early 17th-century base. Inside the building the ceiling-beams are exposed.

The *Moat* is fragmentary.

Condition—of house, good.

a(4). STUBBERS, house, outbuilding, barn, and fish-pond nearly 1 m. W. of the church. The *House* is of three storeys ; the walls are partly of plastered timber-framing and partly of brick ; the roofs are tiled. The E. and W. walls incorporate some late 16th-century brickwork, but the house was otherwise almost entirely rebuilt in the 18th century, and there is a modern block in the S. side. Inside the building are some early 17th-century doors and panelling. The E. staircase is of *c.* 1700 with turned balusters and square newels ; the W. stair-case is of similar date and has heavy twisted balusters and square newels with turned tops and pendants.

The *Outbuilding* adjoins the house on the S.E. and is of late 17th-century date ; the walls are of brick. Inside the building are some original panelled doors and exposed ceiling-beams. The *Barn* is of the 16th century, of five bays, timber-framed and weather-boarded ; the roof is of five bays and is thatched. N.E. of the house is a large fish-pond.

Condition—Of house, good.

b(5). HOUSE and smithy 600 yards E. of the church, is of two storeys, timber-framed and plastered ; the roofs are tiled. It was built in the 15th century with cross-wings at the E. and W. ends ; the W. cross-wing has been destroyed. Inside the building are some exposed ceiling-beams and the E. wing has an original king-post roof-truss.

Condition—Good.

b(6). HOUSE, two tenements and Post Office 100 yards N. of (5), is of two storeys with attics ; the walls are timber-framed ; the roofs are tiled. It was built probably in the 16th century with a cross-wing at the E. end. There is a 17th-century extension at the W. end, possibly on the side of an earlier cross-wing. The chimney-stack has early 17th-century diagonal shafts on a rectangular base with a moulded capping. Inside the building some of the timber-work is exposed, and in the cross-wing is an original cambered tie-beam with curved braces.

Condition—Good.

---

63. NORTH SHOEBURY. (F.d.)

(O.S. 6 in. lxxix. S.W.)

North Shoebury is a small parish 3 m. E.N.E. of Southend. The church is the principal monument.

Ecclesiastical :—

(1). PARISH CHURCH OF ST. MARY (Plate, p. xxxii) stands on the W. side of the parish. The walls are of ragstone-rubble with some flint ; the dressings are of Reigate and other limestone ; the roofs are tiled. The church was built during the course of the 13th century, beginning with the *Chancel c.* 1230, the S. arcade of the *Nave c.* 1250, the lower part of the *West Tower* probably late in the 13th century. The N. wall of the Nave was rebuilt about the middle of the 14th century, and the top stage of the tower was added or rebuilt in the 14th or 15th century. The former S. aisle was destroyed at some uncertain date and the arcade built up ; the filling of the middle bay is probably mediaeval. The *South Porch* was added in the 18th century. The church has been restored in modern times.

Amongst the fittings the fragment carved with a cross is noteworthy.

Architectural Description—the Chancel (32½ ft. by 20¾ ft.) has an E. window all modern except the splays and segmental rear-arch ; below it is a moulded internal string-course of the 14th century returned about 5 ft. along the side walls. In the N. wall are three 13th-century lancet-windows with hollow-chamfered rear-arches. In the S. wall are three similar lancet-windows, all partly restored, and at the W. end a "low-side" window of one light with a rounded head, widened from a lancet-window ; E. of it is a 13th-century doorway with chamfered jambs and two-centred arch. The partly restored chancel-arch is probably of the 14th century, and is two-centred and of two chamfered orders, the outer continuous and the inner resting on attached semi-octagonal shafts with modern capitals and bases ; the S. shaft is also modern.

The *Nave* (32 ft. by 21 ft.) has a 14th-century N. wall with three windows ; the easternmost is of two trefoiled lights with a quatrefoil in a two-centred head ; the other two windows are each of two trefoiled ogee lights with tracery in a square head ; between them is the N. doorway with chamfered jambs and two-centred head. In the S. wall is a mid 13th-century arcade of three bays with two-centred arches of two chamfered orders ; the columns are octagonal with moulded capitals and bases and the responds have attached half-columns. The middle bay was blocked probably in the 15th century when the roof was renewed, and the other bays have later blocking containing a modern window and doorway ; the base of the first column has been restored.

The *West Tower* (8¼ ft. square) is of three stages, undivided externally, with a boarded pyramidal "lantern" on the top. The late 13th-century tower-arch is two-centred and of one chamfered order. In the W. wall is a wide lancet-window of the 13th century. The second stage has a rectangular opening in the W. wall. The bell-chamber has no windows and is probably a later addition or rebuilding.

The *Roof* of the nave is of the 15th century, with two king-post trusses with curved braces and traceried spandrels ; the king-posts have moulded capitals and bases, four-way struts and a central purlin, the last is modern ; the N. wall-plate is moulded and embattled, and the S. plate, in the E. bay, is moulded ; the roof has four large head-corbels, probably of the 14th century, reused.

Fittings—Chest : In tower—with slightly cambered lid, lock-plate and two staples, late 16th-century. *Font :* square Purbeck marble bowl with fleurs-de-lis in relief in the spandrels of the top surface, moulded underside and base for one central and four side-shafts, late 12th-century ; square stem with four attached shafts, later. *Glass :* In nave—in three N. windows, in heads and tracery, grisaille foliage (Plate, pp. xliv–v), yellow oak leaves and borders, 14th-century, partly *in situ. Lockers :* In chancel—in N. wall, rectangular with rebated edges, possibly 13th-century ; in E. wall, behind communion table, small square recess with rebated edges and a boarded back, possibly 14th-century. *Painting :* On chancel-arch, remains of red colour, and on the soffit indications of outline of the wood tympanum. *Paving :* In chancel, below altar-step, pavement of square

red tiles with traces of patterns and glazing, mediaeval ; in porch, red tiles, possibly 17th-century. *Piscina :* In chancel—with hollow-chamfered two-centred head and destroyed trefoiled cusping, 14th-century, round drain with mutilated corbel below, 13th-century, bowl broken. *Plate :* includes cup and cover-paten of 1568. *Miscellanea :* In nave—fragment (Plate, p. 25) of head-stone or coffin-lid with richly ornamented cross-head and below the capitals GRE., late 12th or early 13th-century. Under communion table, fragments of 13th-century moulded voussoirs, some with remains of red and black colour.

Condition—Good.

Secular :—

(2). GATEHOUSE and moat at Moat House, 300 yards S.S.W. of the church. The *Gatehouse* is of two storeys, timber-framed and weather-boarded, and was built probably in the 16th century ; it has an entrance archway in the middle and the upper storey projects on the N. side.

The *Moat* is dry on one side.

Condition—Of gatehouse, fairly good.

(3). NORTH SHOEBURY HALL, 60 yards S. of the church, is of two storeys with attics ; the walls are partly of brick and partly of weather-boarded timber-framing ; the roofs are tiled. It was built in the 16th or early in the 17th century and has an original chimney-stack at the W. end with a moulded capping and modern shafts.

Condition—Good.

———

OCKENDON, see NORTH OCKENDON and SOUTH OCKENDON.

———

64. ORSETT. (C.d.)

(O.S. 6 in. [a]lxxvi. S.W. [b]lxxxiii. N.E. [c]lxxxiv. N.W.)

Orsett is a parish and village 4 m. N. of Tilbury. The church, " Bishop Bonner's Palace " and Hall Farm are the principal monuments.

Ecclesiastical :—

[e](1). PARISH CHURCH OF ST. GILES AND ALL SAINTS stands in the middle of the village. The walls are of flint and ragstone-rubble with some Barnack and pudding-stone ; the N.W. tower is mainly of brick. The dressings are of Reigate and other limestone ; the roofs are tiled and the spire weather-boarded. The *Nave* is of mid 12th-century date and incorporates the original 12th-century chancel. A N. aisle of three bays was added *c.* 1230, and about the same time a N. chapel was added to the 12th-century chancel, which may then have been lengthened. About 1330–1340 the present *Chancel* was built beyond

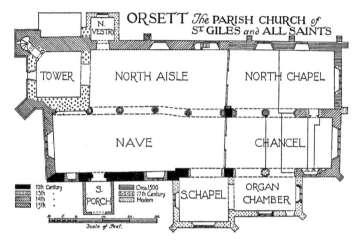

ORSETT *The* PARISH CHURCH *of* S^T GILES *and* ALL SAINTS

N. VESTRY

TOWER

NORTH AISLE

NORTH CHAPEL

NAVE

CHANCEL

S. PORCH

S. CHAPEL

ORGAN CHAMBER

12th Century
13th ,,
14th ,,
15th ,,

Circa 1500
17th Century
Modern

Scale *of* Feet.

the former chancel, which was then thrown into the nave, a connecting bay being inserted between the nave arcade and the 13th-century arch N. of the original chancel; at the same time the 13th-century chapel was abolished and the whole of the *North Aisle* rebuilt and widened. In the 15th century the *North-West Tower* was added, encroaching on the aisle, the W. wall of the nave was rebuilt and the *South Porch* added. About 1500 the *North Chapel* was added. In 1610 much of the tower was rebuilt, and extensive repairs or additions to it were made in 1674. The *Organ Chamber*, *South Transept* and *North Vestry* are modern, and the S. porch has been mostly rebuilt.

Architectural Description—The *Chancel* (39¼ ft. by 18¼ ft.) has an E. window of *c.* 1330–40 and of four trefoiled lights with tracery in a two-centred head with a moulded label, all partly restored. In the N. wall is a late 15th or early 16th-century arcade of two bays with two-centred arches of two moulded orders springing from an octagonal column and semi-octagonal responds with moulded capitals and hollow-chamfered bases. In the S. wall is an early 14th-century window of two trefoiled lights with tracery in a two-centred head with a moulded label; the tracery is partly restored; the S. arcade is modern. There is no chancel-arch.

The *North Chapel* (39 ft. by 21 ft.) has the lower part of the N. and E. walls roughly diapered with flint and ragstone; the E. window is modern. In the N. wall are two windows, the eastern of *c.* 1500,

and of two cinquefoiled lights with vertical tracery in a two-centred head with a moulded label; the western is like the S. window of the chancel, but the tracery has been partly restored; at the W. end of the S. wall is a shallow buttress which probably marks the N.E. angle of the original church.

The modern *Organ Chamber* incorporates in the E. and S. walls two reset and partly restored windows of the same date and similar in design to that in the S. wall of the chancel.

The *Nave* (62¾ ft. by 18½ ft.) has a N. arcade (Plate, p. 37) of five bays, but the westernmost bay now forms a recess, being blocked by the S. wall of the W. tower. The arches are two-centred; the first and the three westernmost are of the 13th century and of two orders, the outer plain and the inner chamfered; the third and fourth arches have plain labels; the westernmost arch and possibly the easternmost arch have been rebuilt and the labels cut back; the second arch is of the 14th century and of two moulded orders with an additional hollow-chamfered order on the S. side; this order is corbelled out on the E. side and on the W. is carried on a carved head-corbel. The E. respond is semi-octagonal and has a partly restored capital and a moulded base partly cut away and repaired in cement; the first two piers are of 14th-century date and have grouped shafts with moulded capitals and bases; the third and fourth piers are circular and the W. respond semi-octagonal, all with moulded capitals and bases. The deflection in the line of the N. wall, in the second bay, is due to the different widths of the early chancel and nave, which joined at this point. In the S. wall is a modern arch and two windows; the eastern is of late 14th-century date and of three ogee cinquefoiled lights with tracery in a square head with a damaged label and head-stops, one of which is modern; the western window is of mid 14th-century date and of two cinquefoiled lights with tracery in a two-centred head with a restored moulded label. Between the windows is the S. doorway (Plate, p. 161), of c. 1160, with a semi-circular arch of two orders, the outer square and the inner carved with cheveron orna-ment and carried on attached shafts with carved capitals and chamfered bases; the abaci are con-tinued along the wall-face and support a label carved with billet-enrichment; the opening has a flat segmental head with small rolls at the angles, and the tympanum is filled with a sunk panel carved with triangular diaper-work. The break in the S. wall marks the entrance of the original chancel. The W. wall has been largely refaced, and the W. window, copied from the late 15th-century original, has been restored except for the rear-arch and parts of the label and outer jambs.

The *North Aisle* (50¼ ft. by 20¼ ft.) has in the N. wall two 14th-century windows, each of two trefoiled lights with a quatrefoil in a two-centred head with a moulded label; the dressings have been repaired in cement; immediately W. of the eastern window is the doorway to the 15th-century rood-loft staircase; it is two-centred, with rebated jambs and head; the stairs are cut through the W. splay of the window and land on the middle of the sill; the 14th-century N. doorway has moulded jambs, two-centred head and label, repaired in cement.

The modern *North Vestry* incorporates some old material.

The *North-West Tower* (16½ ft. square) is of three stages, with a plain parapet and embattled turret; it is surmounted by a pyramidal spire. The lower part of the tower is partly of rubble and of 15th-century date; the E. wall and parts of the other walls are of 17th-century brick. In the E. wall is a round-headed archway with plain plastered imposts and keystone. In the wall above are three un-finished inscriptions, one, "Valentine Carey Deane of S. Paules and parson of Orset gave to this steeple," dates the rebuilding c. 1610; the other inscriptions record the names of other contributors to the tower; above the modern W. doorway is an early 17th-century brick window of three four-centred lights in a square head. The second stage has, in the S. wall, a doorway to the roof with a two-centred head; in the W. wall is a 17th-century brick window of two four-centred lights in a square head with a moulded label. The bell-chamber has in each wall a square-headed window of two four-centred lights with a moulded

label, all repaired in cement. On the S. side of the parapet is the date 1678. The spire is of 1694.

The *South Porch* has been rebuilt, but retains a 15th-century roof of two bays with a moulded cambered tie-beam, king-post, four-way struts, central purlin, braced collar-beams and old rafters.

The *Roof* of the chancel is plastered except the early 16th-century N. and S. wall-plates, which are moulded and embattled. The roof to the N. chapel and aisle is probably of early 17th-century or earlier date and is divided into six bays by chamfered tie-beams; the eastern part of the S. wall-plate is carried on shaped stone corbels; the W. tie-beam rests on square moulded corbels built into the tower wall. The roof of the nave (Plate, p. 37) is of five bays, with moulded tie-beams supported on curved braces with traceried spandrels; the third, fourth, and fifth tie-beams have king-posts with two-way struts and a central purlin, parts of which and the cross-struts have been cut away; across the W. end is a collar with curved braces below forming a two-centred arch; the wall-plates are moulded and embattled; the first two bays are of the 16th and the remainder of the 15th century.

Fittings—*Brasses* and *Indents*. Brasses: In chancel—on N. wall, (1) to Robert Kinge, Parson, 1584, inscription and shield-of-arms; on floor, (2) to Thomas Latham, 1485, and Jane his wife; figures of children, son in long loose gown and two daughters wearing butterfly head-dresses, etc., part of inscription and head of son worn away. In tower, (3) inscription recording bene-faction of Thomas Hotofte, 1495. In vestry, loose, (4) group of six girls, 16th-century. See also Monu-ment (2). Indents: In chancel—forming seat to sedilia, (1) fragment of Purbeck marble slab, with marginal inscription in Lombardic letters, 13th-century. In nave—(2) two large figures with inscription-plate, two groups of children and shield; (3) defaced; (4) inscription-plate; (5) two figures, inscription-plate and two small indents; (6) similar to (5), but figures smaller; (7) figure of woman with inscription-plate. In N. aisle—(8) half figures of man and woman with inscrip-tion-plate. *Chests:* In chancel, of oak, with front of four linen-fold panels with shaped brackets under, end rails carried down to form legs; lid with moulded frame planted on to form panel, late 16th-century. In N. aisle, of oak (Plate p. xliii), with grooved marginal enrichment on front, back and ends, and remains of iron bands, late 16th or early 17th-century, bottom missing, lid in one piece, from older 'dug-out' chest, 13th-century. *Font* (Plate, pp. xlii–iii): octagonal bowl with alternate faces carved with rosettes and shields, one charged with *an archbishop's pall and cross*, prob-ably for the archbishopric of Canterbury, one with *one roundel and a label* possibly for Archbishop Courtenay, the two others each with *a cross;* the

NORTH OCKENDON CHURCH.
Glass in E. window of N. Chapel; 13th, 14th and
15th-century and modern.

SOUTH SHOEBURY CHURCH.
Recesses in S.E. angle of Nave; early 13th-century.

ORSETT CHURCH.
In N. Chapel ; of Sir John Hart, 1658.

WOODHAM FERRERS CHURCH.
Monument of Cecilie, wife of
Edwin Sandys, Archbishop of
York, 1610 : erected 1619.

LITTLE WARLEY CHURCH.
Of Mary Strutt, daughter of Thomas Chapman, 1658.

STANFORD-LE-HOPE CHURCH.
Recess in N. wall of Chancel, 14th-century ;
and Altar-tomb, c. 1500.

RAYLEIGH CHURCH.
In S. Chapel ; early 16th-century.

buttresses, stem and hollow-chamfered base, c. 1500. *Glass :* In nave—in S.E. window, six quatrefoils with rosettes and borders, four partly restored, 14th-century ; in head of middle light, miscellaneous fragments, 15th-century. In N. aisle—in N.E. window, part of border of swastikas and a few oak-leaf quarries, etc., 14th-century ; in middle window, in top quatrefoil, rosette with foliage, portion of border and some oak-leaf quarries, 14th-century. *Monuments* and *Floor-slabs.* Monuments : In N. chapel—against N. wall, (1) to Sir John Hart, 1658, white marble altar-tomb (Plate, p. 105) with black marble moulded bases and top slab, on tomb recumbent effigy, in civil costume, flanked by Ionic columns supporting an entablature with carved frieze and curved pediment, five shields-of-arms ; against S. wall, (2) rectangular Purbeck marble panel with arched recess having trefoiled spandrels and small side shafts ; in panel, brass of kneeling figure of man in civil costume, scroll, and indents of Trinity and inscription-plate, c. 1535. Floor-slabs : In chancel —(1) to Jane, wife of William Gilbert, 1639, with two shields-of-arms ; (2) to William Gilbert, 1640, with two shields-of-arms ; (3) to Matthew Styles, 1652, with shield-of-arms ; (4) to Jane Sonds, 1686. In N. chapel—(5) to John . . . . . , 1658. In nave—(6) to Theophilus Bustard, 1668, and Margaret (Halfhid) his first wife, 1653, with shield-of-arms. In N. aisle—(7) to John Brown, 1597. *Niche :* In N. chapel—in S.W. corner, with lancet-head, much restored. *Painting :* In N. aisle—on W. end of N. wall, traces of long staff and small figure, probably St. Christopher and the Christ Child, late 15th or early 16th-century. *Piscina :* In chancel—with chamfered jambs and trefoiled head with moulded label and quatrefoiled drain, jambs repaired in cement and sill of drain carried along to seats of adjoining sedilia, 14th-century ; shelf modern. *Plate :* includes cup and cover-paten of 1575, flagon of 1677 engraved with inscription and shield and date, 1678, salver of 1677 and dated the same year, and salver of 1688, dated 1705. *Pulpit* (Plate, p. 4) : panelled sides in two tiers with enriched frieze, dentilled cornice and carved shield-of-arms, base and stairs modern ; against the wall at back of stairs, richly carved and arcaded panelling with fluted pilasters at the sides ; in upper panel initials IS.–R.I., in the frieze the date 1630. The pulpit is said to have been brought from Bletchingley. *Screen :* Between N. aisle and N. chapel—mostly modern but incorporating 15th-century traceried heads to the upper panels, lower part of the cornice, and close lower panelling, pierced with two quatrefoils and a trefoil. *Sedilia :* In chancel—of three bays with stepped seats and moulded two-centred arches with moulded labels, springing from Purbeck marble shafts with moulded capitals and bases, 14th-century. *Sundials :* Two, on E. jamb of S.

doorway, triangular with three radiating sinkings. *Weathervane :* On spire, of wrought iron with initials I.B.–I.F. and date 1694. *Miscellanea :* In vestry—two pots said to have been dug up in the churchyard, also rowel-spur, probably 16th-century. In nave—stone mortar.

Condition—Good.

Secular :—

ᵉ(2). " BISHOP BONNER'S PALACE," ring and bailey earthwork, ¼ m. N.W. of the church. The work consists of a circular enclosure (200 ft. internal diameter) surrounded by a ditch about 50 ft. wide. To the N. is an oblong bailey enclosed by a well-defined ditch ; on the N. side the defences are strengthened by a second ditch. The work is said to be the site of a palace of the bishops of London, but the only remains of buildings is a fragment of rubble foundation on the N.W. side of the ring-work. In a wood 200 yards to the W. is a large oblong fish-pond.

Condition—Fairly good.

ᵉ(3). ORSETT HALL, ½ m. E.N.E. of the church, has been practically rebuilt, but a room in the S.E. corner of the building has a mid 17th-century plaster ceiling and a stone fireplace (Plate, p. 97). The ceiling is divided by a ceiling-beam into two bays subdivided by moulded ribs into panels of varying form with small pendants at the main intersections and sprigs of foliage, cherubs-heads and rosettes in the panels. The fireplace has moulded jambs and four-centred arch and is flanked by strapwork pilasters with terminal figures supporting an overmantel of two arched bays divided by similar pilasters and carved with figures of Hope and Charity ; the entablature is enriched with heads and arabesques with birds. In the hall is some original panelling.

Condition—Good.

MONUMENTS (4–22).

The following monuments, unless otherwise described, are of the 17th century and of two storeys, timber-framed and plastered or weather-boarded ; the roofs are tiled or thatched. Some of the buildings have exposed ceiling-beams or original chimney-stacks.

Condition—Good, or fairly good, unless noted.

ᵉ(4). *Birch Terrace*, house (Plate, pp. xl–i), three tenements, 100 yards E. of the church, has a 16th-century cross-wing at the S. end. The upper storey projects at the W. end of the cross-wing and has exposed timber-framing.

ᵉ(5). *Crown House*, formerly inn, 30 yards S.W. of the church, has an original chimney-stack on the N. with the initials and date $\frac{M}{I\,D}$ 1674 (?).

Inside the building are some old battened doors.

Condition—Poor.

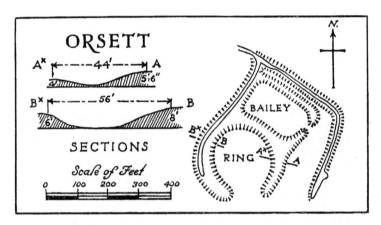

e(6). *Cottage,* S.W. of (5) on S. side of road, has an original panelled door.

Condition—Bad.

e(7). *Cottage,* E. of (6).

Condition—Bad.

e(8). *House,* and shop, E. of (7), has cross-wings at the E. and W. ends.

e(9). *Church House,* now post-office, E. of (8), has a cross-wing at E. end with the upper storey projecting in front. Inside the building is an original battened door.

e(10). *Barrington's Farm,* house, 1200 yards S.E. of the church, was built late in the 17th or early in the 18th century, but has been refaced with modern brick. Inside the building is an original battened door.

e(11). *Cock Inn,* 280 yards S. of (10).

e(12). *Seaborough Hall,* nearly 1¼ m. S.S.E. of the church, has a cross-wing at the W. end. Inside the building are some old battened doors.

Condition—Poor.

e(13). *" Five Chimneys,"* house, two tenements, about ¾ m. S.S.W. of the church, was built late in the 17th or early in the 18th century.

Condition—Bad.

e(14). *Cottage,* at N.W. side of Orsett Heath, nearly 1¼ m. S.S.W. of the church, was built late in the 17th or early in the 18th century.

b(15). *Kempsters,* house, 1 m. S.W. of the church, has a cross-wing at the N. end and has been partly refaced with brick.

b(16). *House,* at S.E. angle of cross-roads at Baker Street, ¾ m. W.S.W. of the church, was built probably in the 16th century and has a cross-wing at the W. end. The upper storey projects at the N. end of the cross-wing.

b(17). *Mill House* (Plate, pp. xl–i), 70 yards W. of (16), has a later addition on the S. The upper storey projects on part of the N. front. Inside the building the early 18th-century staircase has a close string, turned balusters and square newels.

b(18). *Greygoose Farm,* house, 1½ m. W.S.W. of the church.

e(19). *Hill House,* 700 yards W.S.W. of the church, has a two-storeyed porch on the S. front with a hipped roof.

e(20). *Hall Farm,* house and " cage," about 400 yards N.W. of the church. The *House* has been rebuilt except for the early 16th-century E. portion (Plate, p. xxxiv), which is a good example of exposed timber-framing. The upper storey projects and is gabled at the E. end, and each storey has an original window of eight lights with pointed heads ; at the base of the gable is a moulded and enriched beam and the barge-boards are also moulded. On the S. side is an original moulded ceiling-beam.

The " *Cage* " or lock-up has been re-erected E. of the house. It is a timber-framed structure (8 ft. by 5 ft.) with a hipped roof. It has a small two-light window fitted with iron bars and a battened door.

e(21). *House,* ¼ m. E. of (20), has a cross-wing at the E. end.

Condition—Poor.

*(22). *Lorkins*, house, 1¼ m. N. by E. of the church, was built in the 15th century and has a cross-wing at the W. end. The upper storey projects at the S. end of the cross-wing on curved brackets; at the base of the gable is a moulded bressummer. Inside the building the main block has been divided into two storeys, but retains its original king-post roof.

Unclassified :—

*(23). DENEHOLES in Hangman's Wood, mostly in Little Thurrock parish (*q.v.*).

---

65. PAGLESHAM. (F.c.)

(O.S. 6 in. (*a*)lxx. N.E. (*b*)lxxi. S.W.)

Paglesham is a parish on the N. bank of the Roach, 6 m. N.E. of Southend-on-Sea.

Ecclesiastical :—

*(1). PARISH CHURCH OF ST. PETER stands in the village. The walls are of stone, with some flint and Roman brick; the roofs are tiled. The *Chancel* and *Nave* contain some 12th-century work, but in the 15th century the S. wall of the chancel and the greater part of the N. and S. walls of the nave were rebuilt, and the chancel-arch was widened and partly rebuilt at the same time. The *West Tower* was added early in the 16th century. The church was extensively repaired and the chancel walls refaced in 1883; at the same time the upper parts of the N. and S. walls of the nave were refaced or rebuilt. The *North Vestry* and *South Porch* are modern.

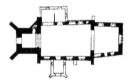

Architectural Description—The *Chancel* (18 ft. by 17½ ft.) has an early 15th-century E. window partly restored and of three cinquefoiled lights with tracery in a two-centred head with a moulded label. In the N. wall are two modern windows. In the S. wall are two much restored early 16th-century windows; the first a single square-headed light; the second of two cinquefoiled lights in a square head with a moulded label; between the windows is a doorway, probably of the same date, with hollow-chamfered jambs and rounded head. The chancel-arch, two-centred and of one plain order, was probably rebuilt in the 15th century with reused material; the lower parts of the responds are of 13th-century date, and the wall above the springing has a set-back of 4 in.

The *Nave* (37½ ft. by 22¾ ft.) was mostly rebuilt in the 15th century, but a few feet of the lower part at the E. end of the N. wall are of 12th-century date. In the N. wall, at the E. end is a modern window; further W. is a window all modern except the early 16th-century splays and rear-arch; the early 16th-century N. doorway, now opening into the modern vestry, has moulded jambs and two-centred head with a moulded label; at the E. end of the wall are parts of the jambs of a blocked doorway to the rood-loft staircase. In the S. wall are three modern windows incorporating some reused stones in the splays and in one of the rear-arches, head-stops and parts of a moulded label with carved flowers. Between the second and third windows is an early 16th-century doorway with moulded jambs and two-centred head with a moulded label.

The *West Tower* (11¼ ft. by 10 ft.) was built early in the 16th century and is of three stages, with an embattled parapet (Plate, pp. xxxii-iii). The tower-arch is two-centred and of three hollow-chamfered orders, the inner one being carried on semi-octagonal responds with moulded capitals and bases. The W. doorway has moulded jambs and two-centred head with a moulded label; the W. window is of three cinquefoiled lights with vertical tracery in a two-centred head·with moulded external jambs and label. The second stage has in each wall a window of one trefoiled light with a square moulded label. The bell-chamber has in each wall a square-headed window of two cinquefoiled lights in a square head with a defaced moulded label.

Fittings—*Bells*: three, 1st by John Dier, 1598; 2nd by Charles Newman, 1693; 3rd no inscription, possibly early 18th-century. *Brass Indents*: In S. porch—(1) of inscription-plate; (2) of figure and inscription-plate. *Chairs*: In chancel—two, of oak elaborately carved (Plate, p. xlii), late 17th-century. *Chest*: In vestry—of oak, plain and made up of 13th century and later woodwork, including Italian carved poker-work panel in the back, 16th-century. *Coffin-lid*: S. of tower, large fragment, carved with part of stem of raised cross, possibly 13th-century. *Doors*: In S. doorway— of ridged battens with hollow-chamfered ribs planted on, two strap-hinges and lock-plate, early 16th-century, ribs partly restored. In tower—in W. doorway, of battens with fillets planted on and strap-hinges, 15th-century; in ground-stage door-way of stair-turret, of studded feathered battens with two strap-hinges, 15th-century; in second-stage doorway of stair-turret, of vertical battens fixed to horizontal ones, with two strap-hinges, ring - handle and circular plate, 15th-century. *Monuments*: In churchyard—S. side of S. porch, (1) to Richard Hagman, 1681, shaped head-stone with skull, cross-bones and fleur-de-lis. S. of tower (2) to John Stiltamen, 1714, head-stone. *Piscinae*: In chancel, S. of E. window, with square projecting bowl in shape of scalloped capital with central drain, c. 1150; stem modern. In nave, at E. end of S. wall, with hollow-chamfered jambs and cinquefoiled head, sexfoiled drain and mortice for shelf, 15th-century, partly mutilated. *Plate:* includes cup and cover-paten of 1568, with bands of engraved ornament, etc. *Scratchings:* In nave, on dressings to N. and S. doorways and in tower, on dressings to tower-arch and W. doorway, masons' marks.

Condition—Good.

Secular :—

HOMESTEAD MOATS.

a(2). At West Hall, nearly ¾ m. W. of the church.

b(3). At East Hall, about ½ m. E.S.E. of the church.

MONUMENTS (4–7).

The following monuments are, unless otherwise described, of the 17th-century, and of two storeys, timber-framed and plastered or weather-boarded ; the roofs are tiled. Some of the buildings have original chimney-stacks and exposed ceiling-beams. Condition—Good.

b(4). *Church Hall*, 50 yards E. of the church, is of brick. It has a late 18th-century addition on the N. and has been much altered.

b(5). *House*, now four tenements, 50 yards S. of (4), is of two storeys with attics. The W. wing was built early in the 17th century, and to it was added on the E., late in the same century, an L-shaped extension.

b(6). *Plough and Sail Inn*, at Eastend, nearly 1¼ m. S.E. of the church, is a small central-chimney type of building with modern additions at the back. Inside the building is a 17th-century battened door.

b(7). *House*, now five tenements, 100 yards N. of (6), is of one storey with attics. It has 18th-century additions at either end.

Unclassified :—

b(8). RED HILLS, at East Hall, about ½ m. E.S.E. of the church. There is another at South Hall, about ¼ m. S. of East Hall.

66. PITSEA. (D.d.)

(O.S. 6 in. *(a)*lxix. S.W. *(b)*lxxvii. N.W.)

Pitsea is a small parish 9 m. W.N.W. of Southend-on-Sea.

Ecclesiastical :—

b(1). PARISH CHURCH OF ST. MICHAEL stands near the middle of the parish. The *West Tower* was built early in the 16th century and is ashlar-faced with dressings of Reigate stone. The rest of the church was rebuilt in 1871.

Architectural Description—The *West Tower* (8 ft. square) is of three stages, undivided externally

(Plate, pp. xxxii–iii), and with an embattled parapet and carved gargoyles at the angles. In the E. wall is a doorway with chamfered jambs and two-centred arch. The W. window is of one square-headed light. The second stage has in the W. wall a similar window. The bell-chamber has in the E. wall a square-headed loop; the other three sides have each a window of one trefoiled light with a square moulded label.

Fittings—*Bells:* three ; 1st and 2nd by John Wilnar, 1636 ; 3rd by Henry Jordan, 15th-century and inscribed " Sancte Petre Ora Pro Nobis." *Brass:* In chancel—on S. wall, to Elizabeth (Raye) wife of John Purlenant, 1588, inscription only. *Font:* octagonal bowl with moulded lower-edge, plain stem and hollow-chamfered base, early 16th-century. *Plate:* includes cup of 1568, and stand-paten of 1692, with shield-of-arms of Sir Thomas Moyer. *Scratchings:* on E. doorway of tower, masons' marks, early 16th-century.

Condition—Of tower, good.

Secular :—

b(2). PITSEA HALL, 350 yards S.W. of the church, is of two storeys with attics and cellar. The walls are of plastered timber-framing and the roofs are tiled ; the cellar, which is under the W. end of the house, is of brick. It was built late in the 16th century, and has a later N.W. addition and a modern extension on the W. The upper storey projects on the E. end of the N. front and has a moulded bressummer with a shaped bracket at the E. end. Inside the building some of the principal beams of the ground-floor rooms are exposed.

Condition—Good.

a(3). GREAT CHALVEDON HALL, about 1 m. N.N.E. of the church, is of two storeys with attics. The walls are of plastered and weather-boarded timber-framing ; the roofs are tiled. It was built in the first half of the 16th century and, though there appears originally to have been another wing on the W., the existing 16th-century building· is of E-shaped plan, with the wings extending towards the N. There are modern extensions on the N. On the S. front are three gables. The main chimney-stack has grouped diagonal shafts on a rectangular base ; in the W. wall at the first-floor level is a blocked doorway with a segmental-pointed head. Inside the building much of the timber-framing is exposed, and many of the rooms have open-timber ceilings. The main fireplace on the ground-floor has a moulded and cambered head. The attic storey above the staircase has a blocked two-light window with moulded mullions, and on the first floor are several 16th-century doors. The roof over the E. wing has cambered tie-beams and collars, and that over the W. wing has a cambered tie-beam with heavy curved braces.

Condition—Good.

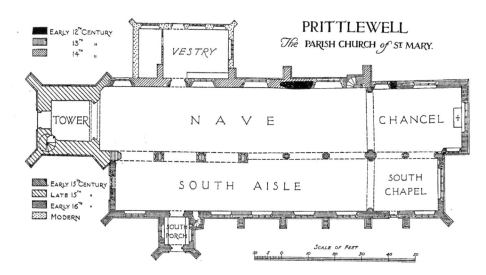

EARLY 12TH CENTURY
13TH "
14TH "

PRITTLEWELL
The PARISH CHURCH *of* ST MARY.

EARLY 15TH CENTURY
LATE 15TH "
EARLY 16TH "
MODERN

VESTRY

TOWER

N A V E

CHANCEL

SOUTH AISLE

SOUTH
CHAPEL

SOUTH
PORCH

SCALE OF FEET

67. PRITTLEWELL. (F.d.)

(O.S. 6 in. [a]lxxviii. N.W. [b]lxxviii. N.E.
[c]lxxviii. S.E.)

Prittlewell is a parish on the N. side of the
Thames Estuary. It includes the town of Southend-on-Sea. The principal monuments are the
church, Priory and Porters.

Ecclesiastical :—

[b](1). PARISH CHURCH OF ST. MARY stands in the
village. The walls are of ragstone-rubble with a
little flint; the dressings are of Reigate and Kentish
ragstone; the roofs are covered with lead and
slates. The N. wall of the chancel, and perhaps
part of the N. wall of the nave, appear to date
from the beginning of the 12th century, and the
S. wall of the *Nave* above the arcade is of rather
later date. At this period the church appears to
have had a central tower. In the second half of
the 13th century the three W. bays of the S.
arcade, with probably a fourth further E., were
built and a S. aisle added. The N. wall of the
nave appears to have been rebuilt at some uncertain
period, possibly the 14th century. The *West
Tower* was added *c.* 1470. *C.* 1500–30 the church
was much altered, the *Chancel* largely rebuilt,
the *South Chapel* added, the S. arcade of the
nave extended E. on the site of the former central

tower, a clearstorey added to the corresponding
portion of the N. wall, the *South Aisle* rebuilt
and widened and the *South Porch* added. The
church was restored in modern times, when the
North Vestry was added.

The church is of considerable architectural
interest from its variety of styles. Among the
fittings the S. door and the well preserved coffin-lid
are noteworthy.

The *Chancel* (33 ft. by 22 ft.) has an E. window
all modern except the early 16th-century hollow-
chamfered splays and four-centred rear-arch. In
the N. wall are two windows, the eastern is modern
except the early 16th-century splays and four-
centred rear-arch; the western is also modern
except for the 15th-century splays and hollow-
chamfered segmental rear-arch; this window is
set low in the wall; between the windows is the
W. part of an early 12th-century round arch
probably a doorway, partly of Roman brick and
partly of ragstone; it is visible both inside and
outside. In the S. wall is a 15th-century window
of two cinquefoiled lights in a segmental head,
all modern externally. Further W. is an early
16th-century arcade of two bays with two-centred
arches of two orders, the outer moulded and the
inner hollow-chamfered; the octagonal column
has concave faces and moulded capital and base;
the responds have attached half-columns. The

early 16th-century chancel-arch is generally similar to the S. arcade, but with slightly different mouldings ; the outer order is probably of 13th-century material reused.

The *South Chapel* (24 ft. by 19 ft.) has an E. window, modern except for the early 16th-century splays and rear-arch. In the S. wall are two windows ; the eastern is modern except the splays and two-centred rear-arch, which are probably of the 15th century, reset ; the western window is modern except the early 16th-century splays and four-centred rear-arch ; below it is a doorway, modern except the early 16th-century splays and four-centred rear-arch. The early 16th-century W. arch is similar to the chancel-arch except that it is four-centred.

The *Nave* (100 ft. by 23½ ft.) has a square portion at the E. end, separately roofed and no doubt indicating the position of the former central tower. In the N. wall are four lower windows ; the eastern is modern except the early 16th-century W. splay and segmental-pointed rear-arch ; the second is modern except the splays and two-centred rear-arch, which are possibly of the 14th century ; the third is modern except the early 16th-century splays and segmental-pointed rear-arch ; the westernmost window is of early 16th-century date, partly restored and of three cinquefoiled lights in a square head ; E. of the easternmost window is the early 16th-century rood-loft staircase ; the lower doorway has rebated jambs and a modern head, and there are faint traces of the blocked upper doorway ; further E. is part of a 15th-century splay of a doorway or window ; above the head of the easternmost window is the E. part of the relieving-arch of an earlier window ; E. of the head of the second window is part of the rear-arch of an earlier pointed window ; the N. doorway is of early 15th-century date with modern jambs and chamfered two-centred arch. The wall of the two E. bays (representing the former central tower) is carried up as a clearstorey and has two early 16th-century windows, modern externally and each of two trefoiled lights in a square head. The S. arcade is of six bays (Plate, p. 110) ; the three eastern bays are of early 16th-century date and of detail similar to the chancel-arch ; the three W. bays are of the 13th-century, with two-centred arches of one chamfered order ; the three W. columns are octagonal with moulded capitals and bases, octagonal to square on plan ; the W. respond has an·attached half-column ; above the two W. piers of the 13th-century work are two 12th-century windows (Plate, p. 110), each of one round-headed light and blocked when the arcade was built but now partly opened-out again ; there are parts of a similar window above the third pier from the E. ; the comparatively low level of these windows implies that the 12th-century nave was aisleless ; the two E. bays of the wall are carried

up as a clearstorey and have two windows similar to those of the N. clearstorey.

The *South Aisle* (17½ ft. wide) has a modern embattled parapet but old carved heads at the level of the string-course. In the S. wall are five windows all modern except the early 16th-century splays and four-centred rear-arches ; between the fourth and fifth windows is the early 16th-century S. doorway with moulded jambs, two-centred arch and label ; further E. is a small early 16th-century doorway to the staircase to the room above the porch ; it has moulded jambs and four-centred head. In the W. wall is a window similar to those in the S. wall ; below it is an early 15th-century doorway, now blocked, and with moulded jambs, two-centred arch and label.

The *West Tower* (14½ ft. square) is of the 15th century, and was finished *c.* 1470 ; it is of four stages with a moulded plinth and embattled chequer-work parapet with octagonal turrets at the angles continued down to the base of the bell-chamber and capped with crocketed pinnacles (Plate, p. 97). The two-centred tower-arch is of three orders, the two outer chamfered and continuous and the inner resting on attached shafts with moulded capitals and bases. The W. window is modern except the splays and two-centred rear-arch ; the W. doorway has moulded jambs and two-centred arch in a square head with a defaced label and spandrels enclosing two shields, one with a cross of St. George and one defaced ; flanking the doorway are two carved head-corbels. The doorway to the turret-staircase, in the splayed S.W. angle, has moulded jambs, two-centred arch and label ; above it is a second doorway with rebated and chamfered jambs and two-centred arch ; it is now blocked, but formerly opened on to a ringing-gallery, of which four corbels remain. Flanking the W. window externally are two much-weathered niches with two-centred heads and square moulded labels. On the S. wall of the ground-stage, externally, is a row of corbels, of doubtful purpose, but resembling those of a pent roof. The N., S. and W. walls of the second stage have each a window of two cinquefoiled lights in a square head with a moulded label ; except for the N. window all have been completely restored externally below the label. The N. and S. windows are much-weathered niches with cinquefoiled heads and square labels. The third stage has in both the E. and W. walls a window of two cinquefoiled lights in a four-centred head with a moulded label ; there are modern clock-faces in the N. and S. walls. The bell-chamber has in each wall a window of three cinquefoiled lights with intersecting tracery in a four-centred head with a moulded label ; the S. and W. windows are much restored.

The *South Porch* is of early 16th-century date, and of two storeys with an embattled parapet of

NORTH OCKENDON : PARISH CHURCH OF ST. MARY MAGDALENE.
Monuments in the N. Chapel to the Poyntz Family ; 17th-century.

PRITTLEWELL : PARISH CHURCH OF ST. MARY.
Interior from S. Aisle, showing S. Arcade of Nave ; E. half, early 16th-century, W. half,
13th-century ; disused windows over, 12th-century.

PRITTLEWELL: (2). PRITTLEWELL PRIORY.
Roof of upper room in W. Range ; 15th-century.

PRITTLEWELL: (3). PORTERS.
Interior of Hall, showing Panelling, early 16th-century, and Fireplace, late 16th-century.

flint chequer-work. The four-centred outer arch-way is of two moulded orders, the outer continuous and the inner resting on attached shafts with moulded capitals and bases ; there is also a moulded label ; the archway has been much restored in cement. The upper storey has a window of one four-centred light in a square head, restored in cement. The side walls of the lower storey have each a window of two cinquefoiled lights in a square head with a moulded label, all much decayed ; higher up in the W. wall is a plain loop.

The *Roof* of the ground-stage of the tower has moulded main timbers, plain joists and a square bell-way, all of the 15th century.

Fittings—*Coffin-lid :* In nave—in N.W. angle, with hollow-chamfered edge and raised cross, 13th-century. *Door* (Plate, pp. 4-5) : In S. doorway—of five upright panels with embattled rails, panels carved with trefoiled ogee arches and crocketed finials, quatrefoils in lowest tier, early 16th-century. *Font:* octagonal bowl with concave panelled faces, six carved with, a rose (twice), a heart with two crossed spears, a shield with *a cheveron between three fleurs-de-lis*, a defaced crucifix and a dimidiated Tudor rose and pomegranate, square stem with attached shafts at angles having moulded bases, early 16th-century. *Glass :* In S. chapel—in E. window, twelve panels with figure-subjects, (*a*) Elijah's sacrifice ; (*b*) the Virgin and Child enthroned ; (*c*) Christ and St. John the Baptist ; (*d*) the Building of the Temple ; (*e*) Jesse enthroned with his Tree behind ; (*f*) Christ before Caiaphas ; (*g*) Christ appearing to the disciples after the Resurrection ; (*h*) David and the Anointing of Solomon ; (*i*) Elisha and the Shunammite's son ; (*j*) The Temptation (Plate, pp. xliv-v) ; (*k*) the Ecce Homo ; (*l*) the Three Children in the fiery furnace ; glass all foreign ; (*f*) and (*g*) possibly 17th-century, rest 16th-century. *Monuments :* In nave—on N. wall, (1) to Mary (Cocke) wife of Richard Davies, 1623, alabaster and black marble tablet with side pilasters and achievement-of-arms. In churchyard —E. side, (2) to Dorothy Freeborne, 1641, and Samuel her husband, 1658 (?), table-tomb. *Niche :* In S. chapel—in E. wall, with head broken away, date uncertain. In nave—in face of W. pier of arcade, small with four-centred head, 15th-century. See also Architectural Description, under Tower. *Panelling :* In nave—framed on N. wall, two long portions of oak panelling, probably from chest, (*a*) upper part of winged beast or beasts with intertwined necks ; (*b*) elaborate window-tracery, both probably foreign, *c.* 1500. *Piscina :* In S. chapel—in S. wall, with flat cinquefoiled head, drain broken, *c.* 1500. *Plate :* includes large cup of 1668. *Stoup :* In S. porch—with four-centred head, bowl destroyed, *c.* 1500. *Miscellanea :* In churchyard—fragments of window-tracery, worked stones, etc., 15th and early 16th-century.

Condition—Good, but much decay in external stonework ; porch recently restored.

Secular :—

b(2). PRITTLEWELL PRIORY, house, walls and foundations, 550 yards N. of the church. The Priory was founded for Cluniac monks as a cell to Lewes, at the end of the 11th or beginning of the 12th century. It was dissolved in 1536. Of the existing remains the N. wall of the *Frater* was built late in the 12th century. The remaining parts of the W. range are apparently of the 15th century. There is no evidence of the date of the foundations and remaining fragments of the church. The church and E. range were destroyed probably soon after the dissolution. The W. and S. ranges were turned into a house and very much altered. Extensive 18th-century or modern additions were made on the W. side. The building has recently been completely restored, the Frater cleared and extended to its original length, and the site of the church excavated.

The *Walls* are mainly of rubble repaired and partly refaced with modern brick. The roofs are tiled.

The foundations of the *Church* are very indeterminate as to the E. end ; the nave, however, had a S. aisle, of which the foundations of two rectangular piers have been uncovered. A long stretch of foundation on the N. side may indicate a sleeper-wall under the N. arcade or a N. wall.

The *Cloister* (88 ft. E. to W. by 87 ft. N. to S.) is bounded on the N. by a rubble wall which is mainly a part of the S. wall of the church considerably patched ; there are slight indications of the position of the western processional entrance.

The *Frater* (76 ft. by 26 ft.) has modern walls built on the old foundations, except on the N. side. In this wall is a late 12th-century door-way (Plate, p. 121), considerably restored, with a two-centred arch of two moulded orders enriched with cheveron and dog-tooth ornament ; the moulded jambs have each a restored free shaft with moulded and foliated bell-capital and square abacus ; above is an offset for the cloister roof, and further E. one original corbel of the same roof. Near the middle of the wall externally is a patch of brick-blocking with one stopped jamb of stone on the W. side and possibly representing the lavatory. Higher in the wall is a range of small pointed windows all modern except one, which has a moulded trefoiled head, shafted splays with moulded imposts and a moulded rear-arch with dog-tooth ornament. Reset on the internal wall further W. is a section of a large moulded arch with nail-head ornament. The roof of the frater is mainly of early 15th-century date, with king-post trusses, moulded tie-beams, rebated king-posts and four-way struts.

The *West Range* has on the ground-floor two barrel-vaulted chambers and half of a third probably of 15th-century date ; in the S. wall of the southernmost is a 15th-century doorway with a

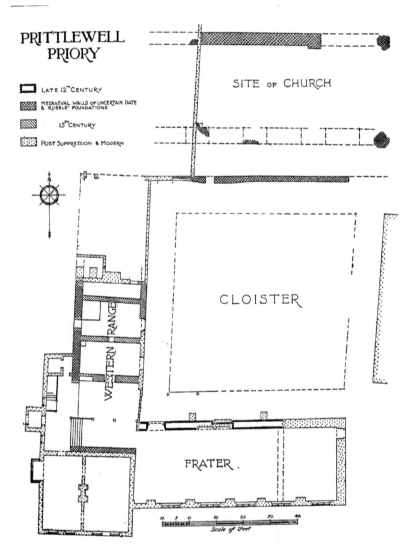

PRITTLEWELL
PRIORY

LATE 12ᵀᴴ CENTURY
MEDIAEVAL WALLS OF UNCERTAIN DATE & RUBBLE" FOUNDATIONS
15ᵀᴴ CENTURY
POST SUPPRESSION & MODERN

SITE OF CHURCH

CLOISTER

WESTERN RANGE

FRATER.

Scale of Feet

four-centred head. The upper floor of the W. range is timber-framed, with modern windows of the old design and a 15th-century roof (Plate, p. 111) of five bays with two original king-post trusses, double chamfered tie-beams, octagonal king-posts with moulded capitals and bases and four-way struts ; the rafters are smoke-blackened. At the N. end is a reset 16th-century fireplace with moulded jambs and four-centred arch in a square head.

Preserved in the building are many worked and moulded stones from the 12th to the 15th century, including coupled column-caps, cusped panelling, dog-tooth ornament, etc. There is also a stone coffin.

Condition—Good.

ᵉ(3). PORTERS, house (Plate, p. 114), 70 yards S. of All Saints' Church, is of two storeys with attics and basement. The walls are of brick with some stone dressings ; the roofs are tiled. Parts of the house are of early 16th-century date, but it was completed or extensively rebuilt towards the end of the same century. The original house was built probably on a half H-shaped plan with the cross-wings extending towards the S., but the space between the cross-wings was apparently filled in at the rebuilding and an entrance porch built on the N. front. In the 17th century a small addition was made on the middle of the W. front, and there are traces of a corresponding addition on the E. side ; modern alterations include the building of a porch at the S.W. corner.

Elevations—The N. Front has a moulded plinth, which is continued round the building, and is gabled at either end. The E. gable has an original transomed and mullioned window to both the ground and first floors and a three-light window to the attics ; the W. gable is similar, but the two lower windows are of four lights. The porch has a square-headed entrance with a moulded oak frame with moulded base and stops set in a brick opening with splayed jambs and head ; in each of the side walls is a two-light window of brick ; the inner doorway is chamfered but otherwise similar to the entrance, but set in chamfered brick, and has an original door of three long panels. Lighting the hall are two late 16th-century windows, one of three the other of five transomed lights, but the windows to the upper floors of the central block are modern, as is the gable of the porch. On the E. Front is a rectangular chimney-stack with three diagonal shafts. The S. Front is similar in arrangement to the N. front, but only the windows in the gables and those in the main block are original. The W. Front has three original windows and an original chimney-stack with three diagonal shafts. The chimney-stack in the middle of the main block has three detached diagonal shafts.

Interior—The Hall (Plate, p. 111) has exposed ceiling-beams, and in the S. wall is a late 16th-century stone fireplace (Plate, p. 65) with a straight-sided four-centred head and small shields and carved leaves in the spandrels, above the opening is a frieze carved with masks and acanthus leaves which terminate in half-figures supporting a cartouche of strapwork. The walls are lined with early 16th-century linen-fold panelling with some modern work and incorporating five early 16th-century panels of foreign workmanship (probably French), each carved in bold relief with the figure of a king and retaining traces of colour. In the early 17th-century panelled screen at the W. end of the hall are two doorways with flat heads and arched angles, carved spandrels and fluted pilasters at the sides. At the S. end of the 'screens' is a moulded square-headed doorway with a 17th-century door. The room in the S.E. angle of the house has a fireplace of similar design to that in the hall but with a less elaborately carved frieze. Adjoining the modern E. staircase is a central-newel staircase with a double row of early 17th-century turned balusters at the first-floor landing ; the 17th-century door to the cellar stairs has large strap-hinges. The Kitchen has the timber-framing and ceiling-beams exposed ; the fireplace has a wide four-centred head, and the door has an old fleur-de-lis hinge and a grating. On the First Floor, the rooms in the E. wing and above the hall have fireplaces of similar design to that in the S.E. room on the ground-floor, but with varying detail. The room above the kitchen has a fireplace with a moulded four-centred arch and in the E. wall a moulded square-headed doorway. The roofs are of collar-beam type with braced purlins; that over the main block has curved braces to the principals.

Condition—Good.

MONUMENTS (4–12).

The following monuments, unless otherwise described, are of the 17th century, and of two storeys, timber-framed and plastered ; the roofs are tiled. Some of the buildings have original chimney-stacks and exposed ceiling-beams.

Condition—Good.

ᵇ(4). House, now two shops (Plate, p. xl), on W. side of North Street, 50 yards W. of the church, was built early in the 16th century on a half H-shaped plan with the cross-wings extending towards the W. A cart-way through the N. end of the central block was made probably at some later date. The upper storey of the cross-wings originally projected on the E. front and at the W. end of the N. wing, but two of these projections have been underbuilt. Inside the building some of the constructional timbers are exposed.

H

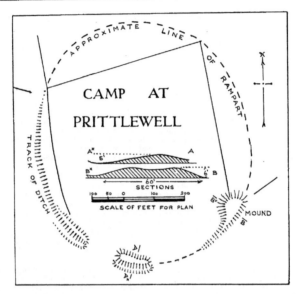

b(5). *Shop*, 20 yards S. of (4) is a fragment of a 16th-century house which was added to, on the E. side, in the following century. On the S. side of the earlier building the timber-framing is exposed, and in the party wall is a blocked three-light window with moulded frame and mullions.

b(6). *Deeds Cottages*, house (Plate, pp. xl–i), now a bank and shop, at corner of North Street and West Street and immediately S. of (5), is of weather-boarded timber-framing. It was built in the 16th century, but has been much altered.

a(7). *Great Folly*, house, about 1½ m. W. of the church, has been much altered, and added to on the S. and W. Inside the building is an original staircase, now blocked.

a(8). *Coleman's Farm*, house, nearly 1 m. N.W. the church, has modern additions on the N. and S.

a(9). *Whitehouse Farm*, house, nearly 1 m. N.N.W. of the church, has modern additions on the E. The upper storey projects on the W. front.

b(10). *Temple Farm*, house, about 1 m. N.N.E. of the church, has timber-framed walls partly weather-boarded and partly covered with plaster. The main part of the building is of 16th-century date and L-shaped on plan with the wings extending towards the S. and E., but it has been considerably altered and added to. Inside the E. wing of the house is an original doorway with a four-centred head.

b(11). *Hamstel*, house, nearly 1¼ m. E. of the church, has modern additions on the N.

b(12). *Cooper's Farm*, house, about 1 m. N.E. of the church, was built probably c. 1600. The upper storey projects at the back. Inside the building two rooms are lined with early 17th-century panelling and there is an original stone fireplace with moulded jambs and four-centred head.

Unclassified :—

b(13). CAMP, S.E. of Fossett's Farm, 1 m. N.E. of the church, is situated on ground which slopes gently towards the N. and is not far from the head of a creek of the River Roach. It is roughly elliptical on plan, and measures about 800 ft. from N. to S. and 650 ft. from E. to W.; at the S.E. corner is an irregularly-shaped mound. The defences consisted of a rampart and dry ditch, but though the outline can be traced as an undulation in the fields for the greater part of its circumference, it is only at the S.W. corner that the rampart and ditch are well defined.

Condition—Fairly good; the ditch on the W. side is gradually being filled in, and the mound, which is said to have been considerably lowered, is enclosed in a small plantation.

North Front.

South Front.

PRITTLEWELL: (3). PORTERS. Early 16th-century and later.

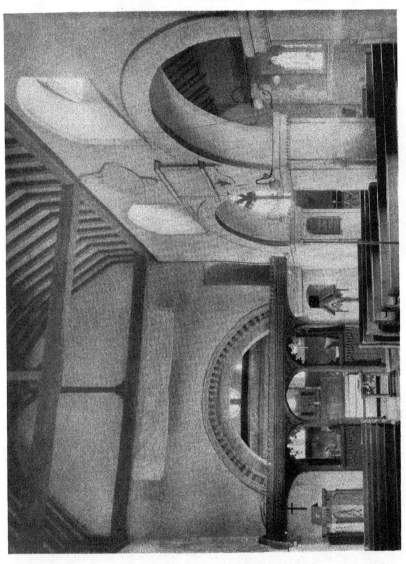

RAINHAM: PARISH CHURCH OF SS. HELEN AND GILES.

Chancel arch, 12th century; widened during 16th cent. Wall arches N. of arch, 13th century. S. Arcade, c. 1170;

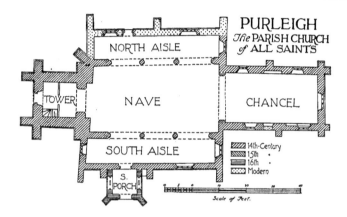

PURLEIGH
The PARISH CHURCH
of ALL SAINTS

NORTH AISLE

TOWER   NAVE   CHANCEL

SOUTH AISLE

14th-Century
15th
16th
Modern

S. PORCH

Scale of Feet.

68. PURLEIGH. (E.b.)

(O.S. 6 in. [a]lxi. N.E. [b]lxii. N.W.)

Purleigh is a parish 3½ m. S. of Maldon. The church is the principal monument.

Ecclesiastical —:

[b](1). PARISH CHURCH OF ALL SAINTS stands about the middle of the parish. The walls are of ragstone, septaria and flint rubble. The chancel and tower have courses of 14th-century bricks with a partly glazed surface ; the porch is of red brick ; the dressings are of limestone ; the roofs are tiled. The whole church, consisting of *Chancel, Nave, North* and *South Aisles* and *West Tower,* was rebuilt in the 14th-century, with the possible exception of the W. wall of the nave ; the work was begun early in the century, the tower being the latest part undertaken. Early in the 16th century the *South Porch* was added. In the 18th century the N. and W. walls of the N. aisle were rebuilt. The church was restored in the 19th century, when the chancel-arch and the upper part of the S. arcade were reconstructed and the walls of the aisles partly rebuilt.

Architectural Description—The *Chancel* (34 ft. by 13 ft.) has a 14th-century E. window of three cinquefoiled lights with tracery in a two-centred head with moulded rear-arch and labels. In the N. wall are two 14th-century windows, each of two cinquefoiled lights with a sexfoiled spandrel in a two-centred head with moulded rear-arch and labels. In the S. wall are two similar windows, and between them is a doorway probably of the same date, now blocked. The four-centred chancel-

arch is of two chamfered orders ; the responds have moulded capitals ; the work is of the 15th century, reconstructed in modern times.

The *Nave* (47 ft. by 24 ft.) has an early 14th-century N. arcade of three bays with two-centred arches of two chamfered orders ; the octagonal columns have moulded capitals and bases and the responds have attached half-columns. Below the capitals of the E. respond and the easternmost pier are carved shields of the arms of Brianzon— *gyronny of twelve pieces with a bend over all,* both mutilated. The S. arcade is of similar date and detail to the N. arcade, except that the orders of the arches die on to octagonal *tas-de-charge ;* the arches have been partly reconstructed. There is a set-off in the W. wall, which may indicate that the lower part is of earlier date than the 14th century.

The *North Aisle* (8 ft. wide) has a 14th-century E. window of two cinquefoiled ogee lights with a cusped spandrel in a two-centred head with moulded labels and rear-arch. In the N. wall are two windows, the eastern is of late 14th-century date, much restored, and of two cinquefoiled ogee lights with tracery in a square head with a moulded label ; the western window is of the 15th century, much restored, and of two cinquefoiled lights with vertical tracery in a segmental head with a moulded label ; between the windows is the 14th-century N. doorway with jambs and two-centred arch of two orders, one moulded and one chamfered ; the label is moulded.

The *South Aisle* (9 ft. wide) has an E. window similar to the E. window of the N. aisle, but with head-stops to the labels. In the S. wall is a window similar to the corresponding window in the N.

aisle and also much restored; further W. is the 14th-century S. doorway, with jambs and two-centred arch of two moulded orders with a moulded label and head-stops. In the W. wall is a window all modern except the splays and moulded rear-arch.

The *West Tower* (12½ ft. square) is of mid 14th-century date and of four stages with an embattled parapet. The lower part has alternate courses of knapped flint and ragstone, and the buttresses have small crosses in knapped flint, with flowered ends. The two-centred tower-arch is of two chamfered orders, the inner dying on the responds. The W. doorway has moulded jambs, two-centred arch and label with head-stops. The N., S. and W. walls of the second stage have each a window of two trefoiled lights with a quatrefoil in a two-centred head with a moulded label and head-stops. The N., S. and W. walls of the third stage have each a window of two trefoiled ogee lights with tracery in a two-centred head with a moulded label. The bell-chamber has in each wall a similar window. On the E. wall is the weathering of the former roof of the nave.

The *South Porch* is of red brick and of early 16th-century date. The outer archway has chamfered jambs and four-centred arch. The timber-framed gable is mostly modern, but incorporates parts of a moulded tie-beam. In the E. wall is a window of two four-centred lights in a four-centred head. In the W. wall is a window of one four-centred light. The *Roof* of the porch is of early 16th-century date and has moulded tie-beams, wall-plates, plain collar-beams and restored central purlin.

Fittings—*Bells*: five, 2nd to 5th by Miles Graye, 1636. *Brasses*: In chancel—(1) to Margaret (Rande), wife of John Freake, rector, 1592, inscription only; (2) to Cecily, widow of Edmund Freake, bishop of Worcester, 1599, inscription only; (3) to John Freake, B.D., rector of Purleigh and archdeacon of Norwich, 1604, inscription only; *Chest*: In N. aisle—iron-bound, 17th-century. *Communion Rails*: with moulded rail and turned balusters, late 17th or early 18th-century. *Door*: In S. doorway—of nail-studded overlapping battens with strap-hinges and domed scutcheon-plate, 14th-century. *Glass*: In chancel—in E. window, fragments of border, etc.; in N. and S. windows, tabernacle-work, borders, etc., *in situ*, 14th-century. In N. aisle—in E. window, roundel in black and white foliage in spandrel, *in situ*, probably late 14th-century; in N. windows, tabernacle-work, crowns and fragments of border, late 14th-century, *in situ*. In S. aisle—in E. window, leopard's head (Plate, pp. xliv-v) and foliage, 14th-century; in S. window, tabernacle-work, late 14th-century. *Locker*: In chancel—in N. wall, rectangular recess, date uncertain. *Monument* and *Floor-slab*: Monument: in churchyard — S. side, to John Strange, 1688, brick table-tomb with three

achievements-of-arms. Floor-slab: In chancel—now covered by seating, but said to be to Elizabeth Burton, 1624. *Piscinae*: In chancel—with moulded jambs and cinquefoiled head, partly restored, quatrefoiled drain, 14th-century. In S. aisle—in S. wall, with triangular head and broken drain, 15th-century. *Pulpit*: hexagonal, angles enriched with fruit and foliage, enriched panels to sides, carved and moulded cornice, staircase with turned and twisted balusters, tapering stem and moulded base, c. 1700. *Recess*: In chancel—in N. wall, with moulded segmental-pointed arch, 14th-century, label destroyed, probably tomb-recess. *Sedilia*: In chancel—in range with piscina, of three bays with moulded jambs and cinquefoiled heads, 14th-century, partly restored. *Table*: In tower—with turned legs and plain rails, 17th-century. *Miscellanea*: In chancel—in recess, small stone inscribed S.H. ob. Jan. 3, 1712–13 Ag. 48; on sill of N.E. window, carved and moulded stones, head-stop to label, 14th-century; stone with cheveron ornament, 12th-century; fragments of patterned tiles; loose quatrefoil of glass similar to that in N.E. window of N. aisle. Condition—Good.

Secular :—

b(2). MOATED MOUND, 350 yards S.S.W. of the church, is flat-topped and about 250 ft. in diameter at the base. It is surrounded by a ditch with a strong rampart on the counter-scarp, except on the N. side. There are slight indications of two short lengths of rampart extending towards the N. Condition—Fairly good.

a(3). HOMESTEAD MOAT at Wickham's Farm, about 2¼ m. W. of the church.

b(4). BARONS, house, about 250 yards N. of the church, is of two storeys, timber-framed and plastered; the roofs are tiled. It was built probably in the 17th century and has cross-wings at the E. and W. ends. Inside the building some of the ceiling-beams and joints are exposed. Condition—Good.

---

69. RAINHAM. (A.d.)

(O.S. 6 in. *(a)*lxxiv. S.E. *(b)*lxxv. S.W.)

Rainham is a parish and village 5 m. E. of Barking. The church is the principal monument.

Ecclesiastical :—

a(1). PARISH CHURCH OF SS. HELEN AND GILES stands in the village. The walls are of septaria and flint-rubble, with limestone dressings; the roofs are tiled. The whole church, including *Chancel, Nave, North* and *South Aisles* and *West Tower*, was built c. 1170. The N. wall of the chancel, from its thickness and material, was probably

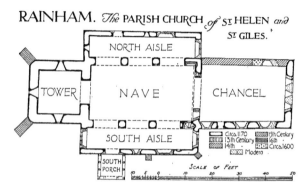

RAINHAM. *The* PARISH CHURCH *of* Sⁱ HELEN *and* Sⁱ GILES.

rebuilt in the 13th or 14th century, and at some period the chancel-arch was widened. The top stage of the tower was built in the 13th century, but was largely reconstructed in the 16th century, when the diagonal buttresses were added to the lower part. There appears to have been a 15th-century vestry on the N. side of the chancel, but it no longer exists. The church was restored in the 19th century and the *South Porch* is modern.

The church is of considerable architectural interest.

Architectural Description—The *Chancel* (31½ ft. by 19¾ ft.) has in the E. wall three round-headed windows, all modern except some reused stones in the outer splays of the outermost windows ; above them is a circular window flanked by two round-headed windows, all restored externally, but with 12th-century splays and rear-arches ; below the circular window are traces of the two-centred rear-arch of a window, probably of the 15th century. In the N. wall is a single-light window, all modern except some stones in the W. splay ; E. of it is part of the E. splay of a window, of uncertain date ; W. of the existing window is a blocked doorway, probably of 15th-century date, with a segmental-pointed rear-arch on the outside face. In the S. wall are three lancet-windows, all modern except the 13th-century splays and rear-arches of the two W. windows and the W. splays of the easternmost ; E. of the easternmost window, which also replaces a former larger window of the 14th century, is the E. splay and part of the round head of a destroyed 12th-century window ; between the two western windows is a late 12th-century doorway (Plate, p. 120) with a semi-circular arch of two orders enriched with cheveron ornament and with a label carved with nail-head ornament ; the jambs have each an attached shaft with the capital

carved with water-leaf and a grotesque face ; the lower parts of the jambs have been restored. The late 12th-century chancel-arch (Plate, p. 115) has probably been widened ; the slightly distorted semi-circular arch is of two orders on the W. face, the inner plain and the outer with cheveron ornament ; there is a shallow chamfered label on the W. face ; the responds have scalloped capitals and moulded abaci continued along the E. face as a string-course ; N. of the W. face is a moulded 13th-century wall-arch with a moulded label, a similar arch adjoins it on the N. wall of the nave ; under the first wall-arch is a loop-squint to the nave, now blocked ; S. of the chancel-arch the lower part of the wall has been cut back on the W. side, and in it is a 15th-century squint with a segmental-pointed head ; above it the abacus of the chancel-arch is continued, as a string-course, to meet the label of the E. arch of the S. arcade ; above this is the early 16th-century upper doorway to the rood-loft staircase ; it has a square head with a wood lintel.

The *Nave* (39 ft. by 20 ft.) has N. and S. arcades (Plate, p. 115) of *c.* 1170, with round arches of one plain order with chamfered labels on the nave side and towards the S. aisle ; the square piers have chamfered plinths and scalloped capitals with moulded abaci ; the piers have attached shafts at the angles, each with a moulded band except the northern shafts of the N. arcade and the S. shaft of the S.E. respond ; the responds are half-piers, but the W. responds have no shafts ; the mouldings of the capitals and abaci are continued along the W. wall and returned round the tower-arch. The clearstorey has on each side three windows with 12th-century angles to the splays and segmental-pointed rear-arches, probably of the 13th century ; the 17th or 18th-century outer stonework, of pointed oval form, is possibly a restoration of a 13th-century enlargement of the original openings, and has a cusp cut in the middle of each side.

The *North Aisle* (7¼ ft. wide) has an E. window, all modern except the rear-arch and N. splay, which are probably of late 15th or early 16th-century date. In the N. wall are two windows, the eastern of the 14th century and of two trefoiled ogee lights in a square head with a moulded label; the western window is a single 12th-century light with a round head; further W. is the 12th-century N. doorway, with a segmental arch and the W. jamb of brick, both of *c.* 1600; it has a round rear-arch and moulded imposts. In the W. wall is a window similar to the western window in the N. wall.

The *South Aisle* (7½ ft. wide) has an E. window all modern except some stones in the two-centred rear-arch which are possibly of the 14th century. In the N. wall, E. of the arcade, is the early 16th-century lower doorway to the rood-loft staircase, with a rebated wooden frame and square head. In the S. wall are two windows similar to the corresponding windows in the N. aisle, but the western one is entirely modern and the other largely restored; further W. is the S. doorway, all modern except the splays, rear-arch and part of a round 12th-century inner order; one internal voussoir is carved with diaper ornament. In the W. wall is a window all modern except part of the splays, which are possibly of the 14th century.

The *West Tower* (15½ ft. square) is of three stages externally but of two storeys internally; it has a 16th-century embattled parapet of brick and a low pyramidal roof. The 12th-century tower-arch is of one plain round order and the responds have imposts continued round from the arcades. The N., S. and W. walls have each a 12th-century window of one round-headed light, restored externally. The bell-chamber has in each wall two narrow brick windows, probably of the date of the parapet; one window on the W. is blocked.

The *Roof* of the chancel is of the 15th century, and of two bays with tie-beams, king-posts with four-way struts under a central purlin and wall-plates with modern cornices. The modern gabled roof of the S. aisle incorporates some old material.

Fittings—*Bells:* three; 1st by Thomas Bartlet, 1618; 2nd and 3rd by John Hodson, 1670. *Brasses:* In chancel—(1) to Mary, wife of Anthony Ratcliffe, 1630, inscription only; (2) to Katherine, widow successively of George Frith and Robert Hollden, 1612, achievement-of-arms and inscription. In nave—(3) of civilian in fur-lined gown and wife in pedimental head-dress, *c.* 1500, with two shields-of-arms—(*a*) *a griffon* quartering *a molet* impaling a defaced charge quartering *a cheveron engrailed*

between *three molets;* (*b*) *a griffon* impaling *a cheveron engrailed between three molets;* (4) in S. aisle—of woman in butterfly head-dress, *c.* 1480, and two shields-of-arms—(*a*) *a griffon charged with three bars;* (*b*) *a molet and a border,* indent of figure of husband and inscription-plate. *Chest* (Plate, p. xliii): In N. aisle—covered with leather and iron strap-work and with semi-hexagonal lid, three hasps, 16th-century. *Coffin-lids:* In churchyard—W. of tower (1) coped, with remains of raised lozenges; (2) and (3) with moulded edges and remains of crosses, all 13th-century, much damaged. *Door:* In N. doorway of three battens with remains of one ornamental iron hinge, late 12th or early 13th-century. *Font:* roughly circular bowl with chamfered under-edge and two projecting lobes, one broken, for fastening, 12th-century; octagonal stem with trefoil-headed panels on four sides and panelled buttresses on the other four, chamfered base, 15th-century. *Locker:* In chancel—in S. wall, with rebated jambs and triangular head, date uncertain. *Niches:* In nave—in E. pier of N. arcade, small and plastered, with four-centred head, date uncertain. In E. respond of S. arcade, with rough arched head, plastered back, date uncertain. *Paintings:* In chancel, on N. wall, remains of red foliage and on N. jamb of N. window traces of red border. In nave—on N. and S. walls, parts of conventional running borders in red, 13th-century; on W. wall, considerable remains of similar ornament, and on either side of tower-arch remains of 14th-century quatrefoils enclosing flowered crosses; on S. wall at E. end, remains of red paint on both arcades and remains of masoned lines and sexfoils on rear-arches of clearstorey windows. *Piscina:* In S. aisle—foliated head of pillar-piscina, late 12th or early 13th-century, now set on a modern corbel in front of an ancient square recess. *Plate:* includes cover-paten of 1563, cup of 1652 with baluster stem, and stand-paten of 1713, dated 1714. *Scratching:* On wall of rood-loft staircase, large drawing of ship with two masts, 16th-century. *Screen* (Plate, p. 115): Between chancel and nave—incorporates 15th or early 16th-century lower halves of moulded muntins and door-posts, the latter buttressed, and moulded middle rail. *Seat:* In chancel—chair partly made up of old work, including a 15th-century bench-end with a crouching lion on the shoulder, and half a popey-head, also seat-board and moulded top-rail of back.

Condition—Good.

Secular :—

b(2). DAYMNS HALL (Plate, pp. 56–7), 2½ m. E.N.E. of the church, is of two storeys with attics; the walls are of brick; the roofs are tiled. It was built in the 17th century, and is of L-shaped plan with the wings extending towards the S. and E. Both wings have a band-course between the storeys and a moulded cornice below the parapet ; the E. wing has three gables with moulded copings. In the E. end is a window with an original moulded wooden frame. The S. doorway has an original door of nine moulded panels. Inside the building are exposed ceiling-beams and a door of moulded battens.

Condition—Good.

ᵃ(3). COTTAGE, two tenements, opposite the church, is of two storeys, timber-framed and weather-boarded ; the roofs are tiled. It was built in the second half of the 17th century, and has exposed ceiling-beams and internal timber-framing and an original chimney-stack.

Condition—Good.

---

70. RAMSDEN BELLHOUSE. (D.c.)

(O.S. 6 in. ⁽ᵃ⁾lx. S.E. ⁽ᵇ⁾lxviii. N.E.)

Ramsden Bellhouse is a parish 2½ m. E. of Billericay.

Ecclesiastical :—

ᵇ(1). PARISH CHURCH OF ST. MARY (Plate, pp. xxxviii–ix) stands about the middle of the parish. The tower or belfry and the S. porch are timber-framed. The *West Tower* or belfry is of the 15th century, and the *South Porch* is perhaps of late 14th-century date. The rest of the building is modern.

Architectural Description—The *West Tower* is timber-framed, and consists of a central rectangular structure with the roof carried down over annexes on the N. and S. There is a third annexe on the W. side with a pent-roof. Placed astride the main roof is the timber bell-chamber, surmounted by a short octagonal spire. The main structure rests on four oak posts with curved braces and modern added struts. In the W. wall of the W. annexe is a 15th-century oak doorway with moulded jambs and four-centred arch in a square head with spandrels carved with foliage, a rose and a shield. The bell-chamber has in each wall a two-light window with modern pointed heads.

The *South Porch* is timber-framed, and probably of late 14th-century date. The outer archway is two-centred and is flanked by openings with ogee heads. The gable has foiled barge-boards and the side walls have modern diamond-shaped mullions. The roof has one tie-beam with curved braces, old rafters and a central purlin.

The *Roof* of the chancel has three tie-beams, the two western with plain king-posts ; the middle tie-beam has early 16th-century twisted foliage ornament ; the westernmost is probably of the 15th century and the easternmost probably of the 17th century. The 15th-century roof of the nave is of three bays with four king-post trusses, chamfered tie-beams and one plain and three

rebated king-posts, one with moulded base ; the tie-beams have mortices for braces, except the easternmost, which is probably of later date.

Fittings—*Bells :* three ; 1st by William Land, 1615 or 1618 ; 2nd by William Lambert, 1638 ; 3rd by Richard Phelps, 1711. *Chairs :* In chancel —two, with carved backs and front rails, twisted posts, early 18th-century. *Chest :* In nave—large and heavily bound with iron, lid in two portions, each with five strap and three link-hinges, four hasps and staples, two handles at ends and two handles to lids, probably mediaeval. *Door :* In W. doorway of tower—of battens with fillets planted on, late 15th or early 16th-century. *Font :* octagonal stem and moulded base, 15th-century, bowl and part of base modern. *Font-cover :* of wood with eight voluted supports to turned middle-post, late 17th or early 18th-century. *Plate :* includes Elizabethan cup of 1562 with two bands of engraved ornament, small paten of about the same date, also engraved but without foot. *Recess :* In nave—reset in N. wall, with stop-moulded jambs, trefoiled and sub-cusped head and quatrefoiled spandrels, moulded cornice above, late 14th-century, probably piscina or stoup.

Condition—Good, mostly rebuilt.

Secular :—

ᵇ(2). HOMESTEAD MOAT, at Cox Green, 1,500 yards N.N.W. of the church.

ᵃ(3). CHITHAM'S FARM, house and moat, about 1¼ m. N.W. of the church. The *House* is of two storeys, timber-framed and plastered ; the roofs are tiled. It was built probably in the 16th century with a central block and N. and S. cross-wings, but has been much altered and added to on the S. and W. The upper storeys of both the cross-wings originally projected on the E. front, but the upper storey of the S. wing has been underbuilt. Inside the building one small room has exposed ceiling-beams.

The *Moat* entirely surrounds the house.

Condition—Of house, good, much altered.

ᵇ(4). BARN, at Ramsden Bellhouse Hall, N.W. of the church, is timber-framed and weather-boarded, with a thatched roof, and was built probably in the 17th century. The barn has two porches on the S. side.

Condition—Poor.

ᵇ(5). STABLE, at E. end of churchyard, is of the 17th century, timber-framed and weather-boarded ; the roof is thatched.

Condition—Fairly good.

ᵃ(6). HOUSE, on S. side of the road to Billericay, nearly 1¼ m. N.N.W. of the church, is of two storeys, timber-framed and plastered ; the roofs are tiled. It was built probably in the 16th century, and now consists of a rectangular block with an E. cross-wing and a staircase block in the S.W. angle, to which has been added a modern wing extending towards the S. The base of the chimney-stack at the E. end is original, and inside the building some of the timber-framing is exposed.

Condition—Fairly good, much altered.

71. RAMSDEN CRAYS. (C.c.)

(O.S. 6 in. (a)lx. S.E. (b)lxviii. N.E.)

Ramsden Crays is a parish 2 m. E. of Billericay.

Ecclesiastical :—

b(1). PARISH CHURCH OF ST. MARY stands near the middle of the parish. The church has been entirely rebuilt in modern times, but incorporates some old work. In the S. wall of the chancel is a window with two 15th-century cinquefoiled heads to the lights and part of the moulded label of the same date. The N. wall of the nave has two windows, both with old splays and rear-arches; the eastern window has also jambs and head of two trefoiled lights with a moulded label, all of c. 1400. In the S. wall are two old windows, the eastern of the 15th century and of two cinque-foiled lights in a square head with a moulded label and modern jambs, mullion and sill; the second window is similar but smaller and the label is partly modern; between them is the early 15th-century S. doorway, with moulded jambs and two-centred arch. In the W. wall is a modern window with old head-stops. The nave has a 15th-century roof with moulded plates and three tie-beams with king-posts having four-way struts. The bell-turret at the W. end stands on four 15th-century posts, with heavy braces forming two-centred arches and square framing above to support the turret.

Fittings—Bells : two, inaccessible, but said to be 2nd by Thomas Bartlet, 1617. Font : octagonal bowl and stem, entirely retooled and of doubtful date.

Condition—Rebuilt.

Secular :—

b(2). HOMESTEAD MOAT, at Parsonage Farm, immediately S. of the church.

a(3). HUNT'S FARM, about 1½ m. N. of the church, is of two storeys, timber-framed and plastered; the roofs are tiled. It was built pro-bably in the 17th century on an L-shaped plan with the wings extending towards the S. and W. The main chimney-stack is original. Inside the building some of the rooms have exposed ceiling-beams.

Condition—Good, considerably altered.

72. RAWRETH. (D.c.)

(O.S. 6 in. lxix. N.E.)

Rawreth is a parish on the S. side of the Crouch, 6 m. E. of Billericay. The church is the principal monument.

Ecclesiastical :—

(1). PARISH CHURCH OF ST. NICHOLAS stands on the W. side of the parish. The walls are of rag-stone with limestone dressings; the roofs are tiled. The S. arcade of the Nave, the W. wall of the North Aisle and the West Tower are all of mid 15th-century date. The rest of the church, including Chancel, Organ Chamber, North Porch and N. arcade, has been rebuilt in modern times, but incorporating the old materials.

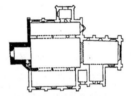

Architectural Description—The Nave (36½ ft. by 21 ft.) has a 15th-century S. arcade of three bays with modern arches; the eastern column is modern, the western is octagonal with a moulded capital and base; the responds have attached half-columns, and all considerably restored.

The North Aisle has reset in the N. wall the cinquefoiled head of a 15th-century window.

The West Tower (9½ ft. square) is of 15th-century date and of three stages, with an embattled parapet. The two-centred tower-arch is of two orders, the outer moulded and continuous and the inner chamfered and dying on to the side walls. The W. doorway has moulded jambs and modern head, above it is a window modern except the 15th-century splays and rear-arch. The second stage has in the S. wall a square-headed window. In the W. wall is a window of two trefoiled lights in a square head with a moulded label. The bell-chamber has in each wall a similar window with a defaced label.

The North Porch is modern, but incorporates reused material, including the head of a 15th-century window of two trefoiled lights, reset in the E. wall.

Fittings—Bells : two; 1st probably by John of Hadham, early 14th-century and inscribed "Jam Tempus Est"; 2nd uninscribed but probably of the same date. Brasses : In S. aisle—on S. wall (1) to Rebecca (Warde), wife of Robert Listney, 1602, inscription only; on W.

SOUTH OCKENDON: PARISH CHURCH OF ST. NICHOLAS.
North Doorway; late 12th-century, re-set in the 15th century.

RAINHAM: PARISH CHURCH OF SS. HELEN AND GILES.
North Doorway of Chancel; late 12th-century.

SUTTON: PARISH CHURCH OF ALL SAINTS.
South Doorway; early 13th-century—partly restored.

PRITTLEWELL: (2). PRITTLEWELL PRIORY.
Doorway in N. wall of Frater; late 12th-century—partly restored.

wall (2) to Richard Hayes, 1600, inscription only.
See also Monument (1). *Chest:* In S. aisle—of
hutch-type with shaped feet, iron bands and
three hasps, 16th-century. *Font:* modern, but
incorporating old cylindrical stem. In churchyard—octagonal bowl with arcaded sides and sunk
in ground, 12th or 13th-century. *Monuments:*
In S. aisle—on S. wall (1) to Edmund Tyrell, 1576,
Purbeck or Sussex marble tablet with attached
side-columns and a round head with mixed Classic
and Gothic ornament, brass kneeling figures of
man in plate-armour and wife, inscription and
three brass shields-of-arms. In churchyard—W.
of tower (2) to John Trent, 1703, flat slab with
moulded edge. *Paving:* In chancel—eight squares
of Purbeck marble. *Stoup:* in N. porch—stone
mortar, set in wall.
Condition—Poor, many cracks owing to subsi-
dence.

Secular :—

HOMESTEAD MOATS.

(2). At Rawreth Hall, ¾ m. E.S.E. of the church.

(3). At Raymond's Farm, 600 yards S.S.E. of
the church.

(4). At Chichester Hall, ½ m. S.S.W. of the
church.

(5). At Beeches, about 1 m. N.E. of the church.

(6). At Tryndehayes, about 1 m. E. of the
church.

---

73. RAYLEIGH. (E.c.)

(O.S. 6 in. lxix. S.E.)

Rayleigh is a parish and small town 6 m. N.W.
of Southend-on-Sea. The church and the castle
are the principal monuments.

Ecclesiastical :—

(1). PARISH CHURCH OF THE HOLY TRINITY
stands in the village. The walls are mainly of
ragstone-rubble, with much flint in the chancel and
south chapel and some brick; the S. porch is
entirely of brick; the dressings are of limestone
and Roman brick; the roofs are covered with
tiles and lead. The *Chancel* was built probably
early in the 12th century. During the 15th
century the *West Tower* was built and the *Nave*
rebuilt and probably lengthened up to the tower ;
the *North Chapel*, and *North* and *South Aisles*
were built, with the *North Vestry*, probably late
in the same century. *C.* 1517 the *South Chapel*
was built by William Alleyn, and about the same
time the *South Porch* was added. The church
has been restored in modern times, when the N.
vestry was enlarged.

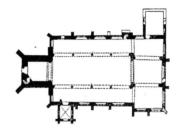

Architectural Description—The *Chancel:* (20½ ft.
by 16¾ ft.) has 12th-century E. quoins of Roman
brick and stone. The almost completely restored
15th-century E. window is of four cinquefoiled
lights in a square head with a moulded label ;
below it, towards the S., is a 15th-century doorway, now blocked, and with a four-centred head
and square moulded label ; in the gable is a window
of one trefoiled light. In the N. wall is a late
15th-century four-centred arch of two hollow-
chamfered orders, the outer continuous and the
inner resting on attached shafts with moulded
capitals and bases. In the S. wall is a similar
arch, probably of early 16th-century date, but the
responds are completely covered with modern
cement. The 15th-century four-centred chancel-
arch is of two continuous moulded orders.

The *North Chapel* (21¼ ft. by 12 ft.) has a 15th-
century E. window of four cinquefoiled lights
with vertical tracery in a two-centred head. In
the N. wall is a much-restored 15th-century
window of three cinquefoiled lights in a three-
centred head ; further E. is a 15th-century doorway with moulded jambs and two-centred arch.
In the W. wall is a 15th-century arch, two-centred
and of two hollow-chamfered orders dying on to
the walls.

The *North Vestry* is of the 15th-century ; the
northern half is a modern extension. In the E.
wall is a window of two plain lights in a square
head. The attic above has a small rectangular
window in the N. wall.

The *South Chapel* (20¼ ft. by 15 ft.) is of early
16th-century date, and has an E. window of four
cinquefoiled lights in a square head. In the S.
wall are two windows, each of three cinquefoiled
lights in a square head ; the eastern window is
blocked externally. In the W. wall is a four-
centred arch of two hollow-chamfered orders
dying on to the side walls ; on the N. side the
wall is splayed back and the arch rests on moulded
corbelling.

The *Nave* (57 ft. by 20½ ft.) has 15th-century
N. and S. arcades, each of four bays with two-
centred arches of two moulded orders ; the
columns have each four attached shafts with

moulded capitals and bases ; the S.E. respond has a round attached shaft, but the others have attached semi-octagonal shafts with concave faces and moulded capitals and bases.

The *North Aisle* (10 ft. wide) is of the 15th century, and has in the N. wall four three-light windows, all completely covered in cement and plaster ; below the westernmost is a blocked doorway with hollow-chamfered jambs and two-centred head ; at the E. end of the wall is the rood-loft staircase ; the lower doorway has rebated jambs and four-centred head ; the upper doorway has a cusped and sub-cusped head of reused early 15th-century work. In the W. wall is a 15th-century window of two cinquefoiled lights with vertical tracery in a two-centred head.

The *South Aisle* (9½ ft. wide) is of the 15th century, and has in the S. wall four windows, all of three cinquefoiled lights and covered with cement externally ; the two eastern have four-centred heads with labels and stops carved with a head and angels holding shields with crosses ; the third is probably a 17th-century restoration, and has a three-centred head with a moulded label ; the westernmost has a square head and a moulded label ; below this window is the reset 13th-century S. doorway with a two-centred arch of two orders, the inner chamfered and continuous and the outer moulded and resting on shafts with defaced capitals and bases ; the 15th-century label is moulded. In the W. wall is an early 16th-century window of three pointed lights in a square head.

The *West Tower* (14 ft. square) is of the 15th century and of three stages, with an embattled parapet and an embattled turret rising above it (Plate, pp. xxxii–iii). The two-centred tower-arch is of two continuous chamfered orders. The W. window is of three cinquefoiled lights with tracery in a two-centred head with a restored label ; below it is a row of shields, one with the arms of Vere and the rest now defaced ; the W. doorway has moulded jambs and two-centred arch in a square head with a moulded label and cusped spandrels. The N., S. and W. walls of the second stage have each a window of one trefoiled light ; above the W. window is another window of two cinquefoiled lights in a square head with a restored label. The bell-chamber has in each wall a window similar to that last described.

The *South Porch* (Plate, p. xxxviii) is of early 16th-century date and of red brick with a crow-stepped embattled parapet with a trefoiled corbel-table. The outer archway has chamfered jambs, four-centred arch and label ; above it is a niche with a four-centred head and set in a square outer order. The side walls have each a window of two four-centred lights in a square head with a moulded label. The porch is covered by a brick vault with chamfered diagonal and wall-ribs springing from moulded corbels in the angles.

The *Roof* of the chancel has been much restored, but incorporates some old timbers. The early 16th-century roof of the N. chapel is of two bays, with moulded principals forming two-centred arches and trussed-rafters. The 15th-century roof of the nave is of six bays, partly restored, and with five king-post trusses. The S. chapel and N. and S. aisles have old rafters, including some early 16th-century moulded beams and joists in the N. aisle.

Fittings—*Bells :* eight ; 5th by Thomas Bullisdon, early 16th-century and inscribed " Ihus " and " Sancta Margareta Ora Pro Nos " ; 6th by Robert Burford, probably early 15th-century, and inscribed " Sit Nomen Domini Benedictum " ; 7th by John Hodson, 1657. *Brass and Indents*— Brass : In N. aisle—of John Barrington, 1416, and Thomasin, his wife, 1420, figures of civilian and wife, head of male figure and inscription lost. Indents : In N. aisle—(1) of priest in doctor's cap, and inscription-plate. In S. porch—(2) defaced. In W. tower—(3) of figure and inscription-plate. *Chest :* In S. aisle—dug-out with two hinges, lock and three hasps, mediaeval. *Consecration Crosses :* In nave—flanking tower-arch, black painted formy crosses in circles, 15th-century, that on S. repainted. *Door :* In tower—in staircase doorway, of overlapping battens with straphinges and sexfoiled handle-plate, 15th-century. *Font :* In S. aisle half of square Purbeck marble bowl with round-headed panels in sides, late 12th-century. *Gallery :* In tower—cross-beam, wall-posts and braces of former ringing-gallery ; front of beam with Jacobean ornament and spandrels of braces with cusped ornament, early 17th century, floor removed. *Glass :* In N. chapel —in E. window, small rose and other fragments, early 16th-century. In N. aisle—in W. window, fragments in tracery. *Monuments :* In S. chapel— against S. wall, (1) recessed wall-monument (Plate, p. 105) of freestone, consisting of base with three cusped and traceried panels, two enclosing shields ; slab with moulded edge ; recess in wall above with square-headed canopy with cusped and panelled soffit and side-shafts with moulded capitals and bases ; at back five shallow niches with ogee traceried heads and moulded pedestals, remains of foliated cornice with cresting and two shields, early 16th-century. In churchyard—S. of church (2) to Richard Ransford, 1677, head-stone ; E. of church—(3) to Avis Croft, 1712, head-stone. *Niches :* On tower—in S.W. buttress, with triangular head and square moulded label, 15th-century, half-restored. See also S. porch. *Piscina :* In N. chapel—in S. wall, with three-centred head and round drain, c. 1500. *Plate :* includes large cup of 1681 dated 1683 and stand-paten of 1681. *Royal Arms :* In tower—on N. wall, of Queen Anne before the Union. *Screen* (Plate, pp. 4–5) : In W. arch of N. chapel—with entrance and four side-bays, entrance with four-centred head and vertical tracery above, side-bays with cinquefoiled heads and tracery, moulded head-beam, *c.* 1500, cresting and lower panels modern. *Scratching :* On jamb of S. doorway—date 1638. *Miscellanea :* In S. aisle—capital of 15th-century column. In S. porch—sections of columns of grouped shafts, supporting benches.

Condition—Good, but stonework of windows much decayed.

Secular :—

(2). THE CASTLE, mount and bailey (Plate, p. xxxvii), appears to be identical with that built about the end of the 11th century by Suene, son of Robert Fitz-Wimarc. It appears to have fallen into disuse in the 13th century or even earlier, and was ruinous in the 14th century (V.C.H., 1, p. 300, *Essex Arch. Soc. Trans.*, N.S., XII; Morant, 1, p. 273). No masonry now stands above ground, but recent excavations have disclosed considerable quantities of stone and rubble in the inner bailey and on the N.E. slope of the mound.

The work is of special interest as a strong and well-preserved example of its type.

The castle is situated in a commanding position on a spur overlooking the valley of the Crouch, and depends for its defence to a great extent on the natural contours of the ground. The plan consists of a strong keep-mound with a bailey to the E. and an outer bailey on the same side. Both the mound and the inner bailey are surrounded by a deep dry ditch having on the N. and W. a strong outer bank with traces of an external ditch. The defences of the outer bailey are now represented by a scarp dropping into the gardens of the modern houses to the E., and by slight traces of ditches at the S.E. corner. From the foundations disclosed it appears that the inner bailey was enclosed within a stone wall, which probably continued up the causeway to the mound, and the rubble on the slope of the mound may be part of the keep which had been thrown down from the summit. The approach to the mound is by a causeway on the S. side, and the entrance to the inner bailey appears to have been through

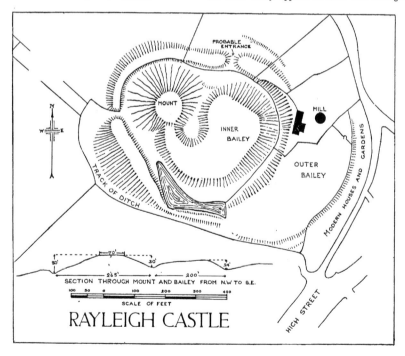

SECTION THROUGH MOUNT AND BAILEY FROM N.W TO S.E.

SCALE OF FEET

RAYLEIGH CASTLE

the rampart on the N. and along the eastern ditch of the mound. The mound is 50 ft. high above the ditch on the N.W. side and is 260 ft. long by 150 ft. wide, surrounded by a ditch which is 24 ft. below the scarp on the E. side. The dimensions of the outer bailey are not recoverable. Condition—Good.

MONUMENTS (3-8).

The following monuments, unless otherwise described, are of the 17th century, and of two storeys, timber-framed and plastered or weatherboarded ; the roofs are tiled. Some of the buildings have exposed ceiling-beams and original chimney-stacks.

Condition—Good, or fairly good.

(3). *Rectory*, house, N. of the church, was built in the 16th century or possibly earlier, with a central block and N. and S. cross-wings, but has been much altered and added to. The upper storey of the S. wing originally projected on the E. but has been underbuilt. Inside the building the curved braces supporting the bressummer of the projecting storey are visible.

(4). *Mount Pleasant Cottages*, range of tenements, 100 yards W. of the church, has modern additions at the. back. Inside the building some of the timber-framing is exposed, and one of the tenements has a wide open-fireplace.

(5). *House*, now three tenements, on N.W. side of road, 120 yards S.W. of the church, was built in the 16th century, and has modern additions at the back. The upper storey projects on the S.W. front. Inside the building some of the rooms have moulded ceiling-beams.

(6). *Cottage*, now offices, opposite (5).

(7). *Three Horseshoes Inn*, now tenements, 150 yards N.E. of the church.

(8). *Rayleigh Lodge*, 1,200 yards E.S.E. of the church, was built probably in the 16th century, but has been much altered and added to. Inside the building one of the ground-floor rooms is lined with early 17th-century panelling and has an encased ceiling-beam with curved braces. The timber-framing is partly exposed in the upper storey, together with a braced tie-beam.

----

74. RETTENDON. (D.b.)

(O.S. 6 in. (*a*)lxi. N.E. (*b*)lxi. S.W. (*c*)lxix. N.W.)

Rettendon is a parish about 7 m. E.N.E. of Billericay. The church is the principal monument.

Ecclesiastical :—

(1). PARISH CHURCH OF ALL SAINTS stands at the S. end of the parish. The walls are of ragstone-rubble with some flint, septaria and pudding-stone ; the dressings are of Reigate stone, and the

roofs are covered with tiles and slate. The *Nave* is of uncertain date, the earliest detail being the S. doorway, of c. 1200. Early in the 13th century the *Chancel* was rebuilt and probably lengthened. In the 15th century the *North Aisle* and arcade, the *West Tower* and the *North Chapel* and *Vestry* were added ; the chancel-arch was probably removed at the same period. The church has been restored in modern times, when the S. walls of the chancel and nave were refaced, the pyramidal spire added, and the *South Porch* rebuilt with some old material reused.

The two-storeyed Vestry or Priest's House is interesting, and among the fittings the carved 12th-century slab and the 15th-century bench-ends are noteworthy.

Architectural Description—The *Chancel* (36½ ft. by 19¾ ft.) has an E. window all modern except the 13th-century shafted splays and moulded rear-arch and label. In the N. wall is a window of one pointed light opening from the upper storey of the vestry ; further W. is a 15th-century doorway with moulded jambs and four-centred arch in a square head with a moulded label ; the late 15th-century arch to the N. chapel is two-centred and of two hollow-chamfered orders ; the responds have attached semi-octagonal shafts with concave faces and moulded capitals and bases ; further W. is an opening about. four feet above the floor with a round head. In the S. wall are two windows, both modern except for the splays and rear-arch of the western, which are possibly of the 14th century ; between them is a modern doorway ; at the E. end of the wall is a blocked window.

The *North Vestry* is of the 15th century and of two storeys, with a chimney-stack against the N. wall. The ground-storey has in the E. wall a modern window. In the W. wall is a doorway to the staircase with hollow-chamfered jambs and four-centred arch. The upper storey has in the E. wall a modern window and the sill of a 15th-century window. In the N. wall is a small square-headed window ; E. of the modern fireplace is a blocked doorway, formerly approached by an external stair. In the S. wall are two wide recesses with flat two-centred heads. In the W. wall is a doorway from the staircase, with a four-centred head.

The *Nave* (44½ ft. by 20 ft.) has a late 15th-century N. arcade of three bays with two-centred arches of two hollow-chamfered orders ; the octagonal columns have concave faces and moulded capitals and bases ; the responds have attached half-columns. In the S. wall are three windows, each of three lights and all modern except for the reset 15th-century rear-arches and splay-stones ; between the two western windows is the S. doorway of c. 1200, partly restored and with chamfered jambs and two-centred arch with a chamfered label.

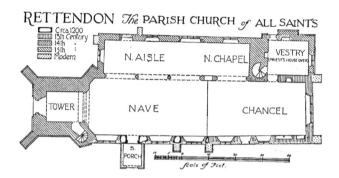

RETTENDON *The* PARISH CHURCH *of* ALL SAINTS

Circa 1200
15th Century
14th
15th
Modern

N. AISLE   N. CHAPEL   VESTRY
PRIEST'S HOUSE OVER

TOWER   NAVE   CHANCEL

S. PORCH

Scale of feet.

The *North Chapel* and *Aisle* (12 ft. wide) has in the N. wall three windows, the easternmost and westernmost are each of the 15th century and of two cinquefoiled lights in a square head with a moulded label; the middle window is modern except for the reset 14th-century splays and part of the moulded label with stops carved as a beast and a serpent with a human head; W. of the windows is the blocked N. doorway, with chamfered jambs, possibly of the 13th century reset, and a modern head. In the W. wall is a window similar to the westernmost window in the N. wall, but with a restored label; above it is a single-light window, modern externally.

The *West Tower* (11 ft. square) is of the 15th century and of three stages with an embattled parapet. The two-centred tower-arch is of three hollow-chamfered orders; the chamfered responds have each an attached shaft with moulded capital and base. The W. window is of two four-centred lights with uncusped tracery in a two-centred head with a moulded label; below it is the W. doorway, with moulded jambs, two-centred arch and label; both doorway and window are set in a recess with a two-centred head. The second stage has in the E. wall a square-headed opening to the roof of the nave. In the N. wall is a window of one four-centred light with a square moulded label. In the S. wall is a window of one cinque-foiled light in a square head with a moulded label. The bell-chamber has in each wall a two-light window with a square head and a moulded label; the lights of the E. window are four-centred and the others cinquefoiled.

The *Roof* of the N. aisle is of late 15th-century date and of four bays with moulded and curved braces to the collar-beams, forming two-centred arches; the wall-plates are moulded.

Fittings—*Bells:* six; 6th by Samuel Newton and John Peele, 1704. *Brackets:* In chancel—on S. wall, of stone, moulded and with trumpet-stem knotted at the end, 13th-century. In vestry —in N. wall, semi-octagonal and hollow-chamfered, 15th-century. *Brasses:* In chancel—on N. wall— (1) to Margaret, wife of [George] Hayes, 1552. In N. aisle—(2) of Richard Humfrie, 1607, in civil dress with kneeling figures of three sons; (3) of Richard Cannon, 1605, in civil dress; on loose slab (see Monument (1)), (4) of civilian and two wives, *c.* 1535, with group of three sons and four daughters, indents of a third wife, two groups of children and inscription-plate. *Chest:* In vestry —of hutch-type with old lock-plate and hinge, 17th-century. *Coffin-lid:* In vestry—at head of turret-staircase, with hollow-chamfered edge and remains of raised cross, 13th-century. *Font:* octagonal bowl with moulded under-edge, plain stem and moulded base, 15th-century. *Locker:* In chancel—in N. wall, with rebated reveals and triangular head, probably 14th-century. *Monuments* and *Floor-slab*—Monuments: In N. aisle— (1) loose slab (Plate, p. 25), probably part of former monument, with later brass (4) set in it, cable-moulded edges and between them on each side bands of conventional foliage, birds, etc., late 12th-century. In churchyard—S. of church—(2) to James Stillemen (?), 1694, table-tomb; (3) to Ambrose S . . . ., 1684, slab. Floor-slab: In N. aisle—to William Humfrey, 1628. *Piscina:* In chancel (Plate, p. xlv)—with moulded and trefoiled head with a moulded label, dog-tooth ornament and foliated stops, octofoiled drain, early 13th-century. *Plate* (Plate, p. xlvi): includes cup of 1562 with two bands of engraved ornament and a stand-paten of 1641, given in 1642. *Seating:* In chancel—incorporated in modern work six elaborately traceried panels with heads of several others, also ten bench-ends, nine with carved popey-heads (Plate, p. 5), some having carved badges—the eagle and child (eagle missing), bear and ragged staff, two apes, a lion and a dog, also a fir-cone, late 15th-century. *Sedilia:* In chancel (Plate, p. xlv)—of two bays with hollow-chamfered trefoiled heads with moulded labels and mask-stops, 13th-century, jambs and shaft modern. *Miscellanea:* In N. aisle—fragment of square bowl of 12th-century font. Incorporated in external walling, fragments of window tracery, etc., 14th-century.

Condition—Good.

Secular :—

b(2). BARN (Plate, p. xli), at Rettendon Place, 100 yards N.E. of the church, is of two storeys with brick walls and a tiled roof. It was built in the 16th century, and has a modern extension at the E. end. The E. and W. walls are gabled, and each has within the gable a blocked three-light window. The S. wall has three gables, with blocked windows in two of them. The roof is divided into five bays by queen-post trusses.

Condition—Good.

MONUMENTS (3–6).

The following monuments, unless otherwise described, are of the 17th century and of two storeys, timber-framed and plastered ; the roofs are tiled. Some of the buildings have original chimney-stacks and exposed ceiling-beams.

Condition—Good.

b(3). *Pound Farm,* house, about 1¼ m. N.N.W. of the church, was built in the 16th century with a cross-wing at the N. end, and has two modern additions on the N. and S. The upper storey of the cross-wing projects on the E. front, and the main chimney-stack has four grouped shafts set diagonally.

a(4). *Hyde Hall,* farmhouse, about 2¼ m. N.N.E. of the church, has been added to on the E. and W. and considerably altered.

c(5). *Cottage,* 750 yards W. of (4), is of central-chimney type with a modern extension at the back.

c(6). *Hawk Inn,* S. of Battlesbridge Station, nearly 1 m. S.E. of the church, is a small rectangular building of 16th-century date, which has been added to on the N., E. and W.

---

75. ROCHFORD. (F.c.)

(O.S. 6 in. (a)lxx. S.W. (b)lxx. S.E.)

Rochford is a parish and small town on the N. bank of the river Roach, 3 m. N. of Southend-on-Sea. The church and Rochford Hall are the principal monuments.

Ecclesiastical :—

a(1). PARISH CHURCH OF ST. ANDREW (Plate, p. 126) stands to the W. of the town. The walls are of ragstone-rubble with some flint and septaria in the chancel walls, and squared rubble in the S. aisle, porch and stair-turret of the tower; the N. chapel and the W. tower are of red brick; the dressings are of Reigate and other limestone; the roofs are covered with tiles and lead. The thickness of the E. wall of the nave and of the N. wall W. of the arcade seem to indicate remains of early work. The *North Aisle* was added in the first half of the 14th century, and there was perhaps· a S. aisle of the same date. Late in the 15th century the *Chancel,* the N. and S. arcades of the *Nave* and the *South Aisle* were rebuilt, the *South Porch* added, and the tower stair-turret begun. Early in the 16th century the *North Chapel* was added and the *West Tower* completed. The church has been much restored and the *Organ Chamber* is modern.

The W. tower is a good example of early 16th-century brickwork.

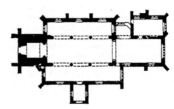

Architectural Description—The *Chancel* (33½ ft. by 17½ ft.) is probably of the 15th century ; the lower part of the walls are of stone and the upper of flint-rubble, but the work is probably all of the same date, as it continues also round the buttresses. The E. window is partly restored, and of five cinque-foiled lights with vertical tracery in a two-centred head with a moulded label of late 15th-century date. In the N. wall is a modern arch ; further E. is an early 15th-century doorway with moulded jambs and two-centred arch in a square head with quatrefoiled spandrels enclosing small heads ; the moulded label has one head-stop ; E. of the doorway is an early 16th-century squint with a square head, brick reveals and stone inner jambs. In the S. wall are two windows, all modern except the splays and segmental rear-arches, which are probably of the 15th century ; further W. is a narrow modern opening into the S. aisle. The chancel-arch is modern except for some reused stones in the responds.

The *North Chapel* (22 ft. by 12 ft.) is of early 16th-century date and of red brick. The E. window is of stone and of three pointed lights in

ROCHFORD : PARISH CHURCH OF ST. ANDREW.   From the South-West.
West Tower, early 16th-century ;   S. Aisle and S. Porch, late 15th-century.

ROCHFORD: ROCHFORD HALL. *c.* 1540–50.
From the North-East.

STIFFORD: (2). FORD PLACE.
Gables from the South-East, with initials and date, 1655.

a segmental-pointed head with a moulded label. In the N. wall are two windows, each of two plain square-headed lights with a moulded label; between them is a fireplace with hollow-chamfered jambs and four-centred arch in a square head; the N. wall has two projecting plastered gables, probably of late 16th or early 17th-century date. In the S. wall is a large recess with a four-centred head, now partly blocked. In the W. wall is a doorway with moulded jambs, four-centred arch and label.

The *Nave* (49 ft. by 17¼ ft.) has 15th-century N. and S. arcades, each of three bays with two-centred arches of two chamfered orders; the octagonal columns have moulded capitals and bases and the responds have attached half-columns. The clearstorey has no ancient features.

The *North Aisle* (10 ft. wide) has in the E. wall an early 14th-century window of three cinquefoiled ogee lights with net tracery in a square head. In the N. wall are two windows, all modern except the splays and rear-arches, which are probably of the 14th century; between them is the 14th-century N. doorway, with moulded jambs, two-centred arch and label with defaced stops; it is now blocked. In the W. wall is a late 15th or early 16th-century window of two trefoiled lights in a square head with a moulded label, partly of brick.

The *South Aisle* (11 ft. wide) has an embattled parapet of chequer-work. In the E. wall is a 15th-century window of three cinquefoiled lights with vertical tracery in a two-centred head with restored label and mullions. In the N. wall, E. of the arcade, is the 15th-century lower doorway to the rood-loft staircase; it has rebated jambs and two-centred head. In the S. wall are two 15th-century windows, each of two cinquefoiled lights in a square head and modern externally except the jambs; between them is the 15th-century S. doorway, with moulded jambs, two-centred arch and label. In the W. wall is a 14th-century window of one cinquefoiled ogee light in a square head; further N. is the late 15th-century doorway to the tower staircase, with hollow-chamfered jambs and two-centred head.

The *West Tower* (11 ft. square) is of c. 1500 and of red brick; it is of three stages, with an embattled parapet and an octagonal turret rising above it and much diapering in black brick; the lower part of the turret is of stone and of 15th-century date. The two-centred tower-arch is of three continuous chamfered orders; the inner order is interrupted by moulded capitals and bases, the former being of whitewashed brick or stone. High up in the S. wall of the ground-stage, inside, is a blocked opening with a moulded segmental arch of stone; it is probably a 15th-century doorway from the stair-turret. The W. window is of three cinquefoiled lights with vertical tracery in a two-centred head with a moulded label; the W. doorway has moulded jambs, four-

centred arch and label; above it is a rectangular sunk panel containing a stone shield—*a chief indented* for Butler, Earl of Ormonde. The N., S. and W. walls of the second stage have each a window of one pointed light, more or less restored. The bell-chamber has in each wall a window of two cinquefoiled lights in a square head and all modern externally except the heads of the E. window and part of the heads of the N. window.

The *South Porch* is of late 15th-century date, and has a chequer-work parapet like that of the S. aisle. The two-centred outer archway is of two moulded orders, the outer continuous and the inner resting on attached shafts with moulded capitals and bases; the label is moulded. The side walls have each a window of two cinquefoiled lights in a square head, partly restored. In each angle of the porch is a moulded corbel for a projected vault.

The *Roof* of the N. aisle is flat-pitched, and may incorporate some old timbers. The roof of the S. aisle is largely modern, but incorporates some 15th-century timbers, and there are three 15th-century stone head-corbels. The floor of the first stage of the tower has early 16th-century moulded beams and a square bell-way in the middle.

Fittings—*Brass*: In nave—of Mary Dilcok, 1514, small figure of woman in pedimental head-dress; indents of scroll and figures of Virgin and Child. *Coffin-lid*: In S. porch—with moulded edges and raised cross, probably 13th-century. *Communion Rails*: with twisted balusters, c. 1700. *Doors*: In chancel—N. door (modern) has two old strap-hinges, probably 15th-century. In tower—in lower doorway to turret-staircase at W. end of S. aisle, of nail-studded battens, fillets planted on and strap-hinges, late 15th-century; in upper doorway of same staircase, of battens with strap-hinges, same date. *Monuments*: In churchyard—N. side—(1) to Richard Knight, 1702, table-tomb; (2) to Stephen Jackson, 1706, table-tomb; N. of tower—(3) to John Fortescue, 1710, and Anne, his wife, 1709, table-tomb; (4) to Ralph Desbrow, early 18th-century table-tomb. *Piscinae*: In chancel—with cinquefoiled head, label cut back, late 14th or early 15th-century, modern sill. In S. aisle—in S. wall, with moulded jambs and rounded head, broken round drain, 15th-century. *Plate*: includes large cup and cover-paten of 1705. *Scratching*: In chancel—on jamb of S.W. window, the name and date—Samuel Purkis, 1642. The doorways to the rood-loft staircase, and the tower stair-turret have masons' marks common to one another.

Condition—Good.

Secular :—

ª(2). ROCHFORD HALL, house (Plate, p. 127) and boundary walls, 110 yards W.N.W. of the church. The *House* is of two storeys with attics; the walls

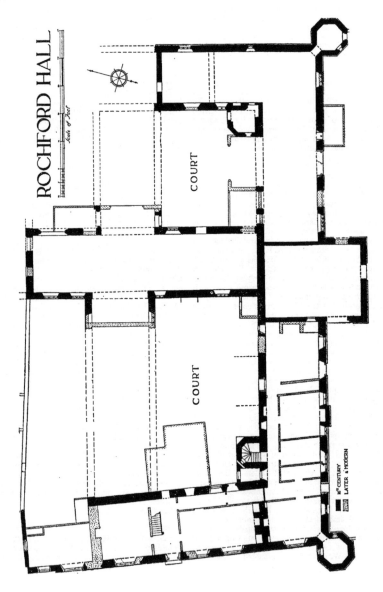

are of rubble and brick; the roofs are tiled. It was formerly one of the largest houses in the county, with at least three if not four courtyards, and was built *c.* 1540–50. The whole of the S. part of the house has been entirely destroyed; the surviving buildings of the western courtyards have been reduced in height and turned into barns, etc. The only part remaining to the full height consists of the two wings meeting at the N.E. angle. The walls generally are covered with a thin coat of plaster, which must always have been the case, as the mixed rubble and brickwork of the walls is evidently not intended to be exposed.

The house is of much interest as the wreck of a very large 16th-century mansion.

The *E. Elevation* has four original gables with the stumps of pinnacles at the apexes. All the existing windows are modern, but the blocked openings of a number of square-headed windows are visible, with labels cut back flush with the wall. At the N.E. angle is an octagonal turret with remains of an embattled parapet and some original windows with square-moulded labels.

The *N. Elevation.* Only the E. part stands to the full height, and has four gables, each with a single octagonal chimney-shaft rising from the apex; three of these shafts retain their moulded caps. The original windows have all been wholly or partly blocked, and are similar in form to those on the E. side. To the W. of the wing just described is a rectangular projecting bay, formerly the central feature of the N. front. It is ruined to the ground-storey, and has remains of an original opening in the W. wall and a low brick arch in the N. wall, possibly for a drain and now blocked. The remainder of the N. front is standing one storey high and is used as barns. In it are some original windows, one of four round-headed lights in a square head, and an original wide door or archway with a four-centred head. At the N.W. angle is the lower storey of an octagonal turret similar to that at the N.E. angle.

W. Elevation. The remaining part contains two old windows similar to those already described.

The house has been so completely gutted that it is impossible to determine the original arrangement of the main rooms or to identify the site of the great hall or main entrance. The only feature of interest inside the house is the spiral staircase of solid oak treads.

The *N.E. Courtyard* has in the N.E. angle an octagonal stair-turret (Plate, pp. 56–7) brought out to square at the base. It contains some original single-light windows and has remains of an embattled parapet with a moulded string. There was formerly a projecting building in the middle of the N. side, now destroyed, but with a blocked fireplace-opening with a three-centred head at the first-floor level. There are traces and part of the base of another but quite small projection on the

W. side. Various original windows remain, all with rounded heads to the lights in a square outer order. The central block, now of cruciform plan owing to the partial destruction of the cross-arm, has a number of original windows, and on the W. side at the S. end a wide four-centred and moulded arch (Plate, pp. 56–7); the responds have attached shafts with moulded capitals. There is another four-centred archway of smaller size in the S. wall of the adjoining cross-wing. At the S. end of the main block, in a wall formerly internal, are two recesses, both with four-centred arches in square heads; one has the spandrels enriched with blank shields with an inlaid filling.

The *N.W. Courtyard* has a semi-octagonal turret in the N.W. angle, and there are a number of original windows and four doorways with four-centred heads.

The outer *Boundary-wall* towards the road is original, and has black-brick diapering. Outside it is part of an original drain with a four-centred brick covering, at the side of the road. Other boundary walls are probably original.

Condition—Poor, partly ruinous.

MONUMENTS (3–10).

The following monuments, unless otherwise described, are of the 17th century, and of two storeys, timber-framed and plastered; the roofs are tiled. Some of the buildings have original chimney-stacks and exposed ceiling-beams. Condition—Good or fairly good, unless noted.

a(3). *Almshouses* (Plate, pp. 56–7), four tenements on N. side of Church Street, 340 yards N.N.E. of the church, were founded by Robert Rich, Lord Warwick, early in the 17th century, and form a long rectangular block of red brick, one storey high, with two projecting gabled bays on the front. The bases of three chimney-stacks are old, but the solid door and window-frames have apparently all been renewed.

b(4). *The Forge*, on N. side of Church Street, 160 yards S.E. of (3), has an 18th-century addition on the N. and a later W. wing, to the N. of which, lighting the first floor, is an original window of two lights with solid frame and mullion.

b(5). *Range of shops and tenements* (Plate, p. xl), on E. side of South Street, 180 yards N. of Salt Bridge. The gabled cross-wing at the N. end is probably of 16th-century date, but the rest of the building is of the 17th century.

b(6). *House* (Plate, p. xxxv), 40 yards N. of (5), was built in the 15th century with a central hall open to the roof, and N. and S. cross-wings. Late in the 16th or early in the following century a first floor was inserted in the hall, and there is a modern addition at the back. The upper storey of the N. wing originally projected on the W. front, but has been underbuilt; it retains the curved supporting braces at either end. The chimney-stack to the N. wing is of four shafts on a cruciform plan set diagonally; the chimney to the hall-block is rectangular. Inside the building some of the rooms have exposed ceiling-beams. The hall was in two bays with a central king-post truss, now visible on the first floor; the tie-beam was supported on curved braces, which still show in the lower room. In this room is an open fireplace. The roof over the S. wing is in four bays with king-post trusses with curved braces.

[b](7). *House,* on N. side of road, opposite N. end of North Street, was probably built in the 17th century, but is of at least two periods. The S. front has three gables.

Condition—Poor.

[b](8). *House* (Plate, pp. xxxiv–v), now two tenements, adjoining (7) on the E., has a projecting upper storey at the E. end. The central chimney-stack has a moulded capping to the base.

[b](9). *King's Hill,* house, 120 yards S.E. of (8), has a W. cross-wing, possibly of 16th-century date, to which was added in the 17th century an E. block, thus making a building of T-shaped plan. To it have been added modern extensions on the N. Inside the house, at the top of the staircase, are five turned balusters of late 17th-century date.

[a](10). *House,* at Stroud Green, about 1 m. W.N.W. of the church, is of one storey with attics, and was built in the 16th century. It has a cross-wing at the W. end and a modern N.W. addition.

---

76. RUNWELL. (D.c.)

(O.S. 6 in. [(a)]lxi. S.W. [(b)]lxix. N.W.)

Runwell is a parish about 5 m. E. of Billericay. The church and Fleming's Farm are the principal monuments.

Ecclesiastical :—

[b](1). PARISH CHURCH OF ST. MARY stands in the S.W. angle of the parish. The walls are of ragstone-rubble, with some pudding-stone, brick and flint; the dressings are of limestone; the roofs are tiled. The S. arcade of the *Nave* is of *c.* 1200, but the rest of the church, including the N. wall of the nave, the *South Aisle, North* and *South Porches* and *West Tower,* were built or rebuilt during the course of the 15th century. The church has been restored in modern times, when the *Chancel* was rebuilt and extended towards the E. and the *South Vestry* added.

The timber N. and S. porches are interesting.

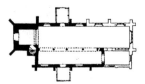

Architectural Description—The *Chancel* is modern, but reset in the E. wall is a 15th-century window of three trefoiled lights in a four-centred head with a moulded label. Reset in the N. wall are two 15th-century windows, each of two trefoiled lights in a square head with a moulded label. In the S. wall, E. of the nave-arcade is a 15th or early 16th-century squint with a square head.

The *Nave* (37¾ ft. by 15½ ft.) has in the N. wall two 15th-century windows, both of two cinque-foiled lights in a square head with a moulded label; between them is the 15th-century N. doorway, with chamfered jambs, two-centred arch and moulded label; below the western window is a rough segmental-pointed relieving-arch. The S. arcade is of early 13th-century date, and of four bays with two-centred arches of two chamfered orders; the columns are cylindrical, with moulded capitals and bases, and the square chamfered responds have chamfered imposts; the arcade shows evidence of reconstruction, the second column being out of place.

The *South Aisle* (9 ft. wide) has a modern opening in the E. wall, and above it is a modern window with reused 15th-century stones. In the S. wall are two windows similar to those in the N. wall of the nave; between them is the 15th-century S. doorway, with chamfered jambs and two-centred arch.

The *West Tower* (11 ft. by 12¼ ft.) is of the 15th century, and of three stages with an embattled parapet, an embattled turret rising above the S.E. angle and a short shingled spire (Plate, pp. xxxii–iii). The two-centred tower-arch is of three hollow-chamfered orders; the two outer die on to the splayed responds and the inner rests on attached shafts with moulded capitals and bases. The W. window is of the 14th century, reset, and of three cinquefoiled lights with intersecting tracery in a two-centred head with a moulded label. The W. doorway has moulded jambs, two-centred arch and label. The second stage has in each wall a window of one trefoiled light with a square moulded label. The bell-chamber has in each wall a window of two lights in a square head with a moulded label; the heads of the lights on the E. and W. are cinquefoiled, and of those on the N. and S. trefoiled.

The *North Porch* (Plate, p. xxxix) is of late 15th-century date, timber-framed, and of two bays on dwarf brick walls. The three-centred outer archway has spandrels carved with foliage and the name in black-letter Iohes Okashott ; flanking it are two bays with cinquefoiled and traceried heads ; above the cross-beam in the gable is a king-post, carved on the face with a shallow panel and a rosette. The side walls have each six open lights with traceried heads similar to those flanking the entrance ; those on the E. are modern restorations. The roof has a middle king-post truss with curved braces springing from moulded and carved brackets and a central foliated boss.

The *South Porch* (Plate, p. xxxix) is of similar date and construction to the N. porch, but rests on a plinth of stone and flint. The four-centred outer archway is flanked by open lights with cinquefoiled ogee heads and tracery ; the moulded cross-beam supports a king-post with a pointed niche cut in the outer face. The side walls have each six lights similar to those flanking the entrance, but the heads on the W. side and three of those on the E. are modern. The middle king-post truss has curved braces forming a four-centred arch ; the wall-plates are moulded.

The *Roof* of the nave incorporates some old timbers ; that of the S. aisle is probably of the 15th-century partly restored ; it has braced collar-beams forming round arches and a moulded wall-plate on the S. side. The spire is a timber-framed construction of the 15th century.

Fittings—*Bells :* ·four—1st, 2nd and 3rd by Robert Mot, 1591. *Brass* and *Indent* Brass : see Monuments (1). Indent : In tower—of inscription-plate and two shields. *Coffin-lids :* In chancel—(1) of Purbeck marble with double hollow-chamfered edge and raised ornamental cross, 13th-century. In S. porch—(2) tapering slab of Purbeck marble. Sawn up and used in plinths of S.W. buttresses of aisle—(3) two with moulded edges. *Doors :* In S. doorway—of nail-studded battens with strap-hinges, 15th-century. In tower—in doorway to turret, with strap-hinges, 15th-century. *Font :* octagonal bowl with moulded under-side, plain stem and modern base, 15th-century ; old base now in Rectory garden. *Glass :* In vestry—in E. window, two roses, two whole and two half quarries with ornamental design and a border of leafage and coloured glass, 15th-century. In S. aisle—in E. window, fragments of foliage and border and four roundels of coloured glass, 13th or 14th-century. *Monuments* and *Floor-slab :* Monuments : In chancel—on N wall—(1) of Eustace Sulyard, 1547, and Margaret, his wife, 1587, tablet with side pilasters and pediment, on slab—brasses of man in plate-armour and woman in ruff, etc., kneeling at prayer-desk and three shields-of-arms ; on S. wall—(2) to Edward Sulyard, 1692, white marble tablet with achievement-of-arms. Floor-slab : In tower—to Thomas Sulyard, 1634, with shield-of-arms. *Piscinae :* In S. aisle—in S. wall, with chamfered jambs and

square head, round drain, 15th-century ; further W. similar, 15th-century, reset. *Plate* (Plate, p. xliv) : includes cup of 1562, with band of engraved ornament, and cover-paten of the same date. *Poor-box :* In nave—of oak hollowed out, with slotted

Runwell Poor-box.

iron plate in top, iron-bound lid and four iron discs nailed on, 15th or 16th-century. *Scratchings :* On tower-arch and splays of windows in second stage of tower, various masons' marks. *Stoup :* In N. porch—with round bowl, cut back, probably 15th-century. *Sundial :* On W. jamb of S. doorway—scratched sundial, stone reset.

Condition—Good, except tower.

Secular :—

b(2). FLEMING'S FARM, house and outbuildings, 1½ m. N.N.W. of the church. The *House* is a fragment of a much larger house of late 16th or early 17th-century date (said to have been destroyed by fire), and is of two storeys with attics ; the walls are of brick and the roofs are tiled. It is rectangular on plan, with a large rectangular bay projecting on the N.W. front, and has a modern extension on the S.W. and a smaller addition on the N.E. On the *N.W. Elevation* (Plate, p. 132) the projecting bay is gabled and has a moulded coping with pointed finials on moulded bases at the apex and on the kneelers. Lighting the ground-floor is a five-light window with a single-light window on the return ; both have moulded heads, jambs, mullions and transom. The first floor has a large window of similar detail but with two transoms, and a single-light window on both returns. The *N.E. Elevation* has two gables, the N. one of which is similar to the gable just described but with a modern coping. The chimney-stack is original and has three diagonal shafts with oversailing tops.

Inside the building, the front room on the ground-floor (now the kitchen) has two moulded ceiling-beams, and some of the beams in the ceiling and the timber-framing in the walls of the back room are exposed. In the window to the kitchen is some 16th-century glass, with a mutilated cartouche of the arms of Sulyard and pieces of ruby, yellow, brown, blue and white glass, some in the form of foliage. The staircase has some original panelling on both the ground and first floors, and in the room above the kitchen is a stone fireplace with a moulded, four-centred head and jambs. In the attic is an original fireplace with a square head.

The *Outbuilding* stands to the N. of and is of about the same date as the house. It is of one storey, built of brick and rectangular on plan and has a two-centred doorway and a three-light square-headed window with moulded head, jambs, transom and mullions. The door is of four panels with moulded and nailed-studded framing.

Condition—Of house, good.

*(3). GIFFORD'S FARM (Plate, pp. xxxiv–v), about 1¼ m. N. of the church, is of two storeys, timber-framed and plastered, with tiled roofs. It was built in the 16th century on a T-shaped plan, with cross-wing at the N. end, but the roof of the S. wing has been raised and both wings have small modern additions. The upper storey of the cross-wing projects on the E. front ; it is supported on curved brackets, and has below a slightly projecting bay-window of four lights with diamond-shaped mullions. On the N. front is a blocked window of three lights with diamond-shaped mullions, and an original chimney-stack ; in the W. end of the S. wall of the cross-wing is a blocked window similar to the one in the N. wall. Inside the building some of the rooms have exposed ceiling-beams. The roof over the N. wing has a queen-post truss, with curved braces to the tie-beam and curved wind-braces.

Condition—Good.

*(4). CHURCH END, house (Plate, pp. xl–i), 600 yards N.W. of the church, is of two storeys with attics, timber-framed and plastered ; the roofs are tiled. It was built in the 17th century on an L-shaped plan with the wings extending towards the N.W. and S.W. ; the additions on the back and side are modern. On the N.E. side is an original chimney-stack, the top of which has been rebuilt. Inside the building some of the rooms have exposed ceiling-beams.

Condition—Good.

---

77. ST. LAWRENCE (NEWLAND). (G.b.)

(O.S. 6 in. (*a*)lv. S.W. (*b*)lv. S.E. (*c*)xiii. N.W.)

St. Lawrence is a parish on the S. of the Blackwater estuary and 5½ m. N. of Burnham-on-Crouch.

Ecclesiastical :—

*(1). PARISH CHURCH OF ST. LAWRENCE was entirely rebuilt in 1878, but contains from the old church the following :—

Fittings—*Piscina :* In nave—in N. wall, with moulded jambs and two-centred head, round drain, 14th-century. *Plate :* includes large pewter flagon with inscription and date 1700.

Condition—Rebuilt.

Secular :—

*(2). MOYNES FARM, house and moat, 1¼ m. S. of the church. The *House* is of two storeys, timber-framed and weather-boarded ; the roofs are tiled. It was built *c.* 1595, the date on a wooden panel inside the house. The room is panelled to half its height and has a moulded ceiling-beam.

The *Moat* surrounds the house.

Condition—Of house, fairly good.

*(3). ST. LAWRENCE HALL, 150 yards S.S.E. of the church, has been rebuilt except for a gabled cross-wing of the 16th or 17th century. It is of two storeys, timber-framed and plastered ; the roof is tiled. The upper storey projects at the N. end. Inside the building is an original window with bar-mullions and now blocked.

Condition—Good.

*(4). WEST NEWLANDS, house, about 1¼ m. S.W. of the church, is of two storeys, timber-framed and plastered and partly weather-boarded ; the roofs are tiled. It was built probably in the 17th century, and has an original chimney-stack with three diagonal shafts.

Condition—Good, much altered.

---

78. SANDON. (D.b.)

(O.S. 6 in. liii. S.W.)

Sandon is a parish 3 m. S.E. of Chelmsford. The church is the principal monument.

Ecclesiastical :—

(1). PARISH CHURCH OF ST. ANDREW (Plate, p. 133) stands at the N. end of the parish. The walls are of pudding-stone and flint-rubble with some Roman bricks ; the tower and S. porch are of brick ; the dressings are of limestone and brick ; the roofs are tiled. The *Chancel* and *Nave* were built in the 12th century. The chancel-arch was rebuilt probably late in the 13th century. The N. arcade was built and the *North Aisle* added about the middle of the 14th century. Probably in the 15th century the chancel was extended about 5 ft. to the E. Early in the 16th century the *West Tower* and the *South Porch* were added. The church has been restored in modern times, when the walls of the N. aisle were heightened

The brick tower and S. porch are interesting, and among the fittings the pillar-piscina, communion table and pulpit are noteworthy.

RUNWELL : (2). FLEMING'S FARM. Late 16th or early 17th-century.
North-West Front.

SANDON: PARISH CHURCH OF ST. ANDREW. 12th-century and later.

From the South-East; Windows, late 13th to early 16th-century; Tower and S. Porch, early 16th-century.

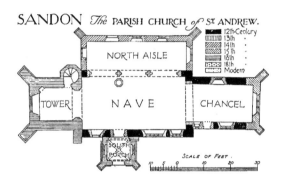

SANDON *The* PARISH CHURCH *of* S.T ANDREW.

NORTH AISLE

TOWER | N A V E | CHANCEL

SOUTH PORCH

SCALE OF FEET.

Architectural Description—The *Chancel* (22 ft. by 13¾ ft.) retains in the N. and S. walls the Roman brick quoins of the 12th-century chancel. The early 15th-century E. window is much restored, and of three cinquefoiled lights with modern tracery in a two-centred head. In the N. wall is a late 13th or early 14th-century window of two pointed lights in a two-centred head with a moulded label. In the S. wall are two windows, the eastern uniform with that in the N. wall and the western a 'low-side,' but modern except for the moulded splays and rear-arch; this window has a casement with a 17th-century iron catch; between the windows is a partly restored 14th-century doorway with double chamfered jambs, two-centred arch and moulded label. The late 13th-century chancel-arch is two-centred and of one plain order with moulded imposts, partly destroyed; above the arch is a round-headed opening, now blocked.

The *Nave* (38¾ ft. by 19¼ ft.) has original 12th-century quoins at the E. angles. The mid 14th-century N. arcade is of three bays with two-centred arches of two moulded orders; the columns are of quatrefoil plan, the N. and S. shafts being of semi-octagonal form, all have moulded capitals and bases; the responds have attached half-columns, and the base of the W. respond is square. In the S. wall are three windows; the easternmost is of early 16th-century date and of two rounded lights in a square head; above it are two modern lights of similar form; the second window is modern, and the westernmost has a modern frame set in place of a partly destroyed 13th-century window; E. of it is the 14th-century S. doorway, with chamfered jambs, two-centred arch and a moulded label with head-stops.

The *North Aisle* (10½ ft. wide) has in the E. wall a window all modern except the splays and

rear-arch. In the N. wall are two windows, both modern except for the splays and rear-arch of the eastern, which incorporates a 12th-century voussoir; further W. is the 14th-century N. doorway, now blocked, and with double chamfered jambs, moulded two-centred arch and modern label. In the W. wall is an 18th-century window set in an old opening with a 14th-century moulded label.

The *West Tower* (12 ft. square) is entirely of early 16th-century date and of red brick; it is of three stages, the two lower undivided externally, and has an extensive diapered decoration in black brick, including two large crosses on the W. face of the top stage, numerous crosses of St. Andrew and various ornamental lozenges; the embattled parapet rests on a corbel-table of small arches. The four-centred tower-arch is of three plain orders; the responds are splayed. The W. window is of three pointed lights with uncusped tracery in a two-centred head; the W. doorway has a four-centred head, and has been converted into a window. The N. and S. walls of the second stage have each a window of one pointed light. The bell-chamber has in each wall a window of two pointed lights set in an elliptical outer arch.

The *South Porch* (Plate, p. xxxviii) is of early 16th-century date and of red brick with a crow-stepped parapet resting on a corbel-table of trefoiled arches. The outer archway has chamfered jambs and moulded two-centred arch and label; above it is a wide niche or panel with an ogee head; flanking the niche are two large crosses of St. Andrew in black headers. The side walls have each a window of two pointed lights with a spandrel in a round head. The porch has a brick vault with diagonal chamfered ribs springing from angle-shafts with moulded bases. On each side is a seat resting on two segmental arches of brick.

The *Roof* of the chancel is boarded, and is divided into panels by 15th-century moulded ribs ; the wall-plates are also moulded. The roof of the nave is modern except the 15th-century eastern truss, which has moulded hammer-beams and curved braces enclosing traceried spandrels, under a modern collar-beam.

Fittings—*Bells :* five ; 1st and 2nd by John Hodson, 1653. *Brasses :* In chancel—(1) part of slab with two scrolls and two shields-of-arms (a) *on a chief indented three roundels, a border,* for Latham, (b) Goldsmiths' company, indents of heads of two figures and marginal inscription, *c.* 1510 ; on N. wall, (2) of Patrick Fearne [1588], parson of the parish, kneeling figures of man in fur-lined gown and wife in wide-brimmed hat, scrolls and inscription-plate, all set in panel. *Communion Table :* with four legs at angles and three along the middle, all turned as columns and supporting arches, side rails each with three turned acorn-pendants, one turned pendant in middle of front and back rails, late 17th-century. *Doors :* In doorway of chancel—with moulded panels and pedimental head, possibly late 17th-century. In S. doorway—modern, but with three strap-hinges, 15th-century. In N. doorway—of feathered battens with one strap-hinge, probably 15th-century. In tower—in doorway to turret staircase, of feathered battens with strap-hinges, probably early 16th - century. *Font :* octagonal with moulded lower-edge to bowl, probably early 16th-century. *Glass :* In chancel—in S.E. window, various detached pieces, including four shields-of-arms— (a) *argent three bends azure, on a chief sable two lions or face to face* (Plate, pp. xliv–v), for St. Gregory ; (b) *ermine a cheveron sable with three crescents or thereon* for Doreward (Plate, pp. xliv–v) ; (c) *gules a cheveron ermine between three fleurs-de-lis or* (Plate, pp. xliv–v) and (d) Darcy, 15th and 16th-century, but (d) restored and (b) of doubtful antiquity. In W. window of porch—fragmentary shield of the arms (a). *Monuments :* In chancel—on N. wall, (1) to Anne, wife of Brian Walton, D.D., rector, 1640, alabaster and black marble tablet ; on S. wall, (2) to Deborah, wife of Samuel Smith, " pastor of this congregation," 1647, tablet. *Panelling :* In chancel—incorporated in quire stalls, seven panels with incised scroll-work, also one fluted panel in prayer-desk, early 17th-century. Reset under stairs to pulpit, two arcaded panels with foliage, early 17th-century. *Piscinae :* In chancel—with chamfered jambs and two-centred head, round drain, 13th-century ; pillar-piscina (Plate, p. xlv) with shaft ornamented with spiral fluting and beading, base with cheveron ornament and capital carved with interlacing design, 12th-century, found in N.W. buttress in 1904. *Plate :* includes flagon of 1624, given in 1688, and cup and cover-paten of 1628. *Pulpit :* octagonal with buttresses and pinnacled angles, moulded and crested

top-rail, pierced and traceried lower rail, each face with cusped and traceried heads and linen-fold panel, trumpet-stem with moulded ribs and octagonal post with moulded and crested capital and moulded base, late 15th-century (Plate, p. 79).

Condition—Good.

Secular :—

MONUMENTS (2–5).

The following monuments, unless otherwise described, are of the 16th-century, and of two storeys, timber-framed and plastered ; the roofs are tiled. Some of the buildings have original chimney-stacks and exposed ceiling-beams.

Condition—Good or fairly good.

(2). *Sandon Place,* house and outbuildings, on opposite side of the road, N.E. of the church. The *House* has a slated roof and was built probably in the 16th century, but conclusive evidence has been entirely lost in modern alterations. The plan appears to have originally been half H-shaped, with cross-wings extending towards the N., but the space between them has been filled in by a modern addition and the roof over the central block has probably been raised. The upper storey of the cross-wings projects on the S. front. The chimney-stack to the central block is of late 16th or early 17th-century date. Inside the building some of the timber-framing shows in the walls ; at the back of the house and in the wall on the W. side of the central chimney is a doorway with a three-centred head ; in the staircase is a blocked window.

The *Outbuilding* W. of the house is of brick with diaper-work in black headers. Inside the building, in the walls, are some small recesses with four-centred heads.

(3). *Cottage,* 100 yards E. of (2), is a small rectangular building, partly refaced with brick. On the E. side is an original chimney-stack (Plate, p. 57) with an embattled base and moulded capping surmounted by grouped diagonal shafts.

(4). *Mayes Farm,* house, 1,150 yards E.S.E. of the church, is built on an L-shaped plan, with the wings extending towards the N. and W. The upper storey projects on the S. of the E. front. The main doorway is original, and has moulded jambs and four-centred head with sunk spandrels and retains an original door with moulded fillets and drop-handle. The chimney-stack at the junction of the wings has grouped diagonal shafts.

(5). *House,* on N. side of road at Woodhill, about 1¼ m. E. of the church, is probably of 15th or early 16th-century date, and has a cross-wing at the E. end. The main block is of one storey with attics and has the middle part of the S. wall carried up in a gable. The chimney-stack has a rectangular base with a moulded capping surmounted by grouped diagonal shafts.

SHOEBURY, see NORTH SHOEBURY and SOUTH SHOEBURY.

79. SHOPLAND. (F.c.)

(O.S. 6 in. lxxviii. N.E.)

Shopland is a small parish on the S. bank of the River Roach, 3 m. N.E. of Southend-on-Sea. The church and Beauchamps are the principal monuments.

Ecclesiastical :—

(1). PARISH CHURCH OF ST. MARY MAGDALENE stands on the E. side of the parish. The walls are of rubble covered with cement and rough-cast ; the dressings are of limestone ; the roofs are tiled and the bell-turret boarded. The *Nave* was built early in the 12th century. The *Chancel* was rebuilt and widened in the 13th or 14th century. The *South Porch* was added early in the 15th century and the bell-turret in the 16th century. The timber S. porch is interesting, and amongst the fittings the font is noteworthy.

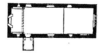

Architectural Description—The *Chancel* (21½ ft. by 18¾ ft.) has an E. window all modern except the plastered splays and two-centred rear-arch, which are possibly of the 14th century. In the N. wall is a doorway with a four-centred rear-arch, probably of the 15th century ; it is blocked and not visible externally. In the S. wall is a 14th-century window of one cinquefoiled light, set in a cemented lancet-shaped opening, probably of the 13th century. There is no chancel-arch.

The *Nave* (39½ ft. by 19 ft.) has in the N. wall two windows, the eastern of the 15th century, of two cinquefoiled lights with vertical tracery in a square head having a moulded label with defaced head-stops ; the splays have small carved head-stops at the springing level ; the western window is a single small early 12th-century light with a round head ; between the windows is the blocked N. doorway ; it is not visible externally, but has a hollowed chamfered rear-arch, probably of the 14th century. In the S. wall are two windows, the eastern is of the 14th century, and

of two cinquefoiled lights with tracery in a square head ; the western window is similar to the corresponding window in the N. wall, but is blocked; further E. the outlines of a similar window are visible internally ; the 14th-century S. doorway has moulded jambs, two-centred arch and label with head-stops. In the W. wall is a window probably all modern. The bell-turret, at the W. end of the nave, stands on four oak posts with curved braces, probably of the 16th century.

The *South Porch* (Plate, p. 137) is of early 15th-century date, timber-framed and of two bays. The square-headed outer archway is flanked by ogee-headed openings ; above the moulded lintel are three ogee-headed niches, the middle one having a number of round mortice-holes at the back ; the western niche contains remains of a carved head, cut back. The side walls have in the outer bay three cinquefoiled lights with traceried heads. The wall-plates and tie-beams are moulded, and the ties, which are steeply cambered, have curved braces.

The *Roof* of the chancel is possibly of 14th or 15th-century date and of trussed-rafter type, ceiled on the soffit ; the plates are hollow-chamfered. The nave has three late 14th-century king-post trusses ; two tie-beams and the plates are moulded ; the slender king-posts of the two western trusses are octagonal and have moulded capitals and plain bases.

Fittings : Bells : Inaccessible, but said to be by Peter Hawkes, 1608. *Brass :* In nave—slab partly under pews [of Thomas Stapel, 1371], serjeant-at-arms, mutilated figure in armour with pointed bascinet, camail, etc., knee-cops and legs below missing, indents of marginal inscription and cinquefoiled crocketed canopy and shields, fragment of inscription remaining at top. *Coffin-lid :* In nave—as threshold of S. doorway, with hollow-chamfered edge, probably 13th-century. *Doors :* In chancel—in blocked doorway, roughly framed door, 17th or 18th-century. In nave—in N. doorway, possibly 15th or 16th-century. *Font* (Plate, pp. xlii–iii) : Square bowl, S. face with interlacing arcade of round arches resting on shafts with moulded capitals and 'hold-water' bases ; W. face with three trefoiled arches with flattened shafts having similar capitals and bases, roses in the spandrels and fleur-de-lis cusp-points to the middle bay ; E. and N. faces each with three large incised fleurs-de-lis and two formy crosses in circles, stem consists of a middle and four side shafts with moulded caps and bases, early 13th-century. *Glass :* In chancel—in tracery of E. window, numerous fragments, partly old and including crowns, foliage, borders, heraldic mantling and drapery, 13th, 15th and 17th-century. In nave—in S. window, yellow oak-leaf ornament in tracery, late 14th-century, *in situ. Monument :* In churchyard—slab to William Haker, yeoman, 1639. *Paving :* In nave—numerous small tiles with remains of glaze, one with a crown, mediaeval. *Piscina :* In chancel—with chamfered jambs and trefoiled head, sexfoiled drain, 14th-century. *Plate :* includes cup of 1683. *Seating :* In nave—one bench with a shaped standard and rail, of the 16th century, partly repaired. Another with 17th-century bench-ends. *Sedile :* In chancel—in S. wall, wide recess with chamfered jambs and two-centred arch, 14th-century.

Condition—Good, much restored except N.E. window of the nave, which is badly decayed.

Secular :—

(2). HOMESTEAD MOAT, at Butler's Farm, 1,100 yards N. of the church.

(3). HOUSE, now two tenements, 50 yards W. of the church, is of two storeys with attics ; the walls are of timber-framing, partly plastered and partly weather-boarded ; the roofs are tiled. It was built in the 17th century, and has a modern addition at the back. On the E. front are two gabled dormer-windows, and the central chimney-stack is original. Inside the building there are some exposed ceiling-beams in the ground-floor rooms.

Condition—Good.

(4). BEAUCHAMPS, house (Plate, p. 136), ½ m. E. of the church, is of two storeys, timber-framed and plastered ; the roofs are tiled. It is a long rectangular building of *c.* 1688, with a two-storeyed porch on the E. front. On the E. front there are considerable remains of elaborate pargeting, the lower storey being treated in the form of rusticated masonry, the upper with scrolls, swags and fruit-ornament and the date 1688 in Roman figures with a large rose above (Plate, p. 152). At the eaves-level is a modillioned cornice, which is continued round the porch. The central chimney-stack is original, but the upper part of the chimney-stack at the N. end of the house has been rebuilt. Inside the building the southernmost room has a fine plaster ceiling divided into two bays by a cased beam. In each bay is a large elliptical wreath (Plate, p. 152) of laurel leaves and berries and with a pendant of fruit and flowers in the centre surrounded by four cherubs' heads alternating with rosebuds ; outside the wreath at either end of the ceiling are roses and fleurs-de-lis.

Condition—Good.

(5). FOX HALL, 750 yards S S.E. of the church, is of two storeys with attics ; the walls are timber-framed and weather-boarded ; the roofs are tiled. The cross-wing at the E. end of the house and the E. end of the main block are the remains of a 15th-century building, the W. end of which was rebuilt in the 16th century. There is a modern addition on the E. The upper storey of the cross-wing projects on the S. front and is supported on

two curved brackets, and on the W. front is a 16th-century chimney-stack with crow-stepped offsets and an oversailing cap. Inside the building the ceiling-beams in the ground-floor rooms of the E. wing are exposed, and in the W. cross-wall is a blocked doorway with a four-centred head. Springing from the side walls of the room occupying the W. end of the former hall are two curved braces which probably supported the tie-beam of the original hall roof. In this room is a wide 16th-century fireplace with a four-centred head. The roof over the E. wing has an original tie-beam with a mortice for a king-post.

Condition—Good.

────────

80. SOUTH BENFLEET. (D.d.)

(O.S. 6 in. [(a)]lxxvii. N.W. [(b)]lxxvii. S.W.)

South Benfleet is a small parish on the N. bank of the Thames, opposite Canvey Island, 6 m. W. of Southend-on-Sea. The church is the principal monument.

Ecclesiastical :—

[a](1). PARISH CHURCH OF ST. MARY THE VIRGIN stands in the centre of the village at the S. end of the parish. The walls are of ashlar, rubble, Roman brick and flint ; the roofs are covered with tiles and lead. The walls of the nave and aisles contain a considerable quantity of squared ragstone and septaria, possibly reused Roman material. The W. end of the *Nave* is of mid 12th-century date. About the middle of the 13th century the chancel-arch was rebuilt. *C.* 1300 a S. aisle was added, and the *West Tower* was built probably shortly after. In the middle of the 15th century the *Chancel* was rebuilt with the chancel-arch, and the S. arcade and aisle rebuilt. Late in the same century the *South Porch* was added. *C.* 1500 the *North Aisle* was added, and the clearstorey is of the same date. In the 17th century minor repairs were carried out, and in recent years the church has been restored and the floor of the nave lowered by about two feet.

The church is of considerable architectural interest, the S. porch being an unusually good piece of timber work.

Architectural Description—The *Chancel* (35¼ ft. by 22 ft.) has a modern E. window, but a segmental relieving-arch to a pre-existing one shows externally and internally. In the N. wall are two 15th-century windows restored in cement, and each of two cinquefoiled lights with vertical tracery in a two-centred head. In the S. wall are two similar windows ; between them is a 15th-century doorway with chamfered jambs and two centred head restored in cement. The early 15th-century

SHOPLAND: (4). BEAUCHAMPS.
East Front, with pargeting, dated 1688.

SHOPLAND:
PARISH CHURCH OF ST. MARY MAGDALENE.
South Porch ; early 15th-century.

SOUTH BENFLEET :
PARISH CHURCH OF ST. MARY THE VIRGIN.
South Porch ; late 15th-century.

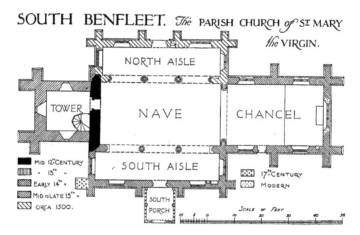

SOUTH BENFLEET. *The* PARISH CHURCH *of* St MARY *the* VIRGIN.

chancel-arch is two-centred and of two hollow-chamfered orders; the mid 13th-century responds are semi-circular, with three attached shafts with continuous moulded capitals and bases; the responds were perhaps reset and the former arch widened early in the 15th century. Above the arch, showing externally, are three small blocked windows of 16th-century date with rounded heads.

The *Nave* (44½ ft. by 22½ ft.) has N. and S. arcades, each of three bays. The N. arcade is of *c.* 1500, with two-centred arches of two chamfered orders; the columns have each four attached shafts with moulded capitals and bases; the responds have attached half-columns. A set-back in the walling at the level of the respond caps indicates the cutting away and rebuilding of the earlier work. The S. arcade was rebuilt in the 15th century, and has two-centred arches of two chamfered orders resting on octagonal piers and semi-octagonal responds, all with moulded capitals and bases; the capitals of the responds and of the second pier are reused work of *c.* 1300 from a former arcade. Some of the stones have masons' marks. In the W. wall is a 12th-century doorway with a semi-circular head and jambs of two chamfered orders with mutilated impost-mouldings. Higher up are two blocked 12th-century windows, each of a narrow round-headed light with wide splays. The clearstorey has on each side three late 15th-century windows, each of two cinquefoiled lights in a square head with a moulded label; below the level of the sills on each side are four carved stone corbels, two being grotesque heads, and the others the symbols of the evangelists.

The *North Aisle* (43½ ft. by 10¼ ft.) is of *c.* 1500, and has an embattled parapet. In the E. wall is a window of two cinquefoiled lights with a quatre-foil in a four-centred head. In the N. wall are two windows; the eastern is of three cinquefoiled lights in a four-centred head; the western is similar to the window in the E. wall; between the windows is the blocked N. doorway, with moulded jambs and two-centred head. E. of this is the rood-loft staircase, with square-headed upper and lower doorways. In the W. wall is a window of two lights similar to those in the N. and S. walls of the chancel. All the windows and the doorway have moulded labels.

The *South Aisle* (10 ft. wide) had an embattled parapet with a grotesque head at the S.E. angle. The four windows are all of mid to late 15th-century date and uniform with that in the W. wall of the N. aisle; between the two windows in the S. wall is a 15th-century doorway (Plate, p. 140) with moulded jambs and two-centred head.

The *West Tower* (16¼ ft. by 14½ ft.) is probably of early 14th-century date, and is of three stages undivided externally, with an internal spiral staircase of timber having an octagonal newel. The ground-stage has in each external wall a window of one trefoiled light with a square head. The second stage has in the S. and W. walls a similar window. The bell-chamber has an opening in the E. wall communicating with the roof but now blocked. The N., S. and W. walls have each a square-headed window of two trefoiled lights with a square defaced label.

The *South Porch* (12 ft. by 10 ft.) is of timber and of 15th-century date (Plate, p. 137). The E. and W. sides are each divided into two bays by slightly projecting buttresses. The upper part of each bay has modern mullions and tracery. The outer archway is two-centred with traceried spandrels; above the moulded beam at the base of the gable are three panels divided by buttresses and each having a traceried head and partly restored; above the panels is a moulded and embattled cross-beam, and one moulded barge-board is old. The roof (Plate, p. 140) is of two bays with curved principals, a middle hammer-beam truss and a tie-beam against the N. wall. All the main timbers are moulded and embattled, and the hammer-beams, purlins, tie and collar-beams have curved braces with traceried spandrels.

Fittings—*Bells :* five; 1st by John Hodson, 1664; 3rd, by John Walgrave, inscribed "Nomen Magdalene Campana Gerit Melodie," 15th-century; 4th by Miles Graye, 1676; 5th by John and Henry Wilner, 1636; bell-frame, 17th-century. *Bracket :* In S. aisle—on E. wall, square, moulded stone bracket, 15th-century. *Brass :* In chancel—on S. wall, to William Card[inal], 1568, inscription only. Some fragments of a canopy and the stem of a bracket of *c.* 1400 from this church are now preserved in Colchester Museum. *Coffin-lid :* In nave—at E. end, tapering slab with double-chamfered edge, raised foliated cross and mutilated marginal inscription in French; the base is broken away, late 13th-century. *Consecration-crosses :* On N.W. buttress to W. tower, small stone cross with Roman-brick filling; on each of the S.W. and W. buttresses similar Roman-brick cross with flint-filling. *Font :* circular Purbeck-marble stem, 13th-century or earlier, rest modern. *Glass :* In the E. and N.W. windows of the N. aisle are some 14th and 15th-century fragments of quarries and borders. *Monument and Floor-slabs :* Monument in churchyard—S.W. of the tower, table-tomb with illegible inscription and date 1695. Floor-slabs : In chancel—(1) to Sir William Appleton, Bart., 1705, and Dorothy, his wife, 1719, with achievement-of-arms. (2) to William, 1685, and John, 1689, sons of Sir William Appleton, with achievement-of-arms. *Niches :* In N. aisle—in N.E. corner, (1) square-headed and set diagonally in angle : in E. respond of S. arcade—(2) shallow, with pointed head, 15th-century ; in S. aisle—in S. wall, (3) with moulded jambs and three-centred head, deeply projecting semi-octagonal shelf, 15th-century. *Paving :* In N. aisle, at W. end—large cream-coloured tile with large quatrefoil in black inlay, date uncertain. *Piscinae :* In chancel—with moulded jambs and cinquefoiled arch in square head, 15th-century. In N. aisle—with chamfered segmental-pointed head and round drain, 15th-century. In S. aisle—in S. wall, with moulded

jambs, trefoiled ogee head and sexfoiled drain, 14th-century. *Plate :* includes cup of 1576 with band of engraved ornament and cover-paten of the same date. *Stoup :* In S. porch, E. of doorway—segmental-headed recess with broken basin, 15th-century. *Sundial :* On W. jamb of S. doorway to chancel, scratched dial.

Condition—The walls have some bad cracks (since repaired), particularly the W. wall of the S. aisle. The S. porch is breaking away from the S. wall of the S. aisle, and the S. arcade is giving at the first pier.

Secular :—

MONUMENTS (2–9).

The following monuments, unless otherwise described, are of the 17th century and of two storeys, timber-framed and plastered or weatherboarded; the roofs · are tiled. Some of the buildings have original chimney-stacks and exposed ceiling-beams.

Condition—Good or fairly good, unless noted.

b(2). *Hoy Inn*, 50 yards S. of the church, was built late in the 15th or early in the following century, with a central hall and E. and W. crosswings ; in the 16th century an upper floor was inserted in the hall, and in recent years it was added to on the N. and E. At the E. end of the original hall is a late 16th-century chimney-stack, the upper part of which has been rebuilt. The main beams in the ceilings of the ground-floor rooms are exposed, and the middle room has moulded wall-posts with carved and moulded braces dividing it into two bays. In the room above is a moulded wall-plate and the end of a moulded tie-beam which has been cut away.

b(3). *Anchor Inn*, 50 yards E. of (2), was built possibly in the 16th century, but has been much altered. The upper storey projects on the S. front.

b(4). *Cottage*, two tenements, E. of (3). Condition—Poor.

b(5). *Cottage*, three tenements, 200 yards E. of (4), was built probably in the 16th century with a cross-wing at the W. end.

b(6). *Cottage*, 150 yards S.S.W. of the church.

b(7). *House*, 30 yards S. of (6), is of T-shaped plan with the cross-wing at the N. end, and is of early 17th-century date or possibly earlier ; there are modern additions at the W. end of the cross-wing.

a(8). *Great Tarpots*, house, about 1½ m. N.N.W. of the church, is of two storeys with attics. It was built in the 17th century on an L-shaped plan with the wings projecting towards the N. and E. and has small modern additions.

Condition—Good.

ᵃ(9). *Jarvis Hall*, house, outbuilding and barn about 1¼ m. N.N.E. of the church. The *House* has been completely altered. The *Outbuilding* E. of the house is of brick and is now of two storeys only; it formed part of a larger building, of which foundations have been found. In the E. wall is an original window of three lights with a square head; in the W. wall is a blocked window. The *Barn* N.W. of the house is of the 16th century and of five bays with queen-post roof-trusses. Condition—Poor.

Unclassified :—

ᵃ(10). DANISH CAMP. Although no definite earthworks remain, the churchyard and adjoining land, bounded on the N. and W. by the backwater from Benfleet Creek, is probably the site of Hasten's Camp mentioned in the Anglo-Saxon Chronicle under A.D. 894. This is suggested by the position and formation of the ground, and the theory is strengthened by the fact that considerable remains of burnt ships and human skeletons were found when the railway bridge was built over the mouth of the backwater, *c.* 1855. (*Essex Arch. Soc. Trans.*, N.S., VIII, p. 236.)

81. SOUTH FAMBRIDGE. (E.c.)

(O.S. 6 in. lxx. S.W.)

South Fambridge is a small parish on the right bank of the Crouch, 6 m. N. of Southend-on-Sea.

Ecclesiastical :—

(1). PARISH CHURCH OF ALL SAINTS was rebuilt in 1846. The plate is now at Ashingdon (*q.v.*).

Unclassified :—

(2). RED HILLS, N. of Fambridge Hall, about ½ m. N. of the church.

___

82. SOUTH HANNINGFIELD. (D.b.)

(O.S. 6 in. lxi. S.W.)

South Hanningfield is a parish 4 m. N.E. of Billericay.

Ecclesiastical :—

PARISH CHURCH OF ST. PETER (Plate, p. xxxviii–ix) stands on the E. side of the parish. The walls are of rubble, mostly covered with plaster; the 12th-century work appears to be of coursed herring-bone type; the dressings are of limestone; the roofs are tiled. The *Nave* was built probably early in the 12th century; the N. wall of the *Chancel* may be of the same date, but is without distinctive features. Late in the 14th or early in the 15th century the

South Porch was added, but this has been largely if not entirely rebuilt. Probably in the 15th century the nave was extended about 12 ft. to the W., and the timber bell-turret is of this date. The church has been restored in modern times, when the whole of the S. and most of the E. wall of the chancel have been rebuilt in brick.

Architectural Description—The *Chancel* (22 ft. by 14½ ft.) has no ancient features.

The *Nave* (49½ ft. by 21 ft.) has in the N. wall two windows, the eastern is a 13th-century lancet, much decayed externally, and the western is of the 12th century and of one round-headed light; further W. is the 15th-century N. doorway, now blocked and with moulded jambs, four-centred arch and label; about 6 ft. W. of the doorway is a joint showing the termination of the 12th-century work. In the S. wall are two windows, the eastern is of the 15th century and of two cinque-foiled lights in a square head with a moulded label; the western window is a 13th-century lancet similar to that in the N. wall; further W. is the early 15th-century S. doorway, with double hollow-chamfered jambs and two-centred arch and having a deep draw-bar socket in the W. jamb. In the W. wall is a window all modern except perhaps the opening. The bell-turret at the W. end of the nave stands on four 15th-century posts with curved and partly restored braces.

The *South Porch* incorporates most of the late 14th or early 15th-century two-centred outer archway, the framing above it, the foiled barge-boards and most of the timbers of the king-post roof.

The *Roof* of the nave has 15th or 16th-century chamfered tie-beams with curved braces.

Fittings—*Bell :* inaccessible, but said to be by Anthony Bartlet, 1664. *Door :* In S. doorway—(Plate, pp. 4–5) of feathered battens with strap-hinges having cross-pieces and ends of mill-rind type, triangular drop-handle, probably late 14th or early 15th-century. *Floor-slab :* In chancel—to John and Thomas Tabor, 1678. *Font :* plain octagonal bowl with moulded under-edge, plain stem and base, probably late 15th-century, perhaps partly retooled. *Glass :* In nave—in N.E. window, fragments made up with modern glass, late 13th and 14th-century; in S.E. window, fragments including border of foliage *in situ* and several quarries with sprigs of foliage, 15th-century; in S.W. window, quarries with foliage, probably *in situ*, 13th or

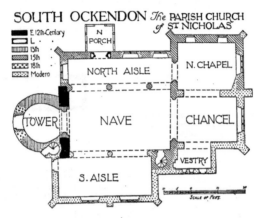

SOUTH OCKENDON *The* PARISH CHURCH *of* ST NICHOLAS

early 14th-century. *Painting :* In nave—in splays and rear-arch of S.E. window, remains of foliated scroll-ornament, 15th-century. *Plate :* includes cup of 1562, with bands of engraved ornament. *Stoup:* In nave—E. of S. doorway, remains of recess.

Condition—Fairly good, but some slight cracks in nave and some stonework decayed.

---

83. SOUTH OCKENDON. (B.d.)

(O.S. 6 in. [(a)]lxxv. S.E. [(b)]lxxxiii. N.W. [(c)]lxxxiii. N.E.)

South Ockendon is a parish and small village 3 m. N.N.W. of Grays Thurrock. The church is the principal monument.

Ecclesiastical :—

[a](1). PARISH CHURCH OF ST. NICHOLAS stands on the S. side of the green in the middle of the village. The walls are of flint and stone-rubble ; the dressings are of Reigate stone ; the roofs are tiled. With the exception of the circular *West Tower*, which was added *c.* 1230–40, to a building probably of early 12th-century date, practically the whole of the church was rebuilt late in the 15th century, when the *North Aisle* and *Chapel* were added, a late 12th-century N. doorway being reset in the N. wall of the aisle. In 1744 the western part of the tower fell and was subsequently rebuilt. The *Chancel* and N. chapel were extensively restored in 1866, when much of the N. aisle was rebuilt, the *South Aisle, South Vestry, North Porch* and tower stair-turret were added and the building generally repaired.

The circular W. tower is of interest, and the N. doorway is a good example of 12th-century work. The monument to Sir R. Saltonstall, an early

17th-century Lord Mayor of London, is a good specimen of its type.

Architectural Description—The *Chancel* (22¼ ft. by 16¼ ft.) is, with the exception of the W. wall, completely modern. The chancel-arch is of late 15th-century date and of two hollow-chamfered orders, the outer continuous, the inner carried on responds of the same section with moulded capitals and hollow-chamfered bases.

The *North Chapel* (22 ft. by 17 ft.) has an embattled parapet. In the N. wall are two windows, each of a single cinquefoiled light with a square traceried head ; both are possibly of the 15th century, but very much restored. In the W. wall is a 15th-century two-centred arch of similar detail to the chancel-arch, but the responds, carrying the inner order, have moulded bases.

The *Nave* (37½ ft. by 21¾ ft.) has a N. arcade of two whole bays and one half bay, the apex of the arch of the latter abutting against the E. wall. The arches are two-centred and of two hollow-chamfered orders ; the piers are octagonal and the W. respond semi-octagonal, and all have moulded capitals and bases of similar detail to the W. arch of the N. chapel. At the N.E. end the angle of the E. wall is chamfered to mitre with the outer order of the easternmost arch, but the quoins in the wall are of earlier date than the arcade. The original N.W. angle of the nave is visible externally. Above the arcade is a clearstorey with three 15th-century windows, modern externally, and each of two cinquefoiled lights under a four-centred head. At the E. end of the S. wall is a 15th-century doorway to the rood-loft staircase, with hollow chamfered jambs and two-centred arch ; the upper doorway also has a two-centred head, but is blocked. The S. arcade and clearstorey are modern.

SOUTH BENFLEET: PARISH CHURCH OF ST. MARY THE VIRGIN.
Interior of South Porch, late 15th-century; South Doorway, mid 15th-century.

SOUTH OCKENDON : PARISH CHURCH OF ST. NICHOLAS.
Monument in N. Chapel of Sir Richard Saltonstall, 1601.

The *North Aisle* (9¼ ft. wide) is lighted by modern windows. The reset N. doorway (Plate, p. 120) is of late 12th-century date and of three moulded orders, elaborately carved with enriched cheveron ornament, and having a moulded label carved with billet enrichment. The outer order of the jambs has keeled angle rolls and square imposts ; the second has detached shafts with spiral mouldings enriched with pellet and dog-tooth ornament ; the inner order has attached columns with keeled angle-rolls to the adjoining reveals. The shafts and jambs have continuous carved capitals, partly restored moulded abaci and modern bases ; the whole doorway has been considerably restored.

The *West Tower* (internal diameter 13½ ft.) is in four stages, of which the two uppermost are largely modern (Plate, pp. xxxii–iii). The tower-arch, of *c.* 1230–40, is two-centred and of two chamfered orders, the inner carried on semi-circular attached shafts with moulded capitals and bases ; the upper member of the capital is continued round the respond as an impost ; the outer order is moulded on the E. side. The 15th-century W. doorway has jambs and two-centred head of two hollow-chamfered orders with a restored moulded label ; above the doorway is a brick window, all modern except the reused sill. The second stage has, low down on the E. side, two blocked openings with semi-circular heads ; above are two large corbels, probably marking the level of a previous floor. On the N. side is a small 13th-century window with a square head and modern internally. On the W. side is a brick window similar to that below.

Fittings—*Brasses* and *Indents*. Brasses : In N. chapel—on E. wall, (1) to Gilbert Saltonstall, 1585, with four shields-of-arms ; on N. wall, (2) (Plate, p. 56) [of Sir Ingram Bruyn, 1400] with part of figure, head and helm missing, black-letter inscription on breast, " Ecce nunc in pulvere dormio sed scio quod redemptor meus vivit," upper halves of two side shafts and fragments of arch and canopy, two shields-of-arms—*a mill-rind cross* quartering *lozengy* (?) ; on W. wall, (3) of Margaret Barker, 1602, figure in dress of period, with shield-of-arms ; on floor, (4) to Gilbert Saltonstall, 1585, with shield-of-arms. Indents : In N. chapel, mostly hidden by the organ, of brasses (2) and (3). *Chest* : In N. chapel (Plate, p. xliii)—bound with broad iron bands, two ring-handles at each end, and one lock, 14th-century or earlier. *Coffin-lid* : In N. chapel —13th-century tapering slab of Purbeck marble with double hollow-chamfered edge. *Hour-glass stand* : attached to pulpit, wrought-iron, 17th-century. *Monuments* and *Floor-slab*. Monuments : In N. chapel—on E. wall, (1) to Philip Saltonstal, 1668, erected 1670 by his widow Alice, mural monument of marble, with side columns, entablature with broken pediment and achievement-of-arms ; against N. wall, (2) of Sir Richard Saltonstall, 1601, Lord

Mayor of London, erected by Suzanne (Poyntz), his wife ; alabaster and marble wall-monument (Plate, p. 141) on double base with two arched recesses above, flanked by Corinthian columns supporting an entablature with elaborate achievement-of-arms ; in recesses kneeling figures of man in armour and wearing the mayoral cloak and chain, and lady in furred gown, ruff and widow's veil ; below figures of six sons and nine daughters separated by prayer-desk ; against W. wall, (3) to George Drywood, 1611, and Elizabeth (Samson), his first wife, 1595, black and white marble tablet flanked by Ionic pilasters supporting an entablature and achievement-of-arms. In churchyard—N. of tower, (4) to Thomas Elderton and Alse, his wife, both 1703, head-stone. Floor-slab : In N. chapel —to Sir William How, 1650 (?), black marble slab with inscription and three shields-of-arms. Condition—Good.

Secular :—

[a](2). RECTORY, house and moat, 450 yards S.S.W. of the church. The *House* is of two storeys with attics ; the walls are of plastered timber-framing ; the roofs are tiled. The middle part of the house is of 17th-century date, but has 18th-century and modern additions on all sides and has been much altered. The central chimney-stack is original and has four rebuilt shafts set cross-wise on a rectangular base.

The *Moat* surrounds the house.

Condition—Of house, good, much altered.

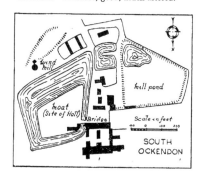

[a](3). SOUTH OCKENDON HALL, gatehouse, barn, moat and mill-ponds, 900 yards E.N.E. of the church. The present house is modern, but, judging from the remains of the walling to the gatehouse which stands at the N.E. corner of the moat, the original house must have been a building of considerable importance. A length of about 40 ft. of the outer wall of the *Gatehouse* is standing, with the remains of an entrance 9½ ft. wide. It is 3 ft. thick and has

two offsets. The lower part of the wall, to the height of about 20 ft., is of coursed Reigate stone and of mediaeval date, and the upper part of *c.* 1700, is brickwork. Across the moat, leading to the gatehouse, is a bridge, all modern except the lower part of the retaining wall on the W. side, which is of limestone-rubble.

The *Barn* (Plate, p. xli) stands outside, at the N.E. corner of the moat, and has brick walls with internal timber-construction ; the roof is partly tiled and partly slated. It is of eleven and a half bays with side-aisles and has two projecting porches on the S. side. It was built late in the 15th or early in the 16th century, but the two easternmost bays are of later date. The roof rests on heavy squared posts and braced main purlins and has braced tie-beams and king-posts supporting a central purlin below the collars to the principal rafters.

The *Moat* surrounded the original house and is exceptionally large and well-preserved.

The *Mill-ponds* are marked by three large shallow depressions in the ground, and the S. arm of the moat was also probably used in connection with the mill. A windmill now stands on the site.

Condition—Of gatehouse, good, but fragmentary ; of barn, good.

MONUMENTS (4–13).

The · following monuments, unless otherwise described, are of the 17th century, and are of two storeys, timber-framed and plastered or weather-boarded ; the roofs are tiled. Some of the buildings have original chimney-stacks and exposed ceiling-beams.

Condition—Good.

ᵃ(4). *Royal Oak*, inn and tenement, on E. side of the green, 100 yards N. of the church, is of weather-boarded timber-framing and built on a half H-shaped plan with the cross-wings extending towards the E. The N. wing and N. half of the central block are of 15th-century date, and the S. half is a 17th-century addition or rebuilding. The S. chimney-stack is of T-shaped plan and of 17th-century date. Inside the northern half of the building the beams are of much heavier timbers than in the southern half, and on the first floor some of the timber-framing is exposed. In the N. wing is a blocked window of four lights with diamond-shaped mullions, and the roof is of the king-post type with curved braces and central purlin.

ᵃ(5). *Street Farm*, two tenements, 160 yards N.W. of the church, has modern additions at the back.

ᵃ(6). *House* and shop, at S.W. corner of the green, 80 yards N.W. of the church, has been partly refronted with brick. The S. end is a cross-wing of a 15th-century house, the major part of which was apparently rebuilt in the 17th century ;

there are modern additions at the back. The roof of the S. wing has been heightened on the S. side, and in the W. wall is an original door of three nail-studded and moulded battens with two shaped wrought-iron hinges. Inside the building, below the ceiling in the first floor of the S. wing, is an original cambered tie-beam with the foot of a king-post.

ᵃ(7). *Inn*, 50 yards W. of (6).

ᵃ(8). *House*, now four tenements, 60 yards S. of (6), is of two storeys with attics. The walls are of weather-boarded timber-framing, and there are additions at the back. The chimney-stack is original, and has a square base with a moulded capping surmounted by four shafts set diagonally on a cross-shaped plan ; on the front of the base is a sunk panel.

ᵃ(9). *Quince Tree Farm*, on W. side of the road, 60 yards S. of (2), is of two storeys with attics. The E. end of the N. wing of the present building is part of a house of early 16th-century date. The S. wing was added or rebuilt in the 17th century, and a modern addition on the W. side of the N. wing makes the present plan T-shaped. The upper storey of the N. wing projects on the E. and is supported on two curved brackets.

ᵃ(10). *Glasscocks Farm*, on S. side of the road, 660 yards W. of the church, is of L-shaped plan with the wings projecting towards the N.W. and S.W. and has modern additions at the back.

ᵇ(11). *Little Belhus*, house and garden wall, about ¾ m. S.W. of the church. The *House* is of two storeys with attics and is timber-framed and weather-boarded. It was built in the latter part of the 16th century on a half H-shaped plan with a two-storeyed porch on the N. front and with the cross-wings extending towards the S. It has, at the S.W. corner, a small later addition. Above the roof of the central block is a small bell-turret. The N. *Front* is gabled at either end and has, at the W. end of the central block, a gabled porch, the upper storey of which projects on all sides. The doorway to the porch is four-centred with sunk spandrels, and in each of the side walls is a four-light window with chamfered jambs and mullions. The inner doorway has a moulded frame and a door of eight panels with moulded rails and muntins. On the *S. Front* is an original window of two lights with diamond-shaped mullions, and there are two original chimneys, one with two and the other with three diagonal shafts. At the N. end of the *W. front* is another original chimney-stack, and further S. a panelled door similar to the inner door of the porch. Inside the building, the ground-floor room of the E. wing has a stone fireplace with a frieze carved in a series of circular and diamond-shaped foliated panels, in the centre one of which is a small blank shield. The four-centred arch has been cut away to form a square head. The room is lined with early 17th-century panelling and has an original doorway with a moulded frame. In the passage on the N. side of the central block is a similar doorway with a panelled door. Three of the rooms on the first floor are lined with early 17th-century panelling, and at the head of the staircase is a panelled door. The two rectangular gardens, one on the N. and the other to the S. of the house, are both enclosed by 16th-century brick walls. In the W. wall E. of the entrance gateway are two segmental-headed niches, and in the E. wall of the S. garden is a four-centred opening in a square head.

ᵃ(12). *Gateway and wall*, at Groves Barns, about ¾ m. N.N.E. of the church, are built of brick with some tile and are of late 16th-century date. There is about 100 ft. of walling, 7 ft. high with a chamfered base and projecting coping with a blocked gateway 9 ft. wide in the middle. The gateway is in the form of a semi-circular rusticated arch springing from moulded imposts and flanked by pilasters with moulded capitals and bases which rest on plinths and support a wide entablature, the upper part of the cornice of which has either been demolished or was never built. Over the pilasters are triglyphs, and the spandrels to the arch are rusticated.

ᵉ(13). *Great Mollands*, house, about ¾ m. E.S.E. of the church, is timber-framed and weather-boarded and has 18th-century and modern additions at the E. end.

Unclassified :—

ᵃ(14). MOUNDS, three, at South Ockendon Hall, on the edge of a steep scarp overlooking Mar Dyke. The first stands 160 yards N. of the moat, and is 150 ft. in diameter at the base and about 17 ft. high, with a flat summit. It is surrounded by a dry ditch.

The second stands about 200 yards S. of the moat, and is about 130 ft. in diameter at the base and 10 ft. high ; the northern part of the mound has been removed.

There was formerly a third mound in the vicinity.

Condition—Of N. mound, good ; of S. mound, bad.

---

84. SOUTH SHOEBURY. (F.d.)

(O.S. 6 in. lxxix. S.W.)

South Shoebury is a small parish including the town of Shoeburyness, 3¼ m. E. of Southend-on-Sea. The church and Manor House are the principal monuments.

Roman :—

(1). A Roman kiln was discovered in 1892 about 300 yards W.N.W. of (5). It consisted of a furnace with an oven above it, a platform 18 in. square and 4 in. above the furnace forming the floor of the latter. The roof and walls were domed, about 5 ft. high and 4–5 ft. in diameter, and made of the sandy loam in which it was built, worked up into clay about 2 in. thick and burnt. When it fell into disuse in the Roman period it became a grave. Human bones and red and black potsherds were found inside it, and an urn containing bones just outside it. The burial had been disturbed (*Essex Arch. Soc. Trans.*, N.S., IV, p. 202 ff.).

(2). Another kiln, probably Roman, was discovered in 1895 nearly 500 yards S. of (1) and 17 yards S.W. of the War Department's forty-fifth boundary-stone. It was a little over 5 ft. high and 3 ft. in diameter and originally dome-shaped. The circular floor of the oven (2–3 in. thick) rested on an inverted cone-shaped pedestal 16 in. high and narrowing to a diameter of 1½ ft., and was heated from the furnace below by eight equidistant circular holes, 2–3 in. in diameter, in the circumference ; from the furnace a circular flue 8–9 in. in diameter passed round it and extended from it for 5 ft. or more, first, apparently, going below the furnace level and then ascending. It was probably a flue connecting the furnace with an outside stoke-hole, as in a New Forest kiln (H. Sumner, *A descriptive account of Roman pottery sites at Sloden*, etc., p. 19), but it may have been just a chimney. It should be noted that the potsherds found in the oven were Late Celtic rather than Roman, but were thought to have been brought with the surface-soil and to have fallen in through the broken dome.

Two other kilns of a similar type are said to have been found in the same field, and other evidence of occupation during the Roman period has been noted in the neighbourhood.

(See *Sectional Preface*, p. xxxviii ; and H. Laver, *Essex Arch. Soc. Trans.*, N.S., VI, p. 13 ff. ; Sir C. H. Read, *Proc. Soc. Antiq.* (2 s.), XVI, 40 ff.)

Ecclesiastical :—

(3). PARISH CHURCH OF ST. ANDREW stands on the W. of the town. The walls are of ragstone-rubble except the tower, which is of flint-rubble ; the dressings are of Reigate and other limestone ; the roofs are tiled. The *Chancel* and *Nave* were built about the middle of the 12th century. The West Tower was added early in the 14th century. The *South Porch* was added in the 15th century. The church was restored in the 19th century, and the *South Vestry* is modern.

The chancel-arch, with its flanking recesses, is an interesting feature.

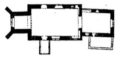

Architectural Description—The *Chancel* (21 ft. by 14½ ft.) has an E. window of *c.* 1400 and of three cinquefoiled lights with tracery in a segmental-pointed head with a moulded label. In the N. wall is a mid 12th-century window of one round-headed light with diapered spandrels to the external head; further W. is a modern recess. In the S. wall are two windows, the eastern similar to that in the N. wall but unornamented; the western window is a 13th-century lancet, restored externally; partly below the eastern window is a doorway of doubtful date with plain jambs and a modern head; W. of the eastern window, externally, is a 13th-century mask-corbel, as though to support a pent roof. The mid 12th-century chancel-arch is round and of two orders, the outer moulded and the inner with cheveron ornament; the responds have a plain inner order and attached shafts to the outer order with capitals, one scalloped and one of cushion form; the moulded abaci are continued round as imposts and are partly ornamented with diapering.

The *Nave* (34¾ ft. by 19¾ ft.) has in the E. wall flanking the chancel-arch two recesses; that on the N. is of late 13th-century date and has a chamfered two-centred arch springing on the N from a moulded bell-corbel with a voluted termination, which also carried the arch of a similar recess in the N. wall, now altered; the S. recess (Plate; p. 104) is higher and of early 13th-century date; it has a moulded two-centred arch springing on the N. from an attached keeled shaft with moulded capital and base and on the S. from a large square corbel with a moulded capital and a square cone-shaped termination ending in a volute; this corbel forms the support of another arched recess in the S. wall with a W. jamb similar to the N. jamb of the adjoining recess. In the N. wall is a 15th-century window of two cinquefoiled lights with tracery in a two-centred head with a moulded label, and the head of a muzzled bear and a lion-headed monster as stops; further E. is the 15th-century rood-loft staircase, the lower doorway has rebated jambs and segmental-pointed head and the upper has a plastered segmental head and is blocked; the 12th-century N. doorway is of one plain order with moulded imposts and a round head. In the S. wall are three windows, the easternmost is set in the recess above described, and is of late 14th-century date and of two trefoiled lights with a quatrefoil in a two-centred head with a moulded label; the second window is a 13th-century lancet with a trefoiled head and a

weathered label; the westernmost window is modern except for the much-restored 15th-century splays, the rear-arch and the carved stops to the external label; the 12th-century S. doorway has a round arch of two orders, the inner plain and the outer moulded and with a billeted label; the outer order of the jambs has attached shafts with scalloped or cushion capitals, moulded abaci and simple bases, the E. shaft has been repaired in 16th or 17th-century brick.

The *West Tower* (9¾ ft. square) is of three stages, undivided externally, and with an 18th-century brick parapet. The 14th-century tower-arch is two-centred and of two chamfered orders dying on to the side walls; the E. angles of the jambs have small traceried stops. The 14th-century W. window is of two trefoiled lights with star-shaped tracery in a two-centred head. The second stage has a square-headed opening in the W. wall. The bell-chamber has in both the E. and W. walls an early 14th-century window of one trefoiled ogee light. The N. and S. walls have each an 18th-century window with a round head of brick.

The *South Porch* is of the 15th century, and is timber-framed with old main timbers and a middle king-post truss with curved braces; the front and mullions have been restored.

The *Roof* of the chancel has 15th-century moulded wall-plates. The 15th-century roof of the nave has three king-post trusses; the three tie-beams are moulded and the wall-plates moulded and embattled; the octagonal king-posts have moulded capitals and bases, and the curved braces to the tie-beams have traceried spandrels and spring from roughly moulded square capitals. Against the E. wall is a 15th-century arched principal, and below it a moulded beam of the same date.

Fittings: *Plate:* includes a cup with a short stem, probably Elizabethan, but without marks and with a band of engraved ornament round top, and a paten of 1630, the gift of Elizabeth Goodwine. *Recesses:* In nave—see Architectural Description. *Miscellanea:* In nave—carved stone head, possibly label-stop, 14th-century.

The churchyard has an old N. wall of rubble.

Condition—Fairly good, but much ivy on tower.

Secular :—

(4). CAMP. Supposed to be that constructed by the Danish leader Hasten *c.* 894. Little remains of the defences, as the site has been built over by the Artillery Barracks, etc. Rampart Street marks the N.E., and about 70 yards of rampart with traces of an external ditch extends from Smith Street in a S.W. direction. Excavation has shown the ditch to have been originally 40 ft. wide and 9 ft. deep. A bank near the magazine marks the western angle of the camp. The original plan of the camp is problematical, as the sea has encroached on the S.E. side. Length approximately 500 yards from N.E. to S.W.

Condition—Fragmentary.

(5). Manor House, or Suttons, 1¼ m. N.E. of the church, is of two storeys with attics ; the walls are of brick and the roofs are tiled. It was built *c.* 1681. The S.E. front has a modillioned eaves-cornice and a brick band between the storeys. The windows are symmetrically arranged and the doorway has an original shell-hood. The hipped roof has small dormers, the middle one having a segmental pediment ; the roof is finished with a lead flat surmounted by a square bell-turret. The weather-vane has the initials and date F.M.R. 1681. Inside the building there is some 17th-century panelling, and the staircase has original turned balusters and moulded string.

The garden has brick walls of the same date as the house.

Condition—Good.

(6) House, at cross-roads, 1 m. N.E. of the church, is of two storeys ; the walls are of brick and the roofs are tiled. The house was built *c.* 1673, the date on a brick tablet or panel on the E. end ; the tablet has an eared architrave and a dentilled pediment and bears also the initials $^{M}_{F\ R}$ and two hearts. There is a brick band between the storeys and the windows have solid frames ; on the E. side is a small oval window, now blocked.

Condition—Good.

---

85. SOUTHCHURCH. (F.d.)

(O.S. 6 in. lxxviii. S.E.)

Southchurch is a small parish on the S. coast of the county adjoining Southend-on-Sea on the E. The church is interesting.

Ecclesiastical :—

(1). Parish Church of the Holy Trinity stands on the S. side of the main road. The walls are of ragstone and flint-rubble, coursed in S. wall of the nave ; the dressings are of limestone ; the roofs are tiled and the bell-turret weather-boarded. The *Nave* was built about the middle of the 12th century. The *Chancel* was rebuilt about the middle of the following century. The chancel-arch and bell-turret are of the 15th-century. The church was restored in the 19th century, when the *South Porch* was added. A new church was built in 1906 N. of the old building, the N. wall of the nave being replaced by an arcade and its windows and doorway reset in the modern nave.

The two 12th-century doorways are interesting, and among the fittings the Easter Sepulchre is noteworthy.

Architectural Description—The *Chancel* (30½ ft. by 16½ ft.) has an E. window all modern except the 14th-century splays and rear-arch. In the N. wall is a mid 13th-century lancet-window, partly restored and now opening into the modern church ; further W. is a modern arch. In the S. wall are three windows, of which the eastern-most and westernmost are mid 13th-century lancets, the westernmost being a ' low-side ' and having traces of the ironwork and fixings of a former shutter ; the middle window is modern except the 14th-century moulded splays and rear-arch ; further W. is a doorway, all modern except the splays. The 15th-century chancel-arch is two-centred and of two chamfered orders, the outer continuous and the inner resting on semi-octagonal attached shafts with moulded capitals and hollow-chamfered bases.

The *Nave* (40½ ft. by 19 ft.) has a modern N. arcade of three bays ; E. of it is the rood-loft staircase ; the lower doorway has rebated jambs, but the head is covered by a monument. In the S. wall are two windows, the eastern is a mid 13th-century lancet, restored externally ; the western is of 14th-century date and of two cinque-foiled ogee lights with tracery in a segmental head and moulded splays ; further W. is the mid 12th-century S. doorway with round arch of two orders, the outer moulded and the inner plain ; there is a line of zig-zag ornament between the two orders, and the label is chamfered ; the jambs have each a round shaft with moulded base and scalloped capital with a moulded abacus continued round the inner order. In the W. wall is a window, all modern except the 14th-century splays and rear-arch. The bell-turret stands over the W. part of the nave, and is probably of the 15th century ; it stands on eight chamfered oak posts with curved braces. Reset in the N. wall of the modern nave are three old windows, two of the 14th century and similar to the western window in the S. wall of the old nave, and one a plain 12th-century round-headed light. Reset in the W. wall is the former N. doorway ; it is of mid 12th-century date and generally similar to the S. doorway, but with a billety label, zig-zag ornament to the outer order of the arch and cushion capitals to the side shafts. Over the doorway is a reset corbel-head of the 12th century.

Fittings—*Bell :* inscribed " Johannes," probably by Geoffrey of Edmonton, early 14th-century. *Door :* In S. doorway—of modern battens on an old frame, drop-handle, pierced scutcheon-plate

and strap-hinges, 15th-century. On modern W. door of modern nave—two strap-hinges, 15th-century. *Easter Sepulchre :* In chancel—in N. wall, recess with moulded jambs and flat segmental-pointed arch, cusped and sub-cusped, late 14th-century. *Indent :* In chancel—of half figure, probably of a priest, and marginal inscription with separate capitals, much defaced, early 14th-century. *Locker :* In chancel—in N. wall, rectangular recess, date uncertain. *Monuments* and *Floor-slab.* Monuments: In chancel—in N. wall below Easter Sepulchre, (1) recess with cusped and sub-cusped segmental arch in a square head with sunk spandrels, altar-tomb with modern slab, front with seven cinquefoil-headed panels, late 14th-century; in S. wall, (2) recess with moulded and depressed ogee arch, jambs each with attached shaft with moulded capital and base, probably tomb-recess, 14th-century, much restored and probably reset. In churchyard—(3) to John Buxton, 1702, table-tomb. (4) to Christopher Parsons, 1713, table-tomb. Floor-slab : In nave—to Henry Moore, 1678, and to Henry Moore, junior, 1689. *Piscinae :* In chancel—with moulded head and attached shafts to jambs with moulded capitals and bases, round drain and shaft, 13th-century, head modern. In nave—on sill of second window, double scalloped capital of pillar-piscina with square drains, 12th-century. *Plate :* includes cup and cover-paten of 1682. *Sedile :* sill of S.E. window of nave carried down to form seat. *Sundials :* on jambs of two windows on S. side of chancel, two scratched dials.
Condition—Good.

Secular :—

(2). SOUTHCHURCH HALL and moat, 1,050 yards S.W. of the church. The *House* is of one storey with attics ; the walls are of plastered timber-framing ; the roofs are tiled. It was built probably in the middle of the 14th century, and is of L-shaped plan with the wings extending towards the S. and E. and has modern additions on the S. On the N. front are four gabled dormers. In each side of the N. porch is the traceried head of a trefoiled ogee light, not *in situ.* The chimney-stack at the E. end of the house is original, and on the W. side of the S. wing is an original stack with stepped offsets and two diagonal shafts. Inside the building some of the rooms have exposed ceiling-beams, and in the N.W. room is a stone fireplace with a segmental head.
The large *Moat* surrounds the house, but is now dry.
Condition—Of house, good.

(3). SAMUEL'S FARM, house and moat, about 1 m. E. of the church. The *House* is of two storeys ; timber-framed and refaced with modern brick ; the roofs are tiled. It was built probably in the

17th century on a rectangular plan, but a modern addition on the S. makes the present plan L-shaped. One of the chimney-stacks is original and has three grouped diagonal shafts ; inside the building some of the timber-construction is exposed.
The *Moat* surrounds the house.
Condition—Of house, good.

(4). BOURNESGREEN FARM (Plate, p. xxxv), now two tenements, at Bournes Green, nearly ¾ m. E. of the church, is of timber-framing, partly plastered and partly weather-boarded ; the roofs are tiled. It was built, possibly in the 16th century, on a half H-shaped plan with the cross-wings projecting towards the W. In the 17th century a first floor was inserted in the hall, and the S. wing has a later extension on the W. The upper storey of the S. wing projects on the E. front, and in the roof of the central block are two dormer-windows. The chimney-stack in the middle of the central block is of 17th-century date. Inside the building some of the ceiling-beams are exposed.
Condition—Good.

———

86. SOUTHMINSTER. (G.b.)

(O.S. 6 in. (ᵃ)lxiii. N.W. (ᵇ)lxiii. S.E.)

Southminster is a parish and village 8½ m. S.E. of Maldon. The church is the principal monument.

Ecclesiastical :—

ᵃ(1). PARISH CHURCH OF ST. LEONARD stands in the village. The walls are of septaria and mixed rubble, with some Roman brick ; the dressings are of limestone ; the roofs are covered with slates. The *Nave* was built early in the 12th century, and the lower part of the *West Tower* may be of the same date. In the 15th century the nave was heightened, the upper part of the tower built and the *North Porch* added. The church has been restored in modern times, when the *Chancel* and *Transepts* were added and the walls of the nave again raised.

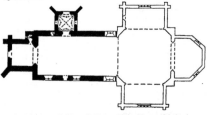

Architectural Description—The *Nave* (58 ft. by 28 ft.) has in the N. wall a modern window and an upper range of two 15th-century windows, both of three trefoiled lights in a square head ; the

SOUTHMINSTER: PARISH CHURCH OF ST. LEONARD.
Stone Vault of North Porch; 15th-century.

STANFORD-LE-HOPE : PARISH CHURCH OF ST. MARGARET.
Interior from N. Aisle, showing N. Arcade of Nave, 13th-century ; S.E. Arch and Window, late
12th-century ; S. Arcade and Clearstorey, 14th-century.

WEST THURROCK : PARISH CHURCH OF ST. CLEMENT.
Interior, showing N. Chapel and N. Arcade of Nave, 13th-century ; N. Arcade of Chancel, early
14th-century : and Chancel-arch, late 14th-century.

early 15th-century N. doorway has moulded jambs, reset two-centred arch and label ; further W. is a 15th-century doorway, leading to the room over the porch : it has hollow-chamfered jambs and two-centred head. In the S. wall are three windows in the lower range ; the easternmost is modern, and the westernmost is of the 15th century, and of two cinquefoiled lights with vertical tracery in a square head with a moulded label ; the middle window is also of the 15th century and of two cinquefoiled lights with a quatrefoil in a four-centred head with a moulded label ; W. of it is the early 12th-century S. doorway, with plain jambs and imposts and round head ; there is an upper range of four 15th-century windows, each of three trefoiled lights in a square head.

The *West Tower* (16 ft. square) is of three stages, with an embattled parapet in flint and stone chequer-work. The 15th-century tower-arch is two-centred and of three continuous chamfered orders ; above it is a blocked round-headed opening. In the E. wall is a carved corbel, probably of the 12th century. In the S. wall is a window, probably of the 12th century and now blocked. The partly restored 15th-century W. doorway has double chamfered jambs and two-centred head ; above it is a window of the same date, partly restored, and of two cinquefoiled lights under a square head with a moulded label. The second stage has in the S. wall a 15th-century window with a trefoiled head. The bell-chamber has in each wall a 15th-century window of two trefoiled lights in a four-centred head.

The *North Porch* is of the 15th century, and of two storeys with a moulded plinth and an embattled parapet. The two-centred outer archway is of two moulded orders, the outer continuous and the inner resting on attached shafts with moulded capitals and bases ; the moulded label has head-stops ; above it are three niches, each with buttressed jambs, cusped crocketed and finialed canopies and moulded sills carved with heads and angels. The side walls have each two windows, those to the lower storey being of two cinquefoiled lights with tracery in a four-centred head with a moulded label and head-stops ; the upper windows are each of two cinquefoiled lights in a square head with a moulded label and head-stops. The lower stage has a stone vault with moulded ribs and bosses, carved with foliage, half-angels and a Trinity with two supporting figures ; the vault springs from angle-shafts with moulded and embattled capitals and moulded bases (Plate, p. 146).

Fittings—*Bells :* six and clock-bell ; 5th by James Bartlet, 1684, clock-bell, same date. *Brasses and Indents.* Brasses : In chancel—(1) to [William Harris, high sheriff of Essex, 1556] shield and plate with Latin verses only remaining ; (2) of man in civil costume and wife, *c.* 1560, with arms of city

of London, other parts missing. In nave—(3) of John King, 1634, figure in civil dress and two shields-of-arms. Indents : In N. porch—two slabs with defaced indents. *Chest :* In tower—square, iron-bound, probably 16th-century. *Consecration Crosses :* In nave—on splays of S. doorway, two incised crosses formy in circles, upper one probably 12th-century. *Door :* in staircase to upper room of porch, of overlapping battens with strap-hinges, 15th-century. *Font :* octagonal bowl with moulded edge and quatrefoiled panels enclosing flowers ; stem with quatrefoiled and cinquefoiled-headed panels, quatrefoiled base, with square flowers, late 15th-century. *Niches :* see N. porch. *Plate :* includes cup of 1568 with band of incised ornament. *Seating :* In chancel—two bench-ends with popey-heads, 15th-century. *Sundial :* On E. jamb of S. doorway—scratched dial.

Condition—Fairly good.

Secular :—

ᵃ(2). MANOR HOUSE, on S. side of main street, E. of the church, is of two storeys, timber-framed and plastered ; the roofs are tiled. It was built probably in the 17th-century, with cross-wings at the E. and W. ends.

Condition—Good, much altered.

ᵃ(3). HOUSE and shops, opposite (2), is of two storeys, timber-framed and plastered ; the roofs are tiled. It was built in the 16th or 17th century, and has cross-wings at both the E. and W. ends. The upper storey projects at the W. end of the house.

Condition—Good.

ᵃ(4). SPRATT'S FARM, house, ¼ m. N. of the church, is of two storeys, timber-framed and plastered ; the roofs are tiled. It was built probably early in the 17th century, and has three gables on the S. front. The original chimney-stack has three grouped hexagonal shafts.

Condition—Good.

Unclassified :—

ᵇ(5). RED HILL, S. of Newmoor Plantation, 1¼ m. S.E. of the church.

STAMBRIDGE, see GREAT STAMBRIDGE and LITTLE STAMBRIDGE.

87. STANFORD-LE-HOPE. (C.d.)

(O.S. 6 in. ⁽ᵃ⁾lxxvi. S.E. ⁽ᵇ⁾lxxxiv. N.E.)

Stanford-le-Hope is a parish and village on the N. bank of the Thames, 5 m. N.E. of Tilbury. The church and Manor Farm are the principal monuments.

Ecclesiastical :—

ᵇ(1). PARISH CHURCH OF ST. MARGARET stands in the middle of the village. The walls are of ragstone-rubble with some flint ; the dressings are

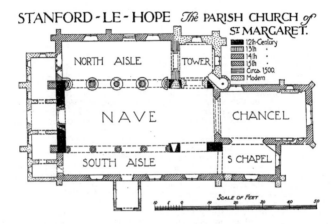

STANFORD - LE - HOPE *The* PARISH CHURCH *of* ST MARGARET.

of limestone ; the roofs are covered with tiles and lead. The *Nave*, with N. and S. aisles, was built *c*. 1180, and shortly after a N. tower was added. In the 13th century most of the N. arcade was rebuilt. In the 14th century the *Chancel* and *North* and *South Aisles* were rebuilt, the S. arcade rebuilt except the E. bay, and the clearstorey and a S. chapel added. In the 15th century the *South Chapel* was largely rebuilt, and the *South Porch* was added in the 16th century. The church has been restored in modern times, when the *North Tower* and the upper part of the chancel walls were rebuilt, the S. porch reconstructed and the *West Vestries* added.

The church is of some architectural interest, and among the fittings the sedilia are noteworthy.

Architectural Description—The *Chancel* (31¾ ft. by 17 ft.) has an E. window all modern except the reset 14th-century splays and rear-arch. In the N. wall are two windows, the eastern of the 14th century, restored externally, and of one trefoiled ogee light with tracery in a two-centred head ; the 15th-century western window is of two cinquefoiled lights in a square head with a moulded label. In the S. wall is an archway of *c*. 1320, two-centred and of two chamfered orders ; the responds have grouped attached shafts with moulded capitals and bases ; further E. is a window all modern except the 14th-century rear-arch and parts of the jambs, mullion and splays. The 14th-century chancel-arch is two-centred and of two continuous hollow-chamfered orders ; it incorporates 13th-century material.

The *South Chapel* (20 ft. by 10¾ ft.) has a 15th-century E. window, partly restored and of two cinquefoiled lights in a flat triangular head with a moulded label. In the S. wall is a 15th-century window of two cinquefoiled lights in a square head ; further W. is a blocked 15th-century doorway with a segmental-pointed rear-arch. The 14th-century W. archway is two-centred and of one chamfered order dying on to the walls.

The *Nave* (55 ft. by 20 ft.) has in the E. wall N. of the chancel-arch the upper doorway from the rood-loft staircase ; it is of the 15th century and has a square head ; at a rather lower level N. and S. of the arch are two corbels for the former rood-loft. In the N. wall is a modern arch to the tower, incorporating some old stones and a head-stop ; further W. is a blocked 12th-century window with a round head and restored splays ; the 13th-century N. arcade (Plate, p. 147) is of four bays with two-centred arches of two hollow-chamfered orders ; two of the columns are round and one octagonal with moulded capitals and bases ; the responds have attached half-columns, round on the E. and octagonal on the W. At the E. end of the S. wall is one bay of the late 12th-century arcade, with a two-centred arch of one moulded order and moulded imposts ; W. of it is a round-headed window of the same date, much restored ; the 14th-century S. arcade is of four bays with two-centred arches of two chamfered orders ; the columns are octagonal, with moulded capitals and bases ; the responds have attached half-columns. The 14th-century clearstorey has three windows on the N. side and five on the S., all are of quatrefoil form and have been extensively restored. The W. wall has an internal set-back marking the extent of the 12th-century work; the W. window and doorway are modern except for the 14th-century splays and rear-arches.

The *North Tower* (12 ft. square) is modern except for the reset moulded impost of an arched recess in the E. wall, which is of the 13th century, and the W. archway, which is two-centred and chamfered and has 13th-century moulded imposts; the inner order is modern.

The *North Aisle* (14½ ft. wide) has in the N. wall two 14th-century windows, each of two trefoiled ogee lights with tracery in a two-centred head with a moulded label; between them is the 14th-century N. doorway, with moulded jambs and two-centred arch; it is now blocked. In the W. wall is a window all modern except the 14th-century splays and rear-arch; below and to the S. of it is a small square-headed window, originally of the 13th century, but much restored.

The *South Aisle* (8 ft. wide) has in the S. wall three windows; the two eastern are of *c.* 1500, and each of two cinquefoiled lights in a square head with a moulded label; the partly restored westernmost window is of the 15th century, and of two trefoiled lights in a square head with a moulded label; E. of it is the 14th-century S. doorway, with moulded jambs, two-centred arch and label. In the W. wall is a much-restored window of one trefoiled light; below it are a modern window and doorway.

The *South Porch* is of the 16th century, much altered and reconstructed; the heads of the E. and W. openings have the mortices of diamond-shaped mullions. The outer entrance is modern.

The *Roof* of the N. aisle is largely modern, but incorporates a cambered tie-beam, probably of the 17th century; on the S. side are shaped stone corbels. The first floor of the tower has restored beams and wall-plates. The pent roof of the S. aisle has three western bays of the 14th century, with moulded principals and purlin and two bosses carved with a geometric design. The roof of the S. porch incorporates two moulded tie-beams with curved braces, moulded wall-plates and plain rafters and collars.

Fittings—Bracket: In S. chapel—in E. wall, two corbels placed together to form bracket. *Brass Indent:* See Monument (1). *Coffin:* In tower—stone coffin with shaped head and fragments of ridged lid, 13th-century. *Consecration Cross:* In chancel—reset in N. splay of E. window, incised formy cross in circle. *Door:* In S. doorway—of nail-studded, ridged battens, 15th or 16th-century, restored. *Font:* bowl, octofoiled on plan, capitals on under-side with defaced foliage, round stem with eight small shafts and moulded base, Purbeck marble, early 13th-century, top part of bowl

restored. *Font-cover:* of octagonal ogee form with crocketed ribs, 17th or 18th-century, modern finial. *Inscription:* In nave—on first column of S. arcade, scratched inscription—" William Burnel 1581 curate of Stanford." *Locker:* In tower—in N. wall, round-headed recess, rebated for door, 13th-century, below it a corbel carved with a crowned head, 14th-century. *Monuments* and *Floor-slabs.* Monuments: In chancel—on N. side, (1) wall-recess (Plate, p. 105) with cinquefoiled ogee arch with moulded label, head-stops (one modern) and crocketed gable over, with carved finial, jambs flanked by panelled buttresses terminating in crudely carved finials, 14th-century, E. buttress modern; set in recess, altar-tomb with sides and ends panelled with sub-cusped quatrefoils enclosing blank shields and upright panels with cinquefoiled heads, Purbeck marble slab with moulded edge and indent of brass inscription, in wall at back, indent of kneeling figure and scroll, *c.* 1500. In S. chapel—in N.E. angle, (2) to Sir Heneage Fetherstone, Bart., 1711, and Mary (Benet), his wife, 1710, large white marble tablet flanked by Ionic columns with pediment and blank shield-of-arms; on S. wall, (3) to Anna Maria (Williamson), wife of Henry Fetherstone, 1689–90, grey and white marble tablet with Ionic side columns and shield-of-arms; (4) to Heneage Fetherstone, 1711, and Frances (Western), his wife, 1746, white marble tablet with fluted Doric pilasters and shield-of-arms. In N. aisle—on E. wall, (5) to Richard Champion, 1599, alabaster and black marble tablet with side pilasters, pediment and achievement-of-arms; on N. wall, (6) to . . . . Champion, late 16th or early 17th-century, alabaster and marble tablet with Corinthian side columns, broken pediment and shield-of-arms. Floor-slabs: In S. chapel—(1) to Anna Maria Fetherstone, 1689–90, with achievement-of-arms. In S. aisle—(2) to Thomas Aleyn, 1677, rector, with achievement-of-arms. *Panelling:* In N. aisle, early 17th-century panelling incorporated in chest. *Piscinae:* In chancel—with moulded jambs, trefoiled head and moulded label with leaf finial, sexfoiled drain, 14th-century. In S. chapel—in S. wall, with chamfered jambs and two-centred head, semi-round drain, 14th or 15th-century. *Plate:* includes cup of 1709 with baluster stem and dated 1710, stand-paten probably of same date. *Screen* (Plate, pp. 4–5): under W. arch of S. chapel —of seven bays with septfoiled ogee heads, oak-leaf finials and tracery, moulded mullions; embattled head and coved cornice, late 14th or early 15th-century, lower panels modern. *Sedilia:* In chancel —of three stepped bays, with moulded two-centred arches and labels with head-stops, columns between the bays with moulded capitals and bases, responds with attached half-columns, horizontal label above, returned down the responds, 14th-century. *Stoup:* In S. aisle—E. of S. doorway, semi-octagonal

bowl with moulded under-side, 15th-century. *Miscellanea :* Against N.E. buttress of chancel, strap-hinge, probably 15th-century.
Condition—Good.

Secular :—

MONUMENTS (2–10).

The following monuments, unless otherwise described, are of two storeys, timber-framed and plastered ; the roofs are tiled. Some of the buildings have exposed ceiling-beams and original chimney-stacks.
Condition—Good, unless noted.

b(2). *Barn*, at the Rectory, S.W. of the church, is of weather-boarded timber-framing with some brick ; the roof is partly thatched and partly tiled. It was built early in the 17th century with a S. porch, and late in the same century was extended eastwards. It is divided into seven bays by queen-post trusses with curved braces to the tie-beams.

b(3). *House*, 100 yards E.N.E. of the church, is of L-shaped plan with the wings extending towards the S. and E. and a staircase in the angle. It was built in the 15th century, the roof over the S. wing heightened possibly in the 17th century, and there are small modern additions at the back. In the N. wall is a blocked two-light window with diamond-shaped mullions. Inside the building some of the original beams are partly exposed. The roof of the N. wing is divided into three bays by cambered tie-beams, one of which retains its king-post with two-way struts and curved braces.
Condition—Bad.

a(4). *Hassenbrook Hall*, house and garden wall, about ½ m. N. of the church. The *House* is an early 17th-century brick building of Z-shaped plan with the main front facing the S.E. It was built, according to Morant, in the reign of James I by Cuthbert Fetherstone, but has been considerably altered and partly refaced with modern brickwork. There are three original chimney-stacks and at the E. corner an original window, now blocked, with moulded head, jambs and mullions.
Three brick walls to the garden on the S.E. side of the house are original. In the S.E. wall is a four-centred doorway (Plate, p. 64) with moulded jambs in a square head. It is surmounted by a triangular pediment with a moulded coping and has in the tympanum a circular opening. There is, adjoining the house, a four-centred doorway, and at intervals in the walls are small niches with circular heads.

a(5). *House* (Plate, p. 57), 150 yards N.E. of (4), is of T-shaped plan, with the cross-wing at the S. end. The cross-wing was built probably late in the 16th century and the N. block added in the

following century ; on the front is a small modern addition. The main chimney-stack is original and of grouped diagonal shafts on a rectangular base.

a(6). *Moore Place*, house, about ¾ m. N.N.E. of the church, is of two storeys with attics, and was built in the 17th century on a H-shaped plan with N. and S. cross-wings. It has been much altered, and has modern additions on either side of the central block. In the N. wall are two original windows, each of three transomed lights. Inside the building one of the rooms has an open fireplace.

a(7). *Potter's Farm*, house and barns, about 1½ m. N.N.E. of the church. The *House* is of two storeys with attics, and was built possibly in the 17th century on an L-shaped plan with the wings extending towards the N.E. and N.W. It has been much altered, entirely refaced with brick, and has modern additions on the W.
The brick barn to the N.E. of the house has a S.E. porch and a number of loop-holes in the N.W. and S.E. walls. It was built probably in the 17th century and is now a ruin.
The weather-boarded barn to the S.E. of the house is now used as a chapel, and has cambered tie-beams with curved struts supporting the purlins.

a(8). *Oak Farm*, house and walling, about 1 m. E.N.E. of the church. The *House* is of brick, and was built early in the 17th century on an L-shaped plan, with the wings extending towards the N.E. and N.W.; it has a small modern addition on the N. ; the N.W. wing has been partly refaced with modern brick. The upper part of the main chimney-stack has been rebuilt. Inside the building is some exposed timber-framing, and there are three battened doors of early 17th-century date. E. of the house is some old brick walling.

b(9). *Ivywall Farm*, house, 1,100 yards E. of the church, was built in the 15th century on a half H-shaped plan with a central hall and E. and W. cross-wings extending towards the S. ; an upper floor has since been inserted in the hall. On the E. wall is a 16th-century chimney-stack with an octagonal shaft. In the S. wall of the hall is a blocked doorway. Inside the building some of the timber construction is exposed, and there are some moulded ceiling-beams. The doorway between the hall and E. wing has a four-centred head, and in the E. wing is a similar blocked doorway. The roof over the hall is divided into two bays by an original king-post truss. The cambered tie-beam is supported on curved braces which form a four-centred arch, and the king-post has four-way struts. The roof over the W. wing is of three bays and of similar construction, but the king-posts have two-way struts to the central purlin.

b(10). *Manor Farm* (Plate, pp. xxxiv–v), house previously known as Cabborns, ½ m. S.S.E. of the church, is of two storeys, with a cellar under part of the building. It was built in the 15th century, with a central hall and N.E. and S.W. cross-wings, the latter extending towards the S.E. only, and the former on both sides of the hall. Late in the 16th or early in the 17th century a first floor was inserted in the hall, when the roof was raised and the S.E. wall carried up in two gables. Late in the 17th century a N.W. staircase was added and a porch built at the S. end of the hall. The upper storey of the S.W. wing projects on the S.E. The main chimney-stack at the N.E. end of the hall is of late 16th or early 17th-century date, and of five diagonal shafts set on a rectangular base with a moulded capping. Inside the building the hall on the ground-floor is divided into two bays by a heavy ceiling-beam supported on curved brackets. The 'screens' were at the S.W. end of the hall, and in the wall dividing them from the cross-wing are two doorways with two-centred heads, one of which has been partly blocked In the N.W. wing of the hall is a similar doorway, and there are some 17th-century doors, some of battens and some panelled. In the cellar some of the timber-construction is exposed, and the main ceiling-beam is supported on heavy curved brackets. All the roofs are of the king-post type, with cambered tie-beams and curved struts to the king-posts.

At the S.W. corner of the farm buildings is some 16th-century brickwork.

88. STEEPLE. (F.b.)

(O.S. 6 in. [a]lv. S.W. [b]lxiii. N.W.)

Steeple is a parish on the S. side of the Blackwater estuary, 6 m. E.S.E. of Maldon. Stanesgate Priory is the principal monument.

Ecclesiastical :—:

[a](1). PARISH CHURCH OF ST. LAURENCE formerly stood 150 yards S. of Steeple Hall, where the churchyard is still enclosed. The new church was built in 1882 on a site 600 yards further E., and incorporates much of the old building material. In the W. wall of the vestry are two 12th-century head-stops, and in the N. wall of the nave is a late 14th-century window of two cinquefoiled lights with a quatrefoil in a two-centred head with a moulded label. The late 14th-century S. doorway has moulded jambs, two-centred arch and label with head-stops.

Fittings—*Bell :* by Miles Graye, 1636. *Font :* octagonal bowl with moulded under-edge, blank shields on alternate sides, 15th-century. *Glass :* In nave—in old window, small fragments. *Piscina :* In chancel—pillar-piscina with square drain and spirally fluted shaft, 12th-century.
Condition—Rebuilt.

[a](2). STANESGATE PRIORY, ruin, N. of Stanesgate Abbey Farm, 1¾ m. N. of the church. The walls are of septaria and other rubble with dressings of limestone. The Cluniac priory was founded probably early in the 12th century by Ralph, son of Brian, as a cell to Lewes Priory. The church became ruinous early in the 14th century, when part of the N. wall was rebuilt and the body shortened at both ends. The priory was dissolved in 1525, and the church was subsequently used as a barn; it is now partly roofless, and has numerous sheds abutting on to its four sides.

The 12th-century windows on the S. of the nave are interesting.

Architectural Description—The *Church* (72 ft. by 18 ft.) is now a plain rectangle, but there are slight indications of a former transept on the N. side, and there was certainly a chancel or apse E. of the present E. wall. There are also traces of foundations apparently indicating that the 12th-century nave extended about 25 ft. further W. than at present. The E. wall is a filling, apparently modern, between the 12th-century responds of a former arch; the responds are of two plain orders on the E. face. At the N.E. angle is a heavy diagonal buttress, probably of the 14th century, and indicating that the former chancel or apse no longer existed at that date. The N. wall has on the E. end, externally, a short length of 12th-century string-course. In this wall are remains of three 14th-century windows, the middle one was of two lights, and has a two-centred head with a moulded label; the westernmost window was of two lights, and has remains of tracery in a two-centred head with a moulded label; further W. is an 14th-century doorway with moulded jambs and segmental arch and partly blocked; in the middle of the wall is a wide modern opening, and immediately E. of it is a slight set-back with remains of 12th-century quoins which may be the western internal angle of a former N. transept. In the western part of the S. wall (Plate, p. xxxiii) are three blocked round windows of the 12th century; the easternmost has been partly destroyed by a modern opening, and the westernmost must have been impinged upon by the inserted 14th-century W. wall. E. of the modern opening is a 13th-century recess, perhaps reset, with jambs and two-centred arch of two plain orders; still further E. is a blocked 15th-century doorway showing only externally and having a four-centred head. There is a second blocked doorway below and between the two western round windows. The W. wall has been largely destroyed.

The *Roof*, now rapidly falling to pieces, has rough king-post trusses, probably of the 16th century.

Fittings—*Piscina :* In S. wall—at E. end, with part of moulded jamb and two-centred head,

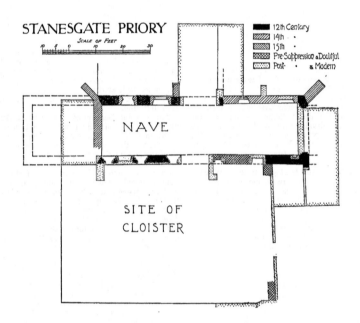

STANESGATE PRIORY

SCALE OF FEET

■ 12th Century
▨ 14th · ·
▧ 15th ·
▨ Pre-Suppression & Doubtful
▭ Post· · & Modern

NAVE

SITE OF
CLOISTER

14th-century. *Miscellanea :* reused in 14th-century
repairs, sections of 12th-century shafting, etc.

The domestic buildings lay to the S. of the
church, and the start of a thick wall adjoins the
S. wall 17 ft. W. of the E. end. This was probably
the E. wall of the E. range of the cloister.

Condition—Ruinous and in a dangerous state of
decay.

Secular :—

b(3). HOMESTEAD MOAT at Batt's Farm, ¾ m.
S.E. of the church.

a(4). STANESGATE ABBEY FARM, house (Plate,
p. 57) S of (2), is of two storeys, timber-framed
and weather-boarded ; the roofs are tiled. It was
built probably late in the 16th century, and has
18th-century additions on the S. and E. The
central chimney-stack has grouped diagonal shafts.
Inside the building are original exposed ceiling-
beams and a stone fireplace with moulded jambs
and a four-centred head.

Condition—Of 16th-century part, ruinous.

89. STIFFORD. (B.e.)

(O.S. 6 in. lxxxiii. N.E.)

Stifford is a parish and village 2 m. N. of Grays
Thurrock. The church and Ford Place are the
principal monuments.

Ecclesiastical :—

(1). PARISH CHURCH OF ST. MARY THE VIRGIN
stands on the S. side of the main road towards the
middle of the parish. The walls are of flint and
ragstone-rubble, with some pudding and iron-
stone in the rebuilt S. aisle ; the dressings are of
Reigate and other limestone ; the roofs are tiled.
Part of the N. wall of the *Nave* is of 12th-century
date. In the middle of the 13th century the
South Chapel was added to the chancel, and *c.*
1260–70 the *South Aisle* was added and the S.
arcade of the nave built ; the *West Tower* was built
probably about the same time. In the 14th
century or possibly earlier the *Chancel* was largely
rebuilt and probably extended eastwards. At
some subsequent date the S. arcade was repaired

PARGETING AND PLASTERWORK.

Part of Ceiling of S.E. room ; c. 1655.

STIFFORD : (2). FORD PLACE.

Ceiling of S.W. room : Panel in N.W. angle ; late 17th-century, with allegorical figure of Winter.

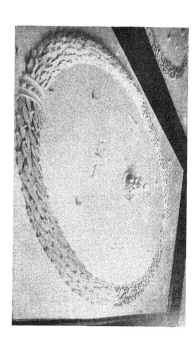

Part of Ceiling of southernmost room.

Detail of Pargeting on E. Front, with date 1688.

SHOPLAND : (4). BEAUCHAMPS, 1688.

Ceiling of S.E. Room ; *c.* 1655.

Ceiling of S.W. Room ; late 17th-century.
STIFFORD : (2). FORD PLACE.

and reset. The S. aisle has been rebuilt more than once, and the archway between it and the S. chapel widened. The church was restored in the 19th century, when the *North Porch* was built.

Architectural Description—The *Chancel* (26½ ft. by 14¼ ft.) has in the E. wall a three-light window and in the N. wall two two-light windows, all modern except the splays and rear-arches. In the S. wall is a rebuilt two-centred archway to the S. chapel of mid 13th-century date and of two chamfered orders ; the outer dies on to the wall and the inner springs on the E. from a semi-octagonal respond with moulded capital and base and on the W. from a shaped corbel. The chancel-arch is modern.

The *South Chapel* (19¼ ft. by 15 ft.) has in the E. wall (Plate, p. 53) three graduated lancet-windows, modern externally ; they are grouped internally under three trefoiled rear-arches, each of one chamfered order and carried on attached shafts with moulded capitals and bases. In the S. wall are three lancet-windows, all modern except the recut splays and the reset trefoiled rear-arch of the first window. In the W. wall is a low two-centred arch of two chamfered orders abutting on the N. wall and springing from a plain chamfered respond on the S. Above the arch is a lancet-window, all modern except the two-centred rear-arch and splays.

The *Nave* (33½ ft. by 18½ ft.) has in the N. wall a wide two-centred recess in which is set a modern lancet ; further W. is a two-light window with a square head, all modern except the hollow-chamfered splays and a moulded internal label of late 14th or early 15th-century date ; the partly restored 12th-century N. doorway has an arched head of two plain orders, the inner segmental with a plastered tympanum and the outer semi-circular with a moulded label ; the jambs are chamfered and have moulded imposts ; W. of the doorway is a modern window. The S. arcade is of *c.* 1260–70 and of two bays with segmental-pointed arches of two chamfered orders ; the middle column is circular, with a moulded capital and base ; the outer order is continued down the responds and the inner is carried on short shafts with moulded capitals and crowned head-corbels (Plate, p. 161).

The *South Aisle* (31¼ ft. by 12 ft.) has been rebuilt, but incorporates some old material. In the S. wall are two windows, the eastern modern

except for the splays and two-centred moulded rear-arch of *c.* 1260 ; the western window is also modern except for the splays, the moulded lintel and the corbelled capital which supports it on the W., which are all of *c.* 1260.

The *West Tower* (11¼ ft. by 10¾ ft.) is of three stages, and is surmounted by a shingled broach-spire. The two-centred tower-arch is of late 15th-century date and of two chamfered orders ; the inner order is carried on semi-octagonal responds with moulded capitals and bases, while the outer is continuous on the E. side. The late 13th-century W. window is of a single trefoiled light. The second stage has in each wall a modern window, that in the E. wall communicating with the roof. The bell-chamber has in each wall a late 13th-century window of one trefoiled light.

All the *Roofs* are modern, but that over the nave incorporates some 15th-century timbers, including a hollow-chamfered tie-beam, octagonal king-post with moulded capital and base, and four-way struts.

Fittings—*Bells :* three ; 1st and 2nd by John Clifton, 1633 and 1635 respectively. *Brasses and Indent.* Brasses : In chancel—(1) of Ralph Perchehay, rector of Stifford, *c.* 1380, half-figure (Plate, p. 160) of priest in mass vestments. In nave—(2) figure of priest in shroud holding a heart inscribed "ihs" ; indent of scroll and inscription-plate, late 15th-century. In S. chapel, reset on E. wall, (3) of John Ardalle, 1504, and Anne, his wife, figure of man in long furred gown, belted at the waist, and of woman in pedimental head-dress, etc., four shields-of-arms, (*a*) *a cheveron between three stars* for Ardalle, (*b*) *a cheveron,* (*c*) *crusily a lion,* (*d*) *three bulls' heads ;* (4) of Ann, daughter of Thomas Lathum, 1627, figure of woman in costume of period ; (5) of Elizabeth, wife of Thomas Lathum, 1630, figure of woman in costume of period ; (6) of William Lathum, 1622, and Suzan (Sampson), his wife, 1622, both figures with ruffs and cloaks with pendant sleeves, woman with conical hat and farthingale, three shields-of-arms. Indent : In chancel—on S. side, partly hidden, Purbeck marble slab with indents of marginal inscription in Lombardic capitals, to David de Tillebery, early 14th-century. *Chairs :* In chancel—two, with carved backs and arms, carved and turned legs and rails, late 17th-century. *Chest :* of boards bound with three iron straps, probably 16th-century. *Door* (Plate, pp. 4–5) : In N. doorway, of nail-studded battens, probably 16th-century on later framing ; reset on front, three iron straps, the upper and lower attached to crescent-shaped hinges, and all with scroll-shaped ends, also small shaped scutcheon-strap of similar workmanship, early 13th-century, iron catch and lock-plate, 17th-century. *Font :* square bowl with slightly tapering sides, carried on central stem of three grouped shafts with plain capital and base; four round corner-columns with moulded capitals and bases, 13th-century, partly recut. *Hour-glass stand:* fixed to the pulpit, 17th-century. *Monuments* and F*loor-slabs.* Monuments: In W. tower—on N. wall, (1) to Sir Nathaniel Grantham, 1708, Elizabeth (Kenwrick), his wife, 1711, and Martha, their daughter, 1703, white marble cartouche supported by weeping cherubs, at base a skull and above a defaced achievement-of-arms; (2) to Anne (Robinson), wife of James Silverlock, 1642; Elizabeth, wife successively of Cornelius Speering, Sir Richard Higham and James Silverlock; also to her son John Speering and her daughter Katherine; also to Sarah, wife of Robert Strode and afterwards of James Silverlock; inscription set in an alabaster frame with flanking consoles, and moulded base with curved brackets; on cornice, inscription to James Silverlock, 1667, with broken pediment above and a shield-of-arms. In churchyard—on E. wall of chancel, (3) to James Robertson, rector of Stifford, 1709, head-stone with shield-of-arms. *Floor-slab:* In chancel—to Anthony Bradshawe, 1636, Judith, his wife, 1641, and William, their son, 1649. *Painting:* In nave, on E. respond of S. arcade, corbel (Plate, p. 161) coloured in patterns of black, red and gilt, with the carved head, forming the terminal, painted with the same colours, the hair and crown being gilded; on the respond, round the corbel, remains of a design of red rosettes on a black ground and contained within a border, late 13th or early 14th-century, lower part probably a later addition. *Plate:* includes cup and cover-paten of 1627, dated 1628, flagon of 1665, with the arms of Silverlock and inscription, and a stand-paten of 1683. *Pulpit:* of oak, octagonal, with shallow Doric pilasters on corners, and three sides with panels in form of arched recesses with responds and keystones; on one side the date 1611; base modern. *Stairs:* In W. tower—with solid wedge-shaped treads and old newel-post at bottom.

Condition—Good, but the W. tower is greatly overgrown by ivy.

Secular :—

(2). FORD PLACE, house, outbuildings and walls, 1,150 yards W.N.W. of the church. The *House* is of two storeys with attics; the walls are partly of brick and partly of plastered timber-framing; the roofs are tiled. It was rebuilt *c.* 1655 on an irregular plan with cross-wings at the N. and S. ends and a second wing on the N. Part of the S. wing has since been destroyed and the S. side refaced. There are modern additions on the W. and N. sides. The E. side of the main block and the S. side of the adjoining cross-wing are of red brick with a heavy cornice and a series of plain 'Dutch' gables; the cornice on the main block is supported by two brick pilasters with moulded

capitals and standing on corbelled projections; one gable has a sunk panel with the initials $\begin{smallmatrix} S \\ I\,M, \end{smallmatrix}$ probably for James Silverlock and his wife; the second gable has the date 1655 (Plate, p. 127). A gable on the cross-wing has the initials R.S. The 'Dutch' gables are continued round the N. cross-wings, but without the cornice (Plate, pp. 56–7).

Inside the building the S.E. room has an original plaster ceiling divided into four bays by moulded trabeations enriched with guilloche ornament; the panels have elaborate strapwork with a rosette in the middle of each. The S.W. room has a rich plaster ceiling of late 17th-century date, divided into two main compartments and six panels; the main trabeation has running foliage, and the panels are surrounded by a band of bay leaves enclosing wreaths of oak leaves and fruit and flowers alternately; the four wreaths at the corners of the room have figures representing the four seasons; the other two have repainted shields-of-arms (Plates, pp. 152, 153). Several other rooms have original ceiling-beams, and there is a doorway, formerly external, with a moulded and carved architrave and a panelled door.

The *Gardener's Cottage,* formerly stables, is of 17th-century date, much altered and rebuilt. The walls round the house and garden are largely of 16th-century brickwork.

Condition—Good.

MONUMENTS (3–10).

The following monuments, unless otherwise described, are of the 17th century, and of two storeys, timber-framed and plastered or weatherboarded; the roofs are tiled or thatched. Some of the buildings have original chimney-stacks and exposed ceiling-beams.

Condition—Good or fairly good.

(3). *Dog and Partridge Inn,* 520 yards W. by S. of the church, has an 18th-century extension on the E. Inside the building is some original panelling.

(4). *House,* two tenements, 150 yards E. of (3), has cross-wings at the E. and W. ends. The upper storey projects at the S. end of the E. cross-wing.

(5). *House,* two tenements, 200 yards E.N.E. of (4), was built probably late in the 17th or early in the 18th century.

(6). *House,* three tenements, 40 yards E. of (5), was built probably early in the 18th century.

(7). *Cottage* (Plate, pp. xl–i), 20 yards N.E. of (6), was built probably early in the 18th century.

(8). *Cottage* (Plate, pp. xl–i), 20 yards E. of (7). Inside the building are some old battened doors.

(9). *Cottage,* two tenements, opposite church, was built probably early in the 18th century.

(10). *Cottage* (Plate, pp. xl–i), two tenements, opposite (6).

90. STOCK. (C.b.)

(O.S. 6 in. (ᵃ)lx. N.E. (ᵇ)lx. S.E.)

Stock is a parish and small village about 5 m. S. of Chelmsford. The church is the principal monument.

Ecclesiastical :—

ᵇ(1). PARISH CHURCH OF ALL SAINTS stands in the village. The walls are of mixed rubble with some freestone and pudding-stone ; the dressings are of limestone ; the belfry and porch are timber-framed ; the roofs are tiled and the spire shingled. The earliest detail in the church is of the 14th century, but it is probable that the walls of the *Nave* are of earlier date. In the second half of the 15th century the N. arcade was built and the *North Aisle* added ; at the same date, or perhaps a little earlier, the timber *Belfry* and *South Porch* were added. The *Chancel* was rebuilt in 1847–8 and the *North Vestry* added.

The timber belfry is of considerable interest, with its W. doorway, over which are original oak traceried windows.

Architectural Description—The *Nave* (44 ft. by 22 ft.) has a 15th-century N. arcade of four bays with two-centred arches of two hollow-chamfered orders ; the columns are octagonal and have moulded capitals and hollow-chamfered bases ; the E. respond has an attached half-column ; the W. bay is about half the width of the others. In the S. wall are three windows, apparently all modern ; between the two western is the partly restored S. doorway ; it is probably of late 14th-century date, and has jambs and two-centred arch of two orders, the outer moulded and the inner chamfered. In the W. wall is a late 14th-century doorway with moulded jambs and two-centred arch.

The *North Aisle* (13¼ ft. wide) has in the E. wall a modern arch ; S. of it is a reset 15th-century doorway with hollow-chamfered jambs and two-centred arch. In the N. wall are two 15th-century windows, each of two cinquefoiled lights under a square head with a moulded label ; further W. is the N. doorway, similar to the S. doorway, but with a moulded label. In the W. wall is a window uniform with those in the N. wall ; above it are two 15th-century windows, each of one cinque-

foiled light and probably reset ; between them is a grotesque corbel, also reset.

The *Belfry* (Plate, p. 156) is of two stages, both weather-boarded ; the lower has a surrounding aisle with a pent roof ; the upper has a short octagonal spire and a gabled projection on the E. side. The main structure stands on four oak posts with curved braces to each stage. The central square has curved diagonal principals, each with a cusp-point near the base and meeting at a boss in the middle carved with a grotesque face. The N. and S. walls of the aisle have each a 15th-century window of oak and of three trefoiled lights with tracery in a four-centred head. The 15th-century W. doorway (Plate, p. 157) has moulded jambs and two-centred arch in a square head with traceried spandrels ; above it is a range of three square lights filled with cusped tracery. At N.E. angle of the ground-stage is a post with the initials R.R., E.H., 1683, probably the date of repairs and of the addition to the E. of the bell-chamber.

The *South Porch* is timber-framed and of 15th-century date. It has a four-centred outer archway in a square head with panelled spandrels ; above it is a moulded cross-beam, and in the gable are five panels, the middle one having a trefoiled head ; one of the open lights flanking the archway and those in the side walls are fitted with slender 18th-century balusters. The roof has moulded plates and tie-beams with curved braces and plain king-posts ; the foiled barge-boards are much weathered.

The *Roof* of the N. aisle is of the 15th century and of three bays with king-post trusses ; the wall-plates are moulded and embattled and the tie-beams moulded or hollow-chamfered ; they support king-posts with hollow-chamfered struts springing from attached buttresses.

Fittings—*Bells :* three ; 3rd by John Diar and Robert Wickes, 1577, bell-frames old. *Brass :* In nave—on S. wall, of Richard Twedye, 1574, figure of man in armour and achievement-of-arms set in a black marble slab, formerly a small altar-slab, cut down, but with two consecration-crosses at the lower angles. *Chairs :* In chancel— two with elaborately carved high backs and carved legs, also two stools of same workmanship, possibly late 17th-century. *Door :* In N. doorway— modern, but having one ornamental hinge and scutcheon-plate with drop-handle, probably 15th-century. *Font :* octagonal bowl with moulded lower edge, plain stem and base, probably 15th-century. *Font-cover :* flat, of oak, with middle post having acorn terminal and four shaped supports, probably early 18th - century. *Floor-slab :* In chancel—to Giles Alin or Aleyn, 1677, with shield-of-arms. *Panelling :* In tower—late 16th and 17th-century, forming partition to vestry. *Seating :* In N. aisle—three bench-ends with popey-heads and front standards or buttresses with moulded caps, strings and bases and remains of carved figures on tops, 15th-century.

Condition—Good, much restored.

Secular :—

b(2). ALMSHOUSES, four tenements, 140 yards W. of the church, were founded by Richard Twedye in the second half of the 16th century. The present building forms a long rectangular block of red brick one storey high, with a tiled roof, and is of late 17th-century date. It has two original chimney-stacks (Plate, pp. 56–7).

Condition—Good.

a(3). COTTAGE, 400 yards N.E. of the church, is of one storey with attics. The walls are of plastered timber-framing and brick ; the roofs are tiled. It was built probably late in the 17th century on a rectangular plan and has an original chimney-stack. Inside the building the ceiling-beams are exposed.

Condition—Bad.

b(4). COTTAGE, on W. side of the road, about ¾ m. S. of the church, is of one storey with attics. The walls are of timber-framing partly plastered and partly weather-boarded ; the roofs are tiled. It was built in the 17th century with two gabled dormers on the E. front and has an original chimney-stack of two diagonal shafts. Inside the building the ceiling-beams are exposed.

Condition—Fairly good.

Unclassified :—

b(5). MOUND, about 600 yards S.S.W. of the church, is about 55 ft. in diameter at the base and from 2 ft. to 3 ft. high. It is planted with trees of considerable age and is not surrounded by a ditch.

---

91. STOW MARIES. (E.b.)

(O.S. 6 in. lxii. N.W.)

Stow Maries is a parish on the left bank of the Stour and 6 m. S. of Maldon.

Ecclesiastical :—

(1). PARISH CHURCH OF ST. MARY (Plate, pp. xxxviii–ix) stands on the N. side of the parish. The walls are of rubble and brick with dressings of limestone ; the roofs are tiled and lead-covered. The *Chancel* was built probably in the 14th century. The *Nave* was probably rebuilt in the 15th century. Early in the 16th century the walls of the nave were heightened in brick. The *Bell-turret* is of uncertain date. The church has been restored in modern times, when the *North Vestry* and *South Porch* were added and part of the S. wall of the nave rebuilt.

Architectural Description—The *Chancel* (24 ft. by 18¾ ft.) is probably of 14th-century date, but all the details are modern, including the chancel-arch.

The *Nave* (39½ ft. by 18 ft.) has an early 16th-century crow-stepped E. gable of brick. The N. wall has a brick parapet resting on a trefoiled corbel-table of early 16th-century date. In the N. wall is a 15th-century window, partly restored and of three cinquefoiled lights with vertical tracery in a four-centred head with a moulded label and stops carved with angels playing musical instruments ; further W. is the 15th-century N. doorway, with moulded jambs and a reset segmental-pointed head with a moulded label with head-stops ; at the E. end of the wall is the rood-loft staircase, both doorways having two-centred heads of the 15th century. In the S. wall is a modern window ; further W. is the blocked S. doorway. In the W. wall is a modern window.

Fittings—*Bell :* one by Miles Graye, 1686. *Brass :* In chancel—of Mary (Cammocke), wife of William Browne, 1602, figure of woman, three sons and four daughters and a shield-of-arms. *Font :* octagonal stem with trefoil-headed panels and moulded base, 15th-century. *Niche :* In nave—in N. wall, with cinquefoiled head and quatrefoiled spandrels, 15th-century, much defaced. *Piscinae :* In chancel—with trefoiled ogee head and septfoiled drain, 14th-century. In nave—in S. wall, with four-centred head and square drain, early 16th-century.

Condition—Good.

Secular :—

(2). STOW HALL (Plate, p. 57), 200 yards N.N.W. of the church, is of two storeys, timber-framed ; the roofs are tiled. It was built probably early in the 17th century, and has a large modern addition on the S. side. The original central chimney-stack has a square base and grouped shafts, cruciform on plan. Inside the building are exposed ceiling-beams.

Condition—Good.

Unclassified :—

(3). MOUNDS, near head of creek and within the sea-wall, about 1½ m. S.W. of the church. Several large mounds of irregular shape and apparently of tipped material, but without trace of red earth. Possibly connected with mediaeval salt-workings.

Condition—Good.

STOCK: PARISH CHURCH OF ALL SAINTS.
From the South-West, showing the 15th-century Belfry.

STOCK: PARISH CHURCH OF ALL SAINTS.
West Doorway and Window of Belfry; 15th-century.

92. SUTTON. (F.c.)

(O.S. 6 in. lxxviii. N.E.)

Sutton is a small parish on the S. bank of the Roach, 2 m. N. of Southend-on-Sea. The church is interesting.

Ecclesiastical :—

(1). PARISH CHURCH OF ALL SAINTS (Plate, p. xxxii) stands about the middle of the parish. The walls are of ragstone-rubble with dressings of Reigate and Barnack-stone ; the roofs are tiled, and the bell-turret is boarded. The *Chancel* and *Nave* were built in the first half of the 12th century ; the *Bell-turret* was built in the 15th century, and the *South Porch* added c. 1633. The S. doorway is a good example of 13th-century work and the S. porch is interesting as a dated example.

Architectural Description—The *Chancel* (18½ ft. by 18¼ ft.) has three ·modern lancet-windows in the E. wall. In the N. wall is a window all modern externally, but with 12th-century splays ; it has been lengthened. In the S. wall is a window uniform with that in the N., but with only the E. splay of the 12th century ; further W. is a taller lancet-window, mainly old externally ; at the E. end of the wall is a partly restored 13th-century doorway with chamfered jambs and two-centred arch ; it is now blocked. The 12th-century chancel-arch is semi-circular and of two orders on the W. face, the inner plain and the outer roll-moulded ; the responds have each a flat half-round · attached shaft with moulded bases, modern capitals and moulded abaci carried round as imposts.

The *Nave* (38 ft. by 22¼ ft.) has in the N. wall two windows, the eastern is modern and the western is a single round-headed light of the 12th-century, restored at the base ; below and to the W. of it is the 12th-century N. doorway, with plain jambs and round arch and a heavy oak balk as a threshold ; it is disused and now forms a cupboard. In the S. wall are two windows uniform with those in the N. wall, but the western is only slightly restored externally ; the early 13th-century S. doorway (Plate, p. 121) has a two-centred arch of three moulded orders and a damaged chamfered label ; the moulded jambs, also of three orders, have each one attached and two free shafts with moulded capitals and bases ; the E. jamb, except

two of the bases, and the middle W. shaft are modern ; the splays have attached keeled shafts with moulded capitals and partly restored on the E. side. In the W. wall is a window all modern except the splays and rear-arch, which are possibly of the 14th century ; below it are traces, externally, of a former doorway.

The *Bell-turret*, at the W. end of the nave, stands on four posts with curved braces and curved framing above the cross-beams, all of the 15th century ; there are also four inner posts added at a later period, probably in the 17th century.

The *South Porch* is of timber, and has a round outer archway with a key-block and sunk spandrels carved with the date 1633 ; the mouldings of the W. post have a high carved stop. The side walls have each a square opening, now blocked, and having three free and two half-balusters all symmetrically turned.

The *Roof* of the chancel is of the 15th century, with one king-post truss, chamfered main timbers and old trussed-rafters ; the square king-post has a moulded capital and base and four-way struts. The roof of the nave is of the same date and character, and has three king-post trusses and old flat trussed-rafters.

Fittings—Bell : one, inaccessible, but said to be by John Clifton, 1638. *Coffin-lid* : In church-yard—S. of church, with moulded edge and semi-octagonal lower end, Purbeck marble, 13th-century. *Communion Rails* : with turned balusters and heavy top rail, late 17th-century, probably brought from elsewhere and adapted to present position. *Communion Table* : with heavy turned legs and shaped brackets, c. 1660. *Doors* : In N. doorway—disused, of overlapping battens with one old strap-hinge, 15th or 16th-century. In S. doorway—with old inner and modern outer battens. *Floor-slab* : In churchyard—S. side, to John Staple, 1661. *Font* : square bowl with five shallow pointed panels on each side, 13th-century, stem, base and half the bowl modern. *Painting* : In chancel—on splays of 12th-century windows, remains of decoration in red and yellow bands. *Panelling* : In porch—with partly fluted and partly plain frieze, early 17th-century, three carefully cut names on W. side—Charles Hobson, 1647, Samuell Purchas, 1647, and . . . . ard Britridge (16)47. *Plate* : includes a cup of 1601 with baluster stem. *Seating* : In chancel and W. tower—several plain benches of the 16th century, considerably repaired. Also others with shaped standards of late 17th-century date.

Condition—Good.

Secular :—

(2). SUTTON HALL, 140 yards E. of the church, is of two storeys with attics. The walls are of brick and timber-framing partly plastered and partly weather-boarded ; the roofs are tiled. It was built in the 16th century on an L-shaped plan with the wings extending towards the N. and W. and has 17th-century and modern additions in the angle. The walls were largely refaced with brick in the 18th century, and modern alterations include the removal of a staircase which projected at the S. end of the E. front. The chimney-stacks are rectangular, but have been partly rebuilt, and there is a small gable on the S. end of the E. front with moulded barge-boards. Inside the building some of the rooms have exposed ceiling-beams, and in one room on the ground-floor is some 17th-century panelling. There is similar panelling on the first floor and a door with ' cocks-head ' hinges. The roof over the middle part of the front block is original and has cambered tie-beams with curved struts supporting the purlins, but the other roofs are for the most part modern, though incorporating some old timbers.

Condition—Good, much altered.

(3). THE RECTORY, on E. side of the road, 350 yards S. of the church, is of two storeys, timber-framed and plastered ; the roofs are tiled. It is a small early 17th-century building, L-shaped on plan, with the wings extending towards the S. and E., and has modern extensions on the N., E. and S. In the E. wall of the S. wing of the original building is a partly blocked window of three lights. There is one original chimney-stack. Inside the building two of the main ceiling-beams of the ground-floor are exposed but the others are cased.

Condition—Good.

(4). TEMPLE FARM, now two tenements, on S. border of the parish, 1,000 yards S.S.W. of the church, is of two storeys, timber-framèd and plastered ; the roofs are tiled. It is a rectangular building of early 17th-century date, much altered externally. Inside the building some of the ceiling-beams are exposed, and parts of the timber-construction are visible on the first floor.

Condition—Good.

---

93. THUNDERSLEY. (E.c.)

(O.S. 6 in. lxix. S.E.)

Thundersley is a parish about 6 m. W.N.W. of Southend-on-Sea. The church is the principal monument.

Ecclesiastical :—

(1). PARISH CHURCH OF ST. PETER stands near the middle of the parish. The walls are of ragstone-rubble with some flint, Roman brick, pudding-stone, etc. ; the dressings are of limestone ; the roofs are tiled. The *Chancel* is of uncertain date. The *Nave*, with *North* and *South Aisles*, was built *c.* 1200. The *Bell-turret* was added in the 15th

century. The *South Porch* was added in the 18th century. The church has been restored in modern times, when the chancel was largely rebuilt and the *Organ Chamber* added.

The arcades of the nave have interesting early 13th-century foliage.

Architectural Description—The *Chancel* (19½ ft. by 15 ft.) has modern E. and N. windows. In the S. wall is a round-headed doorway and a square-headed single-light window, all covered with cement but probably old. There is no chancel-arch.

The *Nave* (35 ft. by 14 ft.) is of early 13th-century date, and has N. and S. arcades of three bays with two-centred arches of two hollow-chamfered orders ; the columns and responds are alternately round and octagonal, with moulded capitals (Plate, p. 161) carved with conventional foliage of various designs and moulded bases. The 15th-century W. window is of three cinquefoiled lights with vertical tracery in a two-centred head with a moulded label ; below it is a 15th-century doorway with chamfered jambs and three-centred arch and now blocked. The bell-turret at the W. end of the nave is of the 15th century, and stands on four oak posts with braced cross-beams and added uprights.

The *North Aisle* (6½ ft. wide) has three modern windows. The 14th-century N. doorway has chamfered jambs and two-centred arch.

The *South Aisle* (6¼ ft. wide) has a modern E. window. In the S. wall are two 15th-century windows, partly restored, and each of two trefoiled lights in a square head with a moulded label ; between is a doorway entirely covered with modern cement.

The *South Porch* is modern, but incorporates some old timbers.

The *Roof* of the nave is of the 15th century and of the braced collar-beam type with two king-post trusses ; the soffit of the E. tie-beam is grooved for a former boarded tympanum. The roof is continued down over the aisles.

Fittings—*Bells :* two, inaccessible, but said to be 1st uninscribed ; 2nd by Robert Mot, 1588. *Font :* octagonal bowl with quatrefoiled panels enclosing square flowers, of doubtful antiquity. *Funeral-helm,* etc. In nave—on S. wall, helm, 16th or early 17th-century, and sword, later. *Glass :* in S. aisle—in S.E. window, two quarries

with conventional ornament and fragments of tabernacle work, foliage, etc., 15th-century. *Plate :* includes cup with band of engraved ornament and cover-paten of 1569. *Miscellanea :* In N. aisle— moulded bracket or corbel, 13th - century, and another fragment not *in situ.*
Condition—Good.

Secular :—

MONUMENTS (2 and 3).

The following monuments are of two storeys and of the 17th century. Both have exposed ceiling-beams and tiled roofs.
Condition—Good.

(2). *House,* now three tenements, at junction of roads nearly ½ m. E. of the church, is of weather-boarded timber-framing. It is of the central-chimney type with modern extensions; the chimney-stack is original.

(3). *Great Wyburns,* house, 1¾ m. E. of the church, is of plastered timber-framing. It was built on an L-shaped plan with the wings extending towards the N. and W., but has been much altered and added to.

———

THURROCK, see GRAYS THURROCK, LITTLE THURROCK and WEST THURROCK.
TILBURY, see EAST TILBURY and WEST TILBURY.

94. TILLINGHAM. (G.b.)

(O.S. 6 in. (a)lv. S.E. (b)lxiii. N.E.)

Tillingham is a parish and village 6 m N.N.E. of Burnham-on-Crouch.

Ecclesiastical :—

a(1). PARISH CHURCH OF ST. NICHOLAS (Plate, p. xxxii) stands in the village. The walls are of septaria and flint-rubble with limestone dressings; the roofs are tiled. The *Nave* was built in the 12th century. Early in the 13th century the *Chancel* was rebuilt and lengthened. In the 14th century the chancel-arch was rebuilt, a S. aisle built and the *West Tower* added. The church was restored in the 19th century, when the *South Aisle* was rebuilt and the S. arcade opened out and possibly reconstructed and the *South Porch* and *North Vestry* added.

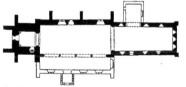

Architectural Description—The *Chancel* (43¼ ft. by 17 ft.) has in the E. wall three 13th-century

lancet-windows, all modern externally. In the N. wall are three similar lancet-windows, the two eastern modern externally and the westernmost with a segmental-pointed rear-arch; there is also a modern opening to the Vestry. In the S. wall are three 13th-century lancet-windows; between the two western is a blocked doorway of the 13th century with a segmental rear-arch and not visible externally. The 14th-century chancel-arch is two-centred and of two chamfered orders; the responds have attached semi-octagonal shafts with moulded capitals.

The *Nave* (52¼ ft. by 21 ft.) has in the N. wall two windows all modern except for the splays and rear-arches; between them is the early 12th-century N. doorway, of one plain order and a segmental head supporting a diapered tympanum enclosed by a round arch. The mid 14th-century S. arcade is of four bays with two-centred arches of two chamfered orders; the octagonal columns have moulded capitals and bases, and the responds have attached half-columns, considerably restored.

The *West Tower* (12 ft. by 11 ft.) is of the 14th century and of three stages with an embattled parapet and a S.E. stair-turret rising above it. The two-centred tower-arch is of three chamfered orders, of which the inner is continued down the responds. The W. window is of two trefoiled lights with a quatrefoil in a two-centred head with a moulded label and head-stops; the W. doorway has double hollow-chamfered jambs and two-centred arch. The second stage has in the N., S. and W. walls a modern window. The bell-chamber has a modern window in each wall.

Fittings—*Bells :* six; 2nd by William Culverden, *c.* 1500 and inscribed "Sancte Luca"; 3rd by Henry Jordan, mid 15th-century and inscribed "Johannes Est Nomen Eius"; 4th by John Darbie, 1684; 5th by Henry Pleasant, 1707. *Brasses :* In chancel—on S. wall, (1) of Edward Wiot, 1584, kneeling figure in cloak and trunk-hose, with shield-of-arms. In S. aisle—(2) to John Wakeman, 1584, inscription only. *Chairs :* In chancel—two, with carved backs and legs, early 18th-century. *Doors :* In turret-staircase to tower, two, of overlapping battens with strap-hinges, 15th-century. *Font :* square bowl with conventional foliage in relief, late 12th-century. *Monument :* In churchyard—S. side, to Charles Cockett, 1714, table-tomb, with shield-of-arms. *Piscina :* In chancel—with moulded jambs and two-centred head, moulded bases to jambs and octofoiled drain, chamfered shelf, 13th-century. *Plate :* includes large cup dated 1616. *Sedilia :* W. of piscina, of three bays with two - centred arches, middle bays on shouldered corbels, 13th-century. *Miscellanea :* Built into walls of S. aisle, various architectural fragments, 12th-century and later.
Condition—Good.

Secular :—

MONUMENTS (2–7).

The following monuments, unless otherwise described, are of the 17th century and of two storeys and timber - framed and plastered or weather-boarded ; the roofs are tiled. Some of the buildings have original chimney-stacks and exposed ceiling-beams.

Condition—Good or fairly good, unless otherwise noted.

a(2). *Stowe's Farm*, house, 600 yards W.S.W. of the church, was built in the 16th century, and has a modern addition on the N. side. The upper storey projects at the E. end of the original block.

a(3). *West Hyde*, house (Plate, pp. xl–i), 1¼ m. W. of the church, has an original central chimney-stack with three grouped diagonal shafts. Inside the building is an early 18th-century fireplace with a heavy moulded architrave.

b(4). *Reddings*, house (Plate, p. xxxv), 1,500 yards S.W. of the church, was built probably early in the 16th century, with cross-wings at the E. and W. ends. The upper storey projects at both ends of the E. wing. On the N. side is a chimney-stack with one diagonal shaft. Inside the building is some exposed timber-framing and a door of 16th-century panelling.

b(5). *Hill House*, house, 500 yards W. of (4), was built probably in the 16th century, and has a cross-wing at the W. end. One chimney-stack has two 17th-century diagonal shafts.

a(6). *Bridgemans*, house (Plate, pp. xl–i), nearly 1¼ m. E.S.E. of the church, has a cross-wing at the E. end. The upper storey projects at the S. end of the cross-wing.

Condition—Poor.

b(7). *Midlands*, house, 1,500 yards S.S.E. of the church, was built probably in the 16th-century, and has two original chimney-stacks, both with grouped diagonal shafts. There are large modern additions.

Unclassified :—

b(8). RED HILL, E. of Jerry's Farm, about 1½ m. S E. of the church. Now levelled.

---

95. UPMINSTER. (B.d.)

(O.S. 6 in. *(a)*lxvii. S.W. *(b)*lxxv. N.W. *(c)*lxxv. S.W.)

Upminster is a parish and village about 2½ m. S.E. of Romford. The principal monuments are the church, Upminster Hall and Great Tomkyns.

Ecclesiastical :—

b(1). PARISH CHURCH OF ST. LAURENCE stands in the village. The walls are of mixed rubble with limestone dressings ; the roofs are covered with lead and slates. The *West Tower* is of *c.* 1200 ;

the bell-chamber is probably of rather later date. The N. arcade of the *Nave* is of early 14th-century date. A N. chapel was added in the 15th century. The church was much altered in 1771, and again in 1862, when the *Chancel, North Chapel, North Aisle* and *South Porch* were practically rebuilt, except perhaps the core of some of the walls ; at the same time the S. wall of the nave was refaced or rebuilt.

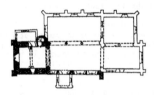

Architectural Description—The *Chancel* (26 ft. by 16 ft.) and *North Chapel* (22½ ft. by 19 ft.) have no ancient features.

The *Nave* (36¾ ft. by 18½ ft.) has a 14th-century N. arcade of three bays with two-centred arches of two chamfered orders ; the columns are of quatrefoil plan with moulded capitals and bases ; the W. respond has an attached half-column ; the E. respond is modern and the easternmost arch has been widened. The other details of the nave are modern.

The *North Aisle* (17¾ ft. wide) has no ancient features.

The *West Tower* (19½ ft. by 15½ ft.) is of three stages, with clasping buttresses to the ground-stage and a pyramidal roof surmounted by a small timber lantern and spire (Plate, pp. xxxii–iii). The two lower stages are of early 13th-century date, and the top stage was added rather later. The two - centred tower - arch is of two chamfered orders with chamfered imposts and bases to the responds. The N. and S. walls have each a single light lancet-window, that on the N. being blocked and having below it a modern door-way ; E. of this is an original doorway, to the stair-turret, with a round head. In the W. wall is a window of two trefoiled lights with tracery in a two-centred head, all modern externally. The floor of the stage above is supported on a heavy beam resting on two chamfered posts with moulded bases and other oak framework, all of the 15th century. The N., S. and W. walls of the second stage have each a lancet-window, restored externally. The bell-chamber has in each wall a window of two lights, all modern externally, but with old splays and rear-arch and a semi-circular relieving-arch on the external face. All these windows have relieving-arches.

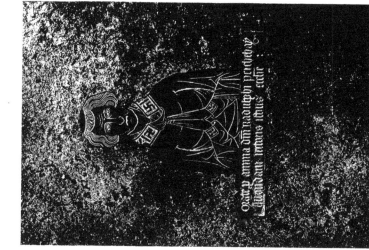

STIFFORD : PARISH CHURCH OF ST. MARY
THE VIRGIN.

Brass of Ralph Perchehay ; c. 1330.

AVELEY : PARISH CHURCH OF ST. MICHAEL.

Brass of Ralph de Knevynton ; c. 1370.

(Approximately one-sixth full size.)

DETAILS OF CARVED STONEWORK.

MOUNTNESSING CHURCH.
Capital, N. Arcade ; mid 13th-century.

MUCKING CHURCH.
Capital, S. Arcade ; early 13th-century.

THUNDERSLEY CHURCH.
Capitals of N. and S. Arcades ; early 13th-century.

STIFFORD CHURCH.
Corbel and Capital, E. respond of S. Arcade ;
1260-70.

ORSETT CHURCH.
South Doorway ; part of E. jamb and head ;
c. 1160.

Fittings—*Bells :* three ; 1st by John Kebyll, late 15th-century and inscribed " Sancte Gabrile Ora Pro Nobis " ; 2nd by Robert Mot, 1583 ; 3rd probably by Richard Holdfeld, and dated 1602. *Brasses :* In N. aisle—on N. wall, (1) to Hamlett Clarke and Alice, his second wife, 1636, widow of William Lathum, inscription only ; (2) of [Elizabeth (de la Felde), wife of Roger Dencourt, 1455] figure of woman in horned head-dress with mantle, etc., dog at feet ; (3) of Geerardt D'Ewes, 1591, figure of man in plate-armour with restored inscription-plate ; (4) of Grace, daughter of William Latham, 1626, figure of woman in costume of period ; on W. wall, (5) figure of man in civil dress, of *c.* 1530, with fur-lined gown, etc., palimpsest on back, part of figure of bishop or abbot, 15th-century ; (6) to John Stanley, 1626, inscription only. In N. aisle—on E. wall, (7) of Nicholas Wayte, 1542, and Ellyn (Dencort), his wife, figures of man in fur-lined gown and woman with pedimental head-dress, palimpsest on back of both effigies, parts of large figure of bishop or abbot, Flemish work of *c.* 1480, palimpsest on inscription part of another inscription ; (8) figure of woman, *c.* 1560, holding a book. *Chair :* In chancel—with late 17th or early 18th-century panelled back and seat, rest modern. *Doors :* In tower—in lower doorway to turret staircase, panelled door, probably 15th or 16th-century, with early 13th-century ornamental hinge refixed ; in doorway to second stage, with hollow - chamfered frame and fillets and strap-hinges, 15th-century. *Font :* octagonal bowl with moulded edges, each side with quatrefoiled panel enclosing a foliated boss, stem with trefoil-headed panels, moulded base, late 15th-century. *Glass :* In N. chapel—in N.E. window, collection of glass, mostly of 1630, the date occurring in both lights, consisting of helms with crests of Lathum and elaborate mantling, four shields-of-arms, including those of Dencourt and Fngaine, other miscellaneous pieces, among them four enamel-painted quarries of the 17th century, made up with modern glass. *Monuments* and *Floor-slabs.* Monuments : In N. aisle—on N. wall, (1) to Elizabeth (Goodlad), wife of Thomas Dugdale, 1701, also to an infant daughter, 1701, and to Mary, 1674, William, 1678, and Abraham Goodlad, 1685, white marble tablet with shield-of-arms. In churchyard—E. of church, (2) to Joseph Bryan, 1695, head-stone ; (3) to Mrs. Ann Collentt, 1710, head-stone. *Plate :* includes 17th-century cup, probably of 1608, an alms-dish of 1686 and a stand-paten of 1704. *Screen :* In W. arch of N. chapel—incorporates some fragments of late 15th or early 16th-century tracery. *Stall front or desk :* with shaped end and moulded rail and book-rest, one standard with remains of popey-head and carved and panelled front edge, other standard not rising above desk, early 16th-century.
Condition—Good, mostly rebuilt.

Secular :—

b(2). HOMESTEAD MOAT at New Place, 550 yards E. of the church.

b(3). UPMINSTER HALL, house (Plate, pp. xxxiv–v) and moat, 1,500 yards N.N.E. of the church. The house is of two storeys with attics ; the walls are of plastered timber-framing and the roofs are tiled. It was built in the second half of the 16th century with a Hall and projecting cross-wings on the N. and S., a N.W. block was added in the 18th century ; further extensions have since been made, the external walls refaced and the interior much altered. On the W. front the first floor of the wings and porch at the S. end of the Hall projects ; the bres-summer of the S. wing is moulded, and the porch gable has carved barge-boards and a carved and moulded pendant. The porch is entered through a four-centred arch, now cased in modern woodwork. On the E. front the projecting upper storey to the original N. wing has been partly underbuilt. The Hall chimney-stack has diagonal shafts on a rectangular base with a moulded capping, the N.W. stack has two similar shafts. Inside the house some of the timber-framing is exposed, and in the Hall are some moulded beams. The roof of the N. wing has a queen-post truss with curved wind-braces to the side purlins, and in that over the Hall are some cambered tie-beams.
The *Moat* is fragmentary.
Condition—Of house, good.

a(4). GREAT TOMKYNS, house (Plate, p. xxxiv) and barn, about 2 m. N.N.E. of the church. The *House* is of two storeys, timber-framed and plastered ; the roofs are tiled. It was built in the 15th century on a rough half H-shaped plan with the wings projecting to the N. Modern alterations include an addition between the wings, an extension of the W. wing and the gallery rebuilt at the E. end of the Hall. Except on the N. front the timber-framing is exposed. On the S. *Elevation* the upper storey of the cross-wings projects. There is an original window of four lights with flat mullions on the W. side of the entrance doorway, and in the E. wall is a similar window of two lights. An original first-floor window at the S. end of the W. front is of five lights with moulded frame, transom and mullions. Interior—The Hall is open to the roof, and has in the E. wall (Plate, p. 65) two doorways with moulded frames, one of which retains its original four - centred arch, the timber - framing in the walls of the ground-floor rooms and in some of those on the first floor is exposed ; some of the rooms have exposed ceiling-beams. Over the E. wing the roof is in four bays and has two cambered tie-beams with curved braces ; all of unusually heavy timbers. The tie-beams of the roof over the W. wing have shaped wall-posts supporting them and curved braces which form flat two-centred arches.

The *Barn*, S. of the house, is of 17th-century date, and is built of weather-boarded timber-framing and has a thatched roof. The roof is in three bays with braced ties and purlins (Plate, p. xli).

Condition—Of house, good.

MONUMENTS (5–12).

The following buildings, unless otherwise described are of the 17th century, and of two storeys, timber-framed and covered with plaster ; the roofs are tiled or thatched. Many of the buildings have exposed ceiling-beams and original chimney-stacks.

Condition—Good or fairly good.

b(5). *High House*, 100 yards S.E. of the church, is of two storeys with attics. It was built late in the 16th century on a rectangular plan and has large modern additions at the back and sides. The W. front has a projecting porch of three storeys, carried on four columns having moulded capitals and modern cased bases, and has a modillioned pediment and cornice. At the eaves-level of the main building is a modillioned cornice which stops against the projecting porch, and above it the wall is carried up in three pointed gables. The central chimney-stack is original and has small V-shaped projections at the sides.

b(6). *Hoppy Hall*, house, about 400 yards S. of the church, is of two storeys with attics. Inside the building are some fragments of early 17th-century panelling and two battened and one panelled door of the same period.

b(7). *Park Corner Farm*, house, about 1 m. S.W. of the church, is of two storeys with attics. It was built in the 16th century ; the house has since been extended on the N. and W., probably in the 18th century. The two 17th-century chimney-stacks have diagonal shafts. Inside the building the roof is of collar-beam construction with curved wind-braces to the purlins.

e(8). *High House*, at Corbet's Tye, now two tenements, nearly 1 m. S. by E. of the church, is of two storeys with attics. The original building has been considerably added to and altered. The central chimney-stack is original and has four diagonal shafts. In one of the ground-floor rooms is an elaborate mantelpiece of *c.* 1700. On either side of the fireplace two turned balusters support a frieze carved with cherubs' heads, dolphins, and figures ; the overmantel is divided into three bays by twisted Corinthian columns ; in the centre of each bay is a shaped panel, carved with a cherub's head.

e(9). *Cottage*, 60 yards S.W. of (8). The walls are partly weather-boarded. The original chimney-stack has three diagonal shafts.

e(10). *House*, now three tenements, 150 yards E. of (8). The middle block is possibly of 15th-century date, but the rest of the building is of the 18th-century. The N. front has a projecting upper storey supported by heavy carved brackets.

e(11). *Great Sunnings*, house, 300 yards S.S.E. of (10), is of two storeys with attics. The W. end has a projecting upper storey carried on a moulded bressummer. The original central chimney-stack has six diagonal shafts on a square base. Inside the building, one room on the ground and three on the first floor are panelled in oak and have carved mantelpieces of *c.* 1600.

e(12). *Cottage* at Chafford Heath, about ¾ m. S. of (10).

---

96. VANGE. (D.d.)

(O.S. 6 in. lxxvi. N.E.)

Vange is a small parish on the N. bank of the Thames estuary, 8 m. N.E. of Grays Thurrock.

Ecclesiastical :—

(1). PARISH CHURCH OF ALL SAINTS stands towards the S.W. side of the parish. The walls are of ragstone-rubble with some septaria and flint ; the dressings are of limestone ; the roofs are tiled. The *Nave* was built in the 12th century or earlier. Late in the 14th or early in the 15th century the W. wall of the nave was rebuilt and the N. and S. walls partly rebuilt ; the side walls of the *Chancel* are perhaps of the same date. In the 18th century the E. wall of the chancel was rebuilt. The church has been restored in modern times, when the *South Porch* was added.

Architectural Description—The *Chancel* (18 ft. by 16 ft.) has an 18th-century E. wall with bands of brick alternating with stone. The E. window is modern, but is set in an 18th-century opening. In the S. wall is a modern window. The late 11th or early 12th-century chancel-arch is semi-circular and plain.

The *Nave* (39½ ft. by 21½ ft.) has in the N. wall a 15th-century window of two trefoiled lights in a square head with a moulded label ; further W. is the early 14th-century N. doorway, with chamfered jambs and two-centred head ; the doorway is now blocked. In the S. wall is a window similar to that in the N. wall, and further W. is the S. doorway of *c.* 1400, with moulded jambs and two-centred head ; at the E. end of the wall is the late 15th-century rood-loft staircase, with a pointed lower doorway and a square-headed upper one ; immediately W. of the staircase is a blocked single-light window, probably of the 12th century. In the W. wall is a 14th or 15th-century window with a two-centred head and moulded label ; the mullion and tracery have been removed.

The *Roof* of the nave is of the 15th century, and has moulded and embattled wall-plates and three king-post trusses. The bell-turret was apparently rebuilt in 1816.

Fittings—*Communion Rails :* incorporate some 17th-century work, including four uprights with shaped tops. *Font* (Plate, pp. xlii–iii) : plain square bowl with rough zig-zag lines on E. face and carved foliage in spandrels of top surface, cylindrical stem and defaced base for four angle shafts, 12th-century, shafts modern. *Glass :* In E. window, two small panels, one showing a crucifix in a churchyard, Flemish or German, late 16th-century, and one, also foreign, showing a man preaching in a church, 17th-century, also a shield-of-arms of Denmark impaling the royal arms of Queen Anne before the union. *Monuments :* In chancel—on N. wall (1) to George Maule, 1667, pastor of the church, alabaster and black marble tablet with moulded frame and achievement-of-arms ; (2) to Mary (Champneis), wife of George Maule, 1659, and Charles, their only child, marble tablet with strapwork frame and achievement - of - arms. *Plate :* includes a repaired cup of 1568 with band of engraved ornament, lid probably of the 17th century, and stand-paten also of the 17th century. *Royal Arms :* On front of modern gallery —of William III, dated 1689, painted on wood. Condition—Good.

Secular :—

(2). HILL FARM, house, 1,050 yards N.N.E. of the church, is of two storeys, timber-framed and weather-boarded ; the roofs are tiled. It was built probably in the 17th century and has small modern additions. Condition—Good.

(3). MERRICKS, house and barn, nearly ¾ m. E.N.E. of the church. The *House* is of two storeys and of brick and timber-framing ; the roofs are tiled. It was built probably in the 16th century with a W. cross-wing, but has been considerably altered and added to and partly refaced with brick. Inside the building some of the timber-framing, ceiling-beams and roof-timbers are exposed.

The *Barn* (Plate, p. xli) stands to the N.W. of the house, and is of late 16th or early 17th-century date. It is of weather-boarded timber-framing with a thatched roof, and has on the E. side a porch with a projecting gable supported by straight braces. Internally the roof is divided into five bays by queen-post trusses.

Condition—Of house good (barn now fallen down).

WAKERING, see GREAT WAKERING and LITTLE WAKERING.

WARLEY, see GREAT WARLEY and LITTLE WARLEY.

97. WENNINGTON. (A.d.)

(O.S. 6 in. [a]lxxxii. N.E. [b]lxxxiii. N.W.)

Wennington is a small parish 6½ m. E.S.E. of Barking. The church is the principal monument.

Ecclesiastical :—

[b](1). PARISH CHURCH OF SS. MARY AND PETER stands in the N. part of the parish. The walls are of mixed rubble, mostly ragstone ; the dressings are of limestone ; the roofs are tiled. There is a reset doorway of the 12th century, but the earliest detail *in situ* is of the first half of the 13th century, when the *Chancel, Nave* and a S. aisle were built. The *North Aisle* was added early in the 14th century, and the *West Tower* late in the same century. The S. aisle was destroyed at some uncertain date and its arcade walled up. The church was restored in the 19th century, when the *South Aisle* was rebuilt, the S. arcade opened out, and the *Organ Chamber* and *North Porch* added.

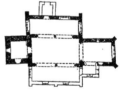

Architectural Description—The *Chancel* (21½ ft. by 14 ft.) has an E. window, all modern except the splays and rear-arch, which are possibly of early 14th-century date. In the N. wall is an early 13th-century window of one light and modern externally. In the S. wall is a window of a single light and modern except for the 13th or early 14th-century splays and rear-arch ; further W. is a modern arch. The 15th-century chancel-arch is four-centred and of two moulded orders ; the outer order is continuous, the inner carried on attached shafts with moulded capitals and bases.

The *Organ Chamber* is modern, but reset in the E. wall are the head and imposts of a 12th-century doorway ; the head is round and has diapered ornament, and the imposts are chamfered ; reset in the same wall are the sill of a window and a 15th-century stone shield with the crossed keys of St. Peter.

The *Nave* (35 ft. by 18 ft.) has an early 14th-century N. arcade of two bays with two-centred arches of two chamfered orders, carried on an octagonal pier and semi-octagonal responds with moulded capitals and bases ; the bases to the responds are modern, and that to the pier has been mostly restored. The S. arcade is of mid 13th-century date and of two bays with two-centred arches of two chamfered orders ; the middle column is circular, the responds semi-octagonal, all with moulded capitals and bases, but the capital to the W. respond is modern. In the W. wall, now opening into the W. tower, is an early 13th-century lancet-window rebated on the outside for a shutter. Below it is a late 14th-century doorway from the tower with moulded jambs and four-centred head.

The *North Aisle* (11¼ ft. wide) has three windows, all completely rebuilt, and a N. doorway all modern except the inner splays and rear-arch.

The *West Tower* (12 ft. square) is of late 14th-century date and of three stages with an embattled parapet. In the S. wall is a late 15th or early 16th-century doorway with rebated and hollow-chamfered jambs and four-centred arch. The W. window is of one trefoiled light. The second stage has in the N., S. and W. walls a window of one square-headed light. The bell-chamber has in each wall a window similar to the W. window.

The *Roof* of the chancel is of the 14th or 15th century, with a central king-post truss and chamfered wall-plates. The roof of the nave is in three bays with chamfered wall-plates and king-post trusses with cambered tie-beams, two-way struts to the king-posts and central purlin.

Fittings—*Bells* : one by Anthony Bartlet, 1662 ; bell-frame, 17th-century. *Brass Indents* : In S. aisle—(1) tapering slab with marginal inscription in single capitals, to THOMAS ATTNOK (or Atenok), much defaced, early 14th-century. Under altar-table—(2) of woman, two shields and inscription-plate over. *Chairs* : In chancel —two with carved backs, turned legs and rails, late 17th-century. *Chest* (Plate, p. xliii) : In N. aisle—of hutch-type with broad stiles terminating at base in feet of roughly ogee shape ; side rails to lid chamfered with original slots for pin-hinges, now replaced by two wrought-iron strap-hinges, 13th-century, part of lid later. *Doors* : In N. doorway—divided into panels by moulded fillets, with strap-hinges, early 16th-century. In tower—in E. doorway, of overlapping battens, with strap-hinges, 16th-century. *Font* : octagonal bowl of Purbeck marble, plain octagonal stem and hollow chamfered base, 13th-century. *Font-cover* (Plate, p. 104) : of oak,

octagonal, with moulded edge and strap-work cresting, middle post with curved supports, first half of the 17th century. *Hour-glass stand* (Plate, p. 104) : In nave—on N.E. respond, of wrought-iron with ornamental foliations, 17th-century. *Monument* : In N. aisle—on S. wall, of Henry Bust, parson of the parish, 1624, Margaret (Bardolphe), his wife, and Henry, their son, 1625, alabaster tablet with kneeling figure of man at prayer-desk and son, one shield-of-arms. *Piscinae* : In chancel—with chamfered jambs and two-centred head, semi-circular drain, 13th-century. In N. aisle—in S. wall, with trefoiled ogee head, broken drain, 14th-century. *Pulpit* (Plate, p. 4) : of oak, hexagonal, with arabesque pilasters at angles and arabesque arched panel with jewel impost and base blocks in each face, and panel with similar carving above and below, early 17th-century. *Seating* : In N. aisle—bench with carved popey-heads. In tower—one bench-end and two desk-ends with variously carved popey-heads, 15th or early 16th-century. *Staircase* : In two upper stages of tower—of oak with solid treads, probably 15th-century.

Condition—Good.

Secular :—

a(2). HOUSE, 460 yards W.N.W. of the church, is of two storeys, timber-framed and weather-boarded ; the roofs are thatched. It was built probably early in the 17th century, and has an 18th-century extension on the W. Inside the building the original ceiling-beams are exposed.

Condition—Good.

b(3). NOAK HOUSE, now tenements, 800 yards S.E. of the church, is of two storeys, timber-framed and plastered ; the roofs are tiled. It was built in the 17th century, and has cross-wings at the E. and W. ends. Inside the building are exposed ceiling-beams.

Condition—Poor.

---

98. WEST HANNINGFIELD. (D.b.)

(O.S. 6 in. *(a)*lx. N.E. *(b)*lxi. N.W.)

West Hanningfield is a parish and scattered village 4 m. S. of Chelmsford. The church, the Meeting House and Elm Farm are interesting.

Ecclesiastical :—

b(1). PARISH CHURCH OF SS. MARY AND EDWARD stands E. of the village. The walls are of flint and pebble-rubble and pudding-stone ; the chancel is mostly of brick, and the tower is timber-framed ; the dressings are of limestone and the roofs are covered with slates and lead. The *Nave* is probably of the 12th century, but there is little evidence of this remaining. About 1330 the *South Chapel* and *Aisle* were added. The timber *Belfry* was

WEST HANNINGFIELD *The* PARISH CHURCH

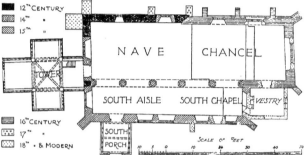

added late in the 15th century, and probably early in the 16th century the *Chancel* was rebuilt and lengthened; the *South Porch* was added about the same time. The church has been restored in modern times and the *South Vestry* added.

The timber belfry is interesting from its cruciform plan.

Architectural Description—The *Chancel* (34 ft. by 20 ft.) has a modern E. window set in the blocking of a larger and earlier window of doubtful date. In the N. wall are two early 16th-century windows of brick, the eastern is of three four-centred lights under a square head with moulded jambs and label ; the western window has a square head and moulded label, but has been fitted with a wooden frame of two lights. In the S. wall is a modern doorway. There is no chancel-arch.

The *Nave* (37½ ft. by 20 ft.) has in the N. wall two 18th-century windows, both with modern wooden frames; the opening of the eastern is of uncertain date; the western has a semi-circular rear-arch probably of the 12th century ; below it is a blocked doorway, probably of the 14th century, with chamfered jambs and two-centred head. The S. arcade is of *c.* 1330 and of five bays, of which one and a half are included in the chancel ; the two-centred arches are of two chamfered orders, and have perhaps been rebuilt at a later date ; the octagonal columns have moulded capitals and bases and the responds have attached half-columns. In the W. wall is a window probably of the 14th century, but fitted with a modern wooden frame ; further S. is a doorway, probably of the 15th century and with moulded jambs and two-centred arch.

The *South Chapel* and *Aisle* (10 ft. wide) has in the E. wall a window, now blocked, the splays and segmental rear-arch are probably of the 14th

century. In the S. wall are four windows of the 14th century with two-centred heads ; the three westernmost have moulded labels with head-stops, and all have 18th-century jambs and modern wooden frames ; between the two easternmost windows is a doorway with hollow-chamfered jambs and segmental-pointed head, made up of reused material ; the 14th-century S. doorway has double chamfered jambs and two-centred arch with a moulded label and head-stops. In the W. wall is a window similar to those in the S. wall but with plastered stops.

The *Belfry* (29 ft. by 24 ft.) is of late 15th-century date and of cross-shaped plan ; the whole structure (Plate, pp. xxxviii–ix) is weather-boarded, and the arms of the cross are of two stages and have low-pitched gabled roofs ; the central portion is carried up one stage higher and finished with an octagonal spire, splayed off at the base. The ground-stage (Plate, pp. xxxviii–ix) of the central portion has curved braces to the cross-beams, forming two-centred arches, and an inserted floor, probably of the 16th or 17th century, at the level of the second stage ; this stage has curved diagonal braces meeting at the centre in a key-block, carved on the soffit with a grotesque face. The timbering of the spire and the studding of the outer walls is modern.

The *South Porch* is timber-framed and of early 16th-century date on 18th-century dwarf brick walls. The outer archway is two-centred. The side walls are each of two bays, each divided into three lights with cinquefoiled heads. The roof has curved braces to the collars and curved wind-braces.

The *Roof* of the nave is ceiled, but has two 15th-century king-post trusses ; the octagonal king-posts have moulded capitals and bases.

Fittings—*Bells* : four, all by Miles Graye, 1676, bell-frame old. *Brasses* and *Indents*. Brasses : In chancel—(1) to John [Clouville or Clonville] and Margerie (Alyngton), his wife, 16th-century, two shields-of-arms and fragments of marginal inscription in marble slab with moulded edge. In S. aisle—(2) of Isabel Clouvill, and John, her son, 1361, half-figure of woman in veiled head-dress and inscription in French, indent of second half-figure. Indents : In chancel—(1) of half-figure of priest and inscription-plate, 15th-century. In S. aisle—(2) of two figures and inscription-plate, 15th-century. *Chest* (Plate, p. xliii) : In nave—long dug-out (8 ft.), heavily iron-bound, lid in two parts with drop-handles, two hasps and money-slot, 13th or 14th-century. *Communion Table* : with heavy turned legs and fluted upper rail with small carved brackets, early 17th-century. *Rails* : with heavy balusters alternately turned and twisted, late 17th-century. *Doors* : In nave—in W. doorway, of feathered battens, with strap-hinges, 15th-century. In S. doorway—of moulded overlapping battens with strap-hinges, oak stock. lock and old drop-handle, 14th or 15th-century- *Floor-slab* : In nave—to John F . . . . , marginal inscription with Tudor rose at each angle, 16th or 17th-century, much worn. *Font* (Plate, pp. xlii–iii) : octagonal bowl, probably cut down and having sunk ornament on faces, moulded lower edge with carved ball-flowers and heads, moulded necking, stem with trellis ornament and roundels, probably all 14th-century ; base of larger font, let into ground, with setting and mouldings for a central and four angle shafts, Purbeck marble, c. 1200. *Glass* : In chancel—in N. window, two small heads of women and a Tudor rose, 16th-century. In S. aisle—in third window, shield-of-arms of Clouville—*two cheverons with five nails on each*, 15th-century. *Panelling* : In S. aisle—round organ—late 16th or early 17th-century panelling. *Piscina* : In S. aisle—in S. wall, with moulded jambs and ogee head, round drain, 14th-century. *Plate* : includes cup and a stand-paten of 1709, the former with the date 1710. *Stair* : In tower—of solid oak balks, probably 16th-century.
Condition—Fairly good, but some cracks in walls.

Secular :—

a(2). THE MEETING HOUSE (Plate, p. 32), formerly known as Fullers, 1¼ m. W.N.W. of the church, is of two storeys with attics. The walls are of plastered timber-framing and the roofs are tiled. It was built in the second half of the 16th century on an L-shaped plan with the wings extending towards the N. and E. and a small central-newel staircase in the angle. In recent years it has been considerably restored and the walls refaced with sham half-timbered work and modern additions made at the back.

The paintings on the walls and roof of the attics in the W. wing are of considerable interest. There are three original chimney-stacks with grouped diagonal shafts, modern at the top ; a few original windows with moulded mullions remain. Inside the building there are two original doorways to the entrance passage with moulded framing, one carved with the initials C. (S ?). There is also reused panelling of late 16th-century date. On the upper floors much of the timber-construction is exposed, and two of the rooms have stone fireplaces with flat four-centred heads. The walls and roof of the two rooms in the attics in the W. wing are decorated with panels painted in brown, black and white enriched with grotesque figures, animals, centaurs, fishes, etc., with borders of conventional and interlacing foliage (Plate, p. 166). In one panel is the date 1615, and there is a shield of Skynner impaling Folkes or Fulke and Bowyer.
Condition—Good.

MONUMENTS (3–10).

The following monuments, unless otherwise described, are of the 17th century and of two storeys, timber-framed and plastered ; the roofs are tiled. Some of the buildings have original chimney-stacks and exposed ceiling-beams.
Condition—Good or fairly good unless noted.

b(3). *Pynning's Farm*, ½ m. S.W. of the church. The walls are partly of brick and the roof is covered with slate. It appears to have been practically rebuilt in the 18th-century except the early 17th-century central chimney-stack, which is of cross-shaped plan and set diagonally.

b(4). *Cottage*, on N. side of road, 720 yards W. of the church, is of timber-framing, partly plastered and partly weather-boarded. It appears to be the wing of a 16th-century house, and has a small modern addition at the back.
Condition—Bad.

a(5). *Compasses Inn*, at cross-roads, 270 yards W.S.W. of (4), is a small rectangular building with modern additions on the N.E. and W.

a(6). *House*, now two tenements, 80 yards S.S.W. of (5), is timber-framed and weather-boarded, and is probably of late 16th-century date. The upper storey projects on the W. front.

a(7). *Slough House Farm*, on S. side of road, 1,500 yards W. of the church, is built on an H-shaped plan with E. and W. cross-wings. The cross-wings are gabled and on the N. front retain their original barge-boards, those to the W. gable being foiled and to the E. gable carved with sunk tracery.

W. side of N. Room.

E. side of S. Room.

WEST HANNINGFIELD: (2). THE MEETING HOUSE (formerly Fullers).
Paintings in Attics of W. Wing; c. 1615.

WEST THURROCK : PARISH CHURCH OF ST. CLEMENT. From the North-West.

*(8). *Kent's Farm*, on E. side of road, 400 yards N.W. of (7), is of timber-framing, partly plastered and partly weather-boarded. It was built probably in the 16th century, and has a cross-wing at the S. end, the upper storey of which projects on the W. front.

*(9). *Elm's Farm* (Plate, pp. xxxiv–v), 1 m. W.N.W. of the church, was built probably in the 16th century on an L-shaped plan with the wings extending towards the W. and N. It was remodelled early in the 17th century, and in the last century the W. bay of the S. wing was destroyed, except for the base of the walls. The *S. Front* is in two bays with projecting gables at the eaves-level, each supported on two brackets carved in the form of grotesque figures. The E. gable has early 17th-century moulded barge-boards with a moulded pendant at the apex, and below each gable is a bay-window with an original moulded brick base. The main and N. chimney-stacks are of the 17th century, and have six and three grouped diagonal shafts respectively. Inside the building the staircase has some early 17th-century flat-shaped balusters, refixed, and there are some others outside the E. doorway. Lying in the garden is a carved figure from the destroyed gable.

*(10). *Hill Farm*, about 1½ m. N.W. of the church, is of one storey with attics. The walls are of weather-boarded timber-framing. It has a cross-wing at the S. end and an 18th-century addition on the N.

---

99. WEST HORNDON. (B.c.)

(O.S. 6 in. lxvii. S.E.)

West Horndon is a parish 3 m. S.E. of Brentwood. It was united to Ingrave, ecclesiastically, in 1712, and the site of the former church is S. of that of the Old Hall.

Secular :—

(1). FOUNDATIONS of brick on the site of the Old Hall about the middle of the parish.

Unclassified :—

(2). MOUND, called "Pigeon Mount," 200 yards W. of (1), is about 100 ft. in diameter and 12 ft. high.
Condition—Good.

(3). MOUNDS, two, 100 yards E. and W. of Thorndon Hall respectively, are probably pieces of landscape-gardening.
Condition—Good.

100. WEST THURROCK. (B.c.)

(O.S. 6 in. lxxxiii. S.W.)

West Thurrock is a parish adjoining Grays Thurrock on the W. The church is interesting.

Ecclesiastical :—

PARISH CHURCH OF ST. CLEMENT (Plates, pp. 147, 167) stands in the S.E. corner of the parish on the N. bank of the Thames. The walls are of flint and ragstone-rubble with dressings of Reigate stone ; parts of the tower are of brick ; the roofs are tiled. The 12th-century church, as shown by excavation in 1912, consisted of an aisleless chancel (conterminous with the later nave) a round nave and a W. porch. The *North* and *South Aisles* were begun c. 1200, the arcades being a little later in date. In the middle of the 13th century a *Chancel* with *North* and *South Chapels* was built to the E. of the pre-existing chancel, which was then converted into part of the nave. In the 14th century the arcades between the chancel and N. and S. chapels were rebuilt and the S. chapel was lengthened. The rebuilding of the chancel-arch followed, and the aisle walls of the nave appear to have been raised about the same time. The circular nave was taken down late in the 15th century and a massive *West Tower* built in the centre of it. In 1640 the tower was repaired. The S. aisle was repaired in 1711, to which date may be assigned the brick buttresses on the S. wall and perhaps the S. doorway ; the top stage of the tower was added or rebuilt in the 18th century. The S. chapel, which is now used as a vestry, was rebuilt late in the 18th or early in the 19th century, and the E. wall of the chancel was largely reconstructed during a recent restoration.

The church is of particular interest as one of few churches in the country that are known to have had a circular nave.

Architectural Description—The *Chancel* (34 ft. by 16½ ft.) has in the E. wall a window, all modern except the two-centred rear-arch and the dressings to the splays, which are of the second half of the 13th century. In the N. wall is a 13th-century single-light window with a trefoiled head ; externally it is repaired with cement. The N. arcade is of early 14th-century date, and of two bays with two-centred arches of two chamfered orders ; the octagonal piers and semi-octagonal responds have moulded capitals and bases. In the E. end of the S. wall is a single-light window similar to the corresponding one in the N. wall but entirely modern externally ; further W. is a 13th-century doorway with a two-centred head ; it was blocked in the 14th century, when the S. chapel was extended ; the S. arcade is similar to the N. arcade. The late 14th-century chancel-arch is built over

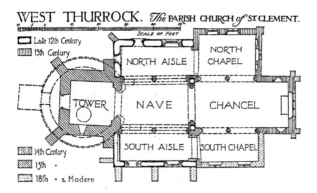

WEST THURROCK. *The* PARISH CHURCH *of* ST CLEMENT.

SCALE OF FEET

☐ Late 12th Century
▥ 15th Century

NORTH AISLE   NORTH CHAPEL

TOWER   NAVE   CHANCEL

▨ 14th Century
▧ 15th .
▦ 18th . & Modern

SOUTH AISLE   SOUTH CHAPEL

the E. wall of the original chancel and is two-centred and of two chamfered orders, the inner being of reused 13th-century stones ; the semi-octagonal responds have moulded capitals and bases ; the greater part of the base to the S. respond has been cut away.

The *North Chapel* (20¾ ft. by 14¾ ft.) has in the E. wall a 13th-century window of two trefoiled lights with a quatrefoil in a two-centred head with a moulded label ; below the window, internally, is a moulded string-course, partly broken away ; a set-back in the wall a few inches above the window marks the line of the original roof. In the N. wall is an early 14th-century window of two trefoiled lights with tracery in a two-centred head ; further W., and set in the lower part of a 13th-century window, of which the quatrefoil remains in the head, is a 14th-century window of two cinquefoiled lights with tracery in a square head ; the hollow-chamfered rear-arch springs from moulded corbels. The archway into the N. aisle is of mid 13th-century date and of one chamfered order ; the N. respond has stop-chamfered angles and a moulded impost, cut off flush with the wall-face on either side ; on the S. the arch springs from à moulded impost carried on two shaped corbels.

The *South Chapel* (21 ft. by 10 ft.) has modern E. and S. walls. The archway to the S. aisle is of the same date and similar detail to the corresponding archway into the N. aisle ; it has been strengthened on the W. by a modern arch, which hides the W. corbel on the N. respond ; the E. corbel is broken away.

The *Nave* (25 ft. by 16¾ ft.) occupies the site of the original chancel, but is slightly wider, the centre lines of the arcades coinciding with the respective outer faces of the side walls. The N. arcade is of early to mid 13th-century date and of two bays with two-centred arches of two chamfered orders springing from a circular column, semi-octagonal E. respond and semi-circular W. respond ; all with moulded capitals and bases ; the E. respond has been partly cut away. The 13th-century S. arcade is similar but somewhat later than the N. arcade, with different detail ; it has possibly been reconstructed in the 14th century, partly with the old material ; the E. respond is semi-circular.

The *North Aisle* (10¼ ft. wide) has in the N. wall a two-light window, all modern except the two-centred rear-arch and some of the dressings to the splays, which are of the 14th century. The N. doorway is of c. 1200, but, with the exception of the chamfered inner order of the two-centred head and the segmental rear-arch, has been rebuilt. In the W. wall is an original window of a single pointed light ; the sill is modern. On the outside face of the W. wall can be seen the level of the original roof.

The *South Aisle* (9½ ft. wide) has in the S. wall a two-light window, all modern except the moulded two-centred rear-arch and the recut dressings to the jambs, which are of the 14th century ; the S. doorway is of the 18th century except for the chamfered splays and segmental rear-arch. In the W. wall, above a set-back at the level of the springing of the S. arcade, is the N. jamb of a blocked window of c. 1200.

The *West Tower* (15½ ft. square) is of three stages with an embattled parapet. The walls are of alternate bands of Reigate stone and knapped flint, except the top stage, which was added in 1640 and is of brick. Internally it is in two storeys, the lower subdivided by a modern gallery. The late 15th-century tower-arch is two-centred and of two chamferéd orders springing from semi-octagonal responds with moulded capitals and mutilated bases, the arch has two modern orders on the W. side. In the S. wall is a window of one trefoiled light. In the W. wall is a late 15th-century doorway with moulded jambs and two-centred head ; above it is a partly restored window of the same date and of two cinquefoiled lights in a square head. The second stáge has in the W. wall a similar window to the one below. The 18th-century bell-chamber has in the E. and S. walls a single, and in the N. and W. walls a two-light window, each with a segmental head. The tower stands partly on and partly within the foundations of the 12th-century round nave, which had an internal diameter of 25 ft. Within the area a round founda- tion, probably of a large font, was found, and there were traces of the former existence of a timber W. porch.

Fittings—*Bells :* three, by John Clifton, 1632. *Brasses* and *Indents.* Brasses : In chancel— (1) of Humphrey Heies, 1584, and his son, 1585, with figures of man and son in civil dress and long punning inscription in Latin ; almost entirely hidden by seating ; (2) to Katherine (Heies), wife of . . . Redinge, 1591, with indent of woman. Indents : under altar—of Nicholas Ferobaud [Dean of Hastings College, *c.* 1315], half-figure of priest with foliated cross under, resting on a beast, marginal inscription in Lombardic capitals. *Coffin :* In N. chapel—under effigy, of Purbeck marble, with shaped head and three drain holes, 13th-century. *Coffin-lids :* In N. chapel—at E. end, (1) of Purbeck marble with raised foliated cross and moulded edge, probably belonging to coffin described above, much defaced, 13th-century ; (2) of Purbeck marble, upper part only, with double hollow-chamfered edge, 13th- century. *Communion Rails :* of oak, with moulded top and bottom rails, turned balusters in shape of small Doric columns with moulded band round middle, thicker balusters at ends and middle, 17th- century. *Doors :* In N. aisle—in N. doorway, of feathered battens, late 15th-century. In S. aisle —in S. doorway, of oak with pointed head and nail-studded battens with moulded ribs on heavy trellis-framing, 15th-century. *Font :* octagonal bowl with moulded edge and under-side, on each face in square panel a quatrefoil containing shields alternating with a rose, a four-leaved flower, Agnus Dei and a sun ; stem panelled and base moulded, 15th-century. *Glass :* In chancel—in head of E. window, miscellaneous fragments including foliage and tabernacle-work, late 13th or early 14th-century ; in N. window a number of quarries, with rosettes and borders, late 13th-century. In N. chapel—in E. window,

in quatrefoil of head, small portion of subject with two men and a woman, in three lower foils, diapered glass with foliated pattern, late 13th or early 14th- century. In second window in N. wall, in traceried head of each light, small flower, *in situ,* 14th- century ; in quatrefoil in head of window, foliated design, late 13th-century. In N. aisle—in N. window, fragments of drapery and crossed hands of a figure, 14th-century. In S. aisle—in S. window, small tonsured head, 14th-century. *Monuments* and *Floor-slabs.* Monuments (Plate, p. 172) : In N. chapel, formerly in S. chapel—(1) of [Sir Christopher Holford, 1608], on modern base, alabaster reclining effigy of man in plate-armour of the period, orna- mented with arabesques, badly mutilated ; (2) of wife of above, on similar base, alabaster figure of woman in close-fitting bodice, farthingale and widow's hood, figure partly defaced. Floor-slabs : In chancel—S. side, (1) to William Clarke, 1630 ; (2) to Elizabeth Tibballs, 1674. *Niches :* In N. chapel—two on either side of E. window with two-centred heads and square jambs, mid 13th- century. *Painting :* In nave—on S. respond of S. arcade, remains of red paint. *Panelling :* In vestry—on E. and S. walls, with fluted frieze, early 17th-century. *Piscinae :* In chancel (Plate, p. xlv)—in S. wall, with trefoiled head and gabled label, two sexfoiled drains with funnel- shaped corbels terminating in knot, stone shelf above, 13th-century. In N. chapel, in E. wall, with hollow-chamfered jambs and pointed tre- foiled head, septfoiled drain and slot above for shelf, 14th-century. *Plate :* includes cup of 1564. *Tiles :* In N. chapel—reset on N. wall numerous pattern-tiles, fleur-de-lis, foliated designs, eagle and a leopard, early 14th-century. *Miscellanea :* In S. aisle—in W. wall, square stone with sunk circular panel with some geometrical pattern in the middle. In N. aisle—above N. doorway, crowned head with curled hair, 14th-century. In W. tower, above W. window, rectangular panel, much worn.

Condition—Fairly good.

— — —

101.. WEST TILBURY. (C.e.)

(O.S. 6 in. [a]lxxxlv. S.W. [b]lxxxix. N.W.)

West Tilbury is a parish and village on the N. side of the Thames, 1½ m. N.E: of Tilbury town. The church and Tilbury Fort are the principal monuments.

Roman :—

(1). Roman tiles, flint blocks, potsherds, bones and oyster-shells were found in the excavations for the Central Dock at Tilbury in 1883. They were scattered over an area of 40 yards or more, lying on a mossy, grass-grown surface 7 ft. below the modern surface (*Arch. Journ.,* XLII, p. 276).

Incineration burials have been found near the ancient ferry at West Tilbury and opposite Low Street Manor Way in Mucking Marsh (*Ib.*, p. 276–7 ; XXIX, p. 187).

On the banks of the Thames, about 1 m. E. of Tilbury Fort, much Roman pottery, including 1st-century 'Samian,' has been picked up ; some of it is now in Grays Thurrock Free Library. It should evidently be connected with the site noted under East Tilbury.

Ecclesiastical :—

(2). PARISH CHURCH OF ST. JAMES stands S. of the village. The walls are of flint and ragstone-rubble with dressings of limestone ; the roofs are tiled. The *Chancel* and *Nave* were built late in the 11th or early in the 12th century. The chancel was lengthened in the 14th century, and the nave was widened towards the N. perhaps at the same period. In 1879 the nave was lengthened towards the W., the *West Tower*, *North Porch* and *Vestry* added, and the church generally much restored and partly rebuilt.

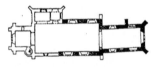

Architectural Description—The *Chancel* (28½ ft. by 14 ft.) has an E. window all modern except the 14th-century splays and rear-arch. In the N. wall are two windows, the eastern of the 14th century with a two-centred rear-arch and now blocked ; the western window is modern ; above the latter is part of a round-headed late 11th or early 12th-century window ; at the W. end this and the S. wall have some herring-bone facing of the same date. In the S. wall are two windows, both modern except for the 14th-century splays and rear-arch of the eastern window. The chancel-arch is modern. The floor of the chancel has been considerably raised.

The *Nave* (38½ ft. by 20½ ft.) has been largely refaced except for some herring-bone masonry in the S. wall similar to that in the chancel. There are no other ancient features except part of a round-headed window of late 11th and early 12th-century date and the reset 13th-century splays and rear-arch of the third window in the S. wall.

The *North Vestry* and *Porch* are modern, but incorporate much old material, including a square-headed window.

Fittings—*Bells* : five—1st by James Bartlet, 1694 ; 3rd by John Wood, 1692 ; 4th by Thomas Bartlet, 1621, 5th probably same date as 3rd.

Brass Indent : In nave—defaced marginal inscription in Lombardic capitals, 14th-century. *Coffin-lid* : In nave—with moulded edge and raised cross, 13th-century. *Piscina* : In chancel—with tre-foiled ogee head, 14th-century. *Recess* : In chancel —in S. wall, with chamfered jambs and two-centred head, date uncertain. *Stoup* : reset in buttress, on N. side of chancel—with two-centred head, bowl destroyed.

Condition—Good, much altered.

Secular :—

b(3). TILBURY FORT, on the river-side on the W. boundary of the parish, was apparently rebuilt in the 17th century, and is of quadrangular form with salient bastions at the angles and a double moat. Considerable lengths of the rampart walls are of 17th-century brick, but the only buildings which are more or less unaltered are the gatehouse and a small chapel.

The *Gatehouse* on the S. side of the fort is of two storeys with an attic ; the walls are of brick, fronted on the S. with stone, and the roofs are tiled. It was built *c.* 1682. The S. front (Frontis-piece) has a wide elliptical arch with moulded imposts and a voluted key-stone ; the spandrels are carved with trophies of arms. Flanking the arch are panelled bays with engaged Ionic columns supporting a continuous entablature, in the middle of which is a panel inscribed "Carolus II Rex Ao. Reg. XXXIV." The upper storey has a panelled centre-piece with a round-headed niche in the middle and flanked by engaged Corinthian columns supporting an entablature and segmental pediment with the royal Stuart arms in the tympanum ; the side-pieces masking the base of the gable are elaborately carved with trophies of cannon and arms. The gate itself is of two folds with strap-hinges, five ranges of panels in each and a wicket in the E. fold. The inner archway (Plate, p. 64) is of brick and semi-circular with panelled spandrels ; the plain jambs and imposts are of stone.

The *Chapel* on the N. side of the fort is a small 17th-century building of brick with a pyramidal tiled roof. In the W. wall is a plain doorway, and in the N. wall is a wide constructional arch springing from the ground-level.

Condition—Fairly good.

MONUMENTS (4–7).

The following monuments, unless otherwise described, are of the 17th century and of two storeys, timber-framed and plastered or weather-boarded ; the roofs are tiled. Some of the buildings have original chimney-stacks and exposed ceiling-beams.

Condition—Good or fairly good, unless otherwise noted.

ᵃ(4). *West Tilbury Hall,* house and barn, N.W. of the church. The *House* is of L-shaped plan with the wings extending towards the S. and W. It has been much altered, and there are modern extensions on the E. Inside the building some of the timber-framing is exposed.

The *Barn,* N.W. of the house, is of the 16th century and of seven bays with a thatched roof of queen-post type.

Condition—Of house, poor.

ᵃ(5). *Marshall's Farm,* house (Plate, p. xxxv), three tenements, 550 yards N. of the church, was built in the 16th century with cross-wings at the N. and S. ends. The upper storey projects at the E. end of both cross-wings. Inside the building the S. wing has a queen-post roof-truss.

ᵃ(6). *Condovers,* house, 650 yards E. of the church, was built in the 15th century with a cross-wing at the N. end and a southern extension of early 17th-century date. The upper storey projects at the E. end of the cross-wing.

Condition—Poor.

ᵃ(7). *Polwicks,* house, 150 yards E.N.E. of (6), has been refronted with modern brick. Under the house is an original cellar of brick.

Unclassified :—

ᵃ(8). EARTHWORKS, S. and W. of the church and Hall, are obscured by gravel diggings and farm buildings. They stand at the edge of an escarpment overlooking the levels towards the river and cover the neck of a promontory. The churchyard stands upon a slight mound suggesting the site of an early camp, whilst a bastion-like projection towards the west gives the work a mediaeval appearance. S.W. of the church is a length of rampart with an internal ditch which turns at right angles towards the N., and appears to be of later date than the other works.

Condition—Imperfect.

---

102. WICKFORD. (D.c.)

(O.S. 6 in. ⁽ᵃ⁾lxix. N.W. ⁽ᵇ⁾lxix. S.W.)

Wickford is a parish and village 4 m. E. of Billericay.

Ecclesiastical :—

ᵃ(1). PARISH CHURCH (dedication unknown) stands E. of the village. It was entirely rebuilt in 1876, but reset in the E. wall are parts of the jambs and mullions of an old window. Reset in the N. wall of the vestry is a 15th-century window of two trefoiled lights.

The *Roof* of the chancel is of late 15th or early 16th-century date and flat-pitched ; it is of two bays with moulded main timbers and joists ; the plates have two rows of carved cresting, and there are carved flower and foliage bosses at the intersections of the purlins and intermediates ; the tie-beams have curved braces with shields in the spandrels.

Fittings—*Bells :* two, both by Kebyll, 15th-century and inscribed, 1st, " Sancta Katerina Ora Pro Nobis " and, 2nd, " Sit Nomen Domini Benedictum." *Font :* octagonal bowl with moulded under-edge and base, plain stem, 15th-century, probably partly recut.

Condition—Rebuilt.

Secular :—

ᵃ(2). HOMESTEAD MOAT, at the Rectory, on opposite side of the road, 100 yards S. of the church.

MONUMENTS (3–7).

The following monuments, unless otherwise described, are of two storeys, timber-framed and weather-boarded, with tiled roofs. Some of the buildings have exposed ceiling-beams and original chimney-stacks.

Condition—Good or fairly good.

ᵃ(3). *House,* now three tenements, on N.W. side of the main road, 800 yards W. N.W. of the church, is of timber-framing partly plastered and partly weather-boarded. It was built in the 17th century on a rectangular plan with a central chimney-stack and has modern additions at the back. The chimney-stack has two diagonal shafts.

ᵇ(4). *Great Broomfields,* house, about 1 m. S.S.W. of the church, is of one storey with attics and is of L-shaped plan with the wings extending towards the S. and E. The S. wing is of 16th-century date and the N.E. wing was added in the following century ; there are modern additions on the E. On the W. front there are two gabled dormers and a gabled porch ; the 17th-century chimney-stack has two diagonal shafts.

ᵃ(5). *Wick Farm,* house and barn, ½ m. S.S.W. of the church. The *House* is of T-shaped plan, the N. cross-wing being of early 17th-century date and the S. wing a later addition.

The *Barn* stands to the S. of the house and is of 17th-century date. It has a S. porch and is divided into five bays by queen-post trusses ; the tie-beams to the two middle trusses have curved braces.

^a(6). *Shot Farm*, house (Plate, pp. xl–i), now two tenements, and barn, 1 m. E. of the church. The *House* was built in the latter half of the 16th century, and is of L-shaped plan with the wings extending towards the S. and W. and has a modern addition on the N. The S. chimney-stack is octagonal and has two octagonal shafts with moulded bases. Inside the building some of the timber-construction is exposed and some of the rooms have open-timber ceilings. On the ground-floor is an original doorway with a four-centred head. In the first floor are two exposed tie-beams, one with curved braces.

The *Barn* (Plate, p. xli), S.W. of the house, is timber-framed and weather-boarded and has a thatched roof. It is of the same date as the house and is divided into six bays by queen-post trusses and has two E. porches with projecting gables.

^a(7). *House*, now two tenements, 60 yards N.E. of (6), is of one storey with attics. It is a fragment of a 15th-century house, and has at the S.W. end a large 17th-century chimney-stack surmounted by four shafts on a cruciform plan set diagonally. In the roof is a king-post truss with cambered tie-beams and curved braces to the king-post.

---

103. WOODHAM FERRERS. (E.b.)

(O.S. 6 in. ^(a)liii. S.E. ^(b)lxi. N.E. ^(c)lxi. S.E.)

Woodham Ferrers is a parish and village 6 m. S.W. of Maldon. The church, Bicknacre Priory and Edwin's Hall are the principal monuments.

Ecclesiastical :—

^b(1). PARISH CHURCH OF ST. MARY stands at the S. end of the village. The walls are of mixed rubble with dressings of limestone ; the roofs are tiled. The *Nave* was built *c.* 1260–70 with N. and S. aisles, and the *Chancel* was rebuilt *c.* 1290. Early in the 14th century the *North* and *South Aisles* were rebuilt. In the 15th century the *South Porch* was built, and late in the same century a W. Tower was added. This tower fell in 1703, was rebuilt in brick in 1715, but has since been removed, and now only the stumps of the side walls remain. The church was repaired in the 19th century, when the E. wall and the E. wall of the S. aisle were largely rebuilt and the *North Vestry* added.

Architectural Description—The *Chancel* (33 ft. by 21½ ft.) has a modern E. window. In the N. wall is a late 13th-century window, modern externally, but with old splays and two-centred

rear-arch ; further E. is a 13th or 14th-century doorway with chamfered jambs and two-centred arch. In the S. wall are three windows, the easternmost is of late 15th-century date and of three cinquefoiled lights in a square head ; the other two windows are uniform with that in the N. wall, but the head of the western is lower ; between them is a modern doorway. The mid 13th-century chancel-arch is two-centred and of two chamfered orders ; the responds have each an attached round shaft with moulded capital and base partly cut away ; the chancel-arch was perhaps reconstructed in the 14th century or at a later date.

The *Nave* (46½ ft. by 22½ ft.) has a N. arcade of *c.* 1260 and of three bays with two-centred arches of two chamfered orders ; the columns and responds have moulded capitals and bases and are alternately octagonal and round ; the E. respond is grooved for a former parclose. The S. arcade is similar to the N., with slightly differing mouldings and the E. column and respond are octagonal and the W. column and respond round. The clearstorey has on each side three windows, modern externally, but with 13th or 14th-century splays.

The *North Aisle* (8¼ ft. wide) has an E. window all modern except the 14th-century splays and rear-arch. In the N. wall are two 14th-century windows, both of two trefoiled ogee lights with tracery in a two-centred head with a moulded label ; further W. is the late 14th-century N. doorway, with modern jambs and moulded two-centred arch ; between the windows is the rood-loft staircase, with 14th-century upper and lower doorways, both with two-centred heads and now blocked. In the S. wall, E. of the arcade is the early 16th-century passage to the later rood-loft, with steps and a four-centred roof composed of stepped arches. The W. window is modern except parts of the 14th-century splays and rear-arch.

The *South Aisle* (8¼ ft. wide average) has an E. window, all modern except the 14th-century splays and rear-arch. In the S. wall are two windows similar to the corresponding windows in the N. aisle but all modern externally ; further W. is the 15th-century S. doorway, with moulded jambs, two-centred arch and label. In the W. wall is a window uniform with the corresponding window in the N. aisle.

The *West Tower* has been destroyed except for the stumps of the side walls where they adjoin the W. front and the two buttresses, which form part of the front and have a moulded plinth and panels of flint-inlay. The late 15th-century tower-arch is two-centred, but only the inner hollow-chamfered order remains in position ; the responds have each one chamfered and two hollow-chamfered orders and an attached shaft with moulded capital and base.

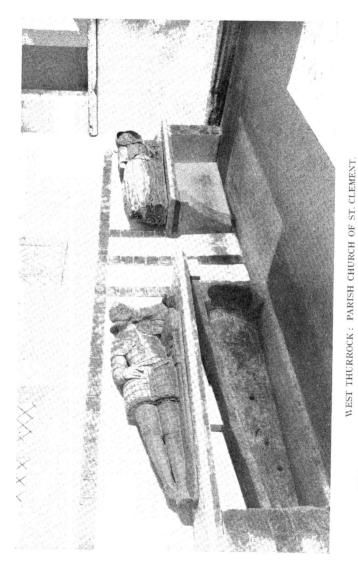

WEST THURROCK: PARISH CHURCH OF ST. CLEMENT.

Effigies in N. Chapel [of Sir Christopher Holford, 1608, and his wife] and Stone Coffin, 13th-century.

WOODHAM FERRERS: BICKNACRE PRIORY; *c.* 1250.
Remains (W. Arch of Crossing) from the South-East.

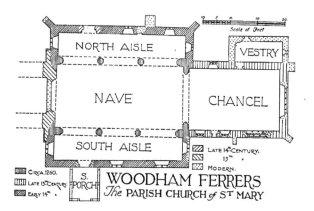

NORTH AISLE

VESTRY

NAVE

CHANCEL

SOUTH AISLE

LATE 14ᵗʰCENTURY.
15ᵗʰ
MODERN.

CIRCA.1260.
LATE 13ᵗʰCENTURY.
EARLY 14ᵗʰ.

S. PORCH

WOODHAM FERRERS
The PARISH CHURCH *of* Sᵀ MARY

Scale of Feet

The *South Porch* is timber-framed and incorporates a few 15th-century posts.

The *Roof* of the chancel is of trussed-rafter type and of uncertain date. The roof of the nave is also of trussed-rafter type with two tie-beams and modern plates. The 14th-century flat pentroof of the N. aisle has moulded main timbers. The roof of the S. aisle is similar, but with chamfered main timbers; it is possibly of the 14th century. The 15th-century roof of the S. porch is of two bays with king-post trusses and moulded wall-plates.

Fittings—*Chest :* In S. aisle—of hutch type, dated 1708. *Door :* In S. doorway—with moulded fillets and frame, planted on, 15th-century. *Font :* plain octagonal bowl with moulded under-edge, 14th-century. *Glass :* In chancel—in S.E. window, two shields of (1) France (ancient) and (2) England, 14th-century, partly patched with other old glass. *Monument* and *Floor-slabs.* Monument (Plate, p. 105) : In chancel—of Cecilie (Willford), wife of Edwin Sandys, Archbishop of York, 1610, erected by her son, Sir Samuel Sandys, 1619, coloured alabaster and black marble wall-monument with kneeling figure of lady at prayer-desk, Corinthian side-columns and entablature, figure of Time on W., back and hood of monument carved as a trellis of flowers and foliage, at top two draped figures supporting lozenge-of-arms, cartouche-of-arms below main figure. *Floor-slabs :* In churchyard—against W. wall of nave (1) to Cecile Sandys, 1610, see monument ; (2) to George Sheillto, with shield-of-arms, late 17th-century. *Niches :* In nave—in E. respond of N. arcade, two, one with a trefoiled

and one with a triangular concave head ; in E. respond and first pier of S. arcade, three, all with trefoiled heads, 15th-century. *Paintings :* In nave—above chancel-arch, large Doom in black and red colour, Christ the Judge in middle seated on a rainbow with angels on right and souls below, hell's mouth in right lower corner, scrolls with black-letter inscriptions, one reading, " Surgite incriminati ad judicium dei," 15th-century ; rough outline of canopies with figures on first column of S. arcade and black outline of head on second column, and traces of foliage on capitals of same arcade ; traces of colour on niches. *Plate :* includes large cup and paten of 1668. *Piscinae :* In chancel—double (Plate, p. xlv), with moulded jambs and trefoiled head, middle pier with moulded capital and base, bases also to jambs, one sexfoiled drain, mid 13th-century. In S. aisle—with pointed head and damaged sexfoiled drain, 14th-century. *Seating :* In chancel—four benches with moulded rails and buttressed standards with carved popey-heads, 15th-century, partly restored. *Sedilia :* In chancel —of three bays with hollow-chamfered jambs, with four-centred heads, horizontal moulded cornice over, early 16th-century. *Stoup :* In S. porch, with segmental head, probably 15th-century.

Condition—Good.

ᵃ(2). BICKNACRE PRIORY, ruins, 2¼ m. N.N.W. of the church. The walls are of iron pudding-stone rubble with some brick ; the dressings are of Reigate and a harder limestone. The priory

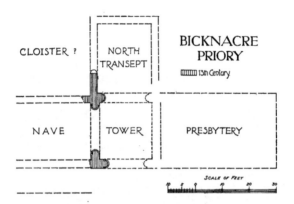

CLOISTER ? NORTH TRANSEPT

BICKNACRE PRIORY

▥ 13th Century.

NAVE TOWER PRESBYTERY

SCALE OF FEET

was founded *c.* 1175 by Maurice Fitz-Geoffrey for Austin canons. The remaining part of the church is apparently of *c.* 1250. The house was always a poor one, and came to an end in 1507 by the death of the last canon.

Architectural Description—The existing remains consist only of the W. arch of the crossing of the church with the adjoining responds of the N. and S. arches. There are doubtful indications in the turf of a chancel extending 65 ft. E. of the existing arch.

The *Crossing* (20 ft. N. to S.) has a W. arch (Plate, p. 173) of *c.* 1250, two-centred and of two chamfered orders, with a relieving-arch immediately above it of alternate bricks and pebbles; the moulded responds have each a large attached round shaft with moulded capitals and base. The former N. and S. arches have similar responds, but the arches have been destroyed; the S. responds have been partly repaired in brick. There are definite indications in the turf of a N. Transept extending about 25 ft. N. of the crossing, but there are no visible traces of the S. arm. W. of the S. arch on the outer face is a heavy corbel for a former roof, indicating the former existence of a S. aisle or chapel on this side communicating with the S. transept without any intermediate arch. Part of a respond has been reset in the remaining part of the W. wall of the N. transept.

The *Nave* (20¼ ft. wide) is represented only by the stumps of the walls on the N. and S. On the N. side is part of the splay of a doorway or window. As there is evidence of an aisle on the S. and none on the N. of the nave, it is probable that the cloister and domestic building lay to the N. of the church.

Condition—Of existing ruins, fairly good.

Secular :—

HOMESTEAD MOATS.

b(3). At Woodham Hall, nearly 1½ m. N.N.W. of the church.

b(4). At Hobclerk's Farm, about ¾ m. N. of the church.

c(5). At Champion's Hall, nearly 1 m. S.S.E. of the church.

b(6). EDWIN'S HALL, house and moat, 1,500 yards E. of the church. The *House* is of three storeys; the walls are of brick and the roofs are tiled. It is said to have been built by Edwin Sandys, Archbishop of York, in the latter part of the 16th century. The original plan no doubt consisted of a central block with cross-wings at the E. and W. ends, but the E. cross-wing has been destroyed. The S. front has an original bay-window to the main block, of two storeys with moulded mullions and transoms; the third storey of the block is lit by three mullioned and transomed windows. Adjoining the W. wing is a two-storeyed porch with an original outer archway of stone with a four-centred head and sunk spandrels. The end of the W. wing has a modern bay-window. Extending further W. is a two-storeyed wing with two original windows. At the back of the house are four original windows and a large original chimney-stack with five shafts, of which the middle one is set diagonally; two gables further W. have moulded barge-boards. Inside the building three rooms are lined with 17th-century panelling, and one room has a panelled overmantel with fluted pilasters. In the second storey are two original stone fireplaces with moulded jambs and flat four-centred heads with carved spandrels;

one fireplace has a panelled and carved frieze above it. The top storey contains some original turned balusters.

The *Moat* surrounds the house with a strong inner enclosure with a weaker enclosure outside it.

Condition—Of house and moat, good.

MONUMENTS (7–11).

The following monuments, unless otherwise described, are of the 17th century and of two storeys, timber-framed and plastered ; the roofs are tiled. Some of the buildings have original chimney-stacks and exposed ceiling-beams.

Condition—Good or fairly good.

^b(7). *House* (Plate, pp. xxxiv–v), three tenements, E. of the churchyard, was built probably in the 16th century and has been refaced with brick. It has a cross-wing at the S. end. The upper storey projects at the E. end of the wing.

^b(8). *House*, N. of (7), has a cross-wing at the S. end and has been partly refaced with brick.

^b(9). *Allenshill Farm*, house, 80 yards N. of the church, has an original chimney-stack with three grouped shafts, set diagonally.

^b(10). *Dyer's Farm*, house, ¾ m. N.N.W. of the church.

^b(11). *Quilter's Farm*, house (Plate, p. 57), ¾ m. W. of (10), has an original chimney-stack with grouped diagonal shafts.

Unclassified :—

^e(12). MOUNDS, two, 1¾ m. S.E. of the church, and within the sea-wall near the head of a creek. They are of irregular shape and resemble the mounds in the parish of Stow Maries. Probably connected with mediaeval salt workings.

Condition—Good.

----

104. WOODHAM MORTIMER. (E.b.)

(O.S. 6 in. ^(a)liii. S.E. ^(b)liii. S.W.)

Woodham Mortimer is a small parish 2 m. S.W. of Maldon. The Hall is the principal monument.

Ecclesiastical :—

^b(1). PARISH CHURCH OF ST. MARGARET stands towards the N.E. side of the parish. The walls are mainly of septaria with some reused freestone in the rubble. The dressings are limestone. The church has been entirely rebuilt except part of the

S. wall of the nave, which is of early 12th-century date.

Architectural Description — The *Chancel* is modern, but incorporates in the S. wall a 15th-century window of one cinquefoiled light, with modern jambs ; further W. are the reset splays and rear-arch of a restored 14th-century window.

The *Nave* has in the S. wall part of the reset splays of a 14th or 15th-century window ; further W. in the 12th-century wall is the S. doorway, modern externally, but with a round 12th-century rear-arch having remains of red colour on the plastered soffit ; further W. is a 12th-century window of one round-headed light, but much restored. In the W. wall are the reset splays of a 14th-century window.

The North Chapel, Vestry, N. Aisle and S. porch are entirely modern.

Fittings—*Bells* : three ; 1st by Miles Graye, 1657 ; 2nd by John Danyell, 15th-century and inscribed " Johannes Est Nomen Ejus " ; 3rd by Miles Graye, 1612. *Brass* : In chancel—of Dorothy, daughter of Giles Alleine, 1584, figure with head missing, inscription beginning—" A little impe here buried is " and shield-of-arms. *Communion Table* : with carved top-rail, shaped brackets and turned legs, early 17th-century, made up with modern work. *Floor-slab* : In N. chapel—against E. wall, to Nathaniel Smith, M.A., rector of the parish, 1693. *Font* : round bowl, octagonal stem with ogee-headed panels, moulded base, stem and base late 15th-century, bowl earlier. *Panelling* : Incorporated in pulpit and organ-case, pieces of carved panels and rails, early 17th-century. *Piscina* : In chancel—modern recess, plain cushion capital with drain of pillar-piscina, 12th-century. *Plate* : includes a cup without marks, but with an Elizabethan stem and a bowl probably of later date.

Condition—Good, mostly rebuilt.

Secular :—

^b(2). WOODHAM MORTIMER HALL, E. of the church, is of three storeys ; the walls are mostly of brick, but partly of plastered timber-framing ; the roofs are tiled. The timber-framed wing at the back is probably of the 16th century. The front block, of brick, was added early in the 17th century, and has four curvilinear ' Dutch ' gables, one of which crowns a small projecting bay. At the back is an original brick gable rising above the older block and containing a blocked window of three lights with moulded mullions. The two chimney-stacks, at the ends of the front block, have modern diagonal shafts. Inside the back wing are some exposed ceiling-beams, and there is a central purlin in the roof. There are also some old battened doors.

Condition—Good.

ᵃ(3). Hill Farm, house, about ½ m. S.W. of the church, is of two storeys, timber-framed and plastered; the roofs are tiled. It was built probably early in the 17th century, and the upper storey projects at the N. end.
Condition—Good.

ᵃ(4). Nursery Farm, house, two tenements, 700 yards W. of (3), is of two storeys, timber-framed and plastered; the roofs are tiled. It was built late in the 16th or early in the 17th century, and has an original chimney-stack (Plate, p. 57) with two tall octagonal shafts. Inside the building there are two late 17th or early 18th-century fireplaces with pilasters and panelled friezes; one has a roughly executed painting of the Fire of London.
Condition—Good, much altered.

ᵃ(5). Tyndales, house, 1,100 yards W. of (4), is of two storeys, timber-framed and plastered and partly refaced with modern brick; the roofs are tiled. It was built in the 16th century, and has an original chimney-stack (Plate, p. 57) with a crow-stepped offset and three diagonal shafts. The stack at the W. end has an original base.
Condition—Good, much altered.

GREAT BADDOW CHURCH,
Corbel and capital, N. arcade,
13th-century.

ESSEX ARMORIAL.

THE family arms given are those that occur in the four volumes of the Essex Inventory dating from before the year 1550. It is thought that the inclusion of this Essex "Armorial" will be of some interest to students, the blazon given in each case being the usual recognized form, though variations in some instances will be found under the individual monuments. The arms (before 1550) of certain well-known families not blazoned (although identified) in the Inventories are here added for the sake of completeness.

E. E. DORLING.

(D') ADELEIGH (?)—*checky or and sable.*
ANLE, or INLE (? = DE LISLE)—*or a fesse between two cheverons sable.*
ARCHDEACON—*argent three cheverons sable with a label gules.*
ARDALL, ·E—*argent a cheveron between three stars gules.*
ARDERNE—*paly or and gules a chief argent with three lozenges gules therein on the middle lozenge a chess-rook or.*
ARUNDEL—*sable six swallows argent.*
    See also Fitzalan, Earl of Arundel.
ASPALL—*azure three cheverons or.*
AYLMER—*argent a cross sable between four Cornish choughs.*
AYLOFFE—*sable a lion or collared gules between three crosses formy or.*
BADLESMERE—*argent a fesse between two gemel-bars gules.*
BALDRY—*sable a cheveron or between three demi-griffons ermine with three martlets gu es on the cheveron.*
BARDOLF—*azure three cinqfoils or.*
    See also Phelips, Lord Bardolf.
BARDWELL—*gules a leaping goat argent horned or.*
BARETT—*barry of four argent and gules parted and countercoloured.*
BATEMAN—*sable six sleeping lions argent.*
BAUD—*gules three cheverons argent.*
BAYNARD—*gules three cheverons ermine with a label of five points or.*
BEAUCHAMP (of Bedford)—*quarterly or and gules a bend sable.*
BEAUMONT—*azure flory and a lion or.*
BEDELL (?)—*argent a cheveron between three molets gules.*
BEELEIGH ABBEY—*argent six fleurs-de-lis azure.*
BELHOUSE—*argent crusily sable with three lions gules.*
BENDISH—*argent a cheveron sable between three rams' heads razed azure.*
BERDEFIELD—*argent a bend azure with three fleurs-de-lis or thereon.*
BERNARD—*argent a bear rampant sable muzzled or.*
BERNERS—*quarterly or and vert with a crescent for difference.*
BIGWOOD—*argent a chief gules with two crescents or therein.*
BOHUN (of Hereford)—*azure a bend argent cotised or between six lions or.*
BOHUN (of Northampton)—*as Bohun of Hereford with three molets gules on the bend.*
BOLEBEC—*vert a lion argent.*
BORGATE—*paly argent and sable.*
BORROW—*azure three fleurs-de-lis ermine with a crescent for difference.*
BOURCHIER—*argent a cross engrailed gules between four water-bougets sable.*
BOURGUYLON—*quarterly or and gules a bend sable charged with three rings or.*
BOUTETORT—*or a saltire engrailed sable.*
BOVILL—*quarterly or and sable a crescent for difference.*
BRAY—*argent a cheveron between three roundels sable with a border engrailed gules.*
BRAYBROKE, ROBERT, Bishop of London—*argent seven voided lozenges and a border gules.*
BRAYBROOK—*argent six voided lozenges gules.*
BRETON—*azure two cheverons or with two molets or in chief.*
BRIANZON (?)—*gyronny of twelve pieces with a bend over all.*
BRIDGES, or BRUGES—*argent on a cross sable a leopard's head or.*
BROTHERTON, THOMAS OF—*England with a label argent.*
BROUGHTON—*argent a cheveron between three molets gules.*
BROWNE—*azure a cheveron between three scallops or a border gules.*
BROWNE (of Beechworth)—*sable three lions passant in bend between two double cotises argent.*
BRUGES—*see* Bridges, above.
BRUYN—*azure a mill-rind cross or.*
BURGH, DE (Earl of Ulster)—*or a cross gules.*
BURLEY—*gules two bars gobony argent and azure.*
BURNELL, or LOVELL—*argent a lion sable with a golden crown in a border azure.*
BUTLER—*azure a cheveron between three covered cups or with a crescent for difference.*
BUTLER (Earl of Ormonde)—*or a chief indented azure.*
CANTERBURY, ARCHBISHOPRIC OF—*azure a cross-staff argent with its cross or and over all a pall argent charged with four crosses formy fitchy sable.*
CARMINOW—*azure a bend or with a label gules for difference.*

M

CHANCEAUX—*argent a cheveron between three rings gules.*
CHIDEOCK—*gules a scutcheon in an orle of martlets argent.*
CLARE—*or three cheverons gules.*
CLOPTON—*sable a bend ermine between two cotises dancetty or.*
CLOVILLE, or CLOUVILLE—*argent two cheverons sable powdered with cloves or.*
COBHAM (of Cobham)—*gules a cheveron or with three lions sable thereon.*
COBHAM (of Sterborough)—*gules a cheveron or with three stars sable thereon.*
COGGESHALL—*argent a cross between four scallops sable.*
COLBROKE—*sable a lion argent and over all a fesse or with three crosses formy fitchy sable thereon.*
COLT, -E—*argent a fesse azure between three galloping colts sable.*
COMYN (of Badenoch)—*azure three sheaves of cummin or.*
CORNEY—*argent a cheveron between three hunting-horns sable with a ring for difference.*
COURTENAY (Archbishop of Canterbury)—*or three roundels gules and a label azure charged for difference with three mitres or.*
CROSBY—*sable a cheveron ermine between three rams argent.*
CUTTE, -S—*argent a bend engrailed sable with three roundels argent thereon.*
DANET—*sable sprinkled with drops argent a quarter ermine.*
DARCY—(a) *argent three cinqfoils gules.*
　　„　　(b) *argent a fesse engrailed between three cinqfoils gules.*
DE LA POLE—*see* Pole, *below.*
DE BURGH—*see* Burgh, *above.*
DELAMORE—*argent six martlets sable.*
DEYNCOURT—*argent billetty and a fesse dancetty sable.*
DINELEY—*argent a fesse and in chief a molet between two roundels all sable.*
DOREWARD, DORWARD, or DURWARD—*ermine a cheveron sable with three crescents or thereon.*
DUNMOW PRIORY—*sable a cross argent between four molets or.*
ELDERBEKE—*gules three cheverons ermine.*
ELY, SEE OF—*gules three crowns or.*
ENGLOWES—*argent a cheveron sable between three billets ermine.*
EREBY—*argent fretty and a quarter sable.*
ESMERTON—*argent a bend cotised sable with three molets argent on the bend.*
EVESHAM ABBEY—*azure a chain with a padloch cheveronwise between three mitres argent.*
FASTOLF—*quarterly or and azure a bend gules with three crosses crosslet argent thereon.*
FELTON—*gules two lions passant ermine crowned or with a molet for difference.*
FELTON (of Playford)—*or a bend azure cotised gules with three roundels argent on the bend.*
FERMOR, or FERMOUR—*argent a fesse sable between three lions' heads razed gules with three anchors or on the fesse.*
FIENNES—*azure three lions or.*
FITZ BARNARD—*vair a chief gules with two pierced molets or therein.*
FITZ LANGLEY—*argent a fesse between three oak-leaves vert.*
FITZ LEWES—*sable a cheveron between three trefoils argent.*
FITZ OTES—*bendy or and azure a quarter ermine.*
FITZ RALPH—*or three cheverons gules each charged with three fleurs-de-lis argent.*
FITZ WARINE—*quarterly fessewise indented argent and gules.*
FITZALAN (Earl of Arundel)—*gules a lion or.*
FITZWALTER—*or a fesse between two cheverons gules.*
FITZWILLIAM—*lozengy argent and gules a border azure bezanty.*
FLAMBERT—*gules a cheveron engrailed argent charged with three dolphins vert.*
FOX—*party vert and sable a cross potent argent.*
FYNDORNE—*argent a cheveron between three crosses formy fitchy sable.*
GENEVILE, DE—*azure three open horse-brays or a chief ermine with a demi-lion gules therein.*
GERNON—(a) *pily wavy argent and gules.*
　　„　　(b) *argent three piles wavy gules.*
GOSHALM (?)—*azure crusilly or a cross argent.*
GREENE, or GRENE—*gules a lion parted fessewise argent and sable crowned or.*
GREGORY, ST.—*or three bend gules a chief or with a host between two lions gules face to face.*
GRENVILLE—*vert a cross argent with five roundels gules thereon.*
GREVILLE—*sable a cross engrailed and a border engrailed or with five roundels sable on the cross.*
GREY (of Wilton)—*barry argent and azure a label of five points gules.*
HARPER—*argent a lion gules and a border engrailed sable with a molet on the lion for difference.*
HARSICKE—*argent a chief indented sable.*
HARTISHORN—*azure a cheveron between three harts' heads cabossed argent.*
HAWKWOOD—*argent a cheveron sable with three scallops argent thereon.*
HEATH—*argent three roundels sable each charged with a crosslet argent.*
HELION—*gules fretty argent a fesse or.*
HEVENINGHAM—*quarterly or and gules a border engrailed sable charged with eight scallops argent and a martlet sable for difference.*
HOLLAND—*azure flory and a leopard rampant argent.*
HORNBY—*argent three bugle-horns stringed gules.*
HOWARD—*gules a bend between six crosslets fitchy argent.*
HUNTINGDON—*argent fretty sable a chief gules with three molets or therein.*
INLE—*see* Anle, *above.*
KILLINGMARSH—*party fessewise ermine and ermines a lion countercoloured.*
KIRKEBY—*azure six lions argent and a quarter or with a molet gules therein.*
LANGLEY—*paly argent and vert.*
LATHAM, LATHOM, or LATHUM (of North Ockendon)—*or a chief indented azure charged with three roundels argent within a border gobony ermine and azure.*

LEVENTHORPE—*argent a bend gobony gules and sable cotised gules.*
LILLING—*gules three fishes swimming within a border engrailed argent.*
LISLE, ARTHUR PLANTAGENET, VISCOUNT—*France and England quarterly quartering de Burgh and Mortimer with a baston sinister azure over all.*
LOVAINE—*gules billetty and a fesse or.*
LOVELL—*see Burnell above.*
LUCY—*gules crusily and three luces argent.*
MACWILLIAM—*party bendwise argent and gules three roses countercoloured.*
MARNEY—*gules a leopard rampant argent.*
MARTEL—*gules three hammers or handles argent.*
MONOX—*argent a cheveron sable between three oak leaves vert with three bezants on the cheveron and a chie' gules with a martlet between two anchors argent therein.*
MONTAGU—*argent a fesse indented of three points gules.*
MONTCHENSY—*barry of ten azure and argent.*
MONTHERMER—*or an eagle vert.*
MORTIMER—*barry or and azure a scutcheon argent a chief or with two pales and three gyrons azure therein.*
MOUNTFORT—*bendy or and azure a border gules.*
NORBURGH—*gules a chief ermine.*
NORRIS—*argent a cheveron between three falcons' heads razed sable.*
NORTHWOOD—*ermine a cross engrailed gules.*
  ,,   (of Shalford)—*Northwood with a boar's head sable in the quarter.*
PAGENHAM—*quarterly or and gules.*
PARR, KATHERINE—*argent two bars azure and a border engrailed sable quartered with the augmentation or on a pile gules three roses of York between six of Lancaster.*
PERVENT—*gules three crescents argent.*
PEVERELL—*vairy azure and or.*
PEYTON—*sable a cross engrailed or with a molet argent in the quarter.*
PHELIPS, LORD BARDOLF—*quarterly argent and gules with an eagle sable in the quarter.*
PICOT (?)—*sable billetty or a griffon argent.*
POLE, DE LA—*azure two bars wavy or.*
POWLET—*sable three swords pilewise argent hilts or.*
POYNINGS—*barry or and vert a bend gules.*
POYNTZ—*barry of eight gules and or with a molet sable for difference.*
PRAYERS—*gules a bend argent cotised or.*
PYRTON—*ermine a cheveron engrailed azure with three leopards' heads or thereon.*
RADCLIFFE—*argent a bend engrailed sable.*
RATISDON—*azure six scallops argent.*
RAYMOND (of Hunsdon)—*sable a cheveron argent between three eagles argent and a chief argent with three martlets sable therein.*
ROBERTS—*argent three pheons sable a chief sable with a running greyhound argent therein collared gules.*
ROCHFORD—*quarterly or and gules a border engrailed sable.*
ROKELL—*gules a fesse indented ermine between three martlets argent.*
ROLF—*argent a raven sable.*
ROOS—*gules three lions argent (crowned azure ?).*
SACKVILLE—*quarterly or and gules a bend vair.*
ST. OSYTH ABBEY (later arms)—*parted cheveronwise in chief a ring between a mitre and a crozier.*
SAMFORD—*barry wavy argent and azure.*
SCALES—*gules six scallops or.*
SCARGILE—*ermine a saltire engrailed gules with a fleur-de-lis or for difference.*
SCOTT (of Rotherfield)—*party indented argent and sable a saltire countercoloured.*
SCROPE—*azure a bend or with a crescent for difference.*
SERGEAUX—*argent a saltire sable between twelve cherries gules.*
SEYMOUR, JANE—*quarterly : 1 and 4, or on a pile gules between six fleurs-de-lis azure three leopards of England ; 2 and 3, gules a pair of wings or.*
SHAW, or SHAA—*argent a cheveron between three lozenges ermines.*
SHELDON—*azure a cross or.*
SIBLES—*gyronny or and azure four martlets countercoloured.*
SKELTON—*azure a fesse between three fleurs-de-lis or.*
SPELMAN—*sable powdered with roundels argent and two flanches argent.*
STAFFORD—*or a cheveron gules.*
STAFFORD, ANNE, COUNTESS OF (daughter of Thomas of Woodstock)—*Stafford impaling France (modern) quartering England and Bohun all within a border argent.*
STANYE—*argent a bend cotised sable.*
STERNE (of Essendon)—*or a cheveron sable between three crosses paty sable.*
SULYARD—*argent a cheveron gules between three pheons reversed sable.*
SUTTON—*or three cheverons sable.*
SWINBURNE, or SWYNBORNE—*gules crusily and three boars' heads argent.*
TEY—*argent a fesse between three martlets in the chief and a cheveron in the foot azure with a crescent for difference.*
THOMAS—*sable three left-hand gauntlets argent.* (Gunter borne by Thomas.)
TILTY ABBEY—*argent a cross gules with five fleurs-de-lis or thereon.* (N.B.—These are also the arms of Duresme of Essex, temp. Edward I.)
TIPTOFT—*argent a saltire engrailed gules.*
TUNSTALL (Bishop of London)—*sable three combs argent.*
TRUSBUT—*gyronny azure and ermine.*
TRUSSELL—*argent fretty gules with bezants at the crossings of the fret.*

TYRRELL, or TYRELL—*argent two cheverons azure and an engrailed border gules.*
UFFORD—*sable a cross engrailed or.*
URSWIK, or URSWYK—*argent on a bend sable three lozenges argent each charged with a saltire gules.*
VALOINES—*paly wavy argent and gules.*
VENABLES—*azure two bars argent.*
VERE—*quarterly gules and or with a molet argent in the quarter.*
WAKE—*or two bars gules with three roundels gules in the chief.*
WAKERING, JOHN, Bishop of Norwich (1416–1425)—*azure a pelican or in chief a mitre.*
WALDEGRAVE—*party argent and gules with a border gules.*
WALDEN—*sable two bars with three cinqfoils argent in the chief.*
WALDEN ABBEY—*azure a bend argent cotised or between two molets or with three scallops argent on the bend.*
WARREN—*checky or and azure a border engrailed argent.*
WARENNE (Earl of Surrey)—*checky or and azure.*
WELBECK—*argent a cheveron gules between three lozenges sable with three martlets or on the cheveron.*
WENTWORTH—*sable a cheveron between three leopards' heads or.*
WESTON—*argent a fesse sable and a border engrailed gules.*
WILFORD—*party or and gules a cheveron between three leopards' heads with three crescents on the cheveron all countercoloured.*
WINGFIELD—*argent a bend gules with three pairs of wings argent on the bend.*
WINSLOW—*ermine a cheveron engrailed ermines.*
WISEMAN—*sable a cheveron ermine between three coronels argent.*
WOLLEY—*vert a fleur-de-lis or between two wool-packs argent with two flanches argent each with a wolf azure therein.*
WOODHALL—*argent a mill-rind cross gules.*

MASONS' MARKS IN ESSEX.

THE Masons' marks shown below come from various parts of the County. They are often found on 12th-century masonry but none have been observed in Essex on work earlier than the 14th century, and these are not numerous. They are common in 15th-century work and are cut on the surfaces of responds, piers, soffits, and often on the moulded faces themselves. An interesting group at High Easter includes a master mark (fig. 4) on practically all of the stones of the N. arcade, accompanied by a variety of secondary marks (fig. 5), perhaps those of the working masons. The more complicated marks—such as figs. 9, 11, 16, 29, etc. —are possibly only developments of earlier marks, each successor to the use of a mark adding a line or two to distinguish it from that of his predecessor.

No. of Illustration.	Name of Church.				Part of Structure on which found.	Date of Part of Structure on which found.
1	LITTLE HORKESLEY	..	..	..	Tower Arch and N. splay of W. window in Aisle	c. 1340.
2	FORDHAM	..	..	..	Chancel arch and arcade voussoirs	Mid 14th-century.
3	ASHELDHAM	..	..	..	Arch of N. doorway in Nave	14th-century.
4	HIGH EASTER	..	..	..	N. arcade of Nave (principal mark)	c. 1400.
5	,, ,,	..	..	..	,, ,, (other marks)	,,

MASONS' MARKS IN ESSEX—*cont.*

No. of Illus-tration.	Name of Church.	Part of Structure on which found.	Date of Part of Structure on which found.
6	BARKING (ST. MARGARET'S)	Chancel. S. arcade, E. arch	Early 15th-century.
7	,, ,,	,, ,, W. arch	,, ,,
8	,, ,,	,, ,, W. respond	,, ,,
9	CHELMSFORD (CATHEDRAL)	S. Chapel. W. arch into S. Aisle	15th-century.
	MALDON (ALL SAINTS')	Chancel. S. arcade	,,
	COLCHESTER (ST. PETER'S)	Arcades	,,
	WITHAM	N. arch of Chancel	Late 15th-century.
10	BARKING (ST. MARGARET'S)	Nave. S. arcade	15th-century.
11	GREAT DUNMOW	Nave. N. wall, E. window	,,
12	BARKING (ST. MARGARET'S)	Nave. S. arcade	,,
13	MALDON (ALL SAINTS')	Chancel. N. wall arcade	Late 15th-century.
	ROCHFORD	Doorway to Rood-loft and Tower Stair-turret	15th-century.
	PITSEA	E. doorway to Tower	Early 16th-century.
14	ROCHFORD	Doorway to Rood-loft and Tower Stair-turret	15th-century.
	S. BENFLEET	S. arcade	,,
	CANEWDON	S. doorway	Early 16th-century.
	CORRINGHAM	N. arcade	,, ,,
	PAGLESHAM	S. doorway	,, ,,
	RETTENDON	Nave. N. arcade	Late 15th-century.
15	RUNWELL	Tower arch	,, ,,
16	WEST HAM	W. respond and on voussoirs of S. arcade	*c.* 1400.
17	CHELMSFORD (CATHEDRAL)	Chancel. S. arcade	*c.* 1420-30.
	RUNWELL	Tower arch	Late 15th-century.
	PAGLESHAM	N. doorway	Early 16th-century.
18	RETTENDON	Nave. N. arcade	Late 15th-century.
	S. OCKENDON	N. arcade	15th-century.
	PAGLESHAM	Tower arch and W. doorway	Early 16th-century.
19	S. OCKENDON	N. arcade	15th-century.
20	RETTENDON	Door to Vestry, N. wall of Chancel	Late 15th-century.
21	,,	Archway to N. Chapel	,, ,,
22	,,	Nave. N. arcade	,, ,,
23	TERLING	Nave. S. arcade	15th-century.
	WITHAM	Outer order of S. arcade of Chancel	Late 15th-century.
24	GREAT COGGESHALL	All arcades	15th-century.
25	ROCHFORD	Nave arcades	,,
26	DEDHAM	Arcade piers, doors and window jambs	*c.* 1500.
27	WITHAM	W. arch of S. Chapel and W. arch of N. Chapel	Late 15th-century.
28	PAGLESHAM	Tower arch, N. and S. doorways	Early 16th-century.
29	LITTLE TOTHAM	Tower Arch	16th-century.
30	WITHAM	Voussoirs of S. arcade of Chancel	Late 15th-century.

J. W. BLOE.

MOULDINGS IN ESSEX.

THE sections of stone mouldings shown on the two following pages are but a few of the outlines selected from the Commission's records, and while not intended to be fully representative of the wealth of detail in the County it is hoped that they may serve as part evidence for the dates given and incidentally may be useful as a guide to the student of architecture.

They are drawn to a uniform scale and have been arranged approximately in chronological order following the dates assigned to them in the Commission's Reports. Surface decoration is indicated in only a few cases. The examples are all taken from parish churches excepting those from Waltham Abbey, Little Dunmow Priory, and Beeleigh Abbey.

J. W. BLOE.

183

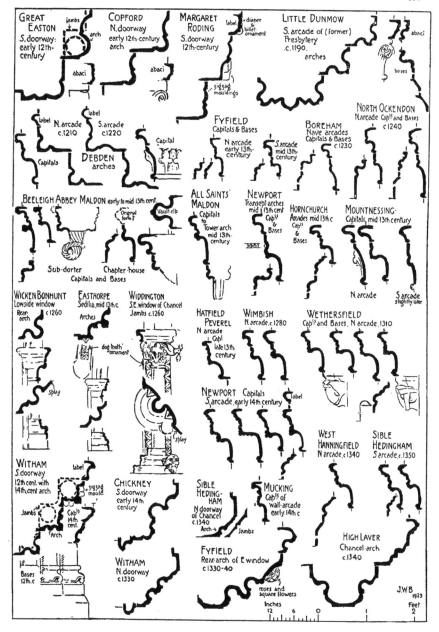

GREAT EASTON
S. doorway:
early 12th century

jambs
arch

abaci

COPFORD
N. doorway,
early 12th-century
arch

abaci

MARGARET RODING
S. doorway
12th-century

label
diaper & billet ornament

zigzag mouldings

LITTLE DUNMOW
S. arcade of (former) Presbytery .c.1190.
arches

abaci

bases

NORTH OCKENDON
N arcade Cap.ll and Bases
c.1240

label
N. arcade
c.1210

label
S. arcade
c.1220

Capital

DEBDEN
arches

Capitals

FYFIELD
Capitals & Bases

N arcade
early 13th century

S. arcade
mid 13th century

BOREHAM
Nave arcades
Capitals & Bases
c.1230

BEELEIGH ABBEY MALDON early to mid 13th cent.

Original form?

Vault-rib

Sub-dorter
Capitals and Bases

Chapter-house
Capitals and Bases

ALL SAINTS MALDON
Capitals
to
Tower arch
mid 13th century

NEWPORT
Transept-arches
mid 13th cent
Cap.ll & Bases

HORNCHURCH
Arcades mid 13th c
Cap.ls & Bases

MOUNTNESSING.
Capitals, mid 13th century

N. arcade

S. arcade
slightly later

WICKEN BONHUNT
Lowside window
Rear-arch
c.1260

splay

EASTHORPE
Sedilia, mid 13th c.
Arches

dog-tooth ornament

WIDDINGTON
S.E. window of Chancel
Jambs c.1260

splay

HATFIELD PEVEREL
N arcade
Cap!
late 13th century

WIMBISH
N arcade, c.1280

WETHERSFIELD
Cap.ls and Bases, N arcade, 1310

NEWPORT Capitals
S. arcade, early 14th century

label

WEST HANNINGFIELD
N arcade, c.1340

SIBLE HEDINGHAM
S arcade, c.1350

WITHAM
S. doorway
12th cent. with
14th cent arch

label
zigzag mould

Jambs

Cap.ls
14th cent.

Arch

Bases
12th c

CHICKNEY
S. doorway
early 14th century

WITHAM
N. doorway
c.1330

SIBLE-HEDING-HAM
N doorway of Chancel
c.1340
Arch
Jambs

MUCKING
Cap.ls of wall-arcade
early 14th c

FYFIELD
Rear arch of E window
c.1330-40

roses and square flowers

HIGH LAVER
Chancel-arch
c.1340

J.W.B.
1923

Inches
12   6   0
Feet
2

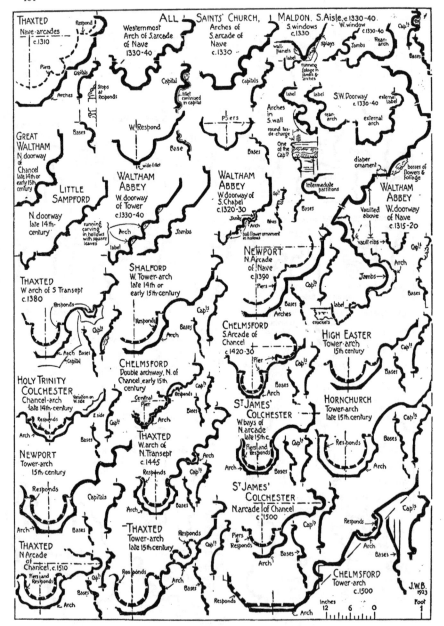

LITTLE BADDOW: PARISH CHURCH OF ST. MARY THE VIRGIN.

Wall Painting in Nave of St. Christopher ; 15th-century (discovered 1922).

ADDENDA ET CORRIGENDA.

THE following list of Addenda and Corrigenda has been divided into its appropriate volumes for greater convenience of reference.

The Addenda consist of descriptions of such monuments as have been inadvertently omitted from the inventories already published and of further particulars (which have transpired since publication) concerning monuments already described.

With regard to the Corrigenda, the Commission is fortunate in that its labours, in one direction, have coincided with those of the Diocesan Committee on Church Plate. The investigation of this subject is one of considerable difficulty, from the frequent effacement or semi-effacement of the hall-marks, from the comparative difficulty of access, and from the impossibility of ensuring by personal investigation that the tally is complete. With regard to the last two disabilities, the Diocesan Committee has perhaps had greater opportunities than the Commission and it has been thought wise therefore to accept, in general, their conclusions (where these differed from these of the Commission's investigators) as the results of a longer, closer and more detailed investigation of the subject than was possible in the case of the Commission.

In the Corrigenda the reference letters refer to the column of the page referred to, and the number following to the number of the line from the head of the page.

VOL. I.

p. xxvii, Illustration — Saffron Walden (136) : for " Clapton's " read " Cloptons."

p. xxxii, 29 : delete reference to Great Saling cup and paten.

Ashdon—p. 7 (a) 31 : for " Thomas " read " Richard."

p. 7 (a) 32 : for " Ann " read " Grace."

p. 7 (a) 35 : for " Swynford " read " Borgate."

Broxted—(5) *Wood Farm :* Recent alterations to the interior of the building revealed a wide fireplace in one of the ground-floor rooms with a small triangular-headed recess in the brickwork at the back and an old wooden chimney-seat on one side. Two other rooms were found to have original brick fireplaces, one with moulded, the other with chamfered jambs and both with four-centred heads. On the upper surface of the wall opposite the former fireplace, below the later plaster, a band of elaborate pargeting was discovered. It is divided horizontally by narrow ribs into three rows of panels ; the top and bottom rows are enriched with sprays of foliage with arms, etc., and the middle with panels of scroll-work alternating with large two-handled vases of flowers in high relief.

Bulmer—(1) *Parish Church*—Plate : add cup of 1632 and stand-paten of 1690, given in 1841.

Castle Hedingham—p. 50 (b) 38 : for " Clare " read " Archdeacon."

p. 50 (b) 41 : for " Fitzhamon " read " Bolebec."

Clavering—p. 69 (b) 49 : for " Seree " read " Serle."

Eisenham—p. 83 (b) 31 : delete alms-dish.

Great Easton—p. 126 (a) 21 : for " Hall " read " Hull."

Great Maplestead—(1) *Parish Church*—Coffin-lid : fragment of, recently found at Monks Lodge and now replaced in church, slightly coped with broad central filet, with interlacing knot-ornament on the side, 11th-century, probably pre-Conquest.

p. 129 (a) 21 : delete " except the E. window, which is probably of the 12th century."

p. 129 (a) 33 : for " both " read " the eastern."

Great Saling—p. 133 (a) 1 : for " 1559 " read " 1573."

Great Sampford—p. 136 (a) 19 : for " Laud " read " Land."

Halstead Urban—The Chapel of Adams' Brewery in Trinity Street nearly ¼ mile W.S.W. of the parish church contains the following late 17th-century fittings from the destroyed church of All Hallows the Great, Thames Street, London. *Font :* of white marble with baluster stem and moulded and reeded bowl ; carved oak *Cover* of octagonal form with ogee capping ; *Reredos* with two round-headed panels, the

HALSTEAD URBAN—*cont.*
whole flanked by Corinthian columns supporting an entablature, broken pediment and three urns and two Corinthian columns flanking the chancel-arch. There is also an oak *Communion-rail* with twisted balusters, said to have come from St. George's Church, Deal.

Little Bardfield—p. 171 (b) 8 : for " Laud " read " Land."

Little Chesterford—(1) *Parish Church*—Plate : add cup and cover-paten of 1630.

Little Maplestead—*Cottage* at Pearmans Hill, ¾ m. S.W. of the church, is of two storeys, timber-framed and plastered. It was built in the 16th century and repaired by one Thomas Porter early in the 18th century. His initials, T.P., and the date 1703 appear over the dormer windows.

Little Sampford—p. 187 (a) 33 : for " three " read " six."

p. 187 (a) 36 : for " Hall " read " Hawkwood."

Manuden—(1) *Parish Church*—Plate : add paten of 1711 with shield-of-arms.

Newport—(11) *The Priory* has, in a room at the N.E. end of the house, traces of 17th-century colour-decoration on one of the walls. A frieze about 13 inches deep has a design reminiscent of Tudor cresting in black outline on a white ground and the wall below was originally covered with a pattern of foliage and flowers outlined in black with dark green leaves ; one of the flowers is of reddish-brown colour.

Pentlow—p. 209 (b) 36 : before " three covered cups " insert " a cheveron between."

Radwinter—(1) *Parish Church*—Plate : The chalice bears the town mark of Hertogenbosch (Bois-le-Duc), Holland, with an inscription indicating that it belonged to the church at Driel, with the date 1541. Another chalice recently presented to the church is probably 16th-century Galician (Spanish) work ; the paten accompanying it has a small medallion with a figure of St. Francis.

p. 215 (a) 26 : for " Wall " read " Wale."

Saffron Walden — (57) *Almshouses :* The foundation possesses a mazer-bowl with silver mountings of 1507 and engraved with figures of the Virgin and Child.

(115) *House* on E. side of Gold Street was recently repaired, revealing a portion of the original moulded bressummer carved with running vine ornament and the initials I.H. and A.H.

Shalford—p. 263 (a) 29 : the date 1562 should apply to the cup only.

Sible Hedingham—(1) *Parish Church*—Plate : add por-
ringer of 1658.
Stebbing—p. 282 (a) 52 and 53 : for " Smith " read
" Sorell."
Takeley—p. 300 (a) 35 : for " Calverden " read " Culverden."
Toppesfield—(1) *Parish Church :* The W. gallery has
encased posts and a front of late 17th-century panelling probably brought from elsewhere and adapted to
fit its present position ; the staircase is of late 16th-
century detail but of deal and is probably a copy of a
century later.

.Toppesfield—*cont.*
(7) *The Rectory :* The timber-framed barn is of the
16th century and is of six bays with braced tie-beams
and wind-braced purlins.
Ugley—(1) *Parish Church*—Plate : add cup of 1632
(Norwich marks) dated 1744.
Wethersfield—p. 335 (a) 23 : for " possibly for Henry
Wentworth........his first wife," read " probably
for Sir Roger Wentworth, 1539 and Ann (Tyrell) his
wife." (Alter plate title, p. 333, accordingly.)
p. 335 (a) last line : for " 1561 " read " 1560."
Wickham St. Paul's—(1) *Parish Church*—Plate : add cup
of 1562 with incised ornament.

VOL. II.

p. xxxiv, 38 : for " Fairfield " read " Fairstead."
p. xxxviii, 9 : for " Toppingale " read " Toppinghoe."
Abbess Roding—*Mound* at road-fork at Green Hill,
600 yards N. of the church.
Black Notley—p. 21 (a) 37 : after " Cottage " insert
" (Plate p. 128)."
p. 21 (b) 4 : delete plate reference.
Illustration p. 128 : for Black Notley "(16)" read
" (14)."
Boreham—p. 23 (b) 31 : for " Chancellor " read " Canceller."
Braintree—(1) *Parish Church*—Plate : add flagon dated
1711.
Chignall (Smealey)—p. 45 (a) 47 : delete " of 1597."
Chigwell—p. 47 (b) 56 : for " 1559 " read " 1607," and for
" cup and paten of 1633 " read " cup and paten of
1632."
Chingford—p. 50 (b) 14 : for " 1699 " read " 1698."
Chipping Ongar—p. 52 (b) 56 : for " 1697 " read " 1705."
Dagenham—(1) *Parish Church*—Plate : add alms-dish of
c. 1700.
Doddinghurst—p. 56 (a) 16 : for " 1589 " read " 1598."
p. 57 (a) last line but one : delete " of 1567."
Epping Upland—p. 63 (b) 31 : delete description of bells
and read " 2nd to 5th by John Waylett, 1707 ; 6th
by Robert Oldfield, 1611."
p. 64 (b) 1 : for " 1639 " read " 1638."
Great Canfield—(1) *Parish Church*—Plate : add a paten
dated 1681.
Great Ilford—(2) *Hospital Chapel*—Plate : add stand-
paten of 1703.
Great Leighs—p. 100 (b) 49 : for " 1560 " read " 1680."
Great Parndon—(1) *Parish Church*—Plate : includes cup
of 1562 and stand-paten dated 1635.
Great Waltham—Illustration, p. 96 : for "(21) Ashcote
Farm " read " (24) Garnetts Farm."
p. 105 (b) 2 : for " Waldegrave " read " Walgrave."
p. 108 (b) 13 : delete plate reference.
p. 108 (b) 33 : after " Garnetts' Farm " insert " (Plate
p. 96)."
Greensted (juxta-Ongar)—(1) *Parish Church*—Plate : includes a stand-paten of 1699, with shield-of-arms.
Hatfield Broad Oak—p. 119 (a) 33 and 34 : delete reference
to carved angels.
(15) *House,* formerly the Town Farm, has recently had
some of the timber-construction exposed inside the
central block. The S. room in the former Hall has
on a post in the N. wall, in addition to the date 1630,
the initials I.H. and a carved rose and molet ; in
the opposite wall is an original doorway with a four-
centred head, and above are some remains of conventional painted decoration of 17th-century-date. The
moulded wall-plates on either side of the original Hall
remain, and in the roof is an original king-post truss
with cambered tie-beam supported by curved braces
in the form of a four-centred arch, and an octagonal
king-post with moulded cap and base and four-way
struts. There is another original king-post truss over

HATFIELD BROAD OAK—*cont.*
the solar wing. In the lintel of one of the ground-
floor rooms are mortices for four diamond-shaped and
one central flat mullion with a groove for a shutter,
and in the passage above the kitchen is a window,
now blocked, with two diamond-shaped mullions.
High Ongar—p. 132 (b) 34 : for " 1696–7 " read " 1683."
Ingatestone—(1) *Parish Church*—Plate : includes cup of
1675.
p. 137 (a) 20 : for " Hawkins " read " Hawkes."
Kelvedon Hatch—p. 142 (b) 44 : for " 1675 " read " 1676."
Lambourne—p. 143 (a) 46 and p. 144 (b) 20 : for " Alridge"
read " Abridge."
p. 144 (a) 20 : before " 1565 " insert " 1559 or."
Latton—p. 147 (b) 29 : for " Woolley " read " Wollaye."
Leaden Roding—(1) *Parish Church*—Plate : add flagon of
1699 and stand-paten of 1709.
Little Baddow—(1) *Parish Church*—Painting (Plate, Vol. iv,
p. 184) : On N. wall of nave, opposite S. doorway, of
St. Christopher carrying the Child-Christ. The Saint
wears a green cap and tunic and red cloak, leans upon a
light green staff, flowered at the top with green leaves
and red berries, and wades through water in which are
fishes, etc. ; the Child-Christ is nimbed, wears a green
garment, holds an orb surmounted by a cross with
pennant and is seated on the left shoulder of the Saint.
On W. side is a chapel with bell and turret and figure
of hermit holding lamp ; on E. side faint traces of
another figure with conical head-dress and holding an
object in right hand ; background of red powdered
with conventional flowers ; upper part of painting is
in good state of preservation but lower part much
worn. It is probably of 15th-century date but superimposed upon earlier work, of which faint traces are
visible in places representing rectangular blocks of
masonry in double purple lines. It has recently been
exposed, having been plastered over since 1749.
Loughton—(8) *Yew Tree Cottage* and a cottage adjoining on
the S.W., 270 yards N. by E. of (7), are of two storeys.
The walls are of timber-framing partly plastered and
partly weather-boarded ; the roofs are tiled. The
cottages were built late in the 16th or early in the 17th
century and have small modern additions at the back.
At either end is a massive chimney-stack with splayed
offsets ; the upper courses of both stacks have been
rebuilt. One of the first-floor windows has a lead
casement probably of 17th-century date. There is
a large exposed ceiling-beam and some plain battened
doors with wood latches.
Condition—Poor.
(9) *White House,* N.W. side of Church Hill, 50 yards N.E.
of St. John's Road, is of two storeys with attics. The
walls are of brick covered with cement ; the roofs are
tiled. The house was built in the latter part of the
16th century but has been much altered and added to
in the 18th and 19th centuries. The walls are covered
with modern cement and towards the N.E. end of the

LOUGHTON—*cont.*
White House—cont.

house is an original chimney-stack of six grouped octagonal shafts, now cemented over. Inside the building are some exposed beams, and one bedroom has an early 18th-century wood chimney-piece with moulded architrave and shelf. In the attic is a brick fireplace with chamfered jambs, segmental arch and an iron grate with thick bars, all of late 17th or early 18th-century date.

Condition—Good.

(10) *Priors*, Trap's Hill, house, barn and outbuildings, 100 yards S.E. of (4). The house is of two storeys, timber-framed and plastered; the roofs are tiled. It was built in the second half of the 16th century and a front or S.W. wing was added in the latter part of the 18th century; about the same time a farmhouse adjoining on the N. was built. The S.W. front of the original building, now overlooking the yard, is weather-boarded and the first floor projects on curved brackets. On the first floor is an original four-light window with moulded mullions and lead casements. On the S.E. front the door to the kitchen is nail-studded and has long hinges with shaped ends. On the N.E. front is a large chimney-stack. Inside the building some of the timber-construction and ceiling beams are exposed. In the Hall is a small cupboard with a linenfold panel, probably refixed, and in the upper floor an old battened door. Some of the roof timbers are exposed and the roof over the N.W. wing is of the central purlin type with curved struts.

The *Barn* and three outbuildings, 20 yards S. of the house, are of weather-boarded timber-framing with tiled roofs. They are probably of late 17th-century date but have been partly renewed.

Condition—Of house, good; of outbuildings, fairly good.

(11) *Beech House*, on S.E. side of High Road, 200 yards N. of (5), is of two storeys; the walls are of brick; the roofs are covered with tiles and slates. The house was entirely rebuilt in the 18th century, but incorporates some beams and fittings of earlier date. On the N.W. front is a recessed brick panel with the following inscriptions, W.R.M. 1648 I R AGE 4. A room on the first floor is lined with early 17th-century panelling and has an oak chimney-piece of the same date, said to have come from Chigwell Hall. The overmantel is in three bays with broad Ionic pilasters carved with festoons of fruit; above is an entablature with a dentilled cornice, acanthus brackets over each pilaster and draped swags over each bay; in each bay is a shouldered and eared panel with carved scrolls; the shelf has carved panels and swags; the fireplace has a stone surround with moulded edges. In the kichen are four plain battened doors with long hinges, and on the upper floor is a late 17th-century door. At the top of the stairs are several plain and one shaped flat baluster.

Condition—Good.

Low Leyton—p. 167 (a) 41: for ' William" read" Philip."

(7) *Forest House*, now used as an annexe to Infirmary and stables, 1¼ m. N.E. of St. Mary's church. The house is of three storeys with cellars; the walls are of brick covered with cement; the roofs are covered with slates. It was built *c.* 1700 and has considerable 18th and 19th-century alterations and additions. The elevations have no original features. Inside the building the Entrance Hall has a plastered ceiling divided into panels by moulded beams with a large octagonal panel in the middle painted with an allegorical group representing Abundance. The Entrance Hall and many of the rooms are lined with original panelling. The main staircase rises in three

LOW LEYTON—*cont.*
Forest House—cont.

flights round a central well to the first floor and has plain strings, moulded handrail, short twisted balusters and square newel-posts with turned pendants. The secondary staircase is of similar character but of simpler detail. On the ground floor of the modern extension is some panelling of *c.* 1600. Removed from the house and reset in the hall of the modern Infirmary is a marble fireplace with a carved and moulded shelf supported by tapering pilasters with busts of female figures in classical drapery. The stable stands to the N.W. of the house and is a rectangular building of two storeys; the walls are of brown bricks with red brick doorways; the roofs are tiled. The middle part of the S.E. front projects and the modillioned eaves-cornice is carried up over it in a pointed pediment. The quoins are rusticated, and at the first-floor level is a plain projecting string. The windows are rect-angular and the roof is hipped.

Condition—Of house and stables, good, the former much altered.

Magdalen Laver—p. 169 (a) 39: for " 1683 " read " 1663."

Maldon St. Peter—(3) *Beeleigh Abbey* : Rough rubble and brick foundations have recently been found 82 feet W. of the existing eastern range. They probably represent the N.W. angle of the cloister formed by the junction of the S. wall of the church with the E. wall of the western range.

p. 178 (b) 15: for " Jacob " read " James."

Margaretting—p. 185 (a) 37: for " 1450 " read " 1550."

Moreton—(1) *Parish Church*—Plate: add stand-paten of 1706.

p. 190 (a) 1: delete " alms-dish of 1648 with shield-of-arms."

Netteswell—p. 196 (b) 7: for " arms " read " Anno."

North Weald Bassett—(1) *Parish Church*—Plate: add cover-paten of 1567.

Norton Mandeville—p. 200 (a) 16 to 18: delete "an early 17th-century cup"; for " given in " read " of "; delete " and without date-mark."

Pleshey—(3) *The Castle* : Excavations undertaken on the mount in 1922 revealed the foundations of walls enclosing a rectangular space about 63½ feet by 62½ feet from which on the N., E. and W. were, at irregular intervals, various rectangular projections and lengths of walling. The foundations are of various dates and different materials, the thinness of the walls and the general arrangement do not indicate any great antiquity, and possibly no part of the building is older than the 14th century. (See *Essex Arch. Soc. Trans.*, N.S., XVI, 190, with plan.)

Romford Urban—(1) *Parish Church*—Plate: add paten of 1707.

Roxwell—Illustration p. 247: for " Screens," " 17th-century " read " Skreens," " late 16th-century."

Stapleford Abbots—p. 222 (b) 43: large paten of 1688 not 1687.

Theydon Bois—*Roman* : In the grounds of Birch Hall, under the lawn, is a brick wall supposed to be Roman. Fragments of undoubted Roman brick with pink mortar attached have been picked up on the site. (Information from Mr. Miller Christy.)

Theydon Garnon—(1) *Parish Church*—Plate: add cover-paten of same date as cup (1562).

Theydon Mount—p. 234 (b) 50: for ' 1614" read '" probably of 1587."

Waltham Holy Cross—p. 243 (b) 19: for " (Champnon) his wife " read " (Champarnon) his mother."

Woodham Walter—p. 270 (b) 30: delete" Giles' or."

VARIOUS PARISHES.

Forest of Waltham Boundary Stones.

The earlier stones are probably those erected in 1642 by the Commissioners after a Perambulation of Waltham Forest following an Act of Parliament passed in 1641. They now stand on concrete bases having been re-erected in 1909.

(a) *Richards Stone.*—Navestock Parish, N.E., corner of Curtis Mill Green, about 1¼ m. E.N.E. of St. Mary's church, Stapleford Abbots.

(b) *Navestock Stone,* Navestock Parish, on N. side of Bourne Brook, 630 yards S. of (a).

(c) *Park Corner Stone,* between Dagenham and Romford Parishes, on E. side of hedge between fields, 300 yards W.N.W. of Havering Lodge. On E. face remains of

inscription in Roman capitals, ...ORN....STONE; top of stone broken.

(d) *Marks Stone.*—Dagenham Parish, on E. side of Whale bone Lane, 770 yards S. of road junction at Marks Gate. On W. face remains of inscription in Roman capitals, MA....STONE. At side, later stone, probably 18th-century, with inscription.

(e) *Warren Stone,* on E. side of cart-track, in field 230 yards E. of (4). On W. face remains of inscription, Sept. 8. 164..

(f) *Forest Bounds Stone,* on E. side of Whalebone Lane, 840 yards S. of (d). On W. face remains of inscription ....T BO..NDS. At side, later stone, with inscription.

(g) *Havering Stone,* on N. side of London—Romford Road, 460 yards E. of Whalebone Lane, with defaced inscription, Sept. Octav 170....of. Be....

VOL. III.

p. xxvii, 16–17 : delete reference to inscription at Jedburgh.

p. xxxi, 33 : for " West Stockwell " read " East Stockwell."

p. xxxiii, Illustration—Stanway, fireplace : for " 17th " read ' 16th."

Alphamstone—p. 4 (a) 33 : for " 17th " read " late 16th."

Ardleigh—p. 6 (b) 57 : for " former " read " latter."

Boxted—(1) *Parish Church*—Plate : add, a restored 17th-century cup.

Bradwell (juxta-Coggeshall)—p. 13 (b) 29 : for "Beancock" read "Beaucock."

Brightlingsea—p. 17 (a) 39 : for " 1505 " read " 1514." p. 17 (b) 39 : for " 1620 " read " 1560."

Chapel—(1) *Parish Church*—Plate : add an Elizabethan Cup.

Colchester—(1) *Roman Remains :* (a) W. of the place marked (13) in the plan of Roman remains a mosaic pavement was recently uncovered and has since been removed to the Castle Museum. The ornament consists of panels, bands of guilloche pattern and geometric designs ; the mosaic was surrounded by a broad band of plain red tesserae and nearly half the whole design was recovered. In the neighbourhood of the pavement several foundations of walls at varying depths have been encountered and their further excavation is now pending.

(b) Mosaic pavement (Plate, Vol. iv, p. 185), found 1923, in garden approximately 130 yards S. of East Hill House, surrounded by red border (about 19 feet square in all) with central square divided into nine rectangular panels by strips of cable pattern ; centre panel encloses circle containing four heart-shaped leaves shaded from red to white ; four of the remaining panels are square and contains geometric patterns ; each of the others contains a small dolphin and a composite sea-beast in black, red, white and yellow colours ; in S.E. corner the pavement has collapsed into a pit of uncertain depth and purpose.

Walls.—Recent examination of the interior of the bastion at the S.E. corner of the wall behind Priory Street showed it to be of hollow construction and a later addition to the Roman wall. The face of the wall was badly ruined before the addition was made, and the tower is carried down a long way below the earlier footings. This evidence renders it improbable that the bastions are Roman work, and though it is insufficient to give a precise date to their building it suggests that they were probably added to strengthen the wall in mediæval times and served as buttresses as much as for defensive purposes.

p. 33 (b) 38 : for " early 17th-century " read " of 1658."

(3) *Parish Church* of *Holy Trinity*—Plate : add a·stand-paten of 1710.

(4) *Parish Church* of *St. James*—Plate : add an alms-dish of 1692.

(13) *Parish Church, Lexden*—Plate : add cover-paten of 1670.

Dedham—p. 82 (a) 50 : for " W." read " R." p. 82 (b) 20 and 49 : for " Roger " read " Rogers."

Earls Colne—p. 87 (b) 18 and 19 : for " Clare " and " FitzHamon " read " Archdeacon " and " Bolebec." p. 88 (a) 6 : for " Eileston " read " Elleston." p. 88 (b) 10 : delete " for Coucy."

East Mersea—*Roman :* A piece of tessellated pavement was given to the Colchester Museum by an inhabitant of this parish about 1832. The site from which it came is quite uncertain. (Information from Dr. P. Laver.)

Fingringhoe—p. 101 (b) 18 : for " 13th " read " 14th."

Frating—p. 104 (b) 34–5 : delete Plate.

Great Braxted—(1) *Parish Church*—Monument : on S. wall outside, to Countess de la Vall, wife of Sir William Ayloff, 1683, with shield-of-arms.

Great Clacton—p. 115 (a) 11 : for " Larry Roris " read " Lany Rous."

Great Coggeshall—(2) *Parish Church*—Plate : add stand-paten of 1702.

Lamarsh—(11) *Chestnut Lodge :* Inside the building a room on the ground-floor has a moulded ceiling-beam with carved shield stops with *three chevrons.*

Langham—p. 150 (b) 43 : for " Arqlus " read " Charles."

Lawford—(2) *Lawford Hall :* In the dining-room is a stone mantelpiece of c. 1580 with shields of Waldegrave and Wilberforce.

Little Bentley—(1) *Parish Church*—Plate : add cover-paten probably of same date as cup.

Little Clacton—(1) *Parish Church*—Brass : In nave—to William Hubbard and his three wives, Rose, Jane and Joice, inscription only, late 16th-century.

Little Wigborough—(1) *Parish Church*—Plate : add Elizabethan cup with incised ornament.

Markshall—p. 178 (b) 51 : for " Poynings " read "Poyntz."

Pattiswick—(1) *Parish Church*—Brass : In organ-chamber, to Briant Dacre, 1638, inscription only. Plate : includes cup and cover-paten of 1702–3 recently restored to the church.

Thorrington—(1) *Parish Church*—Plate : add stand-paten of 1702.

Tolleshunt Major—p. 223 (b) 12 : after " 17th " add " or early 18th."

Twinstead—(1) p. 224 (b) 13 : for " 16th " read " 15th."

West Bergholt—(1) *Parish Church*—Plate : add Elizabethan cup, much altered.

West Mersea—*Roman :* Early in 1923 remains of walls of Roman brick were found in the garden of a house on the E. side of the road about 200 yards N. of the church.

Wivenhoe—p. 234 (a) 5 : for " 1729 " read " 1725."

Wormingford—p. 236 (a) 46 : for " coat impaling " read " impaled coat " and delete " a lion rampant." p. 236 (a) 47 : for " Clare " read " Baud." p. 236 (b) 10 : for " Hoskyns " read " Poynings."

GLOSSARY

OF THE MEANING ATTACHED TO THE TECHNICAL TERMS USED IN THE INVENTORY.

Abacus.—The uppermost member of a capital.

Alb.—Long linen robe, with close sleeves ; worn by clerks of all grades.

Alettes or **Allettes.**—In armour, plates usually rectangular, of metal or leather covered with cloth or other light material, fastened by a lace to the back or sides of the shoulders ; they commonly display armorial bearings ; worn c. 1275 to c. 1325.

Altar-tomb.—A modern term for a tomb of stone or marble resembling, but not used as, an altar.

Amess.—Fur cape with hood, and long tails in front ; worn by clerks of the higher grades.

Amice.—A linen strip with embroidered apparel, placed upon the head coifwise by a clerk before vesting himself in an alb, after which it is pushed back, and the apparel then appears like a collar.

Ankar-hold.—The dwelling house of an ankorite or recluse.

Apparels.—Rectangular pieces of embroidery on alb, amice, etc.

Apse.—The semi-circular or polygonal end of a chancel or other part of a church.

Arabesque.—A peculiar kind of strap-ornament in low relief, common in Moorish architecture, and found in 16th and 17th-century work in England.

Arcade.—A range of arches carried on piers or columns.

Arch.—The following are some of the most usual forms :—
Segmental :—A single arc struck from a centre below the springing line.
Pointed or two-centred :—Two arcs struck from centres on the springing line, and meeting at the apex with a point.
Segmental-pointed :—A pointed arch, struck from two centres below the springing line.
Equilateral :—A pointed arch struck with radii equal to the span.
Lancet :—A pointed arch struck with radii greater than the span.
Three-centred, elliptical :—Formed with three arcs, the middle or uppermost struck from a centre below the springing line.
Four-centred, depressed, Tudor :—A pointed arch of four arcs, the two outer and lower arcs struck from centres on the springing line and the two inner and upper arcs from centres below the springing line. Sometimes the two upper arcs are replaced by straight lines.
Ogee :—A pointed arch of four or more arcs, the two uppermost or middle arcs being reversed, i.e., convex instead of concave to the base line.
Relieving :—An arch generally of rough construction, placed in the wall above the true arch or head of an opening, to relieve it of some of the superincumbent weight.
Stilted :—An arch with its springing line raised above the level of the imposts.
Skew :—An arch not at right angles laterally with its jambs.

Archbishops' Vestments.—Buskins, sandals, amice, alb, girdle, stole, fanon, tunic, dalmatic, chasuble, pall ; gloves, ring, mitre ; an archbishop carries a crosier but, in later times, holds a cross-staff for distinction.

Architrave.—A moulded enrichment to the jambs and head of a doorway or window opening ; the lowest member of an entablature (q.v.).

Argent.—In heraldry, white or silver, the latter being the word used in mediaeval English blazonry.

Armet.—*See* " Helmet."

Arming Doublet.—Sleeved coat worn under armour ; 15th and 16th centuries.

Arming Points.—Laces for attaching parts of armour together.

Arris.—An edge or angle.

Articulation.—The joining of several plates of armour to form a flexible defence.

Ashlar.—Masonry wrought to an even face and square edges.

Aumbry.—*See* ' Locker.'

Azure.—In heraldry, blue.

Baberies.—The " childlike conceits " and other carvings on the underside of misericords.

Badge of Ulster.—A silver scocheon charged with a red hand upraised, borne in the arms of baronets of England, Ireland, and the United Kingdom.

Bailey.—A court attached to a mount or other fortified enclosure.

Bainbergs.—Shin guards of plate-armour or leather.

Ball-flower.—In architecture, a decoration peculiar to the first quarter of the 14th century, consisting of a globular flower of three petals enclosing a small ball.

Banded Mail.—Mail shown with narrow bands, between rows of rings ; construction uncertain.

Bar.—*See* " Fesse."

Barbe.—Pleated linen covering for chin and throat, worn by widows and women under vows.

Barbican.—An advanced protective work before the gate of a town or castle, or at the head of a bridge.

Barbican Mount.—A mound advanced from the main defences to protect an entrance.

Barge-board.—A board, often carved, fixed to the edge of a gabled roof, a short distance from the face of the wall.

Barnack stone.—A shelly oolitic limestone ; from Barnack, Northamptonshire.

Barrel-vaulting.—*See* " Vaulting."

Barrow.—A burial mound.

Barry.—In heraldry, an even number of horizontal divisions in a shield, normally six, but sometimes four or eight. When a greater and indefinite number of divisions appear the word **Burely** is used.

Bascinet.—Steel head-piece worn with camail, sometimes fitted with vizor.

Baston.—*See* " Bend."

Battled.—In heraldry, the edge of a chief, bend, bar, or the like drawn in the fashion of the battlements of a wall.

Bead.—A small round moulding.

Bell-capital.—A form of capital of which the chief characteristic is a reversed bell between the neck moulding and upper moulding ; the bell is often enriched with carving.

Bend.—In heraldry, a band aslant and across the shield, commonly from the dexter chief. A narrow bend over other charges is called a **Baston.** The baston with the ends cut off, drawn in the other direction across the shield is a mark of bastardy in post-mediaeval heraldry. A field or charge divided bendwise into an equal number of parts, normally six, is said to be **bendy.**

Bendwise.—In the direction of a bend.

Bendy.—In heraldry, divided bendwise into an equal number of divisions, normally six.

Berm.—A platform on the slope of a rampart.

Besagues.—Small plates worn in front of the arm-pits.

Bevor.—Plate-defence for chin and throat.

Bezant.—In heraldry, a gold roundel or disc.

Billet.—In heraldry, a small oblong figure ; also in architectural ornament chiefly used in the 11th and 12th centuries.

Billety.—In heraldry, a field or charge powdered with billets.

Bishops' Vestments.—Same as an archbishop's, but without pall, and a bishop carries a crosier, and not a cross.

Bolection-moulding.—A moulding raised above the general plane of the framework of the door or panelling in which it is set.

Border.—In heraldry, an edging round a coat-of-arms, whether simple or quartered.

Boss.—A projecting square or round ornament, covering the intersections of the ribs in a vault, panelled ceiling or roof, etc.

Bouget or **Water-bouget.**—A pair of leather bottles, borne as a heraldic charge.

Bowtell.—A continuous convex moulding ; another term for roll-moulding.

Brace.—In roof construction, a subsidiary timber inserted to strengthen the framing of a truss. *Wind-brace*, a subsidiary timber inserted between the purlins and principals of a roof to resist the pressure of the wind.

Brassart.—Plate-armour defence for the arm.

Bressummer.—A beam forming the direct support of an upper wall or timber-framing.

Brick-nogging.—The brick-work filling the spaces between the uprights of a timber-framed building.

Brick-work.—*Header* :—A brick laid so that the end only appears on the face of the wall.
Stretcher :—A brick laid so that one side only appears on the face of the wall.
English Bond :—A method of laying bricks so that alternate courses on the face of the wall are composed of headers or stretchers only.
Flemish Bond :—A method of laying bricks so that alternate headers and stretchers appear in each course on the face of a wall.

Brigandine.—Coat of padded cloth and very small plates (of metal).

Broach-spire.—*See* " Spire."

Broach-stop.—A half-pyramidal stop against a chamfer to bring out the edge of a stone or beam to a right angle.

Buff Coat.—Coat of heavy leather.

Burgonet.—*See* " Helmet."

Buskins.—Stockings reaching to the knee ; worn by archbishops, bishops, and mitred abbots.

Butterfly Head-dress.—Large, of lawn and gauze on wire, late 15th-century.

Buttress.—A mass of masonry or brick-work projecting from or built against a wall to give additional strength.
Angle-buttresses :—Two meeting, or nearly meeting, at an angle of 90° at the corner of a building.
Diagonal-buttress :—One placed against the right angle formed by two walls, and more or less equi-angular with both.
Flying-buttress :—A butting arch transmitting thrust from a wall to an outer buttress.

Cable-moulding.—A moulding carved in the form of a cable.

Camail.—Hood of mail ; first worn attached to hauberk, then separate from it with tippet of mail over shoulders, and, in the 14th century, attached to bascinet.

Cambered (applied to a beam).—Curved so that the middle is higher than the ends.

Canonical Quire Habit.—Surplice, amess, cope.

Canopy.—A projection or hood over a door, window, etc., and the covering above a tomb or niche ; also the representation of the same on a brass.

Cantilever.—A beam supported at a point short of one end, which end carries a load, the other end being fixed.

Canton.—A word applied in modern heraldry to the Quarter which is commonly given less space than in the older examples.

Caryatid.—Pillar carved as a woman.

Casement.—1. A wide hollow moulding in window jambs, etc.
2. The hinged part of a window.
3. The sinking for a brass in a slab.

Cassock.—Long, close-sleeved gown ; worn by all clerks.

Cellarer's Building or **Cellar.**—In monastic planning that part of the Convent under the control of the cellarer containing store-rooms, wine-vaults, etc. In Cistercian monasteries it also included the Frater and Dorter of the Lay brethren (conversi). Its ordinary position in all orders was on the W. side of the cloister.

Central-chimney Type of House.—*See* " Houses."

Chamfer.—The small plane formed when the sharp edge or arris of stone or wood is cut away, usually at an angle of 45° ; when the plane is concave it is termed a *hollow chamfer*, and when the plane is sunk below its arrises, or edges, a *sunk chamfer*.

Chantry-chapel.—A small chapel usually occupying part of a large building, specially attached to a chantry.

Chasuble.—A nearly circular cape with central hole for head, worn by priests and bishops at mass. It is put on over all the other vestments.

Chausses.—Leg-defences of mail.

Checky.—In heraldry, a field or charge divided into squares or checkers.

Cheveron.—In heraldry, a charge resembling a pair of rafters of a roof ; sometimes used decoratively.

Chief.—In heraldry, the upper part of the shield. Cut off from the rest of the field by a horizontal line and having its own tincture, it becomes one of the charges of the shield, covering a space which occupies from a third to a half, or even more of it.

Chrismatory.—A box containing the holy oils for anointing.

Chrisom-child.—Child swaddled in a chrisom-cloth.

Cinquefoil.—1. *See* " Foil."
2. An heraldic flower of five petals.

Clearstorey.—An upper storey, pierced by windows, in the main walls of a church. The same term is applicable in the case of a domestic building.

Close-helmet.—*See* " Helmet."

Clunch.—A local name for the lower chalk limestone, composed of chalk and clay.

Cockatrice.—A monster with the head and legs of a cock and the tail of a wyver.

Coif.—Small close hood, covering head only.

Collar-beam.—A horizontal beam framed to and serving to tie a pair of rafters together some distance above the wall-plate level.

Combed Work.—The decoration of plaster surfaces by ' combing'" it into various patterns.

Console.—A bracket with a compound curved outline.

Cope.—A processional and quire vestment shaped like a cloak, and fastened across the chest by a band or brooch ; worn by clerks of most grades.

Coped-slab.—A slab of which the upper face is ridged down the middle, sometimes hipped at each end.

Cops, Knee and Elbow.—Knee and elbow defences of leather or plate.

Corbel.—A projecting stone or piece of timber for the support of a superincumbent weight.

Cotises.—In heraldry, pairs of narrow bands, in the form of bends, pales, fesses, or cheverons, and borne accompanying one of those charges on each side of it.

Counter-coloured.—In heraldry, term applied in cases where the field and charges exchange tinctures on either side of a dividing line.

Counter-scarp.—The reverse slope of a ditch facing towards the place defended.

Courtyard Type of House.—*See* " Houses."

Cove.—A concave under-surface.

Cover-paten.—A cover to a communion cup, sometimes used as a paten.

Credence.—A shelf, niche, or table on which the vessels, etc., for mass are placed.

Crest, cresting.—1. A device worn upon the helm. 2. An ornamental finish along the top of a screen, etc.

Crockets.—Carvings projecting at regular intervals from the vertical or sloping sides of parts of a building, such as spires, canopies, hood-moulds, etc.

Crosier, or Pastoral Staff.—A tall staff ending in an ornamental crook carried as a mark of authority by archbishops, bishops, and heads of monastic houses, including abbesses and prioresses.

Cross.—In its simplest form in heraldry, a pale combined with a fesse, as the St. George's Cross ; there are many other varieties, of which the following are the most common :—*Crosslet*,—with a smaller arm crossing each main arm ; *Crosslet fitchy*,—having the lowest arm spiked or pointed ; Crosslet *flowered* or *flory*,—having the arms headed with *fleurs-de-lis* ; *Crosslet formy*,—arms widening from the centre, and square at the ends. The old forms of the crosslet have, as a rule, the arms ending as in trefoils with rounded petals ; *Plain crosses*,—with four equal arms not extending to the edges of the shield ; *Moline* (or *mill-rind*), —with the arms split or forked at the ends ; *Paty*,—as

Cross—*cont.*
a cross *formy*, but with the arms notched in two places at the ends, giving them a form which may approach that of a blunt head of a *fleur-de-lis* ; *Potent* (or *Jerusalem*),—having a small transverse arm at the extreme end of each main arm ; *Tau* (or *Anthony*),— in the form of a T.

Cross-loop.—Narrow slits or openings in a wall, in the form of a cross, generally with circular enlargements at the ends.

Cross-staff.—Staff terminating in a cross ; carried before archbishops, who are usually shown holding it on effigies, brasses, etc.

Cross-vaulting.—*See* " Vaulting."

Crow-stepped.—A term applied to gables, the coping of which rises in a series of steps.

Crusily.—In heraldry, covered or powdered with crosslets.

Cuirass.—Breast and back plates of metal or leather.

Cushion-capital.—A cubic capital with its lower angles rounded off to a circular shaft.

Cusps (*cusping, cusped heads, sub-cusps*).—The projecting points forming the foils in Gothic windows, arches, panels, etc. ; they were frequently ornamented at the ends, or *cusp-points*, with leaves, flowers, berries, etc.

Dagging.—Cutting of edges of garments into slits and foliations.

Dalmatic.—The special vestment at mass of a deacon ; a loose tunic of moderate length, slit up sides, with wide sleeves and fringed edges.

Dance.—In heraldry, a fesse or bar drawn zigzagwise, or **dancetty.**

Deacons' Vestments (Mass).—Amice, alb, stole (worn over left shoulder), dalmatic, and fanon.

Demi-brassart.—Plate-defence for outside of arm.

Dexter.—In heraldry, the right-hand side of a shield as held.

Diaper.—Decoration of surfaces with squares, diamonds, and other patterns.

Dimidiated.—In heraldry, applied to the halving of two shields and joining a half of each to make a new shield.

Dog-legged Staircase.—Two flights of stairs in opposite directions.

Dog-tooth Ornament.—A typical 13th-century carved ornament consisting of a series of pyramidal flowers of four petals ; used to cover hollow mouldings.

Dormer-window.—A vertical window on the slope of a roof, and having a roof of its own.

Dorter.—In monastic buildings, the common sleeping apartments or dormitory.

Double-ogee.—*See* " Ogee."

Dovetail.—A carpenter's joint for two boards, one with a series of projecting pieces resembling doves' tails fitting into the other with similar hollows ; in heraldry an edge formed like a dovetail joint.

Drawbar.—A wood bolt inside a doorway, sliding when out of use into a long channel in the thickness of the wall.

Dressings.—The stones used about an angle, window, or other feature when worked to a finished face, whether smooth, tooled in various ways, moulded, or sculptured.

Drip-stone.—*See* " Hood-mould."

Easter Sepulchre.—A locker in the north wall of a chancel wherein the Host was placed from Good Friday to Easter Day, to typify Christ's burial after His crucifixion. A temporary wooden structure in imitation of a Sepulchre with lights, etc., was often placed before it, but in some parts of the country this was a more permanent and ornate structure of stone.

Eaves.—The under part of a sloping roof overhanging a wall.

Embrasures.—The openings, indents, or sinkings in an embattled parapet.

Enceinte.—The main outline of a fort.

Engaged Shafts.—Shafts cut out of the solid or connected with the jamb, pier, respond, or other part against which they stand.

Engrailed.—In heraldry, edged with a series of concave curves.

Entablature.—In Classic or Renaissance architecture, the horizontal superstructure above the columns or jambs of an opening, consisting of an *architrave, frieze,* and *cornice.*

Ermine or Ermines.—The fur most frequently used in heraldry; white powdered with black tails. Other varieties are sometimes found, as sable ermined with silver, and in more modern heraldry, gold ermined with sable, and sable ermined with gold.

E Type of House.—*See* " Houses.'

Fanon.—A strip of embroidery probably at one time a handkerchief, held in the left hand, or worn hanging from the left wrists by bishops, priests and deacons. It is often called a maniple.

Fan-vaulting.—*See* " Vaulting."

Fascia.—A plain or moulded board covering the plate of a projecting upper storey of timber, and masking the ends of the cantilever joists which support it.

Feretory.—A place or chamber for a shrine.

Fesse.—In heraldry, a horizontal band athwart the shield. When more than one fesse is borne they are known as **Bars.**

Finial.—A formal bunch of foliage or similar ornament at the top of a pinnacle, gable, canopy, etc.

Fitchy.—*See* " Cross."

Flanches.—In heraldry, the side portions of a shield, bounded by convex lines issuing from the chief.

Foil (*trefoil, quatrefoil, cinquefoil, multifoil,* etc.).—A leaf-shaped curve formed by the cusping or feathering in an opening or panel.

Foliated (of a capital, corbel, etc.)—Carved with leaf ornament.

Fosse.—A ditch.

Four-centred Arch.—*See* " Arch."

Frater.—The refectory or dining-hall of a monastery.

Fret or Fretty.—In heraldry, a charge formed of a number of bastons drawn from each side of the shield, and interlaced like lattice-work. In modern heraldry, the charge of a fret takes the form of a narrow saltire interlacing a voided lozenge, while the word *Fretty* is kept for the older form.

Frieze.—The middle division in an *entablature,* between the architrave and the *cornice;* generally any band of ornament or colour immediately below a cornice.

Funeral helm.—A trophy, in the form of a crested headpiece, carried at the funerals and placed over the tombs of important personages.

Fusil.—In heraldry, a word applied to the pieces into which a fesse is divided by engrailing or indenting.

Gable.—The wall at the end of a ridged roof, generally triangular, sometimes semi-circular, and often with an outline of various curves, then called *curvilinear.*

Gadlings.—Spikes or knobs on plate-gauntlets.

Galleted or garretted Joints.—Wide joints in rubble or masonry into which thin pieces of flint or stone have been inserted.

Gambeson.—Garment of padded cloth worn under hauberk or as sole defence.

Gardant.—In heraldry, an epithet of a beast whose full face is seen.

Gargoyle.—A carved projecting figure pierced to carry off the rain-water from the roof of a building.

Gimel-bar or Gemel-bar.—In heraldry, a pair of narrow bars lying close to one another.

Gipon.—Close-fitting vest of cloth, worn over armour *c.* 1350 to *c.* 1410.

Gobony.—In heraldry, checkers or panes of a metal alternating with a colour, or either with a fur.

Gorget.—Plate defence for neck and throat.

Greek Cross.—A plain cross with four equal arms.

Griffon or Griffin.—A winged monster with the fore parts of an eagle, and the hinder parts of a lion.

Groining, Groined Vault.—*See* " Vaulting."

Guige.—Strap from which shield was suspended.

Guilloche-pattern.—An ornament consisting of two or more intertwining wavy bands.

Gules.—In heraldry, red.

Gussets.—Pieces of flexible armour placed in gaps of plate defences.

Gyronny or Gironny.—In heraldry, the field of a shield divided into six, eight or more gussets meeting at a point in the middle.

Haketon.—Studded, stiffened or quilted body-defence, of cloth, leather and metal, with moderately long skirts.

Half-H type of House.—*See* " Houses."

Hall and cellar type of House.—*See* " Houses."

Hammer-beams.—Horizontal brackets of a roof projecting at the wall-plate level, and resembling the two ends of a tie-beam with its middle part cut away; they are supported by braces (or struts), and help to diminish lateral pressure by reducing the span. Sometimes there is a second and even a third upper series of these brackets.

Hatchment.—A heraldic display in a rectangular frame. commonly set lozenge-wise.

Hauberk.—Shirt of chain or other mail.

Helm.—Complete barrel or dome-shaped head-defence of plate.

Helmet.—A light headpiece; various forms are: Armet, Burgonet, close Helmet, all similar in principle.

Hipped roof.—A roof with sloped instead of vertical ends. *Half-hipped,* a roof whose ends are partly vertical and partly sloped.

Hood-mould (*label, drip-stone*).—A projecting moulding on the face of a wall above an arch, doorway, or window; in some cases it follows the form of the arch, and in others is square in outline.

Houses.—These are classified as far as possible under the following definitions :—
1. *Hall and cellar type* :—Hall on first floor ; rooms beneath generally vaulted ; examples as early as the 12th century.
2. *H type* :—Hall between projecting wings, one containing living rooms, the other the offices. The usual form of a mediaeval house, employed, with variations, down to the 17th century.
3. *L type* :—Hall and one wing, generally for small houses.
4. *E type* :—Hall with two wings and a middle porch ; generally of the 16th and 17th centuries.
5. *Half-H type* :—A variation of the E type without the middle porch.
6. *Courtyard type* :—Houses built round a court ; sometimes only three ranges of buildings with or without an enclosing wall and gateway on the fourth side.
7. *Central-chimney type* :—(Rectangular plan), small houses only.

Impaled.—*See* " Parted."

Indent.—The sinking or casement in a slab for a monumental brass.

Indented.—In heraldry, notched like the teeth of a saw.

Infirmary.—In monastic planning a distinct block of buildings, generally including a hall, misericorde, kitchen and chapel, and devoted to the use of the infirm or aged.

Invected.—In modern heraldry, edged with a series of convex curves.

Jambs.—1. The sides of an archway, doorway, window, or other opening.
2. In heraldry, legs of lions, etc.
3. In armour, plate-defences for lower leg.

Jazerine.—Armour of small plates on leather or cloth.

Keep.—The great tower or stronghold in a castle ; of greater height and strength than the other buildings.

Keystone.—The middle stone in an arch.

King-post.—The middle vertical post in a roof-truss.

Kneeler.—Stone at the foot of a gable.

Label.—*See* " Hood-mould." In heraldry, a narrow horizontal band (lying across the chief of a shield), from which small strips, generally three or five, called *pieces*, depend at right angles.

Lancet.—A long narrow window with a pointed head, typical of the 13th century.

Latin Cross.—A plain cross with the bottom arm longer than the other three.

Latten.—A term applied to the alloy of copper, zinc, etc., used in the manufacture of memorial brasses, etc.

Lenten Veil.—A cloth or veil hung across the chancel or presbytery between the stalls and the altar, during Lent.

Leopard.—In heraldry, a lion showing its full face ; always passant (unless otherwise emblazoned), as in the three leopards of England.

Lierne-vault.—*See* ' Vaulting.'

Linces, linchets or lynchets.—Terraces on a hill-side formed by the gradual banking of ploughed earth between the main furrows.

Linen-fold panelling.—Panelling ornamented with a conventional representation of folded linen.

Lintel.—The horizontal beam or stone bridging an opening.

Lion.—In heraldry, face in profile and (unless otherwise emblazoned) always rampant.

(8220)

Liripipe.—Long tail of cloth attached to hooded tippet of the 14th century ; the whole finally developed into a form of turban called *Liripipe head-dress.*

Locker (*Aumbry*).—A small cupboard formed in a wall.

Loop.—A small narrow light in a turret, etc. ; often unglazed.

Louvre *or* **luffer.**—A lantern-like structure surmounting the roof of a hall or other building, with openings for ventilation or the escape of smoke, usually crossed by slanting boards to exclude rain.

Low-side window.—A grated, unglazed, and shuttered window with a low sill, *i.e.*, within a few feet of the floor, in the N. or S. wall of the chancel near its W. end, probably the window at which the sacring bell was rung.

Lozenge.—In heraldry, a charge like the diamond in a pack of cards.

L type of house.—*See* ' Houses.'

Luce.—In heraldry, a fish (pike).

Lychgate.—A covered gateway at the entrance of a churchyard, beneath which the bier is rested at a funeral.

Mail Skirt.—Shirt of chain mail worn under traces and tuiles.

Mail Standard.—Collar of chain mail.

Manche, Maunche.—A lady's sleeve with a long pendent lappet ; a heraldic charge.

Maniple.—*See* " Fanon."

Mantle or Mantling.—In heraldry, a cloth hung over the hinder part of a helm ; the edges were fantastically dagged and slit.

Martlet.—A martin, shown sometimes in heraldry without feet.

Mask-stop.—A stop at the end of a hood-mould, bearing a distant resemblance to a human face ; generally of the 12th and 13th centuries.

Mass Vestments.—These included the amice, alb, and girdle (which were worn by all clerks) to which a sub-deacon added the tunicle and fanon, a deacon the dalmatic, fanon and stole (over one shoulder only) and the priest the fanon, stole (over both shoulders) and chasuble. Bishops and certain privileged abbots wore the tunicle and dalmatic under the chasuble, with the mitre, gloves, and ring, and buskins and sandals. Archbishops used the pall in addition to all the foregoing. Bishops, abbots, and archbishops alike carried crosiers, and in the same way, but an archbishop had likewise a cross carried before him for dignity, and he is generally represented holding one for distinction. The mass vestments were sometimes worn over the quire habit, and the hood of the grey amess can often be seen on effigies hanging beyond the amice apparel at the back of the neck.

Mazer.—A bowl, generally for drinking, made of maple wood and often mounted in silver.

Merlon.—The solid part of an embattled parapet between the embrasures.

Mezzanine.—A subordinate storey between two main floors of a building.

Mill-rind (*Fer-de-moline*).—The iron affixed to the centre of a millstone ; a common heraldic charge. In early heraldry the name given to the mill-rind cross, or cross moline.

Misericord.—1. An indulgence in the form of a folding seat of a quire-stall, having a broad edge or bracket on the underside, which can be used as a seat by the occupant when standing during a long office.
2. In monastic planning, a small hall, generally attached to the Infirmary, in which better food than the ordinary was supplied for special reasons.

Mitred Abbots' Vestments.—Same as a bishop's.

Modillions.—Brackets under the cornice in Classic architecture.

Molet.—In heraldry, a star of five or six points, drawn with straight lines. When the lines are wavy it is called a *Star*. A molet with a round hole in the middle is called a *Rowel*.

Morse.—Large clasp or brooch fastening cope across the breast.

Mullion.—A vertical post, standard, or upright dividing an opening into lights.

Muntin.—The intermediate uprights in the framing of a door, screen, or panel, butting into or stopped by the rails.

Mutules.—In Classic and Renaissance architecture, small flat brackets under the cornice of the Doric order.

Nasal.—Plate of a headpiece to protect nose.

Nebuly.—Heraldic term for a line or edge, following the fashion of the mediaeval artists' conventional cloud.

Neck-moulding.—The narrow moulding round the bottom of a capital.

Newel.—The central post in a circular or winding staircase; also the principal posts at the angles of a dog-legged or well-staircase.

Nogging.—The filling, generally of brick, between the posts, etc., of a timber-framed house.

Ogee.—A compound curve of two parts, one convex, the other concave; a *double-ogee* moulding is formed by two ogees meeting at their convex ends.

Or.—In heraldry, gold; a word which, like *argent*, was established in English blazon in the second half of the 16th century.

Orders of Arches.—Receding or concentric rings of voussoirs.

Oriel Window.—A projecting bay-window carried upon corbels or brackets.

Orle.—In heraldry, a term used to describe a voided scocheon, or a number of small charges, as martlets or the like.

Orphreys.—Strips of embroidery on vestments.

" Out of the Solid."—Mouldings worked on the styles, rails, etc., of framing, instead of being fixed on to them.

Oversailing Courses.—A number of brick or stone courses, each course projecting beyond the one below it.

Ovolo moulding.—A Classic moulding forming a quarter round in section.

Pale.—In heraldry, a vertical band down the middle of a shield.

Palimpsest.—1. Of a brass: reused by engraving the back of an older engraved plate.
2. Of a wall-painting: superimposed on an earlier painting.

Pall.—1. In ecclesiastical vestments, a narrow strip of lambswool, having an open loop in the middle, and weighted ends; it is ornamented with a number of crosses and forms the distinctive mark of an archbishop; it is worn round the neck, above the other vestments.
2. A cloth covering a hearse.

Paly.—In heraldry, a shield divided by lines palewise, normally into six divisions, unless otherwise emblazoned.

Panache.—A plume or bush of feathers worn on the helm.

Pargeting.—Ornamental plaster work on the surface of a wall.

Parted or Party.—In heraldry, a term used when a shield is divided down the middle. When two coats of arms are marshalled, each in one of these divisions, the one is said to be party or parted with the other, or in the words of the later heraldry, to be impaling it. The word *party* or *parted* is also used for other specified divisions, as *party bendwise*.

Parvise.—Now generally used to denote a chamber above a porch.

Passant (of beasts, etc.).—In heraldry, walking and looking forward—head in profile.

Pastoral Staff.—*See* " Crosier."

Paten.—A plate for holding the Bread at the celebration of the Holy Communion.

Paty (*cross*).—*See* " Cross."

Pauldron.—Plate-defence for the shoulders.

Pediment.—A low-pitched gable used in Classical and Renaissance architecture above a portico, at the end of a building, and above doors, windows, niches, etc.; sometimes the middle part is omitted, forming a " *broken* " *pediment*.

Perk.—A perch on which to hang vestments.

Pheon.—In heraldry, a broad arrow-head.

Pilaster.—A shallow pier attached to a wall.

Pile.—In heraldry, a triangular or wedge-shaped charge, issuing from the chief of the shield unless otherwise blazoned.

Piscina.—A basin with a drain, set in or against the wall to the S. of an altar.

Plinth.—The projecting base of a wall or column, generally chamfered or moulded at the top.

Popey.—The ornament at the heads of bench-standards or desks in churches; generally carved with foliage and flowers, somewhat resembling a *fleur-de-lis*.

Portcullis.—The running gate, rising and falling in vertical grooves in the jambs of a doorway.

Pourpoint.—A body defence of cloth or of leather, padded or quilted.

Powdered.—In heraldry, a shield or charge with small charges scattered indiscriminately thereon is said to be powdered with them.

Presbytery.—The part of a church in which is placed the high altar, E. of the quire.

Priests' Vestments (*Mass*).—Amice, alb, girdle, stole crossed in front, fanon, chasuble.

Principals.—The chief trusses of a roof, or the main rafters, posts, or braces, in the wooden framework of a building.

Processional Vestments.—Same as canonical.

Pulvinated Frieze.—In Classical and Renaissance architecture, a frieze having a convex or bulging section.

Purlin.—A horizontal timber resting on the principal rafters of a roof-truss, and forming an intermediate support for the common rafters.

Purple or Purpure.—One of the colours in heraldry.

Pyx.—Any small box, but usually a vessel to contain the reserved Sacrament.

Quarry.—In glazing, small panes of glass, generally diamond-shaped or square, set diagonally.

Quarter.—In heraldry, the dexter corner of the shield; a charge made by enclosing that corner with a right-angled line taking in a quarter or somewhat less of the shield and giving it a tincture of its own.

Quartered or Quarterly.—A term which, in its original sense, belongs to a shield or charge divided crosswise into four quarters. After the practice of marshalling several coats in the quarters of a shield had been established, the quarters themselves might be quartered for the admission of more coats, or the four original divisions increased to six or more, each being still termed a quarter.

Quatrefoil.—In heraldry, a four-petalled flower. *See* also "Foil."

Queen-posts.—A pair of vertical posts in a roof-truss equi-distant from the middle line.

Quillon.—Bars forming cross-guard of sword.

Quilted Defence.—Armour made of padded cloth, leather, etc.

Quire-habit.—In secular churches : for boys, a surplice only over the cassock ; for clerks or vicars, the surplice and a black cope-like mantle, partly closed in front and put over the head, which was exchanged for a silk cope on festivals ; canons put on over the surplice a grey amess. In monastic churches, all classes, whether canons regular, monks, friars, nuns, or novices, wore the ordinary habit with a cope on festivals.

Quoin.—The dressed stones at the angle of a building.

Ragged, Raguly.—In heraldry, applied to a charge whose edges are ragged like a tree trunk with the limbs lopped away.

Rampant (of beasts, etc.).—In heraldry, standing erect on one foot, as if attacking or defending.

Rampart.—A mound or bank surrounding a fortified place.

Rapier.—Cut and thrust sword.

Razed.—Of a head, etc., in heraldry, having a ragged edge as though torn off.

Rear-arch.—The arch on the inside of a wall spanning a doorway or window-opening.

Rear-vault.—The space between a rear-arch and the outer stonework of a window.

Rebate (*rabbet, rabbit*).—A continuous rectangular notch cut on an edge.

Reliquary.—A small box or other receptacle for relics.

Rerebrace.—Plate or leather defence for upper arm.

Rere-dorter.—The common latrine of a monastic house.

Reredos.—A hanging, wall, or screen of stone or wood at the back of an altar or daïs.

Respond.—The half-pillar or pier at the end of an arcade or abutting a single arch.

Revetment.—A retaining wall of masonry against a bank of earth.

Roll-moulding *or* **Bowtell.**—A continuous convex moulding cut upon the edges of stone and woodwork, etc.

Rood (*Rood-beam, Rood-screen, Rood-loft*).—A cross or crucifix. The *Great Rood* was set up at the E. end of the nave with accompanying figures of St. Mary and St. John ; it was generally carved in wood, and fixed on the loft or head of the rood-screen, or in a special beam (the *Rood-beam*), reaching from wall to wall. Sometimes the rood was merely painted on the wall above the chancel-arch or on a closed wood partition or tympanum in the upper half of the arch. The *Rood-screen* is the open screen spanning the E. end of the nave, shutting off the chancel ; in the 15th century a narrow gallery was often constructed above the cornice to carry the rood and other images and candles, and it was also used as a music gallery. The loft was approached by a staircase (and occasionally

ROOD—*con.*

by more than one), either of wood or in a turret built in the wall wherever most convenient, and, when the loft was carried right across the building, the intervening walls of the nave were often pierced with narrow archways. Many of the roods were destroyed at the Reformation, and their final removal, with the loft, was ordered in 1561.

Roundel.—In heraldry, a round plate or disc of any tincture other than gold.

Rubble.—Walling of rough unsquared stones or flints.

Rustic work, rusticated joints.—Masonry in which only the margins of the stones are worked.

Sabatons or Sollerets.—Articulated plate-defences for the feet.

Sable.—In heraldry, black.

Salade or Sallet.—Light steel headpiece, frequently with vizor.

Saltire.—In heraldry, an X-shaped cross ; also called St. Andrew's cross.

Sanctus-Bell.—A small bell, usually hung in a bell-cot over the E. gable of the nave, or in the steeple, and rung at the Elevation of the Host during mass. The name is also applied to small bells of post-Reformation date.

Scallop.—A shellfish, a common charge in heraldry.

Scalloped capital.—A development of the cushion-capital in which the single cushion is elaborated into a series of truncated cones.

Scapple, to.—To dress roughly, of masonry or timber.

Scarp.—A vertical or sloping face of earth in a ditch or moat, or cut in the slope of a hill, facing away from the place which it helps to defend.

Scribe.—A term applied to timber cut or fitted to an irregular surface or moulding.

Scroll-moulding.—A rounded moulding of two parts, the upper projecting beyond the lower, thus resembling a scroll of parchment.

Scutcheon or Scocheon.—1. A shield, a charge in heraldry, *Voided Scutcheon*, a scutcheon whose border alone is seen ; termed in modern heraldry an *Orle.*

2. A metal plate pierced for the spindle of a handle or for a keyhole.

Sedilia (sing. *sedile*, a seat), sometimes called presbyteries.—The seats on the S. side of the chancel, quire, or chapel near the altar, used by the ministers during the Mass.

Septaria.—Nodules of hardened clay from the upper Tertiary formations, used as building material during the Roman and, to a less extent, during the mediaeval period.

Sexpartite vault.—*See* "Vaulting."

Shaft.—A small column.

Shafted jambs.—A jamb containing one or more shafts either engaged or detached.

Shell-keep.—A ring wall cresting a castle mount and sometimes enclosing buildings.

Shingles.—Tiles of cleft timber, used for covering spires, etc.

Sinister.—In heraldry, the left-hand side of a shield as held.

Slip-tiles.—Tiles moulded with a design in intaglio which was then filled in, before burning, with a clay of a different colour.

Slype.—A mediaeval term for a narrow passage between two buildings ; generally used for that from the cloister to the cemetery of a monastic establishment.

Soffit.—The under side of a staircase, lintel, cornice, arch, canopy, etc.

Soffit-cusps.—Cusps springing from the flat soffit of an arched head, and not from its chamfered sides or edges.

Solar.—An upper chamber in a mediaeval house adjoining the daïs end of the Hall, and reserved for the private use of the family.

Sollerets.—*See* " Sabatons."

Spandrel.—The triangular-shaped space above the haunch of an arch ; the two outer edges generally form a rectangle, as in an arched and square-headed doorway ; the name is also applied to a space within a curved brace below a tie-beam, etc., and to any similar spaces.

Spire, Broach-spire, Needle-spire.—The tall pointed termination covered with lead or shingles, the roof of a tower or turret. A *Broach-spire* rises from the sides of the tower without a parapet, the angles of a square tower being surmounted, in this case, by half-pyramids against the alternate faces of the spire, when octagonal. A *Needle-spire* is small and narrow, and rises from the middle of the tower-roof well within the parapet.

Splay.—A sloping face making an angle more than a right-angle with the main surface, as in window jambs, etc.

Springing-line.—The level at which an arch springs from its supports.

Sprocket-pieces.—Short lengths of timber covering the end of roof-rafters to flatten the angle of pitch of the roof at the eaves.

Spurs.—*Prick :* in form of plain goad ; early form. *Rowel :* with spiked wheel ; later form.

Squinch.—An arch thrown across the angle between two walls to support a superstructure, such as the base of a stone spire.

Squint.—A piercing through a wall to allow a view of an altar from places whence it could otherwise not be seen.

Stages of Tower.—The divisions marked by horizontal string-courses externally.

Stanchion, stancheon.—The upright iron bars in a screen, window, etc.

Stole.—A long narrow strip of embroidery with fringed ends worn above the alb by a deacon over the left shoulder, and by priests and bishops over both shoulders.

Stops.—Projecting stones at the ends of labels, string-courses, etc., against which the mouldings finish ; they are often carved in various forms, such as shields, bunches of foliage, human or grotesque heads, etc. ; a finish at the end of any moulding or chamfer bringing the corner out to a square edge, or sometimes, in the case of a moulding, to a chamfered edge. A splayed stop has a plain sloping face, but in many other cases the face is moulded.

Stoup.—A vessel, placed near an entrance doorway, to contain holy water ; those remaining are usually in the form of a deeply-dished stone set in a niche, or on a pillar. Also called *Holy-water Stones*, or *Holy-water Stocks.*

String-course.—A projecting horizontal band in a wall ; usually moulded.

Strut.—A timber forming a sloping support to a beam, etc.

Style.—The vertical members of a frame into which are tenoned the ends of the rails or horizontal pieces.

Sub-deacons' Vestments (*Mass*).—Amice, alb, tunicle, fanon.

Surcoat.—Coat, usually sleeveless, worn over armour.

Swastika.—A peculiar cruciform figure, each arm of which is bent to form a right angle.

Tabard.—Short loose surcoat, open at sides, with short tab-like sleeves, sometimes worn with armour, and emblazoned with arms ; distinctive garment of heralds.

Table, Alabaster.—A panel or series of panels of alabaster carved with religious subjects and placed at the back of an altar to form a reredos. The manufacture was a distinctively English industry of the 14th, 15th and early 16th centuries, centred at Nottingham.

Taces or tonlets.—Articulated defence for hips and lower part of body.

Tas-de-Charge.—The lower courses of an arch or vault-springer, when the joints are horizontal and not radial with the curve.

Terminal figure.—The upper part of a carved human figure growing out of a column, post, or pilaster, diminishing into the base.

Tie-beam.—The horizontal transverse beam in a roof, tying together the feet of the rafters to counteract the thrust.

Timber-framed building.—A building of which the walls are built of open timbers and covered with plaster or boarding, or with interstices filled in with brick-work.

Totternhoe stone.—Clunch from Totternhoe, Bedfordshire.

Touch.—A soft black marble quarried near Tournai and commonly used in monumental art.

Tracery.—The ornamental work in the head of a window, screen, panel, etc., formed by the curving and interlacing of bars of stone or wood, and grouped together, generally over two or more lights or bays.

Transom.—A horizontal bar of stone or wood across the upper half of a window-opening, doorway, or panel.

Trefoil.—In heraldry, a three-lobed leaf with a pendent stalk.

Tressure.—In heraldry, a narrow flowered or counter-flowered orle, often voided or doubled, as in the arms of the Kings of Scots.

Trimmer.—A timber, framing an opening in a floor or roof.

Tripping.—Applied, in heraldry, to stags, etc., walking or passant.

Truss.—A number of timbers framed together to bridge a space or form a bracket, to be self-supporting, and to carry other timbers. The *trusses* of a roof are generally named after a peculiar feature in their construction, such as *King-post, Queen-post, Hammer-beam*, etc. (*q.v.*).

Tuiles.—In armour, plates attached to and hanging from the edge of taces, or tonlets.

Tunicle.—Similar to dalmatic.

Tympanum.—An enclosed space within an arch, doorway etc., or in the triangle of a pediment.

Types of Houses.—*See* " Houses."

Vair.—In heraldry, a fur imitating grey squirrels' skins, usually shown as an alternating series, often in rows, of blue and white bell-shaped patches. If of other tinctures it is called *vairy*.

Vallum.—A rampart.

Vambrace.—Plate-defence for lower arm.

Vamplate.—Funnel-shaped hand-guard of lance.

Vaulting.—An arched ceiling or roof of stone or brick, sometimes imitated in wood. *Barrel-vaulting* (sometimes called *waggon-head-vaulting*) is a continuous vault unbroken in its length by cross-vaults. A *groined vault* (or cross-vaulting) results from the intersection of simple vaulting surfaces. A *ribbed vault* is a framework of arched ribs carrying the cells which cover in the spaces between them. One bay of vaulting, divided into four quarters or compartments, is termed *quadripartite*; but often the bay is divided longitudinally into two subsidiary bays, each equalling a bay of the wall supports; the vaulting bay is thus divided into six compartments, and is termed *sexpartite*. A more complicated form is *lierne-vaulting*; this contains secondary ribs, which do not spring from the wall-supports, but cross from main rib to main rib. In *fan-vaulting* numerous ribs rise from the springing in equal curves, diverging equally in all directions, giving fan-like effects when seen from below.

Veil.—A sweat-cloth attached to the head of the crosier. (*See also* "Lenten Veil.")

Vernicle.—A representation of the face of Christ printed on St. Veronica's handkerchief.

Vert.—In heraldry, green.

Vestments (ecclesiastical).—*See* alb, amess, amice, apparels, archbishops' vestments, bishops' vestments, buskins, canonical quire habit, cassock, chasuble, cope, crosier, cross staff, dalmatic, deacons' vestments, fanon, mitred abbots' vestments, morse, orphreys, priests' vestments, processional vestments, quire habit, sub-deacons' vestments, stole, tunicle.

Vizor.—Hinged face-guard of bascinet, salade, close helmet, etc.

Voided.—In heraldry, with the middle part cut away, leaving a margin.

Volute.—A spiral form of ornament.

Voussoirs.—The stones forming an arch.

Vowess.—A woman, generally a widow, who had taken a vow of chastity, but was not attached to any religious order.

Waggon-head-vault.—*See* 'Vaulting.'

Wall-plate.—A timber laid lengthwise on the wall to receive the ends of the rafters and other joists.

Warming-house.—In monastic planning, an apartment in which a fire was kept burning for warmth.

Water-bouget.—*See* "Bouget."

Wattle and daub.—An old form of filling in timber-framed buildings.

Wave-mould.—A compound mould formed by a convex curve between two concave curves.

Weather-boarding.—Horizontal boards nailed to the uprights of timber-framed buildings and made to overlap; the boards are wedge-shaped in section, the upper edge being the thinner.

Weathering (to sills, tops of buttresses, etc.).—A sloping surface for casting off water, etc.

Weepers.—Small upright figures, generally of relatives of the deceased, placed in niches or panels round the sides of mediaeval tombs; occasionally also represented on brasses.

Well-staircase.—A staircase of several flights and generally square, surrounding a space or "well."

Wimple.—Scarf covering chin and throat.

Wyver or Wyvern.—A dragon-like monster with a beaked head, two legs with claws, and tail sometimes coiled in a knot. The earlier examples show wings.

COMBINED INDEX.

For the general headings and the method used in compiling this Index readers are referred to the three Reports of the Index Committee printed in the previous volumes on Essex. The recommendations of this Committee were considered and adopted by the Commission.

How to use the Index. This Index is a combined one covering the four volumes on Essex. The volume in which each individual parish is scheduled is indicated by the figure in bold type which directly follows the name of the parish.
1 = Essex North-West (1916); **2** = Essex Central and South-West (1921); **3** = Essex North-East (1922); **4** = Essex South-East (1923).
The figure (or figures) in brackets and in light-face type which directly follows the number of the volume refers to the number of the monument within the parish. Thus—Abberton Hall, Abberton **3** (2) indicates that the parish of Abberton is scheduled in Volume 3 and that Abberton Hall is the monument numbered (2) in that parish.
The parishes are printed alphabetically so far as each volume is concerned and this in itself is an index.
Page references have been given when considered necessary, those in Roman figures being to the Sectional Preface and County Survey.
* An asterisk denotes an addition or correction, and the reference in question will be found in the Addenda et Corrigenda (**4** pp. 185–8), under the volume and parish concerned.

* *See Addenda et Corrigenda, pp. 185–8, under this Volume and Parish.*

Instructions how to use this Index given on page 198.

* *See Addenda et Corrigenda, pp. 185-8, under this Volume and Parish.*

Instructions how to use this Index given on page 198.

* See Addenda et Corrigenda, pp. 185-8, under this Volume and Parish.

Instructions how to use this Index given on page 198.

Armour : *cont.*

FUNERAL-HELMS AND HELMETS :

15th-century : Witham **2** (1) (*Plate* **2** p. 85)

16th-century :

Barking **2** (2) ; Bocking **1** (1) ; Bradfield **3** (1) ; Bradwell (juxta-Coggeshall) **3** (1) ; Castle Heding- ham **1** (3) ; East Horndon **4** (1) ; Faulkbourne **2** (2) ; Good Easter **2** (1) ; Grays Thurrock **4** (1) ; Great Hallingbury **2** (2) ; Little Bentley **3** (1) ; Magdalen Laver **2** (1) ; Springfield **2** (1) ; Stapleford Abbots **2** (1) ; Steeple Bumpstead **1** (2) ; Theydon Garnon **2** (1) ; Wethersfield **1** (1) ; Willingale Doe **2** (1) ; Witham **2** (1) (*Plate* **2** p. 85)

16th or 17th-century :

Danbury **4** (1) ; Thundersley **4** (1)

circa 1600 :

East Ham **2** (2) ; Rivenhall **3** (2) (*Plate* **3** p. 133)

17th-century :

Bradwell (juxta-Coggeshall) **3** (1) ; Cressing **3** (1) ; Dagenham **2** (1) ; Great Bardfield **1** (1) ; Hempstead **1** (1) ; Latton **2** (2) (fragments) ; Navestock **2** (1) ; Witham **2** (1) (*Plate* **2** p. 85)

GAUNTLETS :

16th-century : Castle Hedingham **1** (3)

Undated : Grays Thurrock **4** (1)

SWORDS :

Undated : Grays Thurrock **4** (1) ; Thundersley **4** (1)

Armours, Good Easter **2** (6)

Arms, shields-of-, blazoned, *see under* **Heraldry**

Armstrong, Jane, *see* **Luther 2**

Arnold's Farm, Lambourne **2** (5)

„ „ Mountnessing **4** (4)

Arrowsmith, arms : North Weald Bassett **2** (1)

Arrowsmith, Thomas, rector of the parish, 1705–6, and Margaret, his wife, 1702, floor-slab to : North Weald Bassett **2** (1)

Arundel, arms : Layer Marney **3** (1) (glass) (*Plate* **3** p. 192) ; *see also* **Fitzalan, Earl of Arundel**

Ascension, The, glass : Stisted **3** (1)

Asfeldens, Berners Roding **2** (3)

Ash, *see under* **Inns**

Ash Farm, Weeley **3** (6)

Ash Ground, Good Easter **2** (17)

Ashcote Farm (formerly), Great Waltham **2** (21)

Ashdon 1 pp. 4–9 ; **4** p. 185

Ashdon Place, Bartlow End **1** (1) (*Plate* **1** p. xxv)

Asheldham 4 pp. 2–3

Ashen 1 pp. 9–10

Ashen :

Thomas, 1684, and Frances, his wife, 1694, tablet to : Horndon-on-the-Hill **4** (1)

Thomas, John, William, John and Richard, 17th- century floor-slab to : Horndon-on-the-Hill **4** (1)

Ashen House, Ashen **1** (3)

Ashfield, Great Canfield **2** (10)

Ashingdon 4 pp. 3–4

Ashlings, Magdalen Laver **2** (3)

Ashlyns, site of, High Ongar **2** (2)

Ashman's Farm, Woodham Walter **2** (5)

Ashwell Hall, Finchingfield **1** (46)

Aspall, arms : Wimbish **1** (1) (glass)

Assandun, Battle of, *see* **Ironside, Edmund**

Asser :

George, 1674, and Susanna, his wife, 1658, table-tomb to : Barling **4** (1)

George, 1683, and ———, his wife, late the wife of Thomas Wright, 1686, floor-slab to : Barling **4** (1)

Assers, Good Easter **2** (12)

Atkyns, arms : Waltham Holy Cross **2** (1)

Atkyns, Francis, 1640, floor-slab to : Waltham Holy Cross **2** (1)

Attnok, *or* **Atenok,** Thomas, indent of early 14th-century marginal inscription to : Wennington **4** (1)

Attridges, High Roding **2** (10)

Aubyns, Writtle **2** (12) (*Plate* **2** p. 272)

Audley, *or* **Awdeley :**

Arms : Colchester **3** (11) ; Saffron Walden **1** (1) (3)

Motto : Saffron Walden **1** (1)

Audley, *or* **Awdeley :**

Catherine, wife of Robert, 1641, floor-slab to : St. Michael's, Berechurch, Colchester **3** (11)

Sir Henry, and Anne (Packington), his wife, monument to, erected 1648 : St. Michael's, Berechurch, Colchester **3** (11) (*Plate* **3** p. 97)

Robert, floor-slab to : St. Michael's, Berechurch, Colchester **3** (11)

Robert, 1624, monument to, erected by Katherine (Windsor), his wife : St. Michael's, Berechurch, Colchester **3** (11)

Thomas, Lord, K.G., Lord Chancellor, 1544, altar-tomb to : Saffron Walden **1** (1)

Thomas, 1584, and John, 1588, brass to : St. Michael's, Berechurch, Colchester **3** (11)

Audley End, see Saffron Walden **1**

Audley End House, Saffron Walden **1** (3) (*Plates* **1** pp. xxxiv–v, 234–8) ; 17th-century painting of, at Bower Hall, Steeple Bumpstead **1** (5)

Augustine, St., of Hippo :

CARVING (on pulpit) ; White Colne **3** (1)

GLASS : Maldon St. Peter **2** (3) (*Plate* **2** p. xxxv)

PAINTING (on screen) : Foxearth **1** (1)

Augustinians, *see* AUSTIN CANONS, *under* **Religious Houses**

Aurelius, M., coin of : Colchester **3** (1 D.)

Austin, arms : Ingatestone and Fryerning **2** (1)

Austin, *or* **Austen :**

Frances, wife of James, 1698, and James, 1699, floor-slab to : Ingatestone and Fryerning **2** (1)

Henry, servant of the Earl of Carlisle, 1638, brass to : Waltham Holy Cross **2** (1)

Austin Canons, *see under* **Religious Houses**

Austin's Lane, see Harwich **3**

Aveley 4 pp. 4–10

Avenant, Nicholas, 1599, slab to : West Ham **2** (1)

Avenue House, Witham **2** (18)

Awdeley, *see* **Audley,** *above*

Axe and Compasses, *see under* **Inns**

Aylet, arms : Great Braxted **3** (1) ; Great Coggeshall **3** (2) ; Heybridge **3** (1) ; Rivenhall **3** (2)

Aylet, -t :

Elizabeth (Freshwater), wife of William, 1690, floor-slab to : Heybridge **3** (1)

Jeremy of Doreward Hall, 1657, floor-slab to : Riven- hall **3** (2)

"John Aylet Gave Me In The Vorchup Of The Trinitie Ao. 1523," inscription on bell : Leaden Roding **2** (1)

John, 1707, and Mary, his wife, 1730, floor-slab to : Bocking **1** (1)

Judith (Gaell), 1623, wife of Robert, LL.D., brass to : Feering **3** (1)

Robert, LL.D., 1654, tablet to : Great Braxted **3** (1)

Thomas, 1638, brass to : Great Coggeshall **3** (2)

Thomas, 17th-century floor-slab to : Great Coggeshall **3** (2)

Aylmer, arms : Harlow **2** (2)

Aylmer, Thomas, 1518, and Alys, his wife, brass of : Harlow **2** (2)

* See Addenda et Corrigenda, pp. 185–8, under this Volume and Parish.

Instructions how to use this Index given on page 198.

* See Addenda et Corrigenda, pp. 185–8, under this Volume and Parish.

Instructions how to use this Index given on page 198.

* See *Addenda et Corrigenda, pp. 185–8, under this Volume and Parish.*

Instructions how to use this Index given on page 198.

Instructions how to use this Index given on page 193.

Beaumont :
Elizabeth, widow of William, Viscount Beaumont and Lord Bardolfe, and wife of John, Earl of Oxford, 1537, brass of : Wivenhoe **3** (1)
William, Viscount Beaumont and Lord Bardolfe, 1507, brass of : Wivenhoe **3** (1)
Beaumont-cum-Moze 3 pp. 7–8
Beaumont Hall, Beaumont-cum-Moze **3** (3) (*Plate* **3** p. 234)
Beavis Hall, Langford **2** (6)
Beazley End, see Wethersfield **1**
Beckingham Hall, Tolleshunt Major **3** (3) (*Plate* **3** p. 230)
Becklandwood Farm, Earls Colne **3** (28)
Beckman, John, parson, 1628, also Elizabeth ——, 1611, brass and floor-slab to : Little Burstead **4** (1)
Beckwith, Frances, see **Hervy 2**
Beddall's End, see Braintree. **2**
Bedell, arms : Writtle **2** (1)
Bedell :
Family, brass probably of *c.* 1500 : Writtle **2** (1)
Thomasin, widow of John, see **Thomas 2**
Bedeman's Berg Cell, Writtle **2** (2)
Bedfords, Good Easter **2** (14)
Bedlar's Green, see Great Hallingbury **2**
Bedynfeld, Phillippe, see **Darcye 3**
Beech House, Loughton **2** (11)*
Beeches, Rawreth **4** (5)
Beeleigh Abbey, Maldon St. Peter **2** (3) (*Plates* **2** pp. 176, 178, 179, 182, 183) ; *see also* **4** p. 187
Beeleigh Abbey, arms : Maldon All Saints **2** (1) (corbel)
Beggarshall Coppice, Hatfield Broad Oak **2** (41)
Belchamp Otton 1 pp. 14–16
Belchamp St. Paul's 1 pp. 16–18
Belchamp Walter 1 pp. 18–21
Belhouse, arms : Aveley **4** (6) (glass)
Belhus, Aveley **4** (6) (*Plates* **4** pp. 9, 56–7, 64–5)
Belitha, Anne, see **Dyer 1**
Bell, see under **Inns**
Bell, arms, Writtle **2** (1)
Bell :
Alice, wife of Robert, 1646, floor-slab to : St. Leonards at-the-Hythe, Colchester **3** (10)
Edward, 1576, brass of : Writtle **2** (1)
Bell House (*or* Mannocks), High Easter **2** (28)
,, ,, Romford Urban **2** (9) (*Plate* **2** p. 128)
Bellame, arms : East Mersea **3** (1)
Bellame, Lieut. Col. Edward, 1656, tablet (painted wooden panel) to : East Mersea **3** (1)
Belfries and Bell-towers, etc., timber, *see under* **Towers**
Bellfounders and Foundries : [1]
BAGLEY, JAMES (1710–1717) : Doddinghurst **2** (1)
BAGLEY, MATTHEW (1693–1716) : Woodford **2** (1)
BARTLET, ANTHONY (1649–1675) : Burnham **4** (1) ; Chingford **2** (1) ; Chipping Ongar **2** (2) ; Hempstead **1** (1) ; Hornchurch **4** (1) ; Hutton **4** (1) ; Little Laver **2** (1) ; North Weald Bassett **2** (1) ; South Hanningfield **4** (1) ;· South Weald **2** (1) ; Stanford Rivers **2** (1) ; Toppesfield **1** (1) ; Wennington **4** (1)
BARTLET, JAMES (1675–1700) : Aveley **4** (1) ; Bocking **1** (1) ; Broxted **1** (1) ; Hockley **4** (1) ; Lambourne **2** (1) ; Maldon St. Peter **2** (2) ; Southminster **4** (1) ; West Tilbury **4** (2)
BARTLET, THOMAS (1616–1631) : Aveley **4** (1) ; Chadwell **4** (2) ; Corringham **4** (1) ; East Horndon **4** (1) ; Fobbing **4** (1) ; Laindon **4** (1) ; Little Parndon **2** (1) ; Rainham **4** (1) ; Ramsden Crays **4** (1) ; West Tilbury **4** (2) ; Willingale Doe **2** (1)

Bellfounders and Foundries : *cont.*
BIRD, JOHN (15th century) : Copford **3** (1) ; Halstead Urban **1** (1) ; High Easter **2** (1) ; Laindon **4** (1) ; Little Bardfield **1** (1) ; Little Horkesley **3** (1) ; Pebmarsh **3** (1) ; Stondon Massey **2** (1) ; Twinstead **3** (1)
BOWLER, RICHARD (1587–1603) : Birdbrook **1** (1) ; Colchester **3** (2) ; Fairsted **2** (1) ; Halstead Urban **1** (1) ; Markshall **3** (1) ; Shalford **1** (1) ; Tolleshunt Knights **3** (2) ; Witham **2** (1) ; Wormingford **3** (1)
BRACKER, AUSTIN (16th century) : Alphamstone **3** (1)
BREND OF NORWICH, JOHN (1564–1582) : Birdbrook **1** (1)
BRISTOL FOUNDRY : Chrishall **1** (1)
BULLISDON, THOMAS (*c.* 1500) : Aldham **3** (1) ; Dengie **4** (1) ; Mountnessing **4** (1) ; Rayleigh **4** (1) ; Weeley **3** (1)
BURFORD, ROBERT (1392–1418) : Ardleigh **3** (1) ; Bowers Gifford **4** (1) ; Dedham **3** (1) ; Faulkbourne **2** (2) ; Great Henny **3** (1) ; Little Bromley **3** (1) ; Margaretting **2** (1) ; Mount Bures **3** (1) ; North Benfleet **4** (1) ; Rayleigh **4** (1) ; Weeley **3** (1)
BURFORD, WILLIAM (1373–1392) : Bowers Gifford **4** (1) ; Dovercourt **3** (2) ; Eastwood **4** (1)
BURY FOUNDRY : Alphamstone **3** (1) ; Fingringhoe **3** (1) ; Great Horkesley **3** (1)
CARTER, JOSEPH (1607–1609) : Stanford Rivers **2** (1)
CARTER, WILLIAM (1609–1616) : High Ongar **2** (1) ; Stapleford Tawney **2** (1) ; Willingale Doe **2** (1)
CHURCH, *or* CHIRCHE, REIGNOLD (?–1498) : Liston **1** (1)
CHURCH, *or* CHIRCHE, THOMAS (1498–1527) : Ashdon **1** (5)
CLARKE, JOHN (1599–1621) : Downham **4** (1) ; Little Burstead **4** (1) ; Roxwell **2** (1) ; Tilty **1** (1) ; Wimbish **1** (1)
CLIFTON, JOHN (1632–1640) : East Horndon **4** (1) ; Horndon-on-the-Hill **4** (1) ; Lambourne **2** (1) ; Little Burstead **4** (1) ; Stifford **4** (1) ; Sutton **4** (1) ; Theydon Mount **2** (1) ; West Thurrock **4** (1) ; Willingale Doe **2** (1)
CROWCH, ROBERT (15th century) : Little Clacton **3** (1)
CULVERDEN, WILLIAM (*c.* 1500) : Aveley **4** (1) ; Elsenham **1** (1) ; Margaretting **2** (1) ; Takeley **1** (1) ; Tillingham **4** (1) ; Wicken Bohunt **1** (1)
DANYELL, JOHN (15th century) : Cranham **4** (1) ; Great Easton **1** (1) ; Great Holland **3** (1) ; Great Maplestead **1** (1) ; Great Wigborough **3** (1) ; Heybridge **3** (1) ; Sible Hedingham **1** (1) ; Theydon Bois **2** (1) ; Wix **3** (1) ; Woodham Mortimer **4** (1)
DARBIE, JOHN (1656–1685) : Ardleigh **3** (1) ; Beaumont-cum-Moze **3** (1) ; Bocking **1** (1) ; Colchester **3** (6) ; Dedham **3** (1) ; Great Dunmow **1** (1) ; Great Tey **3** (1) ; Heybridge **3** (1) ; Ramsey **3** (1) ; Tillingham **4** (1)
·DAWE, WILLIAM (also known as WILLIAM FOUNDER) (1385–1418) : Aldham **3** (1) ; Brightlingsea **3** (3) ; Frating **3** (1) ; Netteswell **2** (1) ; Pleshey **2** (2)
DIER, DIAR, *or* DYER, JOHN (1575–1600) : Barling **4** (1) ; Berners Roding **2** (1) ; Corringham **4** (1) ; Elsenham **1** (1) ; Great Canfield **2** (1) ; Little Baddow **2** (1) ; Paglesham **4** (1) ; Stock **4** (1)
DODDES, ROBERT (last half of the 16th century) : Wimbish **1** (1)
DRAPER, THOMAS (*c.* 1574–1595) : Copford **3** (1) ; Halstead Urban **1** (1) ; Stambourne **1** (1)
ELDRIDGE, BRYAN (1640–1661) : Great Dunmow **1** (2)
FOUNDER, William, see DAWE, *above*
GARDINER, THOMAS (1709–1760) : Belchamp Walter **1** (1) ; Boxted **3** (1)
GEOFFREY OF EDMONTON (*c.* 1303 ?) : Southchurch **4** (1)

* See Addenda et Corrigenda, pp. 185–8, under this Volume and Parish.

[1] *The dates assigned to these Bellfounders and Foundries are for the most part taken from Church Bells of Essex (1909), by C. Deedes and H. B. Walters.*

Instructions how to use this Index given on page 198.

* *See Addenda et Corrigenda, pp. 185–8, under this Volume and Parish.*

Instructions how to use this Index given on page 198.

See Addenda et Corrigenda, pp. 185–8, under this Volume and Parish.

Instructions how to use this Index given on page 198.

* See Addenda et Corrigenda, pp. 185-8, under this Volume and Parish.

Instructions how to use this Index given on page 198.

See Addenda et Corrigenda, pp. 185–8, under this Volume and Parish.

O

Instructions how to use this Index given on page 198.

Instructions how to use this Index given on page 198.

See Addenda et Corrigenda, pp. 185–8, under this Volume and Parish.

Instructions how to use this Index given on page 198.

See Addenda et Corrigenda, pp. 185–8, under this Volume and Parish.

Instructions how to use this Index given on page 198.

* See Addenda et Corrigenda, pp. 185–8, under this Volume and Parish.

Instructions how to use this Index given on page 198.

Brasses, Monumental : *cont.*
INSCRIPTIONS, etc. : *cont.*
16th-century :
Althorne **4** (1) ; Aveley **4** (1) ; Barking **2** (2) ;
Barnston **2** (1) ; Belchamp St. Paul's **1** (1) ;
Bobbingworth **2** (1) ; Bradfield **3** (1) ; Braintree
2 (1) ; Chigwell **2** (2) ; Colchester **3** (11) ; Colne
Engaine **3** (1) ; Corringham **4** (1) ; Downham
4 (1) ; East Ham **2** (2) ; East Mersea **3** (1) ;
Elmdon **1** (1) ; Felsted **2** (1) ; Finchingfield **1** (1) ;
Fingringhoe **3** (1) ; Goldhanger **3** (2) ; Gosfield
1 (1) ; Great Bardfield **1** (1) ; Great Coggeshall
3 (2) ; Great Hallingbury **2** (2) ; Great Waltham
2 (1) ; Great Warley **4** (1) ; Harlow **2** (2) ;
Harwich **3** (1) ; Hatfield Peverel **2** (1) ; Hempstead **1** (1) ; Hornchurch **4** (1) ; Hutton **4** (1) ;
Lawford **3** (2)* ; Layer Marney **3** (1) ; Leigh
4 (1) ; Little Clacton **3** (1) ; Littlebury **1** (2) ;
Low Leyton **2** (2) ; Mountnessing **4** (1) ; Navestock **2** (1) ; North Ockendon **4** (1) ; Orsett
4 (1) ; Pitsea **4** (1) ; Purleigh **4** (1) ; Rayne
1 (1) ; Rettendon **4** (1) ; Roxwell **2** (1) ; Sheering
2 (1) ; Shelley **2** (1) ; South Benfleet **4** (1) ;
South Ockendon **4** (1) ; ' South Weald **2** (1) ;
Southminster **4** (1) ; Stanford Rivers **2** (1) ;
Stapleford Tawney **2** (1) ; Strethall **1** (1) ;
Tillingham **1** (1) ; Toppesfield **1** (1) ; Thorrington
3 (1) ; Ugley **1** (1) ; Waltham Holy Cross **2** (1) ;
Walthamstow **2** (1) ; West Hanningfield **4** (1) ;
West Thurrock **4** (1) ; Woodford **2** (1)
17th-century :
Abbess Roding **2** (1) ; Alphamstone **3** (1) ;
Bobbingworth **2** (1) ; Bocking **1** (1) ; Borley
1 (1) ; Bradfield **3** (1) ; Bradwell-juxta-Mare **4**
(2) ; Braintree **2** (1) ; Broomfield **2** (1) ; Broxted
1 (1) ; Chadwell **4** (2) ; Cranham **4** (1) ; Creeksea
4 (1) ; Danbury **4** (1) ; East Ham **2** (2) ; East
Hanningfield **4** (1) ; Feering **3** (1) ; Finchingfield
1 (1) ; Fingringhoe **3** (1) ; Foxearth **1** (1) ; Great
Chesterford **1** (3) ; Great Coggeshall **3** (2) ; Great
Dunmow **1** (1) ; Great Easton **1** (1) ; Great
Henny **3** (1) ; Great Wigborough **3** (1) ; Great
Yeldham **1** (1) ; Hatfield Broad Oak **2** (1) ;
Heybridge **3** (1) ; High Ongar **2** (1) ; High Roding
2 (1) ; Horndon-on-the-Hill **4** (1) ; Kelvedon
Hatch **2** (1) ; Leigh **4** (1) ; Little Baddow **2** (1) ;
Little Burstead **4** (1) ; Low Leyton **2** (2) ;
Messing **3** (1) ; Navestock **2** (1) ; Newport **1** (1) ;
North Fambridge **4** (1) ; Pattiswick **3** (1) ;
Pebmarsh **3** (1) ; Purleigh **4** (1) ; Rainham **4** (1) ;
Rawreth **4** (1) ; Saffron Walden **1** (1) ; Shalford
1 (1) ; St. Osyth **3** (2) ; South Weald **2** (1) ;
Stanford Rivers **2** (1) ; Stansted Mountfitchet **1** (2) ;
Stebbing **1** (1) ; Steeple Bumpstead **1** (2) (coffin-
plate) ; Takeley **1** (1) ; Thaxted **1** (2) ; Tolleshunt
D'Arcy **3** (1) ; Twinstead **3** (1) ; Upminster
4 (1) ; Wakes Colne **3** (1) ; Waltham Holy Cross
2 (1) ; Willingale Spain **2** (1) ; Woodford **2** (1)
Early 18th-century (before 1715) :
Latton **2** (2) ; Leigh **4** (1)
PALIMPSEST :
14th-century : Tolleshunt D'Arcy **3** (1)
circa 1400 : Tolleshunt D'Arcy **3** (1)
circa 1460 and *circa* 1500 : Ingatestone and
Fryerning **2** (2)
15th-century :
Aveley **4** (1) ; Strethall **1** (1) ; Tolleshunt D'Arcy
3 (1) ; Upminster **4** (1) ; Walthamstow **2** (1)
16th-century : Wimbish **1** (1) (now in British
Museum)

Brasses, Monumental : *cont.*
PALIMPSEST : *cont.*
Undated :
Colchester **3** (4) ; Fingringhoe **3** (1) ; Stondon
Massey **2** (1)
MISCELLANEOUS :
CANOPIED BRASSES :
14th-century :
Aveley **4** (1) ; Chrishall **1** (1) ; Little Horkesley
3 (1) (*Plate* **3** p. 171) ; Stondon Massey **2** (1)
(remains)
circa 1400 : South Benfleet **4** (1) (fragments now
in Colchester Museum)
15th-century :
Great Bromley **3** (1) ; Little Horkesley **3** (1)
(*Plate* **3** p. 171) ; South Ockendon **4** (1) (remains)
16th-century :
Loughton **2** (1) ; Wivenhoe **3** (1)
FLEMISH BRASSES :
14th-century :
Aveley **4** (1) ; Tolleshunt D'Arcy **3** (1)
15th-century :
Aveley **4** (1) ; Upminster **4** (1)
Undated :
Colchester **3** (4) ; Stondon Massey **2** (1)
SHIELDS ONLY :
13th-century : Little Leighs **2** (2)
15th-century :
Gosfield **1** (1) ; Hatfield Peverel **2** (1) ; Horn-
church **4** (1) ; Little Leighs **2** (2) ; Maldon All
Saints **2** (1)
circa 1500 : Hornchurch **4** (1)
16th-century :
Bradwell-juxta-Mare **4** (2) ; Faulkbourne **2** (2) ;
Hornchurch **4** (1) ; Ingatestone and Fryerning
2 (1) ; Stanford Rivers **2** (1) ; Tolleshunt D'Arcy
3 (1) ; Walthamstow **2** (1)
17th-century :
East Ham **2** (2) ; Margaretting **2** (1) ; Writtle
2 (1) (on Weston tomb)
Undated : Little Horkesley **3** (1)
SHROUD BRASSES :
15th-century : Stifford **4** (1) (priest)
16th-century : Little Horkesley **3** (1) (woman)
UNCLASSIFIED :
14th-century : Tolleshunt D'Arcy **3** (1) (Apostles,
etc.)
15th-century : Stanford Rivers **2** (1) (swaddled
infant)
circa 1500 :
Elmstead **3** (1) (hands holding a heart) ; Hornchurch **4** (1) (group of five boys)
16th-century :
Aveley **4** (1) (children) ; Little Ilford **2** (1) (school-
boy) ; Orsett **4** (1) (group of six girls) ; Sandon
4 (1) (scrolls and shields) ; Woodham Mortimer
4 (1) (child)
17th-century :
Great Chesterford **1** (3) (swaddled infant) ;
Woodham Walter **2** (1) (death's head)
INDENTS :
Alresford **3** (2) ; Ashdon **1** (5) ; Bardfield Saling **1** (1) ;
Barking **2** (2) ; Barling **4** (1) ; Basildon **4** (1) ;
Beaumont-cum-Moze **3** (1) ; Belchamp Walter **1** (1) ;
Birdbrook **1** (1) ; Blackmore **2** (1) ; Black Notley
2 (1) ; Bocking **1** (1) ; Boreham **2** (1) ; Bradfield **3** (1) ;
Bradwell (juxta-Coggeshall) **3** (1) ; Bradwell-juxta-
Mare **4** (2) ; Bulphan **4** (1) ; Burnham **4** (1) ; Canew-
don **4** (1) ; Chadwell **4** (2) ; Chelmsford **2** (2) ;
Chignall **2** (2) ; Chingford **2** (1) ; Chipping Ongar

See Addenda et Corrigenda, pp. 185–8, under this Volume and Parish.

Instructions how to use this Index given on page 193.

* *See Addenda et Corrigenda, pp. 185–8, under this Volume and Parish.*

Instructions how to use this Index given on page 198.

---

* See Addenda et Corrigenda, pp. 185–8, under this Volume and Parish.

Instructions how to use this Index given on page 198.

Bull, *see under* **Inns**
Bullisdon, Thomas, *see under* **Bellfounders**
Bullock, arms : Faulkbourne **2** (2)
Bullock -e :
Sir Edward, 1644, tablet to : Faulkbourne **2** (2)
Henry, 1609, brass to : Great Wigborough **3** (1)
Henry, 1628, floor-slab to : Great Wigborough **3** (1)
Bulls Bridge Farm, Hempstead **1** (28)
Bull's Farm, Radwinter **1** (5)
Bulls Lodge, Boreham **2** (5)
Bullstead Farm, Great Burstead **4** (11)
Bulmer 1 pp. 45–47 ; **4** p. 185
Bulphan 4 pp. 16–17
Bulstrode, arms : Lawford **3** (2) (glass)
Bumpstead, *see* **Helion Bumpstead 1** *and* **Steeple Bumpstead 1**
Bundish Hall, Shelley **2** (2)
Burdocke, John, 1601, John, his son, and others later, floor-slab to : Leigh **4** (1)
Bures 3 pp. 18–19 ; *see also* **Mount Bures 3**
Burford, Robert and William, *see under* **Bellfounders**
Burgh, arms : Thaxted **1** (2) (glass)
Burgh, Hubert de, Hadleigh Castle built by : *see* Sectional Preface **4** p. xxxvii
Burgoyne, arms : Great Yeldham **1** (1)
Burgoyne, Susanna (Bastwick), wife of Dr. Burgoyne, 1685, tablet to : Great Yeldham **1** (1)

Burgundy, arms : Stondon Massey **2** (1) (brass) ; Witham **2** (1) (tiles)
Burkitt, arms : Dedham **3** (1)
Burkitt :
Martha (Wilkinson), wife of William, 1698, floor-slab to : Dedham **3** (1)
William, minister of the Church, 1703, tablet to : Dedham **3** (1)
Burley, arms : Castle Hedingham **1** (1) (Vere tomb)
Burnell, arms : Aveley **4** (6) (glass)
Burnel, " William Burnel 1581 Curate of Stanford," scratched inscription : Stanford-le-Hope **4** (1)
Burnham 4 pp. 17–19
Burnham Hall, Burnham **4** (2)
Burnt Hall, site of, Matching **2** (5)
Burnt House, Chickney **1** (5)
Burnt House Farm, Earls Colne **3** (27)
,, ,, ,, Shalford **1** (28)
,, ,, ,, Wimbish **1** (31)
Burnt Houses, Hornchurch **4** (24)
Burntwood End, see Saffron Walden **1**
Burrough, Thomas, 1600, brass to : Eastwood **4** (1)
Burrow, -s, *or* **Burrowes :**
A——, 1710, floor-slab to : Broxted **1** (1)
Elizabeth, widow, 1698, floor-slab to : Wendens Ambo **1** (2)
John 1694, and Thomas, 1780, floor-slab to : Great Sampford **1** (1)
Burstead, *see* **Great Burstead 4** *and* **Little Burstead 4**
Burstead House, Great Burstead **4** (14)
Burton, Elizabeth, 1624, floor-slab to : Purleigh **4** (1)
Burton End, see Stansted Mountfitchet **1**
Bury, The, Clavering **1** (12)
Bury, arms : Little Wakering **4** (1)
Bury, Bradford, 1675, slab to : Little Wakering **4** (1)
Bury Cottage, The, Felsted **2** (25)
Bury Farm, Felsted **2** (26)
Bury Foundry, *see under* **Bellfounders and Foundries**
Bury Lodge, Stansted Mountfitchet **1** (41)
Bush Elms, Hornchurch **4** (23)
Bush End, see Hatfield Broad Oak **2**
Bush Farm, Little Sampford **1** (22)
Bushes, Magdalen Laver **2** (5)
Bushett Farm, Great Bardfield **1** (48)
Bust, arms : Wennington **4** (1)
Bust, Henry, parson of the parish, 1624, Margaret (Bardolphe), his wife, and Henry, their son, 1625, monument of : Wennington **4** (1)
Bustard, arms : Orsett **4** (1)
Bustard, Theophilus, 1668, and Margaret (Halfhid), his first wife, 1653, floor-slab to : Orsett **4** (1)
Busts, *see* **Effigies**
Butcher, John, vicar of the parish, 1707, head-stone to : Feering **3** (1)
Butcher Row, see Saffron Walden **1**
Butchers' Company, arms : Halstead Rural **1** (4)
Butler, arms : Pentlow **1** (1) (Felton tomb) ; Theydon Garnon **2** (1)
Butler, Earl of Ormonde, arms : Rochford **4** (1) (W. Tower)
Butler :
Amphillis, *see* **Wyld 2**
Francis, *see* **Felton 1**
Richard, 1688, floor-slab to : Theydon Garnon **2** (1)
Sarah, *see* **Jeffrey 2**
Butler's Farm, Saffron Walden **1** (7)
,, ,, Shopland **4** (2)
Butlers Hall, Bulmer **1** (4)
Buttles Farm, Great Waltham **2** (52)
Buttles Farm, Great Dunmow **1** (43)
Butts Green Farm, Clavering **1** (29)

* *See Addenda et Corrigenda, pp. 185–8, under this Volume and Parish.*

Instructions how to use this Index given on page 198.

* See Addenda et Corrigenda, pp. 185–8, under this Volume and Parish.

Instructions how to use this Index given on page 198.

* *See Addenda et Corrigenda, pp. 185–8, under this Volume and Parish.*

Instructions how to use this Index given on page 198.

* See Addenda et Corrigenda, pp. 185–8, under this Volume and Parish.

Instructions how to use this Index given on page 198.

* *See Addenda et Corrigenda, pp. 185-8, under this Volume and Parish.*

Instructions how to use this Index given on page 198.

* See Addenda et Corrigenda, pp. 185–8, under this Volume and Parish.

Instructions how to use this Index given on page 198.

See Addenda et Corrigenda, pp. 185–8, under this Volume and Parish.

Instructions how to use this Index given on page 198.

Clare, arms: Blackmore 2 (1) (roof); Colchester 3 (16) (tile); North Ockendon 4 (1) (glass); Thorrington 3 (1)
Clare, John, 1564, and his two wives, Joan and Katherine (Pirton), brass to: Thorrington 3 (1)
Claredown Farm, Belchamp St. Paul's 1 (13)
Clarence, see under Inns
Clarence, Philippa, daughter of Lionel, Duke of, arms: Great Bardfield 1 (1) (glass)
Clarendon, see under Inns
Claret Hall, Ashen 1 (4)
Clarke, -e, or Clerk, -e, arms: Kelvedon 3 (2); Tilbury-juxta-Clare 1 (1); Wanstead 2 (2); Writtle 2 (1)
Clark, -e, or Clerk, -e :
    Abraham, 1700, slab to: Kelvedon 3 (2)
    Elizabeth, daughter of John, 1712, head-stone to: Epping Upland 2 (2)
    Hamlett, and Alice, his second wife (widow of William Lathum), 1636, brass to: Upminster 4 (1)
    John, senior, 1681-2, and Anne, his wife, 1692, tombstone to: Tilbury-juxta-Clare 1 (1)
    John, 1706, floor-slab to: Writtle 2 (1)
    John, 1712, and Elizabeth, daughter of John, 1712, head-stone to: Epping Upland 2 (2)
    John, 1719, and Mary, his wife, 1711, floor-slab to: Wanstead 2 (2)
    Joseph, see Youngman, alias Clerk 1
    Thomas, initials of, on bressummer: Great Coggeshall 3 (31)
    William, 1630, floor-slab to: West Thurrock 4 (1)
    William, 1666, tablet to: Harwich 3 (1)
Clarke, John, see under Bellfounders
Clark's Cottage, Great Waltham 2 (22)
Clark's Farm, Ardleigh 3 (13)
    ,,   ,,   Belchamp Walter 1 (9)
    ,,   ,,   Kelvedon 3 (54)
Claudius, coins of: Colchester 3 (1 D. and E.)
Claudius House, Colchester 3 (154)
Clavering 1 pp. 67-75; 4 p. 185
Clavering Castle, Clavering 1 (2)
Clavering Farm, Clavering 1 (5)
Clavering Place, Clavering 1 (7)
Clavering's Farm, Halstead Rural 1 (2)
Clayhall Farm, Great Ilford 2 (3)
Claypit Farm, Birch 3 (7)
Claypits, Saffron Walden 1 (153)
Claypits Farm, Thaxted 1 (1) (32)
Clees Hall, Alphamstone 3 (4)
Clements Hall, Hawkwell 4 (3)
Clerk, -e, see Clark, -e, above
Cleves, Duchy of, arms: Stondon Massey 2 (1) (brass)
Clifton, John, see under Bellfounders
Clitherow, Judith, see Cory 4
Clock House, Boreham 2 (11)
    ,,   ,,   Braintree 2 (67)
    ,,   ,,   Great Dunmow 1 (2) (Plate 1 p. 133)
Clock House Farm, Little Sampford 1 (14)
Clocks :
    circa 1500: Colchester 3 (10) (clock-face)
    17TH-CENTURY: Great Dunmow 1 (2)
    EARLY 18TH-CENTURY (before 1715): Felsted 2 (1)
Clock-works :
    EARLY 18TH-CENTURY (before 1715): Felsted 2 (1)
Clodmore Hill, see Arkesden 1
Clonville, see Clouville, below
Clopton, arms: Halstead Rural 1 (4) (glass); Ingrave 4 (1) (Fitz Lewes brass)
Clopton :
    Frances, daughter of Thomas, 1675, floor-slab to: Chignall 2 (2)
    Mary, see Coker 2

Clopton Hall, side of, Great Dunmow 1 (4)
Cloptons, Saffron Walden 1 (136) (Plate 1 p. xxvii)
Clopton's Farm, Great Dunmow 1 (42)
Close House, The, Saffron Walden 1 (29)
Clovile, or Clouville, arms: Finchingfield 1 (1) (font); West Hanningfield 4 (1)
Clouville (or Clonville) :
    John, and Margerie (Alyngton), his wife, 16th-century brass to: West Hanningfield 4 (1)
    Isabel and John, her son, 1361, brass of: West Hanningfield 4 (1)
Club Room, The, Ashdon 1 (13)
Cluniac Monks, see under Religious Houses
Coach and Horses, see under Inns
Coale, John, 1673, slab to: Wethersfield 1 (1)
Coat : Part of boy's leather coat (for bound apprentice under the Aleyn bequest), probably 17th-century: Little Waltham 2 (1)
Cobbins Farm, Burnham 4 (3)
Cobbs Farm, Fordham 3 (6)
    ,,   ,,   Goldhanger 3 (3)
    ,,   ,,   Great Hallingbury 2 (19)
    ,,   ,,   Manuden 1 (7)
Cobham (of Cobham), arms: Chrishall 1 (1) (de la Pole brass)
Cobham (of Sterborough), arms: Little Dunmow 1 (1) (Fitz Walter tomb)
Cobham, Joan, daughter of John de, see Pole, de la, 1
Cobler's Green, see Felsted 2
Cock, see under Inns
Cocke, -e :
    Mary, see Davies 4
    William, 1619, pastor of the church, and Anne, his wife, 1625, stone to: St. Giles' Church, Colchester 3 (9)
Cock and Bell, see under Inns
Cock and Pye, see under Inns
Cock and Rather Shop (now Post Office), High Easter 2 (15)
Cock Green, see Felsted 2
Cockerelles, site of, Noak Hill 2 (2)
Cockerill, Sarah, 1679, floor-slab to: Holy Trinity Church, Colchester 3 (3)
Cockett, arms: Tillingham 4 (1)
Cockett, Charles, 1714, table-tomb to: Tillingham 4 (1)
Codham Mill, Wethersfield 1 (49)
Coffins and Coffin-lids and slabs : see also Sectional Preface 1 p. xxxii
Coffins :
    LEAD, 17th-century: Hempstead 1 (1)
    STONE :
        Mediaeval: Berden 1 (4); Dunton (Wayletts) 4 (1); East Tilbury 4 (2); Great Bardfield 1 (1); Little Dunmow 1 (1); Maldon St. Peter 2 (3); Prittlewell 4 (2); Stanford-le-Hope 4 (1); Stapleford Tawney 2 (1); West Thurrock 4 (1); Wix 3 (1)
Coffin-lids and slabs :
    PRE-CONQUEST (POSSIBLY 11th - CENTURY): Great Maplestead 1 (1)*
    12TH-CENTURY :
        Elsenham 1 (1); Stapleford Tawney 2 (1); Witham 2 (1)
    12TH OR 13TH-CENTURY: North Shoebury 4 (1) (perhaps head-stone) (Plate 4 p. 25)
    13TH-CENTURY :
        Aythorpe Roding 2 (1); Berden 1 (1); Birdbrook 1 (1); Brightlingsea 3 (3); Chelmsford 2 (2); Colchester 3 (5); Dovercourt 3 (2); East Horndon 4 (1); East Tilbury 4 (2); Faulkbourne 2 (2); Feering 3 (1); Gestingthorpe 1 (1) (fragments); Good Easter 2 (1) (Plate 2 p. 103); Great Bentley

* See Addenda et Corrigenda, pp. 185-8, under this Volume and Parish.

Instructions how to use this Index given on page 198.

Coffin-lids and slabs : *cont.*
13TH-CENTURY : *cont.*
3 (1) ; Great Dunmow 1 (1) ; Great Horkesley 3 (1);
Great Maplestead 1 (1) ; Great Tey 3 (1) ; Greensted
(juxta-Ongar) 2 (1); Harlow 2 (2) ; Heybridge 3 (1) ;
Hornchurch 4 (1) ; Ingatestone and Fryerning 2 (2) ;
Langham 3 (1) ; Little Bentley 3 (1) ; Little Dunmow
1 (1) ; Little Horkesley 3 (1) ; Little Leighs 2 (1) ;
Little Yeldham 1 (1) ; Margaret Roding 2 (1) ; Mun-
don 4 (1) ; Paglesham 4 (1) ; Prittlewell 4 (1) ;
Rainham 4 (1) ; Rettendon 4 (1) ; Rivenhall 3 (2) ;
Rochford 4 (1) ; Runwell 4 (1) ; Saffron Walden 1 (1) ;
St. Osyth 3 (4) ; Salcott 3 (2) ; Shopland 4 (1) ;
South Benfleet 4 (1) ; South Ockendon 4 (1) ; Stan-
way 3 (2) ; Sutton 4 (1) ; Tolleshunt Major 3 (1) ;
Wakes Colne 3 (1) ; West Mersea 3 (4) ; West
Thurrock 4 (1) (*Plate* 4 p. 172) ; West Tilbury 4 (2) ;
Wickham Bishops 2 (1) (fragments) ; Witham 2 (1) ;
Wrabness 3 (1)
13TH OR 14TH-CENTURY :
Aveley 4 (1) ; Barling 4 (1) ; Waltham Holy Cross
2 (1)
circa 1300 :
Great Dunmow 1 (1) ; Little Dunmow 1 (1)
14TH-CENTURY :
Arkesden 1 (1) ; Clavering 1 (1) ; Navestock 2 (1) ;
Newport 1 (1) ; Pebmarsh 3 (1) ; Shalford 1 (1)
15TH-CENTURY : Wethersfield 1 (1)
MEDIAEVAL :
Berden 1 (1) ; Berners Roding 2 (1) ; Birch 3 (1) ;
Blackmore 2 (1) ; Dengie 4 (1) ; Great Canfield 3 (1) ;
Langham 3 (1) ; Little Hallingbury 2 (1) ; Mar-
garetting 2 (1) ; Nazeing 2 (1) ; Ridgewell 1 (2) ;
Sheering 2 (1) (fragments) ; Stapleford Tawney 2 (1) ;
Thorrington 3 (1) ; Tolleshunt Major 1 (1) ; West
Bergholt 3 (1) ; Willingale Doe 2 (1)
Coffin-plates :
17th-CENTURY :
Colchester 3 (9) ; Steeple Bumpstead 1 (2)
Coffin-stools :
17TH-CENTURY :
Little Horkesley 3 (1) ; Stebbing 1 (1)
Coft Hall, Little Bardfield 1 (9)
Cogan, Mrs. Christian, 1710, floor-slab to : Barking 2 (2)
Cogesale, *see* **Coggeshall,** *below*
Coggeshall, *see* **Great Coggeshall 3** *and* **Little Coggeshall 3**
Coggeshall, arms : Ashdon 1 (5) (Tyrell tomb) ; East
Horndon 4 (1) (Tyrell tomb) ; Little Sampford 1
(1) (glass) ; Shalford 1 (1) (font)
Coggeshall, *or* **Cogesale :**
Alice, *see* **Tyrell 4**
Elizabeth, *see* **Bourchier 1**
Elizabeth, *see* **Watson 1**
Thomas, 1421, brass said to be of : Springfield 2 (1)
Coggeshall Abbey, Little Coggeshall 3 (2) (*Plates* 3 pp.
166, 167)
Coggeshall Hall, Little Coggeshall 3 (3)
Coke, arms : Great Totham 3 (1)
Coke, Elizabeth (Pilborough), wife of Richard, 1606, and
Elizabeth, their daughter, wife of Thomas Wilde,
brass of : Great Totham 3 (1)
Coker, James, 1702, and Mary (Clopton), his wife, 1720,
floor-slab to : Black Notley 2 (1)
Colbey, Anne, *see* **Browning 2**
Colbroke, arms : Castle Hedingham 1 (1) (Vere tomb) ;
Earls Colne 3 (1) (W. Tower)
Colchester 3 pp. 20–74 ; 4 p. 188
Colchester, arms : West Ham 2 (1)

Colchester :
Helen, *see* **Bourchier 1**
Henry, 1700–1, and Penelope, his wife, 1719, tablet to :
West Ham 2 (1)
Colchester Castle : Colchester 3 (18) (*Plates* 3 pp. 51,
54, 55, 58, 59, 62)
Colchester Club (formerly **White Hart Inn**), Colchester
3 (20)
Colchester Hall, Takeley 1 (5)
Cold Norton 4 p. 25
Coldblows, North Benfleet 4 (2)
Coldhall Farm, Panfield 1 (2)
Coldharbour Farm, Tilty 1 (6)
Cole :
Danyell, 1642, last Bailiff and first Mayor of Colchester,
floor-slab to : St. Peter's Church, Colchester 3 (8)
Elizabeth, *see* **Drake 3**
John, inscription for (" 1566 I.C.") on ceiling-beam :
Markshall 3 (2)
John ?, Alderman 16—, and Anne ? (Thurston ?), his
wife, 1668, floor-slab to : St. Peter's Church, Col-
chester 3 (8)
Cole End, *see* Wimbish 1
Cole End Farm, Wimbish 1 (26)
Cole's Farm, Belchamp Otton 1 (5)
Colebrand, Richard, 1674, Dean and Rector of Bocking,
brass to : Bocking 1 (1)
Coleman, Mary, *see* **Johnson 2**
Colemans Farm, Faulkbourne 2 (14)
,, ,, Prittlewell 4 (8)
Coleward Farm, Burnham 4 (9)
Colford, Agnes, *see* **Makyn 2**
Colickey Green, Woodham Walter 2
Collard :
Nicholas, 1680, floor-slab to : Barnston 2 (1)
William, 1688, and Judeth, his wife, 1665, floor-slab
to : Barnston 2 (1)
William, 1698, floor-slab to : Barnston 2 (1)
Collecting-shovel :
17TH-CENTURY : Epping Upland 2 (2)
Colleges, *see under* **Religious Houses**
Collentt, Mrs. Ann, 1710, head-stone to : Upminster 4 (1)
Collier's Hatch, Stapleford Tawney 2 (2)
Collins, *see* **Collyn,** *below*
Collins Farm, Aythorpe Roding 2 (5)
Collops Farm, Stebbing 1 (65)
Collopsbarn, Great Tey 3 (31)
Collyn, arms : Takeley 1 (1)
Collyn, *or* **Collins :**
Ann, wife of Richard, 1670, floor-slab to : Boreham 2 (1)
Hannah, *see* **Knollis 1**
John, 1639, " coryphaeus " of the parish, brass to :
Broxted 1 (1)
Mary, wife of John, 1714, floor-slab to : Fyfield 2 (1)
Richard, 1678, gentleman harbinger to Charles II, and
his two infants, Christopher and Elizabeth, floor-
slab to : Boreham 2 (1)
Samuel, M.D., 1670, brass to : Braintree 2 (1)
William, 1684, floor-slab to : Takeley 1 (1)
Colne, *see* **Colne Engaine 3 ; Earls Colne 3 ; Wakes Colne
3 ;** *and* **White Colne 3**
Colne Engaine 3 pp. 74–76
Coleford House, Earls Colne 3 (23)
Colshill, arms : Chigwell 2 (2)
Colshill, Thomas, 1595, and Mary (Crayford) his wife,
1599, monument to : Chigwell 2 (2)
Colston, Elizabeth, *see* **Hicks 2**
Colt, -e, arms : Roydon 2 (1) ; Stambourne 1 (1) (glass) ;
Waltham Holy Cross 2 (1)

* *See Addenda et Corrigenda, pp. 185–8, under this Volume and Parish.*

Instructions how to use this Index given on page 198.

Colt, -e :
John, 1521, Elizabeth (Eldrington) and Mary (Anle ?), his wives, brass of : Roydon **2** (1)
Margaret (Heath), 1602, wife successively of John Ducket, John Swift and Henry Colt ; also John Swift and Richard, his son, 1601, tablet to : Roydon **2** (1)
Thomas, 1471, and Johanne, his wife, brass of ; Roydon **2** (1)
Thomas, 1559, and Magdalen, his wife, tablet with brasses of : Waltham Holy Cross **2** (1)

Colville Hall, White Roding **2** (13) (*Plate* **2** p. 44)

Commandments, The, painted on board and dated 1580 : Wimbish **1** (1)

Common Hill, see Saffron Walden **1**

Communion Rails :
circa 1600 : Hazeleigh **4** (1)
17TH-CENTURY :
Ashdon **1** (5) ; Great Burstead **4** (4) (*Plate* **4** p. 53) ; High Ongar **2** (1) ; Laindon Hills **4** (1) ; Leaden Roding **2** (1) ; Little Warley **4** (1) (gate probably from) ; Shalford **1** (1) ; Stanford Rivers **2** (1) ; Stapleford Tawney **2** (1) ; Sutton **4** (1) ; West Hanningfield **4** (1) ; West Thurrock **4** (1)
INCORPORATING 17TH-CENTURY WORK : Vange **4** (1)
17TH OR 18TH-CENTURY :
Purleigh **4** (1) ; Thaxted **1** (2) ; Ugley **1** (1)
circa 1700 :
Basildon **4** (1) ; Little Bromley **3** (1) ; Rivenhall **3** (2) ; Rochford **4** (1) ; Terling **2** (1) ; Theydon Garnon **2** (1)
EARLY 18TH-CENTURY (before 1715) :
Beaumont-cum-Moze **3** (1) ; Belchamp Otton **1** (1) ; Birdbrook **1** (1) ; Colchester **3** (8) (reused in gallery-staircase) ; Great Waltham **2** (2) ; Hatfield Broad Oak **2** (1) (*Plate* **2** p. 118) ; Maldon St. Mary **2** (1) ; Pentlow **1** (1) ; Stebbing **1** (1)

Communion Tables :
see also Sectional Preface **3** p. xxxiii
16TH-CENTURY :
Felsted **2** (24) ; Terling **2** (1) ; Newport **1** (1) (16th-century panels incorporated in modern table)
16TH OR 17TH-CENTURY :
Alphamstone **3** (1) ; High Roding **2** (1)
circa 1600 : Asheldham **4** (1)
17TH-CENTURY :
Abberton **3** (1) ; Aveley **4** (1) ; Barnston **2** (1) ; Belcham St. Paul's **1** (1) ; Bocking **1** (1) ; Bradwell (juxta-Coggeshall) **3** (1) ; Chickney **1** (1) (now forming chest) ; Chignall **2** (2) ; Clavering **1** (1) ; Colchester **3** (2) (7) (8) ; Cressing **3** (1) (*Plate* **3** p. xxxii) ; Downham **4** (1) ; Easthorpe **3** (1) ; Elmstead **3** (1) ; Fairsted **2** (1) ; Farnham **1** (1) ; Finchingfield **1** (1) ; Great Bromley **3** (1) ; Great Chesterford **1** (3) ; Great Horkesley **3** (1) ; Great Oakley **3** (1) ; Great Tey **3** (1) ; Great Waltham **2** (2) ; Hatfield Broad Oak **2** (1) ; Henham **1** (1) ; High Laver **2** (1) ; Ingatestone and Fryerning **2** (1) ; Ingrave **4** (1) ; Laindon Hills **4** (1) ; Langley **1** (1) ; Latchingdon **4** (1) ; Lawford **3** (1) ; Layer Marney **3** (1) ; Leaden Roding **2** (1) ; Lindsell **1** (1) ; Little Baddow **2** (1) ; Little Bentley **3** (1) ; Maldon St. Mary **2** (1) ; Manuden **1** (1) ; Messing **3** (1) ; Moreton **2** (1) ; Mount Bures **3** (1) ; Newport **1** (1) ; Norton Mandeville **2** (1) ; Pattiswick **3** (1) ; Pentlow **1** (1) ; Pleshey **2** (2) ; Ridgewell **1** (2) ; Saffron Walden **1** (1) ; Sandon **4** (1) ; Sutton **4** (1) ; West Hanningfield **4** (1) ; Wethersfield **1** (1) (forming cupboard) ; Wickham St. Paul's **1** (1) ; Woodham Mortimer **4** (1)

Communion Tables : *cont.*
circa 1700 :
Basildon **4** (1) ; Steeple Bumpstead **1** (2)
17TH OR 18TH-CENTURY : Ugley **1** (1)
EARLY 18TH-CENTURY (before 1715) :
Beaumont-cum-Moze **3** (1) ; Berden **1** (1) ; Margaretting **2** (1) ; Stanford Rivers **2** (1) ; Stebbing **1** (1) ; White Roding **2** (2)

Compasses, *see under,* **Inns**

Compton, Henry, Bishop of London :
ARMS : Colchester **3** (4) (glass) ; Harlow **2** (2) (glass)
INITIALS OF (on panel from early 18th-century pulpit) : Colchester **3** (6)

Comyn of Badenock, arms : Aveley **4** (3) (glass)

Comyns, arms : Dagenham **2** (1) ; Writtle **2** (1)

Comyns :
Anne (Gurdon), wife of John, 1705, floor-slab to : Writtle **2** (1)
Richard, floor-slab to : Writtle **2** (1)
Capt. Richard, 1700, table-tomb to : Dagenham **2** (1)
Dr. Thomas, 1656, floor-slab to : Dagenham **2** (1)

Condovers, West Tilbury **4** (6)

Conduit-head :
16TH-CENTURY : Little Leighs **2** (2) (*Plate* **2** p. 160)

Coneyfield Wood, Messing **3** (23)

Connier, *see* **Conyers,** *below*

Conservative Club, Great Burstead **4** (24)

Constable's Farm, Foxearth **1** (11)

Constantine, coins of : Great Burstead **4** (1) ; Low Leyton **2** (1) ; Stanway **3** (1)

Constitutional Club, Braintree **2** (45)
 "   "   Great Coggeshall **3** (28)

Convent School, Colchester **3** (192) (*Plates* **3** p. 101)

Conway, Helegenwagh, daughter of Lord, *see* **Smith 2**

Conyers, arms : Walthamstow **2** (1)

Conyers, *or* **Connier :**
Dorothy, *see* **Waldegrave 2**
Mary, wife of John, 1701–2, and Tristram, their son, 1711, floor-slab to : Walthamstow **2** (1)
Tristram, 1684, and Winifred (Gerard), his wife, 1694, tablet to : Walthamstow **2** (1)
William, 1659, tablet to : Walthamstow **2** (1)
" (W)ylyam and Benet his wife," portion of inscription : Epping Upland **2** (2)

Conyers, *or* **Cowards Farm,** Wimbish **1** (21)

Conysby, Marthagnes, *see* **Hicks 2**

Cooch, John, 1711, floor-slab to : Creeksea **4** (1)

Cooe (?), " Robert Cooe " ? name painted on W. wall of tower, Brightlingsea **3** (3)

Cooke, arms : Great Burstead **4** (4) ; Romford Urban **2** (1)

Cooke :
Sir Anthony, 1576, preceptor to Edward VI, and Anne (Fitzwilliams), his wife, monument of : Romford Urban **2** (1) (*Plate* **2** p. 203)
Sir Anthony, 1576, tablet to : Romford Urban **2** (1)
Elizabeth, daughter of John, 1713, head-stone to : Margaretting **2** (1)
John, son of John, 1708, head-stone to : Margaretting **2** (1)
Robert, *see* **Holmes 2**
Ursula (Thresher), wife of John, 1705, and their daughter, Ursula, 1703, tablet to : Great Burstead **4** (4)

Cook's Hall, West Bergholt **3** (2)

Cooksmill Green, see Writtle **2**

Cooksplace, Leigh **4** (3)

Coombs, Little Stambridge **4** (3)

Cooper, arms : Danbury **4** (1·

Cooper, Samuel, 1677, floor-slab to : Danbury **4** (1

Cooper's End, Elmdon **1** (23)

Cooper's Farm, Prittlewell **4** (12)

* *See Addenda et Corrigenda, pp. 185–8, under this Volume and Parish.*

Instructions how to use this Index given on page 198.

Coopersale House, Epping **2** (2)
Cootes' Farm, Steeple Bumpstead **1** (30)
Copford 3 pp. 76–78
Copford Hall, Little Bardfield **1** (6)
Coppin, Lettice, *see* **Tyrell 2**
Copthall Lane, see Thaxted **1**
Corbet, Bridget, *see* **Darcy 3**
Corbets Tye, see Upminster **4** .
Cordwainer's Hall, London, 17th-century stone steps and balustrades, originally the entrance to: Wethersfield **1** (2)
Cornell, Thomas, Church Windows inserted by bequest of, *c.* 1527 : Ashdon **1** (5)
Corney, arms : Thaxted **1** (6) (glass)
Cornish Hall, Finchingfield **1** (4)
Corringales, Hatfield Broad Oak **2** (34)
Corringham 4 pp. 25–27 .
Corsellis, *or* **Corselis,** arms : Great Ilford **2** (3) ; Layer Marney **3** (1)
Corsellis :
Mary, *see* **Abdy 3**
Mary, *see* **Maynard 2**
Nicholas, 1674, monument to : Layer Marney **3** (1)
Cory, arms : Danbury **4** (1) ; Hutton **4** (1)
Cory :
Robert, D.D., 1704, rector and prebendary of St. Paul's, floor-slab to : Danbury **4** (1)
Thomas, 1656, prothonotary of the Court of Common Pleas, also Judith (Clitherow), his wife, 1663, tablet to : Hutton **4** (1)
Cotcroft, Kelvedon **3** (49)
Cotton, Luce, *see* **Tallakarne 1**
Cotton's Farm, Finchingfield **1** (44)
Council Offices, Great Burstead **4** (27)
Court House, Barking **2** (5)
     ,,   ,,   Walthamstow **2** (8)
Courtenay, Archbishop of Canterbury, arms : Orsett **4** (1) (font)
Courts, Aveley **4** (17)
Covenbrook Hall, Stisted **3** (20)
Cow Farm, Doddinghurst **2** (12)
Coward's Farm, *or* **Conyers,** Wimbish **1** (21)
Cowell's Farm, Lindsell **1** (5)
Cowicks, Sheering **2** (11)
Cowland :
John, Sarah, his wife, Susannah, and John, table-tomb to, erected 1712 by Sarah Cowland : North Ockendon **4** (1)
John, 1700, floor-slab to : Woodford **2** (1)
William, 1687, floor-slab to : Aythorpe Roding **2** (1)
Cowless Hall Farm, Radwinter **1** (30)
Cox's Farm, Elsenham **1** (16)
Cox Green, see Ramsden Bellhouse **4**
Cox Hall, Great Dunmow **1** (46)
Coys, arms : Hatfield Peverel **2** (1)
Coys, Daniel, 1673, floor-slab to : Hatfield Peverel **2** (1)
Cozens Farm, High Ongar **2** (5)
Crabb's Farm, Kelvedon **3** (55)
Crabtree Farm, Great Bentley **3** (3)
Cracherode, arms : Faulkbourne **2** (2)
Cracherode, Cracherod, *or* **Cracheroad :**
Elizabeth, 1693–4, floor-slab to : Faulkbourne **2** (2)
John, 1534, and Agnes, his wife, brass of : Toppesfield **1** (1)
Sarah, 1705, widow, floor-slab to : Little Yeldham **1** (1)
Thomas, 1701, floor-slab to : Little Yeldham **1** (1)
William, 1585, and Elizabeth his wife, 1587, brass to : Toppesfield **1** (1)
Cracknell's Farm, Little Bardfield **1** (7)
Cradle House, Markshall **3** (4)

Craig's Farm, Stambourne **1** (7)
Crakanthorpe, Mary, wife of Samuel, 1709, slab to : Bocking **1** (1)
Cramers Green, see Great Tey **3**
Crane (wooden) :
circa 1700 : Harwich **3** (2)
Crane :
Henry, 1436, brass to : Walthamstow **2** (1)
Thomas, 1654, tablet to : Kelvedon **3** (2)
Cranes, Nevendon **4** (2)
Cranes and Hooks, *see* RACKS AND HOOKS, *under* **Ironwork**
Cranham 4 pp. 27–28
Cranham Hall, Cranham **4** (3)
Craske, Robert, 1712, Dorothy, his wife, and three children, head-stone to : Mayland **4** (1)
Crawedene, Thomas de, monument to, *c.* 1340 : Fobbing **4** (1) (*Plate* **4** p. 48)
Crawley, Thomas, 1559, brass to : Elmdon **1** (1)
Crawley End, see Chrishall **1**
Crawley's, Netteswell **2** (9)
Crayford, Mary, *see* **Colshill 2**
Creeksea 4 p. 28–29
Creeksea Hall, Creeksea **4** (3)
Creeksea Place, Creeksea **4** (2) (*Plates* **4** pp. 56–7)
Crepping Hall, Wakes Colne **3** (5)
Cressing 3 pp. 78–80
Cressing Temple 3 (3)
Cresswell Farm, Sible Hedingham **1** (5)
Cricketers, *see under* **Inns**
Crippings, High Easter **2** (5)
Cripps, Susanna, wife of William, 1714, and William, 1752, table-tomb to : Barling **4** (1)
Crix Farm, Hatfield Peverel **2** (4)
Croft :
Avis, 1712, head-stone to : Rayleigh **4** (1)
Anne, *see* **Smith 2**
Croft Lane, see Great Waltham **2**
Cromps, High Easter **2** (8)
Cromwell, Jane, daughter of Sir Oliver, *see* **Pallavicine 2**
Crooke :
Anne, *see* **Walton 4**
James, 1707, rector of the parish, floor-slab to : Stondon Massey **2** (1)
Crooked Billet, *see under* **Inns**
Crosbe, *or* **Crosby,** arms : Theydon Garnon **2** (1) (W. Tower)
Crosbe, Sir John, Knight, inscription recording building of church steeple by : Theydon Garnon **2** (1)
Cross Farm, Finchingfield **1** (49)
Cross Lees, Moreton **2** (5)
Cross Keys, *see under* **Inns**
Crosse :
Elizabeth, 1667, widow of Steven, floor-slab to : Pebmarsh **3** (1)
Thomas, 1634, floor-slab to : Pebmarsh **3** (1)
Crosses :
see also Sectional Preface **1** p. xxx ; **2** p. xxxiv
PART OF SHAFT OF SAXON CROSS : Barking **2** (2)
12TH-CENTURY CARVED STONE SHAFT, POSSIBLY PART OF CROSS : Castle Hedingham **1** (1)
LATE 12TH OR 13TH-CENTURY ROOD IN STONE : Barking **2** (3) (*Plate* **2** p. 7)
CALVARY : Marks Tey **3** (1)
CHURCHYARD :
15th-century : Great Coggeshall **3** (2) (remains of)
CONSECRATION :
12th-century : Southminster **4** (1)
13th-century :
Brightlingsea **3** (3) ; Little Coggeshall **3** (1) (possible)

* *See Addenda et Corrigenda, pp. 185–8, under this Volume and Parish.*

Instructions how to use this Index given on page 198.

Crosses : *cont.*
  CONSECRATION : *cont.*
    14th-century :
      Fingringhoe **3** (1)*; Sheering **2** (1) ; West Mersea **3** (4)
    15th-century : Rayleigh **4** (1)
    Undated :
      Bulmer **1** (1) ; Fairsted **2** (1) ; Great Canfield **2** (1) ;
      Great Sampford **1** (1) ; Helion Bumpstead **1** (1) ;
      South Benfleet **4** (1) ; Stanford-le-Hope **4** (1) ;
      Toppesfield **1** (1)
  GABLE :
    14th-century :
      Ashdon **1** (5) (bases of) ; Bardfield Saling **1** (1)
      (base) ; Great Bardfield **1** (1) (base) ; Great
      Dunmow **1** (1) (base) ; Hadstock **1** (2) (base) ;
      Tilty **1** (1) ; West Bergholt **3** (1) (remains of) ;
      Wimbish **1** (48) ; Writtle **2** (1) (remains of)
    15th-century : Belchamp Otton **1** (1) (base)
    Mediaeval : Little Dunmow **1** (1)
    16th-century : Boxted **3** (1) (remains of)
    Undated : Tilty **1** (1)
  PROCESSIONAL :
    17th-century (possibly) : Broxted **1** (1)
Crouch House, Gestingthorpe **1** (9)
Crouchman's Farm, Ulting **2** (9)
Crouch, Robert, *see under* **Bellfounders**
Crow Green, South Weald **2** (17)
Crown Barn, *or* **Garden Fields,** Great Coggeshall **3** (1)
Crow's Farm, Writtle **2** (18)
Crow's Green, see Bardfield Saling **1**
Crowgate, Great Waltham **2** (49)
Crown, *see under* **Inns**
Crown and Thistle, *see under* **Inns**
Crown or Pigtails Farm, Romford Rural **2** (5)
Crown House, Newport **1** (7) (*Plate* **1** p. 203)
    „   „   Orsett **4** (5)
Crownway Wood, Wimbish **1** (9)
Crucifix, Doddinghurst **2** (1)
Crucifixion, The :
  CARVINGS : Colchester **3** (18) ; Great Coggeshall **3** (2)
    (back of recess) ; Newport **1** (1) (on Communion
    table) ; Noak Hill **2** (1)
  GLASS : Great Bardfield **1** (1) ; Hornchurch **4** (1) (frag-
    mentary) ; Noak Hill **2** (1)
  PAINTINGS : Hatfield Peverel **2** (1) ; Little Easton **1** (1) ;
    Newport **1** (1) (chest) (*Plate* **1** p. 200)

Crush, Thomas, 1670, floor-slab to : Roxwell **2** (1)
Crush's Farm, Hutton **4** (4)
Crypts, Bone-holes, *or* **Charnels :**
  13TH-CENTURY : Saffron Walden **1** (1)
  14TH-CENTURY : Fyfield **2** (1) ; Maldon All Saints **2** (1) ;
    Waltham Holy Cross **2** (1)
  16TH-CENTURY : Colchester **3** (8)
  UNDATED : Newport **1** (1) (recess possibly entrance to) ;
    Thaxted **1** (2)
Cuckoos, Little Baddow **2** (9)
Cudworth, Damaris, 1695, widow of Ralph, Master of
  Christ's College, Cambridge, tablet to : High
  Laver **2** (1)
Cuffley, Nathaniel, 1676 (?) slab to : St. Leonard's Church,
  Lexden, Colchester **3** (13)
Cullum, arms : Great Dunmow **1** (1)
Cullum, Mary (Wiseman), wife of Thomas, 1662, framed
  canvas panel with painted inscription to : Great
  Dunmow **1** (1)
Culverden, William, *see under* **Bellfounders**
Culvert's Farm, Boreham **2** (21)
Cumins, Elizabeth, *see* **Nightingale 1**
Cunobeline, coins of : Latton **2** (1) ; Colchester **3** (1 D.)
Cupboards, *see under* **Furniture**
Cupper's Farm, Witham **2** (47)
Cupolas (bell) on houses :
  17TH-CENTURY : Great Dunmow **1** (2)
  EARLY 18TH-CENTURY (before 1715) : Gosfield **1** (3)
    (*Plate* **1** p. 104)
Curd Hall, Little Coggeshall **3** (1 A) (4)
Curls, Clavering **1** (8)
Curwen, Mabel, *see* **Twedy 1**
Cust Hall, Toppesfield **1** (4) ; carvings, etc., from : Great
  Maplestead **1** (2)
Cutlands, Nazeing **2** (15)
Cutler's Green, see Thaxted **1**
Cutte, arms : Arkesden **1** (3) ; Thaxted **1** (6) (glass)
Cutte :
  Sir John, part of Horham Hall built by, in the 16th
    century : Thaxted **1** (6)
  Richard, 1592, and Mary (Elrington), his wife, 1593,
    monument to, erected by their eldest son, Richard :
    Arkesden **1** (1)
  Audrey (=Aetheldreda), *see* **Poyntz 4**

Dacre, Briant, 1638, brass to : Pattiswick **3** (1)*
Dael Holme (formerly **Mill House**), Dedham **3** (4)
Dagenham 2 pp. 55–56 ; **4** p. 186
Dagnetts' Farm, Black Notley **2** (4)
Dagworth Farm, Pebmarsh **3** (10)
Dagworth Manor House, site of, Elmdon **1** (3)
Dairy Farm, Finchingfield **1** (33)
d'Albini, *see* **Albini**
Dale of Clavering, arms : Berden **1** (4) (glass)
Dale Hall, Lawford **3** (3)
Dame Anna's Farm, Fyfield **2** (7)
Danbury 4 pp. 29–33
Danbury Camp, Danbury **4** (10)
Dancote, Allionora, *see* **Poyntz, 4**
Dandies Farm, Eastwood **4** (5)
Danet, arms : Tilty **1** (1)
Danet, Gerard, 1520, " consiliarius " to Henry VIII, and
  Mary, his wife, brass of : Tilty **1** (1)
Daniel in the lions' den, carving (on cupboard) : Castle
  Hedingham **1** (1)

Daniell, John, tablet recording benefactions of, 1695 :
  St. Giles Church, Colchester **3** (9)
Danish Camps, etc., *see* **Pre-Conquest Remains** ; Sectional
  Preface **3** p. xxiv ; *and* County Survey **4** pp. xxviii–ix
Danvale's Farm, Wethersfield **1** (38)
Danyell, John *see under* **Bellfounders**
Darbie, John, *see under* **Bellfounders**
Darby, arms : Walthamstow **2** (1)
Darby, Paul, 1699, floor-slab to : Walthamstow **2** (1)
Darcy :
  ARMS : Maldon All Saints **2** (1) ; St. Osyth **3** (2) (4) ;
    Sandon **4** (1) (glass) ; Tolleshunt D'Arcy **3** (1) (2)
  BADGE : St. Osyth **3** (2) (4)
Darcy of Chich, arms : Springfield **2** (1)
Darcy, -e, D'Arcy, *or* **Darcie :**
  Anthony, J.P., 1540, brass of : Tolleshunt D'Arcy **3** (1) ;
    initials for : Tolleshunt D'Arcy **3** (2)
  Briant, 1587, and Bridget (Corbet), his wife, monument
    to : St. Osyth **3** (2)
  Elizabeth, *see* **Wiseman 2**

---

* *See Addenda et Corrigenda, pp. 185–8, under this Volume and Parish.*

Instructions how to use this Index given on page 198.

* *See Addenda et Corrigenda, pp. 185–8, under this Volume and Parish.*

Instructions how to use this Index given on page 198.

See Addenda et Corrigenda, pp. 185–8, under this Volume and Parish.

Instructions how to use this Index given on page 198.

* *See Addenda et Corrigenda, pp. 185-8, under this Volume and Parish.*

Instructions how to use this Index given on page 198.

Dodington, Margaret, *see* **Whetcombe 2**
Doeg before Saul, glass : Noak Hill **2** (1)
Does, High Easter **2** (29) (*Plate* **2** p. 96)
„   Stanford Rivers **2** (8) (*Plate* **2** p. 129)
Dog and Partridge, *see under* **Inns**
Dog and Pheasant, *see under* **Inns**
Dog-gate (to stairs) :
   18th-century : Wormingford **3** (7)
Dolphin, *see under* **Inns**
Domestic Architecture, *see* **Architecture, Domestic**
Dominic, St., alabaster figure, probably of : Barling **4** (1)
   (*Plate* **4** p. 25)
Domitian, coins of : Faulkbourne **2** (1) ; Hockley **4** (9)
Donyland, *see* **East Donyland 3**
Doom, The :
   GLASS : Stisted **3** (1)
   PAINTINGS : Fairsted **2** (1) ; Waltham Holy Cross **2** (1) ;
      Woodham Ferrers **4** (1)
Doors (most worthy of mention) : (*for Ironwork on doors,*
   see HINGES AND OTHER FITTINGS, *under* **Ironwork**)
   see also Sectional Preface **1** p. xxx ; **2** p. xxxiv ;
      3 p. xxxiii ; **4** p. xlii
   ECCLESIASTICAL :
      11TH-CENTURY : Hadstock **1** (2).
      12TH-CENTURY :
         Castle Hedingham **1** (1) ; Copford **3** (1) ; Heybridge
         3 (1) (*Plate* **3** p. 132) ; Mashbury **2** (1) ; Navestock
         2 (1)
      12TH OR 13TH-CENTURY :
         Eastwood **4** (1) (*Plate* **4** pp. 4–5) ; Little Totham **3**
         (1) (*Plate* **3** p. 132) ; Rainham **4** (1)
      13TH-CENTURY :
         Buttsbury **4** (2) (*Plate* **4** pp. 4-5) ; Eastwood **4** (1)
         (*Plate* **4** p. 45) ; Hadstock **1** (2) ; High Roding
         2 (1) ; Little Leighs **2** (1) ; Navestock **2** (1) ;
         White Roding **2** (2)
      13TH OR 14TH-CENTURY : North Weald Bassett **2** (1)
      circa 1300 :
         Aldham **3** (1) (*Plate* **3** p. 132) ; Colchester **3** (8)
         (*Plate* **3** p. 42)
      14TH-CENTURY :
         Aldham **3** (1) ; Ashdon **5** (1) ; Colchester **3** (5)
         (8) (9) ; Finchingfield **1** (1) ; Fingringhoe **3** (1)
         (*Plate* **3** p. 132) ; Great Bardfield **1** (1) ; Great
         Horkesley **3** (1) ; Great Yeldham **1** (1) ; Maldon
         All Saints **2** (1) ; Ovington **1** (1) ; Purleigh **4** (1) ;
         Shalford **1** (1) ; Sheering **2** (1) ; Wethersfield **1** (1) ;
         White Notley **2** (1) ; Witham **2** (1) ; Writtle **2** (1)
         (*Plate* **2** p. 273)
      14TH OR 15TH-CENTURY :
         Magdalen Laver **2** (1) ; South Hanningfield **4** (1)
         (*Plate* **4** pp. 4–5) ; West Hanningfield **4** (1)
      15TH-CENTURY :
         Ardleigh **3** (1) (*Plate* **3** p. 132) ; Belchamp Walter
         1 (1) ; Braintree **2** (1) ; Burnham **4** (1) ; Canewdon
         4 (2) ; Chelmsford **2** (2) ; Chingford **2** (1) ; Col-
         chester **3** (2) (4) (10) ; Elsenham **1** (1) ; Faulk-
         bourne **2** (2) ; Fobbing **4** (1) ; Gosfield 1 (1) ;
         Great Bromley **3** (1) (*Plate* **3** p. 132) ; Hatfield
         Broad Oak **2** (1) ; Hornchurch **4** (1) ; Langenhoe
         3 (1) ; Latton **2** (2) ; Little Easton **1** (1) ; Little
         Hallingbury **2** (1) ; Little Oakley **3** (1) ; Littlebury
         1 (2) ; Margaretting **2** (1) ; Mashbury **2** (1) ;
         Middleton **3** (1) ; Paglesham **4** (1) ; Ramsey **3** (1) ;
         Tolleshunt D'Arcy **3** (1) ; West Thurrock **4** (1) ;
         Widdington **1** (1) ; Witham **2** (1)
      15TH OR 16TH-CENTURY :
         Hempstead **1** (1) ; Little Waltham **2** (1) ; Upminster
         4 (1) ; Wimbish **1** (1)

Doors : *cont.*
   ECCLESIASTICAL : *cont.*
      circa 1500 :
         Brightlingsea **3** (3) ; Colchester **3** (2) ; Great
         Yeldham **1** (1) ; Inworth **3** (1) ; Strethall **1** (1)
      16TH-CENTURY :
         Basildon **4** (1) ; Brightlingsea **3** (3) ; Burnham **4**
         (1) ; Colchester **3** (10) (11) ; Dedham **3** (1) (*Plate*
         3 p. 42) ; East Mersea **3** (1) ; Gestingthorpe **1** (1) ;
         Great Bromley **3** (1) ; Great Dunmow **1** (1) ; Great
         Sampford **1** (1) ; Hatfield Peverel **2** (1) ; Horn-
         church **4** (1) ; Lawford **3** (1) ; Liston **1** (1) ; Little
         Bromley **3** (1) ; Paglesham **4** (1) ; Prittlewell **4** (1)
         (*Plate* **4** pp. 4–5) ; Saffron Walden **1** (1) ; Salcott
         3 (2) ; Stifford **4** (1) (*Plate* **4** pp. 4–5) ; Thaxted
         1 (2) ; Theydon Garnon **2** (1) ; Waltham Holy
         Cross **2** (1) ; Wennington **4** (1)
      16TH OR 17TH-CENTURY : Great Bromley **3** (1)
      17TH-CENTURY :
         Barking **2** (2) ; Colchester **3** (5) ; Dovercourt
         3 (2) ; Fobbing **4** (1) ; Great Leighs **2** (1) ; Sandon
         4 (1) ; Stapleford Abbots **2** (1)
      EARLY 18TH-CENTURY (before 1715) : Maldon St. Mary
         2 (1)
      UNDATED : Saffron Walden **1** (1)
   SECULAR :
      14TH-CENTURY : Saffron Walden **1** (92)
      15TH-CENTURY :
         Belchamp Walter **1** (5) ; Faulkbourne **2** (3) ; Great
         Yeldham **1** (4) ; Newport **1** (20) ; South Ockendon
         4 (6) ; Thaxted **1** (38)
      15TH OR 16TH-CENTURY :
         Brentwood **2** (2) ; Dedham **3** (2) ; Little Horkesley
         3 (3)
      circa 1500 :
         Great Coggeshall **3** (3) ; Bocking **1** (20) ; Great
         Yeldham **1** (17) ; Tolleshunt D'Arcy **3** (2)
      16TH-CENTURY :
         Aveley **4** (6) (9) ; Bardfield Saling **1** (4) ; Barnston
         2 (3) ; Beauchamp Roding **2** (4) ; Belchamp St.
         Paul's **1** (3) ; Berden **1** (3) ; Bocking **1** (7) (27)
         (34) ; Boreham **2** (20) ; Braintree **2** (9) (10) (45)
         (50) ; Bulmer **1** (4) ; Chelmsford **2** (28) ; Col-
         chester **3** (106) (194) (*Plate* **3** p. xxx) ; Debden
         1 (6) (8) ; Elmstead **3** (3) ; Elsenham **1** (5) ;
         Epping Upland **2** (9) (10) ; Felsted **2** (18) (22) ;
         Finchingfield **1** (3) ; Gosfield **1** (11) ; Great Canfield
         2 (9) ; Great Coggeshall **3** (53) (69) ; Great Leighs
         2 (5) ; Great Waltham **2** (10) (25) (45) ; Halstead
         Rural **1** (1) ; Harlow **2** (15) (*Plate* **2** p. 80) ; Hat-
         field Broad Oak **2** (40) ; Hempstead **1** (21) ; Hen-
         ham **1** (4) ; High Easter **2** (15) ; Hornchurch **4** (3) ;
         Lambourne **2** (3) ; Lindsell **1** (4) ; Little Burstead
         4 (4) (*Plate* **4** p. 65) ; Little Leighs **2** (2) (*Plate* **2**
         p. 160) ; Little Sampford **1** (21) ; Nevendon **4** (5) ;
         Newport **1** (5) ; Pebmarsh **3** (4) ; Roxwell **2** (17) ;
         Saffron Walden **1** (39) (29) (58) (82) ; St. Osyth **3** (7)
         (made up of 16th-century material) ; Sandon **4** (4) ;
         Shalford **1** (4) (5) (24) ; Shelley **3** (4) ; Sible
         Heddingham **1** (13) (30) ; South Ockendon **4** (11) ;
         South Weald **2** (2) (*Plate* **2** p. 246) (5) ; Stansted
         Mountfitchet **1** (16) (32) ; Stapleford Abbots **2** (2) ;
         Stebbing **1** (8) (9) ; Steeple Bumpstead **1** (7) ;
         Thaxted **1** (33) ; Ugley **1** (11) ; Waltham
         Holy Cross **2** (10) ; Wethersfield **1** (3) (24) ; White
         Notley **2** (1) ; Widdington **1** (4) (15) ; Willingale
         Doe **2** (8) ; Wimbish **1** (16) (17) ; Witham **2** (24)
         (44) ; Writtle **2** (12)

* See Addenda et Corrigenda, pp. 185–8, under this Volume and Parish.

Instructions how to use this Index given on page 198.

* See Addenda et Corrigenda, pp. 185–8, under this Volume and Parish.

Instructions how to use this Index given on page 198.

Draytons Farm, Wendens Ambo **1** (13)
Drewe, Elinor, *see* **Kempe 1**
Drury, Anne, *see* **Deane 1**
Drury's Farm, Mountnessing **4** (8)
Dryden House, Great Burstead **4** (29)
Drywood, arms : South Ockendon **4** (1)
Drywood, or **Drywode :**
   George, 1611, and Elizabeth (Samson), his first wife,
      1595, monument to : South Ockendon **4** (1)
   Homphry, 1595, brass to : Hornchurch **4** (1)
   Thomas, 1591, and Anne, his wife, brass of : Horn-
      church **4** (1)
   William, 1602, brass of two wives of : Hornchurch **4** (1)
Duck-decoys, *see under* **Earthworks**
Duck End, see Finchingfield **1**
Duck End Farm, Birchanger **1** (6)
   ,,   ,,   ,,   Lindsell **1** (11)
Duck End Green, see Rayne **1**
Duck Street Farm, Saffron Walden **1** (152)
Ducket, Margaret, widow of John, *see* **Colt, 2**
Duckombe, Alice, *see* **Nevill 2**
Duddenhoe Grange, Wendens Loft **1** (2)
Duffield's Farm, Great Baddow **4** (16)
Dugdale, arms : Upminster **4** (1)
Dugdale, Elizabeth (Goodlad), 1701, wife of Thomas, and
      an infant daughter, 1701, tablet to : Upminster
      4 (1)
Duke of Norfolk, *see under* **Inns**
Duke of Wellington, *see under* **Inns**
Duke of York, *see under* **Inns**
Dukes, Roxwell **2** (17) (*Plate* **2** p. 129)
Dukes Farm, Layer Marney **3** (3)
   ,,   ,,   Willingale Doe **2** (10)
Duke's Head, *see under* **Inns**

Eagle and Child, *see under* **Inns**
Eagle Farm, Birdbrook **1** (15)
Earls Colne 3 pp. 87–90 ; **4** p. 188
Earls Colne Priory, Earls Colne **3** (2)
Earlsbury Farm, Farnham **1** (3)
Earthworks :
   see also Sectional Preface **1** pp. xxi, xxxiii ; **2** pp. xxviii,
      xxxvii ; **3** pp. xxiii, xxxvi ; **4** pp. xxxvii, xlv ; *and*
      County Survey pp. xxv–xxxi
   BURIAL MOUNDS :
      Ashdon (Bartlow Hills) **1** (1) (*Plate* **1** p. 4) ; Col-
      chester **3** (265) ; Great Burstead **4** (32) ; Maldon
      St. Peter **2** (18) ; Shelley **2** (6) ; West Mersea (Mersea
      Barrow) **3** (1)
   CAMPS :
      Asheldham **4** (2) ; Danbury **4** (10) ; Epping Upland
      (Ambersbury Banks) **2** (1) ; Great Hallingbury
      (Wallbury Camp) **2** (1) ; Great Horkesley (Pitchbury
      Ramparts) **3** (20) ; Great Ilford (Uphall Camp) **2** (7) ;
      Littlebury (Ring Hill) **1** (1) ; Loughton (Loughton
      Camp) **2** (1) ; Maldon All Saints **2** (3) ; Prittlewell
      4 (13) ; South Benfleet **4** (10) ; South Shoebury
      4 (4) ; South Weald **2** (18) ; Witham **2** (2)
   CASTLE EARTHWORKS :
      Castle Mounds :
         Berden **1** (1) ; Birch **3** (2) ; Chrishall **1** (2) ;
         Elmdon **1** (2) ; Mount Bures **3** (2) ; Navestock **2** (2) ;
         Stebbing (Stebbing Mount) **1** (3)
      Mounts and Baileys :
         Castle Hedingham **1** (3) ; Chipping Ongar **2** (3) ;
         Great Canfield (Canfield Mount) **2** (2) ; Great
         Easton **1** (2) ;   Pleshey **2** (3) ;   Rayleigh **4** (2)
         (*Plate* **4** p. xxxvii) ; Rickling **1** (2) ; Willingale Doe
         (possibly remains of) **2** (12)

Dumowe, name inscribed on glass : Lindsell **1** (1)   --
Dun, arms : Theydon Garnon **2** (1)   .
Dun, Sir Daniel, 1617, and Joan, his wife, 1640, tablet to :
      Theydon Garnon **2** (1)
Dunche, Mary, *see* **Kirton 2**
Dungeon Farm, Halstead Rural **1** (5)
Dunmow, *see* **Great Dunmow 1** *and* **Little Dunmow 1**
Dunmow Flitch Chair, Little Dunmow **1** (1)
Dunmow Priory, arms : Burnham **4** (1) (S. porch)
" Dunstanus Archiepiscopus," mural inscription : Latton
      2 (2)
Dunton (Wayletts) 4 p. 35
Durlston House, Colchester **3** (66)
Durward, *see* **Doreward** *above*
Dury Falls, Hornchurch **4** (4)
Dutch Cottages, Canvey Island **4** (1) (*Plate* **4** pp. xl–i) (2)
Dutch Fleet, part of church said to have been destroyed
      by, 1667 : East Tilbury **4** (2)
Duton Hill, see Great Easton **1**
Dycotts, Navestock **2** (4)
Dyer, arms : Great Dunmow **1** (1)
Dyer :
   Anne (Belitha), wife of Sir Swinnerton, 1714, floor-slab
      to : Great Dunmow **1** (1)
   Sir John Swynnerton, 1701, tablet and floor-slab to :
      Great Dunmow **1** (1)
Dyer, *or* **Dier,** John, *see under* **Bellfounders**
Dyers' Company, arms : Wanstead **2** (5) (ceiling, etc.)
Dyer's Farm, Woodham Ferrers **4** (10)
Dyke :
   Dorothy, *see* **Robinett 1**
   Mary, *see* **Beale 1**
Dykes, *see under* **Earthworks**
Dynes Hall, Great Maplestead **1** (2)
Dyves Hall, Chignall **2** (4)

Earthworks : *cont.*
   CASTLE EARTHWORKS : *cont.*
      Rings and Baileys :
         Orsett **4** (2) ; Stansted Mountfitchet **1** (3)
      Miscellaneous :
         Clavering **1** (2) ; Colchester **3** (18) ; Hadleigh **4** (2) ;
         Saffron Walden **1** (2)
   DAMS, *see* MILL-DAMS, *below*
   DENE-HOLES :
      Little Thurrock **4** (2) ; Orsett **4** (23)
   DUCK-DECOYS :
      Frating **3** (4) ; Hatfield Broad Oak **2** (42) ; Nave-
      stock **2** (15)
   DYKES OR DITCH-BANKS :
      Colchester (Lexden Earthworks) **3** (265) ; Layer-de-
      la-Haye (Lexden Earthworks), *see* Colchester **3** (265) ;
      Layer Marney **3** (8) ; Ingatestone (Moore's Ditch)
      2 (12) ; Stanway (Lexden Earthworks), *see* Colchester
      3 (265)
   ENCLOSURES :
      Berden **1** (22) ; Great Canfield **2** (12) ; Little Chester-
      ford **1** (13) ; Navestock (Fortification Wood) **1** (4) ;
      Saffron Walden **1** (157) (Repell Ditches); (158) (Grymes'
      Dyke Wood)
   ENTRENCHMENTS :
      Ashdon **1** (35) ; Braintree **2** (76) ; Chignall **2** (11) ;
      Colchester **3** (265) ; East Tilbury **4** (7) ; West Tilbury
      4 (8)
   FASCINE-DWELLINGS : Braintree **2** (76)
   FISH-PONDS :
      Basildon **4** (2) ; Belchamp St. Paul's **1** (2) ; Chrishall
      1 (4) ; Clavering **1** (3) ; East Horndon **4** (2) ; Fyfield
      2 (8) ; Great Bentley **3** (11) ; Hatfield Broad Oak

* See Addenda et Corrigenda, pp. 185–8, under this Volume and Parish.

Instructions how to use this Index given on page 198.

*See Addenda et Corrigenda, pp. 185–8, under this Volume and Parish.

Instructions how to use this Index given on page 198.

* *See Addenda et Corrigenda, pp. 185–8, under this Volume and Parish.*

Instructions how to use this Index given on page 198.

* *See Addenda et Corrigenda, pp. 185–8, under this Volume and Parish.*

Instructions how to use this Index given on page 198.

Instructions how to use this Index given on page 198.

* See Addenda et Corrigenda, pp. 185–8, under this Volume and Parish.

Instructions how to use this Index given on page 198.

* See Addenda et Corrigenda, pp. 185-8, under this Volume and Parish.

Instructions how to use this Index given on page 198.

* See Addenda et Corrigenda, pp. 185–8, under this Volume and Parish.

Instructions how to use this Index given on page 198.

* See Addenda et Corrigenda, pp. 185-8, under this Volume and Parish.

Instructions how to use this Index given on page 198.

* See Addenda et Corrigenda, pp. 185–8, under this Volume and Parish.

Instructions how to use this Index given on page 198.

* See Addenda et Corrigenda, pp 185–8, under this Volume and Parish.

Instructions how to use this Index given on page 198.

* See *Addenda et Corrigenda*, *pp*. 185–8, *under this Volume and Parish.*

Instructions how to use this Index given on page 198.

* *See Addenda et Corrigenda, pp. 185–8, under this Volume and Parish.*

Instructions how to use this Index given on page 198.

* See *Addenda et Corrigenda, pp. 185–8, under this Volume and Parish.*

Instructions how to use this Index given on page 198.

Glass: *cont.*
IN CHURCHES: *cont*
  ENGLISH: *cont.*
    15TH-CENTURY: *cont.*
      2 (1); Henham **1** (1); Hockley **4** (1); Horn-church **4** (1); Horndon-on-the-Hill **4** (1); Inworth **3** (1); Kelvedon **3** (2); Liston **1** (1); Little Bentley **3** (1); Little Burstead **4** (1); Little Horkesley **3** (1); Little Sampford **1** (1); Little Tey **3** (1); Little Waltham **2** (1); Little Warley **4** (1); Magdalen Laver **2** (1); Manuden **1** (1); Margaretting **2** (1); Mashbury **2** (1); Netteswell **2** (1); Newport **1** (1); North Ocken-don **4** (1) (*Plate* **4** p. 104); Orsett **4** (1); Panfield **1** (1); *Pattiswick* **3** (1); Radwinter **1** (1); Ridgewell **1** (2); Roydon **2** (1); Runwell **4** (1); Shalford **1** (1); Shopland **4** (1); South Benfleet **4** (1); South Hanningfield **4** (11); Springfield **2** (1); Steeple Bumpstead **2**; Thaxted **1** (2); Thundersley **4** (1); Tilbury-juxta-Clare **1** (1); Tolleshunt D'Arcy **3** (1); Toppesfield **1** (1); Wakes Colne **3** (1); Wethersfield **1** (1); White Roding **2** (2); Wickham St. Paul's **1** (1); Woodham Walter **2** (1) (*Plate* **4** pp. xliv–v)
    15TH OR 16TH-CENTURY: Great Dunmow **1** (1)
    circa 1500:
      Dedham **3** (1); Greensted (juxta-Ongar) **2** (1) (*Plate* **2** p. xxxv)
    16TH-CENTURY:
      Brightlingsea **3** (3); Bulmer **1** (1); Chignall **2** (1); Dedham **3** (1); Feering **3** (1); Great Burstead **4** (4); Great Ilford **2** (3) (*Plate* **2** p. xxxvii); Great Parndon **2** (1); Great Totham **3** (1); Had-stock **1** (2); Harlow **2** (2); High Roding **2** (1); Hornchurch **4** (1); Laindon **4** (1); Lindsell **1** (1); Little Chesterford **1** (1); Little Ilford **2** (1); Loughton **2** (2); Mashbury **2** (1); Norton Mandeville **2** (1); Pattiswick **3** (1); Rayleigh **4** (1); Ridgewell **1** (2); Saffron Walden **1** (1); Springfield **2** (1); Stambourne **1** (1); Thaxted **1** (2); Tolleshunt D'Arcy **3** (1); Tolleshunt Major **3** (1); West Hanningfield **4** (1); Wethers-field **1** (1)
    16TH OR 17TH-CENTURY:
      East Ham **2** (2); Great Dunmow **1** (1)
    17TH-CENTURY:
      Great Ilford **2** (2); Latton **2** (2); Little Bentley **3** (1); Little Ilford **2** (1); Messing **3** (1); Noak Hill **2** (1); *Pattiswick* **3** (1); Shopland **4** (1); South Weald **2** (1); Upminster **4** (1); Widding-ton **1** (1)
    17TH OR 18TH-CENTURY: Harlow **2** (2)
    EARLY 18TH-CENTURY (before 1715):
      Blackmore **2** (1); Harlow **2** (2); Wenden Lofts **1** (1)
    UNDATED:
      Great Baddow **4** (1); Great Horkesley **3** (1); Little Bromley **3** (1); Noak Hill **2** (1); Steeple **4** (1); Tolleshunt D'Arcy **3** (1)
  FOREIGN (*excluding* HERALDIC GLASS, *for which see below*):
    12TH-CENTURY: Rivenhall **3** (2) (*Plate* **3** p. 193)
    13TH-CENTURY: Rivenhall **3** (2) (*Plate* **3** p. 193)
    14TH-CENTURY:
      Panfield **1** (1); Rivenhall **3** (2)
    14TH OR 15TH-CENTURY: Stisted **3** (1)
    15TH-CENTURY:
      Panfield **1** (1); Rivenhall **3** (2); South Weald **2** (1)

Glass: *cont.*
IN CHURCHES: *cont.*
  FOREIGN: *cont.*
    15TH OR 16TH-CENTURY: Rivenhall **3** (2)
    16TH-CENTURY:
      Easthorpe **3** (1); Great Ilford **2** (2); Hatfield Peverel **2** (1); Layer Marney **3** (1); Panfield **1** (1); Prittlewell **4** (1) (*Plate* **4** pp. xliv–v); Rivenhall **3** (2); Stisted **3** (1); Vange **4** (1)
    16TH OR 17TH-CENTURY:
      Springfield **2** (1); White Notley **2** (1)
    circa 1600: Roxwell **2** (1)
    17TH-CENTURY:
      Chignall **2** (1); Farnham **1** (1); Great Ilford **2** (1); Hatfield Peverel **2** (1); Lambourne **2** (1); Latton **2** (2); Maldon All Saints **2** (1); Manning-tree **3** (1); Noak Hill **2** (1); Prittlewell **4** (1); Rivenhall **3** (2); Springfield **2** (1); Stisted **3** (1); Vange **4** (1); Wenden Lofts **1** (1)
    17TH OR 18TH-CENTURY: Little Burstead **4** (1)
    EARLY 18TH-CENTURY (before 1715): Great Dun-mow **1** (1)
IN HOUSES:
  ENGLISH (*excluding* HERALDIC GLASS, *for which see below*):
    13TH OR 14TH-CENTURY: Walthamstow **2** (12) (*Plate* **2** p. xxxvii)
    14TH-CENTURY:
      Theydon Mount **2** (2); Saffron Walden **1** (4); Walthamstow **2** (12)
    14TH OR 15TH-CENTURY: Saffron Walden **1** (4)
    15TH-CENTURY:
      Halstead Rural **1** (4); Lawford **3** (2); Maldon St. Peter **2** (3) (*Plates* **2** p. xxxv); Markshall **3** (2); Saffron Walden **1** (4); Walthamstow **2** (12); Wickham Bishops **2** (2) (*Fig.* **2** p. 259)
    16TH-CENTURY:
      Aveley **4** (6); Braintree **2** (37); Faulkbourne **2** (3); Great Bardfield **1** (21); Halstead Rural **1** (1); Harlow **2** (15); Ingatestone and Fryerning **2** (3); Laindon Hills **4** (3); Lawford **3** (2); Markshall **3** (2); Pentlow **1** (2); Runwell **4** (2); Stapleford Abbots **2** (2); Thaxted **1** (6)
    16TH OR 17TH-CENTURY: Theydon Mount **2** (2)
    17TH-CENTURY:
      Aveley **4** (6); Laindon Hills **4** (3); Little Burstead **4** (2); Witham **2** (44)
    UNDATED: Little Canfield **2** (4)
  FOREIGN (*excluding* HERALDIC GLASS, *for which see below*):
    16TH-CENTURY:
      Aveley **4** (6); Lawford **3** (2); Saffron Walden **1** (4)
    17TH-CENTURY:
      Arkesden **1** (3); Aveley **4** (6)
    UNDATED: Saffron Walden **1** (4)
HERALDIC GLASS:
  IN CHURCHES:
    ENGLISH:
      14TH-CENTURY:
        Arkesden **1** (1); Bulmer **1** (1); Faulkbourne **2** (2) (*Plate* **2** p. xxxvi); Frinton **3** (1) (*Plates* **3** p. 192); Great Bardfield **1** (1); Great Bur-stead **4** (4) (*Plate* **4** pp. xliv–v); Great Waltham **2** (1); High Easter **2** (1); Little Chesterford **1** (1); Little Sampford **1** (1); Newport **1** (1); North Ockendon **4** (1) (*Plate* **4** pp. xliv–v); Peb-marsh **1** (1); Shalford **1** (1); Springfield **2** (1); Thaxted **1** (2); Wethersfield **1** (1); Widdington Wimbish **1** (1); Woodham Ferrers **4** (1); Wormingford **3** (1) (*Plates* **3** p. 192)

* See *Addenda et Corrigenda, pp. 185–8, under this Volume and Parish.*

Instructions how to use this Index given on page 198.

Glass : *cont.*
HERALDIC GLASS: *cont.*
IN CHURCHES: *cont.*
ENGLISH: *cont.*

15TH-CENTURY :
Arkesden **1** (1) ; Bradwell (juxta-Coggeshall) **3** (1); Clavering **1** (1) ; Copford **3** (1) ; East Horndon **4** (1) (*Plate* **4** pp. xliv–v) ; Great Bromley **3** (1) ; Great Dunmow **1** (1) ; Hatfield Peverel **2** (1) (*Plate* **2** p. xxxvi) ; Henham **1** (1) ; Hornchurch **4** (1) ; Little Ilford **2** (1) ; Little Warley **4** (1) ; Nettleswell **2** (1); Sandon **4** (1) (*Plate* **4** pp. xliv–v) ; Sturmer **1** (1) ; West Hanningfield **4** (1)

15TH OR 16TH-CENTURY :
Great Dunmow **1** (1) ; Sandon **4** (1) (*Plate* **4** pp. xliv–v) ; Steeple Bumpstead **1** (2)

16TH-CENTURY :
Feering **3** (1) ; Great Ilford **2** (2) (*Plates* **2** p. xxxvii) ; Great Parndon **2** (1) ; Harlow **2** (2) ; Hatfield Peverel **2** (1) ; Henham **1** (1) ; High Ongar **2** (1) (*Plate* **2** p. xxxvii) ; Hornchurch **4** (1) ; Layer Marney **3** (1) (*Plate* **3** p. 192) ; Lindsell **1** (1) ; Little Chesterford **1** (1) ; Little Sampford **1** (1) ; Maldon All Saints **2** (1) ; Noak Hill **2** (1) (*Plate* **2** p. xxxvii) ; Sandon **4** (1) ; Springfield **2** (1) ; Stambourne **1** (1) ; Thaxted **1** (2) ; Wethersfield **1** (1) ; Wormingford **3** (1)

16TH OR 17TH-CENTURY :
East Ham **2** (2) ; Little Ilford **2** (1) ; Rivenhall **3** (2)

17TH-CENTURY :
Clavering **1** (1) ; Great Dunmow **1** (1) ; Great Ilford **2** (2) ; Great Waltham **2** (1) ; Hatfield Peverel **2** (1) ; Langley **1** (1) ; Latton **2** (2) ; Little Burstead **4** (1) ; Noak Hill **2** (1) ; North Ockendon **4** (1) (*Plate* **4** pp. xliv–v) ; Stapleford Abbots **2** (1) ; Theydon Mount **2** (1) ; Upminster **4** (1) ; Writtle **2** (1)

17TH OR EARLY 18TH-CENTURY : Harlow **2** (2)

EARLY 18TH-CENTURY (before 1715) :
Colchester **3** (4) ; Hatfield Peverel **2** (1) ; Latton **2** (2) ; Noak Hill **2** (1) ; *V*a$_n$ge **4** (1)

FOREIGN :

16TH-CENTURY :
Great Ilford **2** (2) ; Noak Hill **2** (1)
17TH-CENTURY : Great Ilford **2** (2) ; Lambourne **2** (1) ; Maldon All Saints **2** (1)

IN HOUSES :

ENGLISH :

14TH OR 15TH-CENTURY : Saffron Walden **1** (4)
14TH-CENTURY :
Aveley **4** (6) ; Markshall **3** (2) ; Saffron Walden **1** (4)
16TH-CENTURY :
Aveley **4** (6) ; Berden **1** (4) ; Colchester **3** (231) ; Faulkbourne **2** (3) ; Feering **3** (4) ; Great Maplestead **1** (2) ; Halstead Rural **1** (4) ; Ingatestone and Fryerning **2** (3) (*Plate* **2** p. xxxvii) ; Lawford **3** (2) ; Layer Marney **3** (3) ; Markshall **3** (2) ; Pentlow **1** (4) ; Runwell **4** (2) ; Thaxted **1** (6) ; Theydon Mount **2** (2) ; Widdington **1** (7) ; Wormingford **3** (6)

17TH-CENTURY :
Aveley **4** (6) ; Halstead Rural **1** (4) ; Laindon Hills **4** (3) ; Markshall **3** (2) ; Widdington **1** (7) ; Witham **2** (44)

Glass : *cont.*
HERALDIC GLASS: *cont.*
IN HOUSES: *cont.*
FOREIGN :

16TH-CENTURY :
Braintree **2** (45) ; Lawford **3** (2) ; Theydon Mount **2** (2)
17TH-CENTURY : Arkesden **1** (3)

Glasscock's Farm, South Ockendon **4** (10)
Glebe Farm, Langham **3** (7)
„   „ Thorrington **3** (4)
Globe, *see under* **Inns**
Globe Farm, Farnham **1** (5)
Gloucester, Thomas of Woodstock, Duke of, College of 9 priests founded by, 1393 : Pleshey **2** (2)
Goat and Boot, *see under* **Inns**
Gobert, John, inscription on brass recording benefactions of, 1623 : Hatfield Broad Oak **2** (1)
Gobions, Mucking **4** (4)
God the Father :
CARVING (on chair) : Little Sampford **1** (1)
GLASS : Clavering **1** (1) ; Rivenhall **3** (2)
Godbold, John, 1669, floor-slab to : Hatfield Peverel **2** (1)
Godbolt's Farm, Little Tey **3** (3)
Goddard's Farm, Thaxted **1** (46)
Godd's Farm, Great Sampford **1** (6)
Godebold, Robert, son of, and Beatrice, his wife, Priory founded by, *temp.* Henry I, for Cluniac monks : Little Horkesley **3** (1)
Godfrey :
Elizabeth, wife of Robert, *see* **Scarpe 3**
Richard, 1699, Mary, his first wife, 1683, and Ann, his second wife, 1690, floor-slab to : Clavering **1** (1)
Godfrey's Farm, Radwinter **1** (29)
Godlings Farm, Braintree **2** (57)
Godman, Martha, *see* **Price 4**
Goldacre Farm, Thorrington **3** (8)
Golden Fleece, *see under* **Inns**
Golden Lion, *see under* **Inns**
Golden's Farm, Wethersfield **1** (28)
Golder's Farm, Thaxted **1** (47)
Goldhanger 3 pp. 105–107
Golding :
Elizabeth (West), 1591, wife first of John Buckenham and afterwards of William Golding, brass and remains of former monument to : Belchamp St. Paul's **1** (1)
George, 1617, brass to : Great Henny **3** (1)
William, 1587, brass of : Belchamp St. Paul's **1** (1)
Goldingham Farm, Braintree **2** (65)
Goldington's Farm, Colne Engaine **3** (3)
Goldsmiths' Company, arms : Sandon **4** (1) (brass) ; West Ham **2** (1) (tomb)
Goldstones, Ashdon **1** (34)
Goldwyre, William, 1514, brass of : Great Coggeshall **3** (2)
Good and Evil, Choice between, glass : Lambourne **2** (1)
Good Easter 2 pp. 87–90
Good Hares, Latchingdon **4** (3)
Goodall, Anne, wife of Thomas, 1714, head-stone to : Boxted **3** (1)
Goodeve :
John, 1698, head-stone to : Little Waltham **2** (1)
Sarah, *see* **Hinde 2**
Goodfellows, Tilty **1** (5)
Goodlad :
Elizabeth, *see* **Dugdale 4**
Mary, 1674, William, 1678, and Abraham, 1685, tablet to : Upminster **4** (1)
Richard, 1690, and Elizabeth, his wife, 1712, table-tomb to : Leigh **4** (1)

* *See Addenda et Corrigenda, pp. 185–8, under this Volume and Parish.*

Instructions how to use this Index given on page 198.

* See *Addenda et Corrigenda, pp. 185–8, under this Volume and Parish.*

Instructions how to use this Index given on page 198.

See Addenda et Corrigenda, pp. 185–8, under this Volume and Parish.

Instructions how to use this Index given on page 198.

* *See Addenda et Corrigenda, pp. 185–8, under this Volume and Parish.*

Instructions how to use this Index given on page 198.

Hartishorn, arms : Stambourne **1** (1) (glass, etc.)
Hartridge, Elizabeth, wife of Densc, *see* **Downes 4**
Harvey, *or* **Harve,** arms : Dagenham **2** (1) ; Hempstead **1** (1) ; Low Leyton **2** (2) ; Witham **2** (1)
Harvey, Harvy, *or* **Harve :**
Eliab, 1661 ; Sarah, his daughter, 1655 ; Elizabeth, his daughter, 1656 ; Mary, his wife, 1673 ; Sir Eliab, 1698 ; Eliab, son of Sir Eliab, 1681 ; Elizabeth, wife of Edward, 1695 ; Mary, daughter of the third Eliab and wife of Sir William Whitmore, Bart., 1710 ; monument to : Hempstead **1** (1)
Elizabeth, *see* **Heigham 2**
James, 1627, tablet to : Dagenham **2** (1)
John, 1523, latin inscription concerning : Burnham **4** (1) (S. porch)
Mary (Nevell), 1592, widow of Thomas Smith and wife of Francis Harve, tablet of : Witham **2** (1) (*Plate* **2** p. 251)
Robert, 1695, Rebecka, his wife, 1691, Robert and Thomas, both 1668, Mary and Benjamin, both 1669, floor-slab to : Low Leyton **2** (2)
Sarah, 1655 ; Elizabeth, 1659 ; Eliab, 1661 ; Mary, 1664 ; Mary, 1673 ; Mary, 1677 ; Eliab, 1681 ; Dorothy, 1686 ; E., 1686 ; Dorothea, 1691 ; Matthew, first page of honour to William III, 1692 ; Elizabeth, 1695 ; and M., 1695 ; lead coffins with shaped heads and modelled faces containing the remains of : Hempstead **1** (1)
William, 1657, chief physician to James I and Charles I, discoverer of the circulation of the blood, tablet to : Hempstead **1** (1)
Sir William of Roehampton, 1719, and Bridgett (Browne), his wife, 1701, monument to : Hempstead **1** (1)
Harvey Vault, Hempstead **1** (1)
Harvey's Farm, Ardleigh **3** (11)
„ „ Peldon **3** (3)
Harwich 3 pp. 134–136
Hassenbrook Hall, Stanford-le-Hope **4** (4) (*Plate* **4** p. 64)
Hassobury House, Farnham **1** (19)
Hasten, Camps supposed to be those contracted by the Danish Leader, *c.* 894 : South Benfleet **4** (10) ; South Shoebury **4** (4)
Hatches Farm, Braintree **2** (70)
„ „ Little Burstead **4** (4) (*Plate* **4** p. xxxv)
Hatfield Broad Oak 2 pp. 116–122 ; **4** p. 186
Hatfield Peverel 2 pp. 122–126
Hatfield Priory, Hatfield Peverel **2** (15)
Hatfield Wick, Hatfield Peverel **2** (5)
Hatley's Farm, Felsted **2** (98) (*Plate* **2** p. 97)
Haulsey, William, *see under* **Bellfounders**
Havengore 4 p. 66
Havering-atte-Bower 2 p. 126
Havering Palace, site of, Havering-atte-Bower **2** (1)
Havers :
Clopton, *see* **Fuller 2**
Mrs. Mary, 1679, Maidstone, her son, 1687, and Anne, daughter of John Maidstone, 1698, floor-slab to : Boxted **3** (1)
Hawbush Farm, Cressing **3** (4)
Hawes, Abigail, *see* **Thurkettle 2**
Hawk, *see under* **Inns**
Hawkes, Peter, *see under* **Bellfounders**
Hawkes Cottage, Pattiswick **3** (6)
Hawke's Farm, Little Sampford **1** (5)
Hawkins, arms : Braintree **2** (1) ; Hatfield Broad Oak **2** (1)

Hawkins :
Dorothy, *see* **Scarth 2**
John, Alderman of the City of London, 1633, and John and Abraham, his sons, 1644, monument to : Braintree **2** (1)
John, 1680, and Mary, his wife, 1688, two infant children and Alice Masters, aunt of Mr. Hawkins' father, 1683, floor-slab to : Hatfield Broad Oak **2** (1)
Hawkins-atte-Well, Romford Rural **2** (6)
Hawkin's Farm, Little Sampford **1** (4)
Hawkin's Harvest, Finchingfield **1** (47)
Hawkspur Green, Great Bardfield **1** (41)
Hawkwell 4 p. 66
Hawkwood, arms : Gosfield **1** (1) (label-stop) ; Little Sampford **1** (1) (glass)*
Hawkwood, Sir John, 1394, tomb said to be cenotaph of : Sible Hedingham **1** (1)
Hawkwoods, Sible Hedingham **1** (2)
Hawkwood's Farm, Gosfield **1** (12)
Hayes, Hays, *or* **Heies :**
Humphrey, 1584, and his son, 1585, brass of : West Thurrock **4** (1)
Katherine, *see* **Redinge 4**
Margaret, wife of George, 1552, brass to : Rettendon **4** (1)
Richard, 1600, brass to : Rawreth **4** (1)
Hayles, Epping Upland **2** (4)
Haynes, Mary, *see* **Barlee 1**
Hayrons, High Easter **2** (6) (*Plate* **2** p. 110)
Hazel End, *see* **Farnham 1**
Hazeleigh 4 pp. 66–67
Hazeleigh Hall, Hazeleigh **4** (2)
Head-stones, *see under* **Monuments, Funeral**
Heath, arms : Ingrave **4** (1) (FitzLewes brass)
Heath, Margaret, *see* **Colt 2**
Hedgehall, Great Waltham **2** (5)
Hedges, arms : Theydon Mount **2** (2)
Hedges, Anne, *see* **Smythe 2**
Hedingham, *see* **Castle Hedingham 1** *and* **Sible Hedingham 1**
Heies, *see* **Hayes,** *above*
Heigham, *or* **Heyham,** arms : East Ham **2** (2)
Heigham, Higham, *or* **Heyham :**
Antony, 1540, and Anne, his wife, brass to : Goldhanger **3** (2)
Elizabeth (Harvey), wife of Sir Richard, 1622, brass of and tablet to : East Ham **2** (2)
Elizabeth, widow of Sir Richard, *see* **Silverlock 4**
Lucy, *see* **Stonard 2**
Marie, daughter of Sir Richard, 1621, tablet to : East Ham **2** (2)
Sir Richard, Knight, font given by : East Ham **2** (2)
Thomas, 1531, and Alys, Awdrie, and Frances, his wives, altar-tomb and remains of brasses to : Goldhanger **3** (2)
William, 1620, and Anne (Stoneley), his wife, 1612, tablet to : East Ham **2** (2)
Heila, arms : Castle Hedingham **1** (1)
Heila, Dominic van, of Flanders, 1608, and Wilhelmina (Haleme), his wife, 1605, tablet to : Castle Hedingham **1** (1)
Helen, St. :
GLASS (probably of) : North Ockendon **4** (1) (*Plate* **4** pp. xliv–v)
PAINTING (on screen) : Foxearth **1** (1)
Helion, arms : Finchingfield **1** (1)
Helion Bumpstead 1 pp. 155–157
Helions, Helion Bumpstead **1** (2)
Hempstead 1 pp. 157–161
Hempstead Hall, Hempstead **1** (4)

* See Addenda et Corrigenda, pp. 185–8, under this Volume and Parish.

Instructions how to use this Index given on page 198.

*See Addenda et Corrigenda, pp. 185–8, under this Volume and Parish.

Instructions how to use this Index given on page 198.

* *See Addenda et Corrigenda, pp. 185–8, under this Volume and Parish.*

Instructions how to use this Index given on page 198.

* See Addenda et Corrigenda, pp. 185–8, under this Volume and Parish.

Instructions how to use this Index given on page 198.

Heraldry : *cont.*
ROYAL ARMS: *cont.*
ENGLAND AND FRANCE, etc.: *cont.*
TUDOR (1485–1603) :
Sovereign not identified : East Tilbury **4** (2) (painted) ; Harlow **2** (2) (glass) ; Kelvedon **3** (2) (carved) (*Plate* 3 p. 213) ; Lawford **3** (2) (glass) ; Little Ilford **2** (1) (glass) ; Markshall **3** (2) (glass) ; Saffron Walden **1** (57) (carved) ; Springfield **2** (1) (glass) ; Steeple Bumpstead **1** (10) (carved, apex of roof) ; Thaxted **1** (2) (glass) ; Theydon Mount **2** (2) (glass) ; Waltham Holy Cross **2** (1) (carved) ; Woodford **2** (2) (plaster)
Henry VII : Laindon Hills **4** (3) (glass)
Henry VIII : Boreham **2** (4) (carved) (*Plate* **2** p. 85) ; High Ongar **2** (1) (glass) ; Maldon All Saints **2** (1) (glass) ; Noak Hill **2** (1) (glass) ; St. Osyth **3** (4) (' Bishops' Lodging,'—carved)
Elizabeth : Barking **2** (5) (plaster) ; Boreham **2** (4) (carved) ; Braintree **2** (2) (terra-cotta) (*Plate* **2** p. xxxvi) (17) (plaster) (37) (painted) ; Great Maplestead **1** (2) (glass in bathing-house) ;. Hatfield Peverel **2** (1) (glass)
ENGLAND, SCOTLAND, FRANCE AND IRELAND, 1603– MAY 1ST 1707 (*quarterly* : 1 and 4, *France Modern quartering England* ; 2, *or a lion within a double tressure flowered and counter-flowered gules* for Scotland ; 3, *azure a harp or stringed argent* for Ireland) :
STUART :
Sovereign not identified : Ashingdon **4** (1) (painted) ; Chelmsford **2** (2) (lead panel from roof) ; Finchingfield **1** (1) (painted) ; Fingring-hoe **3** (1) (carved) ; Langley **1** (1) (glass) ; Maldon All Saints **2** (1) (carved) ; Rivenhall **3** (3) (iron fire-back) ; Theydon Mount **2** (2) (carved) ; White Notley **2** (1) (painted)
James I : Roxwell **2** (9) (painted) ; Theydon Bois **2** (1) (painted)
Charles I : Messing **3** (1) (carved) (*Plate* **3** p. 181) ; Mountnessing **4** (6) (iron fire-back)
Charles II : Bradwell (juxta-Coggeshall) **3** (1) (painted) ; Great Baddow **4** (1) (painted) ; Great Tey **3** (1) (painted) ; Ingatestone and Fryerning **2** (1) (painted) ; Laindon Hills **4** (1) (painted) (*Plate* **4** p. 79) ; Little Easton **1** (1) (painted) ; Noak Hill **2** (1) (glass) ; Panfield **1** (3) (plaster) ; Saffron Walden **1** (1) (painted) ; West Tilbury **4** (3) (carved) ; Woodham Walter **2** (1) (painted)
James II : Rivenhall **3** (2) (painted) ; Roxwell **2** (1) (painted)
William III (*Stuart royal arms with a scutcheon of Nassau*) : Colchester **3** (8) (carved) ; Sible Hedingham **1** (1) (carved) ; Vange **4** (1) (painted) ; Witham **2** (1) (carved)
Anne (before the Union with Scotland, *i.e.*, 1702–May 1st 1707) : Basildon **4** (1) (painted) ; Bulphan **4** (1) (painted) ; Cressing **3** (1) (painted) ; Noak Hill **2** (1) (glass) ; Rayleigh **4** (1) (painted) ; Thaxted **1** (2) (painted) ; Vange **4** (1) (glass)
GREAT BRITAIN, FRANCE AND IRELAND, MAY 1ST 1707–1714 (*quarterly* : 1 and 4, *England impaling Scotland* ; 2, *France Modern* ; 3, *Ireland*) :
Anne : Barking **2** (5) (painted) ; Basildon **4** (1) (on Communion cup) ; Great Clacton **3** (1)

Heraldry : *cont.*
ROYAL ARMS: *cont.*
GREAT BRITAIN, FRANCE AND IRELAND, etc.: *cont.*
(painted) ; Great Waltham **2** (2) (painted) ; Hadleigh **4** (1) (painted) ; Kelvedon **3** (2) (painted) ; Toppesfield **1** (1) (painted)
FRANGE ANCIENT : (*azure powdered with fleurs-de-lis or*) : North Ockendon **4** (1) (glass) ; Woodham Ferrers **4** (1) (glass)
FRANCE MODERN : (*azure hree fleurs-de-lis or*) : Aveley **4** (6) (glass) ; St. Osyth **3** (4) (' Bishops' Lodging,'—carved)
HERALDIC GLASS, *see under* **Glass**
HERALDIC PAINTINGS, *see under* **Paintings**
HERALDIC TILES, *see under* **Tiles**
Herberts, Saffron Walden **1** (155)
Herd's Farm, High Laver **2** (6)
Herksted Hall, Steeple Bumpstead **1** (8)
Heron, Thomas, son of Sir John, 1517, brass of : Little Ilford **2** (1)
Heron Gate, see East Horndon **4**
Heron Hall, East Horndon **4** (2)
Heron Pond, East Horndon **4** (2)
Herons, Fyfield **2** (5)
Herris, arms : Creeksea **4** (1) ; Little Burstead **4** (1)
Herris :
Sir Arthur, 1631, brass to : Creeksea **4** (1)
Christopher, 1654, floor-slab to : Little Burstead **4** (1)
Elizabeth, *see* **Walton 4**
Hervy, arms : .Romford Urban **2** (1)
Hervy *or* **Hervey :**
Anne, *see* **Carew 2**
Sir George, 1605, Lieutenant of the Tower, and Fraunces (Beckwith), his wife, monument of : Romford Urban **2** (1) (*Plate* **2** p. 251)
Thomas, 1712, rector of the parish, floor-slab to : Nevendon **4** (1)
Heveningham, arms : Writtle **2** (1) (brass)
Heveningham, Thomasin, see **Thomas 2**
Hewes, Eliza, 1694, head and foot-stones to : Great Burstead **4** (4)
Hewet, Thomas, 1700, slab to : Springfield **2** (1)
Hewitts, Lamarsh **3** (12)
Heybridge 3 pp. 136–138
Heybridge Hall, Heybridge **3** (3)
Heygate, arms : Feering **3** (4) (glass)
Heyham, see **Heigham,** *above*
Hickringill, arms : Colchester **3** (2)
Hickringill, Edmund, 1708, rector of the parish, Anne, his wife, 1708, and Edmund, their son, 1705, floor-slab to : All Saints' Church, Colchester **3** (2)
Hicks, arms : Low Leyton **2** (2)
Hicks :
Marthagnes (Conysby), effigy of : Low Leyton **2** (2)
Sir Michael, 1612, and Elizabeth (Colston), his wife, monument of : Low Leyton **2** (2) (*Plate* **2** p. 150)
Sir William, Bart., 1680, and Sir William, his son, 1703, monument of : Low Leyton **2** (2)
Hide End Farm, Great Easton **1** (19)
High Easter 2 pp. 126–130 (*Plate* **2** p. 81)
High Easterbury, High Easter **2** (16)
High Hall, Fairstead **2** (6)
High House, Upminster **4** (5) (8)
High Houses, Great Waltham **2** (26)
High Laver 2 pp. 130–131
High Laver Grange, High Laver **2** (4)
High Laver Hall, High Laver **2** (2)
High Ongar 2 pp. 131–133 ; **4** p. 186
High Priest, The, glass : Stisted **3** (1)
High Roding 2 pp. 133–136

* *See Addenda et Corrigenda, pp. 185-8, under this Volume and Parish.*

Instructions how to use this Index given on page 198.

* *See Addenda et Corrigenda, pp. 185–8, under this Volume and Parish.*

Instructions how to use this Index given on page 198.

* *See Addenda et Corrigenda, pp. 185–8, under this Volume and Parish.*

Instructions how to use this Index given on page 198.

* *See Addenda et Corrigenda, pp. 185–8, under this Volume and Parish.*

Instructions how to use this Index given on page 198.

* *See Addenda et Corrigenda, pp. 185–8, under this Volume and Parish.*

Instructions how to use this Index given on page 198.

Ironwork : *cont.*
HINGES AND IRONWORK ON DOORS, etc.: *cont.*
13th-century: *cont.*
Totham **3** (1) ; Navestock **2** (1) ; Stifford **4** (1) (*Plate* **4** pp. 4–5) ; Upminster **4** (1) ; Wethersfield **1** (1) ; White Roding **2** (2)
13th or 14th-century : North Weald Bassett **2** (1)
circa 1300 :
Aldham **3** (1) (*Plate* **3** p. 132) ; Colchester **3** (8) (*Plate* **3** p. 42)
14th-century :
Colchester **3** (5) (8) (*Plate* **3** p. 42) ; Fingringhoe **3** (1) (*Plate* **3** p. 132) ; Great Horkesley **3** (1) ; Great Yeldham **1** (1) ; *Purleigh* **4** (1) ; Sheering **2** (1) ; Wethersfield **1** (1) ; White Notley **2** (1) ; Witham **2** (1) ; Writtle **2** (1)
14th or 15th-century :
Buttsbury **4** (2) (*Plate* **4** pp. 4–5) ; Colchester **3** (3) ; Magdalen Laver **2** (1) ; Navestock **2** (1) ; South Hanningfield **4** (1) (*Plate* **4** pp. 4–5) ; Terling **2** (6) ; West Hanningfield **4** (1) ; White Notley **2** (1)
15th-century :
Aldham **3** (1) ; Alphamstone **3** (1) ; Ardleigh **3** (1) (*Plate* **3** p. 132) ; Braintree **2** (1) ; Canewdon **4** (2) ; Castle Hedingham **1** (1) ; Chadwell **4** (2) ; Chingford **2** (1) ; Colchester **3** (2) (4) (5) (10) ; Eastwood **4** (1) ; Elsenham **1** (1) ; Epping Upland **2** (2) ; Faulkbourne **2** (2) ; Fobbing **4** (1) ; Goldhanger **3** (2) ; Great Burstead **4** (4) ; Great Horkesley **3** (1) ; Great Parndon **2** (1) ; Great Wakering **4** (1) ; Great Waltham **2** (1) ; Great Wigborough **3** (1) ; Hadstock **1** (2) ; Hawkwell **4** (1) ; High Easter **2** (1) ; Kirby-le-Soken **3** (1) ; Laindon **4** (1) ; Langenhoe **3** (1) ; Little Bardfield **1** (1) ; Little Oakley **3** (1) ; Little Sampford **1** (1) ; Little Totham **3** (1) ; Little Wakering **4** (1) ; Little Warley **4** (1) ; Margaretting **2** (1) ; Mount Bures **3** (1) ; Paglesham **4** (1) ; Radwinter **1** (1) ; Rayleigh **4** (1) ; Rochford **4** (1) ; Runwell **4** (1) ; Saffron Walden **1** (1) ; Sandon **4** (1) ; South Weald **2** (1) ; South Ockendon **4** (6) ; Southchurch **4** (1) ; Southminster **4** (1) ; Stanford-le-Hope **4** (1) ; Stanway **3** (2) ; Stock **4** (1) ; Takeley **1** (1) ; Terling **2** (1) ; Thaxted **1** (2) ; Tillingham **4** (1) ; Tolleshunt Knights **3** (2) ; Upminster **4** (1) ; West Hanningfield **4** (1) ; Wickham Bishops **2** (1) ; Widdington **1** (1) ; Willingale Spain **2** (1)
15th or 16th-century :
Bradwell (juxta-Coggeshall) **3** (1) ; Dedham **3** (1) ; Little Thurrock **4** (1) ; Little Waltham **2** (1) ; Mundon **4** (1) ; Sutton **4** (1)
Mediaeval :
Great Sampford **1** (1) ; *Pebmarsh* **3** (1) ; Radwinter **1** (1)
circa 1500 :
Brightlingsea **3** (3) ; Colchester **3** (2) ; North Weald Bassett **2** (1) ; Saffron Walden **1** (6) ; Toppesfield **1** (4)
16th-century :
Aveley **4** (6) ; Barnston **2** (1) ; Belchamp Walter **1** (1) ; Booking **1** (6) (7) ; Braintree **2** (9) (45) ; Brightlingsea **3** (3) (4) ; Chignall **2** (1) (2) ; Colchester **3** (3) (10) (11) ; Debden **1** (26) ; East Horndon **4** (1) ; East Mersea **3** (1) ; Epping Upland **2** (2) ; Feering **3** (1) ; Felsted **2** (1) (13) ; Finchingfield **1** (3) ; Gestingthorpe **1** (1) ; Great Bardfield **1** (3) ; Great Burstead **4** (12) ; Great Coggeshall **3** (5) (69) ; Great Dunmow **1** (1) ; Great Leighs **2** (1) ; Great Sampford **1** (1) ; Great Warley **4** (2) ; Halstead Rural **1** (1) ; Halstead Urban **1** (37) ;

Ironwork : *cont.*
HINGES AND IRONWORK ON DOORS, etc.: *cont.*
16th-century : *cont.*
Hempstead **1** (21) ; Henham **1** (4) ; High Laver **2** (1) ; Hornchurch **4** (1) ; Lamarsh **3** (1) ; Lawford **3** (1) ; Layer Marney **3** (1) ; Liston **1** (1) ; Little Bentley **3** (1) ; Little Bromley **3** (1) ; Little ·Burstead **4** (1) ; Little Totham **3** (1) ; Magdalen Laver **2** (5) ; Nazeing **2** (1) ; Newport **1** (1) (5) ; *Paglesham* **4** (1) ; *Pebmarsh* **3** (4) ; Radwinter **1** (6) ; Rayne **1** (4) ; Roxwell **2** (17) ; .Saffron Walden **1** (1) (82) (100) ; St. Osyth **3** (2) ; Sandon **4** (1) (4) ; Shalford **1** (4) (5) (11) (24) ; Shelley **2** (4) ; Sible Hedingham **1** (1) (4) ; South Weald **2** (2) ; Springfield **2** (1) ; Stambourne **1** (1) (6) ; Stansted Mountfitchet **1** (16) ; Thaxted **1** (45) ; Theydon Garnon **2** (1) ; Tilbury-juxta-Clare **1** (1) ; Toppesfield **1** (6) ; Wakes Colne **3** (1) ; Waltham Holy Cross **2** (10) ; Wendens Ambo **1** (2) ; Wennington **4** (1) ; Wethersfield **1** (7) (24) ; Widdington **1** (15) ; Wimbish **1** (16) (33) ; Woodham Walter **2** (1) ; Writtle **2** (1)
16th or 17th-century :
Brentwood **2** (1) ; Colchester **3** (8) ; Great Waltham **2** (25) ; Latton **2** (2) ; Panfield **1** (6) ; Steeple Bumpstead **1** (2)
circa 1600 :
Ashdon **1** (34) ; Finchingfield **1** (4) ; Great Dunmow **1** (2) ; Saffron Walden **1** (4) ; Shenfield **2** (9)
17th-century :
Belchamp Otton **1** (3) ; Black Notley **2** (7) ; Booking **1** (34) (55) ; Boxted **3** (1) ; Braintree **2** (5) ; Castle Hedingham **1** (1) ; Chapel **3** (1) ; Clavering **1** (7) (10) (12) ; Dovercourt **3** (2) ; Great Easton **1** (13) ; East·Tilbury **4** (1) ; Fobbing **4** (1) ; Great Hallingbury **2** (9) ; Great Maplestead **1** (20) ; Halstead Rural **1** (4) (15) ; Hempstead **1** (25) ; Layer Marney **3** (3) ; Little Sampford **1** (14) ; Nazeing **2** (1) ; North Benfleet **4** (5) ; Norton Mandeville **2** (2) ; Pentlow **1** (4) ; Prittlewell **4** (3) ; Ridgewell **1** (9) ; Saffron Walden **1** (4) (16) (125) ; Shalford **1** (14) (15) (33) ; Sheering **2** (6) ; Sible Hedingham **1** (5) ; Stebbing **1** (6) ; Stifford **4** (1) (*Plate* **4** pp. 4–5) ; Stisted **3** (18) ; Sutton **4** (2) ; Thaxted **1** (45) ; West Tilbury **4** (3) ; Wethersfield **1** (11) (19) (63) (65) ; Wimbish **1** (14) ; Witham **2** (17)
circa 1700 : Clavering **1** (10)
18th-century (before 1715) :
Wethersfield **1** (31) ; Wicken Bonhunt **1** (5)
Undated :
Alphamstone **3** (1) ; Ardleigh **3** (11) ; Boreham **2** (9) ; Elmstead **3** (1) ; Finchingfield **1** ·(3) (9) ; Great Easton **1** (23) ; Great Waltham **2** (63) (68) ; Little Dunmow **1** (5) ; Magdalen Laver **2** (1) ; North Benfleet **4** (5) ; *Pentlow* **1** (10) ; Ridgewell **1** (10) ; Shalford **1** (24) ; Sible Hedingham **1** (23) (29) ; Stambourne **1** (5) ; Toppesfield **1** (6) ; West Bergholt **3** (1) ; Wickham Bishops **2** (1)
HOUR-GLASS STANDS :
17th-century :
East Mersea **3** (1) ; Little Bentley **3** (1) ; Norton Mandeville **2** (1) ; South Ockendon **4** (1) ; Stifford **4** (1) ; Thorrington **3** (1) ; Wennington **4** (1) (*Plate* **4** p. 104)
18th-century (before 1715) :
Abbess Roding **2** (1) ; Ingatestone and Fryerning **2** (1)
INN-SIGNS :
Sign-board swung from 17th-century ironwork: Braintree **2** (53)
18th-century frame : Debham **3** (13)

* See Addenda et Corrigenda, pp. 185–8, under this Volume and Parish.

Instructions how to use this Index given on page 198.

* See Addenda et Corrigenda, pp. 185-8, under this Volume and Parish.

Instructions how to use this Index given on page 198.

John, St. :
CARVINGS : Barking **2** (3) (on stone rood) ; Great
Bardfield **1** (1) (on stone screen) (*Plate* **1** p. 106) ;
Great Coggeshall **3** (2) (at back of recess) ; Saffron
Walden **1** (1) (on niche)
GLASS : Lawford **3** (2) ; Maldon St. *Peter* **2** (3) (*Plate*
2 p. xxxv) ; Manningtree **3** (1) ; Noak Hill **2** (1) ;
Springfield **2** (1) ; South Weald **3** (1) ; Stisted **3** (1)
IMAGE : Doddinghurst **2** (1) (on rood-beam)
PAINTINGS : Hatfield Peverel **2** (1) ; Middleton **3** (1) ;
Newport **1** (1) (chest)
SYMBOLS OF : Panfield **1** (1) ; Thaxted **1** (2) ; *see also*
Evangelists, Symbols of the
John the Baptist, St. :
FIGURES OF (on bell) : Margaretting **2** (1)
GLASS : Hatfield Peverel **2** (1) ; Maldon St. Peter **2** (3) ;
Noak Hill **2** (1) ; Prittlewell **4** (1) ; Stisted **3** (1)
HEAD OF : St. Osyth **2** (2) (on font) (4) (carved boss
in Gatehouse of St. Osyth Priory)
Johnson, arms : East Ham **2** (2)
Johnson :
Mary (Coleman), 1634, wife of William, inscription
cut in stone to : East Ham **2** (2)
Warnewood, 1678, daughter of Thomas, floor-slab to :
East Ham **2** (2)
William, 1631, brass to : East Ham **2** (2)

Katherine, St. :
CARVINGS : Danbury **4** (1) (on chair) ; Dedham **3** (1) ;
St. Osyth **3** (2) (arm of angel breaking wheel of) ;
Thaxted **1** (2) (on capital, S. transept)
GLASS : Clavering **1** (1) ; Newport **1** (1) ; Thaxted **1** (2)
PAINTING : East Hanningfield **4** (1) (*Plate* **4** p. 104)
Keble, arms : Great Leighs **2** (1)
Keble, John, Sergeant-at-law, 1699, floor-slab to : Great
Leighs **2** (1)
Kebyll, John, *see under* **Bellfounders**
Keelings, Dengie **4** (3)
Keene, James and Richard, *see under* **Bellfounders**
Keeps :
11TH-CENTURY : Colchester **3** (18) (*Plates* **3** pp. 51,
54–5, 58–9, 62)
12TH-CENTURY :
Castle Hedingham **1** (3) (*Plate* **1** *Frontispiece*) ;
Saffron Walden **1** (2)
Keeres, Aythorpe Roding **2** (10)
Kello, Joseph and Isaac, 1614, brasses to : Willingale
Spain **2** (1)
Kelvedon 3 pp. 140–146 (*Plate* **3** p. 122)
Kelvedon Hatch 2 pp. 142–143 ; **4** p. 186
Kempe, arms : Finchingfield **1** (1) (3) ; Pentlow **1** (1)
Kempe :
George, 1606, John, 1609, and Elinor (Drewe), his wife,
altar-tomb of : Pentlow **1** (1) (*Plate* **1** p. 210)
Jane, *see* **Gardiner 3**
Robert, 1524, and Anne, his wife, altar-tomb with
brass to : Finchingfield **1** (1)
Robert, church roof built at charge of, 1635 : Finch-
ingfield **1** (1)
Robert and Elizabeth, arms and initials of, on rain-
water-heads of 1637 : Finchingfield **1** (3)
William, 1628, and ' Philip,' his wife, 1623, monument
to : Finchingfield **1** (1)
Kemp's Farm, Peldon **3** (4)
Kempsters, Orsett **4** (15)
Kempton, William, 1709, head-stone to : Barking **2** (2)
Kenarley, Margct, wife of James, 1690, and Isaac, their
son, 1705, floor-slab to : St. Osyth **3** (2)

Jolly Boys, Felsted **2** (36).
Jolly Waggoners, *see under* **Inns**
Jonah beneath the gourd (?), carving (on cupboard) :
Castle Hedingham **1** (1)
Jones, Gilbert, 1713, head-stone to : Barking **2** (2)
Jordan and Adam, founders of a Priory of Austin Canons,
1152–1162 : Blackmore **2** (1)
Jordan, *or* **Jurdan,** Henry, *see under* **Bellfounders**
Jordan's Farm, Wakes Colne **3** (11)
Josceline, *or* **Joscelyn,** *see* **Jocelyn,** *above*
Joscelyn's Farm, Great Sampford **1** (30)
Joseph's Brethren casting him into a pit, glass : Aveley
4 (6)
Josselyns, Little Horkesley **3** (3) (*Plates* **3** p. xxx)
„ Mount Bures **3** (8)
Joyce's Farm, Wimbish **1** (55)
Joyner, arms : High Ongar **2** (1)
Joyner, Daniel, 1695, rector of Hockwell, floor-slab to :
High Ongar **2** (1)
Judd, arms : Latton **2** (2)
Judd, -e, Mary, *see* **Altham 2**
Judd's Farm, Stanway **3** (13)
Julius Caesar, *see* **Caesar, Julius**

Kendall, arms : Takeley **1** (1)
Kendall, John, 1679, floor-slab to : Takeley **1** (1)
Kendlemarsh, Richard, and Dennics Barnard, his wife,
arms of : Witham **2** (1)
Kennett, Nicholas, 1713, head-stone to : Great Wakering **4** (2)
Kenningtons, Aveley **4** (4)
Kennloe, Gilbert, 1693, tablet to : Low Leyton **2** (2)
Kentish Farm, Stisted **3** (18)
Kentish's Farm, Sible Hedingham **1** (38)
Kent's Farm, West Hanningfield **4** (8)
Kenwrick, Elizabeth, *see* **Grantham 4**
Kercley (?), George, 1701, head-stone to : Abberton **3** (1)
Killigrews (formerly **Shenfield),** Margaretting **2** (2) (*Plate*
2 p. 270)
Killingmarch, arms : Great Dunmow **1** (1) (glass)
Kindleton, George, 1667, rector of the parish, monument
to : Magdalen Laver **2** (1)
King, -e, arms : Orsett **4** (1) ; Southminster **4** (1)
King, -e :
Anne, *see* **Hill 2**
Edmunde, 1624, tablet to, recording legacy : Halstead
Urban **1** (1)
John, 1634, brass of : Southminster **4** (1)
John, 1657, Elizabeth, his wife, 1661, and Joseph, his
son, 1679, floor-slab to : Chipping Ongar **2** (2)
Martha (Bourne), wife of Thomas, late 17th-century
floor-slab to : Stapleford Tawney **2** (1)
Richard, S. T. P., vicar of the parish and chaplain to
James I, 17th-century tablet to : Toppesfield **1** (1)
Robert, 1584, parson, brass to : Orsett **4** (1)
King Coel's Kitchen, Colchester **3** (265)
King John's Palace, site so called : Writtle **2** (3)
King William, *see under* **Inns**
Kingesmyll, arms : Easthorpe **3** (1)
Kingesmyll :
Anne (Blagrave), widow of George, 1680, floor-slab to :
Easthorpe **3** (1)
Margaret, daughter of George, 1652, floor-slab to :
Easthorpe **3** (1)
King's Arms, *see under* **Inns**
King's Cottage, Elmdon **1** (11)

* *See Addenda et Corrigenda, pp. 185–8, under this Volume and Parish.*

Instructions how to use this Index given on page 198.

* See Addenda et Corrigenda, pp. 185–8, under this Volume and Parish.

Instructions how to use this Index given on page 198.

* See *Addenda et Corrigenda, pp. 185–8, under this Volume and Parish.*

Instructions how to use this Index given on page 198.

* See Addenda et Corrigenda, pp. 185–8, under this Volume and Parish.

Instructions how to use this Index given on page 198.

See Addenda et Corrigenda, pp. 185–8, under this Volume and Parish.

Instructions how to use this Index given on page 198.

* *See Addenda et Corrigenda, pp. 185–8, under this Volume and Parish.*

Instructions how to use this Index given on page 198.

Manor House, Dovercourt **3** (4)
,, ,, Hadstock **1** (3)
,, ,, High Ongar **2** (13)
,, ,, Little Chesterford **1** (2) (*Plate* **1** p. 174)
,, ,, Little Easton **1** (3)
,, ,, Little Laver **2** (4)
,, ,, Roydon **2** (3)
,, ,, Southminster **4** (2)
,, ,, (or **Suttons**), South Shoebury **4** (5)
,, ,, Terling **2** (5) (*Plate* **2** p. 229)
,, ,, Wanstead **2** (3)
,, ,, Wethersfield **1** (2)
,, ,, (or **Spains Hall**), Willingale Spain **2** (4)
Man's Cross Farm, Great Yeldham **1** (8)
Mantell, Robert, Abbey of SS. Mary and Nicholas, (founded for *Premonstratensian* Canons), removed *c.* 1180 from Great Parndon to Beeleigh Abbey by : Maldon St. *Peter* **2** (3)
Mantelpieces, *see* **Fireplaces,** etc.
Mantill's Farm, Copford **3** (7)
Manuden 1 pp. 195–198 ; **4** p. 185
Manuden Hall, Manuden **1** (2)
Manwood Green, see Hatfield Broad Oak **2**
Maples Farm, Great Dunmow **1** (37)
Maplesden (?), Hannah, *see* **Bownd 2**
Maplestead, *see* **Great Maplestead 1** *and* **Little Maplestead 1**
March, Edmund Mortimer, Earl of, *see* **Mortimer 1**
Marchings, Chigwell **2** (13)
Marden Ash, High Ongar **2** (6)
Margaret Roding 2 pp. 182–183
Margaret, St. :
CARVED FIGURE : Dedham **3** (1)
GLASS : Abbess Roding **2** (1)
Margarets, Manuden **1** (10)
Margaretting 2 pp. 183–186 ; **4** p. 187
Margaretting Tye, see Margaretting **2**
Mark, arms : Stondon Massey **2** (1) (brass)
Mark Hall, Latton **2** (6)
Mark, St., symbol of : Tolleshunt D'Arcy **3** (1) (brass) ; *see also* **Evangelists, Symbols of the**
Marke, Ann, widow of Edward, 1621, floor-slab to : Great Wigborough **3** (1)
Market Halls :
15TH-CENTURY : Thaxted **1** (9) (*Plate* **1** p. 310)
16TH-CENTURY :
Barking **2** (5) ; Horndon-on-the-Hill **4** (8) (*Plates* **4** pp. xl, 65) ; Steeple Bumpstead **1** (10) (possibly) (*Plate* **1** p. 310)
Marks, Great Dunmow **1** (8)
Marks Farm, Braintree **2** (69)
Marks Hall, Margaret Roding **2** (4)
,, ,, Markshall **3** (2) (*Plates* **3** p. 180)
,, ,, (site of), Romford Rural **2** (2)
Marks Tey 3 pp. 179–180
Marks Tey Hall, Marks Tey **3** (2)
Markshall 3 pp. 177–179 ; **4** p. 188
Markswood Farm, Little Bardfield **1** (8)
Marlborough Head, *see under* **Inns**
Marney :
ARMS : East Horndon **4** (1) (glass) (*Plate* **4** pp. xliv–v) ; Little Horkesley **3** (1) ; Layer Marney **3** (1)
BADGE : Layer Marney **3** (1)
Marney :
Amic, *see* **Tyrell 4**
Brygete, 1549, wife successively of Thomas Fyndorne and John, Lord Marney, altar-tomb with brass of : Little Horkesley **3** (1)

Marney : *cont.*
Henry, 1523, 1st Lord, K.G., Lord Privy Seal, etc., altar-tomb of : Layer Marney **3** (1) (*Plates* **3** pp. 157, 159) ; Layer Marney Hall begun by early in the 16th century : Layer Marney **3** (2)
John, 2nd Lord, 1525, altar-tomb of : Layer Marney **3** (1)
Sir William, *c.* 1360, altar-tomb of : Layer Marney **3** (1) (*Plates* **3** pp. 158, 159)
Marquis of Granby, *see under* **Inns**
Marr, arms : Boxted **3** (1)
Marr, John, *see* **Carr 3**
Marriage at Cana, The, glass : Aveley **4** (6)
' Marriage Feast ' Room, Matching **2** (13) (*Plate* **2** p. 48)
Marriot, Richard, 1703, and others, monument to : Finchingfield **1** (1)
Marsh, Thomas, 1698, Mary, his wife, 1715, Thomas, their son, 1706, and infant daughters, Mary and Love, floor-slab to : Chelmsford **2** (2)
Marsh Farm, Great Canfield **2** (5)
Marshall, arms : East Donyland **3** (2) ; Finchingfield **1** (1)
Marshall :
Dorothy, wife of Sir John, 1685, floor-slab to : Finchingfield **1** (1)
Elizabeth, 1613, monument of : East Donyland **3** (1)
Lucy, wife of Sir John, 1699, floor-slab to : Finchingfield **1** (1)
Mary, 1627, wife, first of Nicholas Marshall and afterwards of William Graye, brass of : East Donyland **3** (1)
Nicholas, 1621, brass of, erected by Alice (Brooke), his second wife : East Donyland **3** (1)
Marshalls, site of, North Weald Bassett **2** (3)
Marshall's Barn, Writtle **2** (5)
Marshall's Farm, North Weald Bassett **2** (17) (*Plate* **2** p. 128)
,, ,, West Tilbury **4** (5) (*Plate* **4** p. xxxv)
Marshgate, Nazeing **2** (16)
Martel, arms : Great Bromley **3** (1) (glass)
Martels, Great Dunmow **1** (11)
Martin, 1st Vicar of Barking, 1328, floor-slab of : Barking **2** (2) (*Plate* **2** p. 103)
Martin :
Archer, of Jamaica, 1707, floor-slab to : Walthamstow **2** (1)
Thomas, 1672, vicar of the parish, and William, his son, 1664, monument to : Elmstead **3** (1)
Martin, St., at Chenu in Sarthe, glass said to have come from : Rivenhall **3** (2)
Martin's Farm, Berden **1** (10)
,, ,, Margaretting **2** (4)
,, ,, Newport **1** (5) (*Plate* **1** p. 34)
Martin's Hall, Stebbing **1** (42)
Martins Hern, see Stapleford Abbots **2**
Marvel's Garden, Pebmarsh **3** (15)
Mary Cleophas, St., glass : Netteswell **2** (1) (*Plate* **2** p. xxxv)
Mary Magdalene, St. :
GLASS : Liston **1** (1) ; Noak Hill **2** (1) ; North Ockendon **4** (1) (*Plate* **4** p. 104) ; Thaxted **1** (2)
PAINTING (on screen) : Foxearth **1** (1)
Mary the Mother of James, St., glass : Noak Hill **2** (1)
Mary Salome, St., glass : Netteswell **2** (1) (*Plate* **2** p. xxxv) ; Noak Hill **2** (1)
Mary the Virgin, St., *see* **Virgin, The,** *and* **Virgin and Child, The**
Marylands, Kelvedon **3** (52)
Mascalbury, White Roding **2** (12)
Mascalls, Great Baddow **4** (2)

* *See Addenda et Corrigenda, pp. 185–8. under this Volume and Parish.*

Instructions how to use this Index given on page 198.

Mascott's Farm, Copford **3** (5)
Mashbury 2 pp. 186–187
Mashbury Hall, Mashbury **2** (2)
Mason's Marks Illustrated, see **4** p. 181
Master Weaver's House, Southfields, Dedham **3** (2)
Masters, Alice, see **Hawkins 2**
Matching 2 pp. 187–189
Matching Green, see Matching **2**
Matching Hall, Matching **2** (6)
Matching Park, Matching **2** (2)
Matthew, St., glass, probably of : Aveley **4** (6) ; see also **Evangelists, Symbols of the**
Maud (Matilda), Queen (wife of Henry I), benefactress of Secular College founded 1066 by Harold : Waltham Holy Cross **2** (1)
Maud (Matilda), Queen (wife of Stephen), and King Stephen, founders of an Abbey for monks of the Order of Savigny, probably 1140 : Little Coggeshall **3** (2)
Maule, arms : Vange **4** (1)
Maule :
George, 1667, pastor of the parish, tablet to : Vange **4** (1)
Mary (Champneis), wife of George, 1659, and Charles, their only child, tablet of : Vange **4** (1)
Maunsell, Mary, widow of Philip, see **Fortescue 2**
Maurice, see **Morris, -s,** etc., below
Mawkinherds Farm, Barnston **2** (7)
Maxey, arms : Bradwell (juxta-Coggeshall) **3** (1)
Maxey :
Anthony, 1592, and Dorothy (Basset), his wife, 1602, monument of, erected by their son, Sir Henry : Bradwell (juxta-Coggeshall) **3** 1) (Plate **3** p. 97)
Sir William, 1645, Helena (Grevill), his wife, 1653, Grevill, 1648, and William, 1659, their sons, monument to : Bradwell (juxta-Coggeshall) **3** (1)
Mayes Farm, Sandon **4** (4)
Mayland 4 p. 91
Mayn, Alice, see **Caldwell 4**
Maynard, -e :
ARMS : Little Easton **1** (1) ; Walthamstow **2** (1)
CREST : Little Easton **1** (1)
Maynard, -e :
Alse, wife of John, 1584, brass of : St. James' Church, Colchester **3** (4)
Lady Fisher, wife of the Hon. William, 1675–6, floor-slab to : Little Easton **1** (1)
Frances (daughter of William, Lord Cavendish), wife of Sir William, Bart., 1613, tomb of : Little Easton **1** (1)
Sir Henry, 1610, and Susan (Pierson), his wife, tomb of : Little Easton **1** (1) (Plate **1** p. 182)
Henry, 1686, his brothers, Henry and Sir William, Bart., 1685, and Mary (Corselis), their mother, tablet to : Walthamstow **2** (1)
John, 1569, brass to : St. James' Church, Colchester **3** (4)
William, 1640, and Anne (Everard), his wife, 1647, monument to, erected in the 18th century : Little Easton **1** (1) ; flagon given by : Little Easton **1** (1)
William and Mary, children of the Hon. William, 1688, 1687–8, floor-slabs to : Little Easton **1** (1)
Maynard Chapel, Little Easton **1** (1)
Maynard's Farm, Little Sampford **1** (6)
Maypole Farm, Wimbish **1** (12) (56)
Maysent, Judith, 1691, Elizabeth, 1691, John, 1693, Joseph, 1698, Rebecca, 1704, Mary, 1707, John, 1718, children of John ; also Judith, his wife, early 18th-century slab to : Booking **1** (1)
Maze, The, Saffron Walden **1** (159)

Mazengarb, Isaac, 1698, and Mary, his wife, 1714, floor-slab to : Little Wigborough **3** (1)
Mead, -e :
ARMS : Elmdon **1** (1) ; Great Easton **1** (1)
CREST : Great Easton **1** (1)
Mead, -e :
Jane, wife of John, 1626, and John, their son, 1666, floor-slab to : Great Easton **1** (1)
John, of Duton Hill, 1614, brass to : Great Easton **1** (1)
John, 1629, brass to : Finchingfield **1** (1)
John, 1689, and Sarah, his wife, 1722, also Ann, 1758, and Rebecca, her sister, 1763, monument to : Great Easton **1** (1)
John, 1710, floor-slab to : Great Easton **1** (1)
Thomas, 1585, ' secundo justiciaio de banco,' altar-tomb to : Elmdon **1** (1)
Thomas, son of Richard, of Berden, 1653, floor-slab to : Berden **1** (1)
Thomas, son of Sir John, 1678, floor-slab to : Wenden Lofts **1** (1)
Thomasine, wife of Thomas, 1656, floor-slab to : Berden **1** (1)
Measants' Charity, Debden **1** (34)
Medeley, arms : Tilty **1** (1)
Medeley, George, 1562, and Mary, his wife, brass of : Tilty **1** (1)
Meekings Farm, Toppesfield **1** (24)
Meeting House, The (formerly **Fullers),** West Hanningfield **4** (2) (Plates **4** pp. 32, 166)
Meggs, arms : Theydon Garnon **2** (1)
Meggs :
Henry and Thomas, 1670, floor-slab to : Theydon Garnon **2** (1)
Dr. James, 1672, rector of the parish, tablet and floor-slab to : Theydon Garnon **2** (1)
Margaret, wife of James, S.T.P., 1661, floor-slab to : Theydon Garnon **2** (1)
Melaine, Abbey of St. (at Rennes, in Brittany), Priory founded probably c. 1135, as cell to : Hatfield Broad Oak **2** (1)
Melvill, Anne, see **Holbech 2**
Mercers' Company, arms : Lambourne **2** (1) ; West Ham **2** (1) (tomb)
Merchant Venturers, arms : Woodford **2** (2)
Merell, arms : Barking **2** (2)
Merell, Christopher, 1593, and Anne Yardlye, his sister, 1579, brass to : Barking **2** (2)
Merks Hall, White Roding **2** (7)
Merricks, Vange **4** (3)
Merry, arms : Walthamstow **2** (1)
Merry, Mary, wife of Sir Thomas, 1632, monument to : Walthamstow **2** (1) (Plate **2** p. 251)
Merrydeth, Dorothy, daughter of Sir Amos, Bart., 1680, floor-slab to : Margaretting **2** (1)
Mersea, see **East Mersea 3** and **West Mersea 3**
Mersea Island, see **East Mersea 3** and **West Mersea 3**
Mersea Mount, West Mersea **3** (1)
Messing 3 pp. 180–181
Messing Lodge, Messing **3** (11)
Mey, Elizabeth, see **Tedcastell 2**
Michael, St. :
CARVINGS : Braintree **2** (1) (slaying the Dragon) ; Fingringhoe **3** (1) (slaying the Dragon) ; Manning-tree **3** (1) ; St. Osyth **3** (4) (slaying the Dragon)
GLASS : Clavering **1** (1) ; Little Baddow **2** (1) (slaying the Dragon) ; Liston **1** (1) ; Newport **1** (1) (slaying the Dragon) ; Saffron Walden **1** (4) ; Thaxted **1** (2)
PAINTINGS : Copford **3** (1) ; Fingringhoe **3** (1)
Middle Farm, Heybridge **3** (6)
Middleton 3 p. 182

* See Addenda et Corrigenda, pp. 185–8, under this Volume and Parish.

Instructions how to use this Index given on page 198.

* *See Addenda et Corrigenda, pp. 185–8, under this Volume and Parish.*

Instructions how to use this Index given on page 198.

Monuments, Funeral : *cont.*
ALTAR-TOMBS : *cont.*
15TH-CENTURY : *cont.*
Little Dunmow **1** (1) (*Plate* **1** p. 178) ; Little Easton **1** (1) (*Plate* **1** p. xxx); Little Horkesley **3** (1) ; Pleshey **2** (2) ; Rickling **1** (1) ; West Ham **2** (1)
circa 1500 : Stanford-le-Hope **4** (1) (*Plate* **4** p. 105)
16TH-CENTURY :
Arkesden **1** (1) ; Ashdon **1** (5) ; Blackmore **2** (1) ; Boreham **2** (1) ; Borley **1** (1) ; Castle Hedingham **1** (1) (*Plates* **1** p. 50) ; Dedham **3** (1) ; East Horndon **4** (1) ; Elmdon **1** (1) ; Felsted **2** (1) (*Plate* **2** p. 74) ; Finchingfield **1** (1) ; Goldhanger **3** (2) ; Gosfield **1** (1) ; Great Bardfield **1** (1) ; Hatfield Peverel **2** (1) ; Hornchurch **4** (1) ; Ingatestone and Fryerning **2** (1) (*Plate* **2** p. 139) ; Layer de la Haye **3** (1) ; Layer Marney **3** (1) (*Plate* **3** p. 157) ; Little Horkesley **1** (1) ; Pentlow **1** (1) ; Saffron Walden **1** (1) ; St. Osyth **3** (2) (*Plate* **3** p. 197) ; Theydon Garnon **2** (1) ; Theydon Mount **2** (1) (*Plate* **2** p. 235) ; Tolleshunt D'Arcy **3** (1) ; Waltham Holy Cross **2** (1) ; Wethersfield **1** (1) (*Plate* **1** p. 333) ; Witham **2** (1) ; Writtle **2** (1) (*Plate* **2** p. 273)
circa 1600 :
North Ockendon **4** (1) (*Plate* **4** p.100); Rivenhall **3** (2) (*Plate* **3** p. 197)
17TH-CENTURY :
Colchester **3** (11) (*Plate* **3** p. 97) ; East Ham **2** (2) ; Frating **3** (1) ; Great Coggeshall **3** (2) ; Great Waltham **2** (1) ; Ingatestone and Fryerning **2** (1) ; Little Easton **1** (1) (*Plate* **1** p. 178) ; Little Warley **4** (1) (*Plate* **4** p. 85) ; Orsett **4** (1) (*Plate* **4** p. 105) ; Pentlow **1** (1) (*Plate* **1** p. 210) ; Romford Urban **2** (1) ; St. Osyth **3** (2) ; Shenfield **2** (1) ; Stansted Mountfitchet **1** (2) ; Theydon Mount **2** (1) (*Plate* **2** pp. 230, 234) ; Waltham Holy Cross **2** (1)
circa 1700 : Downham **4** (1)
EARLY 18TH-CENTURY (before 1715) : Finchingfield **1** (1)
UNDATED : Ingrave **4** (1) (now used as threshold)
FLOOR-SLABS :
12TH-CENTURY : Barking **2** (2)
circa 1300 : Black Notley **2** (1)
14TH-CENTURY :
Barking **2** (2) (*Plate* **2** p. 103) ; Bradwell (juxta-Coggeshall) **3** (1) ; Hempstead **1** (1) ; Middleton **3** (1) (*Fig.* **3** p. 183)
15TH-CENTURY : East Horndon **4** (1) incised (now a modern raised tomb) (*Plate* **4** p. 40)
MEDIAEVAL : Boxted **3** (1)
16TH-CENTURY :
Ingatestone and Fryerning **2** (1) ; Orsett **4** (1)
16TH OR 17TH-CENTURY : West Hanningfield **4** (1)
17TH-CENTURY :
Aldham **3** (1) ; Asheldham **4** (1) ; ·Aveley **4** (1) ; Aythorpe Roding **2** (1) ; Barking **2** (2) ; Barling **4** (1) ; Barnston **2** (1) ; Beaumont-cum-Moze **3** (1) ; Belchamp Otton **1** (1) ; Belchamp St. Paul's **1** (1) ; Berden **1** (1) ; Blackmore **2** (1) ; Boreham **2** (1) ; Boxted **3** (1) ; Bradwell (juxta-Coggeshall) **3** (1) ; Brightlingsea **3** (3) ; Broomfield **2** (1) ; Broxted **1** (1) ; Bulmer **1** (1) ; Burnham **4** (1) ; Buttsbury **4** (2) ; Castle Hedingham **1** (1) ; Chelmsford **2** (2) ; Chignall **2** (2) ; Chigwell **2** (2) ; Chingford **2** (1) ; Chipping Ongar **2** (2) ; Clavering **1** (1) ; Colchester **3** (2) (3) (4) (8) (9) (10) (11) (12) ; Copford **3** (1) ; Cranham **4** (1) ; Cressing **3** (1) ; Dagenham **2** (1) ; Danbury **4** (1) ; Dedham **3** (1) ; Downham **4** (1) ; East Ham **2** (2) ;

Monuments, Funeral : *cont.*
FLOOR-SLABS : *cont.*
17TH-CENTURY : *cont.*
East Horndon **4** (1) ; Easthorpe **3** (1) ; East Tilbury **4** (2) ; Eastwood **4** (1) ; Elmstead **3** (1) ; Faulkbourne **2** (2) ; Felsted **2** (1) ; Finchingfield **1** (1) ; Gestingthorpe **1** (1) ; Gosfield **1** (1) ; Great Baddow **4** (1) ; Great Braxted **3** (1) ; Great Bromley **3** (1) ; Great Burstead **4** (4) ; Great Canfield **2** (1) ; Great Clacton **3** (1) ; Great Coggeshall **3** (2) ; Great Dunmow **1** (1) ; Great Easton **1** (1) ; Great Horkesley **3** (1) ; Great Leighs **2** (1) ; Great Oakley **3** (1) ; Great Sampford **1** (1) ; Great Waltham **2** (1) ; Great Warley **4** (1) ; Great Wigborough **3** (1) ; Hadstock **1** (2) ; Hatfield Broad Oak **2** (1) ; Hatfield Peverel **2** (1) ; Havering-atte-Bower **2** (1) ; Helion Bumpstead **1** (1) ; Henham **1** (1) ; Heybridge **3** (1) ; High Ongar **2** (1) ; Hornchurch **4** (1) ; Horndon-on-the-Hill **4** (1) ; Ingatestone and Fryerning **2** (1) ; Kelvedon **3** (2) ; Kelvedon Hatch **2** (1) ; Laindon Hills **4** (1) ; Lambourne **2** (1) ; Langham **3** (1) ; Latton **2** (2) ; Lawford **3** (1) ; Leaden Roding **2** (1) ; Leigh **4** (1) ; Little Baddow **2** (1) ; Little Braxted **3** (1) ; Little Burstead **4** (1) ; Little Canfield **2** (1) ; Little Dunmow **1** (1) ; Little Easton **1** (1) ; Little Horkesley **3** (1) ; Little Oakley **3** (1) ; Little Sampford **1** (1) ; Little Thurrock **4** (1) ; Little Totham **3** (1) ; Little Wakering **4** (1) ; Little Waltham **2** (1) ; Little Yeldham **1** (1) ; Loughton **2** (2) ; Low Leyton **2** (2) ; Maldon All Saints **2** (1) ; Maldon St. Mary **2** (1) ; Margaretting **2** (1) ; Mayland **4** (1) ; Mountnessing **4** (1) ; Navestock **2** (1) ; Newport **1** (1) ; North Weald Bassett **2** (1) ; Ovington **1** (1) ; Pebmarsh **3** (1) ; Purleigh **4** (1) ; Quendon **1** (1) ; Ramsey **3** (1) ; Rivenhall **3** (2) ; Roxwell **2** (1) ; Roydon **2** (1) ; Runwell **4** (1) ; Saffron Walden **1** (1) ; St. Osyth **3** (2) ; Shelley **2** (1) ; Sible Hedingham **1** (1) ; South Benfleet **4** (1) ; South Hanningfield **4** (1) ; South Ockendon **4** (1) ; South Weald **2** (1) ; Southchurch **4** (1) ; Springfield **2** (1) ; Stanford-le-Hope **4** (1) ; Stanford Rivers **2** (1) ; Stansted Mountfitchet **1** (2) ; Stapleford Tawney **2** (1) ; Stebbing **1** (1) ; Steeple Bumpstead **1** (2) ; Stifford **4** (1) ; Stisted **3** (1) ; Stock **4** (1) ; Stondon Massey **2** (1) ; Sturmer **1** (1) ; Sutton **4** (1) ; Takeley **1** (1) ; Thaxted **1** (2) ; Theydon Garnon **2** (1) ; Toppesfield **1** (1) ; Twinstead **3** (1) ; Waltham Holy Cross **2** (1) ; Walthamstow **2** (1) ; Wanstead **2** (2) ; Wenden Lofts **1** (1) ; Wendens Ambo **2** (1) ; West Bergholt **3** (1) ; West Ham **2** (1) ; West Thurrock **4** (1) ; Wethersfield **1** (1) ; Wickham Bishops **2** (1) ; Wickham St. Paul's **1** (1) ; Willingale Doe **2** (1) ; Wimbish **1** (1) ; Witham **2** (1) ; Woodford **2** (1) ; Woodham Ferrers **4** (1) ; Woodham Mortimer **4** (1) ; Woodham Walter **2** (1) ; Writtle **2** (1)
17TH OR 18TH-CENTURY : Bulmer **1** (1) ; East Ham **2** (2) ; Little Wigborough **3** (1) ; Stanway **3** (2)
EARLY 18TH-CENTURY (before 1715) :
Barking **2** (2) ; Barnston **2** (1) ; Beaumont-cum-Moze **3** (1) ; Birdbrook **1** (1) ; Black Notley **2** (1) ; Booking **1** (1) ; Boreham **2** (1) ; Broxted **1** (1) ; Chelmsford **2** (2) ; Chigwell **2** (2) ; Colchester **3** (2) (8) (10) ; Creeksea **4** (1) ; Danbury **4** (1) ; Downham **4** (1) ; East Mersea **3** (1) ; Epping Upland **2** (2) ; Felsted **2** (1) ; Fobbing **4** (1) ; Fyfield **2** (1) ; Gosfield **1** (1) ; Grays Thurrock **4** (1) ; Great Braxted **3** (1) ; Great Burstead **4** (4) ; Great Clacton **3** (1) ; Great Dunmow **1** (1) ; Great Easton **1** (1) ; Great

* See *Addenda et Corrigenda, pp. 185–8, under this Volume and Parish.*

Instructions how to use this Index given on page 198.

Monuments, Funeral : *cont.*

FLOOR-SLABS: *cont.*

EARLY 18TH-CENTURY, etc. : *cont.*

Henny 3 (1) ; Great Oakley 3 (1) ; Hatfield Broad Oak 2 (1) ; High Ongar 2 (1) ; Horndon-on-the-Hill 4 (1) ; Ingatestone and Fryerning 2 (1) ; Langham 3 (1) ; Leigh 4 (1) ; Little Burstead 4 (1) ; Little Horkesley 3 (1) ; Little Thurrock 4 (1) ; Little Yeldham 1 (1) ; Loughton 2 (2) ; Magdalen Laver 2 (1) ; Manningtree 3 (1) ; Mountnessing 4 (1) ; Nevendon 4 (1) ; North Ockendon 4 (1) ; North Weald Bassett 2 (1) ; Radwinter 1 (1) ; Rivenhall 3 (2) ; Roxwell 2 (1) ; Saffron Walden 1 (1) ; Sheering 2 (1) ; Sible Hedingham 1 (1) ; South Benfleet 4 (1) ; South Weald 2 (1) ; Springfield 2 (1) ; Stambourne 1 (1) ; Stapleford Tawney 2 (1) ; Stebbing 1 (1) ; Stisted 3 (1) ; Stondon Massey 2 (1) ; Thaxted 1 (2) ; Theydon Garnon 2 (1) ; Waltham Holy Cross 2 (1) ; Walthamstow 2 (1) ; Wanstead 2 (2) ; West Bergholt 3 (1) ; West Ham 2 (1) ; Willingale Doe 2 (1) ; Woodford 2 (1) ; Wormingford 3 (1) Writtle 2 (1)

UNDATED :

Gosfield 1 (1) ; Takeley (coffin-shaped) 1 (1)

HEAD-STONES :

PRE-CONQUEST HEAD-STONE WITH LATER WINDOW CUT IN IT : White Notley 2 (1) (*Fig.* 4 p. xxxi)

12TH OR 13TH-CENTURY HEAD-STONE OR COFFIN-LID : North Shoebury 4 (1) (*Plate* 4 p. 25)

17TH-CENTURY :

Barking 2 (2) ; Basildon 4 (1) ; Blackmore 2 (1) ; Boreham 2 (1) (now floor-slab) ; Canewdon 4 (2) ; Colchester 3 (6) ; East Ham 2 (2) ; Epping Upland 2 (2) ; Feering 3 (1) ; Felsted 2 (1) ; Great Burstead 4 (4) ; Great Coggeshall 3 (2) ; Great Chesterford 1 (3) ; Great Dunmow 1 (1) ; Great Stambridge 4 (1) ; Great Waltham 2 (1) ; Harlow 2 (2) ; Hornchurch 4 (1) ; Ingatestone and Fryerning 2 (1) ; Little Canfield 2 (1) ; Little Waltham 2 (1) ; Margaretting 2 (1) ; Mount Bures 3 (1) ; Paglesham 4 (1) ; Rayleigh 4 (1) ; Stebbing 1 (1) ; Tilbury-juxta-Clare 1 (1) ; Upminster 4 (1) ; Wanstead 2 (2) ; Wivenhoe 3 (1)

circa 1700 : High Easter (oak) 2 (1)

EARLY 18TH-CENTURY (before 1715) :

Abberton 3 (1) ; Arkesden 1 (1) ; Aveley 4 (1) ; Barking 2 (2) ; Belchamp Walter 1 (1) ; Blackmore 2 (1) ; Boxted 3 (1) ; Colchester 3 (6) (13) ; Danbury 4 (1) ; Doddinghurst 2 (1) ; Earls Colne 3 (1) ; East Donyland 3 (1) ; East Tilbury 4 (2) ; Eastwood 4 (1) ; Epping Upland 2 (2) ; Feering 3 (1) ; Fordham 3 (1) ; Great Burstead 4 (4) ; Great Coggeshall 3 (2) ; Great Chesterford 1 (3) ; Great Dunmow 1 (1) ; Great Wakering 4 (2) ; Great Warley 4 (1) ; Hockley 4 (1) ; Kelvedon Hatch 2 (1) ; Laindon Hills 4 (1) ; Langham 3 (1) ; Leigh 4 (1) ; Little Canfield 2 (1) ; Little Wakering 4 (1) ; Little Waltham 2 (1) ; Margaretting 2 (1) ; Mayland 4 (1) ; Mountnessing 4 (1) ; Mundon 4 (1) ; Nazeing 2 (1) ; North Benfleet 4 (1) ; North Ockendon 4 (1) ; Paglesham 4 (1) ; Pentlow 1 (1) ; Rayleigh 4 (1) ; Shenfield 2 (1) ; South Ockendon 4 (1) ; Steeple Bumpstead 1 (2) ; Stifford 4 (1) ; Thorrington 3 (1) ; Upminster 4 (1) ; Walthamstow 2 (1) ; Wanstead 2 (2) ; West Ham 2 (1) ; Wickham Bishops 2 (1)

MURAL :

14TH-CENTURY : Fobbing 4 (1) (*Plate* 4 p. 48)

15TH CENTURY :

Maldon All Saints 2 (1) ; Steeple Bumpstead 1 (2)

Monuments, Funeral : *cont.*

MURAL : *cont.*

circa 1500 : Colchester 3 (7)

16TH-CENTURY :

Ashdon 1 (5) ; Aveley 4 (1) ; Barking 2 (2) ; Belchamp St. Paul's 1 (1) ; Berden 1 (1) ; Berners Roding 2 (1) ; Borley 1 (1) ; Chigwell 2 (2) ; Colchester 3 (8) ; Cold Norton 4 (1) ; Great Bardfield 1 (1) ; Great Hallingbury 2 (2) ; Greensted (juxta Ongar) 2 (1) ; Ingatestone and Fryerning 2 (1) ; Latton 2 (2) ; Lawford 3 (1) ; Little Sampford 1 (1) ; Navestock 2 (1) ; North Ockendon 4 (1) ; Orsett 4 (1) ; Rawreth 4 (1) ; Rayleigh 4 (1) (*Plate* 4 p. 105) ; Romford Urban 2 (1) (*Plate* 2 p. 203) ; Runwell 4 (1) ; Saffron Walden 1 (1) ; St. Osyth 3 (2) ; Stanford-le-Hope 4 (1) ; Stapleford Abbots 2 (1) ; Strethall 1 (1) ; Terling 2 (1) ; Theydon Garnon 2 (1) ; Tolleshunt D'Arcy 3 (1) (*Plate* 3 p. 97) ; Waltham Holy Cross 2 (1) ; West Ham 2 (1) ; Witham 2 (1) (*Plate* 2 p. 251) ; Woodford 2 (1) ; Writtle 2 (1) (*Plate* 2 p. 273)

circa 1600 :

Little Bardfield 1 (1) ; Margaretting 2 (1) ; South Ockendon 4 (1) ; Stanford-le-Hope 4 (1)

17TH-CENTURY :

Abbess Roding 2 (1) ; Arkesden 1 (1) ; Ashen 1 (1) ; Barking 2 (2) ; Barnston 2 (1) ; Birdbrook 1 (1) ; Booking 1 (1) ; Boxted 3 (1) ; Bradwell (juxta-Coggeshall) 3 (1) (*Plate* 3 p. 97) ; Bradwell-juxta-Mare 4 (2) ; Braintree 2 (1) ; Castle Hedingham 1 (1) ; Chelmsford 2 (1) ; Chigwell 2 (2) ; Chingford 2 (1) ; Chrishall 1 (1) (fragment of) ; Clavering 1 (1) ; Colchester 3 (3) (4) (6) (8) (9) (10) (11) (*Plate* 3 p. 97) ; Cressing 3 (1) (*Plate* 3 p. 97) ; Dagenham 2 (1) ; Danbury 4 (1) ; Debden 1 (1) ; Dedham 3 (1) ; Earls Colne 3 (1) ; East Donyland 3 ((1) ; East Ham 2 (2) ; East Horndon 4 (1) ; East Mersea 3 (1) ; Elmstead 3 (1) ; Fairsted 2 (1) ; Farnham 1 (1) ; Faulkbourne 2 (2) ; Finchingfield 1 (1) ; Fingringhoe 3 (1) ; Great-Baddow 4 (1) ; Great Braxted 3 (1) ; Great Canfield 2 (1) ; Great Dunmow 1 (1) ; Great Easton 1 (1) ; Great Maplestead 1 (1) (*Plates* 1 pp. xxx, 130) ; Great Parndon 2 (1) ; Great Warley 4 (1) ; Great Yeldham 1 (1) ; Halstead Urban 1 (1) ; Harlow 2 (2) ; Harwich 3 (1) ; Hatfield Broad Oak 2 (1) ; Helion Bumpstead 1 (1) ; Hempstead 1 (1) ; Heybridge 3 (1) ; High Laver 4 (1) ; Hornchurch 4 (1) ; Horndon-on-the-Hill 4 (1) ; Hutton 4 (1) ; Ingatestone and Fryerning 2 (1) (*Plate* 2 p. 138) ; Kelvedon 3 (2) ; Lamarsh 3 (1) ; Lambourne 2 (1) ; Latton 2 (2) ; Layer Marney 3 (1) ; Leigh 4 (1) ; Little Baddow 2 (1) (*Plate* 2 p. 151) ; Little Easton 1 (1) ; Little Ilford 2 (1) (*Plate* 2 p. 251) ; Little Parndon 2 (1) ; Little Sampford 1 (1) ; Little Totham 3 (1) (*Plate* 3 p. 97) ; Little Waltham 2 (1) ; Low Leyton 2 (2) (*Plate* 2 p. 150) ; Magdalen Laver 2 (1) ; Maldon All Saints 2 (1) ; Manuden 1 (1) ; Markshall 3 (1) ; Mountnessing 4 (1) ; Mucking 4 (1) ; Navestock 2 (1) ; North Ockendon 4 (1) (*Plates* 4 pp. 100, 110) ; Pentlow 1 (1) ; Prittlewell 4 (1) ; Quendon 1 (1) ; Rickling 1 (1) ; Rivenhall 3 (2) ; Romford Urban 2 (1) (*Plates* 2 pp. 102, 251) ; Roxwell 2 (1) ; Roydon 2 (1) ; Runwell 4 (1) ; Saffron Walden 1 (1) ; Sandon 4 (1) ; Shelley 2 (1) ; South Ockendon 4 (1) (*Plate* 4 p. 141) ; South Weald 2 (1) ; Stanford-le-Hope 4 (1) ; Stanford Rivers 2 (1) ; Stifford 4 (1) ; Tendring 3 (1) ; Thaxted 1 (2) ; Theydon

Instructions how to use this Index given on page 198.

Monuments, Funeral : *cont.*
MURAL : *cont.*
17TH-CENTURY : *cont.*

Garnon 2 (1) ; Thorpe-le-Soken 3 (1) ; Tilty 1 (1) ; Tollesbury 3 (2) ; Toppesfield 1 (1) ; Vange 4 (1) ; Wakes Colne 3 (1) ; Walthamstow 2 (1) (*Plate* 2 p. 251) ; Wanstead 2 (2) (*Plate* 2 p. 250) ; Wennington 4 (1) ; West Ham 2 (1) ; Wethersfield 1 (1) ; Wicken Bonhunt 1 (1) ; Willingale Doe 2 (1) (*Plate* 2 p. 102) ; Willingale Spain 2 (1) ; Wimbish 1 (1) ; Witham 2 (1) ; Woodford 2 (1) ; Woodham Ferrers 4 (1) ; Writtle 2 (1) (*Plate* 2 p. 273)

17TH OR 18TH-CENTURY :
Upminster 4 (1) ; Walthamstow 2 (1)

EARLY 18TH-CENTURY (before 1715) :
Ardleigh 3 (1) ; Barking 2 (2) ; Chipping Ongar 2 (1) ; Clavering 1 (1) ; Colchester 3 (7) ; Dagenham 2 (1) ; Dedham 3 (1) ; Felsted 2 (1) ; Great Burstead 4 (4) ; Great Dunmow 1 (1) ; Great Parndon 2 (1) ; Great Waltham 2 (1) ; Hempstead 1 (1) ; High Laver 2 (1) ; High Ongar 2 (1) ; Kelvedon 3 (2) ; Leigh 4 (1) ; Little Easton 1 (1) ; Little Sampford 1 (1) ; Low Leyton 2 (2) ; Maldon All Saints 2 (1) ; North Ockendon 4 (1) (*Plate* 4 p. 100) ; Saffron Walden 1 (1) ; South Weald 2 (1) ; Stanford-le-Hope 4 (1) ; Steeple Bumpstead 1 (2) ; Stifford 4 (1) ; Theydon Garnon 2 (1) ; Theydon Mount 2 (1) ; Wendens Ambo 1 (2) ; West Ham 2 (1)

RECESSES :
13TH-CENTURY :
Danbury 4 (1) ; Little Wakering 4 (1) (possibly)
circa 1300 : Danbury 4 (1)
14TH-CENTURY :
Ashdon 1 (5) ; Belchamp Walter 1 (1) (*Plate* 1 p. 20) ; Chrishall 1 (1) ; Colchester 3 (3) (12) ; Feering 3 (1) ; Great Leighs 2 (1) (*Plate* 2 p. 103) ; Great Sampford 1 (1) ; Laindon 4 (1) ; Langham 3 (1) ; Little Baddow 2 (1) (*Plate* 2 p. 155) ; Little Leighs 2 (1) (*Plate* 2 p. 173) ; Middleton 3 (1) ; Purleigh 4 (1) ; Rickling 1 (1) ; Shalford 1 (1) (*Plate* 1 p. 262) ; Sible Hedingham 1 (1) ; Southchurch 4 (1) ; Stanford-le-Hope 4 (1) (*Plate* 4 p. 105) ; Stansted Mountfitchet 1 (2) ; Thorpe-le-Soken 3 (1) ; Wethersfield 1 (1)
circa 1400 : Little Easton 1 (1) (*Plate* 1 p. xxx)
15TH-CENTURY :
Panfield 1 (1) ; Rickling 1 (1)
16TH-CENTURY :
East Horndon 4 (1)
17TH-CENTURY :
Great Waltham 2 (1) (*Plate* 2 p. 102) ; Little Bentley 3 (1)

SARCOPHAGI :
16TH-CENTURY :
Barking 2 (2) ; Chelmsford 2 (2)
17TH-CENTURY :
Stansted Mountfitchet 1 (2) ; Walthamstow 2 (1) ; West Ham 2 (1)
17TH OR 18TH-CENTURY : South Weald 2 (1)

SLABS ; *see also* FLOOR-SLABS *and* MURAL, *above* :
12TH-CENTURY : Rettendon 4 (1) (*Plate* 4 p. 25)
13TH-CENTURY :
Belchamp St. Paul's 1 (1) ; Faulkbourne 2 (2) ; Hatfield Broad Oak 2 (1)
14TH-CENTURY : Rickling 1 (1)
15TH-CENTURY :
Arkesden 1 (1) ; Little Easton 1 (3)

Monuments, Funeral : *cont.*
SLABS, etc.: *cont.*
17TH-CENTURY :
Castle Hedingham 1 (1) ; Colchester 3 (13) ; Dedham 3 (1) ; Great Coggeshall 3 (2) ; Lawford 3 (1) ; Little Wakering 4 (1) ; Mountnessing 4 (1) ; Rettendon 4 (1) ; Romford Urban 2 (1) ; Shopland 4 (1) ; Wethersfield 1 (1) ; Writtle 2 (1)
EARLY 18TH-CENTURY (before 1715) :
Black Notley 2 (1) ; Bocking 1 (1) ; Colchester 3 (13) ; Kelvedon 3 (2) ; Mountnessing 4 (1) ; Rawreth 4 (1) ; Springfield 2 (1) ; West Ham 2 (1)

TABLETS ; *see* MURAL, *above*
TABLE-TOMBS IN CHURCHYARDS :
17TH-CENTURY :
Alresford 3 (2) ; Barling 4 (1) ; Buttsbury 4 (2) ; Chigwell 2 (2) ; Colchester 3 (2) ; Dagenham 2 (1) ; Dedham 3 (1) ; Doddinghurst 2 (1) ; Eastwood 4 (1) ; Fingringhoe 3 (1) ; Great Coggeshall 3 (2) ; Great Maplestead 1 (1) ; Leigh 4 (1) ; Nevendon 4 (1) ; Prittlewell 4 (1) ; Purleigh 4 (1) ; Rettendon 4 (1) ; South Benfleet 4 (1) ; West Ham 2 (1)
circa 1700 : Great Wakering 4 (2)
EARLY 18TH-CENTURY (before 1715) :
Barling 4 (1) ; Burnham 4 (1) ; Canewdon 4 (2) ; Cold Norton 4 (1) ; Dagenham 2 (1) ; East Ham 2 (2) ; Gosfield 1 (1) ; Harwich 3 (1) ; North Ockendon 4 (1) ; Rochford 4 (1) ; Southchurch 4 (1) ; Tillingham 4 (1) ; Walthamstow 2 (1)

WALL-MONUMENTS ; *see* MURAL, *above*
MISCELLANEOUS :
15TH-CENTURY panels from former monument : Messing 3 (1)
16TH-CENTURY stone panels from former monument : Bradwell-juxta-Mare 4 (2)
Sarsen stone used as late 17TH-CENTURY monument : Chadwell 4 (1)
EARLY 18TH-CENTURY monument in churchyard : Black Notley 2 (1)

Moon's Farm, Walthamstow 2 (10)
Moor Hall, Writtle 2 (8)
Moore, *or* **More,** arms : Barking 2 (4) (More of Cheshire) ; Bocking 1 (1) ; Thaxted 1 (2)
Moore, *or* **More :**
Daniel, son of John, 1631, tablet to : Thaxted 1 (2)
Grisell (Eden), wife of Adrian, 1624, monument to : Bocking 1 (1)
Henry, 1678, and Henry, junior, 1689, floor-slab to : Southchurch 4 (1)
John, son of Edward, one of the cursitors of the Court of Chancery, 1624, brass to : Navestock 2 (1)
Thomas, 1670, tablet to : Barking 2 (2)
William (More *alias* Tayler), 1532, and his grandson, John, five times Mayor of Thaxted, 1619, brass of : Thaxted 1 (2)
Moore Place, Stanford-le-Hope 4 (6)
Moore's Ditch, Ingatestone and Fryerning 2 (12)
Moor's Farm, Felsted 2 (75)
  ,,   ,, Little Totham 3 (2)
Moot Hall, The, Maldon All Saints 2 (5) (*Plate* 2 p. 177)
  ,,   ,,   ,, Steeple Bumpstead 1 (10) (*Plate* 1 p. 310)
Mordaunt, William, 1518, and Anne (Huntingdon), his wife, brass of : Hempstead 1 (1)
More, *see* **Moore,** *above*
Moreton 2 pp. 189–190 ; 4 p. 187
Morice, *see* **Morris,** *below*
Morlands Farm, Wickham St. Paul's 1 (2)

* *See Addenda et Corrigenda, pp. 185–8, under this Volume and Parish.*

Instructions how to use this Index given on page 198.

Morley :
 John, name of, on panel and initials of, on iron gate :
　Halstead Rural **1** (4)
 John, of Halstead, inscription recording purchase of
　land by, 1681 : Great Maplestead **1** (8)
Morley Green, see Arkesden **1**
Morriss, arms : Boreham **2** (1)
Morris, -s, Maurice, or **Morice :**
 Catherine (Pointz), wife of John, early 17th-century
　monument of : North Ockendon **4** (1)(*Plate* **4** p. 110)
 Sir James Pointz, *alias* Morice, see **Pointz 4**
 Capt. John, 1638, tablet to : Wanstead **2** (2)
 Mary, see **Bonnell 2**
 Sarah, wife of Thomas, 1704,head-stone to : Arkesden**1** (1)
 Thomas, LL.B., 1684–5, floor-slab to : Boreham **2** (1)
Morris' Farm, Hadstock **1** (8)
Mors, see **Deth 3**
Mortemer, Mahand de, *c.* 1340, indent of brass-inscription
　to : Tilty **1** (1)
Mortimer, arms : Great Bardfield **1** (1) (glass) ; Shalford
　1 (1) (font) ; Thaxted **1** (2) (glass)
Mortimer, Edmund, Earl of March, and Philippa, his wife,
　daughter of Lionel, Duke of Clarence, arms :
　Great Bardfield **1** (1) (glass)
Mortlock's Farm, Radwinter **1** (38)
Mosaic Pavements, Roman, see under **Roman Remains**
Mose Hall, Ardleigh **3** (10)
Moses, paintings : Chadwell **4** (2) (the finding of) ;
　Gestingthorpe **1** (1)
Mosse, Thomas, 1712, head-stone to : Doddinghurst **2** (1)
Mosse's Farm, Alphamstone **3** (3)
Moss's Farm, Helion Bumpstead **1** (5)
Mot, Robert, see under **Bellfounders**
Mott, Mark, 1691, and Mark, his father, 1694, floor-slab
　to : Wethersfield **1** (1)
Motts, Berners Roding **2** (6)
Motts Green, see Little Hallingbury **2**
Mouldings, Illustrations of, **4** pp. 183–4
Moulsham's Farm, Great Wigborough **3** (4)
Mounds, see under **Earthworks**
Mount and Bailey Castles, see under **Earthworks**
Mount Bures 3 pp. 184–186
Mount Farm, Belchamp Walter **1** (11)
Mount Hill, see Halstead Urban **1**
Mount House, Braintree **2** (76)
 　　,,　　　　,, Henham **1** (7)
 　　,,　　　　,, Pleshey **2** (4)

Mount Pleasant, Dedham **3** (24)
 　　,,　　　　,, Wanstead **2** (4)
Mount Pleasant Cottages, Rayleigh **4** (4)
Mount Thrift, East Horndon **4** (3)
Mountecho Farm, Chingford **2** (2)
Mountfort, arms : Aveley **4** (6) (glass)
Mountnessing 4 pp. 91–93
Mountnessing Hall, Mountnessing **4** (5)
Mountney's, Roxwell **2** (7)
Mount's Farm, Great Saling **1** (6)
Moverons, Brightlingsea **3** (13)
Mowbray, " Gulielm d'Albini Seigneur de Molbray, ceu
　de Mowbray," inscription on glass : Laindon Hills
　4 (3)
Mowden Hall, Hatfield Peverel **2** (2)
Moyer, arms : Low Leyton **2** (2) ; Pitsea **4** (1) (on paten)
Moyer :
 James, 1661, floor-slab to : Leigh **4** (1)
 Lawrence, 1685, and Frances (Alvey), his wife, 1686,
　floor-slab to : Low Leyton **2** (2)
 Sir Thomas, arms of, on paten : Pitsea **4** (1)
Moyne, arms : Steeple Bumpstead **1** (6)
Moynes Farm, St. Lawrence (Newland) **4** (2)
Moyns Park, Steeple Bumpstead **1** (6) (*Plates* **1** pp. 291–2)
Moze Church, site of, Beaumont-cum-Moze **3** (2)
Moze Cross, see Beaumont-cum-Moze **3**
Mucking 4 pp. 94–95
Mucking Hall, Barling **4** (2)
Mudwall, Good Easter **2** (7)
Mudwall Farm, Great Dunmow **1** (6)
Mulberry Green, see Harlow **2**
Mulcaster, Katherine, wife of Richard, parson of the
　church, 1609, brass to : Stanford Rivers **2** (1)
Mullings, John, 1713, head-stone to : Great Coggeshall **3** (2)
Mulsham Hall, Great Leigh **2** (15)
Mundays, Writtle **2** (13) (*Plate* **2** p. 272)
Mundon 4 pp. 95–96
Mundon Hall, Mundon **4** (1)
Munkin's Farm, Bradwell-juxta-Mare **4** (5)
Murrells, Stanford Rivers **2** (5)
Murrell's Farm, Bocking **1** (3)
Musgrave, Dorcas (Bigg), 1610, wife of Thomas, of Norton,
　Yorks, brass of : Cressing **3** (1)
Myddylton House, Saffron Walden **1** (27)
Myldemay, see **Mildmay,** above
Myrtle Cottage (now **The Gables**), Horndon-on-the-Hill
　4 (17)

Nabott's Cottages, Springfield **2** (3)
Napper, Anne (Shelton), wife of William, 1584, brass of :
　Stanford Rivers **2** (1)
Nash Farm, White Roding **2** (14)
Nash Hall, High Ongar **2** (10)
Nativity, The :
 CARVING (on reredos) : Radwinter **1** (1)
 GLASS : Hatfield Peverel **2** (1) ; Roxwell **2** (1)
 PAINTING : Latton **2** (2) ; Little Wakering **4** (1)
Naves (with special features) :
 CIRCULAR :
　Little Maplestead **1** (1) (*Plate* **1** p. 184) ; West
　Thurrock **4** (1) (formerly)
 TIMBER :
　Greensted (juxta-Ongar) **2** (1) (*Plate* **2** p. 113)
Navestock 2 pp. 190–193
Navestock Hall, Navestock **2** (5)
Naylinghurst Farm, Braintree **2** (73)
Nazeing 2 pp. 193–195
Nazeing Park, see Nazeing **2**

Nazeingbury, Nazeing **2** (2)
Neale, Margaret, daughter of John, 1652, slab to : Shelley
　2 (2)
Neave, see **Neve,** below
Nelmes, Hornchurch **4** (3) (*Plates* **4** pp. 71, 75)
Nendick, Hump., of London, 1707, and Mary (Walford),
　his wife, afterwards widow of Capt. Thomas
　Kitching, 1722, slab to : Black Notley **2** (1)
Nero, coins of : Great Coggeshall **3** (1)
Neptune, see under **Inns**
Nether Farm, Abbess Roding **2** (5)
Nether Hall, Gestingthorpe **1** (5)
 　　,,　　　,, Moreton **2** (8)
 　　,,　　　,, Roydon **2** (2) (*Plates* **2** pp. 208, 209)
Netteswell 2 pp. 195–197 ; **4** p. 187
Netteswell Cross, see Netteswell **2**
Netteswell Plantation, Netteswell **2** (5)
Netteswellbury, Netteswell **2** (3) ; panelling possibly from,
　Netteswell **2** (5)

---

* See Addenda et Corrigenda, pp. 185–8, under this Volume and Parish.

Instructions how to use this Index given on page 198.

* See Addenda et Corrigenda, pp. 185–8, under this Volume and Parish.

Instructions how to use this Index given on page 198.

* See Addenda et Corrigenda, pp. 185–8, under this Volume and Parish.

Instructions how to use this Index given on page 198.

* See Addenda et Corrigenda, pp. 185–8, under this Volume and Parish.

Instructions how to use this Index given on page 198.

* See Addenda et Corrigenda, pp. 185–8, under this Volume and Parish.

Instructions how to use this Index given on page 198.

* *See Addenda et Corrigenda, pp. 185–8, under this Volume and Parish.*

Instructions how to use this Index given on page 198.

* See Addenda et Corrigenda, pp. 185–8, under this Volume and Parish.

Instructions how to use this Index given on page 198.

*See Addenda et Corrigenda, pp. 185–8, under this Volume and Parish.

Instructions how to use this Index given on page 198.

* *See Addenda et Corrigenda, pp. 185–8, under this Volume and Parish.*

Instructions how to use this Index given on page 198.

Plaster-work : *cont.*
HERALDIC :
  16TH-CENTURY :
    Aveley **4** (6) (S. front) ; Barking **2** (5) ; Braintree **2** (17) ; Great Waltham **2** (10) ; Saffron Walden **1** (7) ; Stansted Mountfitchet **1** (7)
  17TH-CENTURY :
    Markshall **3** (2) (S. front) ; Panfield **1** (3) ; Radwinter **1** (20) ; Widdington **1** (6) ; Witham **1** (44)
Plateau Camps, *see* **Earthworks**
Plate, Church :
  see also Sectional Preface **1** p. xxxii ; **2** p. xxxvii ; **3** p. xxxv ; **4** p. xliv
  PRE-REFORMATION (before 1547) :
    CHALICES :
      15TH-CENTURY : Mundon **4** (1) (stem)
      16TH-CENTURY : Radwinter **1** (1) (of foreign origin)*
    MAZERS :
      15TH-CENTURY : Colchester **3** (3) (*Plate* 3 p. xxxv)
      16TH-CENTURY :
        Colchester **3** (10) (*Plate* 3 p. xxxv) ; Saffron Walden **1** (57)*
    PATENS :
      16TH-CENTURY :
        Earls Colne **3** (1) (*Plate* 3 p. xxxv) ; Great Waltham **2** (1) (*Plate* 2 p. xxxix) ; Radwinter **1** (1) (of foreign origin)*
  POST-REFORMATION (after 1547) :
    ALMS-DISHES :
      17TH-CENTURY :
        Aveley **4** (1) ; Bulphan **4** (1) ; Colchester **3** (4)* ; Danbury **4** (1) ; Great Baddow **4** (1) ; Great Braxted **3** (1) ; Little Braxted **3** (1) ; Netteswell **2** (1) ; Stapleford Abbots **2** (1) ; Stapleford Tawney **2** (1) ; Thaxted **1** (2) ; Upminster **4** (1) ; Walthamstow **2** (1) ; Widdington **1** (1) ; Witham **2** (1)
      circa 1700 :
        Barking **2** (2) ; Dagenham **2** (1)*
    EARLY 18TH-CENTURY (before 1715) :
      Chelmsford **2** (2) ; Norton Mandeville **2** (1)*
    UNDATED : East Hanningfield **4** (1)
    CANDLESTICKS :
      17TH-CENTURY : Harlow **2** (2)
    CHALICE :
      17TH-CENTURY : Colchester **3** (6) (*Plate* 3 p. xxxv)
    COVER-PATENS :
      16TH-CENTURY (after 1547) :
        Ardleigh **3** (1) ; Arkesden **1** (1) ; Ashen **1** (1) ; Beaumont-cum-Moze **3** (1) ; Belchamp Otton **1** (1) ; Birdbrook **1** (1) ; Black Notley **2** (1) ; Buttsbury **4** (2) ; Chingford **2** (1) ; Colchester **3** (7) ; Cold Norton **4** (1) ; Doddinghurst **2** (1) ; Downham **4** (1) ; Dunton (Wayletts) **4** (1) ; East Ham **2** (2) ; East Horndon **4** (1) ; Easthorpe **3** (1) ; Eastwood **4** (1) ; Elmstead **3** (1) ; Elsenham **1** (1) ; Faulkbourne **2** (2) ; Great Braxted **3** (1) ; Great Saling **1** (1) ; Great Sampford **1** (1) ; Great Tey **3** (1) ; Great Wigborough **3** (1) ; Hadleigh **4** (1) ; Hadstock **1** (2) ; High Roding **2** (1) ; Hornchurch **4** (1) (*Plate* 4 p. xliv) ; Hutton **4** (1) ; Inworth **3** (1) ; Kelvedon **3** (2) ; Layer-de-la-Haye **3** (1) ; Little Braxted **3** (1) ; Little Bromley **3** (1) ; Little Parndon **2** (1) ; Little Tey **3** (1) ; Manuden **1** (1) ; Margaret Roding **2** (1) (*Plate* 2 p. xxxix) ; Marks Tey **3** (1) ; Mayland **4** (1) ; North Benfleet **4** (1) ; North Ockendon **4** (1) (*Plate* 4 p. xliv) ; North Shoebury **4** (1) ; North Weald Bassett **2** (1)* ; Orsett **4** (1) ; Panfield

Plate, Church : *cont.*
  POST-REFORMATION, etc. : *cont.*
    COVER-PATENS : *cont.*
      16TH-CENTURY, etc. : *cont.*
        1 (1) ; Paglesham **4** (1) ; Rainham **4** (1) ; Roydon **2** (1) ; Runwell **4** (1) (*Plate* 4 p. xliv) ; St. Osyth **3** (2) ; Salcott **3** (2) ; Shalford **1** (1) ; South Benfleet **4** (1) ; Strethall **1** (1) ; Theydon Garnon **2** (1)* ; Thundersley **4** (1) ; Tolleshunt D'Arcy **3** (1) ; Ulting **2** (1) ; Weeley **3** (1) ; Wendens Ambo **1** (2) ; Wethersfield **1** (1) ; White Colne **3** (1)
      16TH OR 17TH-CENTURY : Tilbury-juxta-Clare **1** (1)
      17TH-CENTURY :
        Aveley **4** (1) ; Barking **2** (2) ; Chigwell **2** (2) (*Plate* 2 p. xxxix)* ; Clavering **1** (1) ; Colchester **3** (7) (13)*; Corringham **4** (1) ; East Ham **2** (2) ; Great Leighs **2** (1)* ; Great Waltham **2** (1) (*Plate* 2 p. xxxix) ; High Ongar **2** (1) ; Lamarsh **3** (1) ; Lawford **3** (1) ; Leaden Roding **2** (1) ; Little Bentley **3** (1) (*Plate* 3 p. xxxv)* ; Little Burstead **4** (1) ; Little Chesterford **1** (1)* ; Markshall **3** (1) ; Mashbury **2** (1) ; Messing **3** (1) ; Mount Bures **3** (1) ; Roxwell **2** (1) ; Sandon **4** (1) ; Shenfield **2** (1) ; South Weald **2** (1) ; Southchurch **4** (1) ; Springfield **2** (1) ; Stapleford Abbots **2** (1) ; Stifford **4** (1) ; Theydon Garnon **2** (1) ; Wenden Lofts **1** (1) ; West Ham **2** (1) ; Widdington **1** (1) ; Wivenhoe **3** (1)
      EARLY 18TH-CENTURY (before 1715) :
        Colchester **3** (6) ; Foulness **4** (2) (*Plate* 4 p. xliv) ; Great Braxted **3** (1) ; Great Warley **4** (1) ; High Ongar **2** (1) ; Little Horkesley **3** (1) ; Pattiswick **3** (1)* ; Rochford **4** (1)
      UNDATED :
        Great Bentley **3** (1) ; Helion Bumpstead **1** (1) ; Rayne **1** (1)
  CUPS, *see also* CHALICE, *above* :
    16TH-CENTURY (after 1547) :
      Abberton **3** (1) ; Althorne **4** (1) ; Ardleigh **3** (1) ; Arkesden **1** (1) ; Asheldham **4** (1) ; Ashen **1** (1) ; Ashingdon **4** (1) ; Barling **4** (1) ; Beaumont-cum-Moze **3** (1) ; Belchamp Otton **1** (1) ; Birchanger **1** (1) ; Birdbrook **1** (1) ; Black Notley **2** (1) ; Brightlingsea **3** (3)* ; Buttsbury **4** (2) ; Chapel **3** (1)* ; Chingford **2** (1) ; Colchester **3** (7) (10) (*Plate* 3 p. xxxv) ; Cold Norton **4** (1) ; Dagenham **2** (1) (*Fig.* 2 p. 56) ; Dengie **4** (1) ; Doddinghurst **2** (1) ; Downham **4** (1) ; Dunton (Wayletts) **4** (1) ; Earls Colne **3** (1) (*Plate* 3 p. xxxv) ; East Ham **2** (2) ; East Horndon **4** (1) ; East Mersea **3** (1) ; Easthorpe **3** (1) ; Eastwood **4** (1) ; Elmstead **3** (1) ; Elsenham **1** (1) ; Faulkbourne **2** (2) ; Great Braxted **3** (1) ; Great Canfield **3** (1) ; Great Parndon **2** (1)* ; Great Saling **1** (1) ; Great Sampford **1** (1) ; Great Stambridge **4** (1) ; Great Tey **3** (1) ; Great Wigborough **3** (1) ; Hadleigh **4** (1) ; Hadstock **1** (2) ; Hempstead **1** (1) ; High Easter **2** (1) ; High Roding **2** (1) ; Hockley **4** (1) ; Hornchurch **4** (1) (*Plate* 4 p. xliv) ; Horndon-on-the-Hill **4** (1) (*Plate* 4 p. xliv) ; Kelvedon **3** (2) ; Lambourne **2** (1) ; Langley **1** (1) ; Layer-de-la-Haye **3** (1) ; Little Braxted **3** (1) ; Little Laver **2** (1) (bowl) (*Plate* 2 p. xxxix) ; Little Parndon **2** (1) ; Little Tey **3** (1) ; Little Wakering **4** (1) ; Little Waltham **2** (1) (stem) ; Little Warley **4** (1) ; Little Wigborough **3** (1)* ; Manuden **1** (1) ; Margaret Roding **2** (1) ; Margaretting **2** (1) (*Plate* 2 p. xxxix) ; Marks Tey

Instructions how to use this Index given on page 198.

See Addenda et Corrigenda, pp. 185–8, under this Volume and Parish.

Instructions how to use this Index given on page 198.

See Addenda et Corrigenda, pp. 185–8, under this Volume and Parish.

Instructions how to use this Index given on page 198.

* *See Addenda et Corrigenda, pp. 185–8, under this Volume and Parish.*

Instructions how to use this Index given on page 198.

* *See Addenda et Corrigenda, pp. 185–8, under this Volume and Parish.*

Instructions how to use this Index given on page 198.

See Addenda et Corrigenda, pp. 185–8, under this Volume and Parish.

Instructions how to use this Index given on page 198.

Rake (?), Thomas, 1697, head-stone to : East Ham **2** (2)
Rakefairs, Lindsell **1** (7)
Ralph, son of Brian, founder of Stanesgate Priory in the 12th century : Steeple **4** (2)
Rame, Francis, 1617, and Helen, his wife, 1613, monument of : Hornchurch **4** (1)
Rampley, Elizabeth, 1688, floor-slab to : All Saints Church, Colchester **3** (2)
Rampston :
　Robert, 16th-century brass formerly to : Chingford **2** (1)
　Robert, inscriptions recording benefactions of, 1585 : Chigwell **2** (2) ; East Ham **2** (2) ; Low Leyton **2** (2) ; Waltham Holy Cross **2** (1) ; Walthamstow **2** (1) ; Woodford **2** (1)
　Roland, 1598, brass of : Great Parndon **2** (1)
Ramsden Bellhouse **4** pp. 119–120
Ramsden Bellhouse Hall, Ramsden Bellhouse **4** (4)
Ramsden Crays **4** p. 120
Ramsey **3** pp. 191–193
Rande, Margaret, see Freake **4**
Ranks Green, see Fairsted **2**
Ransford, Richard, 1677, head-stone to : Rayleigh **4** (1)
Ranshaw, Philip, son of Rev. Philip, 1691, floor-slab to : Asheldham **4** (1)
Raphael, James, 1686, floor-slab to : Waltham Holy Cross **2** (1)
Ratcliffe, Mary, wife of Anthony, 1630, brass to : Rainham **4** (1)
Rathborne :
　Mrs. Re——, 1689, floor-slab to : Beaumont-cum-Moze **3** (1)
　Rev. James, early 18th-century floor-slab to : Beaumont-cum-Moze **3** (1)
Ratisdon (?), arms : Pentlow **1** (2) (glass)
Raven, see under Inns
Ravens Farm, Little Easton **1** (4)
　,,　　,,　　Woodham Walter **2** (9)
Ravens House, Stansted Mountfitchet **1**. (32)
Ravensfield Farm, Bures **3** (10)
Ravenstock Green, see Saffron Walden **1**
Rawlins, William, and Ann, his sister, 1703, floor-slab to : Magdalen Laver **2** (1)
Rawlinson, John, 1698, floor-slab to : East Tilbury **4** (2)
Rawreth **4** pp. 120–121
Ray, -e :
　Anne, wife of Robert, 1712, head and foot-stone to : Belcham Walter **1** (1)
　Elizabeth, see Purlenant **4**
　George, 1609, brass to : Stansted Mountfitchet **1** (2)
　John, M.A., F.R.S., 1705–6, monument to : Black Notley **2** (1)
　Thomas, 1692, and Dorothy (Glascock), his wife, 1701, floor-slab to : Stansted Mountfitchet **1** (2)
Ray Farm, Ingatestone and Fryerning **2** (11)
Raylands, High Easter **2** (22)
Rayleigh **4** pp. 121–124
Rayleigh Castle, Rayleigh **4** (2) (Plates **4** p. xxxvii)
Rayleigh Lodge, Rayleigh **4** (8)
Rayments Farm, Wimbish **1** (11)
Raymond, arms : Belcham Walter **1** (1) (4) ; Downham **4** (1)
Raymond :
　Philip, of Hunsdon, and Agnes (Sterne), his wife, arms : Belcham Walter **1** (1) (4)
　Sir Thomas, 1683, floor-slab to : Downham **4** (1)
Raymond's Farm, Rawreth **4** (3)
Rayne **1** pp. 218–220
Rayne Hatch Farm, Stisted **3** (19)
Rayne Lodge, Rayne **1** (21)
Rayner, arms : Thaxted **1** (2)

Rayner :
　Elizabeth (daughter of William Swallow), 1693, also to Mary, wife of William, floor-slab to : St. Peter's Church, Colchester **3** (8)
　John, 1679, floor-slab to : Thaxted **1** (2)
　John, 1697, John, 1698, Smethe, 1703, Richard, 1708, Jeremiah, 1714, children of John, floor-slab to : Thaxted **1** (2)
　Thomas, 1674, floor-slab to : Thaxted **1** (2)
　Thomas, 1692, floor-slab to : Thaxted **1** (2)
　Thomas, 1710, floor-slab to : Thaxted **1** (2)
Rawreth Hall, Rawreth **4** (2)
Reading-desks, see Lecterns
Rebow, arms : Colchester **3** (6)
Rebow, John, 1699, and others of later date, monument of, erected by Sir Isaac Rebow : St. Mary's Church, Colchester **3** (6)
Recesses, see under Monuments, Funeral
" Recorders House," Thaxted **1** (15) (Plate **1** p. 313)
Rectory, The, Ashdon **1** (7A)
　,,　　,,　　Barnston **2** (4)
　,,　　,,　　Black Notley **2** (7)
　,,　　,,　　Bowers Gifford **4** (3)
　,,　　,,　　Bradwell-juxta-Mare **4** (4)
　,,　　,,　　Chipping Ongar **2** (13)
　,,　　,,　　Easthorpe **3** (4)
　,,　　,,　　Fobbing **4** (2)
　,,　　,,　　Fyfield **2** (9)
　,,　　,,　　Great Hallingbury **2** (3)
　,,　　,,　　(Old) Great Yeldham **1** (4) (Plate **1** p. xxxiv)
　,,　　,,　　Kelvedon Hatch **2** (6)
　,,　　,,　　Lambourne **2** (4)
　,,　　,,　　Liston **1** (2) ·
　,,　　,,　　Little Burstead **4** (3)
　,,　　,,　　Little Canfield **2** (2)
　,,　　,,　　Little Laver **2** (1A)
　,,　　,,　　Little Sampford **1** (20)
　,,　　,,　　Little Stambridge **4** (1)
　,,　　,,　　Little Yeldham **1** (3)
　,,　　,,　　Little Waltham **2** (3)
　,,　　,,　　Panfield **1** (5)
　,,　　,,　　Pattiswick **3** (4)
　,,　　,,　　Pebmarsh **3** (2)
　,,　　,,　　Quendon **1** (3)
　,,　　,,　　Radwinter **1** (2)
　,,　　,,　　Rayleigh **4** (3)
　,,　　,,　　Shelley **2** (4)
　,,　　,,　　Sible Hedingham **1** (3)
　,,　　,,　　South Ockendon **4** (2)
　,,　　,,　　Stanford-le-Hope **4** (2)
　,,　　,,　　Stapleford Tawney **2** (4)
　,,　　,,　　Sturmer **1** (3)
　,,　　,,　　Sutton **4** (3)
　,,　　,,　　Toppesfield **1** (7) (for barn at, see **4** p. 186)
　,,　　,,　　Twinstead **3** (2)
　,,　　,,　　White Roding **3** (9)
　,,　　,,　　Widdington **1** (7)
　,,　　,,　　Wickford **4** (2)
　,,　　,,　　(Site of old), Willingale Doe **2** (2)
　,,　　,,　　(Old) Willingale Spain **2** (23)
Rectory Cottages, White Roding **2** (9)
Rectory Farm, Gestingthorpe **1** (8)
　,,　　,,　　Littlebury **1** (18)
　,,　　,,　　Manuden **1** (14)
　,,　　,,　　Strethall **1** (3)
Red Cow, see under Inns
Red Hills, see under Earthworks
Red House, Little Yeldham **1** (4)
Red Lion, see under Inns

* See Addenda et Corrigenda, pp. 185–8, under this Volume and Parish.

Instructions how to use this Index given on page 198.

* *See Addenda et Corrigenda, pp. 185–8, under this Volume and Parish.*

Instructions how to use this Index given on page 198.

Instructions how to use this Index given on page 198.

* *See Addenda et Corrigenda, pp. 185–8, under this Volume and Parish.*

Instructions how to use this Index given on page 198.

* See Addenda et Corrigenda, pp. 185–8, under this Volume and Parish.

Instructions how to use this Index given on page 198.

* *See Addenda et Corrigenda, pp. 185–8, under this Volume and Parish.*

Instructions how to use this Index given on page 198.

* See Addenda et Corrigenda, pp. 185–8, under this Volume and Parish.

Instructions how to use this Index given on page 198.

See Addenda et Corrigenda, pp. 185–8, under this Volume and Parish.

Instructions how to use this Index given on page 198.

* See Addenda et Corrigenda, pp. 185–8, under this Volume and Parish.

Instructions how to use this Index given on page 198.

* See Addenda et Corrigenda, pp. 185–8, under this Volume and Parish.

Instructions how to use this Index given on page 198.

* *See Addenda et Corrigenda, pp. 185–8, under this Volume and Parish.*

Instructions how to use this Index given on page 198.

* *See Addenda et Corrigenda, pp. 185–8, under this Volume and Parish.*

Instructions how to use this Index given on page 198.

Smith, *or* **Smyth, -e :** *cont.*
Sir William, 1631, son of Sir William, senior, and his two wives, Helegenwagh (daughter of Lord Conway) and Anne (Croft), altar-tomb of : Theydon Mount **2** (1) (*Plate* **2** p. 230)
Willyam, and Dorcas, his wife, mid 17th-century floor-slab to : Cressing **3** (1)
Smith's Farm, North Benfleet **4** (3)
,,   ,,   Twinstead **3** (4)
Smith's Green, see Debden **1**
,,   ,,   Takeley **1**
Smithy, East Tilbury **4** (6)
Snayn, "Johannes Snayn et Richardus Lynn me fecit," inscription on bell : Maldon All Saints **2** (1)
Snelling, arms : Navestock **2** (1)
Snelling, Ann (Nicholls), wife of Charles, 1623, also Rowland, their child, 1625, tablet of : Navestock **2** (1)
Snell's Farm, Great Henny **3** (7)
Snoreham, site of St. Peter's Church : Latchingdon **4** (2)
Snow, arms : Doddinghurst **2** (1)
Snow, Nathaniel, 16—3, John, 1670 (?), and Nathaniel, 1677, his sons ; also Rhodda, wife of Nathaniel, 1697, table-tomb to : Doddinghurst **2** (1)
Snow's Farm, White Roding **2** (4)
Snowden Fen, Halstead Rural **1** (13)
Soken, *see* **Kirby-le-Soken 3, Thorpe-le-Soken 3,** *and* **Walton-le-Soken 3**
'**Soldiers' Graves,'** earthwork locally known as : East Tilbury **4** (7)
Solme, Precilla, widow of John, *see* **Buckenham 2**
Solomon :
CARVING : Kelvedon **3** (2) (with Queen of Sheba) (possibly)
GLASS : Harlow **2** (2) (incidents in his life) ; Margaretting **2** (1) (*Plate* **2** p. xxxvi) ; Prittlewell **4** (1) (anointing of)
Somerset, Katherine, daughter of Edward, Earl of Worcester, *see* **Petre 2**
Sonds, Jane, 1686, floor-slab to : Orsett **4** (1)
Songar, ——, *c.* 1480, brass of : Clavering **1** (1)
Sorrell, arms : Great Waltham **2** (1)
Sorrell, Sorell, *or* **Soreil :**
Dorothy (Lane), wife of John, 1681, floor-slab to : Stebbing **1** (1)
Joane, *see* **Carowe 2**
John the elder, 1666, floor-slab to : Stebbing **1** (1)*
John the younger, 1671, floor-slab to : Stebbing **1** (1)*
Mary, wife of John, 1652, and her son, John, 1674, floor-slab to : Great Waltham **2** (1)
Sounding-boards :
17TH-CENTURY :
Aveley **4** (1) ; Barling **4** (1) ; East Mersea **3** (1) (*Plate* **3** p. 181) ; Great Baddow **1** (1) (*Plate* **4** p. 4) ; Layer Marney **3** (1) ; Thaxted **1** (2) ; Waltham Holy Cross **2** (1) (now used as table-top)
EARLY 18TH-CENTURY (before 1715) :
Abbess Roding **2** (1) ; Great Coggeshall **3** (2)
South Benfleet 4 pp. 136–139
South Fambridge 4 p. 139
South Hall, Paglesham **4** (8)
South Hanningfield 4 pp. 139–140
South Ockendon 4 pp. 140–143
South Ockendon Hall, South Ockendon **4** (3) (14)
South Shoebury 4 pp. 143–145
South Weald 2 pp. 214–218
South Weald Camp, South Weald **2** (18)
Southchurch 4 pp. 145–146
Southchurch Hall, Southchurch **4** (2)
Southcote, *or* **Southcotte,** arms : Borley **1** (1) ; Witham **2** (1)

Southcote, *or* **Southcotte :**
John, Justice of the Queen's Bench, 1585, and Elizabeth (Robins), his wife, altar-tomb of : Witham **2** (1)
Magdala (Waldegrave), wife of John, 1598, monument of : Borley **1** (1)
Southey Green, see Sible Hedingham **1**
Southey Green Farm, Sible Hedingham **1** (29)
Southfields, Dedham **3** (2) (*Plates* **3** pp. xxx, 84, 85, 100)
,,   Dunton **4** (4)
Southlands, Ulting **2** (4)
Southminster 4 pp. 146–147
Spade Cottage, Little Easton **1** (13)
Spain's Hall, Finchingfield **1** (3) (*Plate* **1** p. 91)
,,   ,,   (or **Manor House),** Willingale Spain **2** (4)
,,   ,,   *see also* **Spaynes Hall,** *below*
Sparhawk, Sarah, *see* **Bridg 3**
Sparke, arms : Great Parndon **2** (1)
Sparke :
Christopher, 1713, tablet to : Great Parndon **2** (1)
Mary (Turnor), widow of Thomas, B.D., 1661, tablet to : Great Parndon **2** (1)
Sparling's Farm, Felsted **2** (78)
Sparrow, arms : Gestingthorpe **1** (1)
Sparrow, John, 1626, monument of : Gestingthorpe **1** (1)
Sparrow's Farm, Debden **1** (41)
,,   ,,   Terling **2** (27) (*Plate* **2** p. 129)
,,   ,,   Twinstead **3** (5)
Spaynes Hall, Great Yeldham **1** (3)
Speering, Elizabeth, widow of Cornelius, and James, their son, *see* **Silverlock**
Spencers, Magdalen Laver **2** (4)
Spelman, arms : Stambourne **1** (1) (glass, etc.)
Spies, Return from Canaan of the, figure-subject on iron fire-backs : Gosfield **1** (3) ; Kelvedon **3** (24)
Spitland, Hempstead **1** (31)
Spoon, *see under* **Plate, Church**
Spooner, Alse, *see* **Sayer 3**
Spoons Hall, Pebmarsh **3** (12)
Spotted Dog, *see under* **Inns**
Spratt's Farm, Southminster **4** (4)
Spread Eagle, *see under* **Inns**
Spriggs, High Ongar **2** (3)
Sprigg's Farm, Ashdon **1** (26)
,,   ,,   Blackmore **2** (13)
,,   ,,   Little Sampford **1** (23)
Spring Farm, Bulphan **4** (2)
,,   ,,   Tolleshunt D'Arcy **3** (4)
Springfield 2 pp. 218–220
Springate Farm, Belchamp Walter **1** (14)
Springham, Mercymight, *see* **Bristowe 2**
Springwell, see Little Chesterford **1**
Squint, illustration of 15th-century : Hadleigh **4** (1) (*Plate* **4** p. 104)
Stace :
John, and Susanna, his wife, 1684, head-stone to : Epping Upland **2** (2)
Nymphas, son of Nymphas, 1709, head-stone to : Epping Upland **2** (2)
Susanna, widow of Nymphas, 1679, head-stone to : Epping Upland **2** (2)
Susanna, daughter of Nymphas, 1680, head-stone to : Epping Upland **2** (2)
Susanna, daughter of Nymphas, ——4, head-stone to : Epping Upland **2** (2)
Stacey :
Edward, 1555, and Katherine, his wife, 1565, tablet with brasses of : Waltham Holy Cross **2** (1)
Julian, *see* **Stafford 2**

* *See Addenda et Corrigenda, pp. 185–8, under this Volume and Parish.*

Instructions how to use this Index given on page 198.

* *See Addenda et Corrigenda, pp. 185–8, under this Volume and Parish.*

Instructions how to use this Index given on page 198.

Stanes :
Mary, wife of Jeffrey, 1709, floor-slab to : Hatfield Broad Oak **2** (1)
Robert, 1712, head-stone to : Great Warley **4** (1)
Stanesgate Priory, Steeple **4** (2)
Stanesgate Abbey Farm, Steeple **4** (4) (*Plate* **4** p. 57)
Stanford Farm, Braintree **2** (74)
Stanford-le-Hope 4 pp. 147–151
Stanford Rivers 2 pp. 220–222
Stanley, arms : Roydon **2** (1) ; Walthamstow **2** (1)
Stanley :
Elizabeth (Dinn), 1589, wife of John, brass of : Roydon **2** (1)
John, 1626, brass to : Upminster **4** (1)
Lady Lucie (Percy), wife of Sir Edward, monument of, *c.* 1630 : Walthamstow **2** (1)
Stanley Hall, Pebmarsh **3** (3)
Stanstead Hall, Halstead Rural **1** (1) (*Plate* **1** p. xxiv)
Stansted Castle, Stansted Mountfitchet **1** (3)
Stansted Mountfitchet 1 pp. 275–280
Stanton's Farm, Black Notley **2** (6) (*Plates* **2** p. 114)
Stanway 3 pp. 207–209
Stanway Hall, Stanway **3** (4)
Stanye, arms : Stambourne **1** (1) (glass, etc.)
Stapel, *see* **Staples,** *below*
Stapleford Abbots 2 pp. 222–225 ; **4** p. 187
Stapleford Tawney 2 pp. 225–226
Staple, -s, *or* **Stapel**
John, 1661, floor-slab to : Sutton **4** (1)
Thomas, 1371, brass of : Shopland **4** (1)
Thomas, 1592, brass of : West Ham **2** (1)
Star and Fleece, *see under* **Inns**
Starlings Green, see Clavering **1**
Staunton, Anfrid de, Church built or rebuilt by, in the 14th century : Alresford **3** (2)
Staresmore, Dorothye, *see* **Strutt 4**
Stebbing 1 pp. 280–288 ; **4** p. 186
Stebbing Green, see Stebbing **1**
Stebbing Green Farm, Stebbing **1** (63)
Stebbing Mount, Stebbing **1** (3)
Stebbing Park, Stebbing **1** (7)
Stedman, John, 169(3 ?), rector of the parish, floor-slab to : Great Warley **4** (1)
Steeple 4 pp. 151–152
Steeple Bumpstead 1 pp. 288–295
Steevens, *or* **Stevens,** Barking **2** (2) ; Maldon All Saints **2** (1)
Steevens, *or* **Stevens :**
Elizabeth, 1700, and Mary, wife of Captain Whitaker, 1698, floor-slab to : Leigh **4** (1)
John, 1677, tablet to : Maldon All Saints **2** (1)
John, 1711, head-stone to : Great Warley **4** (1)
John, 1714, tablet to : Maldon All Saints **2** (1)
Paul, 1675, and Judeth (Reymers), 1697, floor-slab to : Barking **2** (2)
Stephen, arms : Lamarsh **3** (1)
Stephen, Thomas, 1654, tablet to : Lamarsh **3** (1)
Stephen, King, and Queen Maud, founders (probably 1140) of an abbey for monks of the Order of Savigny : Little Coggeshall **3** (2)
Stephen, St. :
GLASS : Great Bardfield **1** (1) ; Maldon All Saints **2** (1) (Martyrdom of)
PAINTING (on screen) : Clavering **1** (1)
Sterne (of Essendon), arms : Belchamp Walter **1** (1) (4)
Sterne, Agnes, *see* **Raymond 1**
Stevens, *see* **Steevens,** *above*
Stevens Farm, Felsted **2** (62)
Stevington End, see Bartlow End **1**
Steward, Mary, *see* **Tallakarne 1**

Stickling Green, see Clavering **1**
Stifford 4 pp. 152–154
Stile, *see* **Style,** *below*
Stilleman, *or* **Stileman :**
" Humferi Low et Henry Stileman Churchwardens Ano D. 1639," inscription on fascia-board : Great Baddow **4** (1)
James, 1694, table-tomb to : Rettendon **4** (1)
John, 1699, floor-slab to : St. Peter's Church, Colchester **3** (8)
Stiltamen, John, 1714, head-stone to : Paglesham **4** (1)
Stisted 3 pp. 210–212
Stisted Hall (the original), 16th-century panelling said to have come from : Stisted **3** (11)
Stisted Hall Park, Stisted **3** (11)
Sto——, Susanah, 16(6 ?)8, floor-slab to : Horndon-on-the-Hill **4** (1)
Stock 4 pp. 155–156
Stock, Richard, 1568, brass to : Ugley **1** (1)
Stock Hall, Matching **2** (10)
  ,,   ,,   Ulting **2** (7)
Stock Village, see Burnham **4**
Stocking Green, see Radwinter **1**
Stocks, Whipping-posts *and* **Pillories :**
PILLORY :
17th-century : Waltham Holy Cross **2** (1) (*Plate* **2** p. 258)
STOCKS :
18th-century :
Doddinghurst **2** (16) (*Plate* **2** p. 258) ; Little Easton **1** (15)
STOCKS AND WHIPPING-POSTS :
16th-century : Waltham Holy Cross **2** (1) (*Plate* **2** p. 258)
17th or 18th-century : Havering-atte-Bower **2** (2) (*Plate* **2** p. 258)
WHIPPING-POSTS :
18th-century (before 1715) : Bradwell-juxta-Mare **4** (7)
Stock's Farm, Berden **1** (2) (15)
Stockstreet Farm, Great Coggeshall **3** (94)
Stockwell Arms, *see under* **Inns**
Stockwell Hall, Little Burstead **4** (2)
Stockwell House, Colchester **3** (107)
Stokes, arms : Walthamstow **2** (1)
Stokes :
Jeremiah, 1708, Elizabeth, his wife, 1707, and Richard, 1696, and Basil, 1710, their sons, floor-slab to : Walthamstow **2** (1)
Thomas, 1701, head-stone to : Great Burstead **4** (4)
Stonage Farm, Little Waltham **2** (6)
Stonard, arms : Stapleford Abbots **2** (1)
Stonard, *or* **Stonnard :**
Francis, 1604, and Lucye (Higham), his wife, 1596, also Henry, his brother, 1555, tablet to : Stapleford Abbots **2** (1)
George, 1558, brass of : Loughton **2** (2)
John, 1541, and Joan and Katheryn, his wives, brass of : Loughton **2** (2)
Stonards Farm, Brentwood **2** (12)
Stondon Hall, Stondon Massey **2** (2)
Stondon Massey 2 pp. 226–227
Stone, Elizabeth, *see* **Leigh 2**
Stone Hall, Little Canfield **2** (4)
  ,,   ,,   Wanstead **2** (5)
Stone, Nicholas, monuments by : Walthamstow **2** (1) (*Plate* **2** p. 251) ; Writtle **2** (1) (*Plate* **2** p. 273)
Stoneham Street, see Great Coggeshall **3**
Stonehill Farm, Roxwell **2** (14)
Stonehouse, arms : Debden **1** (1)
Stonehouse, James, 1638, tablet to : Debden **1** (1)

* *See Addenda et Corrigenda, pp. 185–8, under this Volume and Parish.*

Instructions how to use this Index given on page 198.

*See Addenda et Corrigenda, pp. 185–8, under this Volume and Parish.

Instructions how to use this Index given on page 198.

Sumner, William, 1559, brass of : Harlow **2** (2)
Sun, *see under* **Inns**
Sundials :
  ON CHIMNEY-STACKS :
    17th-century : Stapleford Abbots **2** (3)
    Early 18th-century (before 1715) : Theydon Mount **2** (2)
  MURAL : *see also* SCRATCHED, *below :*
    17th-century :
      Great Maplestead **1** (1) ; Latton **2** (2)
    Early 18th-century (before 1715) :
      Clavering **1** (1) (fragment) ; North Weald Bassett **2** (1)
  PEDESTAL, 17th-century : Boreham **2** (4)
  SCRATCHED :
    Althorne **4** (1) ; Ashingdon **4** (1) ; Boreham **2** (1) ; Burnham **4** (1) ; Castle Hedingham **1** (1) ; Chadwell **4** (2) ; Chickney **1** (1) ; Great Bentley **3** (1) ; Great Braxted **3** (1) ; Great Easton **1** (1) ; Great Horkesley **3** (1) ; High Easter **2** (1) ; Lawford **3** (1) ; Lindsell **1** (1) ; Little Burstead **4** (1) ; Little Thurrock **4** (1) ; Netteswell **2** (1) ; Orsett **4** (1) ; Runwell **4** (1) ; South Benfleet **4** (1) ; Southchurch **4** (1) ; Southminster **4** (1) ; Springfield **2** (1) ; Stanford Rivers **2** (1) ; Thorrington **3** (1) ; Waltham Holy Cross **2** (1) ; Wicken Bonhunt **1** (1) (2)
' **Sunken Way,**' *or* ' **Hollow Way,**' Colchester **3** (265)
Surrex Farm, Feering **3** (6)
Surridges Farm, Steeple Bumpstead **1** (27)
Sussex, Earls of, *see* **Radclif**
Sutton 4 pp. 157–158
Sutton, arms : Halstead Urban **1** (1)
Sutton, -e :
  Margaret, *see* **Bourchier 1**
  Margerie, indent of 14th-century marginal inscription to : Wivenhoe **3** (1)
Sutton Arms, *see under* **Inns**
Sutton Hall, Sutton **4** (2)
Suttons (*or* **Manor House**), South Shoebury **4** (5)
Sutton's Farm, Mucking **4** (6)
Swaine's Farm, Saffron Walden **1** (129)

Swallow :
  Elizabeth, daughter of William, *see* **Rayner 3**
  Thomas, 1712, floor-slab to : Thaxted **1** (2)
Swallows Cross Farm, Doddinghurst **2** (7)
Swan, *see under* **Inns**
Swan, Johanah, wife of Amos, 1704, tablet to : Steeple Bumpstead **1** (2)
Swan's Farm, Radwinter **1** (4)
Swayne's Hall, Widdington **1** (6)
Swift, -e, arms : Roydon **2** (1)
  James, 1713, Mary, his wife, 1720, James and Thomas, their sons, 1713 and 1720, slab to : Bocking **1** (1)
  John, 1570, brass of : Roydon **2** (1)
  John, 1601, and Margaret (Heath), his wife (afterwards wife of Henry Colt), 1602, and Richard, his son, tablet to : Roydon **2** (1)
Swinburne, *see* **Swynborne,** *below*
Swinerton, arms : Stanway **3** (3)
Swinerton, St. John, All Saints Church, Stanway **3** (3), restored by, in the 17th century
Swinfield, Mr., floor-slab to : Waltham Holy Cross **2** (1)
Sword, *see under* **Armour**
Swynborne, *or* **Swinborne,** arms : Finchingfield **1** (1) (Berners tomb) ; Little Horkesley **3** (1)
Swynborne :
  Andrew, 1418, and John, 1430, brass of : Little Horkesley **3** (1)
  Sir Robert, 1391, and his son, Sir Thomas, 1412, Lord of Hammes, Mayor of Bordeaux, and Captain of Fronsac, altar-tomb with brasses of : Little Horkesley **3** (1)
Sydnor, Helen, 1651, daughter of Thomas Leventhorpe, monument to : Great Baddow **4** (1)
Symonds, arms : Great Yeldham **1** (1) ; Halstead Rural **1** (4) (glass) ; Panfield **1** (3) (glass)
Symonds, *see also* **Fitz Symonds :**
  Elizabeth (Quarles), wife of John, 1666, brass to : Great Yeldham **1** (1)
  John, 1692, tablet to : Great Yeldham **1** (1)
  Richard, 1627, and Elizabeth (Plume), his wife, brass of : Great Yeldham **1** (1)
  Thomas, 1705, table-tomb to : East Ham **2** (2)

Tables, *see under* **Furniture ;** *see also* **Communion Tables**
Table-tombs in Churchyards, *see under* **Monuments, Funeral**
Tablets, Mural, *see* MURAL, *under* **Monuments, Funeral**
Tabor :
  John and Thomas, 1678, floor-slab to : South Hanningfield **4** (1)
  William, rector of High Ongar and Archdeacon of Essex, 1611, brass to : High Ongar **2** (1)
Taborsfield Cottage, Bardfield Saling **1** (8)
Taggles, Matching **2** (11)
Tailler, " Humfri Tailler 1631," inscription on brass alms-dish of foreign workmanship : Danbury **4** (1)
Takeley 1 pp. 299–301 ; **4** p. 186
Takeleys, Epping Upland **2** (5)
Talcott, Thomas, 1686, floor-slab to : Holy Trinity Church, Colchester **3** (3)
Tallakarne, arms : Ashen **1** (1) ; Helion Bumpstead **1** (1)
Tallakarne :
  Devereux, 1627, and Mary (Steward), his wife, tablet to : Helion Bumpstead **1** (1)
  Luce (Cotton), wife of John, 1610, tablet to : Ashen **1** (1)
Tan Office, Shalford **1** (35)
Tan Office Cottages, Stisted **3** (6)
Tan Office Farm, Stebbing **1** (35)

Tanfield, arms : Margaretting **2** (1)
Tanfield :
  Daniel, 1695, head-stone to : Margaretting **2** (1)
  Martha, wife of Edmund, *see* **Borrit 2**
  William, and Elizabeth, his wife, monument of, *c.* 1600 : Margaretting **2** (1)
Tanhouse Farm, Ulting **2** (6) (*Plate* **2** p. 128)
Tanner's Cottage, Moreton **2** (2)
Tanner's Farm, Great Dunmow **1** (10)
  ,,   ,,   Stebbing **1** (44)
Tapestry :
  17TH-CENTURY : Ingatestone and Fryerning **2** (3) (probably Dutch)
  circa 1700 : Aveley **4** (6)
  EARLY 18TH-CENTURY : Aveley **4** (6)
  UNDATED : Steeple Bumpstead **1** (7) (now in Saffron Walden Museum)
Tasburgh, Maude, *see* **Cammocke 4**
Tasciovanus, coin of : Latton **2** (1)
Tayler, More, *alias, see* **Moore,** *or* **More 1**
Taylor :
  John, 1713, head-stone to : Great Dunmow **1** (1)
  Capt. Zachariah, 1710, Elizabeth, his wife, 1711, and Priscilla, his daughter, 1698, floor-slab to : West Ham **2** (1)

* *See Addenda et Corrigenda, pp. 185–8, under this Volume and Parish.*

Instructions how to use this Index given on page 198.

* *See* Addenda et Corrigenda, *pp. 185–8, under this Volume and Parish.*

Instructions how to use this Index given on page 198.

* See Addenda et Corrigenda, pp. 185–8, under this Volume and Parish.

Instructions how to use this Index given on page 198.

* *See Addenda et Corrigenda, pp. 185–8, under this Volume and Parish.*

Instructions how to use this Index given on page 198.

* See Addenda et Corrigenda, pp. 185-8, under this Volume and Parish.

Instructions how to use this Index given on page 198.

* See Addenda et Corrigenda, pp. 185–8, under this Volume and Parish.

Instructions how to use this Index given on page 198.

* *See Addenda et Corrigenda, pp. 185-8, under this Volume and Parish.*

Instructions how to use this Index given on page 198.

See Addenda et Corrigenda, pp. 185–8, under this Volume and Parish.

Instructions how to use this Index given on page 198.

* See Addenda et Corrigenda, pp. 185–8, under this Volume and Parish.

Instructions how to use this Index given on page 198.

* See Addenda et Corrigenda, pp. 185–8, under this Volume and Parish.

Instructions how to use this Index given on page 198.

See Addenda et Corrigenda, pp. 185–8, under this Volume and Parish.

Lightning Source UK Ltd.
Milton Keynes UK
UKHW010746261118
332983UK00009B/869/P

9 781528 205863